Foreword

Preserving the Past for the Present

'What do you remember about the community?' was the question we asked of seniors and elders from a broad range of different cultural, socioeconomic, and political backgrounds and perspectives. The question was answered in many different ways: we learned about swimming at the Lakelse Hot Springs, growing up on the South Side, skating in the Horseshoe, witnessing the Terrace Mutiny, and how people feel the community has changed.

Preserving the Past for the Present: An Oral History Project rather ambitiously aimed to collect cultural knowledge, foster intergenerational partnerships, engage seniors and youth in local history, and expand the Heritage Park's narrowly focused pioneer perspective. The project was a way to expand the Heritage Park's collections and operations beyond the chronological and physical limitations of our pioneer-focused heritage site. It took us longer than we expected, but we accomplished all of our initial objectives, occasionally even surpassing our lofty goals.

We collected stories and records about our community that have already proven invaluable. We learned the Sm'algyax words for different seafood and berries, how Gitaus was affected by the Second World War, and about the waves of forestry development. Researchers in the future will find this project to be an important insight into economic history, social history, and the ways the community perceived ourselves. Terrace will be strengthened by this new contribution of cultural knowledge and history: our history is now more nuanced, broader, and richer.

Through the participation of Caledonia Secondary School's History 12 class and the 'Na Aksa Gyilak'yoo School, youth were mentored in local history by seniors and elders. Many of the students were intimidated by the interview process before it began, but just as many came away from the interviews they conducted thrilled to share tidbits they had learned. Many relaxed into the process and realised that the seniors they were interviewing were very similar to them, and they bonded over unanticipated connections. Several of the students continued visiting the seniors and elders long after the interview wrapped up.

For these students, history came alive, and they were thrilled to tell their teachers about how Terrace was so unexciting that floor hockey games were broadcast live on the radio. Seniors, too, had a chance to share their stories and feel like their knowledge was important, to the youth, to Heritage Park, and to the broader community, even though many were resistant to being interviewed at first. Interestingly, most of the women we approached about being interviewed were uncertain about participating, insisting they did not have anything important to contribute. By contrast, most of the men quickly agreed to be interviewed. This underlined the importance that gender expectations have on people's experiences, and underscored our need to ensure that women were equal participants in the project.

By including Sikh Canadian, Chinese Canadian, and Tsimshian voices, among many others, our project has succeeded in expanding the diversity of Terrace's published history. The stories of these and other groups and sectors who have historically gone unvoiced have now been preserved for generations to come. This is, of course, still only a partial record: we cannot hope to convey the entirety of community history in one volume, even one as large as this one is.

The interviews were conducted by volunteers with a diverse range of abilities and skills. Several trained journalists conducted interviews. Interviews were also done by nervous community volunteers, high school students, and even children. The people who were interviewed similarly varied: some were very confident and happy about the process, while many others were nervous and needed to be reassured throughout. As such, the final product is a varied, quilt-like assemblage of stories. Some people submitted photos from their own collections, some were found in Heritage Park's collection, and still others were from other institutions. We have found much richness in people's responses, and we hope you will, too. We also hope you will read the interviews in the context of the project, and be forgiving when things seem abrupt or imperfect.

In a similar vein, we apologize for any spelling inconsistencies, especially in place names. While we tried to be consistent, we worked with over 88 different interviewers, interview subjects, transcribers, and editors, and are certain that errors remain. These are, of course, all our own, and not the responsibility of the volunteer project participants.

Through the long process of Preserving the Past for the Present, we have learned many important lessons. First of all, people speak differently than they write. Because of this, it was disconcerting for many of our participants to see their interview on paper. At the outset, we instructed our transcribers to work verbatim, and to be as close to the raw original as possible. As we proceeded, we realised that we would have to strike a balance between being true to the interview and being fair to the person whose words were being published. We did not want to make the people who so generously agreed to be interviewed for this project feel uncomfortable or inarticulate. Some of the participants, unfortunately, withdrew from the project due to this discomfort. So, we shifted into a harsher editing style, and pulled out repetitions, hesitations, and confused tenses. The full, raw interviews will still be available for future researchers to listen to via the audio recordings. What you read here is an edited version.

We also learned that we were hopelessly optimistic in our timeline. Interviews took weeks if not months to set up, volunteers spent about six to eight hours transcribing each hour of audio, the interviewees took months to edit their transcripts, and editing consumed a lot of our time. Part-time staff worked on the project, piece-mealing it together amidst other projects and programs. This, of course, meant that the greater lengths of time spent on each section exponentially extended the project. It was, overall, much longer than we expected, but we were committed to creating a product that we and the participants could be proud of. This, we hope, is what you will read in the following pages.

Preserving the Past for the Present was, from the outset, very much a community project. It was not an academic project or even a strictly historical project. Instead, it was meant to serve as a cross-section of our community, at an important moment in history, as our community seemed poised to be affected by major industrial development. The project took place during the era of 0% vacancy in the Terrace housing market, when the town was booming and drastic change felt imminent. We felt an underlying push to preserve the feel of our community before more people, businesses, and industrial development moved in. That has not, perhaps, occurred in the way we expected, but major changes have happened and will continue to happen. This is how people felt about the past, present, and future of Terrace in 2013.

A common thread in the interviews was that people came to Terrace for six months, a year, or two years, and then ended up staying for the rest of their lives. There is something about this community that captures people and draws them in. We think, from listening to the wealth of stories we collected in this project, that it is the warmth and resilience of the people. We hope that, through this project, we are able to introduce you to some of the people who make Terrace what it is.

Acknowledgements

We gratefully acknowledge the invaluable contribution of the following people to this collaborative community project:

Transcribers who spent countless hours listening to the audio files and typing these into written transcripts: Allison Bench, Kelsey Callewaert, Katie Chicoine, Ed Curell, Dorian George, Ella Goodlad, Sarah Komadina, Elena Kusaka, Lenard Lindstrom, Krizia McDonough, Estelle Mitchell, Melanie Pollard, Kourtney Scott, Brittany Seymour, and Courtney Smaha.

Editers who helped refine the interviews through multiple working drafts: Sarah Artis, Elena Kusaka, Madeleine Link, Terra Nord, Melanie Pollard and Kelsey Wiebe.

Community Partners who went above and beyond to help set up and organize the interviews: Sasa Loggin, Greer Kaiser, Colleen Austin, Natasha Obzera and Tracey Sam.

Artistic and technical collaborator who worked on cover design, printing layout, and formatting: Terra Nord.

A special thank-you to Maggie Baxter for being an ongoing soundboard throughout the project.

And much appreciation to our funder, New Horizons for Seniors, who made this project possible.

Table of Contents

Community Volunteers

Volunteers were the backbone of this project. Heritage Park put out a call early in the fall of 2013, looking for people interested in preserving the history of their community. We were overwhelmed with the response. Over 25 people put their names forward to help with the project. Some wanted to conduct the interviews. Others preferred to help with the long, tedious work of transcribing them.

Volunteers came with a range in backgrounds. Some stepped forward with a keen interest in local history, others had participated in similar community projects, others brought professional training as journalists. Some were students from NWCC, others were staff or volunteer board members from Heritage Park. All were excited to give their time and energy to preserving local history.

Rod Link sharing interview tips with volunteers during interview training session at Heritage Park. October 2013.

We held two training sessions for those who were interested in interviewing. Rod Link from the Terrace Standard, contributed his time and skill to these events. We gathered in Dix's Dance Hall over two evenings, and Rod shared some practical tips for interviewing gleaned from his years of experience in journalism. Volunteers practiced together and pored over the pages of names of people that had been suggested for interviews.

From there, we approached the elders and seniors with whom volunteers were most interested in having a conversation. Over 42 seniors/ elders participated in these interviews. They graciously shared their time, their pictures, their stories, and their insights and perspectives on life in Terrace over the years.

Volunteers practicing interview skills.

Each interview was unique and created some interesting points of contact in the community. Some volunteers interviewed people they already had a relationship with. These interviews built on established rapports and unfolded like a comfortable, insightful conversation with a longtime friend.

Other interviews created newly meaningful connections. In follow-up chats with volunteers, we heard about: follow-up coffee conversations, return visits and even the delivery of food from one senior after the interviewer had her baby! These were lovely, unexpected, outcomes from the project.

Don Varner Interview
Interviewed by Ted Wilson, 22 November 2013

Don was born in 1944 in Prince Rupert. His father worked as a riveter, helping construct Liberty ships for the American Navy during WWII. The family moved inland and his mother accepted a teaching position at a schoolhouse in Pacific. He attended Skeena Secondary School and later BCIT for Mechanical Engineering, graduating in 1976. Don returned to the northwest to live in Usk, marry, and have a family. He worked at the Department of Highways in surveying, eventually moving to the Forest Service where he was employed until retirement. In the second half of the interview, he provides more details of his childhood in the northwest, and recounts stories told to him by his father. His grandfather Charlie Durham immigrated to Canada from Norway and eventually found himself in Kitselas and Usk. His grandmother, Margaret Evelyn, married Charlie and moved from Norway to Canada. The family eventually built a hotel with a pool hall, a historic site now known as Durham House. In this interview, Don Varner describes in detail his family's early history and life in the northwest post-WWII.

TW: Instead of starting when you were born, let's start with your grandfather Charlie Durham and proceed.

DV: Grandpa was born in Norway about 1862 or so. He was a bit of a rebel and he ran away from home. Went to sea on the Empress of China. He came back to Norway, I gather, to meet again with his true love. A lady by the name of Margaret Evelyn, if I am not mistaken, who was from a fairly wealthy middle class family, the type that had servants in the house. And he took her away and got to Canada. It must have been a terrible shock to her because she came from a house with people who would do what she wanted—servants and so on— not slaves, but servants, maids—and she ended up in Kitselas canyon by herself with Charlie, of course, in a log house by herself. As I say, no help, no family, and she raised a family of five girls, two boys. Must have been a shock to her and she did it with aplomb and dignity. She died in 1948, I believe—I can't remember much about her because I was four years old, but I do remember her speaking to me. Okay, that was my grandmother.

My grandfather was a bit of a rebel; he worked here and there. He was in Montreal [Quebec] and a few other places. He worked for Rogers Sugar Refinery down in Vancouver and was turfed because he was a union man and Mr. Rogers [owner of Rogers Sugar Refinery] didn't like union people. Grandpa was always like that. That's about it for Grandpa. He came back up and lived in Kitselas. They had to move the homestead back when the railroad came in 1913. The railroad spent quite a bit of time around Kitselas because there's four tunnels there and that took a couple of years to get through. They finished that in 1913 and after that, the town of Kitselas kind of declined. It was because of the death of the steamboats—not the death but, you know, there was no need for the steamboats any more. The reason for Kitselas just died away.

About the time before the railroad was completed, there was a lot of business between my grandfather's place, which was on the railroad side, of course, and the town of Kitselas on the other side, where the steamboats tie up and often transfer their freight on the crown line from the foot of the canyon to the head of the canyon. Grandpa had a kind of a ferry service there, but he lost that when he went to Vancouver and George Little stepped in and said he was a better man to do that particular job. So when Grandpa got back from Vancouver, he didn't have a ferry service.

TW: What caused your grandpa to choose Canada as a place to settle?

DV: I will be damned if I know. It was a nice piece of land there and some of the steamboats used to go up there and he spotted it and he decided that would be a nice place. It was on the canyon which was a bottleneck for the steamboats and so on. That's one reason he settled there. Built a house, had a few animals, including a pig named Caruso [laughter], because it sounded like [opera singer Enrico] Caruso apparently.

TW: Not having ever heard the pig or Caruso we can't make comparisons, I guess.

DV: The Durham house at Kitselas was kind of a social place for the railroad people to stop in and visit and, of course, with five girls, you know, it was kind of understandable. Anyway, when the town died out, there was no real reason for the Kitselas establishment any more. They moved to Usk in 1916, I believe. Grandpa built a hotel with a pool hall and they lived there for a number of years. They had the A.Y. Jackson Group of Seven painter stop in there one time and paint a picture of Kitselas Mountain, which was called Usk. We've never been able to find a copy of that picture, but I have had it confirmed by a gallery in Toronto, I believe, that it does exist, but they don't know where it is.

TW: Let's go to your mother's birth.

DV: My mom was born in the canyon in about, God, I can't remember her birth date—about 1912. Does that sound about right? Round about that time. Her midwife was Lizzy Kitselas, the princess I believe, but I think that particular line of native royalty has died out. I'm not sure; I'm not privy to what goes on there.

I've seen her picture; she was a fine-looking woman, a handsome woman. She later took up with an Englishman by the name Dick—Richard Lowrie —who had a homestead around Usk. There is a creek named after him, Lowrie Creek. I don't really remember much about her. I remember when she was getting quite on in years she spoke to me. She said, "Get out of the way, little boy." She couldn't walk very well—very straight—and her eyesight was going. So that's my touch with greatness.

TW: And you said your mother was the first white woman [to live in Kitselas].

DV: No, that would have been—my mother would have been the youngest. The next youngest, Irene Bowie—she was born on a steamboat on the Skeena River. And she was the first white baby on the river between Port Essington and Hazelton. Port Essington was a booming town then and Hazelton was kind of a trading centre, although they did a lot of trading in liquor, because the first steamboat every spring that went up there was generally loaded with booze, as I understand it.

TW: And of course the town of Kitselas that we refer to was called White Kitselas, down the lower end of the canyon. Is that correct?

DV: As far as I know it was just called Kitselas.

TW: Wasn't there a village farther up in the canyon?

DV: There was Kitselas Canyon, but the village which was in a good part on—I guess it kinda spread over the canyon. I never heard it called Kitselas, it was just Kitselas Canyon. But I imagine the town of Kitselas got its name from that. And in recent years, when they closed down the Kitselas station at the canyon and moved it further west towards Terrace, they called that Kitselas, but that wasn't the original Kitselas.

TW: So the building that we see when you walk up the tracks is not where the original was.

DV: Some people call it New Kitselas. They had a very small station in there.

TW: I guess the original Kitselas station was pretty big, if they were building those tunnels there. Okay, now we get to your dad, I guess.

10

DV: Dad, he was born in Pennsylvania and he was a big kid. He worked in a steel mill, a steel mill in Scranton [Pennsylvania] and around there. He worked there for a while and then he left and went up to Canada. It is one of the mysteries of why he left.

He got in trouble with somebody or some girl perhaps. Anyway, maybe he just had itchy feet. He left and he worked up near La Pas [Manitoba] and kind of bummed across the Prairies. Thrown in jail for vagrancy, which they used to do. Throw people in jail for vagrancy and they would go and work in some farmers' field to work off their crime. Dad said it wasn't bad. He had a good time, met a lot of farmers. Some of them were cheap, some fed you really well, some of them you stayed for the summer. One place he worked at, they took a cow and put it up in the second story of the barn. I don't know why but that's what they did.

I gather he had a lot of fun. Because he told me one story about working with this guy who I believe was from Poland. Maybe he was Ukrainian or something; anyway, he didn't have much English, so Dad taught him the names of these various horses and on the teams were various things such as **** and so on. And the family they were working for at that time were Mennonites and quite religious. So he was a poor innocent guy from Europe running these horses and calling them **** and these other names which wasn't very nice of my dad, but too late now. Anyway, he did this, and so on, and eventually came over to Usk. His story was he was looking for a guy who owed him some money. I don't know if that is true or not.

Anyway, he ended up at Usk. He got a job because he was a teamster with horseshoeing and so on. He got a job running a pack train up the Columario Mine and that time he came by the name 'Slim' because the foreman at the mine asked him if he could handle a six-horse team or an eight-horse team. More than a team, anyway. Dad said, "I can drive them as far as I can see them," because that's the way he talked. And this guy said, "You wouldn't be Slim Moorehouse"—who was a famous teamster from back east. Dad said, "Oh, I might be." Oh, that Slim Moorehouse—so he got the name Slim. Although it wasn't him but he was "Slim" forever after.

TW: Even though he wasn't "Slim."

DV: Yeah, he took the name of somebody more famous and made it his own.

TW: What era was it when he was and got thrown in jail?

DV: I think he worked everywhere.

TW: What era, what time?

DV: Oh, pre-Depression. And of course, it was in Usk that he met my mom and they got married. We used to say or he used to say that he married her because she was the only one he knew of that had a job. My mom was a school teacher. Well, it must have worked because they stayed married all their lives to each other.

TW: When was he born?

DV: 1896.

TW: Approximately eight years older than your mom, more than that. You say your mom was born in 1912, so he was about 12 years…

DV: My whole family, there's always been a discrepancy you know a few years between the men and the women. Anyway, that's what happened. Dad died in 1978, New Year's Day.

TW: With a smile on his face?

DV: I don't know—he passed away and I still miss him.

Slim Varner (sitting) and Dick Adams. 1949. Finished loading boxcar of lumber. The Way We Were Collection via Terrace Public Library.

TW: I have people that knew both you and your dad say that you are a carbon copy. Is that true?

DV: No. No way near.

TW: You deny it, do you?

DV: Yeah, Dad was a good man.

TW: Well, there you are, that lets you out. Okay, I guess we get to you.

DV: To me. Well I was born about 10,000 years ago. My birth date is March 10, 1944. I was born in Prince Rupert. My dad at that time—although they'd lived in Usk when the war started—Dad having worked in a steel mill went down to work in the shipyards in Prince Rupert building Liberty ships [cargo ships built in North America during the Second World War. The Canadian version were actually called Park ships]. He was a riveter. That's where my sisters and I were born. I have an older sister born in '41 and a younger sister born in the year after I was—born in '45, I think. Anyway, Dad worked down there. I got meningitis.

Now, this is an interesting thing. When I was about two years old, I got meningitis, which affected my hearing and so on, my sense of balance, my good looks, but apparently I was just on death's door—they thought I was going to die. The doctor told my mother you just have to prepare for the worst. She got home, but in the meantime, my doctor had spoken to an American. There were a lot of American soldiers around at that time. Spoken to an American doctor who was able to get a supply of penicillin which was only for the American forces that were stationed in Prince Rupert.

TW: Now that is interesting, because it was a Canadian who found it.

DV: Anyways, my Canadian doctor got some of this penicillin, gave me a shot and apparently I just leaped out of bed and started running around. [Laughter.] Truthfully, they noticed the difference, so I am grateful to the Americans for that. Good people—my dad of course being an American, I don't know if that had anything to do with it. I think it was just a humanitarian gesture on the part of the American forces.

Anyway, about 1947 or so, we all moved back to Usk. Dad was in logging and being a teamster he had horses and he went logging with horses and he did that for a long time. I think he was probably the last person in this area to depend on horses for logging until he bought an old D4 Cat. He brought it up from the States. In those days, you could bring stuff up from the States for farming, so of course the Cat was for farming—you wouldn't have had a blade or winch on it. When he got it up here, he decided to go logging, so he had a blade and a winch installed and away he went.

TW: He used to pole a lot of logs, too, didn't he?

DV: Well, that is mostly what he did, was push poles. He did other stuff, too.

TW: Poles being the primary source of income. Can you talk a little bit about your childhood in Usk?

DV: My childhood? Still in it, you know. [Laughter.] I didn't know we were deprived. We didn't have TV or public transportation. When you wanted to go somewhere, you walked. It was pretty good—we didn't have restrictions, and we didn't worry about being molested and so on. My parents were happy if I just went in the bush and rode around and came back for supper. Basically that was it. I had chores to do. I had to bring in the wood, feed the chickens, and get the eggs—various other things. My sisters had their things to do, much easier than mine, but still…

TW: Would they concur with that?

DV: I don't see how they could possibly differ. What would they have to do?

TW: Maybe we should send them a copy of this.

DV: Well, we can if you want. Everybody had their stuff they had to do. You would do it and then you were free to do what you wanted. I had friends most of the time. There was other families around.

It's a funny thing; in those days, there was no difference made between whether you were First Nations or anything, you know. You either liked them or you didn't. Everybody was the same, go and visit them in their houses and they come and visit in your house. It didn't seem to be the same segregation as we have now. Not anywhere near the segregation. Maybe I'm wrong because I was a kid—maybe the older people segregated each other, but I know that's not true.

TW: So you would say relationships have deteriorated a little bit in the intervening years?

DV: Maybe it's just my age speaking, yeah, I think relationships have deteriorated.

TW: You once told me you went to school in Pacific?

DV: I went to school in Usk Elementary from grade one to five. That would have been from 1950 to June of '56. In fall of '56 the town of Pacific, a railroad town about 12 miles down the line from Usk, had a number of kids but they didn't have enough to establish a school. I believe there was 14 children needed and they only had 12 or something. So they made an offer to my mom, who was a school teacher—she wasn't practicing then but she still had her papers as a school teacher—if she would come to Pacific with a couple of her kids. They would give her a place to stay in the school house and that's the way it worked. So that is what we did. I went to school in Pacific in 1956/57, I think, if I've got my dates right—in about that time. It only lasted for one year because that was the year they were bringing the diesel engines in, transferring from the steam engines.

Now the steam engines had to have regular stops to re-water and so on and do the various things. They were generally stationed 24, 30 miles apart. Pacific was a divisional point and the next one was in Terrace. They had a big roundhouse in Pacific, they had a water tower, they had an ice house. They used to keep ice for the dining cars. They had a little restaurant there, because I believe it was a half-hour stop for the passengers to go out and have a bite to eat in the beanery.

TW: Of course they needed a roundhouse because the steam engines don't go backwards very well.

DV: I don't know if they minded so much but it is hard to see when you are going backwards.

TW: Diesel engines don't care and what does it matter on a train track.

DV: You should have seen those things—the roundhouse. Great big oily machines and so on. They smelled oily, they smelled like bunker fuel. You couldn't touch it without getting your hands dirty. And spitting steam and so on, it was gorgeous. [Laughter.]

TW: I never heard of a steam engine being called gorgeous. I know people that are aficionados but gorgeous is not a term I've heard before, but anyway.

DV: I got to go in the cabin and it was all brass. Big brass gauges and big levers and so on. Covered in grease, of course.

TW: Just what a small boy loves.

DV: Oh man! But they wouldn't let me take one home. That was Pacific and after that, I came back to Usk. I think there was another year in Usk and then I went to Skeena High School in Terrace starting in '57 I think. The school year '57-'58 was my first year in Skeena. I graduated in '61. My first year was in grade nine.

TW: High school back in those days was nine to twelve?

DV: Yeah.

TW: And then you went on to BCIT [British Columbia Institute of Technology]?

DV: No, I took a couple of years off. Messed around here and there. Did different things. Drove truck. Worked in BC Packing ice plant, Flanders air filter installation, when they were building the pulp mill. Kamyr digesters and so on. Then I went to BCIT. Went there for a year and then I came back to make some more money and then I went back for my final year. Graduated from BCIT, diploma in Mechanical [Engineering] in 1979, June of 1979.

TW: We didn't miss each other by much. I was going to night school then.

DV: What were you in?

TW: I was actually in survey technology. I did it in night school. So our paths wouldn't have crossed. You went from that to...

DV: BCIT was a fairly new establishment then. Nobody even knew what I was trained to do and I had a heck of a time explaining, you know. And going through the unemployment office and they almost got me a job fixing small motors which is not really what mechanical engineering is about. Finally I started with the Department of Highways. It was properly named the Department of Highways, a fill-in job until I could find something better.

Anyway, I got a job on the survey crew and it was all right and then I kinda started getting into it more and I realized that there is a lot more to this than what people think. And then one time, the party chief showed up drunk and started pushing the district tech around and got fired. I kinda lied because I'd been watching him and said I could run an instrument and the district tech knew I was lying through my teeth but he needed somebody. And he took me out and showed me a few of the basics about setting up an instrument, a level to start with and I got used to that and got onto the transit and so on and lo and behold I was the party chief. It was good; I liked it. In those days, I was the only one they'd keep on over the winter and we'd hire engineering aids in the summer. We had a good time. We had a real good crew. We'd go and lay out our line and if things were way ahead of schedule, we'd maybe go and explore around the bush and see if there was a better way to put the road through or looking for gravelly deposits or so on. Yeah, we had a good time.

Anyway, stayed there for 10, 11 years and because I was on top of my pay scale and no place to go, I switched over to the Forest Service. That was properly called in those days the Forest Service, none of this department of this and that and the other thing or ministry. It was the Forest Service. I stayed there for 25 years. That was a good time, too. I found that the people I worked with in the government were all the best people you could hope to meet and the best people you could work with. Very few exceptions.

Varner family pictured with Bill McRae: Kate, Don, John, Slim and Kay with Bill McRae [l-r].
Outside the family home in Usk. Circa 1950. Don Varner Collection.

TW: Me being one of them.

DV: I'm not going to name anyone. [Laughter.] Yeah, it was great. Then I retired in 2007. That's the story of my exciting career.

TW: Do you want to delve into your family career?

DV: My family: I got married in 1976, had two kids, marriage broke up in about 20 years. The kids stayed with me and they are both over in Alberta in around Edmonton. Not that they couldn't stand me, but it's more that there was no work around here for them. That was a bad time, 1990s to 2010. There wasn't that much going on around Terrace. It was pretty hard to get work. So they both moved over there and they are doing well. A boy and a girl.

TW: I guess you talked about what you did in Usk. There wasn't a theatre in Usk.

DV: No, no, Charlie Adam, I believe, did have a theatre. It was located in the Emerson Block on Lakelse Ave, just about where the hotel is now. What do they call that hotel, is it the Inn of the West [Days Inn]?

TW: I think that is what they call it now.

DV: Anyway, across from there. In the old days it was across from the Little House, but that was the Osborne House for a while. Because Osborne took the house and made it into a rooming house. Anyway, that's what it was on the south side of Lakelse Avenue and it was just a big barn-looking building and that is where I saw the "Greatest Show on Earth." When did that come out—in the middle '50s?

TW: Early '50s.

DV: I saw it twice. What a show.

TW: Well, if you lived in Usk, did you come into town to go to the theatre or had you moved into town at that time?

DV: No, more a thing of opportunity. If I happened to be in town. Well, 1950, we'd come to town more or less once a week to go grocery shopping and so on. And then in '57, when I started going to high school, trips were more frequent. So I was in town quite a bit. 'Course I had friends I could stay with. Sometimes they'd come out to Usk and stay there. So that was my experience with the theatre. Then we had the drive-in down towards Braun's Island end of town. That was always kind of neat, too.

TW: I remember you and I saw it being taken down out of the Forest Service office.

DV: Yeah, that's right, yeah. Kind of a shame, you know, what with TV and DVDs and so on, of course theatres are another thing in the past. God, we had a lot of fun in those things. Yes, I know we called it the passion pit, but there were other things, too.

TW: What restaurants were around then? I guess the Inn of the West was around—it was the Lakelse Hotel, wasn't it?

DV: The Inn of the West was the Lakelse Hotel.

TW: Were there any other places like that around town in your youth?

DV: There was the Travellers Café which was sandwiched in, half a block east of the intersection on Kalum and Lakelse so that would be east on Lakelse on the north side of the road. There was a little cafe there which appeared to be about eight feet wide and went the length of the building and so on. That was a good place. They had stools and a counter and that was up against where the cooks and

16

waitresses went in there. I can't remember the name of the people that had it. One of them had worked in the shipyard with my dad.

That's where we used to go. And there was another one down even further east on the south side of Lakelse Avenue. It was on a corner. The door was actually cut out of a bias between—I'm not sure what street it would be. That was a good restaurant. That's the only two I can really remember.

TW: Did you ever go out to the Lakelse Lake in those days?

DV: Oh yeah, we spent a week out there one time and had a hell of a good time. I was about six years old. Of course we took the Old Lakelse Lake Road. It was an hour's drive from Terrace. It was pretty narrow and windy and rough. We went to the cabin one time.

TW: The cabin?

DV: I am not sure where it was—we rented a cabin. I broke my arm when I was about 5 years old. That would have been pinpointed to about 1949. I had this enormous cast on my arm and it was good for hitting my sister with.

TW: Which they greatly appreciated.

DV: It was good for me, maybe not for them. I was a mean little kid—I must have been. I never thought it at that time. No, no, I was just defending myself. [Laughter.]

TW: I think we should send a transcript to them and get their comments. [Laughter.] Any other activities outside the home?

DV: We used to play ball at Usk during the summer. If it wasn't raining, we'd go down to the ball diamond, we called it the ball diamond. It was actually a ball diamond set up back in the Depression days. Dad and a bunch of other guys—they flattened out an area there and set up a screen and had a ball game. Anyway, we used to go down there and play softball. You remember the kind where you get your position established and then when somebody went out everybody would move up—third base, second base, first base, catcher, or whatever it was—do you remember that?

TW: Three people at bat and when you went out to left field and centre field and right field. That way you could use your kids and still make a team.

DV: And if you got a good hitter, you'd more or less have to trip him up or do something—you wouldn't get him out.

TW: We used to have a rule, five hits and you're out.

DV: That was a big thing, we never played football. Why didn't anyone play football? We played ball—real ball.

TW: Do you remember any of the local events that you celebrated like Remembrance Day or Victoria Day, any of those things?

DV: Well we used to have—before the Pioneer Store burnt down in 1951 and even after it was— Christmas concerts, remember those, and the kids would all get up and display their talents and afterwards there'd be a dance if you could find someone to make music and so on. You could always find somebody to get drunk. We used to have those, but they stopped in the middle '50s. They don't seem to go over so well anymore. But I remember those.

TW: Well, you pretty well covered what you remember of downtown Terrace. I guess you remember the L.H. & K. Mill and Pohle Lumber.

DV: What I mostly remember, is holy smokes, they paved the middle lane. Before that, it was all gravel and good parking and then they went and ran a ribbon of pavement right down the middle there. The shoulders were still gravel and so on. Oh, talk about class.

TW: That was '51 when Queen Elizabeth paid a visit?

DV: No, the Queen wasn't in '51, she was much later in 1950s. 1950—I'm not sure when she did come up here, but it was much later than '51. I thought it was 1955—I'd have to look it up. [It was 1959.]

TW: I'm sure it is recorded some place. That was the occasion the street was paved.

DV: I wasn't in Terrace at the time.

TW: Where were you? Oh, you were in Usk. Were your folks members of the Co-op?

DV: I remember the Co-op before it was the big Co-op. It used to be a little one. Bought a pair of gumboots for three dollars. The original Co-op was more or less where the gas station was. Yeah it was up there, right across from the drugstore. You could go across the street and there was the Co-op. Who didn't know the Co-op—that was the big box store in Terrace? 'Course they had the cafeteria upstairs.

TW: That was always a favourite of yours.

DV: Everybody who was anybody in Terrace went to the cafeteria up there. There was more or less a group of people that held court up there—they'd go up there around noon and have their sandwiches. It was a pretty good place to get a decent lunch for a reasonable price. It was a shame when they lost the Terrace Co-op, because there was a lot of people in there you could go and socialize with and they knew you, you know.

TW: It was more than a store.

DV: More than a store. I still got a lot of Co-op tools. What the heck was their brand name? You know what I mean. Lots of tools.

TW: Every once in a while, I still find some tools with Coop labels on it. Back in your youth, what did most people do for work? What was the main employment?

DV: Well, it was logging—this was always logging country. There was logging, there was the railroad, there was the government services, highways, and there was a little bit of mining. But the big one was logging. I don't have the numbers to prove it. But I am sure that over half the people made their living one way or another from the woods.

Especially after 1948, when they issued TFL [Tree Farm License] #1, that was more or less a new thing, and to have Columbia Cellulose have a guaranteed source of wood, it made an awful difference. It wasn't just small-time loggers. Of course, it did drive a lot of small-time loggers out of business, per se. If you weren't logging for Columbia Cellulose, a lot of times you weren't logging, unless you were like my dad, taking poles, and then you worked for Bell Pole. You had a couple of options there. You could always cut down poles and sell them. That was never a problem.

TW: Your dad was mostly a pole logger.

DV: Yeah he was.

TW: Because he was stubbornly independent?

DV: He was a Dutchman—Pennsylvanian Dutch. Yeah, he was. A lot of people he would not work for. Not unless he had... ??

TW: Did one of them sell him a go-devil?

DV: Yeah. [Laughter.]

TW: How did the community interact with the police? I guess Usk didn't have a police force, did it?

DV: No, we hardly ever saw the police. And when we did it was, "Hi, what are you out here for?" I remember oh, it would have been about grade three or so, the police came up to the school to give a talk about—I don't remember what the talk was about—I guess about obeying the law or something. Oh yeah, we just worshipped those police officers. Yeah, it was great. But they wouldn't show us their firearms. They had firearms. Do you remember the old holsters that would flap on? They wouldn't take them out.

TW: Do you remember the impact of Kitimat and Alcan?

DV: No, not really, because it was all taking place way down there. One of my friends had a brother who was working during the days when they were building it. This was back in 1953, and he got a chance to go down there and I was so envious, but that's really the only impact that I saw.

I remember when they opened up the highway—would have been '61. I drove to Kitimat and drove back. I am not even certain of that date. I wasn't old enough to drive—I didn't get a driver's license 'til 1960.

TW: You were the driver, were you?

DV: Yeah, I drove, and my dad drove one car and I drove the other one. I remember, *Whoa, look at this road it's so straight and so smooth and there's no hills hardly.* [Laughter.] I remember Highway 16 between Terrace and Hazelton: sometimes it was impassable because of mud holes, and I remember my dad used to tell this story—which was not true—about this one mud hole which was fairly close to where he was logging and this woman came by and got in the wrong rut and got stuck and Dad came over to help and pull her out with the horses.

He said, "You are the second pregnant woman I pulled out this week." And she said, "I'm sorry sir to inform you that I am not pregnant." "I beg to inform you that you are not out of this hole, either." [Laughter.] I don't believe that is true—I don't think it is true.

TW: Did he ever tell your mother that story?

DV: Oh, that was one of his favourite stories. He told everybody that story. Just like the story how he got the name Slim. Occasionally we'd have company and visitors and they'd ask him how he got the name and all of us kids would groan because we'd heard the story so many times. So this mud hole was one of his stories and probably not true.

TW: Were there any of those major mud holes between Usk and Terrace?

DV: Oh, yeah, there was—let's see, there was one at Swede Creek, there was another one at Edgar Creek. I'm sure there were other ones just developed here and there. Swede Creek is near Gitaus subdivision now. Edgar Creek is on the Terrace side of—I think they call it Fall Creek but the original name was Edgar Creek. Just west of Gossen Creek subdivision. I remember those two and you had to kinda plan your way through them because if you got in the wrong rut or the wrong wallow you were going to be stuck. Yeah, in particular during spring break-up it was pretty bad.

TW: And all the whisky creeks were east of Usk, were they?

DV: I'd like to know if those names were ever really real, but ah—that was a shame when they took down all the sign posts.

TW: You'd better elaborate, because people won't know.

DV: Well, from east of St. Croix there was Dewar's Creek, Johnny Walker Creek, there was Seagram's, probably a couple more. It was just a series of creeks and they were all named after good stuff.

TW: Good Canadian whisky.

DV: Yeah, we didn't have any scotch or things like that or bourbon, God help us. [Laughter.] No, it was just whisky, good honest whisky. And there was a Whisky Creek too. Couldn't think the name of a whisky—just got stuck with whisky.

TW: But they've changed all those names now, have they?

DV: I think a lot of them are just culverts and so on. You go across and you never even know it. Like Scree Creek between Terrace and Amesbury.

TW: You don't know it's there, you don't know it.

DV: So what else have we got?

TW: We've pretty well covered all their questions. Now comes the fun part.

DV: The floodplains.

TW: Do you remember the flood: that's one of the questions here that I didn't touch on.

DV: Oh, yeah the flood—good old floods. The flood of '48 is the first one I remember. I was four years old—our house was up on a bench and Usk Hotel was on the lower part of the bench and I remember sitting on the bank with my dad looking at this hotel. The water was up to the second storey—just about onto the second storey—and the proprietor of the hotel, a gentleman by the name of McGillivray who had a wooden leg, was standing there on the second storey yelling something to my dad about the water, I remember that. That was the '48 flood. There were a couple of minor floods in between. There was one earlier in the mid-'60s, and then the next big one was in '72, which was fairly high. And the last one, of course, was 2006/2007. And that one was strange, because the flood record for the water gauge at Usk showed a certain level of water which was lower than the one in '72. The actual water level was higher. It was measured on a house there that I know and various other places. So, I don't know if the gauge was wonky or what, but anyway, they were all pretty high floods.

TW: What about 1978?

DV: Oh, that was nothing. That was a false flood that was nowhere—it wasn't a real—it was more all the little creeks were running wild but the Skeena River.

Tw: You told me once it took out 25 out of 28 major structures between Terrace and Hazelton.

DV: I tell you that? I was probably lying. But, anyway, it took out a lot of them. But the Skeena River level was not that high. All these little creeks were running wild and I saw them taking out the bridges but the river itself didn't flood, so I don't know how you'd tie that in together, and I know that Lakelse Lake was pretty high, too. I guess it all depends on how you define a flood. I say a flood is when the Skeena River comes way up and I start looking out the door and I say, "Oh—that's a flood." But if it's just Kleanza Creek getting all snarky that's just—that's not a flood, that's just a freshet.

TW: I think we should explain to our listening audience that you live on the bank of the Skeena River.

DV: Yes, I do, so if it comes up high enough you might to be in trouble. One year, actually the projected 200-year flood, flooded my basement.

TW: So you are on the flood plain.

DV: It hasn't so far. 1936, I think. The water was supposed to have been very high and it might have been coming close to my basement but it wouldn't be there yet—who's to say. We've probably lived through a 100-year flood—possibly.

TW: Well, according to the flow gauge things that I've read—'35, '36 and 2007 were much closer to the same, and '48 was slightly less. So that's four floods in 70 years.

DV: Yeah.

TW: So, I don't think any one of them is a 100-year flood.

DV: Most of the floods we get is a 25-year flood, is what I feel.

TW: So we've covered most of the points that I had here—the first four, anyway, that deviate from the provided notes were.

Now could you tell us the story of the man who died with a smile on his face?

DV: Well, I can, but it's not going to involve any names.

TW: That's all we want.

Ted Wilson and Don Varner at Heritage Park. 2013

DV: Some of his descendants may or may not know the story. May or may not want to know the story. Although personally I would be proud. There was a gentleman here in the early days—the country was opening up and he was getting on in years. But every so often when he got in to some money—I'm not sure if it was a pension or whatever, he would go and get a couple bottles of some decent stuff and pick up a few of his lady friends and they would have a party. The party often went on all night to the best of his ability I should say. Apparently he was in bed with a couple of these young ladies discussing philosophy and so on and he passed away with these two young ladies.

TW: Did they go with him or just him?

DV: They were there, they didn't pass away—he did. He passed away from an overdose of philosophy.

TW: I see.

DV: And it must have, how do you say—he must have had a smile on his face. I know I would.

TW: Now tell us your mother's version of your dad's story.

DV: Well, Dad told the story in a little more detail. I believe he gave a few names. There's this other organization that used to go around collecting oral histories and they came up to my mom and dad's apartment. They were staying in the Willows at the time. And Dad, who liked to talk, told them this story. My mother was horrified; although she knew the story to be true, she didn't think it should be spread about, especially with the names attached. So when the transcript came back she made it clear to my father in no uncertain terms that story wasn't going to come out. Of course that is why I'm being kind circumspect.

TW: Your mother's influence is making itself felt.

DV: She's still making it felt. I think maybe my dad is maybe hanging his head. He wouldn't be proud of me. But there it is. I'm not the man my father was.

TW: Or maybe you just learned a little bit more from your mother.

DV: Well, there's always that. Judging from past experience, I'm a slow learner.

TW: Your participation in opening the new bridges.

DV: I didn't really have much to do with that. I did help Martin Kind, I believe, he was the carpenter, that did the form work for the two monuments at the east and west end of the bridge. You know you have plaques on them and I was in charge of making a curtain that you could pull the string and it would roll up and unveil these plaques in all its shiny glory because our then-Premier Bill Bennett was going to come up and open the bridge. I was cautioned by the district manager that I should stay close to the monument—to this plaque—in case Bill Bennett couldn't figure out how to pull this string. [Laughter.] This is true—I was told, "You stay right there and if he seems to be confused, reach over there and pull the string"—which I didn't have to do.

TW: You didn't have to insist.

DV: No, he figured it out himself.

TW: Oh, did he?

DV: Yes—amazing.

TW: Finally, so you can get to your beer with Bob. How did you acquire the name "Mayor of Usk"?

DV: I don't know, I think it was the longest—actually, my dad was occasionally referred to as the Mayor of Usk. Or maybe it's hereditary. The other thing is that I've probably lived in Usk the longest and, I'm not sure, I may even been the oldest person there. I turned 70 in March.

I may be the oldest resident there. If there is anyone older, they haven't lived in Usk as long as I have. I got it covered both ways. The Mayor of Usk business was mostly just talked about among friends in a sarcastic way, I think, but then it got put in the paper there when they unveiled the

22

plaque for the 100th year of the Usk ferry. And I have been trying to live it down since because people point to me and laugh.

Doreen Byng Interview

Interviewed by Sarah Komadina, December 2013

Doreen Byng was born in Viking, Alberta, in 1940. Doreen's grandparents, the Houldens, owned land on Halliwell Ave. and raised their family in Terrace. When Doreen was five months old, her parents returned to Terrace to raise their family here. She remembers how hard her mother worked gardening, canning, ironing, doing laundry by hand, and raising her and her eight siblings. Her mother died when Doreen was only 15 years old. After her mother's passing, her father and siblings moved to Vancouver. However, Doreen decided to remain in Terrace with her grandparents to finish high school. Doreen married when she was 20 years old and had three children. Doreen worked as a stay-at-home mother until her children were teenagers. When she returned to the workforce, she worked for a short time at the library, then for the Cancer Control Agency, and finally as a receptionist for Mills Memorial Hospital. In this interview, Doreen talks about her childhood, her children, her parents, and grandparents. She discusses popular downtown locations, Lakelse Hot Springs, the logging industry, and Terrace's boom-and-bust economy. Doreen also recollects her experiences dealing with sexism growing up in the 1950s and later on as an adult.

SK: Looking at how you came to Terrace, you weren't originally born here. Can you tell me where you were born and how your life started?

DB: Well, actually, my mother came here in 1927 with her parents, and I'm not sure when my father came here. My mother grew up in Terrace. My grandmother Jackson came to Terrace from Alberta for a better climate as a result of illness. But they married here. Their first child was born in Prince Rupert and then they moved back to Viking, Alberta — to where my father came from — and my brother John and I were both born in Viking. [Birthdate: November 6, 1940.] But when I was five months old they came back to Terrace, so I grew up here.

SK: So five months old and growing up in Terrace, so you wouldn't remember anything about Alberta?

DB: Nothing about Alberta, no.

SK: And when you were here, how many siblings did you have growing up in Terrace?

DB: Well, eight actually, because there were nine children in my family.

SK: And what was that like?

DB: It was very busy actually. And it's an advantage in a way to have that many siblings, because you have people that you have things in common with. Of the three older children, we all liked to read a lot and always had company walking to school, and things like that, that were positive.

SK: What was your maiden name?

DB: It was Jackson.

SK: And you are related to the Houlden family?

DB: My mother was a Houlden but she married Ford Jackson, and so we were Jacksons, of course.

SK: Is the Houlden family in Terrace?

DB: My grandparents, when they came here, bought 10 acres on Halliwell [Ave], which is down the street from Uplands School. And they came to Terrace because my grandfather was gassed during the [First World] War and lost a lung. They had been living in Winnipeg and the climate was too severe for him. So they moved to Terrace because they heard that it had a mild climate, and he had a friend here and had the friend buy him property.

In his little write up, Uncle Charlie said he thinks they paid $300 for their 10 acres, and they lived in a little cabin-type place over where the college is now. They had a house built for them on the property on Halliwell, and so that is where my mother grew up. And I'm not sure why my father came to Terrace, but he was working here when he was quite young. And they married and raised a family here. I was the third child in my family.

SK: Third generation to grow up in Terrace?

DB: Well, my grandparents were adults, of course, and they had three children. And my grandmother was pregnant when they came here. So my uncle was born in Terrace, but they weren't born here. They were the first generation here.

Doreen [far left] pictured with her siblings: John Jackson, and Eveline Flint (Jackson). Terrace, 1941. Doreen Byng Collection.

My mother wasn't born here. I think she was about seven or eight years old when she came here. But then, my brothers and sisters and I were born here. Actually, at the time my mother was having children, there was no hospital in Terrace. So women either went to Prince Rupert or to Hazelton, because there was Wrinch Memorial Hospital in Hazelton at the time, founded by the United Church. So you went to either one of these localities 'til after the Second World War. When the army left, they left a hospital and the community used it from that time onward. So one of my sisters was born at home, and I think my brother Bill, who was the sixth child, was born in Prince Rupert. And then my sister Donna and my sister Judy were probably born in the hospital in Terrace.

SK: Do you remember your mom talking about what it was like for Terrace not having a hospital? If something even minor happened, what would they do?

DB: Actually, there was a Doctor Stanley Mills. He was the local doctor, and he had a little two-room building in the centre of town, and he did all sorts of things that doctors wouldn't do now. Like he wouldn't do dentistry, but he would pull out really bad teeth. He would do all of that sort of thing in his office. General practitioners did things like removing tonsils and things like that in the hospital, but I would imagine if you needed real surgery, you went to Prince Rupert.

SK: And now your life here, what schools did you attend here in Terrace?

DB: The elementary school at that time was called Riverside, and it was down where the curling rink is now. And then they built Skeena Junior Secondary. When I was in grade seven we moved into that school, and at that time you went through from grade seven to grade 12 in that school. So it wasn't until later that it was separated into a junior high and then Caledonia Senior Secondary separately. So we went all the way through high school in that school.

Doreen's high school picture. Skeena Secondary School.
Circa 1957. Doreen Byng Collection.

SK: Do you have any memories of that school you would like to share?

DB: It was a very ordinary high school, you know. You had all the usual high school basketball and badminton teams, and volleyball, I imagine. And they had high school dances and things like that. But I can't think of anything specially.

SK: And what sports did you play?

DB: Oh, just badminton.

SK: Did you love it?

DB: Yeah, I really enjoyed it. When you are about five feet tall, it's about the only sport available to you. [Laughs] Because being short doesn't matter in badminton but it certainly matters in everything else.

SK: And did you do any extracurricular activities while you were in school?

DB: Well, I was on the student council, and I was the editor of the high school annual club.

SK: When you were going to school, what were some of the things that you and your friends would do, after school or at school?

DB: Well, a lot of kids those days had after-school jobs and that kind of thing. And one of the things I remember that I was thinking about, when doing this thing... it's hard for girls nowadays to believe, but we were not allowed to wear slacks to school. And most of us walked and we lived near the college on the Bench. And we walked to school and we used to wear slacks underneath our skirts and take them off when we got to school, because in the wintertime it was cold and it was wet and snowy and everything. Can you imagine girls not wearing…? I mean nowadays kids wear anything they want to school and I see kids running around in T-shirts and jeans and going out of the school. And I think, *They must be freezing to death.* But I just think that it's outrageous that girls were treated that way during the '50s.

Skeena High School, circa 1957. Coast Mountains School District Collection.

SK: So would you have to wear skirts during gym and things like that as well?

DB: Well, no. You wore shorts to gym class, but you were not allowed to leave the gym wearing shorts. Nobody was allowed to go up and down the halls wearing shorts or anything. You had to be dressed in a skirt.

SK: And what was the reasoning behind that, do you remember?

DB: I don't know; I suppose they thought it wasn't appropriate for a girl to wear trousers.

SK: And what were your parents doing? Were your mom and dad both working?

DB: My father worked in the woods. He was working in logging, in milling — that sort of thing. My mom was a stay-at-home mother, which most of the moms were when I was growing up. I can't remember any of the mothers of my friends working. In fact, I can remember being really surprised that my friend Louise's mother could drive. Because my mother couldn't drive and it would never occur to her to learn how to drive. But then in those days, most families had one vehicle, or a pick-up, or a car. And Dad took it to work anyway, so a lot of mothers wouldn't have anything to drive even if they could drive.

SK: And for your mom, being a stay-at-home mom, was that good and comforting and nice to have?

DB: Actually, women in those days did so much work at home. Families — almost every family — had a vegetable garden. There was no produce constantly shipped in the way it is now. And people didn't have a vegetable garden because they loved to garden; they had it because they wanted the food.

It is now becoming fashionable again for people to grow a garden, but women like my mother grew a garden. They spent a lot of time doing laundry because they had wringer washer machines and everybody hung their laundry out on a line, and ironed all kinds of clothes. And my mother did a lot of canning. Women then canned fish and fruit from their fruit trees. We had cherry trees and plums and things like that.

So mothers did a huge amount of work, and I would say it was more a necessity than a pleasure. I don't know how a family with eight children could have possibly managed if they didn't have a stay-at-home mother.

SK: And do you remember your mom being super exhausted growing up, or upbeat? What was she like with eight kids and gardening?

DB: I would say more exhausted. She wasn't an organized person, which made it harder. Some women had huge families. There was the Johnston family here that had 16 kids and Mrs. Johnston, I think, was a much more organized person. And I think by the time she had some of the younger children, some of the first children were adults anyway. But actually, we were a fairly large family but we certainly weren't one of the biggest. Lots of families had 10 and 12 kids, so it didn't seem so unusual, whereas now if you had eight children it would seem huge.

SK: And what about growing up into your teenage years? We were talking a little bit of when you moved away from your house before we started the interview and there was a document that was found behind a wall that was returned to you. Do you mind telling me about that?

DB: Oh, actually not at all. It was an honour roll certificate, and in those days, if your marks were high enough and you passed from one grade to the next one, you got an honour roll certificate. I had just stuck it up on the wall in my bedroom. And actually, my mother died when she was 36. And so I was 15, and my father and some of the children moved to Vancouver, but I stayed in Terrace and lived with my grandparents to finish high school. So when I left, I moved out of the house and left this certificate on the wall. And years and years later, my niece moved into that house, and when they went to do a renovation, they found my old certificate on my wall under the gyprock. So she gave it to me, and I was really pleased to see it. I had forgotten all about it; it's from June 23rd, 1955, and so now I have it framed.

SK: And do you remember looking at that, when you were growing up, in your bedroom? Because it would have been on your wall, so you would have been just looking up at the wall.

DB: I know and I didn't think when I left… I didn't really think about the fact that the house would be sold, and if I had thought of that I probably would have taken it with me. But everything happened very suddenly, so it just got left there. But it was really fun having it back, and I am really impressed when I look at it and look at the way the principal probably filled the certificate in. And his writing is really amazing, compared to the handwriting of people nowadays.

SK: And so part of your family moved to Vancouver and you stayed with your grandparents. Did other siblings stay with you?

DB: No. My brother John had stayed in the area but he had moved out on his own and he was working. So we were the only two that stayed here and the rest all left. After I graduated from high school, I got a job working in the local post office and then eventually I married, had children, and was a stay-at-home mom myself.

SK: What was living with your grandparents like?

SB: Actually, I really enjoyed it. They lived downtown rather than on the Bench so I got to play badminton at the local civic centre. And it was interesting because my grandmother was an extremely independent woman with a far more forward attitude than my mother had ever had. So it was interesting living with a woman with a completely different attitude toward life.

Doreen's grandparents, Mabel and Harry Houlden. Pictured here at their home on Halliwell Avenue. Circa 1930s. Doreen Byng Collection.

SK: And what were their names?

DB: My grandfather was Harry Houlden and my grandmother was Mabel Eveline Houlden.

SK: So they were the ones who came from Winnipeg to Terrace?

DB: Yes.

SK: Was going from a household — like a full household and then a household of just you — was that an adjustment?

DB: It was different, in a way, but my grandmother used to have boarders. And at the time I moved in with them, she had two boarders living there. They had both worked in banks and eventually they were transferred on. I was in grade 12 by then, and I think she decided she wasn't going to carry on doing that, so finally there were only the three of us. But then when I started working, I moved out on my own.

SK: And where did you move to?

DB: Oh, my girlfriend and I rented a small house and we lived there for a few months. And eventually she moved to Victoria and I married.

SK: How did that situation go?

DB: About typical. Most kids think that it's going to be wonderful living on their own. We found we weren't used to the fact that you have to make your own meals, and do dishes, and do laundry, and all those sorts of things. I think it's what happens to every 18- or 19-year-old who moves out on their own.

SK: When did you get married?

DB: I was barely 20 actually, and I had met a young man who worked at Finning Tractor in Terrace, and I had only known him for six months. We married. A year later I had my first child, so I had stopped working when I was about five months pregnant. And so I stayed at home and learned how to look after a baby.

SK: And what was that like? I mean, 21 years old…?

DB: I was 21 when David was born. I am 73 now and he is 52, and it's hard to believe he is that old already. But I was very lucky because I actually had three little boys, and they were all quite large babies, and they were all really good. So I never had a cranky, crying baby; they were actually really fun.

SK: You had three boys and what years were they born?

DB: '61, '63, and '65.

SK: And was it a busy household, especially when they were walking around?

DB: When they were tiny, yes, it was. Actually, we had moved from Terrace to Vancouver, and then we moved to Burnaby, and then we moved to Nanaimo; my husband was transferred around. We moved to Nanaimo when Gregory was almost a year old, and then when he was about two-and-a-half, we got transferred back to Terrace. So we came back.

My grandmother had moved into a smaller house, so we actually lived in my grandmother's old house for about a year, and built a house on the Bench and moved into that. So my children grew up on Thomas Street close to Uplands School, so it was really good.

SK: Was that here?

DB: Not in this house.

SK: So you grew up on the Bench as well as your children. So, to have that similarity what does that make you feel to know that?

DB: It was really good, actually, at the time when we built that house. It was on three acres, so we had a little bike trail that they rode through the woods. And they rode around the neighbourhood on their bikes.

Actually Terrace is a really great place for kids to grow up in. At that time, you were allowed to fish for trout in Spring Creek. About the time David was 12, he used to go down and sit and fish. So all of these children that were growing up on the Bench tended to be friends and they had a really good time. I think Terrace is a great place for kids to grow up in.

SK: And for yourself, were you working at all during this time or were you staying at home?

DB: No, I stayed at home until my children were teenagers, and then I went back to work part-time in a library for a year or so, and then I started doing some work for the Cancer Control Agency. And I gradually learned how to type on my own. Usually you go to college for a couple of years and you train to be a medical stenographer. But I just gradually began doing it, and picked it up, and so that is what I did. When I went back to work finally, I worked in patient reception at the hospital, and I worked typing in doctors' offices.

SK: Now going back to work, what was that like?

DB: Well actually, I was quite happy to stay-at-home too, but I had decided to divorce my husband. So he left and I needed to support my family, and so it became necessary to work. So it was really busy, because I wasn't used to working. I was entirely on my own running a house. I had three teenage sons, two dogs, a cat and a budgie bird.

SK: And what year was that?

DB: Actually, I asked him to leave in 1978, and my divorce was finalized in 1980. It takes a long time to get anything through a court system.

SK: And so going back as a woman in the workforce in the '70s/'80s, what was it actually like? Was there any kind of stigma?

DB: Well actually, one of the things I found really interesting is, of course, when you are getting a divorce, you have to hire a lawyer and that sort of thing. And it was a process. And I found I would explain that I had decided to divorce my husband and so on. And I found they invariably said to me, "So I take it then, Mrs. Byng, that you are leaving." And I would say, "No, there are three children and myself and all of the family pets, so we are staying in the family house and he is leaving." There was a real attitude of sorts that the husband had all the rights and ownership and the wife and kids just had to leave and manage as best they can, which of course, having the grandmother that I did, was not my attitude.

SK: And do you think things are different now?

DB: Well, yeah, they are, because most women work now, so it wouldn't have been much of an issue. But even when I was having my children, many wives stayed at home — so you were in an inferior financial position — whereas now there are wives who earn as much as their husbands and sometimes even more, and they would not find it as difficult to support themselves as women in my day did.

SK: So what did your boys do? And what did you do once all of this settled down?

DB: Well, by that time David was 18; he had graduated and he had started working for the Department of Highways, and moved out into his own apartment, and had about the same experience that I did. After some time of living on his own, he came back and said, "Can I please come home?" So he moved back home.

The youngest, Gregory, when he graduated went to Carleton University in Ottawa, so he was a long way from home at 17. He went to the university in Ottawa until he got an honours degree in economics. And then eventually he went to the University in Montreal, and also he went to the University in Paris for a year. Yes, so he had a master's degree in philosophy.

And David, of course, went around being transferred around the province working for the Ministry of Highways. And now he is deputy minister in Victoria, and he works for Shirley Bond who is a Minister of Tourism and Labour and things like that.

And my middle son actually died in a car accident when he was 31.

SK: So we can go into some recreational questions, like some of the restaurants that were popular?

DB: Oh goodness, the only two restaurants that I remember from when I was really young was the cafe called the Silvertip Café, that was run by a Chinese man — and I have no idea what his name was—but it was very popular. And there was a little corner snack bar called the Snack Bar, run by Mrs. Lambly and her husband. She was Flossie Lambly and her husband's name was Geoff, and I'm sure you must have heard about them from other people. Anyway, all the teenagers went there after school. It was really… What was that old television show that had teenagers in it? I can't remember the name of it now. Oh, the guy that started it and eventually became a director.

SK: Fonzie. *Happy Days.*

DB: Yes! *Happy Days.* It was a bit like that. They didn't dance in there, of course, but they had a jukebox, and people bought milkshakes, and that sort of 1950s snack bar. And people went to the Silvertip Café. A lot of adults who went out in the evening went there to have Chinese food and then went home. Those are the only two restaurants that I actually remember from when I was that young.

SK: And also, too, what are some of the other things that were here that may not be here now? Were there arcades or maybe roller skating?

DB: Actually, really early on, when I was in Riverside School, there was a great big civic centre there that was the drill hall for the army. And it had a concrete floor, and kids did roller skate there. Kids brought roller skates to school and roller skated there at noon. And I think it might have burned down eventually. Anyway, it's not there.

But there was a civic centre about where the George Little Park is now. People used to play badminton there at night, and they used to have dances and things, and eventually, I think, that also burned. And we do not have a civic centre now, which is too bad, because it means there isn't an appropriate place for a lot of those things.

SK: Was Terrace smaller when you were growing up than it is now — population-wise?

DB: Oh yeah, it was tiny. Actually I think that it became a village about the time my grandparents moved here, but it was really a small place.

SK: And was there a road to Kitimat then?

DB: No. Those things I am a bit vague about. But actually, when they were building Kitimat, the only way to get to Terrace from Kitimat was by train. So yeah, it's hard to imagine.

SK: Was there a movie theatre here?

DB: Yes, there was actually, and it was down…do you know where Gemma's is now? That's where it was. It was run by a man called Charlie Adam. We all used to go to the show on Saturday afternoon. And I remember when *Cinderella* first came here; my sister Donna was about six, and we were all thrilled at the idea she could go see it. It was *Snow White* because there were dwarves in it.

We thought that Donna would love this movie and she hated the whole thing, and she hated the dwarves, and it was a giant failure. And we were all — as her brothers and sisters — we were all disappointed that she didn't like it.

Actually, I have a picture of Donna and Judy, when they were little; they were very cute when they were little. My sister Judy has Down's Syndrome. But they were really cute and she is now. Judy is exactly 10 years younger than I am, and I'm 73, so she is 63. Most Down's Syndrome people didn't used to live that long, so she has done very well actually, and she lives in Kamloops.

SK: What sibling were you?

DB: I was the third child and Judy was the eighth. And then my sister Doris was born in Prince Rupert, and that was when my mother died. She had a sister named Doris living in Prince Rupert, and Aunty Doris and Uncle Dom took the baby home from the hospital, and they eventually adopted her, so she grew up in Prince Rupert. She is in Calgary now.

SK: One question I did have was about the hot springs. Did you ever go to the Lakelse Hot Springs?

DB: Yes, actually at the time my children were young enough to be taking swimming lessons, the hot springs were open, and I used to take Gregory out there for swimming lessons. And it was actually open, I would say, when I was 19 or so. I don't remember going there particularly because I can barely swim and I hate swimming, but it was there and I remember that one of my friends from the high school worked there.

SK: What were some of the things your friends did?

DB: I think it was more of a tourism type of thing actually, at the time, and I don't remember since I'm not that interested in swimming. I don't honestly remember that much about it other than that it was a great advantage being able to have swimming lessons from the point of view of safety.

SK: Do you remember any significant local events — parading in the streets or anything like town parties?

DB: Not really. A lot of that stopped in a way when the civic centre wasn't available any more. I mean, there were all the usual May Day parades and the November 11th type of thing and so on, but I don't remember anything particularly significant.

SK: Downtown Terrace…you mentioned a little bit about the restaurants, but was there anything down there that you remember that is still there or maybe gone?

DB: Not really. The little house on the corner that was the police station has been there as long as I can remember, and it had all sorts of different things in it over the years, but at least it's still the original old building. Terrace doesn't have a lot of old buildings.

SK: Some of the logging and forestry, when you were growing up, what kind of role did that play for you?

DB: Well, my father worked as a loader, working for a man named Dale who had a little logging outfit, and eventually he and my uncle had a mill together. And that was when my mother died, and within a year or so he decided to move to Vancouver. So that is really the only type of employment he had, so that was about it. And my uncle Alec, of course, had Houlden Logging.

SK: So, would you have witnessed the shutting down of the mill and then, of course, the reopening last year? How did that change over the years when you were growing up, and how did that change the community?

DB: Well, actually, it had a huge influence on the community because logging and milling and those sorts of things were about the only kind of employment. So if IWA [International Woodworkers of America Union] went on strike or something like that happened, the town just shut down in a way.

When I was in grade 12, I got a job working in the store called Five to a Dollar in the summer. But I eventually just got laid off because an IWA strike or something was happening at the time. There just were no customers because if logging wasn't doing well, people just had no work really.

Terrace has always been a boom and bust kind of town, because things would just go really well, and then slow down, and then start up again. It seems to be quite busy right now.

SK: And with that too, how did the community of Terrace interact with Kitselas and Kitsumkalum?

DB: I really wouldn't be aware of that, because when I went through school, there were always First Nations kids in school and we were always friends with them the same way we would have been friends with anybody else. I find all of these things, all of the problems about Aboriginal people and so on, really didn't exist when I was kid because people were always really decent and were all friends with one another. So I don't remember these problems.

SK: And, more generally, how has Terrace changed over the years? Is there anything you would like to point out?

DB: I don't think so, actually. I think in a lot of ways it's the same.

SK: Is there anything else you would like to add about the Houlden family that you think should be recorded?

Terrace Co-op. Mantel Collection.

DB: My grandfather was one of the first people who founded the Terrace Co-op, which went on for years and years. My uncle Alec was very active in it and was the president at times and that sort of thing. Both my uncle Alec and his wife Judy Houlden were very good local citizens. I mean, not only did he do all these things like serving on the board at Terraceview [Lodge] and serving on the hospital board, all the kinds of things he did, but she did all of these things that stay-at-home women did then, like Meals-on-Wheels, and canvassing for Salvation Army.

I remember because she made me help. And she used to do book sales for the local library, and I remember Gregory and I having to go down to the Co-op Friday nights and sell books — this sort of thing. So I would say they were very stalwart local citizens. And that's one thing that people forget: that these women, who were at-home women, they did all these kinds of things for the community. And now, with most women working, it's really hard to find volunteers to do things.

SK: Is the Houlden family still living in Terrace today?

DB: I have cousins who are still here, of course—the Houlden cousins. And my brother John still lives here, and he has two daughters who live here. Yeah, there are quite a few Houldens still here.

SK: Now also growing up in Terrace and staying in Terrace, you moved around a little bit but you came back. So what is comforting about Terrace?

DB: It was very interesting in a way because I was living away for six years, and in that six years I lived in three different places. I've made friends in three different places and I've made friends wherever I moved. When I came back I was really shocked in a way, that people were in small groups, and in the time that I was gone, they really haven't met different people.

I think if you stay in a community all your life, you're very comfortable just having the same group of friends, and in a way, I thought they were missing something. A lot of people came to Terrace but they hadn't made friends with them. And I think it's very interesting to meet new people, and it's a shame to stay in your slot and not mix with new people.

SK: Are you still meeting new people today?

DB: Sometimes. I find that sometimes the older women I've met around here like Mamie Kirby, who must be 91, and Ruth Shannon, who I got to know in the hospital auxiliary… Ruth is 85… And I think for my age, it's really interesting meeting people who are either older than you or younger than you. I would never want to live in one of those retirement communities.

Ernest "Ernie" Edward Sande Interview

Interviewed by Mike Folkema, 21 October 2013

Ernest "Ernie" Edward Sande was born in Terrace on May 15, 1950. His father, Raymond Ernest Sande, worked at the sawmill and in logging. Active in the forestry business for generations, his father operated the Sande Sawmill after the retirement of his grandfather. Ernest attended Kalum School, then graduated from Skeena Junior/ Senior High School. He was active in the high school's swim club, the Hot Springers Swim Club, and he also worked as a lifeguard at Skoglund Hot Springs. After retiring from the sawmill business in 1966, his father worked as a pilot for Trans Provincial Airlines. Ernest was a mechanic's helper for the airline. He attended university and learned to fly. In 1971, the Sande family started their own commercial flying business, BC Yukon Air Service, operating out of Watson, Yukon and Dease Lake, BC. In 1990, Ernie returned to Terrace to take a position with Northern Mountain Helicopters. He describes his career as a pilot, flying both helicopters and fixed-wing aircrafts. In the latter half of the interview, Ernest recalls how life in Terrace has changed since the 1960s. He notes the growth of the recreation and arts industry in Terrace.

MF: Where and when were you born?

ES: I was born in Terrace, May 15th, 1950, in the Red Cross Hospital, which used to be up on the hill off Park Ave. right up against the hill there. It's close to where the swimming pool is now. Those buildings have just recently been demolished here, in the past year.

MF: Can you tell me about your parents?

ES: My dad's name is Ernest Edward Sande. My dad's parents were Ernest Sande and Edna Sande, and they came to Terrace—probably in the early forties, about 1944. It was the sawmill and logging business that brought them here. My dad was born in 1930 while his family was living in Sinclair Mills. Sinclair Mills was a small sawmill town along the Fraser River about sixty miles east of Prince George. My dad was actually born in Prince George as there were no medical facilities in Sinclair Mills. Dad's family came to Terrace—I don't know the exact year but it would have been around '42, '43, '44— somewhere around that time.

My mother's name was Colleen Elizabeth Sande. Her parents were Ed and Eva Whalen, and they first moved to Terrace around 1939. My mother was born in Grand Prairie, Alberta. They came from Alberta initially to Smithers, I think, and then ended up in Terrace around 1939.

MF: And your siblings—can you tell me a bit about them?

ES: I have a sister three years younger, and I have a brother that's 10 years younger. They were both born in the Red Cross Hospital as well. Shortly after my brother was born, Mills Memorial Hospital opened up, but he was born in the old hospital, same one that we were before Mills opened. They are both still living in Terrace.

MF: Can you tell me about your grandfather?

ES: My dad is Raymond Ernest, and I am Ernest Edward, and my granddad Sande, was Ernest Courtland.

MF: And he came to Terrace for the first time in…?

ES: Be around forty-three or forty-four. And that's when he brought the family here.

MF: Your grandfather was always involved with the sawmill/logging business as I recall. What about your parents?

ES: Well, I guess it would be probably 1958 that my granddad Sande retired. At that time my dad took over the running of the sawmill—basically became in charge of it. And then that continued from—I guess it would be until about 1966 when the sawmill shut down. Prior to fifty-eight, my granddad was actively involved in the logging and sawmill operation. My dad was involved as well, but after fifty-eight. Dad could tell you about that. But that was when he retired and Dad basically took over the primary running of the sawmill, or the responsibility for it. After the mill shut down is when he started to fly commercially with Trans Provincial Airlines. He had always been flying, I think since about 1953 or '54 as a private pilot.

On my mom's side, her parents weren't involved in the logging industry to the same extent that we were. Although my grandpa on my mom's side—my mom's father—did work in the sawmill from time to time, a little bit. But he also had a place out at Lakelse and used to have a few cabins in the summer time that he used to rent out. They called it Sunset Cabins. Used to rent boats.

MF: And— growing up in Terrace, what would be a typical day in your childhood?

ES: Well, if we start at school age, my sister and I both went to Kalum School. It is now a resource centre and it's over on the same property where the school board office is and the school district maintenance office is also over there. It's a very old school. I believe my parents went to school in the same area—possibly part of the time in the same building. There also was an old high school over there that I think my dad attended. So both my parents were in school here, as well as myself. I went from grade one to grade seven in Kalum School and from grade eight to grade twelve in Skeena High. It was Skeena Junior/Senior High School at that time.

A typical day for me growing up in my elementary years—I had a good buddy across the road named Don Parmenter. We would go to school during the day and after school we would be out playing football in the field and if we weren't at my parents', hanging around my place, we would be over at his place. And another close friend I had was Dave Taft. I lived down on the corner of Olson and Eby during that time—during my elementary years—and the Tafts lived on the east side of Eby, about half a block away. The Parmenters lived on the west side, maybe about a half a block away. If you lived on the west side of Eby you would attend Kalum School, and if you were on the east side of Eby you would attend Riverside School. So Don and I went to Kalum, and David went to Riverside.

When I got into high school years—at that time there was a swim club started up here in the early sixties. The real moving force behind that was Gordon McConnell. And this is before the days of having a pool in town. So we used to go out to the hot springs and our swim club was called the Hot Springers Swim Club. And that filled a lot of my high school years. I was involved in the swim club—first as a student, and then later I was an instructor and I used to instruct elementary kids on Saturdays and then Wednesdays after school, the high school kids used to come out there. We also had a competitive team. We used to train and then go to local meets in Kitimat and Prince Rupert. I was quite involved with the swim club throughout high school until I graduated in 1968. I guess 1968 was one of the last years that there was a class graduated out of Skeena. And I believe there maybe was one more and then Caledonia opened up. So where I graduated out of Skeena, my sister, who is three years younger, graduated from Caledonia

MF: Do you have any memories of school that you would like to share?

ES: Well, I can remember an interesting one when I was in grade one because we had a fire at the school. We had the main Kalum School and then we had two—I wouldn't really call them portables—I guess today they would be called the portable, but they were small one room buildings that were separate from the main school. And the two grade one classes were in these two portables. I remember the one adjacent to the one I was in caught fire. It was quite a bit of excitement because the fire truck came and there was lots of smoke. And the one thing I remember is the teachers getting everybody outside. This was a fire drill for real—for both the main school and the little schools. The thing that I remember about that was that I knew one of the firemen, so myself and a few of my friends, we waited until the fire truck arrived and we waved at the firemen, and then everybody split. There were teachers chasing kids down the road and everybody just took off. But that was one of the memorable things from elementary school, the fire in grade one. Aside from that I can remember all my teachers, most of them, and being that it was a small town then, there was a lot of kids that I started grade one with, and graduated grade 12 with.

MF: You mentioned your brother and your sister are both still living here in Terrace. Have they moved away, as you did, and come back?

ES: Both of them did for a short period of time. There was a period of time that we had a family flying business. It was in the southeast Yukon and northwest BC from 1971 through to 1988. At different times the whole family was involved in that. But my brother also became an accountant and worked out of Stewart, BC. And then he came back to Terrace and worked for McAlpine as an accountant and more recently—for the past number of years—he has been working as an instructor at Northwest Community College. And likewise, my sister used to work in the family flying business, but she also was going to university and became a pharmacist. She worked for a number of years as a pharmacist in Terrace for Northern Drugs.

MF: What was the name of the flying business?

Ernie and his Stearman at Watson Lake. Ray Sande Collection.

ES: The flying business that we had was B.C. Yukon Air Service. We operated out of Watson, Yukon and Dease Lake, BC. My dad and I were involved in flying locally before we moved north. My first job after graduating from high school, was as a mechanics helper for Trans Provincial Airlines in town here. Trans Provincial operated both from the airport and from a floatplane base on Adel Road, just off First Avenue at Lakelse lake, so I used to split my time between the two places. And that was a summer job for me for the next four years, for about four months each summer. My dad also spent some time as a pilot working for them after he got out of the sawmill business. In 1971, the family moved north to Watson Lake Yukon to run BC Yukon Air Service.

MF: I understand you are retired now.

ES: I did—at the end of 2012, I retired.

MF: So, how did your parents make a living?

ES: Well, probably from when I was born, my dad was involved in the sawmill business—when I was born. And he did that right through until 1966.

MF: And that was always here in Terrace?

ES: That was always here in Terrace. My dad was born in 1930, so when the war years were on, he was too young to be in the war. So the entire time of my living here, right up until the mill shut down, that's what they were involved in, the sawmill business and the logging business.

MF: And then in '66, the sawmill was purchased by which company?

ES: I don't know the exact story of how that went, but basically there were a couple of companies involved in buying it, Skeena Forest Products and Pohle Lumber Company. There were also quite a few timber sales. I don't really know the detailed history about that. But during that time, the mill was basically shut down and then the assets and the property that were involved were purchased by other parties. Once he was out of it, that's when he started to pursue the flying; first as an employee and then he bought the company up in the Yukon, in 1971. And that would be the time when he left Terrace. In fact, we all left Terrace for a number of years, in 1971.

MF: Why did you leave in 1971?

ES: Well, the first couple years I was going to university. At that time I didn't finish a degree; I wasn't sure exactly what I wanted to do. And then I had an opportunity to get involved in the flying business. So in 1971, I moved north and spent 19 years up north involved in the flying.

MF: And can you elaborate a bit more about that? How you spent that 19 years?

ES: When I was going to university was when I started learning to fly. I actually learned to fly down in the lower mainland. I finished most of my commercial license in Terrace here while I was still working for Trans Provincial. And then, during the time that I left Terrace when we had the family business, I was flying fixed wing aircraft. So that would be everything up to and including the size of a twin otter, and it was mostly involved with mining exploration. Some recreational type flying we used to do. And some forestry, more in terms of protection: supported fire camps and some fire patrol, that type of stuff. So that would be in the period when we were gone from Terrace. I did spend one year in Smithers in 1989 and then in 1990 I returned to Terrace. At that time, I had switched from fixed wing flying to helicopters. And so, I flew for the seasons of 1990 through to and including 1994 for Northern Mountain Helicopters out of Terrace. I was working both as a base pilot and actually the last year of 1994 I worked as a contract pool pilot. Which meant I wasn't flying out of Terrace, but rather at various exploration camps, but it was still with Northern Mountain.

MF: Are you still flying?

ES: I quit flying six, seven years ago. We had an aircraft we were flying privately up until that point.

MF: Were you flying both helicopters and fixed-wing at that time still?

ES: During the period from 1990 to 1994, I was flying helicopters commercially, and fixed-wing privately. And then, after 1994, it was only fixed-wing, and only privately.

MF: When did you move back to Terrace, on a more or less permanent basis?

ES: I came back to Terrace in 1990.

MF: And why did you come back?

ES: What actually brought me back was the flying position.

MF: With?

ES: With Northern Mountain Helicopters. Because at that time Terrace was one of about 9 or 10 bases that they [Northern Mountain Helicopters] had.

Ernie Sande & Laurie Thain with the Stearman. (Note of interest: Laurie, an old family friend, is originally from Terrace and was inducted into the B.C. Country Music Association's (BCCMA's) Hall of Fame in 2016. Ray Sande Collection.

MF: Is that company still active?

ES: No, they are not. They were absorbed by Vancouver Island Helicopters, some time after I was working for them. But at that time, when I worked for them, their head office was Prince George. And they were a relatively large company at that time.

MF: Do you remember some of the other people that worked for the company at that time? Going into 1990.

ES: Well, the base manager when I went to work there was Ian Swan. He is now the owner of Quantum Helicopters in Terrace. Prior to my working at Northern Mountain, one of the other base pilots was my brother-in-law, Bruce Chapman. At the time, he got out of flying and decided to pursue a career as a teacher. I basically filled his position when he left. The opportunity was there to fill his position, so for me, coming back to Terrace was something that I wanted to do, because I always liked the town. So when the opportunity came to come back here and fly off one of their bases, which happened to be in Terrace, I took it. And I've been here since.

MF: Did you marry?

ES: I was married and I am divorced. I never had any children from the marriage.

MF: What did you do for fun when you were growing up in Terrace?

ES: Well, at that time, I guess when I would be in my teens—there was a ski hill. It was out on Bornite Mountain. It was kind of a put together by volunteers thing—they had a rope tow up there. Quite often we would go out there with buddies. There was a friend that lived just down the street from us that was quite involved in it. He would pick up usually two or three of us kids to go up there. So quite often the weekends in the winter, we'd be out to Bornite ski hill.

Like I mentioned earlier, one of my big involvements all through my high school years was the swim club. And that was probably something that I did all winter during the school year. There were a couple years that I worked as a lifeguard at the hot springs. At that time it was called Skoglund Hot Springs. That would be during the sixties. It was a different facility then than what is at the hot springs now. The existing swimming pool and resort were not there when I worked there. There were two other pools and a hotel. It was a whole other facility that has since been torn down. Basically if you go out there now, it would be on the other side of the hot pool. Like where the water comes out of the ground. If you go over to the other side there, that's where the resort was that I used to work at. So I was involved in that a couple of summers, as a summer job. And, of course, in the winter time we were out there every Wednesday night and every Saturday. Plus there were a couple years—two, three years—that I was out there every night after school, too. So that was a big thing for me, the swim club.

MF: With Lakelse Hot Springs and the hotel facilities. Why did they take down the ones that you used to use?

ES: Well, I was actually gone when they came down. I don't know the whole story about how that went. I know it was starting to get run-down when I was there.

MF: Run-down in what way?

ES: I think just the facilities were getting a little older. When I first started going out there with the swim club, it was still owned by the Skoglund family. And then they sold the business to—I'm not sure which company, but it wasn't a local company. I remember the last summer that I worked there, it seemed like things were starting to get a little more run-down. And that was about the time that I went north. Some time in the next few years—I don't know when it was that they did it. They built the new resort—or the new pool that exists there now. And at some point the other ones were flattened. But that happened at a time when I wasn't in Terrace, so I don't know exactly.

MF: I guess at that time there wasn't a pool in town.

ES: No there wasn't. That's why our swim club, [the Hot Springers Swim Club], went out there in a school bus. As I said, Gordon McConnell was the one that was really a big push getting the swim club going and keeping it going. There were a number of us that were trying to do a little bit of competing and he used to drive us out there every night in his Volkswagen Beetle. He was pretty dedicated.

MF: I was wondering how you got out there, but that explains it.

ES: Well, there were quite a few of us in one little Beetle.

MF: What restaurants were popular over the years when you were younger?

ES: Okay, well I will have to think about that now. Right across the street from Don Diego's there was one owned by the Wong family, which was a Chinese restaurant. I am just trying to think of what it was called. I think it was called the Silvertip Café. Where there's a bit of a parking lot there now, there were actually buildings all the way down. There was a sports store where the sports store is on the corner. Then there was a pool hall and there was Mac's Barber Shop. A guy named MacKeracher used to run that. That's where I used to get my hair cut when I was a little kid. There was a barber shop in the pool hall. And then, those buildings are gone now with exception to the sports shop, which is still there. Then, right down on the corner was the Rexall Drug Store. That building still stands there. We're talking fifties/sixties.

MF: Early sixties?

ES: Yeah. So, there was that café. I have vague recollections of Flossie Lambly's Corner Cafe. I was pretty young, but I mean there is a vague recollection. I was born in 1950, so that was still going. It would be—I think on the corner where the Tilden people—or National Car Rental—uses the parking lot there. It seems to me that's about where it was. That's a little bit foggy—that memory. But I sort of remember that.

MF: Do you recall attending sporting events in Terrace?

ES: Well, I didn't play soccer or little league. There was little league here during that time. And I believe there was soccer. But for me, the only sport that I got involved in was the swimming. I used to belong—this isn't sporting—but I used to belong to Cubs, when I was younger. And then I belonged to Boy Scouts when I got a little older. Probably right up until around '67, maybe, I was involved in Scouts. Skiing is another one I did, but that wasn't a local team sport type thing.

MF: Were you involved in fishing?

ES: I didn't fish a lot myself. Although during the fifties, my family always had riverboats around. In those days, there were very few people on the river, hardly anybody. The First Nations had their nets out there and a few of them had a few boats, I guess to tend the nets. Through the sawmill, my family were using boats on the river for logging purposes. They used to cut stuff off the islands, up above Kitselas Canyon and then run them by boat through the canyon and down below the canyon. (You can get more information from my dad about that). So, the boats were always around. I got a lot of memories of that as a kid. On weekends, myself and my cousins and my grandparents would be out on the river fishing, as a little kid. It would be a family thing. During my years of growing up as a teenager, I wasn't really all that much into fishing. I spent most of my summers at the lake. In fact, just about all my school years, my summers were spent at the lake. Not in town.

MF: Where would you stay when you were at the lake—at Lakelse Lake?

ES: Well, my parents had a cabin out there. The place where the Hull family is now—there's Lloyd Hull and Gordon Hull and, I guess right about where Lloyd's place is now was about where my parents' cabin was. And that whole piece of property, back to the highway, used to belong to Sande Lumber Mills. Those were just summer places, but we were out there all the time in the summer. And then about 1966, I guess, we moved out there full time. So I lived out there from '66 until the time that I started to go to university in 1970. The place that we lived at that time was the place that my mom's dad and mom had. They used to have a few cabins there. And then when it got to be too much for them, my parents bought it off them and then that's where we lived. So my growing-up years actually kept me at the lake just about the whole time. That meant a lot of water skiing. I had a few friends who were out there. So in addition to the swim club, the other thing that we did a lot of was water skiing.

MF: And you still have a family place at the lake?

ES: It's a different place, but yeah. My brother-in-law and sister and my brother have a place on the west side of Lakelse.

MF: And you are still water skiing?

ES: I did a few years ago. But not as good as I used to be.

MF: Would you leave Terrace to go to visit larger communities, either for business or for recreation?

ES: Well, when I was quite young I can remember going down to the Lower Mainland. My dad had a sister in Burnaby. So for us to go to the big city would be to go to Vancouver. Against say going to Prince George or something like that. I can remember going to Prince Rupert. But Vancouver probably would be the city that we would go to occasionally, just because there were some family ties down there.

MF: And would you fly down there in your own plane—or planes?

ES: Well, no. My dad did fly down there in his own plane, but when I was younger, if we flew down it would be on a commercial plane. Or I went down there on the early ferries. Also by road. I don't know if we ever went to Vancouver by train, but we used to go to Rupert by train.

MF: What do you remember about downtown Terrace? Like where did you buy food? Was there a Safeway then? Or was there some other store?

ES: In the earlier days, I guess when I first start remembering about going shopping, would be at the Terrace Co-op. And I know my parents were some of the earlier members of the Terrace Co-op. I've got memories of going to the Terrace Co-op.

MF: So, your family probably did a lot of shopping at the Terrace Co-op?

ES: Especially in the earlier years. You see, there was a period where we left Terrace for a long time. And a lot of things changed while we were gone. You know, as far as newer stores coming in. But during the fifties and sixties, the store I remember is the Co-op. As far as groceries, I can remember—some of these memories are from when I was fairly young—but there was kind of like a hardware store, I think it was called Johnstone and Michael. And it would be on the corner of Kalum and Lakelse, I guess. And it seems to me, if my memory is right, it would be on the corner where Scotia Bank is, that area there, across from the old police station. And on the main street, I can remember one of the stores we used to go into was called The Hub. There were magazines in there. I think it was a lady named Julie Suracki who had that. A lot of these are memories I have when I was fairly young. And there was a bakery on the main street. And there was men's wear. And there was a second men's wear up there that was Millers. It would be up in the direction of where WCB is now, or Work Safe BC, I guess it is. In that block up there.

MF: If you look back, how do you think the town has changed? Let's say during the time that you have been living in Terrace. What would be the main changes?

ES: Well, if I think back to about 1960—I can remember it was quite a big thing to go to Kitimat, because they had a mall over there. They had a Hudson's Bay store. And they had a good Chinese restaurant. Whereas Terrace never had anything like that in those days.

MF: And that was around 1960?

ES: That was in the sixties. So in the sixties, Terrace had a fairly vibrant downtown core. There were no big box stores here. There was no Wal-Mart. The very first kind of mall that came into Terrace, that I can remember, would be on Lazelle Street, sort of beside where CFTK Radio is right now. I remember—I mentioned Gordon McConnell before, he had a store called Terrace Photo Supply (this is before Sight and Sound). And he sold records in there, and you could get pictures developed. That was in that initial little Lakelse—sort of mini mall you would call it. But aside from that it was more—kind of old style downtown. There weren't the big department stores. You know, there were hardware stores and a few restaurants.

MF: You were looking forward to having more of these larger stores?

ES: Well, I don't know if I was looking forward to it. It's just that it was something we did that was a novelty. It's the same as I grew up without a TV. TV came to Terrace—I believe sometime around 1964. So I grew up listening to CBC radio. And you know, laying awake at night listening to Murder at Midnight and The Fat Man and Rod & Charles on Sunday mornings. And then I remember when TV came here: it was around '63 or '64. It was a big deal and it was a big novelty. And it's like when they put the mall over in Kitimat. But Kitimat never had—still doesn't really have a downtown area. When you look back on it, it was a good time to be in Terrace because my memory of downtown was it was a busy place. There was lots going on the main street. It's just that when something new like that comes, it's a real novelty.

MF: Would you say—from 1960 to 1970 that it was a bit of a boom town?

ES: It was a pretty busy place. I mean, the logging industry was doing pretty well then. You know, my dad could probably give you a little more insight into the reasons why they decided to shut down their mill. But it seemed to me—in my memory—that there was lots of money around, there were lots of jobs. There were also a lot of people in Terrace who used to work in Kitimat but live in Terrace. So, there were a lot of kids that I went to school with, whose parents were, for example, Alcan employees, but they lived and grew up in Terrace. So—yeah, there seemed to be lots of opportunity here. I know there were a lot of people going through school, and getting a job once they got out of school. There was work if you wanted to get it. That's sort of my memory on it. Things may have changed. I remember when things did kind of go flat, you know, later on when I came back. And there's a period of time during the seventies and eighties when, of course, I wasn't around here much. But I remember the seventies as being a pretty good time. There was lots going on. It seemed like everybody had jobs, that I can remember. You know, our parents seemed to all have work.

MF: Would you say that people weren't as concerned about—you know—keeping their jobs because they could find another one fairly easily?

ES: Well, I don't know if I can really answer that one, because in the sixties I was either in school or I was getting out of school and then I was heading off to university. There was summer work and it didn't seem that hard to find a summer job. I wasn't really in the job market yet at that stage. So, those are the memories I have, that it was a pretty good time to be around here.

MF: I was born around the same time as you. And my first visit to Terrace was in 1969; I came with a friend of mine from Ontario. So, it would have been in early June of '69. Both of us got jobs the very first day that we arrived in town; my friend at Pohle Lumber and myself at Skeena Forest Products, the two sawmills here in Terrace. We both kept those jobs for the summer. It was so different than today. That was my memory of it.

ES: Yeah, that was kind of my memory of it. And I wanted to go work for Trans Provincial. So I went and applied for a job and got a job. I wanted to be involved around the airplanes. I sort of have memories of all my friends having jobs. It didn't seem to be as difficult as it is now for kids to get out and sometimes find some work.

MF: What did most people that you knew do for work?

ES: Well, for me, most of the people I was around—or some—were tied to the forest industry.

MF: That, in your opinion then, was the main economic driver in Terrace?

ES: I think it was one of the main ones. I mean, I had friends whose parents did different things. Because I had friends whose parents worked at Alcan. And so, they would work in Kitimat. My best friend's dad had his own business here. He had a business called Skeena Auto-Metal. They did welding and they repaired wrecked cars. That would be the Parmenter family. So, you know, there was other work around here. And other jobs and other businesses, but my family and a lot of the friends I had were in one way either working in the bush or working in the sawmill. It was that way for a lot of my friends, too.

MF: What changes have you seen in the forest industry over the years?

ES: Well, I guess, I have to think about that one. When I left here, my family was getting out of the forest business. And I was actually getting more involved in the aviation business. And then there's a long period of time when I wasn't around. When I came back, I was flying helicopters. So I actually did quite a bit of flying with properties that have to do with the forest industry. And it would be Skeena Cellulose or Skeena Sawmills that I used to fly their employees around. It's hard for me to say what the change would be because I wasn't really involved it in before I left and then when I came back—that's when I started to see it, the way it existed in the 1990s. At that time, it was still very busy around here. It would be the major work for the helicopter company I flew for—would be flying for the forest industry. I stopped flying in 1994 and actually went back to school. So, I went to Vancouver for four years to go back to university. At BCIT and UBC.

MF: To get a degree in?

ES: Well, I started off actually to go back there and further my education as an aircraft structure worker, because I also do aircraft maintenance. I took a course at BCIT for eight months to do with major structural repair. And then I switched from that into education, but in technology education. So then I went and did another year at BCIT. And then a year at UBC. And I ended up with a Bachelor of Education out of UBC. During that period of time—I know things really started to really change in the forest industry around Terrace, after I left. I know when I came back here, things were starting to really deteriorate. You know, there was pulp mill getting in trouble.

MF: What year was that again?

ES: Well, I came back here in '96. And because I came back here and I was involved in education, I wasn't really involved in flying any more or directly with any of the forest industry. But I can remember times when the pulp mill shut down in Rupert and, you know when Eurocan was getting in trouble in Kitimat. And then the SCI [Skeena Cellulose Inc.] was shutting down in Terrace. There was a period of time there when mills were shutting down. I wasn't really involved with doing anything that involved the mills. But I can remember this happening around me. So, there were huge changes here in the last ten or twelve years, after I was not involved with it any more. It was still really busy the last time I was working as a pilot here, in '94. I mean—that's what we did. One way or another we were involved with the forest industry. For just about all the flying off the base here. But there were quite a few years where there wasn't any sawdust being made in Terrace.

MF: In regards to the First Nations, how did the community of Terrace interact with Kitselas and Kitsumkalum?

ES: If I think back to my high school years—going back to grade one and all the way through—there were First Nations students in my classes. But I remember that they were a minority in the classes. So in other words, there were way more non-First Nations than First Nations. And that's sort of my memory of going right through high school, right up to my graduating class. Although I've got some friends who I graduated with that are First Nations that are still in Terrace. But I guess those would be my memories. If I look back through my annuals, through all the classes there were always First Nations kids in the classes. But, there were a lot fewer First Nations, especially into later years.

I did all my schooling in two schools, with the exception of kindergarten. At that time there was a kindergarten run by Vi Siemen. And most of the kids of my generation that went to kindergarten school went through her kindergarten. It was on Kenney Street, not that far from where Kalum School is.

MF: When you were a child, what did you expect or hope to accomplish? Did you have any dreams or ambitions of what you would do for the rest of your life?

ES: I was a little bit unsure when I left here. I, like a lot of the kids in my graduating class, went down to university. In my case, I went to UBC. But I didn't go there with a real clear vision of what I wanted to do. I sort of changed my mind a few different times. I do remember that when I left here, although I got a private pilot's licence the first year I was down in Vancouver, at that time in my life I didn't have a real burning desire to become a commercial pilot. But the opportunity did come up to do that at a time when I was becoming quite interested in it. I ended up taking that avenue. But at the time when I was in high school, that wasn't something that I necessarily planned on doing. There were a couple of different things that I thought of at different times in the first couple of years at university. I was quite interested in geology. And I also thought about forestry at one point. And also education. Another thing I thought about was veterinary school. So what that sort of tells you is I didn't really know what I wanted to do. I had interests and the interests were in some of those areas. But it was probably 25 years later, in the nineties, that I actually went back and finished off post-secondary education. I guess growing up I had lots of interests, but I didn't know what I wanted to do when I was in high school.

MF: Was there any particular person or event that made an impact on your early life?

ES: I think I mentioned a few times, one of the things that was really big for me when I was growing up was the swim club. And I know the time that Gordon McConnell spent with those that were interested in the swim club. So when I think about it, he was quite a big impact in that he made something available as a result of a lot of his efforts. There was an opportunity available for me which I got quite involved in. So that was one thing that I think was a really good positive opportunity for me. Because I not only did it just for fun; there were a number of us here that got our national lifeguard ratings. We were quite involved with the Royal Life Saving Society. So there was a lot of opportunity that we had through the swim club. That was as a result of Gordon McConnell as one of the prime people who did that. So he was one person that was, I think, a positive influence on me.

MF: Okay. As a long-time resident of the Terrace area, what changes have you noticed?

ES: I guess one of the things I can notice from when I was growing up here and then from when I came back here in the nineties, was we started to get more of the big box stores. Like Canadian Tire and Wal-Mart and the Wholesale Club. But a lot of these bigger box stores—to me it seems like the downtown core has struggled a bit because of that. At least that's my opinion. That it's made it a little more difficult for some of the smaller stores to keep up or compete. One of the changes I've noticed is if you walk downtown now—and I walk down there quite a bit—is the downtown area seems to be smaller to me. Some of it, as you remember as a kid, seem bigger than they are, but I mean, if you walk down there, there are a lot of buildings that aren't even there anymore. There are a lot fewer small businesses. So that's one of the big changes that I've noticed. I mean, the town's grown, so a lot of stuff comes, the coffee shops and everything come in and the little malls. But that's probably one of the key things—I guess the downtown core seems smaller to me.

MF: As someone who has lived and learned here, what would you want to share with people newly moving to Terrace?

ES: I think there's a lot of opportunity here for family activities. There's a lot more here now than when I was growing up, as far as activities. There was no hockey arena. There was no swimming pool. There was a curling rink. There was a community centre. But there's a lot of activities available for families, say at the Terrace Recreation Centre. There is a fair bit for people to do. There's a lot of activities that happen during the winter time. One of the things about Terrace that I always thought was really a positive thing, was the fact that there's a lot of different things you can do here very close. For example, a few years back I was involved with White Water Kayaking and I used to ski a lot. I don't do both of those because I have a problem in my neck that I can't do that now. But Terrace is one of the places where you could head out in the morning and go paddle the Kitimat River or the Wedeen or the Copper and then you could head up in the afternoon and go rock climbing. And you can go take a hike in the evening. You could do all of this within minutes of each other. I spent four years in Vancouver, and if you wanted to go for a hike on the North Shore you spent a good part of your time available getting over there and getting back for a little bit of a walk.

So one of the big advantages to Terrace, I think, is the amount of things there are to do outside that are easy to access. Because Terrace has really good paddling. The lake out here is one of the few warm fresh water lakes in the north. That's a fairly good resource for people coming here. There are lots of beaches there. There are public beaches and places that are easy to access. You don't have to have a boat to go swimming. I mentioned the climbing. There's some really good rock climbing around here. We've got a great ski hill. There's some good cross-country. So, for people who are involved in any kind of outdoor activities, Terrace has got it all, in my opinion. We have fishing. All that type of stuff. There's easy access to a lot of different types of activities, and you can do more than one thing in one day. So that's one of the things that I'd say is good. Plus, I mentioned our recreation centre here. There's, you know, a good swim club. There's gymnastics. There's dance. There's social dancing. I was fairly involved with social dancing here a few years ago. There's also a lot of multicultural activities. We used to go to Filipino Night and there were multicultural dinners. So there's a lot of activity for those who want to go out and get involved in it.

MF: Especially on the outdoor recreation side of things?

ES: Yeah, I think that's fairly big. There's a lot of stuff that's easy to access in Terrace. We got a really good cross-country ski trail. So you don't have to be a downhill person. We've got great back-country skiing around here. Plus for the kids—and I don't have kids myself—but there are a lot of activities. There's a lot of soccer here. There's lots of opportunity for kids to do dance. Our school programs here have had band programs and music programs that have been really second-to-none for years. You know, going back to when I was in high school, there was always a band program. I know they struggle sometimes because of budgets, but it always seems to have survived in Terrace because a few people had the vision to get out there and keep things going and raise money when they needed it and whatever. So there's a lot of opportunity in that respect, too, for kids.

Things like music or the arts. I was at one of the openings for an art show here. One of the local bands was playing some music there as well. We have local artists having art showings all the time. So there's a lot available in the arts too, it's not just all sports.

MF: In terms of the questions I planned to ask, I've pretty well gone through them. Are there any other comments that you might want to make at this point?

ES: I'm just trying to think here. I know there's probably a few people I remember when I was growing up—I know that other people have talked about them. But, for example, there was a lady— Vesta Douglas was her name—and she worked as a teacher. She was the principal at one point at Uplands but I can remember growing up when I was in elementary school, my mother always used to take me there every Halloween trick-or-treating. It seemed like every other kid in town was there, too. She was a person who I think was involved a lot—and probably touched a lot of people that had kids. So that's one of the memories I have of growing up, was that I was going to Vesta and Douglas' place. Especially on Halloween. I already mentioned I went to kindergarten here. A lot of people from my age went to the same kindergarten as I did.

MF: So I want to thank you for taking the time to sit down with me here tonight and answer these questions, and provide some background on how you've been involved with Terrace and the community here. So thank you very much for doing that.

ES: Okay, you're welcome.

Faith Wing Interview
Interviewed by Allison Bench, 18 December 2013

Faith Wing was born in Prince Rupert in 1944 and was raised in Gitsegukla. Faith is an elder of the Tsimshian nation, who lives at Kitsumkalum. At the age of 15, Faith began working in a cannery in Port Edward where she worked for the next 45 years. Faith married and had nine children. When Faith and her husband moved to Terrace in 1992, she began teaching kids traditional First Nation arts such as cedar weaving, button blankets, and beading. In this interview, Faith discusses her childhood, her children and husband, working at the fish cannery, and living in Terrace. Faith also talks about how her parents attended residential school and how they refused to subject their children to the same fate. In her interview, she says that 'every time my dad knew they were coming for kids, he would hide us away.'

AB: Where and when were you born?

FW: I was born in Prince Rupert but I was raised out in Gitsegukla. I am part of the Tsimshian Indian First Nation.

AB: And when were you born?

Faith as bridesmaid for her sister's wedding. Port Edward. Early 1960s. Faith and Harvey Wing Collection.

FW: December 11th, 1944.

AB: I guess you were from Prince Rupert. When did you and your family arrive in the Terrace area?

FW: 1992, we moved here. My husband got his status back and he's from Kitsumkalum. That's when we moved back.

AB: Did you have any siblings growing up and what was your relationship like with them?

FW: Well, I had four sisters and two brothers and we got along pretty well. And my maiden name is Vickers.

AB: I guess you grew up in Prince Rupert then?

FW: Well, that's Port Ed [Port Edward] and we would travel back. Port Ed's about the same distance as Kalum; we travelled back and forth. I worked in Prince Rupert at Canadian Fish. I was there for 45 years working at a cannery.

AB: Oh wow. So tell me what it was like growing up in Port Edward.

FW: Oh, it was quiet. It was nice and quiet. You know, do your own thing. It wasn't really comfortable to move here. We moved in 1992 and I met some people, learned how to do stuff that I never learned how to do before, like weaving. I learned that from Sandra Wesley.

AB: And what school did you go to when you were younger?

FW: Port Edward.

AB: And do you have any memories of going to school that you wanted to share or that you think is interesting?

FW: Gee, that was quite a while ago I can't remember everything. The principal we had was Mr. McEwan. Only knew one teacher, was Mr. Winner I think. I can't remember. It was nice. I had a hard time trying to go to school. My parents travelled back and forth from the village into town so they could work during the summer time. So I had a hard time in school, I didn't graduate. I was 18 trying to graduate and I just got to grade seven.

Faith and Harvey Wing on their wedding day. United Church in Prince Rupert. Faith and Harvey Wing Collection.

AB: You said you were married. Tell me about your wedding?

FW: Oh, we had a quiet wedding. It was just me and my husband and a few witnesses. We got married in the United Church in Rupert. And that's 43 years ago.

AB: And how did you meet your husband?

FW: Oh that's the first thing I ask: how did we meet? We were quite young; I was 15 when I met him. We just met and that was it.

AB: And you said you have children?

FW: I bore seven; I adopted two.

AB: So how do you find Terrace as a place to raise a family?

FW: By the time I moved here, I only had two children left, and they moved here with me. The rest were all on their own. But gradually they're all living here with me. It's quite nice: they are scattered all over.

AB: What jobs did you work? I guess you could tell me a little bit about what jobs you worked when you were in Port Edward, and then when you came to Terrace.

FW: Well, I was 15. That's when I started working in a cannery; it had different stuff going on in a cannery. Washing fish, canning, and packing, so I did all that. I worked in the cannery for 45 years. I retired in 2009. And then when I moved here I gradually learned to start teaching kids our culture's weaving, button blankets, beading, and all that. I learned weaving from Sandra Wesley so now I'm teaching it.

AB: So you raised your children in Port Edward?

FW: Yes.

AB: How did you find raising your children there?

FW: It's a small town so it wasn't too bad. But when they started going to school in Rupert they had to go back and forth on the bus, so that was the worst thing, thinking about your kids catching the bus to go home.

AB: What was there to do with children in Port Edward?

FW: It's just like elsewhere, where the teachers and the community get together and do stuff. Like they used to have their own little parades, and vote some kids in for queen and king, there was a lot of stuff going on.

AB: How did your career frame your experiences both in Port Edward and then later in Terrace?

FW: I don't really know how to answer that. I really enjoyed working in the canneries and up here I am more or less really enjoying the work I'm doing. Usually I'm really terrified of speaking in public, but working with kids kind of got me around to start speaking to the public. Usually when I touch a mic I cry right away, so it's a really good experience to go through teaching kids. I have lots of grandchildren: I have 30 grandchildren, and right now I have 10 great-grandchildren.

AB: When you were growing up, what did you do for fun?

FW: I don't think I even had time to enjoy life that much because my parents were working hard and I was raising my sisters. My dad was a fisherman and my mom also worked in a cannery. By the time I started going out I had my first child.

AB: I want to go back to when you were younger, too, because we talked a lot about when you had your own children. Tell me about your parents.

FW: My parents, they had a hard life, too. They went to residential school, and they passed on before all the settlements came in and everything. They didn't really talk much about residential, either. As far as I know, we never did go. And all the kids we were growing up with went. Every time we said, "Well, how come we never went?" they would say, "every time dad knew they were coming for kids, he would hide us away."

AB: And do you remember that?

FW: No. I know some of my first cousins said they were five when they got taken away.

AB: So can you describe a typical day in your household during your childhood?

FW: We really got along as a family. If I see you now and I see you tomorrow we would hug each other, that is kind of the family attitude, and that's how my grandchildren are now, too. There's a lot of love there.

AB: And what did your parents do for work when you were growing up?

FW: Like I said, my mom was in a cannery, and my dad was a fisherman. We'd leave the reserve in May to come work in a cannery. My dad had to fish and we didn't get home 'til late September and that's how our schooling was all buggered up. I would have to go to school in Port Ed for a couple of months, and go back in late October or something like that, because that's how late the salmon run used to run, until late October. Now it's done in the beginning of August or something like that.

AB: Growing up, what kind of expectations were there for girls and boys? Was there anything specific or different?

FW: No, I think we just more or less grew up like everybody. I think the whole community comes together and creates stuff for kids. Port Ed was just a big cannery, one section will be First Nation another section will be for the white and the Japanese and the Chinese. We're all living in different places but we got together as a community.

AB: So your parents worked at the cannery that's now the museum?

FW: No, no, no. That's North Pacific. My parents, we lived in Sunnyside at the beginning, before we moved to Port Ed.

AB: Where did you go to see movies?

FW: They had a movie community right in Port Ed. They had a hall there and weekends they had dances for kids and things like that. So they had a real nice hall there for movies.

AB: And I guess when you end up being that age, where did you end up going for dates?

FW: Go to Rupert, they had bus services and they would just travel to Rupert and back again.

AB: What kind of things would you do specifically? If you were to go on a date to Prince Rupert?

FW: Oh, go to movies, and go out for dinner, and things like that. Or just go pop in, in a bar or whatever. Make sure you make it home on the last bus.

AB: And what restaurants do you remember being popular over the years? I guess when you were either in the Port Edward and Prince Rupert area, or in Terrace when you first got here?

FW: They only had one café there [Port Edward], and that was right in front of our house so it wasn't far to walk, and actually my husband's father had to run it for a while. And then, in Rupert, I liked going to Kings and they sold the nicest hamburger. I like my hamburger.

AB: And so were you involved in any other community activities outside of the home? Like clubs or organizations?

FW: Well, right now I'm involved with a community committee down in Kalum for elders and youths. We do fundraising, we do Salmon Run to make sure the kids have a good Christmas party, so that's what I get involved with down there.

AB: Okay, so were you involved in any activities like that growing up or when you were a young mother?

FW: Oh, not really, we were more or less just cannery workers and that was it and they, the people that ran the cannery like Nelson brothers, they even had the babysitters provided for you. You were never stuck with babysitters; they paid for babysitters.

AB: When you were growing up, did you attend any religious services?

Canfisco Oceanside Plant, Prince Rupert. Photo Credit: Canadian Fishing Company.

FW: I brought my kids to go to the United Church and all that. I can't even remember what they call that church but the preacher and his wife left so we started going to the Anglican Church in Port Ed. I made sure me and my kids always went to church every Sunday but since I moved I don't even know any churches up here.

AB: So what local events do you remember celebrating when you were younger?

FW: Oh, they always had a family thing for the whole community for Port Ed. They had a parade and stuff for kids for racing and all that, and the firemen always had a hose-laying contest. Actually we won that once; we practiced how to throw the fire hose. That's heavy. It was a lot of fun.

AB: These events—did they change over the years?

FW: Oh, they don't even have that any more. I think they actually quit before I moved, you know.

AB: What do you remember about the downtown? Did Port Edward even have a downtown?

FW: No.

AB: What do you remember about downtown Prince Rupert when you were growing up?

FW: Like I said, we were back and forth from Gitsegukla to Port Ed; we more or less didn't really go back to Prince Rupert that often. My husband did and he remembers everything up here, too, because he was born right up in Port Essington, where he's from. But his dad is full Chinese and his mom is a First Nation.

AB: And so what do you remember about downtown Terrace when you first moved here? What's changed about it?

FW: It's changed quite a bit. Especially the mall; you walk in that mall and it feels like you walked into a Vancouver mall. It's really changed. I don't even like going shopping any more; it's too busy. So if I want to shop, I shop first thing in the morning or just before the stores are closed. That's when they aren't busy.

AB: Did you shop at the Terrace Co-op when it was open?

FW: Oh yes. I loved that, yes.

AB: Can you tell me a little bit about it?

FW: They had a café and it was just like a mall, different stuff in little corners. The café was awesome.

Canfisco Oceanside Plant, Prince Rupert. 1960. Canadian Fishing Company Collection.

AB: And so when you were working in Port Edward, what did most people you knew do for work?

FW: Well, it's a cannery. You work on the fish that fishermen delivered to the cannery. You just show up either eight, seven-thirty in the morning. And you don't really have a choice; you're told where to go. So I more or less grew up in a warehouse. That's where I worked. I even ran it. Then when they started working shift work, I would run the warehouse and look after the people working for me. So it was quite nice.

AB: And I don't know if you mentioned earlier but what were the canneries' names?

FW: There's all different kinds. Like in Port Ed was Nelson Brothers; they settled down, said they would combine it with BC Packers in Rupert and then now it's Canadian Fish. So it's all different. But they closed Ocean Side so now they're in the same cannery. All the canneries are shutting down in Rupert. They had quite a bit all over, but now it's just Canadian Fish.

AB: Did a lot of other people work at the cannery?

FW: Oh, yeah, lots. Especially because it's just a summer time job. Sometimes you get to work in March. They were able to work on crabs and shrimps and clams, but now it's just salmon. They cut all the rest down so I moved at just the right time.

AB: How do you feel the community interacts with Kitselas and Kitsumkalum?

FW: Pretty good, I guess? I have no idea what. Because I know quite a bit; I know Kitselas and Kalum were supposed to be combined but now all of a sudden they're separated. But they're the same people; they are all from Port Essington. So Kitselas is all the way over there and Kalum is down there. You know where Tempo is? That's where Kalum is.

AB: So, have you lived in Terrace during any major floods?

FW: Oh, yeah. I had to leave the cannery one year to come up here before they flooded the highway. And the reserve down there was involved with Old Remo. They had to sandbag down there and sandbag around the hall. We had to run around to make sandbags for everybody. My husband had to pack all my stuff out. My daughter used to live up in Thornhill, up in the mountains somewhere up there, so they were packing all my freezers out there, but we never got touched by it.

AB: So, how did the floods impact the community?

FW: It was more or less more panicky than anything, because the flood wasn't even that bad. Not once they got up here, up in the hill here. Just a hall and the band office got it, and they just got it down in the basement. So it wasn't major here.

AB: How important do you think First Nations culture has been in shaping the Terrace community?

FW: Well, I started my role modeling. I go to all the schools, whoever asks for me. It was quite busy when it first started but now it's really dying down; it's really dying down. I work on Friday and I think that's the first day in December. And I think that's the last day of school. So really sad for me. My friend Sandra, she's pretty lucky because she knows she's an artist, she's a carver, and the schools are just demanding for those things right now. Kids want to learn how to carve. So I guess I need to go to carving school.

AB: So growing up, were you involved in politics?

FW: No.

AB: What do you think the perception of the northwest is on a provincial or national level?

FW: I have no idea about that. Because I more or less stay out of it. My husband, he would argue that part so…it's bad enough I have all these kids to look after. Well, I don't look after them; they just made my life at home with all these kids running around.

AB: So Port Edward is where you grew up; how has it changed over the years?

FW: Oh, that is really sad, that part. It has really gone down in Port Ed. Hardly anyone is living there now. Canneries moved. They used to have stores there but now they only have one little corner store. And the school, that's gotten really small. That big school, they had to shut it down because there's hardly any kids there. They more or less had to use a building where the community hall is. There used to be a mall there but now they had to rebuild it. It is now a hall where the classes are. So it's really getting small.

AB: And what about Terrace: I mean, you've only been here since '92, but tell me about what has changed in Terrace over the 30 years, I guess.

FW: Well, where I'm living now has really changed; it's gotten bigger. They have lots of new houses going up, so that part has changed. People have changed. They're getting friendlier. Like when I first moved here nobody knew me so I had to make a name for myself so people would recognize me. I do catering. I go out and meet people. I don't really cater that much but I try to. My husband and I, we cater if people ask for you. We don't try to go out and find it. People come to you and they ask it, but we don't try to go out there. We do Chinese food.

AB: And so when you were a child growing up, what did you expect, what were your dreams, what did you hope to accomplish when you were little?

FW: Well, first off, I really wanted to graduate; I really wanted to graduate, so that's why I stayed in school until 18 and I couldn't pass grade seven. And all these kids are 13, 14 years old passing me by. When I finally passed to grade eight, that's when I finally quit. It was hard going back and forth from the reserve, back and forth. So I think that's why all us Native people didn't really grad at the time, because you were taken out of school on the reserve and some of them weren't even put back in school. But my parents tried to put us in school in Port Ed. We would go to school from May to June. And going to school from the reserve to Port Ed, it was harder; it was different from the reserve—stuff you learned in Port Ed. School was harder. I don't know why it's different.

AB: Was there any particular person or event that really affected your life or made a difference in your life, something really significant that changed you as a person?

FW: Well, here, it's changed me since I moved up here. I'm going out and being shy. When I first moved here, I would stay at home and never go out. The phone never rang; no one ever knocks on your door. So after a while, I started going out meeting friends. I have about five elder ladies down there and we go out to the treaty office and we all sit there. Someone would knit or crochet, and Sandra would weave and we would just sit there and talk. Someone would wait from about seven to 10 doing our craft work because you can't do any craft at home because there's lots to do at home. So we would go out every night to do our crafts. It was quite fun.

AB: As a longtime resident of the Northwest—you've been in Terrace a long time, too— what are some changes you've noticed? I guess what would be the most significant changes that have happened around this area?

FW: I have no idea. I don't really notice everything. The only thing right now I'm really involved in doing is travelling with elders, going to these elders gatherings. I really enjoy that and that's why we do a lot of fundraising, to go down there. We get to go travel in July to an elders gathering down there. We went to Salmon Arm last year and this year is Penticton, so that's a lot of fun.

AB: What would you tell someone who was newly moving to Terrace?

FW: Don't wait until people come—don't wait to go out and enjoy yourself. Go out and meet people, and then you'll feel at home. Because I didn't do that. I just stayed at home and waited for the cannery to call and I would rush down to Rupert. I still worked in Rupert when I moved here and

I would rush back and forth. I would get a call at 10, "Can you be in by midnight?" and I would rush down there. So I was involved with that until 2009.

AB: So are there any other stories that you wanted to share that maybe were significant or big?

FW: I don't know; most important part of my life was when I met my husband and then I had all these kids. And now all my grandchildren: I think half of them have graduated already, and all my kids graduated. My husband and I didn't, but all my kids have, so that's what I really, really enjoy and love. My husband, when we were raising our kids, we got all our kids together and said if anybody graduates you get $1000. He hasn't paid up yet. He's waiting to win the million. So my kids are awesome. If anything happens they all get together and help us out. I have five girls and four boys. But I lost one boy, the one that I adopted. It was quite hard. And right now, one of the girls that grew up with my girls—we're going through hard times right now—she just lost her mother last night. So that's where my girls are, going up to go get her, because she was in Prince George. My kids, when they were growing up, they would always bring someone home, or if they needed a place to stay I would bring them in and raise them for a while, and they would go home when they were ready, so that's a part of how we lived. My daughter is growing up, too. She has got all boys and the boys come around and they stay. And that's how my mom was, so this goes on. Whoever needs to stay just comes in and stays and we can't say anything; we just let them stay, enjoy life for a while and let them go.

AB: So that happened when you were growing up, too?

FW: Yes, my mom was—well, that's where I learned everything, was from my mom. I never asked questions when I was growing up: I just watched, looked, observed. When my mom made bread, I never asked how come you do this, how come; I would just do whatever she did when she was making bread. We were taught to never ask questions. My grandmother—my dad's mother—that's how she raised us. Never asked questions. So I never did ask questions. Whenever my mom made bread I just watched her. Actually, my husband did the same thing with his dad. He just watched his dad cook Chinese food, just watched. Sometimes his dad would chase him out and he would sneak back in and see what he was putting in his cooking. That's how I learned how to cook, just watching my mom. And then people would ask, "Oh, how do you cook that?" Well, you just have to learn. So, at my early age it was okay, but sometimes I thought it was not very good. But I enjoyed my life; I really enjoyed my life growing up with my parents. I never talked back to my parents at all, right up until the day I lost them. That's what I keep telling my grandsons, but they don't listen. And that's how we were brought up. I wouldn't say they never hit us or anything, but they had a rough life. But we tried our best to get along.

AB: When you said they had a bad life, what do you mean by that?

FW: Well, all the First Nations that went to residential school, they did quite a bit of drinking. But they knew when to stop and started doing stuff for us. That was them. I tried my best to look after the rest of my sisters. I was the middle child; I tried to look after the kids when they were busy.

AB: Is there anything else you would like to add that we haven't talked about?

FW: Not really, like you said, like I said, they never used to have a bus service going out to Kalum, but now they do, so that's pretty neat. And there's a lot of stuff: like they have that big hall, they have the big fancy one there that nobody uses. It's supposed to be a basketball thing but there's not enough kids to use it; they just use it for floor hockey now. There's quite a bit of difference there since I moved. They have that big health centre, the really big health centre. I think the building's big, but the inside is small. So that's a difference there. It's more or less just that. But uptown, too, has changed quite a bit, but I can't describe what has changed. At the time that I moved here, I don't think they had McDonalds or Boston Pizza or that. I think they had Dairy Queen. I don't know if they had McDonalds when I moved here? That's like Rupert, they don't have those kinds of things. Well, they have McDonalds; they had a KFC but they shut it down. Dairy Queen got shut down, A&W got shut down. They don't have anything but McDonalds. Prince Rupert has gotten smaller too, not just Port Ed.

AB: Would you say that Prince Rupert has gotten less busy than it once was?

FW: Oh yes, even the stores; a whole bunch of stores are shutting down. They're supposed to be going up again, but I hardly see the difference. Mind you, I don't go up there much any more. I don't like traveling the highway, not if I don't have to. I just stay here. I lost a grandson on that highway. So I really don't like that highway.

Felicisima (Fely) Valdez Interview

Interviewed by Melanie Pollard, 24 January 2014

Felicisima (Fely) Valdez was born in the Philippines in 1937. She recalls spending her childhood playing by the seashore, gathering wild berries, and listening to her family play a variety of instruments. After high school, Fely studied to be a midwife in Manila. Fely met her husband, Eliseo C. Valdez, while working as a live-in midwife. They were married November 20th, 1960, and had four children. Fely desired a better life for her growing family and thought Canada would provide that opportunity. Fely immigrated to Canada in 1973 with her daughter and her youngest son. Her husband and remaining children arrived in Canada two years later. Fely began working at Mills Memorial Hospital in the nursery, but held many positions in her thirty years of employment at the hospital. She was very involved with the Filipino-Canadian Association, and was even one of the founders of the association. In this interview, Fely recollects her family going to Furlong Bay, having picnics, swimming at the hot springs, and travelling to Prince Rupert and Kitimat. She also talks about downtown Terrace, the logging industry, Riverboat Days, and her experiences living in Terrace.

MP: Let's start at the beginning. Where and when were you born?

FV: I was born in the Philippines in a hometown called Abulog, Cagayan, which is in the northern part of the Philippines. I was born on October 26th, 1937.

MP: And tell me a little bit about your parents.

FV: My dad's name is Mariano Ramos. My mom's name is Maria Mappala. My dad worked as a fisherman at times and he also worked as a labourer. He's also a gardener; he loves to garden.

MP: What kinds of things would he garden?

FV: Produce, like vegetables that we can use, and lots of fruit trees.

MP: Not to sell?

FV: Not to sell. But sometimes when we had extra, we would share it with other people.

MP: Nice. And what was a typical day like in your house growing up?

FV: A typical day would be going to school on school days, and on the weekends we'd play around. We'd go out to the seashores or we'd go out to play in the yard. Sometimes, we'd go gather some wild berries or wild fruits from the forest nearby. We played outside. It was always sunny. Even in the rain, we'd go out and play in the rain.

MP: That's wonderful. And how many siblings did you have?

FV: There's seven of us altogether. I'm number five.

MP: Wow.

FV: There are three younger ones after me.

MP: What was your relationship like with all your siblings?

FV: We got along well. We were just happy no matter how hard life was. We were always happy. My family likes music. My dad plays guitar and my brothers are the same. They play guitar and they joined a band where they played wind instruments as well.

MP: That's neat.

FV: Yeah. Trumpets and trombones. My dad is fond of stringed instruments. He also plays violin and banjo.

MP: Did you play something as well?

FV: No. But my sister played harp. We had a harp in the house.

MP: Wow. Beautiful.

FV: Yes, she played the harp. So there was always music. And even here [in Canada], when we visited with my mom and dad — they lived in Nanaimo with my elder sister — we get together and we just sing all evening.

MP: That's so neat. And, how many boys and girls were there in the family?

FV: There are three boys and four girls.

MP: And were there different expectations for the boys than the girls?

FV: Yes, of course. The boys were more in and out of the house than the girls. We stuck around most of the time.

MP: What was expected of you as a girl in the house?

FV: We shared chores in the house. We took turns washing dishes or cleaning house, or running errands. We'd tend to the garden.

MP: Wow. Busy.

FV: Busy. Sometimes we'd go out to the shores and watch the fishermen come in and we'd bring home some fresh catch.

MP: Very fresh.

FV: Yes.

MP: Do you have any memories of the schools you attended?

FV: Yes. In elementary school — we didn't have any kindergarten in the Philippines at the time —I went to a public school. And I was lucky to have spent only five years in my grade school. I was accelerated when I was in grade five. From grade five I went to grade six — two grades in one year.

MP: Wow.

FV: There were three of us in high school at the one time and that was expensive. We all attended public school, but it's not like here where you don't have to pay. Even if it's public school, you had to pay tuition fees.

MP: Wow.

FV: There were three of us in high school and we just had to bear it. Big family. We had to make things work.

MP: No kidding.

FV: Yes.

MP: And you went on to attend college or university?

FV: I went to Manila to study midwifery.

MP: How old were you when you started that?

FV: I was maybe 18 when I finished midwifery. It was an 18-month course, a straight 18 months with no break.

MP: That's busy.

FV: After I had just barely finished my course, somebody needed a midwife for a newborn baby. So I was the first one that had a job.

MP: So you started work right away.

FV: I started working right after graduation.

MP: And how long did you practice?

FV: This is really neat. The father of the President of the Philippines, the late Benigno Aquino Jr., was also a political figure in the Philippines at that time. His sister Mrs. Maur Kichanco was my first employer. I took care of her newborn baby for one year. After that I was hired by another sister, Mrs. Erlinda Vargas, to take care of her newborn baby, too. There was a third sister that wanted to hire me but I said, "I would like to have experience inside the hospital." So I went and worked at Manila Railroad Hospital for a few months before I got married.

MP: I was just going to ask about marriage. So how did you meet your husband?

FV: I met my husband [Eliseo C. Valdez] outside of Manila. I was hired as a live-in midwife for this newborn baby and he just lived across the street from me. On my days off—on the weekend—I'd take the bus to commute to Manila and visit my sister, or my friends and my relatives. Sometimes watch a movie or do some shopping. And he would come on the same bus with me because he just lived across the street. We travelled together.

I think he purposely waited until I got on the bus and then took the same bus. That's how we started getting to know each other. He would invite me: "Let's go see a movie on your next day off." And we developed a relationship.

MP: What kind of things would you do as you were getting to know each other?

FV: His mom and dad would invite me to their place; for a meal, go for a walk.

MP: Oh, nice.

FV: They were very nice people. They were nice to me. They even invited me to visit their hometown, which I did. And that's when I found out my husband was younger than me. He lied to me about his age.

MP: Oh no!

FV: Because one time we were talking and I said, "You know what? I don't want to have a boyfriend that is younger than me." And I think he remembered and he lied about his age. He said we were the same age. When I visited the hometown I asked his dad. I said, "How old is Elly by the way?" That's how I found out the truth. But I can't [take back my 'Yes'].

MP: That's hilarious. When did you get married?

FV: We got married November 20th, 1960.

MP: Tell me a bit about your wedding. We just looked at some beautiful pictures.

FV: Yes. I didn't have to do anything except look after my own personal things. Everything else was arranged by his parents.

MP: Wow. There were some beautiful pictures. How many people were there?

FV: About 60 or so. It was in one of the Catholic churches in Santa Cruz, Manila.

MP: And you all went out afterwards?

FV: We all went out to dinner afterwards at a Chinese restaurant.

MP: Nice. What kind of work did your husband do?

FV: He worked with his dad. Sometimes my father-in-law worked in construction. It was a government job and they would build school buildings or things like that. And he would take him and work with him.

MP: Neat. What brought the two of you to Terrace?

FV: My elder sister and my younger sister were already here in Canada. My older sister lived in Terrace. My other sister lived here, too, in Prince Rupert. So, worried about my growing family… I decided I would do something for the sake of my children and my family and my in-laws.

My father-in-law and mother-in-law were hesitant to let me leave because I had to take two of my kids. My older daughter, the only daughter, was almost 12, and my youngest son was four years old when we came. I asked my sisters to help me come over. I applied for a job at Mills Memorial [Hospital]. It took a long time to process my papers but they were patiently reserving that job for me until I came. So then I left my two middle kids, two boys, with my husband. They stayed with my in-laws. We arrived in Terrace on February 12th, 1973. My husband and my two sons came two years after.

MP: Oh, wow. Two years? Must've been a hard two years.

FV: It was hard. It was a big trial for me because after one year of being here, we were looking to celebrate our first year in Terrace. Unfortunately, my son, who was five years old at the time, got sick — really, really sick — a complication from measles. He had encephalitis and I thought I was going to lose him.

MP: That's so hard.

FV: It was. Being here by myself—my husband wanted to come and I said, "It's not going to help whether you're here or not." And I just prayed hard. "If God wants to take him…" I said. "Rather than to have a very sick child to look after, His will be done." But, luckily, he came out of it. My husband and the two middle boys came in June 1975.

MP: That must've been nice to be all together again.

FV: Yes.

MP: And what was it like to raise kids here in Terrace?

FV: Terrace is a good place to be. Our neighbours were really nice; sometimes I would leave my son with my next-door neighbours who were Portuguese. They were really very nice neighbours.

I didn't have a car at first, and I would be picked up by some friends who were on the same shift as me. They would take me to work and they would take me home after the shift. People were very nice. I find that Terrace is a very good community to raise a family.

MP: What kinds of things were there to do with your children here in Terrace?

Valdez family. Noel, Roger, Eric, Felicisima, Eliseo and Angie Valdez Lafavor [l-r].
Circa 1980s. Felicisima Valdez Collection.

FV: They were active in the school activities. They would go skating with the class. They would go on field trips. My daughter Angie was in the French Exchange Program in High School. We billeted a student from St. Jerome, Quebec for a week. After that, the same family in St. Jerome billeted my daughter. It was a good experience for her which she enjoyed very much.

The boys were involved in different sports like basketball, track and field, rugby, curling, and were also in the school band. They competed in Provincials in track and field events and basketball and were happy to come home with medals and trophies. In high school, Noel (third child, middle of three sons) joined the Katimavik program and had a great experience.

MP: That's neat. Were they involved in community activities, too, the kids?

FV: Yes. They participated in sports. Sometimes they would go out and have picnics with friends. We would go out tobogganing or skating, skiing. I was nervous when they went skiing because I dreaded them getting injured.

MP: Nice. Snow.

FV: Snow! The first time it snowed, my son came out from the church. "Wow! It's snowing!" Everyone was looking at us. That was the first time we saw the snow.

MP: That's so cute. And you worked for many years at Mills [Memorial Hospital].

FV: Full time. For 28 years.

MP: Do you want to tell me a little bit about your work and career there?

FV: I started upstairs. My first job was in the nursery, looking after babies, which I enjoyed. I would come on night shift and, at the time, we would start by giving the babies a bath at midnight. I worked on the wards. I worked everywhere in the hospital until I got the job in Emergency. The schedule suited me because I didn't want to leave my kids at night by themselves.

So I worked days and afternoons. And I think I've worked all over the place within the hospital. Most of the time, I worked in Emergency. At the end, I worked in the lab until I retired.

MP: And how do you think working at the hospital all those years framed how you saw Terrace?

FV: It just came to me. Everything just fell into place. I didn't have any difficulties dealing with the people that came and went. I liked it because you were able to meet people.

MP: I bet.

FV: Even outside of work, when you saw people, when you went anywhere, you seemed to know everybody. Everybody said hi. I may not have remembered their names but I knew them, you know, from the hospital. Sometimes my husband would say, "Do you really know all these people?" And I would say, "Of course!" Because I said hi to everybody and they said hi to me.

MP: And in the times you weren't working, what did your family do for fun here in Terrace?

FV: Sometimes we would go to the park. We'd go to Furlong Bay or the other park, Lakelse Lake [Picnic Site]. We'd do picnics. We'd get together with some friends from Prince Rupert and Kitimat. And we had lots of friends that'd come and go.

MP: Nice. So you enjoyed getting out into the mountains and the lakes here?

FV: Sometimes. Yeah.

MP: That's neat. Did you ever go as a family to the hot springs?

FV: Yes. We did.

MP: How was that?

FV: We enjoyed the hot pool there until my husband had problems with kidney failure. We used to just go there and soak in the hot pool. It was nice. Sometimes, you know, we'd have some meals there. But he had some problems with his kidneys and then he started with dialysis, which kept him from being in a hot pool. Later on, it wasn't working for him, and he was switched to haemodialysis at home [which was done at the hospital].

MP: Oh, I'm sorry to hear.

FV: So, in my life, even after I retired from the hospital, I was still working as a nurse for my husband at home.

MP: Yeah. That requires a lot of compassion, and care, and time.

FV: Yes.

MP: It sounds like you were busy with work and your kids. Were you involved in any other community activities?

FV: We were very much involved with the Filipino-Canadian Association. In fact, we were one of the founders of the association. (It was my husband's desire to celebrate and preserve our Filipino culture and heritage. My husband would often remind our kids to never forget their Filipino culture and traditions). We started meeting with Filipinos in Kitimat in the 1980s, 1981 maybe. We joined a group in Kitimat and Terrace and formed the Filipino-Canadian Association. We almost always participated in the multicultural events and diversity programs.

One of the Filipino-Canadian Association floats in the Riverboat Days parades.
Felicisima Valdez Collection.

MP: Tell me a bit more about why you started that.

FV: We Filipinos value our community and cherish the time we spend together. Most of the time, you know, they would come here. Sometimes we would go to Kitimat. And sometimes Filipinos from [Prince] Rupert came [here]. So this house was always a meeting place.

So we decided, "Okay. Let's have some activities." So we gathered together in Terrace, Kitimat and Rupert. And these last two years, we made it a yearly event where we gather at Furlong Bay. Last year we rented a private place on Lakelse Lake. We play some games. It's fun. Once a year we have a dance, a fundraiser.

MP: Neat.

FV: What we make from that, we donate back to the community. Sometimes we donate to the food bank, sometimes the Women's [Resource Centre]. Sometimes, we send it to the Philippines for typhoon victims or flooding or whatever.

MP: So a very active group?

FV: Yes.

MP: How many would there be at an event like that? How many Filipino families are there?

FV: There's not many Filipino families, but it's open to everybody. We entertain them with our Filipino folk dances and serve some of our ethnic dishes.

MP: Nice. Are there any within the group that play music as well?

FV: Sometimes somebody sings. It's open to everybody. It's not just Filipinos. We invite everybody. You should come.

MP: It sounds like fun. And it's still going.

FV: It used to be Terrace and Kitimat combined. In the summer, we'd camp and we'd play games. The guys would play volleyball, sometimes softball, that type of thing. We rent places in the camp and everybody just has fun. (We would reserve several campsites together for several families, share meals and chat and tell stories until late into the night. One time we were making so much noise with our laughter, the park ranger had to shut us down. We told him we were just telling funny stories. The park ranger told us maybe we should tell sad stories so we could dial down the noise. This is what it's like when we get together. It's always one big party).

MP: That's so neat. And did you attend any religious services here in Terrace?

FV: Very much so.

MP: Can you tell me about your experiences or involvement in them?

FV: I go to the Catholic Church. In fact, I joined the choirs of Terrace Sacred Heart Parish. I'm not a good singer but… the group still wants me to join. It's a good service to the church and the community.

MP: You enjoy it?

FV: I enjoy it.

MP: That's wonderful. And how often would your family leave Terrace?

FV: I would say once or twice a year.

MP: Where would you go or how would you get there?

FV: I go by plane. When my husband was still around, we'd drive so that we could see other places.

MP: In BC or…?

FV: In BC. We also travelled to the [United] States when he was still okay. When he started having health problems, it was hard to travel.

I try to coordinate invitations from my children; they're all over the place. Last year, I was in Nanaimo with my one son. My older sister also lives there.

I was supposed to go to Edmonton this Christmas but I decided not to because I've started having problems with my shoulder. I've completely torn the rotator cuff on my shoulder.

MP: Oh.

FV: And I didn't want to travel in the winter because of [possible] flight cancellations. Right after Christmas, my daughter says, "Okay, when are you coming? Christmas is over. My turn." And I have to visit with them because I have two great-granddaughters.

MP: Wow.

FV: These are their pictures here.

MP: Wow. Beautiful. How many grandkids and how many great-grandkids?

FV: I have six grandkids. [Fely shows the pictures.] These are the two in Nanaimo. This is the one in Calgary — Roger's daughter — and one in Edmonton. These are the two great-grandkids from Edmonton.

MP: That's so neat. And your family in the Philippines? They had a hard time saying goodbye. Did you get back to see them very much over the years?

FV: No. No.

MP: It's hard, eh?

FV: It was hard to travel. [My husband allowed me to visit them] but the problem was, who was going to look after him? Like, when my sister in Nanaimo had surgery on her breast, I went to visit her so I could help her. And, as soon as I left, he ended up in the hospital. Because his potassium went up.

MP: That makes travel very hard.

FV: That's why I couldn't leave. If I took him, it was hard, too — especially when he was on dialysis. You had to pack all your things with you.

MP: I'm sorry to hear.

FV: Yes. It was hard.

MP: So if you think about Terrace and your memories — when you came in 1973 to now — what do you remember about how downtown Terrace was then compared to now? Has anything changed?

FV: Of course. Where that shopping mall is now — the Skeena Mall — that was bare. Hardly anything was there before. That shopping mall wasn't there before. That was where the old Catholic Church used to be. It was a small building. That's what I remember.

The [Terrace] Co-op used to be at the large vacant lot next to where the Western Financial Group building is now on Greig Avenue.

We also shopped at Safeway and Overwaitea Foods. Overwaitea Foods used to be where the government services office is located on Eby Street.

MP: And where did you shop for things like clothes and furniture over the years?

FV: I always shopped at the Co-op (and Woolworth's and Fields for clothes).

MP: What kinds of things would they have there [at the Co-op]?

FV: They had clothing, appliances, too… They had offices in the downstairs part of the grocery store. Most of the time, we were dealing with the Co-op; we had a membership.

MP: That's great. What did most people that you knew do for work?

FV: Most of them worked in logging. There were the mills, the lumber mills which are working still. [Other places to work were] Alcan and Eurocan. My husband started working at Alcan in '75, when he came here, until he retired. So those were the major companies employing most of the people.

MP: How have you seen the logging or forest industry change over time?

FV: It was sad when the economy went down because of the logging industry. It's also sad to see the big mills here gone. That was in the 1990's maybe, when the economy was down.

MP: And how did you see that impact Terrace when that happened?

FV: Most of the people moved away because there were hardly any jobs left in logging at the time. There was a drop in the population but we still stayed. It was home. This is home for us.

Terrace is just a very nice place to live. It's just like one big family. Everybody looks after each other and people are friendly, they're helpful. In fact, when my brother-in-law moved to Kitimat, he made the remark that Terrace is friendlier — the people in Terrace are friendlier than the people in Kitimat. That was his first impression when he moved to Kitimat because he also worked at Alcan.

MP: That's a good experience in Terrace.

FV: It is. And I find that, too. Everybody says hi to everybody and everybody looks after everybody. If you see somebody that needs help, somebody's always there to ask, "How may I help you? Can I do something?"

MP: That's so neat.

FV: It is.

MP: I'm thinking about food. You said your parents were gardeners?

FV: Yes.

MP: Did you also garden when you came to Terrace?

FV: Yes.

MP: What did you grow?

FV: I grow bok choy, zucchini, beans, tomatoes, strawberries.

MP: Nice.

FV: Potatoes, kale…what else? Anything that is easy to grow. I enjoy gardening. I have flowerbeds but last year I didn't do much because of my shoulder. I think that's how I got hurt, because when I went there one afternoon, I started digging and that same night I couldn't move my shoulder.

MP: Oh. Too much digging. Have you seen the [Skeena Valley] Farmers' Market change over the years?

FV: Of course. There's more and more people coming to the Farmers' Market from nearby places; more variety of produce, more food booths, lots of space and beautiful surroundings.

MP: And anything in particular you've seen change there besides the numbers?

FV: Oh, of course. The place. It's a nice place. We have the band shelter there. There's more activities going on. There's more people, more events.

MP: That's so neat. And, besides the Saturdays at the Farmers' Market, are there any other community events that you remember celebrating every year in Terrace?

FV: Riverboat Days is one. And sometimes, when we were young and able to do things, we used to participate. We had a float sometimes and joined the parade.

MP: With the Filipino-Canadian Association?

FV: Yes. In fact, one time we won second prize.

MP: That's fun. What was the float?

FV: The float was a nice long flatbed. We had a water buffalo made out of paper mache, a nipa hut made of grass, and a coconut palm tree. We had boys in costume, all sorts of nice costumes. And they were doing the bamboo dance on the flatbed.

MP: That's amazing. Do you remember any other events throughout the years?

68

FV: Well, there's the Parade of Lights and sleigh rides during the Christmas season. A lot of social events going on at the Theatre or Library grounds. It's nice that there's a place that people can go and watch. A couple of years or so ago, the Fil-Can Association participated in the Diversity Program featuring Filipino food and Filipino folk dances.

MP: Gather together.

FV: Gather together and socialize.

MP: Absolutely. And, more generally, how have you seen Terrace change over the years?

FV: There's more businesses. The stores have spread out. All this side now [the South Side], we have more businesses coming in. It used to be that most of the businesses were downtown.

MP: Any other social changes you've seen?

FV: Yes. A lot of people coming and going because of all the proposed projects in this region and Alcan modernization; an added airline transportation [WestJet]. There's more people coming to the R.E.M. [Lee] Theatre, social gatherings, or sometimes for fundraising. I would go sometimes. I like watching performances.

MP: Yeah. There seems to be more available.

FV: More and more [activities for kids and art displays at the Terrace Public Library].

MP: Any other changes you think you could comment on that you've seen?

FV: There's more. We have our Skeena Mall back; there's more businesses where we can shop. It's not like before when it was so quiet there. But even when that place was empty, my husband used to go there and just walk around. That's where he'd go on walks because he couldn't walk outside. He'd just go back and forth there, meet some friends and chat with them.

MP: So when you were a child back in the Philippines, what did you expect or hope to accomplish in your life?

FV: I wasn't expecting that I would live in Canada this long. I thought maybe I would come here and see what opportunities there were, and maybe save money and go back. But I like it here now.

MP: What is it that you like here, that keeps you here, and makes this place home?

FV: Everybody is treated equally. You can't even see classifications of the poor and the middle class and the rich. Whereas back home, you can see the difference; there's a lot of people that are living in poor areas. You can see a big difference between the poor and the rich [in the Philippines]. Here, you know, everybody has the same privileges. Everybody is treated equally. It's just a friendly atmosphere.

MP: So you didn't expect to be in Canada this long?

FV: I didn't. But I find, you know, it's a good place. And even when my boys were growing up, sometimes they would go out with their friends and come home late. Sometimes, they would stay with their friends, and I worried when they didn't come home. But my husband would always tell me, "Well, we told them that when they go out with their friends and they have something to drink, they shouldn't drive." So they stayed with their friends. And my husband always assured me, "If you don't get a call from the hospital or the police station, they're fine."

MP: They're safe?

FV: They're safe. They're with their friends. We know their friends very well.

MP: Was there any particular person or event that made a big impact on you, on your life?

FV: All I wanted was to give my children a good future. I find that Canada is a good place to be. And even my son, the third one, he was able to travel out of the country. He worked in Russia. He worked in Milan [Italy] and Budapest [Hungary]. And he comes home and says, "Mom, I'm proud to be a Canadian."

MP: Wow. Neat.

FV: Because, you know, when he talks to foreigners, they'll ask him, "Where are you from?" "I'm a Filipino, but I'm Canadian," he says. They have a lot of respect for Canadians.

MP: That's very cool. So, as someone who has lived a lot of years here, what would you want to share with new people that are moving to Terrace?

FV: I'm always telling them, at first, it's hard. You have to adjust. In the long run, it's going to be beneficial. You'll reap the fruit of your sacrifices. You have to sacrifice. Some of them come here and, like me, they leave their family behind.

MP: Yeah. That must be hard.

FV: It is hard. And, I say, you know, just persevere. Soon they will be here to join you. I tell them because, you know, I went through that. I feel like I am their mother. In the Filipino group here, they always look up to me like an elder, you know? Everybody calls me 'Tita', which means auntie.

MP: So you've helped people transition when they move here?

FV: Yes. I made a point of that because I've been through it. I had a good experience and I want them to have the same kind of experience.

MP: What kinds of things do you do to help them?

FV: I always invite them over for meals. (I share what I have. Our home is always open to them.) I give them rides. And I take them to church with me. Every way that I can help, I'm always willing to help them. Because I always keep in mind that I've been there.

MP: And are there any other stories you'd like to share about your time in Terrace?

FV: I like it here. I don't know...

My kids are pulling me in every direction. My son in Nanaimo says, "You should move here, Mom. The weather here is better than Alberta." Because my daughter in Alberta says, "You should move here, Mom. We have a place for you. And Roger is in Calgary so we can always get together." I still have a son that lives here with two grandchildren. And I have a hard time trying to decide where I would like to settle. But, meanwhile, I said, "I'll stick around. I like it here." (I have a strong support system and I am blessed to be part of a wonderful Filipino community.)

MP: Hard to uproot?

FV: It is.

MP: Well, Fely, thank you so much. It's been lovely to talk to you. It's been lovely to hear your story of coming here and living in Terrace.

FV: Well, I tell you, I wish I was able to write a book about my life story.

MP: Yeah? This is the beginning of your book.

FV: Yes! It is a wonderful experience and I'd like to say thank-you!

George Kofoed Interview

Interviewed by Ted Wilson, 27 December 2013

One of eight children, George Kofoed was born in 1933 in Terrace. His mother Agnes Desjardins, from southern Manitoba, moved to Terrace in the 1920s. George's father emigrated from Denmark in 1924. The family lived in the Terrace area, where he and his siblings attended Kitsumkalum School and the family had a small mixed farm. George eventually joined the Royal Canadian Air Force, and spent three years in Ontario and Quebec, with his final post in Gander, Newfoundland.. He married and moved to Terrace in 1955, working for Columbia Cellulose Company of America. During his life, he worked as a powder man, river man, bridge man, tree faller, and fisheries officer. Near the end of the interview, he describes the war effort in Terrace and his early years living in Terrace. He remembers Silvertip and Little Joe's restaurants, Labour Day celebrations, and the social, economic, and infrastructure changes in Terrace during the mid-20th century.

TW: Okay, so it says we're supposed to talk about where you were born, but let's talk about your first ancestors to come here, which you said were your mom and your dad?

GK: Yes, as for the exact years I can't be certain, but my mother and her six sisters and two brothers moved here from southern Manitoba. I guess it was sometime in the 1920s. My father emigrated here from Denmark in 1924, to Terrace, and he married my mother whose name was Agnes Desjardins, in 1929.

TW: Oh, so your mother was part of the Desjardins clan. Now the Desjardins—did just the kids come? Or the parents?

GK: Nope, the whole family came. They married in 1929. My oldest sister was born to them in 1931, and I was born to them in 1933 on April fourth, in Terrace. My mother always said it was a nice sunny spring day.

TW: Well it must not have been too difficult for her if she remembers the weather that well.

GK: Well, who knows? I was born in a house in the bottom of what they now call Kalum Hill; the house is no longer there. And was attended to by a midwife, by the name of—believe it was Williamson, who has long since moved on and probably passed away. I attended school there. Started school when I was six, and I went to the Kitsumkalum School. In 1941 my dad had acquired a piece of property in Thornhill and we moved to Thornhill in 1941.

TW: For the information of people, in this current day and age that's where the Mac's store sits now.

GK: That's where the Mac's store sits now and we were the second residents over there in 1941.

TW: And who preceded you? Do you know?

GK: A family by the name of Paquette, Joe Paquette. He came here, I don't remember the year, but he could not read nor write. He left home when he was I think, 11 years old, left to work in the woods or whatever he could turn his hand to. Anyway, I attended the Kitsumkalum School, which was roughly three miles away and we walked it every day during the school year. There were no buses.

TW: Even from Thornhill?

GK: No, no, that's another part of the story.

TW: Oh okay, we will go back to the bottom of Kalum Hill. So when you say Kalum Hill, that's on Kalum Street?

Kofoed family picture. Back row [l-r]: George Kofoed, Adele Johnson, Dianne Gowe, Betty Jean Touring, Chuck Kofoed, Anne McInnis. Front row [l-r]: Joanne Watson, Charles Kofoed Sr. and Agnes Kofoed [George's parents], Thomas Kofoed. Circa 1960s. George Kofoed Collection.

GK: It's called North Kalum.

TW: Just below where the Terraceview [Lodge] is now?

GK: That's right just where Terraceview is now, and I attended school there, as I said, and then we moved across the river. And there was a school across the river. It was a one-room school but it was declared uninhabitable for school children, I guess, so they condemned it and shut it down. The people that lived over there said, "Okay, then you are going to have to provide a bus." So we went to school in a bus from that day forward. The bus was a nine-passenger Buick Sedan, driven by a fellow with the name George Brooks who had a dine and dance here in Terrace and he drove this taxi on the side. I went to school there until I left in grade 10.

My father got injured in the woods and could not look after the place. We had pigs and chickens and cows, and the wood, and all that good stuff that comes with country living. After he recuperated and was able to go back to work, I did not go back to school. I went to work at the Terrace Co-op. I guess I was what you would call nowadays a "go-for" because I did everything. I went and got bread from the bakery, I helped unload rail cars of grain, I stocked shelves, and I measured things out, weighed them and packaged them and put them on the shelves, and kept the fires going.

TW: Wood heat in those days?

GK: Wood and coal, mostly coal. I would have to say, because the store that I worked in was a reclaimed army building. When the store was started, the stove came with the army building and it was coal-burning. After that, I guess you could say I got itchy feet and wanted to see a little bit more of the world. So I joined the Royal Canadian Air Force, and I spent three years back east in Ontario
72

and Quebec and I had one overseas stint that I would like to claim and that was Gander, Newfoundland.

TW: Okay, so was this prior to 1949? Was it a foreign country?

GK: No, they had just joined and it's worthy of note that the feeling still ran pretty high there pro and con to joining the Confederation. There was many a dance there that ended up in the donnybrook after the happy juice started flowing. After that, I came back to Terrace and I married my first wife.

TW: Oh, your wife is a Newfie?

GK: No, my wife is also from BC. She is from the East Kootenays. And we had one child, born in Trenton, Ontario. So the three of us moved back here in 1955, and I went to work in the woods for Columbia Cellulose Company of America, which was the company that had the tree license here in the area at that time. TFL-1 [Tree Farm Licence 1] and I turned my hand to everything and anything that I could lay my hand to and stay employed. And so, in my wisdom or lack of it, I decided to be as employable as possible. And so I became a powder man, used dynamite. I became a river man and used riverboats, I became a bridge man and built bridges, and —towards the end of my career (because the work was taking me away from my family, which by this time I had six children)—I turned my hand to falling. I ended my career as a faller.

I had made a pledge to myself that when I started to get injured, I would change jobs. So I applied with the Department of Fisheries, got taken on as a fisheries officer, and I spent 15 years at that. My wife, my second wife – by this time I had divorced and married another woman by the name of Elizabeth Gaudi — when I told her I was getting out of the bush and going to find something safer, she breathed a sigh of relief. So when I joined Fisheries, I was shot at, chased with a power saw and an axe—so much for getting a safer job. But, anyway, it was something that I enjoyed, especially the habitat work, and I retired at that job.

TW: And that was when we met!

GK: That's right: you worked for forestry and I was still at fisheries at that time.

TW: You told me once the story of building the Kateen River Bridge in 1961, and it rained a tad.

GK: It did rain a tad. That river rose 12 feet in eight hours and that was the end of the bridge, end of the pile driver, end of all of the structural stuff that we had stacked there ready to put on the bridge.

TW: Oh, it was staged on the edge, took everything?

GK: Yeah, we were halfway across the bridge, halfway across the river with the bridge when it went out.

TW: And that was just below the confluence between the Cranberry and the Kateen.

GK: Just above the confluence.

TW: And you were going across the Kateen?

GK: Yep. Some of the stringers which were spruce logs that were manufactured into stringers, were some 60 feet long and one of them ended up in the schoolhouse at Old Aiyansh, in one door and out the window. That was where it was jammed. That's how high the water came up in Old Aiyansh, and Old Aiyansh had been there for some years, so obviously they had not had water of that magnitude up until then.

TW: I heard from another person that is into history—had said that in 1917 it was there, and that's why you find all those houses up on the bank above. And then over the years they sort of crept back down. But, I don't remember who told me that. It would be interesting to remember who told me that.

GK: Well, the pioneers of that area unfortunately have passed on or they could certainly tell you. Peter Hughan was a pioneer there.

TW: It might have been Herb, his son, who told me that.

GK: Yeah, Herb is gone now, too.

TW: That's right he is, too, son of a gun.

GK: I went to his memorial at his homestead there.

TW: During your years living in Thornhill, what was the road configuration when you first went there? It wasn't what it is now because Highway 16 wasn't there, and originally old Lakelse Lake Road went behind your house.

GK: That's right it went behind the store, and part of the old highway is still there to be seen.

TW: It's an old walking trail now.

GK: Yeah, Highway 16, I believe was all the way through to Hazelton and Smithers by the time we moved over there.

TW: A road of some sort.

GK: Yeah, a road of some sort. The road to Rupert, of course, was another story. There was no highway to Rupert.

TW: The army put that in, didn't they?

GK: The army engineers put that in.

TW: In 1943?

GK: Yeah, there was a bit of a celebration when that took place.

TW: Well, that would have been a bit more of a challenge than just going to Hazelton.

GK: Yeah there was kind of a — I don't know — a scare went through this country in terms of a Japanese invasion. So they wanted not to be trapped in Rupert and be isolated so they pushed rather quickly to have that highway put through. And if we are going to talk about World War II, there's a documentation in the archives in Ottawa of which I now have a copy, of an armored train that used to run from Prince Rupert to Pacific, and it was manned, or person-ed as they say now — to be politically correct — of a platoon of soldiers with an NCO [non-commissioned officer] in charge. I think he was a sergeant and on this train were artillery guns and huge searchlights and the idea behind this was if the Japanese tried to come up the Skeena River by submarine and take out some of the bridges on the railway, and/or the Highway 16, they would be dealing with them. And the train would take two or three days to make the round trip from Rupert to Pacific and back to Rupert, on a regular basis. And that was the brainchild of some colonel back in Ottawa.

TW: So I guess the crew were an artillery regiment — I presume. I had heard that story but I didn't know there were multiple guns. There were several artillery pieces on that train.

GK: Two. I think there was one on each end and a pair of searchlights. And just what calibre those artillery pieces were, I don't know, but I'm sure it's in that document. Yeah, the army days here

74

were quite something. We were a quiet town or village of about 1,500 people, and overnight we had 5,000 troops. And they lived — for the first winter, they lived in tents and it was a typical Terrace winter.

TW: A day like today? Half rain, half slop.

GK: A day like today, half rain, half snow, and below zero temperatures. They got it all. There was a sign, I remember, along that stretch there now where the Back Eddy Pub and the Bavarian Inn are located, there was a sign there that said, 'This place is one block west of hell's half acre.'

TW: So some of them had a sense of humor, eh?

GK: Some of them had a sense of humor. And they had built what they call drill halls, which were huge buildings in which they could train. I guess to get out of the weather. I suppose that's one of the reasons why they had it, but they used to use it to hold movies.

TW: Okay, so it had multiple purposes, dances and the whole bit?

GK: Yep, dances. It had a concrete floor. And they were the same size as the existing aircraft hangar that is up at the airport.

TW: Holy cow; so they weren't little.

Ted Wilson and George Kofoed. 2013.

GK: No, they weren't little, they weren't little. At the end of the war, the land that had been donated, you could say by George Little to the war effort by one dollar, so they said, it was returned to him, and they made a civic centre out of that big drill hall. There was one down there where the curling rink is now. And the other one was up on the Bench above the Bavarian Inn. It's backed in next to the mountain there. It's all built up now, it's all real estate now. I believe that building was torn down — no, I'm wrong. It was one of the hangars at the airport that was torn down and moved to Smithers and it became their community centre in Smithers.

TW: No, of course Smithers wouldn't have had the same military presence that Terrace did.

GK: No, it's strange; you talk to a lot of people that were young along with me at the time, and they don't remember the army at all. Nope they don't. The war seemed to not reach them the same way it did us.

TW: Even though they lived right here in Terrace.

GK: I don't mean the people who lived in Terrace, I mean the people who lived in Smithers, 150 miles away. There was nothing sacred here; the army just literally ran rough shod over the country. I can remember driving the horse to hill our potatoes and for some reason the horse stopped and wouldn't go any farther. My dad walked ahead of the horse to see what the problem was, and there was a guy there on a field radio talking to somebody in another part of the country. There was a maneuver going on and he was all camoed up and everything and we didn't see him.

TW: Oh, really? The horse knew he was there or heard him or something.

GK: Yeah, the horse sensed he was there. I remember that. And there were a lot of old pioneer buildings in this area that were used for target practice, too, by the Army. They just riddled them with small arms fire and stuff.

TW: Yeah, aside from the artillery on the train they didn't have big guns here did they?

GK: Oh, they had a few pieces.

TW: Oh, they did.

GK: Yes, they did and they used to use Terrace Mountain as their backstop. They actually started a few fires because of the moisture content of the existing fuel on the side hills there.

TW: Yeah, the southern exposure it gets pretty dry.

GK: Yeah, they started a few fires.

TW: Did they put them out?

GK: Oh, yeah, they would send a detail up there to put them out. Yeah, anyway, there was lots of activity here during the army days, and there were a few rapes. That's right, and there was a few wives made. Families started here, and after the war was over, they moved back here.

TW: Oh, really? So that was the start of some of the growth in population.

GK: That's right.

TW: Well I looked at air photos from 1938 and 1947 and Terrace probably changed more in the — what was it, three years that the army was here — than it did in any —

GK: It seems they were here longer than that, but I'm sure that's all it was. Well, no, they were here in '40.

TW: Oh, really? Okay. So they had started the training base here before the Japanese… [reference to the Japanese Imperial Army attack on Pearl Harbour, December 7, 1941].

GK: Oh, yes. Oh, no, Pearl Harbour certainly didn't trigger it, but Pearl Harbour certainly sped it up, because they put in an airport, too.

TW: Yeah, I knew that came in '42. What was the road system out towards the rifle range in those days? I'm a little baffled by that because there's an old road right up, as you know, by that hillside there. And there's a sort of an access trail that comes down from about behind the third fairway on the golf course to the big bore range, where it is now.

GK: Well the big bore range—my dad worked on that big bore range. It was constructed by the army.

TW: The original one. Well, I'm talking about the new one that's over to the south. There's a trail if you go just south of the embankment they built there, and the trail that goes up the hill, and I don't know how they got there. This would have been before the fires.

GK: More than likely, but certainly it was put in after the war. I mean, that trail was not put in during the war to my knowledge.

TW: No, no, no this was from the old railroad, the Omenica Railroad, I think they called it?

GK: Okay, that was destined for Kitimat originally. And whether funds dried up or ideas dried up or whatever it was, they discontinued it.

TW: Yeah, in 1904, from what I understand. And I am wondering where were the roads that got them there? Do you recall?

GK: Well, the road that would have got them to that escarpment at the bottom of Copper Mountain (or whatever they call it there), that would have been accessed by the road—by the mining road that used to go up the Copper on the north side. They put a bridge in. Of course they put a bridge in for the highway, and I don't know how far it would have gone after they put that bridge in. But that was the access. There was access, actually, up both sides of the Copper River in those days, where the road went to the Dardanelle Mine, which was 24 miles.

TW: That's what we know as the North Copper.

GK: That's right. And on the other side it was just a trapper's trail.

TW: Oh really? Arthur Clore's?

GK: Arthur Clore, yep.

TW: Okay, so that was just a trail in those days. Well, there must have been some logging there because the TFL [tree farm license] starts in at about 10 kilometre, nine kilometre or something like that. There's a sign there that says. So I would presume…

GK: Pretty much at the mouth of the canyon, isn't it?

TW: Just beyond that, yeah.

GK: Five Mile Creek maybe. That's what it's called?

TW: So below that must have been logged just before the TFL was awarded.

GK: Yeah I don't know who would have done that. There were a number of logging outfits here in the country. George Little was one, Claire Giggey, Haugland and Kerr.

TW: Did they have any sawmills out on the east side of the river?

GK: There was a sawmill, I would say probably about three kilometres up on the Copper on north side, called Baxter's. Baxter had a sawmill there. It's now called Baxter's Riffle.

TW: Oh, that's where that name came from! I fished there lots. I did find remnants of an old truck and some other stuff there. And that was a sawmill, was it? Learn something every day.

GK: And back to the road configuration in there were the rifle ranges. That was all put in by the army. They held maneuvers in there, because that was a flat of jackpine thicker than the hair on a dog's back, and not very tall. And it was a great place for practicing guerilla warfare or whatever.

TW: Yeah, well Terrace was originally, as I understand, an army base to teach mountain warfare.

GK: That's right, there was a mountaineering school here. They lost a few in avalanches too.

TW: Snow, or mud, or rock?

GK: Snow avalanches.

TW: So — originally they started it to have mountain troops for northern Europe.

GK: That's true.

TW: Oh, so there's something new there. Well, you have added to my body of knowledge anyways.

GK: Yep. Well there's lots there; it just trigs a person's memory.

TW: So the army built the road into the rifle range off Old Lakelse Lake Road. Which was the road to Lakelse Lake in those days.

GK: No the road, it wasn't off the Old Lakelse Lake Road, it was off the road that goes towards Copper River. It went in there.

TW: Oh, okay, it was the road that is now the original part of Highway 16.

GK: That's right. Right there where the Northern Motor Inn now sits was the army's garbage dump! Everything went in there. Everything. And got buried.

TW: And got buried. Everything. So you don't know if it's under the building or the parking lot.

GK: Probably the parking lot. They dug pretty deep pits and so most of the stuff is pretty well covered. I call it wet garbage, because it was garbage from the mess halls. And my dad — my dad was no fool. He clued in on all this stuff coming to the dump from the mess halls and so he started raising pigs and leaving barrels out at the entrance to our property there, and the army trucks would come by there with garbage cans full of wet garbage. And when I'm talking wet garbage, I'm talking about bacon and eggs, and pork and beans. Everything you'd ever cared to want to eat. Anyway, they would fill those barrels for us. And he raised quite a bunch of hogs off the garbage — well, sold it to the local stores here. Because of the war effort, that was all done on the QT. And the first cut that was made on any of the cargo was where the government stamp was usually set. So any time that the restaurants here in town, or the meat markets were inspected, that part was always missing. They couldn't tell whether it was government-inspected meat or not. But nobody died! It was quite the thing. Quite the thing.

And my dad when he built over there in the '40s, where the Mac's store sits now, he had to use green lumber because all the good lumber was being sent to the war effort and over the years as the lumber dried out the cracks got bigger and thank god for gyprock.

TW: It was a bit of a drafty house at times, was it?

GK: Yeah, covered a multitude of sins, I guess you could say. And the army — some of the lads there, for something to do they would come over and help Dad build. And it was a pretty good-sized house: 34 x 40.

TW: I remember it. When I first came it was there. It was quite impressive…

GK: Yep, it was more or less done with lumber that wasn't done for export or for the war effort.

TW: Was it rejects? Or was it the stuff that he got ahold of before the army knew it was there?

GK: No, I wouldn't call it rejects. I remember a lot of it was — I know they didn't use particleboard or plywood in those days. It was ship lap — they called it ship lap, and it was green, and the people who produced it here, Claire Giggey, or George Little, they were allowed a certain percentage of it to go for local use. But I mean it was green, it dried out on the house, and shrunk.

TW: In those days they cut mostly spruce?

GK: Spruce and hemlock.

TW: Spruce and hemlock.

GK: And my dad and my uncle, they became partners during the war effort and they actually logged, or felled, the spruce on most of these islands in the lower Skeena and it went into making the Mosquito bombers. Spruce plywood.

TW: I know the Sitka spruce was really in high demand. Because they did use that as spruce plywood and I think plywood was invented for that purpose during the war. A lot of technological happenings.

GK: And then after that, they re-logged the islands again for cottonwood because cottonwood went into making plywood as well.

TW: As a peeler log.

GK: Yeah, there were some pretty big trees and some deep snow in those days. I can remember my dad telling me that on those islands down there at Amesbury, they could shove a seven-foot cross-cut through the snow and just the handle would stick out on the other end. They assumed they were on the ground, maybe? But one saving factor about that sort of logging, as tough as it was, there was not much impact on the landscape because of the deep snow.

TW: Although it probably wasn't the greatest utilization, because you wouldn't get down to the butt of the tree.

GK: No, this is true, they used springboards to get above the swell, eh.

TW: They did, eh? They avoided swell?

GK: Well the problem was the scaler wouldn't scale that particular size. You would put the stick across the tree above the swell. That's where we're going to cut 'em.

TW: That's much easier to cut, if you could call it easier.

GK: Yeah, it was; in the beginning it was all handwork.

TW: That's right, because the power saw didn't come in until the 1950s.

GK: Well they had that in the late '40s, too. They were real brutes to use, hard to start and hard to pack around. Especially — and I, you know, I can't remember my dad ever using snow shoes. As deep as the snow got. He may have used them to get to the tree, but then he took them off.

TW: And he was a faller?

GK: He was a faller. My dad, yeah, he was a carpenter, and he was a faller. He apprenticed in the old country as a stone mason, and also he apprenticed as a baker as well. But he quit baking when he married my mother. He showed her how to do it and then stepped back.

TW: So your enthusiasm for multiple trades comes honestly.

GK: Yes. My mom and dad raised eight of us. Five brothers — sorry, five sisters and two brothers.

TW: How many of them are left in Terrace?

GK: I have two sisters in Terrace and two brothers.

TW: And multiple offspring.

GK: And multiple offspring. I have two that live here, a son and a daughter. One son in Prince George, and Balfour, which is just outside of Nelson. A sister that lives in Alberta, and one in Nanaimo on Vancouver Island. Spread around pretty good. They seem to be pretty happy where they are. I don't know why — this has to be the best place.

TW: Do you recall what restaurants you liked here?

GK: Oh, yes, there were not many of them. There was one called the Silvertip, one called Little Joe's, one called the Seven Come Eleven, and I believe — oh, there was another little one, too, that sprung up later on, that was owned by a couple of pioneers, Flossie and Geoff Lambly—I think they called it The Snack Bar, and it was a favorite hangout for me and my peers when I was a teenager. There was another one too, and it was that fellow that had that contract that carried us to school, George Brooks. He had one that was called the Dine and Dance. It was a popular place for the soldiers. And that was the place to be on a Saturday night if you were able to leave the base. Of course, there was a shortage of partners. Because there were more men in the town than women.

TW: By a pretty significant amount.

GK: Yep, but it was a lively place; he made good money.

TW: Did you go to the hot springs at all?

GK: Very seldom.

TW: It was more of a tourist place, was it?

GK: It kind of had half a life for a while, and then it kind of died when the owner I guess passed on. A fellow by the name of Poe. He actually ran a pipe from the hot springs to a hotel along Lakelse Lake. And he had hot water in the hotel from that hot springs. The only other time I went out there as a young fellow was with the boy scouts, and we bushwhacked through the swamps to get there. There was no trail; everything had grown over since the people who had first developed it had moved on. To get to the hot springs there was no road. The road to Kitimat didn't go in near the hot springs until the mid-'50s.

TW: Was the old Lakelse Lake Road not up there then?

GK: Yes it was; it went as far as the far end of the lake. But the road did not go to the hot springs.

TW: Oh, because it went to the old forestry cabin I know.

Sports in Terrace—I'm sure you were in sports at one point or another.

GK: Oh, growing up, we looked forward to the celebration days like the 24th of May, and the 1st of July, and I think that was just about it. I don't think there was anything else, oh Labour Day, and that was it. I looked forward to them because they used to hold sports days and you would compete for money. Two bits for first, 10 cents for second, and a nickel for third, and that was big money back in those days.

TW: Yeah, it would be. But then where would it come from? Would the local merchants put it up?

GK: Yeah, the local merchants put it up. Local organizations would put it up, put some money in the kitty. It was held for kids; it wasn't held for adults. There was an age limit. The adults, they'd play baseball and stuff like that. Terrace had a pretty good baseball team back in those days. My uncle Ted Johnston played on it.

TW: Oh, Ted was your uncle?

GK: Yes he was. He was married to my mom's older sister.

TW: Well I've read his memoirs; he didn't take your name in vain, anyway. You have a copy, I take it? I would expect that.

GK: Yeah that was pretty much it for sports. Later on in my life, as the town grew, we had our own ball league here. The Terrace Hotel had a ball team sponsored by Cariboo Breweries in Prince George. That was Ben Ginter, I believe.

TW: Oh, was that Ben Ginter?

GK: Yeah. And Augie Geeraert, the local pub owner, he sold his beer, so he was one ball team and I played for the Terrace Legion. And the league — I forget how many games it consisted of; it was quite a few over the summer, and the loser had to buy the beer. And we drank lots more of Cariboo Beer than the other stuff because we would always win. Yeah, we had some good games, some good tournaments. And there was a kind of an inter-city, or town league in those days, too, and we used to compete with Prince Rupert and Smithers.

TW: And that would have been before Kitimat was Kitimat.

GK: That's right, yes.

TW: Where was the shopping done in Terrace, mostly at the Co-op?

GK: The Co-op was kind of a start and stop store. It started in the early days, it was one of the originals, but it died. It didn't exist for quite a number of years until a group got together, some of which my parents belonged to as charter members. They held study sessions and studied the Co-op movement, and the Co-op philosophy and stuff and started another store. And that store was one of those reclaimed army buildings, too. The army barracks. You could buy them fairly cheaply and then you had to move them.

TW: Why was it necessary to move them?

GK: Well, I guess maybe George Little had wanted the land.

TW: So George was selling them, was he?

GK: Well, I don't know the ins and outs of that, but you could pick them up fairly reasonable. The criteria was that you had to move them off the property. So they would build huge timbered sleighs, jack the buildings up, and lower them down on the sleighs. And then with the D-8 Cat rumbling down Lakelse Avenue, pulling these buildings to whoever and wherever they were to go.

TW: And that was before it was paved.

GK: Yes, they never paved any of that before the Queen paid us a visit.

TW: Yes. I've heard that part of the story.

GK: By that time I was Cub Master. I remember standing there with my group being inspected by the Queen.

TW: Oh — I heard she just did a drive through?

GK: Oh, no. She did a walk-about. We all assembled at the airport. When she got off the plane—so when she got off the aircraft, she inspected us. I believe she was pregnant with Charlie at the time, truth be known. But I didn't ask. No. Yeah, they paved from the airport to town, and one block around the town, taking in the post office where it now sits. And that block there, they paved that. She did the circuit, and she used a fellow here by the name of Dave Graf. He had a plumbing outfit in town, and he had a brand new Pontiac Convertible — black. And that was where she did the tour. That was the royal limousine.

TW: And back in those days, most of the work was in the woods was it?

GK: Pretty much, there was mixed farming here for quite a number of years, even orchards, and then of course when the tree farm license was granted to that company, then the woods industry really took off.

Queen Elizabeth II and Prince Philip, Lakelse Avenue, July 18, 1959. Heritage Park Collection.

TW: And made it more profitable to work in the woods.

GK: Yes. There was a disease — came through this country and wiped out the orchards. It didn't wipe them out but it produced a scab on the fruit and nobody wanted to buy it. Nobody wanted to buy fruit with scabs on it. Prior to that — I mean, they used to grow strawberries here and all kinds of fruit. But most people that came here, first they had acreages and they would have mixed farming. When we were growing up on North Kalum we had a big garden, and we had cows, and chickens and pigs. So during the Depression years, we really didn't want for anything, because we grew most of our own food.

TW: And the drought didn't affect this area? The drought that hit the Prairies didn't…

GK: No, you mean the drought of the hungry '30s, as it came to be known? No, no it didn't.

TW: You must have seen lots of changes in the logging industry over the years — well, I mean, you talk about your dad falling trees with the Armstrong saw.

GK: The bush fiddle. Yeah they could make 'em sing. He used to tell me they weren't really sharpened until the sawdust that came out had bark on both ends.

TW: So saw filing in those days was quite an art.

GK: Yeah, he could file his own saws.

TW: Well, yeah, you would have to, because you would only have one cross-cut saw, or two cross-cut saws.

GK: Well, they had falling saws and cross-cut saws, you see. Falling saws were longer.

TW: And they would be the ones with the vertical handles at 90 degrees to the blade. I've seen them. And they'd go through the big spruce around here?

GK: Yep, they had to cut. A scaler would come around, and you would be paid by what the scale showed. The scaler worked for the boss man, whether it was Claire Giggey or George Little.

TW: Worked for the log buyer, in essence.

GK: Yep.

TW: And by the time you get out there was feller bunchers, and high lead loggers.

GK: When I became a faller, there was high-lead logging. The feller bunchers came after I'd quit. I would say I think I left the industry in the late '80s, early '90s. Yeah, they had wooden spars originally, and then of course the steel towers came and they were able to move them around.

TW: And the one they called Big Bertha, across from the Chamber of Commerce, I think.

GK: I think it had a sister happening, it was called the Titanic. Because that thing was so heavy it went right through the road when they tried to move it. It just sunk into the gravel. It took — don't know how many bulldozers, one pushing, one pulling — to make that thing move. It was somebody's pipe dream that never really produced. They pulled it off to one side somewhere near Alice Creek, and it sat on the side of the road until the local heritage society, or I guess, whoever decided to move it to its present location.

TW: But most of the real work was done by Madill spars.

GK: Yeah, that's right. Tank mounted steel towers.

TW: Yeah, I think they were on tank retrievers, weren't they?

GK: Yeah, maybe; all I knew is they kinda looked like a tank; they had tracks. But prior to that they were wooden spars. They were usually able to leave one standing tree on site in some cases, in other cases they had to move them there with two logging trucks in tandem and move the big spruce into place and then they would rig it and raise it. They had about a 12-man crew, on a logging truck with a set of winches on it. It was called 'the goat.' And that would be moved into position to raise the spar.

TW: The function of the goat was to stand the spar up? That would be a complex operation.

GK: Yeah, it was a high-lead hooker from Vancouver Island who really knew his stuff about rigging. That was the head honcho. He stayed here, he lived here. I remember there were a number of different ones over the years. The other guys either retired or moved on to greener pastures or whatever, and it had to be an experienced bona fide hooker from Vancouver Island who knew how to handle big timber.

TW: Local people didn't have that experience?

GK: No, we were green as grass to that. We could horse log or Cat log, but that was something strange to us and didn't come in until the tree farm license was granted. That was in the late '40s, early '50s.

TW: I think '49 was the date I recall on documentation I saw. When did they get to Terrace, because they started in Prince Rupert and worked this way, didn't they?

GK: They were here quite quickly in the early '50s — I would say '52.

TW: And when did they start up the Nass?

GK: At about the same time they started pushing roads. So they started pushing towards the Nass and they developed cut blocks as they went and logged them and of course the original idea was to float the logs to Prince Rupert down the Kalum River. In a bag boom. They bag boomed a lot of them in the Kalum Lake and then towed them down the lake to the outfall of the river. Then they would turn them loose. And they had a catch boom here down at what they call the reload now, where they dewatered them and put them on the rail cars and freighted them to Rupert by rail.

TW: The reload being at the Kitsumkalum Village.

GK: Right where the Tempo gas station is now.

TW: Right behind there. Actually, I think at the moment Valard is using it as a staging area for the power line now. That being 2013. If somebody listens to this five years from now, they will still be confused. When did CN [Canadian National Railway] start operating that quarry in behind here, do you recall? Was it always there as far as you can remember?

GK: I think that started operating about the same time that Columbia Cellulose came here and started pushing the road. Because of their failed attempt at floating the logs to Prince Rupert, they decided they would have to freight them here and a rail spur was put into that area.

TW: And they kept putting the rock there and using it as ballast?

GK: Well, yes, and the company would use some of the rock themselves, too. So they originally started the quarry and then I think a deal between them, CN, and First Nations provided the development of that rock quarry there. It's supposed to be a special kind of rock that breaks a certain way and is ideal for putting under the ties on the railway.

TW: Yeah, it has lots of facets to it that lock together. I can remember — I think it was the first time we met down at Cecil Creek, in Kitimat Valley, and John introduced me to 'Leaveright.' Your partner John Hipp introduced me to Laborite. Picked up a rock and said "What kind of rock is this?" And I thought, *This is a fisheries technician trying to get me to identify a rock? What is going on here?* And then he dropped it and said this is 'Leaveright.' I got the message. I think that was the '80s or something? Late '80s? You must have enjoyed that fisheries work as a keen fisherman.

GK: I did! I did. I didn't enjoy the enforcement work as much as I enjoyed the habitat work. Spawning escapements, helicopter flying, and stuff like that I really enjoyed.

TW: Well, who does like enforcement?

GK: Well, it was a necessary thing at the time.

TW: Yeah, that's true. I always thought it worked better when we cooperated. I used to find it worked best. Like the time we met, just go out to the environmental agencies, and say "This is what I want to do, how would you like to see it done?" And before you already made an application, you knew the parameters, you knew how to put it out there. I can always remember that John asked me one time, "Well, who's doing the work?" "Well, Johnny Wright is doing the work." "Give me that,

Johnny knows what he's doing," and ever since then I knew to put him really high at the top of my list.

GK: Yeah, Johnny was a great guy. I liked working for him.

TW: He was your boss at one time?

GK: Yeah, he was my supervisor because he was construction foreman for quite a while in the Nass and we built a lot of bridges up there. As a matter of fact, it was in '61 when he, my brother, and I, we hiked along the road grade to the bridge site.

TW: Maybe he was the one who told me about Aiyansh getting flooded in 1917 because he was a keen historian.

GK: That's right. Anyway we walked that road to the bridge site and lots of times the water was up to our armpits. We wanted to get back in there to see if the pile driver was still in existence. The day after the storm.

TW: Oh and that would have been cold, too; wasn't it in October?

GK: We were hide bound in that we were going to see what had happened.

TW: And then when you got there, there was nothing to see, everything was gone.

GK: Yes, I remember nobody could go to work because all the roads were flooded and we were all kind of congregating in the cookhouse and the construction superintendent — a fellow by the name of Bill McKabe, he radioed up from Terrace to hear our assessment of the flood — asked, "What about the pile driver?" Well, a fellow by the name of Johnny Jackson, he was pretty quick-witted, before Johnny Wright could answer, he said, "Ever heard of a place called China?"

TW: Wasn't the answer that Mr. McKabe wanted to hear, I think.

GK: No, but that's pretty much where it ended up.

TW: Scattered all over the place in the bush.

GK: I think it hung up in the canyon just below the confluence of the Cranberry and the Kiteen, you know that canyon there before it goes into the Nass, I think that's where it hung up, and that's where the hammer was. And that hammer was I think 4200 pounds.

TW: Yeah, I was going to say, those pile drivers aren't light!

GK: No, they aren't light. But I mean it got down that far. And those streams were raging. They were just raging. I can remember within the days that followed I actually ran a riverboat on the lava beds. That's how high the water was.

TW: Holy Dina! Wow, well for people who haven't been to the lava beds, now you've learned something, and when you go and look at it — I've been there lots, but I find that just blows my mind!

GK: There were standing waves in the canyon there at Canyon City, as high as this house. Easily as high as this house. That water and its attempt to get away was piling up on itself.

TW: I guess that would be the outlet to a lot of backed up water.

GK: It was because of that constriction that the lava beds flooded, eh?

TW: Oh, so it backed up and came around?

GK: That's right. Everything was flooded. And the Skeena River did hardly anything. It's just the way that storm path went though.

TW: In '78 the storm just went up the Copper drainage. And the Skeena drainage — looked at the water gauge reports for both years for both rivers and you would never know looking at one that there was a flood in the other. And it didn't matter you know. So we get some storms come in here and they're not huge as far as width is concerned, but they're very concentrated and it's hard to imagine that until you've seen it happen.

TW: One of these areas we haven't touched on because maybe it didn't happen, or maybe we took it for granted is, how did the Native and the white people get along in the early days?

GK: Very well. Very well. Of course there were no restrictions then. I mean if you wanted half a dozen, or a dozen sockeye for canning, you just let it be known and it would be at your door. And one historical note that I remember very vividly and this is going back before I was even at a school age; my dad had a cedar pole company, and he took cedar poles out of the Kalum Valley. We lived in a camp at what they now call 16 Mile, on the Kalum River. And we spent one Christmas there because we got snowed in. This was prior to '39, those being the '30s. There was an Indian couple who came through and they were heading for town on snowshoes. They had come down as far as our camp at 16 Mile by boat and they had a boatload of fish. And I know to this day it was steelhead. It had to be steelhead. They had netted them. And they said "We can't get any farther with this fish, so do you mind if we store them here?" So they dug a hole in the snow, threw the fish in and buried them. And they said "any time you want a fish, you help yourself." And that Christmas dinner was a stuffed big steelhead. I never forget that, because we couldn't get to town to get groceries or anything, we were snowed in. We ate what was there. I believe it was a family of the Nelsons that were going to Terrace.

TW: Well, did they have a village or something at the lake? Where were they from?

GK: They were coming off their trap line, I would suspect. It was a couple, a man and a woman.

TW: And was the river named after that family?

GK: Yeah, that's right.

TW: Little piece of history to note. What about the other rivers along there, like Alice Creek or Star Creek? Where did those names come from?

GK: I have no idea where they came from. No. They were always named Alice Creek and Star Creek in my memory. Luncheon Creek is another one; I don't know where that one came from, either. And Benoit Creek… Leo Benoit was one of my dad's partners in that cedar pole company.

TW: Yeah, I know Benoit Creek pretty well. I put a culvert in there.

GK: That's an old Terrace family and I don't think there are any of them living around here anymore. That was Marguerite Paquette—that was her maiden name. She married Ivan Benoit, and she still lives here, she lives out on Queensway.

TW: The last question I have is around the changes you've seen over the years. We've touched on some of that with the army base and the army being here and then the Columbia Cellulose coming in. Did it change a lot when Kitimat started to happen?

GK: Well, you have me at a disadvantage there, because when Kitimat started to happen was when I was in the military.

TW: And in terms of annual community events, were there Christmas events?

GK: Yes, there was. Schools put on Christmas concerts, which was a big thing. And there was a Santa Claus and he gave every little kid a bag of candy. And we never knew who the Santa Claus was. Would have been a good idea now but I didn't know then.

TW: It was probably better that you didn't.

GK: Yeah ,there was a local orchestra here too, a dance orchestra. It was a fellow who just recently passed away, Allan Dubeau. He was one of the participants in that orchestra.

TW: So, Terrace has a musical history that goes well before the Northwest Music Festival and the R.E.M. Lee Theatre.

GK: Yeah, they had a band. There's old pictures, I think July 1st pictures of the local band marching. I think our first Scout Master here, Sam Kirkaldy, he was quite musically inclined.

TW: Really, I didn't know that about Sam. I know he had a lot of other talents.

GK: Yeah, he played trumpet, I believe.

TW: Were you aware of the mutiny and what was going on then?

GK: Oh yes, vaguely aware, we weren't allowed to go downtown: it was off-limits.

TW: During that time?

GK: Yes, during that time we were more or less confined to our homes, you know. They had a group here called the Air Raid Wardens and that was put together by the Pacific Coast Militia Rangers, of which Corbin King… he's mentioned in the paper there when they show the veterans on Veterans Day. He was a member of that, and Allan Dubeau's dad was one of the ones that spearheaded that. There was a militia here for Home Defence, I guess you could call it, and they were issued with a bone-dry outfit: pants that could stand in the corner after you took them off, stiff, and the jacket, and a hat with a badge on it and a 30-30 carbine rifle. I was so determined that my dad should join so we could get our hands on a 30-30.

TW: You figured that was the thing to have in those days?

GK: Absolutely that was the thing to have.

TW: When you say 30-30 you mean the old Winchester 94?

GK: The old 94, yep. But he never did; he was kind of funny in a way. I wouldn't call him a pacifist, but he equated the Boy Scouts with the Hitler Youth. He said, "I don't see any difference." Both involved in the war effort, you know. I mean, I don't say I went over his head, I guess you could say I went behind his back, but he didn't like it. But I was a member of the Boy Scouts, and we collected tin foil and all that stuff, and string for the war effort.

TW: Recycling is not new?

GK: No, it wasn't, not in those days. And we were rationed, too. We were rationed big time. But then again we had a lot of those amenities at our fingertips, because we had cows and chickens and all that stuff. My mom took in sewing for the military and all that.

TW: Oh yeah, when the boys needed something mended on their little kit.

GK: Oh yeah, I remember one outfit there had a scarlet wedge sewn into the bottom of his dress trousers.

TW: On the inside seam?

GK: Yep. I can't remember the name of the outfit. I used to know them all. But I remember her doing that for a number of them.

TW: I can imagine that would be quite distinctive when you're marking because you would flash.

GK: It was their dress uniform, not their battle uniform.

TW: Yeah, I realize that, but when you're marching, as you step forward it would be there, and as you step the other leg, it would come and go, catch the eye — very clever.

GK: I should Google it sometime and figure out what outfit that was. There were lots of them here. It was a mountaineering school but we had the artillery, and — I don't think we had the Black Watch here, we had the Winnipeg Grenadiers, and the Irish Fusiliers and others.

TW: Oh yeah, they all came to do a tour here. So when you say there were 3000 military personnel, that was at one time and they keep rotating?

GK: It was five actually, 5000.

TW: Military personnel? Was it military personnel and road builders?

GK: Nope. Well, the engineers, they were military, too. The RCEs, they were engineers. They were the ones who built the road to Rupert.

TW: Well, how did that work because I thought it was Foley, Welch and Stewart that did the work? No?

GK: Nope.

TW: Was it military?

GK: To my knowledge, it was the military. No, Welch, Stewart and Bloedel that was a logging outfit.

TW: Yeah, down on the island.

GK: Yeah, they may have been involved, but not to my knowledge.

TW: Well, I know that's who built the railroad, but I thought I had seen documentation to the effect that they were involved in the road building as well. It may have been that the real engineers managed to contract you.

GK: Well, I can remember some of the army personnel running bulldozers.

TW: Oh really? Well, yeah, that would make sense because I think Johnny Wright learned his bulldozer operations in the army, which always struck me funny because John was smaller than you and the old cable machines — you had to be strong.

GK: Yeah, well I could tell you stories that Johnny told me too but that's not part of this.

TW: Yeah, well unfortunately John is gone so.

GK: Yeah, I really liked John. He was a great guy. We put in a lot of time together.

TW: You know, I don't know any enemies of John. There are some people that were a little cool on him but most people thought he was extremely well-liked.

GK: Yep, he was a square shooter.

TW: He really was. In a lot of ways, he was one of the pioneers, even though he wasn't born here. He came with Columbia Cellulose, I think, didn't he? Or was he here before that?

GK: He was here before that. He was here after 1945. I think he worked for L.H. & K., Little Haugland and Kerr, in the woods.

TW: Actually, that would make sense because he told me about building that piece of the Copper Road below the first canyon. Putting a bulldozer in the river and placing gravel up onto the grade and you being a fisheries officer, George, you know it was full of eggs and fry.

GK: Oh I know, they did the same thing up north, too, on the road to Stewart. They dredged out of the Bear River there or something to make part of that road.

TW: Yeah, they did, that's true. I think it was Ginter, wasn't it?

GK: Oh, yeah, nothing sacred in those days.

TW: We've talked some about how Terrace has changed and annual community events. What about the Great War Veterans Association Hall?

GK: The only story I remember about that it was in 1935, '36, the winter of the big snow. They were holding a dance in the War Veterans Hall and the then-provincial policeman of the day must have had some sort of smarts because he came in and shut the dance down, and later that night the building collapsed.

TW: Under the snow load.

GK: Under the snow load.

TW: And you were quite small then.

GK: Oh, I was small then. But I remember the time my dad took me across the Old Skeena Bridge in '36, because I can remember the noise. That bridge was vibrating from the sound of that water.

TW: Well Corbin King's sister Jenny told me that the end span on the tip of the Thornhill end. went out. And Corbin was trapped out at the lake, and he decided he wanted to get into town, so he was jumping across on the logs that were floating there.

GK: See, they've changed the cross section under that bridge twice now, for the water to get away but yeah, they've taken slices off. They blasted the rock.

TW: Yeah, because it's still probably not under the 200-year flood line.

GK: And that bridge used to turn and go to Queensway because that other road wasn't there. We were talking about road access there.

TW: So where did Lakelse Lake Road and the predecessor to Highway 16, which is I think River Road now through Thornhill, isn't it? Where did they come in? When I came in — there was no Highway 16.

GK: You know that bit of a rental outfit, where Del Holtom lives, well that's part of the old road. Those buildings there, they all face part of the old road that used to come off Queensway.

TW: Oh, so they used to meet down at the bridge, Queensway, and Queensway was the general direction that the traffic went or wanted to go then?

GK: Yep. I mean I said that we were only the second house in Thornhill. There were other houses up Queensway. But we were only the second house on that road there.

TW: Okay, because I know Otto Lindstrom told me once that he and his sister took their family cow across the ferry down there at Remo.

GK: Because that was the only bull in the country.

TW: Was Franks' bull, so they walked it all the way into town because they couldn't go across the rail bridge with a cow, or walk across the highway bridge. Back down to Franks' place. He said the whole distance to where he started to where he ended up was three or four miles; he walked 20 with the cow to get it bred.

GK: Well, there was a German fellow, Paul Hertel, a German-born immigrant who came to the Terrace area in the 1930s. He started a family and had a few head of cattle. He homesteaded up the Zymacord River Valley and when the cow needed to be bred, he used to swim the Skeena at Remo with the cow. There was no ferry then and he would strip off, I was told this — he would strip off, tie his clothes to the top of the cows head on her horns — and he would swim the river with her to the bull and then swim her back. He was quite an athletic guy. Apparently it didn't work out here and he and his family moved to Vancouver Island. His daughter wrote a history of being up there and living down on Vancouver Island. And she came through this country and unfortunately I wasn't here at the time, I mean I wasn't in the military but I must have been working in the Nass or something, and I didn't get to talk to her, but I'd dearly love to talk to her. She wrote a book and I can't remember the name of it now.

TW: Or the name of the people?

GK: Yeah.

TW: Well remember Google and see what you can find George. It might be something to add to the collection.

GK: Yeah, I'm not sure if it would be on Google or not. Yeah, that's really too bad, that's a real disservice because I shouldn't forget people like that.

TW: Well, sometimes our brains get overloaded.

GK: Well, another happening that involved this same fellow, I'm sure his name will come to me. There was a fire up where the Uplands School is. There was a house there, a two-storey house. And it caught fire and there was a young girl trapped upstairs — and the story's told to me by my parents — this same guy ran at the house and managed to hook his fingers on the sill of the window on the second storey, pulled himself up and got the girl out of there. Now I know no details how he got her back out of there. Whether he took the girl and jumped, which is probably what he did because the house was on fire. He couldn't have gone downstairs.

TW: Well okay, George we will move on, in our discussions here, we've covered a lot of stuff like the Queen's visit. Now when you were a child what did you expect or hope to accomplish? What were your childhood dreams?

GK: I don't think I had any dreams…

TW: You were busy living in the moment?

GK: Living in the moment, yeah. I remember once being asked by the school inspector what I wanted to be and I told him I wanted to be a biologist. That was more or less to get him off my back so he could move onto the next student. Because I was not good in school: I was looking out the window too much.

TW: So I guess as a fisheries officer, you got as close as you could to what you told him, as a guy could without being tied to a chair.

GK: I went back to school when I married my second wife. We both took university courses here at the local college, and I got my first year university. I finished my high school and got my first year university. And of course that did me good, I guess my brain had developed more then, and I was more accepting to somebody droning on. I used to work all day, and I would come home and we used to drive to Kitimat to take a course, have dinner and drive back to Terrace.

TW: Oh, the course was in Kitimat?

GK: Some of them were and some of them were here, and then go to work the next day.

TW: Do you remember much about Kitimat in the early days?

GK: We used to go there, when I came back from the armed forces. I was involved again in sports teams and played on the local ball team and we used to go to Kitimat to play ball. We used to drive the odd time to see a hockey game, because there was no arena here in those days, either. And Kitimat had an arena before Terrace did, so other than that no, I never used to go there to fish or anything like that.

TW: It wouldn't really be necessary, would it?

GK: No.

TW: I wanted to talk a little bit about a group, a club that we are both members of, and that is the Rod and Gun Club. In its early days, was it a club or was it different disciplines?

GK: No it was a club. Do you know where the Mac's store is? If you turn onto Old Lakelse Lake Road Drive, as you make that corner where the gas station is now, along the other side.

TW: Oh, by the Copperside store?

GK: On the other side of the road, from the Copperside store, that was the trap range, right against that hill right there.

TW: Okay, sort of where Bill Watson's place was. Sort of by Twin River Timbers.

GK: No, across the road from there. Down in that bit of a depression there, I don't know what that is now. Some construction company's warehouse or something, I don't know. But yeah, you could mine lead there. They had quite a club and a lot of the members were from the Lower Mainland because Columbia Cel was really going big time; they were pushing road. They needed gravel trucks and gravel truck fleets, and a lot of those fellows from the Lower Mainland that belonged to clubs down there they moved up here and they joined the local club here. And it was quite thriving.

TW: And apparently there was a pistol range in the basement of the old police hall?

GK: Yes, and I was a member of that club too. It was the old liquor store. Yeah I competed against RCMP members and CN cops and I never ever had to buy coffee.

TW: Was the rifle range itself being used very much in those days?

GK: It was, it was being used but it was only being used because everybody knew it was there and that was the place to go and shoot and that was a legitimate 100 metres away. Eventually the Rod and Gun Club took it over because it was falling out of disrepair. Well, there were no buildings there?

TW: Just the bunkers. Or the shooting butts, and the berms.

GK: I think it was out to 1000 yards at one time. If you walk back to the bush, I mean a lot of those berms were loaded out. It was an easy supply of gravel. You just go in there with a front-end loader

— it was already pushed up for you — and loaded the wind row. So a lot of those berms disappeared. But it was all cleared way back.

TW: Yeah I've seen pictures of it, and I can go back 400 yards and that berm is at the top of a bank that drops down quite a bit.

GK: Okay, so maybe it wasn't 1000 yards, then.

TW: I don't think—at least it wouldn't have been east-west 1000 yards.

GK: Well, that was pretty much east-west.

TW: It was pretty much all east-west eh? Well, I know there was a photo that showed a 500 yard berm and I paced 500 yards and I was down in that hole.

GK: Is that where that guy has that house with the chain link fence around it?

TW: Not quite that far, but in that area, and it looked like somebody had started to build a berm around there.

GK: Well, you see 1000 yards, that's about a kilometre from where you turn off to go into the rifle range.

TW: Well, you can't see the butts around there because there's a rise in the ground in between.

GK: But I know some of those berms were loaded out.

TW: Well I know one — the 100-yard one is completely gone, because that would have been right in front of the clubhouse. And the 200 is between the clubhouse and the trailer now and it has got holes punched in it and stuff.

GK: And they had a range in behind where the court house is now that used to be a brickyard. There was a vein of clay in there that was suitable for making bricks. They made bricks there. And it was named the Brick Yard in my childhood days. But it was the first rifle range and it was 100 metre because I can remember being able to get a vantage point there and watch them shoot. You know, there's a bit of a dugout there, concrete works. Well that's where the guys would hide with the mobile targets. They would move the bull's eye around and the guys back at 100 metres were shooting at it.

TW: Well, they have the same thing at the rifle range there, or is that what you're talking about?

GK: No, keep going, it's been a long time since I've been there.

TW: The one right against the hill is a concrete wall with compartments in it, and then they've got the gravel all pushed up in the front of it. And that's what you shoot into, is the gravel, and right behind there're places where guys can sit. And then they've got two great big concrete bunkers in there.

GK: We're talking about the big bore range?

TW: Not in the current big bore range but the old one.

GK: No, I know the old one, I've been in there many times.

TW: Yeah, where the trap range is. Okay, George, well, I think we've covered everything that I've wanted to.

Gus (August) Gerdei Interview
Interviewed by Melanie Pollard

August (Gus) Gerdei was born in Austria in 1949. Gus came to Canada in 1970 to attend his brother's wedding. During his visit, he decided to apply to immigrate to Canada. Gus moved to Terrace in 1975 and married the following year. The prospect of opening a business brought Gus to Terrace, and he leased a building on Lakelse Avenue for two years before purchasing it in October 1977. In the two-storey building, Gus operated a restaurant, the Bavarian Inn, in the upstairs and opened a nightclub downstairs called Mozart's Boogie Parlor. He ran the nightclub for 10 years before converting it into the Back Eddy Pub. In this interview, Gus talks about opening and operating his business, playing tennis, and participating in popular local events. He also discusses Terrace's economic past and future in the resource industry. Gus has witnessed Terrace's up-and-down economy over the years and has weathered it with hard work and commitment to his business.

MP: Where and when were you born?

AG: I was born in Austria on October 9, 1949.

MP: What brought your family to Terrace and when did you come?

AG: It's not my family, I came to Terrace by myself. I originally came to Kitchener, Ontario. I was only a visitor. I have a brother there, and I came to his wedding in 1970. We went to immigration and applied for it. I wanted to stay for one year and learn some English and I never went back.

MP: And when did you make the move from Kitchener to Terrace?

AG: Originally I went to Toronto. Then moved to Vancouver, worked in Vancouver for four years, and then came to Terrace in May '75.

MP: Could you tell me a little bit about growing up in Austria, and what that was like?

AG: Well, I did my school years, and in those days it was only eight years. Then I went into a butcher apprenticeship for a year and a half. Then I took a three year cooking apprenticeship for a college degree in the hotel industry.

MP: And you finished that up before coming to Canada?

AG: That's right, yes. I did my army stint and then I came to Canada.

MP: How long did you have to…

AG: Nine months.

MP: And what was school like for you growing up?

AG: It's hard to explain.

MP: Any memories of school that you would want to share?

AG: I don't know what to compare it with — you know, I didn't go anywhere else to school. It was okay, I suppose. I didn't want to go to university, let's put it this way. I wanted to do things with my hands. But, I did okay.

MP: When did you figure out that you loved to cook?

AG: Sort of when I went to my pre-butcher apprenticeship, and then I wanted to become a cook. My father wanted me to become an electrician because he was an electrician.

MP: But you like to work with food.

AG: Yeah, yeah, I chose that industry. And you know, I wanted to travel and the adventure. So that's how pretty much I came to Canada.

MP: That's so neat. And so when you came to Canada how old were you?

AG: 21.

MP: Did you marry at all?

AG: Yeah, I'm married now. And we got married in 1976.

MP: Did you meet in Terrace?

AG: No, we met in Vancouver.

MP: Oh, fantastic. Did you and your wife decide together to move to Terrace then?

AG: Well, I came ahead of time and she followed in June of '75. We got married in April '76.

MP: Here in Terrace?

AG: Yeah, and my wife she's Australian.

MP: Oh, that's really neat. How did you meet?

AG: Well, in a dance club. I always liked dancing and that's how we met.

MP: Oh, that's really lovely. And did you have any children?

AG: No, we didn't have any children.

MP: What brought you specifically to Terrace?

AG: Well, a good friend of mine, we worked together for Hy's in Vancouver, and he had a friend up here that had the VW [Volkswagen] Dealership. He came up here on holiday in '74. We were looking at a restaurant in Vancouver. We wanted to open up a restaurant when he came back. The Bavarian Inn was originally built already, but they only made it for three months and went into receivership. So we were looking at it and started to negotiate. I went back to Europe for three months and we kept in touch and when I came back we flew up here, had a look, made a deal; we leased it for two years and a bit and we bought it in October '77.

MP: Wow, so it was probably a very new building?

AG: Yeah, very new, absolutely.

MP: At the time was there both the Back Eddy and the Bavarian?

AG: No, there was no Back Eddy then. We actually opened up a discotheque, downstairs, it was a nightclub. We opened up a disco, and changed things. Upstairs was the Bavarian Inn, and downstairs we called it Mozart's Boogie Parlor.

MP: Mozart's Boogie Parlor, that's great!

AG: Yeah, kind of corny. But it worked. We were a very busy place.

MP: How long did you have the disco?

AG: Ten years.

MP: Ten years, wow — and why did you decide to change it to the Back Eddy?

The Bavarian Inn Restaurant. 2016.

AG: Well, the nightclub business is a tough business, until three o'clock in the morning, and there is more than one reason. You couldn't do business before 9:30 to 10:00 and it was go, go, go, and you couldn't compete with the hotels. In those days, the hotels changed into more nightclub atmosphere after eight o'clock to be a bonus, and they could be open all day long. So it was very tough to compete. I always wanted to go for like a pub atmosphere, so eventually, in 1990, I was able to get the license and build a pub.

MP: And the vision for upstairs, was it always the Bavarian...?

AG: Well it was called the Bavarian Inn, so we obviously followed with the name. We used to have more of a Bavarian theme then, and more a Bavarian style, or a European Style menu, which over the years we changed dramatically. It's more continental now, even the look.

MP: So you have had a business running in Terrace for a lot of years, how have you seen business change?

AG: Oh, it's changed tremendously. We started in fairly good times, and then the early '80s came which was the high interest rates. We had to be very careful and to work hard at it. And then my partner left in '84, so ever since then, I've been running it myself. And it's got its challenges. By '84, it started turning around and business got considerably better again. Then I had the unfortunate happening in 1990. I had a fire, the roof actually — under the roof, the mechanicals shorted out. So we really didn't have a fire inside, it was just the roof collapsed and that was all. It had to be all gutted and started from the bottom up.

But at the same time, I had my pub license already and I was just at the final stages with the plans and everything. And then, when the fire happened, I just happened to be in Vancouver that day, and I said somebody was choking when they phoned me and left a message in the hotel, and I started with a choke. Anyways I had to come right back. But it just slowed us a little bit down. We opened [the pub] up in April of '91. We were planning for February, but we didn't know that was going to happen. So that's how the pub started then in '91 — April '91.

MP: So a lot of challenges through the years for sure.

AG: Oh, yes, it's not for anybody with a faint heart.

MP: Have there been aspects of having this restaurant and pub that you have really enjoyed, or that have kept you going?

AG: Well, you have to enjoy the business and the people, otherwise you're in the wrong place. I think I have been here almost 39 years, so it speaks for itself. But it's not an easy business to be in: long hours and your lifestyle is very different from most people, because when they party, you have to work. And weddings or whatever function, you just couldn't attend, because we were very busy here.

MP: Interesting. The next question is: what do you do for fun! Do you have time? What do you like to do in Terrace?

AG: Well, I've always had a love for tennis and I would go in the afternoon for two hours, and play tennis and come back to work. It used to be long days for me but I maintained it. I even built my own tennis court in my backyard. So I've been doing that. I have since '92, and we have lots of fun that way. And I play golf.

MP: You find time to do those things.

AG: You have to find time. I didn't always have time for it, a lot of years I do.

MP: If you looked at Terrace over the years what restaurants were popular? If you thought of other restaurants that you worked alongside of, what other restaurants came and went?

AG: Well, a lot of restaurants have come and gone, this is the thing because it is a tough industry. Greek restaurants always did well in Terrace somehow, and also the Chinese restaurants. The rest I guess is franchised places always seem to do well somehow.

MP: And what do you think kept you in business throughout those years and tough times?

AG: Hard work. You just gotta be in your business. That's why I basically never did much … how should I say? Work for service clubs. I never tried to belong to them because I could not give myself to volunteer and do things other people have time for. I didn't because my business was more important and I did have to be here — I could not divide my attention to other things. I guess I am a survivor, and been tough throughout the times in Terrace, a lot of ups and downs, especially come '97, when the whole logging came pretty much to a standstill with the pulp mills closing down in [Prince] Rupert and most mills. That really hurt our business here.

MP: Did you see it start to come back again?

AG: Yeah, in 2011, it started to turn around a bit, and this 2013 second half was pretty good, and hopefully 2014 will be a good year.

MP: Keep improving.

AG: Yeah.

MP: There are a few questions about recreation. Did you and your wife ever get to enjoy the Lakelse Hot Springs at all?

AG: Well, personally, I never went for a swim out there. We've been out there having a few drinks, and dinner when they were still having a nice restaurant there, but that went downhill, and it's a shame because there's so much potential out there. It's somehow not managed properly that way…

MP: Tell me what sports in Terrace you were involved in? You said with golf and tennis.

AG: Yeah, I used to play racket ball and squash, and I used to do that but then my knees started giving out. And I have had to rest in the winter times because I just couldn't handle it any more.

MP: Were you ever into watching sports, too?

AG: Here, not so much here. I like sports on TV.

MP: Yeah, big-league stuff. Any local events that you remember celebrating in Terrace over the years?

AG: Well, the Riverboat Days, we always did our slingers race. We pretty much started that.

MP: What's the slingers race?

AG: All the hotels and restaurants can participate in it, and you do your race — with the tray and the drinks and there's water on it, and there's an obstacle course, and it's fun. Whoever wins gets a trophy.

MP: And they do that every year at the Riverboat Days?

AG: Oh yeah, we have been doing that every year for quite a few years.

MP: How does the Bavarian Inn do?

AG: Sometimes we did well, and sometimes other people did well. We always had the managers race. When I could still run sometimes I would do the running, but then things change, so I didn't do the run anymore.

MP: Do you know any other community events that were celebrated here?

AG: Well, usually we used to participate in the Christmas parade, but we haven't done that for a number of years. Mostly with the Back Eddy crew…

MP: What would that involve? Would you make a float?

AG: Well you would make a float and have your staff on it.

MP: Good promotion.

AG: Yeah, that's basically how it works.

MP: And what do you remember about downtown Terrace? How has the downtown changed over the years you've been here?

AG: Well, Terrace went through a lot of changes and I think it became a very nice town. There's always room for improvement.

MP: When you first arrived what was it like compared to now? What were some of the things you remember?

AG: I don't know how I should put it. I really couldn't compare it. I mean Terrace didn't really grow much in that way, in the outlying areas. If you go down Keith Avenue you see a lot of things happening all the way from the new Bridge right down Keith Avenue. But the downtown core itself hasn't changed that much I think.

MP: That's neat. And what did most people you know do for work over the years? Obviously some in the restaurant business but what were most people doing for work?

AG: Oh, you know, obviously the logging industry used to be big around here, pretty much since '97, and then it went downhill from there on. A lot of people left town, go to Alberta and find work there. Lately people are coming back again with Rio Tinto and all the hydroelectric projects, so it's picking up considerably again and hopefully that's not the end. We're trying to get the LNG [liquefied natural gas] going and the pipelines and such, there's not a lot of people against it and I'm a proponent for it and I think it's all good, for the future.

MP: See where it goes, absolutely. How did the community of Terrace interact with Kitselas and Kitsumkalum?

AG: I think quite well. We became the hub for the whole northwest. It's definitely a win-win situation. A lot of things happened; roads have been improved coming out from all those places and it's definitely a very important aspect to Terrace. The days after the logging when the economy pretty much was thriving from the outlying areas coming shopping and spending lots of money.

MP: Have you seen change over the years in terms of people growing their own food here in Terrace?

AG: Well, I suppose people are getting more and more aware of having their own gardens. That's how we grew up. Everybody had their own garden. Except I don't have my own garden. I have to play tennis, you know?

MP: That's great. Any other changes that you've seen in Terrace throughout the years?

AG: Changes? You get caught up in life and you don't always look at the changes when you're part of the change. It's a hard one to explain.

MP: Easier if you've been away and then come back.

AG: Then you see the difference. Well, the economy has been very volatile and now it's picked up again and hopefully continues that way. It's a good place to live, and hopefully there will be more commerce in the future for the new generations.

MP: What else do you think would help to boost business in Terrace?

AG: Well, we definitely need an open mind for industry because we are such a resource-based economy in the country that we cannot compete with any manufacturing coming out of China. It's just impossible. People think we shouldn't do this and we shouldn't do that. I think it would definitely diminish our standard of living. Basically my life cycle is due at an end; I don't have to worry about it. But I do care for the future for other people and I think it has to be kept in mind that we can't turn everything down because it's not perfect. Life itself is not perfect, and we will never achieve it. I always hear that we shouldn't do this and that. And all the years in Terrace, come to think of it, every time something was proposed it was first people want jobs and then there's a proposal of a steel mill or a copper smelter, and it may not be the right proposal, but first people want it and then when it is in the planning then it's getting to be turned down. Somewhere along the line, there has to be a trade-off. We happen to be here and I think the pipeline is a perfect scenario. The trains are not perfect either; to ship everything by train that goes all beside rivers.

MP: When you look back before you came to Canada when you were a child in Austria what did you expect or hope to accomplish?

AG: Well, I never knew that I would end up in Canada, definitely not. But I do remember in my childhood, an aunt out of Vienna used to give me a few books from Canada, and about the Canada geese. I remember that. And you know, we had some songs about Canada and all that stuff we learned in school about Canada. But I never dreamt I would end up in Canada one day. So, it became 43 years, you know, the year I wanted to come. It's definitely a great country. I still think we are the best country in the world. Economically, politically and it's very important that we keep going that way. We cannot stop, how should I say? Progress.

MP: If you think about your life, was there one particular person or event that made a big impact on your life?

AG: Well, I guess starting my business is definitely one thing. And that becomes your lifestyle, and it's a big impact.

MP: As someone who's lived in Terrace for a lot of years, what is something you want to share with new people that are moving to Terrace?

AG: Give it a few years and you will like it. Especially when you come from a bigger centre, it's tough to get used to a small town like Terrace. We went through the same thing. The first two years were tough in that sense. And then you get used to it and you wouldn't want to go back to the big city.

MP: What is it that you like about Terrace that the big city doesn't offer?

AG: Well, it's the closeness to people and you just have more contact with people, where in the big city you don't have that, definitely not.

MP: I guess the last question, were there any other stories about your time in Terrace that you would like to share?

AG: Terrace has been giving us a good living. So I cannot complain at all. And there's good people here. I don't know what else I should say! It's all good. It's a great place to live, and I probably, if I ever sell, I probably wouldn't leave Terrace, let's put it this way. It's home, it's the feel. You know, I've got everything I want.

Isabelle McKee Interview

Interviewed by Lena Wilson, 21 November 2013

Isabelle McKee was born in July of 1938 in Claxton Cannery. Her father, Gunner Edlund, was a strawberry farmer who came to Canada from Sweden in 1932. Her mother was originally from Old Kitselas. One of three children, Isabelle went to the Indian Day School run by Salvation Army teachers. In 1956, she started working in Prince Rupert, met her future husband, Peter McKee Jr., and had a family. In this interview, she briefly describes the opening of the Highway 16 and her childhood memories of life during WWII, particularly the forced removal of Japanese Canadians from Port Essington. Isabelle remembers the first time indigenous peoples were allowed to vote in federal elections. Her grandmother and mother both voted at Skinner's store in Prince Rupert. Reflecting on the Northwest, Isabelle notes, "It's always been a beautiful place for me."

LW: Where and when were you born?

IM: I was born on July 14, 1938, at Claxton Cannery, BC. Claxton was where some of the people went in the summer months to work in the cannery.

LW: How did your family arrive in Terrace?

IM: Actually, my mother and my grandparents lived in Old Kitselas and my father came to the area in 1936. My mother was born in Kitselas in 1910, just prior to the opening of the railroad, because our tunnels were across the river from there. She was born just before the railroad opened in 1913.

My father came from Sweden in 1932. He worked all across Canada and then he arrived in this area during the flood of 1936 and worked on the railway towards Kwinitsa. And he came and joined one of his friends right up the hill. See, over that ridge over there. He went into partnership with him and they had a farm. He was a strawberry farmer.

LW: When did your mom meet your dad?

IM: I guess it would be the summer of maybe '37. I don't know. He would hire people to come and work for him, to pick strawberries in the summer. She began working there. His name was Gunner Edlund. He's quite well-known in Terrace. A lot of people remember my dad.

LW: Nice. Do you have any siblings?

IM: I have a brother, Melvin. And my sister, Maud, lives in Vancouver.

LW: What was your relationship with your siblings like?

IM: Good. Basically we were for the most part sort of isolated and there were not too many other children. We got along quite well. We just had each other to play with.

LW: How come you didn't have very many children to play with?

IM: Because the village was very small and the population would fluctuate. Sometimes there would be a few people there. The people would go to Terrace and live in Terrace for a little while and return. Sort of like that throughout my growing-up years. There were very few people in Kitselas who stayed and lived there all of the time like we did. Kitselas is across the river known as Endudoon, its ancient name.

Kitselas. Terrace Public Library Collection.

LW: It is a pretty small reserve, eh?

IM: Actually it's not that small. It's quite a big-sized reserve, but it's just isolated. The only way to get there was by train in those years.

LW: So, it wasn't where it is now, at Gitaus?

IM: No. Old Kitselas is across the river there, because we had the reserve there with the railroad tracks. And then we had all the settlers on the other side — the mountain side. There were quite a few settlements up toward the mountain.

LW: That's really interesting. So could you describe a typical day in your household during your childhood?

IM: Well, during the school times we would have to get up early like everybody else and get ready for school. Then we would go off to school, spend a regular day at school, and then come home and have to do chores. Because you had to bring in wood and go down and fetch water. Sometimes we would go to the river, depending on what we were using the water for. All water was from the river or from my grandfather's well. We had the old wells. Wood would have to be sawed with the old cross-cut saw. There were no power saws back then.

LW: Wow. That sounds like a lot of work.

IM: Oh yeah. It was. I didn't realize it then, but now when I think back, it must have been just incredible, the amount of physical work. It had to be done to survive in those days. There was no power out there. We had no gas or oil.

LW: You must have been in good shape?

IM: Oh yeah.

LW: What school did you attend?

IM: The Kitselas School, the Indian day school. It burned to the ground recently.

LW: What was your experience in the Indian Day School?

IM: It was good; I thought it so. The teachers were mostly Salvation Army teachers. Sometimes we would have one that was not. They were all good teachers. It was the one big room. You had from grade one to grade eight, however many children were there. We played ball at recess. That seemed to be everyone's favorite. I hated baseball. I was near-sighted. They didn't know I was near-sighted and I couldn't see very well.

LW: Do you have any memories of school you would like to share?

Isabelle McKee, standing outside one of the cabins her father built in Kitselas.
1955. Isabelle McKee Collection.

IM: I'm not sure that I have any that I want to share at this time. I didn't like to be forced into physical activity. It was one of the things I didn't like. I like to do my own thing.

LW: Were there a lot of people who were half Native and half non-Native when you went to school there? Would you have noticed things like that?

IM: Yeah, there were children from the train station. They had the Kitselas station down the road a little ways and their children came to our school when I was quite small. After that, I guess they went to Terrace although the parents were still at Kitselas. They stayed there until after I left home.

LW: Did you marry?

IM: Yes. I married Peter McKee Jr.. He was an immigrant from Scotland. Arrived in Canada in 1954 — he and his family. They lived in Prince Rupert. That's where I moved to find work. I started working in 1956, so that's where I lived.

LW: In Prince Rupert?

IM: Yes.

LW: How did you meet your spouse?

IM: Back in those days, I guess, we were still teenagers. Your fellow workers would all get together and start meeting each other, meeting people.

LW: Tell me about your wedding. How was your wedding?

IM: The wedding was quite nice, but it was small — mostly just family present. We were married in the Anglican Church and we had a little party down at the Legion — dinner and dancing. My in-laws were a noisy group, singing and arguing.

LW: Did you have any children?

IM: Yes, I had two sons.

LW: How did you find Terrace as a place to raise your family? Did you raise them in Terrace?

IM: No, I raised them in Prince Rupert. That's where they grew up — in Prince Rupert.

LW: When did you move back to Terrace?

IM: In 1991. That's when I moved into this house here. They were encouraging people to come home, so I got to come home.

LW: Nice. What did you do for fun in Terrace?

IM: Well, when we lived in Old Kitselas at a very young age, I remember the war years. And I know I was very young, but I have vivid memories of those years. All of the special holidays, we would walk to Terrace for the celebrations. Sometimes we would walk the railroad tracks from Old Kitselas right to Terrace. I remember when Highway 16 opened. We got to cross the ferry at Copper River and then we walked the new highway. I can remember and I was a small girl. My mom and my grandma, we walked. The tree line was next to the road. I can still see it. The highway as you see it now, this was just a narrow road.

LW: Was it dirt?

IM: It was gravel. It wasn't really just dirt but the trees were so tall that it hemmed you right in. It was just a fantastic walk. It was beautiful. Now you have it fixed on all sides. This was just special.

LW: What special occasions would there be? Like Christmas?

IM: We would stay at home at Christmas time, but there would be like the May holiday – the Queen's Birthday — and July 1st and Labour Day. Those were the three most celebrated ones.

LW: What did they do in town?

IM: They had a lot of activities down at the civic centre. It was down where they have Chances now. We would have races and all sorts of sports. They always had a parade and a big celebration that was just so much fun.

LW: Do you know what restaurants were popular over the years?

IM: Oh yeah. I remember Mrs. Lambly's. We loved Mrs. Lambly's and the corner ice cream shop. And also the little restaurant on Kalum, the Silvertip. I guess you've heard of that. It's an old restaurant.

LW: Oh really. I only know Silvertip as promotions [Silvertip Promotions & Signs].

IM: It was a Chinese restaurant. Everybody went there.

LW: Kinda like Polly's now?

IM: Oh yeah. They cooked everything; the Chinese owner didn't just cook Chinese food. Cook whatever you wanted. He would sit in front of his little cafe. I guess it wasn't quite as busy then.

LW: Did you ever visit the Lakelse Hot Springs?

IM: Yes, when I was really small. There was a trail somewhere, because this was before the road went through. I can't remember how we got there but I remember getting there and we came to this little clearing — my dad, my mom, my grandma, and my brother and sister. And we came to this little place and it was the size of a bathtub now — a regular bathtub — and that was the hot springs. I wasn't kidding; it's what it was. You could see the hot water bubbling out of the ground.

From what I've read in some of the history, there was something there prior to that time. There was a building and something around it. I'm not quite sure what was there. It was like a bathtub with these boards all around the water.

LW: Did you go in?

IM: No. We weren't allowed to go in it then.

LW: How come?

IM: I don't know, maybe fear. Our parents said we might not come back. That was my first memory of the hot springs. I think what was going on at that time, I think my father was looking to purchase it. I wonder where he would be if he had of purchased it at that time, if he had the land.

LW: So what about Lakelse Lake. What can you say about Lakelse Lake?

IM: Lakelse Lake was always very pretty. We would go on special occasions or summer camp. We would go to the church camps in Terrace. That is where we would go to spend our time. Lakelse Lake was a safe place to go with our friends.

LW: Can you tell me more about sports in Terrace? Did you play any? Or village sports?

IM: Sports? No. I didn't like sports.

LW: Do you recall attending any sports events?

IM: Yes, we would go and watch baseball and races — whatever they had. They were fun to watch but I didn't like playing them.

LW: What about fishing?

IM: In Old Kitselas, my grandfather did the fishing. He used the net and a skiff — something they built themselves, not purchased. We had a spot by the river where we would clean the fish, and he would take his share and give my mom a share of the fish. We would go down to the river and we would all pitch in. We would get our little fishing lines and have fun fishing when we were done with our work.

LW: So that was your mom's dad?

IM: Yeah.

LW: Were you involved in any other activities outside of the home? Like clubs or organizations?

IM: Oh yeah. They had a ladies group. They couldn't have too many other activities except for evenings, where you would gather in people's homes, and have fun and play games. Those were nice times.

LW: Did you attend any religious services?

IM: Yes, we had our church. I don't know if it was mandatory.

LW: What church did you attend?

IM: It was the United Church. That was the old Methodist Church in front of the schoolhouse. And we had the Salvation Army down the road.

LW: So it was mandatory from your parents?

IM: I'm thinking it was more government-imposed. From what I remember, the teacher said you have to go.

LW: So you talked a little bit about the special events they had. You talked about the summer ones, like Victoria Day. Do you remember celebrating any other events?

IM: Like in Terrace? The one I remember the most was the opening of the highway. It was during the war years when Highway 16 went through — because the highway was built because of the war. I remember that opening. There was a big celebration at the civic centre.

I remember there was — I don't know if this was the opening of the civic centre then — there was an orchestra, like a big brass band. That was the first time I ever heard a real band. I was flabbergasted. I really enjoyed them — the music and the orchestra.

LW: What do you remember about downtown Terrace?

Isabelle pictured here with her aunties: Rhoda Seymour, Emma Bolton, Isabelle McKee, Beatrice Vermeer [l-r]. In front of the United Church. Circa early 1970s. Isabelle McKee Collection.

IM: Downtown Terrace was very small then. You could walk everywhere. My aunt lived just across from where the forestry building was. It looked so huge then, but it's just a tiny white building, as you drive past the Anglican Church. That was the forestry building. My aunt's house was close by. All the streets were narrow but I thought they were very nice. Some of those old trees are still there.

LW: Cool. Where did you buy food?

IM: We would walk from Old Kitselas and go across the river — the Copper River — and there was Skinner's store. You can still see it on the highway — an old house. But he had a store in front of that. That is where we had to go and get our supplies. We would walk the railroad tracks and carry our groceries home. My mother and other adults carried supplies on packboards.

LW: They had it tough back then.

IM: Oh yeah. It didn't seem we needed as many things as you do now. We just had the basics: flour, sugar, tea.

LW: Where did you go shopping for clothes or furniture?

IM: Usually from the Eaton's catalogue back then. That was our main shopping, by mail.

LW: What about furniture?

IM: Furniture? I don't remember any of us having to purchase any furniture because I think what happened… Just over the hill here, down at the old Gitaus site, there was a Hudson Bay site where the old steamships used to come in during the early 1900's. And they had a big hotel there. I think when they closed down the hotel, the people were able to purchase a lot of the furniture that belonged to the hotel. Because some of our furniture was beautiful. My dad bought beautiful Queen Anne chairs. We had Queen Anne furniture in the middle of the farm, in the middle of the forest. And the same for my grandmother. She had mahogany tables and chairs and buffets. I think this was the same as my other grandma. I always loved that old furniture. Anything old, I just treasure it.

LW: Antiques?

IM: Antique furniture. That was the only place I think they got it from. It wasn't ordinary stuff.

LW: Oh wow. That's awesome. Did you shop at the Terrace Co-op?

IM: Did we go to Terrace to shop? Yeah. We did in the later years, because Mr. Skinner started getting old. He eventually had to close and go out of business. We would go to Terrace and shop, and then we would have to bring everything back on the train. It was a little bit better than walking all the way back from Skinner's store.

LW: What did most people that you knew do for work?

IM: For work, there was not much employment in Old Kitselas. There was the CN [Canadian National Railway Company]. They could only employ about one or two people. My dad worked there for a while and my grandfather worked there for years. Anyone else that wanted to work would go to Terrace and work. Not many opportunities for employment.

LW: Did you have any family members who were farmers? Your dad was a strawberry farmer.

IM: The best strawberries ever. I've never tasted strawberries like his. He just had acres.

LW: Do you miss the strawberries?

IM: Oh yeah. I still go out there but it's all different now. They call it the Hankin Ranch now. That was my dad's farm.

LW: They're not like today's. Today's are kind of flavourless.

IM: They come from California or wherever. They don't taste the same.

LW: What role do you think forestry and logging played throughout the history of Terrace?

Isabelle McKee. November 21, 2013. Photo by Lena Wilson.

IM: It created a lot of changes. But in our village I remember back in, I think '54, they logged out an area up behind the village — up past the graveyard — and there was an actual road from the early years. And there was this area where there was a little bridge. Huge cottonwood trees had sheltered the whole area. The water under the bridge was a few feet deep. Salmon would spawn and come up from the river, up the little creek, and spawn in that area. But once, they logged it out. Now it's just a dry creek. There's nothing in there anymore. It's gone. Even the creek, right to the river, is dry. That was a sad thing to happen.

LW: Did any of your friends or family work in the sawmills or do logging?

IM: In the days prior to when I was born, there was a gentleman from Terrace who had a sawmill just above Old Kitselas, and a lot of the people worked there. Also, I think there was a sawmill on Ferry Island where the people went to work.

LW: How did the community of Terrace interact with old Kitselas and Kitsumkalum?

IM: I don't know if they knew we were there. [Laughter.]

LW: How long did it take you to walk there?

IM: Well, it was eight miles right from where we lived to the bridge. There were no telephones.

LW: I couldn't imagine such a place with no telephones. How did the community interact with the police?

IM: We very seldom saw police in our village.

LW: How did the establishment of Kitimat in the 1950s impact Terrace?

IM: At that time, I was living in Prince Rupert. I remember the opening of the railroad to Kitimat. I think it changed the area a lot. It changed the Lakelse Hot Springs a lot.

LW: Because there was just a trail there?

IM: Yes, and now it was accessible for everyone. Developed it to what we have now.

LW: How did the construction of the new bridge impact the community?

IM: I remember it happening, but I was in Prince Rupert then. I remember there was a new bridge being built. Now I think it's quite nice actually. It's also nice that they kept the old one. It's really special.

LW: So did you have a garden or grow any other fruit other than strawberries?

IM: My dad grew potatoes, vegetables… just about everything we'd need.

LW: Did your friends and neighbors do the same — grow gardens?

IM: Yes, it was necessary. We couldn't survive if we didn't have a garden. Had potatoes every year and there were lots of fruit trees, apple trees, cherry trees.

LW: I love the cherries from here. Actually my landlord has plum trees. They are so good. I'm from Hazelton and you can't grow that stuff there.

How has the [Skeena Valley] Farmers' Market changed throughout the years? Have you been to the Farmers' Market?

IM: I get there when I can. Otherwise, I don't have too much access to it, though I wish I did.

LW: Do you think First Nations culture has shaped Terrace?

IM: No, I don't think we had too much influence shaping Terrace, although now we are a little bit more involved. That wasn't the fault of Terrace, though. It was the government of the day's influence over the way we got to interact with each other.

LW: Were you involved in any politics?

IM: Yes, once upon a time I was.

LW: Oh, really, what did you do?

IM: I just helped with the voting and the elections in Prince Rupert. I remember we [First Nations] were not allowed to vote in federal elections. I remember the first vote; we had to walk to Skinner's store to vote. My mother did, and my grandmother. My grandmother was blind, so my mother had to help her to put her 'X' on a little piece of paper. For my mother, it was so special to be able to go and vote. So to make sure and vote is very important in our family.

LW: That's cool. People just take it for granted now.

IM: We take a lot of things for granted.

LW: I couldn't imagine packing water every time I needed it.

IM: Oh yeah. Now we just turn on the tap and waste it all.

LW: How has Terrace changed over the years?

IM: It's gotten a bit bigger. The old streets are still there, but the buildings have changed.

LW: Looking back when you were a child, what did you hope to accomplish?

IM: Well, back then our little world was kind of limited. Without TV and all those things, you are not really aware of what's out there. I know that I always wanted to work somewhere, to have a job and to buy things.

LW: Me, too. Was there a particular person or event that made an impact on your life?

IM: I think for me, in my very young years — I was just a little kid then — but the Second World War was a traumatic time for us, although we were not directly involved. I remember going to Port Essington with my mom and grandma. We'd go visit her brother in Port Essington. That was the time when the Japanese were removed from Port Essington.

It's so vivid to me. I can still hear the people crying. They were, you know, crying as the Japanese people had to give away all their belongings. My grandmother got a few things. Got old records and came home with a few of their treasures that they had to give away. We are aware of what happened back then. I think what happened to us as a people, Native people, I think it created a fear that maybe we might be next. Because things were really changed after that, and the people became more secretive and more protective of each other.

LW: Like you had to watch your back all the time because there was a fear?

IM: Yeah. Because I really believed that the people believed, that if they can do that to one group of people, we might be the next ones to go.

That was really a sad time. I remember people crying and sobbing. All the people — not just the Japanese. It was all the Native people that lived there. It was frightening for a little child. War was frightening although we were far away from it.

Even in Old Kitselas, we had to cover our windows with blankets just so that we wouldn't be seen in the dark. For the longest time up to my teenage years and far beyond, I had a horrible fear of the sound of airplanes. I could not tolerate the sound of airplanes. It was that scary. Terrace was quite involved in that because they had their training centre for the army here.

LW: What kind of training centre?

IM: It's where they got their basic training, I think. There was a lot of army personnel. That's where the civic centre was. I remember they would actually train along the railroad tracks. You'd be walking along and, all of a sudden, you had to get out of the way because you had this great big huge group of army men running down the road. They didn't stop for anything. They just kept running. You had to get out of the way.

LW: What would you want to share with people newly moving into the area?

IM: I think it's a good area. We have so much beautiful scenery. It's always been a beautiful place for me.

LW: Do you remember anything else about the military years?

IM: I remember the opening of the highway, the Japanese, and the training. I remember food being rationed. Sugar was rationed — a lot of food. Our staples were rationed. You had to have those little coupons to buy anything.

LW: Do you think they gave you enough food to live off of?

IM: We had enough food that we grew ourselves. But staples, like sugar, was scarce. I think flour probably was, too. Butter — you had to have a little coupon for butter and probably other things I can't remember.

Jane Dickson Interview

Interviewed by Estelle Mitchell, 29 November 2013

Jane Dickson was born in Ilkley, Yorkshire, and at the age of seven she moved with her family to West Wales, where she attended school and eventually college for two years to do business training. By the early 1960s, she was working in Cardiff. In 1966, Jane decided to travel abroad, and though planning to visit Australia, she stayed for a year in Vancouver. She eventually found a job at the City of Vancouver, and later as secretarial assistant to the Chief Curator of the Vancouver Centennial Museum in 1968. There she met her husband, Peter. They married in 1970, and in January 1973, Jane and her husband hitchhiked down to South America. They lived in Wales for some time before immigrating to British Columbia two years later. Jane discusses how she and her husband built a life in Terrace in the 1970s. Jane worked at a law office for 38 years. Peter took welding at the college. As one of the board members of the Skeena Diversity Society, Jane was instrumental in developing anti-racist work in Terrace. Describing her involvement in the Multicultural Association and later Skeena Diversity Society, Jane links this with her early experience in Wales and the welcoming atmosphere her mother created through her work. To newcomers, Jane advises, "just go out and find your common interest, go out and find a group that matches who you are and go for it."

EM: So if you don't mind telling us where you were born and a little bit about your parents?

JD: I was born in Ilkley, Yorkshire, and lived in Farnborough, near London. Then when I was seven years old, our family—me, my younger sister, Geraldine, my mother and father, Max and Peggy Davis—moved to Aberporth in West Wales, where my father had been transferred to the Ministry of Defence. My mother and father met in 1943 in a photographic unit in the south of England as my father fixed and fitted up cameras into stripped-down Spitfires for photographic reconnaissance. My mother was one of the film developers.

EM: Okay [laughs].

JD: Aberporth is where I attended primary school and later grammar school in Cardigan until I was 18, the sixth year, which is the first year of college. At school, I found I was good at grass hockey and high jumping, representing Wales in both. Then I went on to business training college in Cardiff for a year to give me a base from which to work, because I really didn't know what I wanted to do. While in Cardiff, I found a job in a law firm and stayed there for a year. That was probably around 1964.

Then, I thought, I want to get out of the city and return to home for a while, which was now in Abercych, a small village of about 400 people near Cardigan, where I spent several of my teenage years, and where we'd moved after living in Aberporth. That's where my mother took on the task of resurrecting the village store and post office and through that, I got to know everyone in the village by taking orders and delivering groceries. I considered this home, even though we were English, and we were generally well accepted as an English family.

This was my first real lesson in terms of acceptance of a different culture. I loved the Welsh people because of their hospitality and their welcoming spirit. I'd be welcomed into their homes and given hot strong tea and Welsh griddle cakes, then when leaving I'd be given a penny or a threepenny bit.

EM: Oh! [Laughs.] How lovely.

JD: …or a sweet. You could drop in and visit and that's why I really started to like people, I think in a way—where I felt that they wanted to know me as well. It makes you realize that it takes a community to draw each one of us out and to be able to speak to one another. So I believe that was where this part of my own personal development and cultural acceptance really started.

110

Jane Dickson on Tresaith Beach in West Wales "where it all started", September 2016. Photo credit: Geraldine Hope.

EM: But, still, it was interesting what you said: it was as an English family living in Wales, that you were so accepted in the community.

JD: Yes, as a family, and the villagers also, we went through that transition of wariness then acceptance from within ourselves as we all wanted to get along, and we were very fortunate in that. I think it was partly because my mother's store created that two-way street of her helping the village by bringing the shop back to life and they very much appreciated that convenience as many villagers didn't have cars; they relied on public transport a lot. I used to help my mother deliver groceries to people's homes and I loved helping her put shopping orders together and keeping the shelves stocked. The other part was my father's very social nature: he was a very tall man among the Welsh, who are a shorter race, and he enjoyed his beer at the local pub, a former cottage called Penrhiw, run by a Welshman, Sam, and his Danish wife, Ulla, who made that another centrepiece of the village!

EM: This was—

JD: Back in the '60s.

EM: You said it was also a post office?

JD: Yes, that's right. It was a combination shop and post office where the elderly would come and cash their pension books and all could buy postage supplies. The local people were very grateful to her for reinstating that service. And so it opened us all up by having this direct and complete contact. Truly wonderful.

EM: It coloured your experience here, then.

JD: It certainly has.

EM: That's good.

JD: And then in early 1966, following college and a couple of years of work, I got itchy feet and decided it was time to move on. I needed to travel. I'd met a friend at college, Margaret, who was now staying with her sister, who was teaching at an all-girls' school in Vancouver and was invited to visit them.

EM: Okay, so now we're looking at Vancouver.

JD: Yes, yes. And I thought, *Oh, why don't I?* [Laughs.] That, in fact, was the beginning of my move, when I decided, *Right, off I go.* I had contemplated going on to Australia at some point because I wanted to see some sunshine but I found plenty in Vancouver and lots of mountains.

EM: British Columbia [laughs].

JD: My mother and father had said, "Okay, this is a birthday gift, we'll pay your way to Canada, or you can have a 21st birthday party. You choose." So, I got all my immigration paperwork together and was successful. I left on October 10th, 1966, travelling over by Cunard ship to Montreal.

EM: Now you're how old about this time?

JD: 21.

EM: 21, there we go. Oh, yes, of course, because it was your birthday.

JD: Then I went by train to Vancouver, but to get from the port to the train, we had to pass through a picket line on a bus. They actually had the police there. I thought, *Where am I coming to?* [Laughs.] *What, this is Canada?* It was very unsettling because people were shouting and waving these things at the bus. We never fully understood what was happening but it felt like a strike, and it was a somewhat alarming welcome to a country. The train journey to Vancouver took three days and four nights of mind-boggling distances, arriving there on October 22nd, 1966, where I was met by Margaret and her sister.

I stayed with them for a year, then decided it was time to go back for a short visit with my mother, father, and sister, Geraldine, the following Christmas (1967). On returning to Vancouver, I found it settled me down. Something had clicked and I thought, *Here I am, I'm staying.* I then continued with my job as Girl Friday with the City of Vancouver.

I worked in the personnel department of City Hall to begin with in 1966, after surviving a series of secretarial skill and IQ tests, which I'd never done before. I filled various positions in different departments scattered around the city that were short-staffed for any reason. That was just the best learning experience … and I bought myself a little Morris Minor convertible to get myself around in.

It was a wonderful way of finding my way around Vancouver, meeting people and learning and adapting to different skills. It was very challenging and satisfying. I couldn't have been luckier for a first job there.

It was fabulous; it really was an excellent introduction. And it's there where I found a permanent position in 1968 as the secretarial assistant to the Chief Curator of the new Museum which opened that same year, and that's where I met my husband, Peter.

EM: Okay. Now this isn't the Museum at the University of British Columbia [UBC]?

JD: No, this was the new Centennial Museum and Planetarium, downtown by the water with the great silver crab outside the front. The H.R. MacMillan Planetarium is above [now the Museum of Vancouver].

EM: Okay, yes. Got you [laughs].

JD: In July 1969, the staff was able to go up to the Planetarium and hear about the landing on the moon.

EM: Oh my goodness, yeah.

JD: "The eagle has landed..." It was a very exciting day to be able to be there. I was then getting to know Peter as he had helped set up the new display galleries and after the Museum opening, he was a gallery attendant while attending art school. He was there long enough to become head gallery attendant, giving us time to get to know one another in the galleries [laughs]—after work of course.

And so that's how we came to stay in Vancouver. We married in 1970. I was still working at the museum all this time and Peter was going to art school, working in the galleries and at the Liquor Control Board. Then, in 1972, after Peter received an Honours Diploma in Painting and we were contemplating whether or not to buy a lot on Bowen Island or do a backpack trip down to South America, we decided we had to travel. So we sold everything [laughs], and climbed onto a Greyhound bus with our loaded backpacks heading south in January 1973.

EM: That's one way to do it!

JD: We travelled down by bus, train, and hitch-hiking.

EM: Oh, lovely.

JD: It took us four months to get to Buenos Aires, with many adventures on the way, as you can imagine. We then flew back to Wales from there, because we wanted to visit the family again. Well, of course, when we arrived back in Wales, we were skint. No money, right? We'd spent it all [laughs]. You do these crazy things. Oh, well…

We were planning on coming back to Canada, but didn't know when or how. So, we started working again that May to save up.

EM: So, now you're in Wales.

JD: 1973 now, we're in Wales. My father had been transferred to another work location but they kept their home in Wales. We looked after their home but didn't actually live in it because we wanted to be footloose and fancy-free. We were a couple of hippies, really. Although we really weren't hippies. We had bought a small 22-foot caravan on their land, which we lived in, so we had our own place and space and our clothes smelled of smoke all the time.

When we got some money saved up, we wrote to the Canadian Embassy in London and said, "We want to go back." They wrote and said, "If you've got all your papers from your first time, you're fine." And that was really good, so in April 1975, we returned on a Polish passenger boat.

EM: Okay, to Vancouver?

JD: Yes, to Vancouver via Montreal again. We crossed the country by train and bus, a great combination because it gives you another perspective on how big Canada really is. Huge. We arrived in Vancouver with nothing but three trunks. We thought, *Right, what do we do?* We had to wait for our trunks—that was all to we had to our names—so we decided that while we were waiting, we'd get on the Greyhound bus and travel around the province and see where we'd like to live, because we weren't going to live in the city again. You want to explore other possibilities. So we bought a couple of small packs and took off for Nelson in the Kootenays; we loved Nelson. We very nearly stayed there because of the Notre Dame University, but found out it was closing that year, so that was a strike against it.

Then on up to Prince George and Grande Prairie then back down and along Highway 16, to visit some old friends who might be visiting Terrace. It was a long shot; we didn't know where they might be staying or anything. We arrived on a lovely spring morning in April 1975 with the cottonwood aroma in the air at the bus depot, which was on Lazelle Avenue where the Service Canada building is now.

EM: Okay. Interesting.

JD: *So, what do we do now? How can we possibly find our friends?* CFTK radio station was right there, kitty-corner to the bus depot, so we thought, *let's see if they can help us.* We spoke to Tim McLean—a very popular DJ in Terrace at the time, we found out later. He said he could put our message on the radio and for us to come back in a couple of hours. So we did just that, and he said, "we've heard from them and here's their phone number."

EM: Oh my goodness [laughs]. Small town.

JD: Small town. Wonderful! And they were staying with Anne Anson out at Lakelse Lake. We stayed with them at the lake for a couple of nights and instead of travelling on to Prince Rupert, we returned to Vancouver on the bus with the intention of coming back, having decided that we liked Terrace with its college and its mountains and remembering that morning arrival on the bus into the delicious aroma of cottonwood sap. Terrace also generally felt raw and unfinished and we liked that. Arriving back in Vancouver, we picked up our three trunks after having bought a VW Beetle to pack them into.

We put one trunk on top of the car and managed to fit two inside, because you could put the back seat down. Went down to the Army and Navy on Hastings, bought a whole bunch of camping gear, and headed north.

EM: Oh!

JD: Actually on our way to Terrace this time. The journey took us a couple of days, beetling along, camping along the way. We had our first introduction to the First Nations peoples at the Seeley Lake campground near Hazelton, because they were patrolling through the campground asking, "Where are you from and who are you?" We felt a little bit intimidated by them at the time, because we hadn't met First Nations people before in that way, right? And that was kind of an intriguing, uncomfortable experience because we did feel vulnerable…

EM: They were checking you out.

JD: They were checking us out, and we didn't feel a hundred per cent safe.

EM: Hm.

JD: But then you see, we were still 'city'—we were people who hadn't been up north before in this way. So, we were really treading new ground and new territory and going into places that we didn't really have any sense of. When we safely arrived in Terrace, we started looking for a place to live and, until we found a place that suited us, we camped at Furlong Bay. It was now early May so it was quite warm.

EM: Now, this is where?

JD: Lakelse Lake, yes; Furlong Bay. We headed out there because of the campground and got ourselves set up. We stayed there about three nights, I reckon. We'd come back into town to check the paper for places to live and finally found a place on Cramer Street, opposite the treed end of Rotary Park at Haugland, which had been lived in by the people we were going to rent from on the same lot, Guy Pratt and his wife Anna. It was a two-room house/cabin with a small caravan tacked onto it. Oh, we like caravans!

EM: Tacked on to the house.

114

JD: Tacked on to the house, pretty well stuck. You walked in and the little cabin part was the living room and bathroom, and the caravan comprised a cozy dining area, kitchen, and a bedroom, which was very cold in the wintertime [laughs]. You should've seen the thickness of the ice on the inside of the window! But we survived.

EM: So, you're on the corner of Cramer and Haugland.

JD: Yes, that's where we started. That was our first home. And we were very happy there. Then Guy and Anna moved to Dover Road and we moved into their place on the same corner.

Anyway, on arriving in Terrace, I found three jobs available, all at law offices. That's where my background is. I'm interested in law and the justice system, and so I thought, let's continue in that direction for the time being and see what happens. I applied for all three jobs and they all accepted me, which then was a challenge as to which one to take. To arrive in a place and have three jobs to choose from is amazing, considering how things are nowadays.

EM: For sure.

JD: I started with Grant & Company, which is where I first worked with Don Brown, which then changed to Grant & Crampton, then to Crampton & Brown, then to Crampton, Brown & Arndt, and now is a separate company called Warner Bandstra Brown.

I can't believe it's been that long I've been doing this, but I like the work and the people I work with. Always good. But, anyway, having a job settled us down, grounded us. Peter is an artist, but he also had a strong background in carpentry and hotels. He was also interested in working with steel, so he decided to take a welding course at Northwest Community College while dishwashing at the Bavarian Inn.

EM: Oh really? [Laughs.] That's kind of—

JD: [Laughs.] That was his first job in Terrace, which he had for a year, evolving into a waiter while there. This is not the direction he wanted to go in, but it was good meeting Gus and Heli, and of course Fritz, who was Gus' partner at the time. That was when they had the Mozart Lounge at the Bavarian, downstairs behind the Back Eddy Pub.

EM: Gus is still there.

JD: Yes. So, when we arrived in '75—we'll go back to that time—the Dudley Little Bridge was just being built. Haugland Avenue was our main access into town, then on to Tetrault, which was paved because of the hospital, then Keith Avenue, which was a mess of potholes because of the huge pole yard there with its cone-shaped wood burner by the overpass and stretching east to Kalum Street. This has all been built on now.

EM: Okay, now were you working with the law office?

JD: Yes, that building where I first worked, with [Ken] Grant & Company upstairs, had doctors' offices downstairs. Dr. Brooks was one of them. It burned down later when we weren't there. It was in the same location as the Terrace and District Credit Union used to be, which is now a fitness centre and other agencies.

EM: Oh, Okay. So Haugland was a more accessible route to town.

JD: It was, but where we lived, on the South Side, it was all unpaved. Hard to imagine now. All I know is that our road, Keefer Street, where we bought our house in 1980, was not paved until the '90s. Haugland was done first so we lived on hole-y roads for quite a few years [laughs].

EM: Hole-y roads. There we go now, Keefer—

JD: [Laughs.] Another thing that struck us was the amount of loaded logging trucks on the roads. It was evident that Terrace was a logging town, it was—I've used this word before—in a very raw state. It just was what it was. There was nothing to finesse it. But there was something very attractive about that. Terrace had no pretensions for being anything other than what it is, a northern forestry town, but it had a certain harmony about it, anyway.

EM: Now was the town a lot smaller—the downtown area?

JD: Definitely. There was an old Catholic Church on the land where the Skeena Mall now stands. There were only two drive-ins at the top end of town near the Bavarian Inn, the Dog 'N Suds and A&W. 4600 block [of Lakelse Avenue] was pretty well the downtown, with parts of Kalum Street south towards the Terrace Hotel and railway, and north towards the Library.

EM: Yeah, like you say: Terrace is what it is. There's no pretension [laughs].

JD: That's right. And, in that way, it has an integrity, an honesty; it's a felt sense that you have. And you wonder why you stay in a place, but there are things you feel at a level that you don't actually understand.

EM: No, it's not until later, maybe in hindsight, that you can—

JD: Yes, that you can think that's what attracted you, but I definitely know that the mountains that surround us and the river were an important part of it for us both.

EM: Oh, of course.

JD: For Peter, for him to be surrounded by these gorgeous mountains, open valleys and wonderful mists and the river, only two blocks away down the hill from our first home—we realized this was just a beautiful place in which to live and you don't feel crowded by the mountains. They support you.

EM: Like, Nelson?

JD: Except that Nelson is more hilly and closed-in, I remember. Terrace has its terraces, which seem to create more space.

EM: Yeah. Now were you sort of recreation-wise?

JD: Ah, that was the first thing we did!

EM: Did you ski, fish—you were outside?

JD: Oh yes. Yes! In June 1975—Okay, now we're settled in, let's meet people. Beautiful place, we've got to get out there. So we joined the hiking club, where we met in people's homes and made strong friendships from that time onwards. Helen Watson, Peter and Sheila Caddy, and Jo Harris were part of that first group we met. It was almost like lift-off, because the people we met wanted to be out and up the mountains. They loved being where they were, and were dead keen to take canoeing trips and walk up mountains [laughs].

EM: Mm-hm. Lovely. So this group—because there is a hiking club, and there was until a few years ago. So that was the beginning—

JD: The hiking club still meets, I believe. It was a very strong group then, probably about 15 people. We'd go on regular hikes for many, many years after that. Probably in to the '90s, and then it tapered off because the hiking group was changing, people were leaving; the dynamics of forestry were affecting the population, which was changing the face of Terrace considerably. People were leaving town for jobs in other towns and provinces.

116

EM: So you saw lots of the area, I imagine—lots of hikes.

JD: We did. We learned about trees, wildlife and local plants, and every year were out picking blueberries, and through all this, you became more familiar and comfortable with where you were. But I was always afraid of bears. My father used to say that he got that feeling there was a bear behind every tree, the way I'd talk.

EM: Didn't have to worry about that in Wales [laughs].

JD: No! The biggest mammal then was a badger and they could get pretty upset. We did run into a couple of bears here, nothing life-threatening—more tantalizing than anything.

EM: What about skiing, or—?

JD: Yes, we skied; we used to go to the old Kitsumkalum Ski Hill off Kalum Lake Road about four or five kilometres north, but even though we had winters with big dumps of snow, the hill wasn't successful, and eventually it was relocated to Shames Mountain—a huge improvement. We more likely skied or snowshoed into town for our groceries and work sometimes because of the deep falls of snow in the '70s and '80s and with not quite the same road clearing capacity we have now.

EM: That would've been quite an adventure [laughs]. I was thinking you'd have to snowshoe back with your groceries.

JD: Yes, we did [both laugh].

EM: One way isn't bad. But, that was in 1977. Okay.

JD: Yeah, '77 I believe. That was a big year when we cut through the pole yard and over the railway tracks.

EM: Okay, yes, yes. A lot more rough and tumble then, eh [laughs]?

JD: It was, and on the west side of the overpass there was another burner, another log yard. So you're literally in the middle of all these logs and logging trucks. Of course, by this time, the Dudley Little Bridge was built, which greatly improved movement and access for logging trucks, but it affected downtown Terrace because of decreased traffic generally.

EM: Now, you were talking about the ski hill, too. So it ended up moving, simply because there was less snow up there at Kitsumkalum?

JD: Yes, over the years, less snow seems to have fallen and so Kitsumkalum Ski Hill was no longer viable. There was another ski hill on Bornite Mountain near Kitselas Canyon which had a small ski lift, but we only went a couple of times. And then, of course, Shames Mountain with its higher elevation came into being sometime around 1990, after Kitsumkalum Ski Hill closed with a consortium of business people who then sold it to the Shames Mountain Co-op in 2011, which had it up and running again and they're handling it very well.

JD: What about the hot springs?

EM: Oh, the hot springs, that's another beautiful thing — in the '70s and '80s it was a very popular close-to-town holiday spot. Occasionally, we'd stay at the hotel there for the weekend and enjoy the hot pool, go for a meal. Just like Esther's Inn in Prince George, but in some ways much better because of its location. Also, it's a lovely way to keep warm in the middle of winter. I remember the local architect, Alan Soutar, re-designed it and it also had a very nice restaurant for a while.

EM: A restaurant?

JD: You'd get a very nice meal there. It was just a wonderful place to go, but it kind of went downhill since then, which is really really sad because the potential of that place is so great. And so many people talk about it. I just wish that something could be done for us in our area to use it to its fullest.

EM: Was there another favourite spot? Tillicum Twin Theatres? What was a Saturday night?

JD: Yeah, we'd go to the movies knowing that we were sitting in a wartime Quonset hut! The seats were hard but these were replaced with softer seats to our relief some years ago [EM laughs]. Seems to me they used to have better movies in town then than they do now, but then possibly movies were better years ago, more stories. But we change…

Also, the R.E.M. Lee Theatre opened the year we arrived, in 1975. We were very lucky – there were many concerts and events organized by the Concert Society and the theatre was always full. It was another great place to meet people and feel part of the community.

EM: It was. Obviously, I know you from your community involvement, but did you start at that time getting involved in community groups?

JD: It took me several years to really settle in and learn about the community and myself and how I fit in. It was in the early '80s that I started to get interested and involved. The public art gallery was my first experience when it had its space in the basement under the back part of the library when Ed Curell was the Librarian, which is where art shows were held then and where Peter held his first show in 1979. I became a board member of the Art Gallery in 1990 after it had been relocated to the front basement of the Library some years before, at a time when it almost folded. I couldn't imagine a community without an art gallery and so, with several others, we managed to keep the doors open. I came off that board in 2012.

It was in 1985 that I first met Nirmal and Rani Parmar, and Kathy Mueller, Linda Lee and Comfort Osei-Tutu who all formed the very first multicultural group in 1984 and were the founding members of Terrace & District Multicultural Association. I joined them as a board member in 1986 when it also became a registered society.

EM: All right, so when you met them, they were already involved in the community?

JD: They were planning and holding community events. In 1986 I went to a Human Rights Day Community Potluck Dinner they were hosting and I liked what they were doing. I believe in people coming together and accepting and respecting each other's cultures, and food really is the best way to do this. I think having my Welsh upbringing gave me that opening to other cultures, even though we didn't meet many other cultures in West Wales as it was very rural, but it opened the door for me through their own kindness and generosity of spirit.

So, back to Terrace. You find that the more people you meet, the more you become a part of the community. At another point in the early '80s, we were involved in the Amnesty International group, but it didn't survive very long because people come and go and it's hard to keep something going with just a few people, as we all know from volunteering, and it being more political as well.

EM: … so, the multicultural aspect has always been there.

JD: It's always been there. The Multicultural Association sponsored and held anti-racism and human rights workshops; we assisted with the Citizenship Ceremony whenever it was held in Terrace; we held the annual multicultural potluck dinner; and I sat as a northern representative on the provincial board of AMSSA [the Affiliation of Multicultural Societies and Service Agencies of BC], an umbrella agency in Vancouver.

EM: Was the Skeena Diversity Society an outgrowth of the Multicultural Association?

JD: Yes, Skeena Diversity came out of the Multicultural Association, which spearheaded the first meeting on June 9th, 2000, with the help of the Department of Multiculturalism. Then, in October 2000, a community-based group of various groups/agencies was formed and named as the Skeena Multiculturalism Project Committee. The work was still supported by volunteers, with the one exception that we could obtain provincial government funding to pay someone to make projects happen and keep us on track. That first project in 2000 dealt with institutional racism in the schools and the workplace. Our first chair was RCMP Inspector Tom Forrest, where our meetings were initially held. Nirmal and I stayed with it all because that was what the original 1984 group and subsequent board members and volunteers had envisioned, in wanting the community to develop partnerships and work together towards a common goal. Also, by involving other groups, the Project Committee as a whole gained credibility. Multiculturalism is an integral part of a community. In helping it to grow and unifying it, Nirmal and I are still on the board of Skeena Diversity, which became a society in 2006 with the Centre opening in February 2010.

EM: So now you're able to access some government grants. And now you can hire someone and open a centre.

JD: Exactly, now we can pull back and be part of a policy governance board, having a say in the way the society is run and supporting all its activities, but not doing the same amount of work. That's now done by Saša Loggin, who we met in the early 2000s, and part-time support staff. Saša joined the Skeena Multiculturalism Project Committee and has participated in just about every role as board chair, coordinator, volunteer, and now our Project Director and the Centre Manager. She's quite the dynamo and has contributed immeasurably to the Centre's growth in providing services for immigrants and newcomers to the community, wherever they are from.

EM: Well, I don't want to wrap up but [laughs] I was just thinking. Here's an interesting question: do you have any advice for the present and future people of Terrace? I mean, in view of this interest of yours. Or is that a bit too general?

JD: Well, I've never forgotten the year we arrived in Terrace and finding the hiking group, with which we could share some fun and also learn about our community and the surrounding area at the same time.

Yes, the hiking group was the beginning for us. We found out about them through the public library. So my advice is, know what interests you and then go out and find those people who would love to welcome you to that activity. That is so important—the welcome—and enjoying shared activities with others. Terrace has always been welcoming, but you have to find the group that speaks to you. Skeena Diversity now has a list of all the agencies and clubs in Terrace so that newcomers can find out who and what club/activity is available in town and say, "oh, look, there's karate, there's a book group, a debating club, origami classes, hiking, soccer, you name it." Because shared activities are where people find those they want to spend time with, and make friends with, and to say, "I like this place, it makes me feel good, I want to stay," which then builds the community and makes it stronger.

So, just go out and find your common interest; go out and find a group that matches who you are, and go for it. You'll never know unless you do it and then have the most wonderful experience of your life.

EM: Well, thank you. I think we could do an interview number two. We could carry right on, couldn't we? [Both laugh.] Thank you very much.

JD: That's great, Estelle. Thank you.

John Chen-Wing Interview

Interviewed by Kelsey Wiebe, 19 December 2013

John Michael Chen-Wing was born in Port-of-Spain, Trinidad, in 1935. Both John's parents were from Canton, China. After his parents passed away at the age of five, his uncles hired a nanny to raise him and his three brothers. At the age of 14, John began attending school at Queen's Royal College in Port-of-Spain. John worked as an order clerk before attaining a job teaching Spanish. These positions afforded him the means to save enough money to attend the University of British Columbia [UBC] in Vancouver, British Columbia. He attended UBC for six years and obtained a degree in Psychology with a major in Zoology and Biochemistry. After completing his practicum in Prince Rupert, John moved to Terrace in 1965 to teach Biology at Skeena Junior Secondary School. John married Alice Uberall in 1970 and they had three children together. John and Alice enjoyed an active life; he recalls the times he spent in Terrace hiking, fishing, and dancing. John was an important figure in the community: he held positions as the president for the Terrace District Arts Council and the Northwest Regional Arts Council. He also held a position as the director of the Northwest Education Foundation from 1987 to 2000. In this interview, John talks about the logging and forestry industry, local politics, and the changes the community has experienced. He also shares stories about his wife and their relationship, his experiences raising children, teaching, and being a minority of Chinese descent.

KW: Could you tell me where and when you were born?

JC: I was born in Trinidad. It's part of the Twin Island Republic — Trinidad and Tobago. I was born in a place called Woodbrook, Port of Spain. Woodbrook is a community within Port of Spain, which is the capital of Trinidad and Tobago. I was born on June 24, which is a Monday, 1935. I grew up there, went to school there, and left when I was 24.

KW: How did your parents go to Trinidad?

JC: Well, I don't have much information about my father. I know he was in Trinidad and went back to China to get married. He came back with his wife by boat. That's when my oldest brother was born in a place called Laventille. That's when they moved to a place in Woodbrook — 112 Roberts Street. That's where I was born and grew up for about 12 years.

KW: Can you tell me a little bit more about your parents?

JC: Both my parents are from Canton [China]. I know much more about my mother because she had three brothers in Trinidad when I was born. I don't know when they came, but they must have come after she came. Both she and my father ran a grocery store, which is where we lived — at 112 Roberts Street.

But my father died when I was four and a half years old, and my mother died when I was five years old. So my uncles eventually hired a lady called Octavia Lovell to look after me and my three brothers. She did a very good job. She was like a nanny — looked after all our needs, fed us, clothed us, took us to church.

She belonged to the Seventh-Day Adventist Church. But I was baptized in the St. Crispin Anglican Church. I think one of the reasons why I was baptized in the St. Crispin Anglican Church was because it was the closest church to where we lived. The Seventh-Day Adventist Church was quite a distance away. But since Octavia Lovell was a Seventh-Day Adventist, she would take us to the Seventh-Day Adventist Church on Saturdays.

She was a very good caregiver. She made sure we were clean and neat, went to school, did things on time, read the Bible, and adhered to some of the dietary restrictions of the Seventh-Day Adventist Church. She was very influential in my early education.

KW: So, what was your relationship like with your siblings? You said you had brothers?

JC: I had three brothers. When I was about 12 years old, my eldest uncle in Trinidad was going to go to China. He wanted us all to go — all of us — so they called us one at a time. I was the second child, and then there was a third, and a fourth. So he called the first one. He didn't mind going; he was sort of adventurous. I said no, because I knew if I did go to China, I probably wouldn't get an education. The third one didn't want to go either. The fourth one was about six or seven years old, and he didn't mind. So, my uncle took the eldest and the youngest of my siblings to go with him.

Two uncles remained who didn't want me to go to school and they kept me home for two years at least. Eventually, I rebelled against not going to school. They said, "Well, if you don't want to work here in the store, then you can't go to school. So you better go and get a job." They sent me to the merchants who supply them with grocery supplies.

One of them was my younger brother's godfather. His name was C. Lloyd Trestrail [the name of his company was C. Lloyd Trestrail Company Ltd.] and he was a Canadian from a Canadian family. He said, "What would you like to do?" I said, "I would much rather go to school." So, he sent his son with me to the Queen's Royal College, which was the only public secondary school in Port of Spain at that time. It was fully supported by government.

I was able to secure a place and they paid my way — paid my school fees, paid for my uniform, paid for my books for four years. And that's how I was able to get a secondary education. [But then] I got transferred to stay with my third uncle who had established his business in the northern part of Port of Spain. It was quite a struggle. I didn't know anyone who was an orphan like me. It started being very hard because there was a conflict between whether I should get an education or not, and they were very much against it.

KW: Yeah. You were always committed to going to school. You always wanted to.

JC: It was very difficult because I had to depend on other people to help me. I had to walk everywhere — walk to school, maybe two or three miles every day. And then I didn't have anywhere to study. So I had to go to the public library or the British Council office — mainly the library — and do all my work. I left my books where I studied because I didn't have any way to move them around. Eventually I got a bicycle.

I got my Cambridge school certificate; those exams are set by Cambridge University. And I got my Cambridge high school certificate. I ended up being an audit clerk for a firm of chartered accountants in Port of Spain, after I left Queen's Royal College. I worked there for about 20 months, and then I got a teaching job in Chaguanas, located in Central Trinidad, which paid almost twice as much.

I saved enough money to eventually come to the University of British Columbia [UBC] in Vancouver. By then, my eldest brother had come back from China, but my youngest brother did not. He was riding a buffalo once and fell down. He fell off of it and had a concussion; he died at age 13.

My eldest brother said we had relatives in Vancouver, and maybe I could go there, and maybe they would help me. But they weren't in any position to help me, and they lived very far away from UBC. So, I stayed on campus, in one of the outlying residences—formerly the training centre. It was part of the army camps that served as residences at that time. That's how I got part of my university education.

I spent six years at university. Initially, I was trying to get into medicine. But, there was no way I could afford that, because I didn't have any means of support. I had committed my mind to becoming a medical doctor or a teacher. So I eventually became a teacher. I came and did my practicum in Prince Rupert, and there was a job opening in Terrace, which is close by. That was the first job I applied for, and I was accepted. So, I was the only biology teacher in Terrace for four years; I replaced someone who was very popular and very well liked, so it was very hard to succeed him. I worked really hard and continued to work really hard, and that made a big difference in establishing myself as a teacher here.

KW: So, did you major in biology then?

JC: Not exactly. I got my credentials in biology and chemistry, and I studied zoology. I also studied botany and geology and other subjects. That's why I took extra time. I was focused on doing pre-med, so I did all the pre-med courses. Eventually, I got my degree plus my teacher training; I got a degree in psychology with Education majors in Biology and Chemistry.

KW: What was it like coming to Vancouver, to UBC, from Trinidad?

JC: Well, it was quite different. The weather was different. And before, I didn't have to do things like operate clothes washing machines. I didn't know how to clean a woolen sweater, so I put it in the hot water in the clothes washer and it shrank. So, it was different in that respect.

Plus, I had to walk quite a bit or take public transit. And also, I had to learn when rain falls in Vancouver, you don't go under shelter. Because in Trinidad, when rain falls, you go under shelter. In 15 minutes, the rain stops falling, and then you can walk and the sun comes out. But here, when the rain falls, it continues drizzling all through the day and night.

KW: Never stops.

JC: Well, that is a big difference, plus the temperature. Once I went on the ferry to Victoria. I was coming back and this person says, "Oh, don't worry. You will soon adapt to the weather."

KW: And then coming to Prince Rupert, must have been different once again.

JC: Well, Prince Rupert was also rainy. It rained almost every day, except weekends, for the three weeks that I was there.

KW: Where you lived in Trinidad, was it a large town, or a small town, or a city?

JC: In Trinidad? Well, Woodbrook is a community; it's self-contained. It had a pharmacy, grocery store, laundry, churches nearby, and had a playing ground. There's a park called Siegert Square. Port of Spain is a series of communities — like St. James, Belmont, Woodbrook, Newtown. That's why I thought eventually towns like Terrace would become self-contained communities where you have playgrounds and schools and so on. People wouldn't need to have cars to move about as much. You could ride your bicycle or walk. It may eventually come to that, but I don't know. There's so much reliance on cars and fossil fuels.

KW: So, I understand that you were taught by the Nobel laureate V.S. Naipaul [Sir Vidiadhar Surajprasad Naipaul]?

JC: V.S. Naipaul. He won a scholarship when he was 16 years old, but I only learned later on the reason why he won the scholarship; it was a special scholarship designed for him. Because the school — Queen's Royal College, the school I went to — misread the regulations for the scholarship exams. So he wrote the wrong exams and didn't qualify. But the government of the day enabled him to get a scholarship called the 'Colonial Scholarship', and he went to Oxford and got his Bachelor of Literature.

He taught me and my name is mentioned in two of his books. One called Letters Between a Father and Son, because his father was never published. His father was a journalist but never had a published book, and V.S. Naipaul wanted to have a published work of his father. The second one was his biography, written by Patrick French. It's called, *The World Is What It Is*, and if you didn't know, that's a quotation from Lady Chatterley by D. H. Lawrence. If you look at one of the pages towards the end, where Lady Chatterley was confiding to her father that she had fallen in love with the gamekeeper, there's this quotation: "The world is what it is."

He was very influential in what I read, because he had sort of directed my reading. Probably I learned quite a bit from him. I wrote to him when he went to Oxford for the first two to three months, but that was about it. I didn't realize when Patrick French interviewed me to be part of this biography that he really wanted to know my opinion about V.S. Naipaul's early works.

They are novels written about Trinidad. One of them is a book called Miguel Street. I read it again after the interview, but I didn't really realize at the time that was why I was being interviewed. Miguel Street is probably a facsimile of Roberts Street, but I couldn't identify anyone in it from that street. I knew a lot of people who lived on that street, especially in the part where I lived that had a pharmacy, laundry, grocery store, and a church. Roberts Street was sort of four corners — more than four corners, about five corners—because it was a three-way street. It went one way, one way, one way, one way. So it was quite interesting.

If I had thought about it, I could have told him that the dialogue didn't seem as if it came from the people who lived on that street. He had a story about this lady, with seven children, which is not unusual for women at that time, even though they were not married. The difference between this woman character and other women would be the seven different fathers. That's what I remember from this book called Miguel Street.

He also wrote another book called The Mystic Masseur, and that was made into a movie that was filmed in Trinidad. He has written other books, but his writing became different afterwards. It became more global. He traveled a great deal in the United States, South America, Africa, India. And he has been to Europe. He was one of three or four people in the Caribbean to win the Nobel Prize in English Literature. But people don't think that that's something to talk about because V. S. Naipaul means very little around here. If I told people that I was mentioned in Naipaul's two books, they would never make any fuss about that.

KW: I was impressed. So you were in Prince Rupert and then a job posting came up in Terrace, and that's how you arrived here?

JC: 1965. I came on the bus when I got hired, because I had to come and find somewhere to live. And I'll say a word about Bert Goulet; Bert Goulet was the reeve of Terrace. Because at that time, Terrace was a district.

I taught at Skeena Secondary School — taught courses in grade 8 but mainly grade 9, 10, 11. And then eventually there was grade 12 Biology. I lived only about a block and a half from the school, so I could just walk. I didn't need a car. That was 1965. I got a car in 1967, January, the only Camaro that was in Terrace — a blue Camaro with a long front body.

KW: Wow. Was it okay on the roads here?

JC: Pardon me?

KW: Were the roads okay for a Camaro?

JC: Yeah. It was a bit like a sports car with a bucket seat. Two doors. You had to bend over to get into the back seat.

KW: What were your impressions of Terrace in 1965?

JC: Well, there were not very many paved streets. And I remember the bus stopping at Lakelse Hotel, which is now Inn of the West. That's where the shopping area was: 4600-block Lakelse Avenue. At the time, there was no Shoppers Drug Mart or Safeway.

Further down, where the Skeena Mall is, that's where the Veritas Church was located, and Veritas Hall. And that's the hall where my wedding took place in 1970. The street that I lived on, Davis Avenue, 4800-block, was paved. But not very many were paved. The road from Terrace to Prince Rupert was partially paved, but the road from Terrace to Hazelton wasn't paved. That's what I remember — it being a dusty town but not very large.

Skeena Secondary School was the only secondary school. There was a school called Riverside. That's where the Legion is. There was a school around there. There was a school probably on Kenney Street, where the school board office is. On the right of the school board office was a school — Kalum School — and all the other schools after that.

KW: How did your career, being a teacher, frame your experiences in Terrace?

JC: Actually, I taught in Trinidad for three years, as I mentioned — Spanish. But when I came to UBC, I got my credentials in biology and chemistry, but I also majored in psychology. I found psychology helped me a great deal, because it helped me to understand how people get along well with each other. And even now, I suggest to people who have conflicts, "Is it worth getting upset about these different things? Is that why you do whatever you do? Is that why you go to church? Or do you go to church to be loved and recognized and so on? If those are things that can be overlooked, then there's no problem."

I learned those things from psychology. I learned it from all the different theories of Jung, and all the other psychologists and psychiatrists. I also learned how to understand people, and their character, and their differences. It also determined how I functioned as a teacher.

One thing that helped me is getting married. This lady who worked in the school board office said, "John, you become a better teacher when you become a parent," and I think she was correct. Because when I became a parent, I could understand how children were treated in school, their experiences. And I learned how to modify my treatment of students from what they told me.

I got married in Terrace on March 28, 1970, but I met my wife-to-be the last Friday of April, 1969. I had a friend who taught in Skeena from '68 to '69, whose wife was a nurse, and my wife was the Director of Nursing at our hospital at that time. She said, "You have got to meet Miss Uberall." So I said, "Oh, I don't know how I'll meet her." And she said, "Oh, there's a nurses' party up at the Keystone Apartments and if you go there on the last Friday evening of April, 1969, you'll get to meet her." So, sure enough, I got to meet her, but just casually. When I was going out to go to my car, she was going out to go to her car. I saw this big green Mercedes Benz that she had brought from Germany. She asked me if I would like to go fishing, and I said, "Oh, no, I can't. That's on a Saturday." I had to go to Prince Rupert to go to a meeting.

I looked in the phone book when I went home and I looked for Ubrow, which I thought was the pronunciation of her name. She was German, but not German-born; her parents were German, but she was born in Saskatchewan. So I looked up Uberall thinking it's U-b-r-o-w and surely there was no name like that in the phone book. I didn't realize it was spelt U-b-e-r-a-l-l.

Eventually, I got a phone call from her in the first week of June, [a message] left at school, to phone her at the hospital. She wanted me to take her out to a banquet when the Premier of BC was coming to visit — W.A.C. Bennett. She told me how to get to her place, and how to get tickets and so on.

And that was our first date. It was held at the community centre which is now burnt down, which was at the west end of George Little Park. We started seeing each other from then on.

Then I went to Hawaii because I was thinking of leaving Terrace at that time – because I felt sort of 'isolated' being in Terrace, because there weren't very many people I knew. I always remembered a book I read by Mordecai Richler, with the truth about being a minority and accepting that it's real. I felt like a minority if I was in Trinidad or Terrace, since I was one of the few Chinese people. That was the sort of thing on Naipaul's mind — because I was the only Chinese student in his class. So that's how I stood out.

This lady I met in the fall of 1968 was going back to Hawaii. She said, "John, you should come to Hawaii. You'll feel much differently because you won't feel part of a minority. Because the Japanese and the Chinese are almost the majority." So I went, and it made a big difference. But she was seeing some professor at that time and when he came back from his holiday, he had already fallen in love with her friend. So that was part of that story. But Alice, who became my wife, used to write me there and we exchanged witticisms. I would write something like "my dear love," and she would say different things like "I'm crazy red" — just little things like that. I showed it to this lady and she said, "Oh, this person's in love with you."

KW: You didn't know?

JC: I thought we were just casually corresponding. She wrote to me and told me I should come back to Terrace and that there was going to be an election at the end of August. I came back a week early from Hawaii. I was there for close to two months. I was already there for six weeks, so I showed up for the election… It was August 30, 1969. And the NDP [New Democratic Party] lost. I didn't think they would expect to win but they won the subsequent election in '72.

I began seeing Alice — Alice Anita Uberall. I would spend a lot of time at her place and one mid-November, she said, "Oh, since you're spending so much time at my place, and you can't seem to get away from me, maybe we should get married." So that's how it happened.

KW: She asked you?

JC: Yeah, she did mention it. She was a very engaging person, and very bright and adventurous. And the thing that sealed the deal in a way, was she took her Mercedes Benz to Kitimat to get it serviced, and they left the cap loose on the radiator, and she had to stop at Onion Lake because all the water from the radiator leaked out. So she had to have it towed back to Kitimat to have it fixed. Since I lived only about two blocks away from the school, I didn't really need my car. I let her use my car for about six weeks.

KW: Your Camaro?

JC: My Camaro.

KW: So that's how it sealed the deal, you said?

JC: That's how we ended up getting engaged. Everywhere she went after that, people thought she was very radiant and happy; they thought she was in love, so they weren't surprised that she was getting married. We got married the Saturday after school was out. Then we went to the Alaska Marine Highway — the ferry from Prince Rupert to Skagway — and then took the train from Skagway to Whitehorse, and then drove. We took the train back to Skagway, took the ferry and came back to Prince Rupert, and drove her Mercedes Benz from Prince Rupert to Terrace just in time for school. So that's about one week.

That was the story. Nine months after, almost to the day, she gave birth on the 23rd of December to our first child, Sara. Kids in school are curious about counting the days, so they counted the days, and, surely, it was right. Then we had a second daughter called Lisa. She was born on October 27, 1973. Our son was born on September 16, 1975, which is a day before Alice's birthday, so we all said that he was her birthday present.

Alice and John with baby Sara. 1971. John Chen-Wing Collection.

KW: So you talked about feeling isolated here, or feeling alone? There weren't many other Chinese Canadian people in Terrace or Trinidad.

JC: No. I grew up alone, so I was used to being alone. So that didn't bother me. It was just interacting. Because people treat you differently than if you're not alone. Like even now if I go out... I went out for dinner last night at the Happy Gang Centre. I know some people there, because I taught their children, and they don't approach me; they just leave me alone. Even people that I know who came after would sit down by themselves. So I just casually meet other people, but I know people don't like being alone. The person who cuts my hair doesn't go anywhere, because she doesn't want to go alone. I would never offer to go, but that's what she said. I noticed that other people, older people, don't like going to concerts, and going out alone. It doesn't bother me because I don't mind being alone.

KW: So there weren't any other Chinese Canadian people here in the '60s?

JC: There were a few more, but I think it never amounted to more than 50 or 60. And there are a lot of Chinese restaurants here, so there must be Chinese people here. But you don't see them in groups; there's no sort of Chinese community. There's more of a Filipino community. At one time, there were probably more Vietnamese people living here. But the first four years I felt different about it — 'til I went to Hawaii.

When I went to Hawaii, there were a lot of Chinese descendants and a lot of Japanese in Hawaii, especially. They're probably not the major population groups: there are probably more Hawaiians than there are Orientals. But there are probably more Filipinos and Portuguese. It's a very different community than Terrace.

126

Terrace had a lot of Southeast Asians, too, but a lot of them have moved out of Terrace as the economy has become different. Because the forest industry employed a lot of South Asians. But the Chinese people… well, the two medical doctors, were Chinese. Most of the restaurant owners are Chinese. And there are some other people who are, but I don't know what they do. There are some from Mainland China doing the tree farm licenses or have access to tree farm licenses, but you don't see too much of them. At least the places I go, you don't see much of them. There were two other Chinese teachers who came after I came, but they were at Caledonia, not at Skeena. But they never stayed.

KW: You stayed because of Alice, right? Or came back?

JC: Well, I came back because I got married here. If I didn't, I probably would have gone. Because a lot of students from Trinidad who came to UBC, stayed in North Vancouver, Surrey, Langley, Burnaby, Vancouver, or Richmond. Some of them went to do other studies in Toronto. In the school I told you about, there were about three or four of us living in BC. There's another one who went to the University of Toronto and got his PhD in Economics. Now he has a job in the University of Toronto. There was another fellow who was in class with me who became a neurosurgeon. He was quite bright; he was top of his class in medicine for four years. He belonged to the Honours' Medical Society, and he's retired now. He came directly from Trinidad to summer school and he did pre-med for a very short time. After two years, he got into medical school, and he became a specialist in neurosurgery. But I don't see very much of them.

I just got a note from a fellow, a phone call. He was wondering about how I was doing, because he read about Bob Erb giving away his money. But he just wanted to know how I was doing. So I told him I was fine. I told him that two of my children are coming [for Christmas]. There will be six of us in the house. I won't be alone, so he doesn't have to worry.

Even if I'm alone, I wouldn't feel that alone because of the other people I know. My wife has an extended family here. She has two sisters who live here, and then the two other sisters are coming from Vancouver and from Surrey. So there will be a large gathering. If you get invited on Christmas Day, there will be 24 of us.

KW: What did you and Alice do for fun when you were in Terrace?

JC: Here? We went hiking, a lot. We used to go to Kleanza Creek. She liked hiking and she liked fishing, but I didn't like fishing. Fishing was not a good fit for me because I get bored easily. And we would go dancing.

KW: Where would you go dancing?

JC: Oh, there was a hall on Lakelse Avenue. I forget what the name was. And then there was dancing at the community centre and…

KW: The Orange Hall on Lakelse? There were a couple different names.

JC: No, not the Orange Hall. It was the community centre. I forget the name. It's demolished since then. We'd go dancing in the arena banquet room, and sometimes at big band dances at Caledonia. And probably there was one at Skeena. Those were the big events because a lot of people who liked dancing would go there.

She liked going hiking. I went hiking once, but I never went back. She always took the children, loaded up the car, and went hiking. They'd go to the Charlottes [Haida Gwaii] on the ferry and drive around. Or they would go down to different parts of BC. She liked driving, and camping, and hiking, and everything else.

KW: Did you guys visit the Lakelse Hot Springs?

JC: Well, it wasn't called Lakelse Hot Springs then. I don't think it was called Lakelse Hot Springs. It was called Skoglund Hot Springs and then it was called Mount Layton Hot Springs. It was much more popular at that time, because it was newer. But now it's not so popular. There used to be New Year's Eve dances at a place called 'Ollie's.' I noticed he died recently.

KW: So, tell me more about your involvement in community organizations outside of school.

JC: Apart from being involved in the NDP in the early years… because I played a major part in the campaign in '72. One of the people I knew called Hartley Dent worked really hard about 18 months before the election. He got elected from '72 to '75 and he got defeated in the subsequent election. He ran against a man called Fred Webber who succeeded him — from the radio and TV station.

KW: But you were also the president of the Arts Council?

John Chen-Wing School Photo, Skeena Secondary School. Circa 1968. John Chen-Wing Collection.

JC: Yes, I was President of the Terrace District Arts Council for quite a number of years – about, I think, from '75 to about 1981. In fact one of the highlights of those years was the building of the R.E.M Lee Theatre, which opened in the fall of 1975. That was the focus of a lot of activities. It brought in a lot of concerts — like the Royal Winnipeg Ballet, which came here several times, the Vancouver Symphony, and the National Symphony Orchestra. We made quite a bit of money. So when I stopped being president, the money that we earned — $30,000 – was donated to the Northwest Education Eighty-Eight Foundation, which is the foundation that provides scholarships to secondary school students.

But I was also president of the Northwest Regional Arts Council, which extended through the whole of the Northwest. We had meetings in Prince George and all over the area. It died down somehow. The arts council survived, but in a different format. They even have a logo now. That's one of my community involvements.

A lot of my involvement from 1969 to 2000 was in the school, with the science fair. I started with the science fair when I first came here in '65. It went on until about 1991, until I stepped down from that. I sponsored the yearbook; I was the coordinator from 1970 to 2000. I also set up the scholarship and awards program from '69 to '72, and then from '78 to 2000. I organized all the awards and scholarships. In fact, the whole format that I set continues on, probably more ably than when I did it.

I also became the director, from 1987 to 2000, of the Northwest Education Eighty-Eight Foundation, which is a foundation that has been set up since 1978. Our cash assets are over $700,000. Not too many people know about it, because they don't publicize themselves too much — even though I suggest they do, but they don't. I'm fairly organized in lots of ways but one. I have a reputation among the parents of the children that I taught. They generally thought that I was a hard-working teacher.

KW: It looks like you were a well-loved teacher from the yearbook reminisces that you brought in.

JC: Those were the people who were engaged. If they weren't engaged and didn't care for biology, they would probably think I was a lousy teacher.

KW: What about local events? Do you remember celebrating different local events?

JC: Oh, when I was involved with the Arts Council, we had annual events. We would have concerts in the street, with young kids dancing and performing outside the library here. But in those things, I wasn't too heavily involved, and I didn't pay too much attention to what was going on. In fact, I can't tell you too much about what's going on in sports, except if it involved the school. Like school games — like track and field, or basketball, or volleyball, or whatever it is. I just make an appearance, to show support.

But some of the things that have happened lately were not that well organized when I first came here. Things like Riverboat Days; that's something that came later on. I know something about the shopping area. The Terrace Co-op played a very prominent role in where I shopped. Because it had insurance, and it had clothing sales and a department store in a way. Quite a big gap was created when they closed down.

KW: Why did they close down?

JC: Well, the big stores coming in and the competition that they faced, they weren't doing very well. And probably they weren't moving with the times. That's the reason why they could not continue.

But with the opening of Safeway and the conversion of Overwaitea to Save-On[-Foods], people gravitate towards those areas. I was a director one year, and one of the reasons why I got to be director was because a lot of the Native people who attended the meeting voted for me. They got me to write my name.

KW: Director of the Co-op Association you mean?

JC: Yeah. But I don't think they really wanted me reelected. That's the feeling I got, but that's probably up for discussion.

KW: What role do you think forestry and logging played throughout the history of Terrace?

JC: Well, I don't know too many people who worked in forestry and logging except for the children whom I taught. When I first came here there were quite a few sawmills, but they would come and go. There was Skeena Sawmills and other sawmills but they come and go. Except the Skeena Sawmills and there's another sawmill that's closed down.

There were several smaller sawmills that were run when forestry was a big industry. The closing of Skeena Cellulose Pulp Mill in Prince Rupert, that had a devastating effect. And the closing of Skeena Sawmills, that also had a big effect because a lot of people worked for them. So, a lot of them would have left town to get jobs elsewhere.

A thing that made a big difference — in 2001, there was a new provincial government and they started moving and centralizing all the services in Prince George. There was a correctional institute here in Terrace, communications, transport, forestry — all those head offices or central offices kept moving east. That had a devastating effect, but you don't hear many people talking about it.

Not giving aid to Skeena Cellulose Pulp Mill because they didn't want to give grants to a private industry had a devastating effect. I think something in regard to forestry legislation . . . logging, forestry companies kept their tree farm licenses even though they were shut down. They were manufacturing sawmills and sawmill locations with their tree farm licenses. That also had a devastating effect on the economy of the Northwest. But I don't hear much discussion about that anymore.

KW: So you noted that First Nations people were electing you for the Co-op board? Did you have a good relationship with First Nations people in Terrace?

JC: In those days, we never spoke in terms of First Nations. I always knew they were First Nations because of who they were. But we never really identified with Kitsumkalum or Kitselas. It's only subsequently when the parents tell me, "Oh, you taught my daughter and we live in Kitselas." I knew more about the people in Kitsumkalum because they're close by. And, largely, I knew that some of them came from there. But before, I never thought in terms of whether they came from — Aiyansh, or Kitsumkalum, or Kitselas. The only connection I had with Kitselas was one of the teachers I taught with in Skeena. [He] talked about petroglyphs that he was making copies of, drawings. Not drawings but...

KW: Rubbings.

JC: Rubbings. And he took interest in that as part of his social studies teaching. He'd take kids out there and they'd do mapping and archaeological digs and so on. That's how I connected. Also, I would go to Kitselas Canyon on hikes. I would take people hiking too. We would also go to Lava Lake — the lava beds — for hiking. I'd take kids, and that's the connection I have.

But there was not so much the sense of them being political entities at that time. Because they weren't that prominent. It was only with the birth of the Nisga'a Nation that all that became very prominent in everyday life. Also, a lot of the Terrace business community depended on First Nations patronage. Because a lot of the trading, shopping and so on — people coming from Aiyansh come here. And you notice quite a big presence of young people working in stores and businesses who are First Nations people. Almost every store you go into.

KW: So just kind of integrated into the fabric of the community. Wonderful. So, have you lived in Terrace during any major floods?

JC: Flood? A lot of major floods took place before I came. There is only one flood I remember, '78, and there were probably subsequent floods then. Because in '78, the roads were closed. I know because the schools were affected, because the roads out of Terrace were closed. And the roads going to Kitimat were closed because of the bridge. But that's about it.

There may have been a flood between '65 and '69, because I remember teachers talking about it because electricity was down for a while. But there wasn't any major effect on people here, just temporary. Planes had to bring in their supplies when the roads were closed, because they depended a lot on trucks bringing in groceries and so on.

I think the major floods took place long before I came. Also, I was not here when Alcan was being built. That was the early '50s. And the dam... I saw a video about it.

KW: So you were on the Arts Council. What role do you think art has played in the community throughout the years?

JC: Well, at one time, concert presentations were not that frequent in Terrace. So a lot of people would go to Kitimat, because Kitimat had more support from industry for the Arts Council's Association; Terrace didn't. Because in Kitimat, Alcan would subsidize a lot of the activities there. But with the opening of the R.E.M Lee Theater, things made a big difference. One of the things that my wife found, was my second daughter wanted to play the violin; violin and string instruments became very prominent in the '90s. So she went to such an extent that she formed a community music school, and what they did was sponsor a violin teacher from Romania to come to Terrace to teach. But things didn't work out too well, because he couldn't adapt to children. Coming from a country where everything is dictated from above, children found it quite hard to be in his class. He didn't last too long.

Ryan, Lisa, John, and Sara [l-r] at Terrace Airport, going to Brentwood School. Circa 1991. John Chen-Wing Collection.

What happened was my daughter really wanted to learn the violin. So after she finished grade 8, she wanted to be sent away to school. She and my wife chose a school in Saanich so she could take a bus to go to conservatory and take violin lessons. But she didn't want to take the bus from far out in Saanich to go to downtown Victoria, so that didn't work out. She spent two years there.

So my son said, when is it his turn to go away to school? By then, my wife had got sick, so she said, "He can go in the fall of 1989." We needed to choose between Shawnigan Lake School and

Brentwood College School. So we chose Brentwood College School. But Brentwood College School said, "We would take him if his sister came too." So she transferred to Brentwood. She spent two years in Brentwood College School.

But while they were there, my wife died in her sleep. The reason I remember that was it was the day after the 'Sandinistas' lost power in Nicaragua. I said to myself, "In order to remember this day, I have to remember what happened the day before." That was a Sunday and she died on the Monday. I shielded them from that. Because my other daughter was in Winnipeg at that time, doing her co-op program work session for one of the telecommunication firms in Winnipeg. My three children managed to attend their mother's funeral on Saturday 3rd March 1990.

KW: You said earlier, before we turned on the recorder, that she started a women's group? Can you tell me about that?

JC: Well, I told you it was called the Terrace Women's Organization — women gathering at the forefront to sort of meet and discuss things. One of the things that they accomplished was getting [to be part of] elections; they took part in the federal election and also local elections, and regional elections. A couple of them ran for school trustee and city council, and Alice ran for the regional district. I think one person got elected to be on city council. Alice got elected to be a Regional District Director in the area that is part of the [Mount Layton] Hot Springs and also part of Kitamaat Village. I think it's Area E but I'm not sure. Her sister became a school trustee and she eventually became chairman. The main objective was to get involved.

KW: And they helped Iona Campagnolo's campaign too?

JC: Yeah. That's another thing they achieved. They probably were the Terrace vanguard for the campaign. One of the people involved got to be involved, in different things. Like one of them became part of the Parole Board federally.

KW: How have you felt our community and region have been represented over the years?

JC: Well, when I first came here, federally, they were represented by the NDP. But provincially, they were represented by the Social Credit until 1972. So from 1972 to 1975 it was NDP. From '75 on until about '79 it was Social Credit again.

Cyril Shelford was the MLA [Member of the Legislative Assembly]. And then from '79 to '83 it was NDP. Because the person Iona Campagnolo defeated ran provincially and he became the MLA. And after that it was reverted back to Social Credit with Dave Parker, and '91 to about 2001, it was NDP again, Helmut Giesbrecht. And 2001 to 2005 was Liberal, and then Robin Austin got elected in 2005 and is still in.

KW: So, do you think it was adequate representation for the concerns and issues of the region over the years?

JC: Well, I think federally, Nathan Cullen, he represents the whole of the Northwest pretty well. And we have three NDP MLAs for the Northwest. The truth is, if they're part of government, they feel they are better represented because they could bring largess. If they aren't part of the government, then they're useless. But I think they provide checks and balances. Even if they are not part of the government, they can still play a role representing the people. When they stop representing the people and engaging the people, they get defeated. But I have a very pragmatic feeling as to who represents us — as long as they don't think they are high and mighty, and think that they can do whatever they want.

It's like my granddaughter. She went last Monday to dinner to her grandmother's and she asked her, "Alice" — she is named after her grandmother — "Alice, what would you like Santa Claus to bring you?" She said, "I don't mind. It can be whatever he wants." She's very pragmatic. I wonder where she gets it from.

KW: She's like you? How many grandchildren do you have?

JC: Three. Three granddaughters. Two of them are coming [for Christmas] — Eloise and Harriet. They all have good memories and are very engaging people, and they like Terrace. So I think it must be the air, not the water. They are quite engaging and assertive.

KW: How do you think Terrace has changed over the years?

JC: It has changed in lots of ways and stayed the same in some ways. It's more developed. We have more of a purpose right now. And we have more shopping, except less variety for menswear and ladieswear.

With the coming of Bob's store [All Seasons Source for Sports], with the building of the new bridge in the '70s…it changed the shopping patterns because people can bypass Terrace. They don't have to come through Terrace. With the Old Bridge, they had to come through Terrace.

We also have the Millennium Trail. That makes a big difference. We also have more paving. But we still have things like deep ditches. I think that should change. All the streets should look very similar, not some having deep ditches and some not. Also the building of the [Sande] Overpass…it's all still very controversial. It seems something is wrong with that overpass. It's not an ideal location. Maybe you should be able to drive along Kalum Street, north-south; they should build an overpass to block off that entry crossing.

Shopping has changed, too, because we have Shoppers Drug Mart and Safeway there now, where the Skeena Mall is. That was all cow barns and just undeveloped land, right in the middle of the city, that area to the north side of Lakelse Avenue, 4700-block and probably 4600-block.

The only shopping centre was the 4600-block Lazelle Avenue and Lakelse Avenue. Now we have the Keith Avenue mall, and we have the mall on Lazelle Avenue — the mini mall — and we have all those fast food joints at the Skeena Mall. That has all changed. In fact, at one time people would go to [Prince] Rupert for restaurants. Or they would go to Kitimat; the Chalet is quite a popular restaurant there. But Terrace didn't have very many eating places. There was one Chinese restaurant, as far as I can remember, called Gim's, but that's no longer there. Then there were a series of small restaurants that came and went. Now we have more Chinese restaurants than any other restaurant.

KW: Did you think Terrace was a good place to raise your children?

JC: Well, it was a good place to raise my children because they didn't experience overt racism, because they grew up among people who accepted them. But when my daughter went to Queen's University in Kingston, Ontario, she started realizing it's a different world there. There was an influx of people from Mainland China, and Singapore, and Hong Kong in Queen's, and some people resented them being there; they made fun of Chinese people.

But she had a lot of Chinese friends too from going there — because she met Chinese students who were born in Toronto or Scarborough. And some of her friends were of Chinese origin. She never thought she was Chinese when she was in Terrace, because she was probably one of the few in class. But no, never thought about it. But I think because I was different — people wouldn't tell me anything — but they probably made fun of my name. So I'd make fun with them in a different way.

You know what I would tell them? I would say, "Chen-Wing, it's chicken wing without an 'ick'." But when my son was at Brentwood playing rugby, they would say, "Chicken Wing, catch the ball." And they said, "Chicken Wing – oops – Chen-Wing." All the boys were called by their surname.

133

KW: So, you just dealt with that humor?

JC: Yeah, that's what I thought it was. But when my back was turned, they would make comments like, "cluck, cluck, cluck" and that sort of thing. But I never really made a fuss because when you make a fuss about things like that, then it becomes a scene. When you don't make a fuss, then they get tired of it.

So I would tell them a joke. Every time after biology class, I would tell them a joke about different things. I did that when I was teaching Spanish. I would give them a joke to translate and the joke would have a theme. There was a joke about a Spanish peasant who had a donkey, and he realized as he was lying on the grass with a twig in his mouth chewing it, "If I stop feeding my donkey, I would make a lot of money." So he stopped feeding his donkey and the donkey died. The punch line was the experiment was successful but the donkey died. That was translated from English to Spanish.

KW: When you were a child, John, what did you expect or hope to accomplish?

JC: Well, I think when I was 10 years old, when I was in elementary school, I planned to qualify for entry to get a Scholarship Exhibition to go to Queen's Royal College. But when my uncle got married, he stopped making a fuss about my going to school. [The school] also did something. The principal of the school I was in wanted to get extra rice because it was during World War II; that was 1945. I had no privileges because I was ridiculed. The next day, I went back to school, and you know what he did? He demoted me from 5A seniors to 5B so I couldn't qualify to get a Scholarship Exhibition.

My not going to school made a big difference. I never went to Queen's Royal College until later. But obviously I was doing well in school; I was the only one of the four brothers who did well in school.

Eventually, I had to work my way to get into university. If everything had gone the way I had expected it to go, my life would have been different. I just spoke to other people. This one lady had quite a few children. She and I became good friends because she took an interest in what I was doing. So we talked about my career. She said, "If you don't get into medicine or you don't get to be a doctor, the next best thing to do is do something that you like."

Since I already had experience teaching at that time, that's what I became. I taught for three years in central Trinidad, and I think I was doing a good job because I worked really hard and the kids did very well. Some of those very kids wanted exhibitions to go to the school, so that made a big difference. I decided if I ever became a teacher, I would work really hard to make sure that I made a big difference in the students' lives. And those students who were willing to be engaged in their education ended up doing very well because they followed my example. But if they didn't follow it, that means they weren't that interested in doing what I intended. But they found other ways of being successful. That is what I expected.

What made a big difference was when I got married, because I didn't expect to get married so easily, because I didn't know that many people. When I met Alice, she was very engaging, so we got along quite well. In fact, the week after we went to this political banquet, she went with one of her colleagues in a Volkswagen car to St. Walburg, Saskatchewan, where she was born, and she sent me a post card marked 'Rebelde'. Do you know Spanish?

KW: A little bit.

JC: 'Rebelde' means rebel. So she had the name 'Rebelde'.

KW: Now that you've known her, do you think that was a fair name?

JC: I think that was a fair description of her. Of her four sisters, I think she was willing to venture out, or else she would not have married me. It didn't bother her in the least. She may have thought

134

about it afterwards, but it didn't bother her at that time being married to someone who was non-Caucasian. It never occurred to her until we started having children, reflecting on what people were thinking and saying to her. They would make fun of her. Say if someone came to visit at work and said, "Alice Chen-Wing," they would expect someone to come down the staircase flip-flopping in their slippers, a Chinese woman. But she wasn't. She wasn't unsure; she was 5'8" and she was commanding. No. She was like that. She was very brave and up to challenges, or else she wouldn't have gone out and help form a women's organization and run for politics — especially in an area that was not too hospitable to her.

KW: As someone who has lived and learned here, John, what would you want to share with people newly moving to Terrace?

JC: My advice would be to get integrated in the community and contribute to the community by getting involved — whether it be children's education, or children's activities, or the neighbourhood. Also try to be a good neighbour to the neighbours around you, because only in times of disaster do people seem to get together.

From July to mid-November 2014, the street I live on was being renovated, so people had to put up with a lot of hardships. It's only then that people started getting together and started saying hello and so on. Otherwise, people take it for granted that all neighbors are going to be very good and helpful. But not all neighbours are like that. People value the community in every way that they can, so that way they can feel secure and everyone can look out for each other.

Julia Little Interview

Interviewed by Merilyn McLeod, 9 November 2013

Julia Little was born in North Battleford, Saskatchewan, in 1918. Julia and her family moved to Houston in 1929, but relocated four years later to Hazelton in the Kispiox Valley. Julia moved to Terrace in 1936, when she was 18 years old. She worked for Riley's Drugs for three years before moving to Ocean Falls with her brother. Julia married Gordon Little in 1941. She and Gordon lived in Kwinitsa for 10 years in the 1940s. Julia shares stories of the remoteness and isolation of living in Kwinitsa. When the timber industry slowed, they decided to move back to Terrace to raise their family of four children. In this interview, Julia talks about her children, downtown Terrace, local events, dating, and other recreation in Terrace. She also shares stories about George Little, the Queen's visit, and the flood of 1936.

MM: Where and when were you born?

JA: North Battleford, Saskatchewan, April 11, 1918.

MM: And tell me about your parents?

JA: My parents farmed. My dad was a farmer. My mother actually was a seamstress and I guess she sewed for just about the whole area all the time. Making things, and remaking things. And we had cattle, horses. That was in Saskatchewan. But then we moved to Houston, BC, in 1929, I guess.

MM: Did you move to Terrace?

JA: We lived in Houston for four years and then we moved to Hazelton out to the Kispiox Valley for farming, for almost four years.

MM: Did you have siblings?

JA: Yes, there were eight in our family. Four boys and four girls.

MM: And when did you arrive in Terrace then?

JA: I came to Terrace in 1936.

MM: What brought your family to Terrace?

JA: My family stayed in Hazelton.

MM: Oh, really?

JL: And my sister Bina was married and lived in Terrace.

MM: Okay. Who was she married to, Julia?

JL: Oh, Gordon Kerr. The electrician. He had a light plant.

MM: Okay, you basically came to Terrace because she was living here.

JL: Well, that was one of the reasons. And then I worked at Mr. Riley's Drug Store. For God, what was it, two or three years? Can't remember. Nobody will know, anyhow.

MM: Mr. Riley, I remember that name. Everybody talks about him. So how old were you when you came here?

JL: I was eighteen.

MM: You worked there for how many years?

JL: I worked here for almost three years. I think that was right. And then my brother and I went to Ocean Falls because we heard there was plenty of work there. Worked in the grocery store. I was the first female worker in the grocery department.

MM: And how long were you there?

JL: Until 1941, when Gordon proposed to me.

In front of Riley's Drug Store: Eric Linney, Julia Simpson, Lorna Smith, Tom Olson, Frances Dover, Ina Smith, Steve Arlington [l-r]. The Way We Were Collection. Terrace Public Library.

MM: In 1941 Gordon proposed. And you met him when you were in Terrace of course?

JL: Oh yes, got together in Terrace.

MM: So when you went off to Ocean Falls, he was…?

JL: I was a year older than him. And I thought, *now this is no good. You know. So I'm going away.* So I went to Ocean Falls. But he followed.

MM: So he proposed. And what year were you married then?

JL: 1941. October 4th.

MM: So you didn't attend school here?

JL: No.

MM: Did you have a big wedding, or was it just a small family thing?

JL: We had quite a nice wedding in Hazelton in the United Church.

MM: How many children did you have?

JL: We had four children. The oldest one, George, died from a car accident in 1962.

MM: Yeah, that was the year I graduated. It was very sad. [Pause.] So how did you find Terrace as a place to raise a family?

JL: Well, I think it was very good. You know, we had everything here pretty well that we needed.

MM: Let's backtrack and talk about the fun you had as kids here and some of the things you did for recreation.

JL: Walk to the bridge!

MM: Walk to the bridge! That was a Sunday activity, was it? Was there a movie house here at that time?

JL: No, but a man lived in Smithers and he used to come here, I don't know, once a week or once a month. I don't know. Probably once a month. And there was a building that he could use as a theatre and so we had a movie. But I was always working on a Saturday night, so I didn't get to go.

MM: So where did you go on dates?

JL: A group of us. We'd walk to the Skeena Bridge.

MM: And took pictures! Lots of pictures.

JL: Some of the boys climbed up to the top.

MM: Were there any restaurants in town that you could go to?

JL: Yeah, Ma Lambly. Between Greig and Lakelse.

Linda Bee [Julia's daughter]: About where the Silvertip used to be.

JL: There were a couple of Chinese restaurants.

MM: Did you ever visit the hot springs?

JL: The hot springs, there was nobody out there then.

MM: No, there wasn't at that point, was there?

JL: No, not until Skoglund came — was the hot springs used at all.

MM: Now, Lakelse Lake, I know you have a cabin on the lake, right? When did you start going out there?

JL: That's where the Littles' had their place. Littles' house, a cabin. Your grandparents had a place.

MM: Yeah. But you had your own cabin out there. Because we used to go visit you in the summer all the time.

JL: Well, that was later.

LB: About '53.

JL: We lived there but Dad had those two cabins built. Dudley had inherited property at the lake. Gordon inherited Kwinitsa.

MM: Right. I wanted to talk about Kwinitsa because I remember that.

JL: You came and visited.

MM: We used to visit. And I remember I always looked forward to going out there to visit because it was a fun place.

138

JL: The trees [laughs]!

MM: Lots of snow.

JL: The bush. And lots of snow.

MM: How long did you live in Kwinitsa?

Kwinitsa Station from the Highway. Spring 1965. Richard Rinaldi Collection.

JL: How long? About 10 years.

MM: Oh really? That long?

JL: Yeah. All through the '40s, pretty well.

MM: In the '40s. What was the reason for being at Kwinitsa?

JL: Because of the sawmill. And there was such good timber out there. But after 10 years, we ran out of timber and had to leave. And that was bad. 10 years, kind of wasted, you know?

MM: You feel that way?

JL: Yeah. Gordon did, too.

MM: Because you were pretty isolated, right?

JL: Oh yes [laughs].

MM: I mean, the highway went by, but there wasn't a lot of traffic on it.

JL: Well, the highway wasn't there until the mid-'40s. And there were people at the stations, every 10 miles in those days, and we used to visit back and forth. The Kwinitsa station was only two miles from us. And a section man would come by every day. And then old Bob the patrolman, he'd come pumping along. He only had one arm and he'd stop at our place and take the car off the track and

139

come in for a cup of tea. George was just a little kid. He'd run out and meet old Bob. And you know, Bob just loved that. He'd say "Cup of tea, Bob?" And Bob would come in for a cup of tea. And during his first cup of tea, he says to me, "Woman, I didn't know your creek runs so clear." So I had to put about six tea bags in one pot of tea for him.

MM: Wasn't strong enough.

JL: He was a good old Scotsman.

MM: What was his name? Bob?

JL: Bob McLean.

MM: So yeah, you would be out there for long stretches without really seeing much of anybody.

JL: Until the highway went through. We went down there in 1941 or something.

LB: '41, right. Mom was a bride when they went to Kwinitsa. Yeah, right after her wedding.

JL: We had nine feet of settled snow on the sawmill platform one March, I forget which one it was. That's how much snow there used to be. But it tapered off. By the time we left there, there wasn't nearly as much. Mid-'40s.

MM: So did you homeschool out there?

JL: Poor George, we sent him into town and he stayed with Victor and Barbara Sherwood for a year. The second year was with the Peekvoot family. And he was so glad to come home every weekend. He was happy there. But he was lonesome. He was raised out in the bush, and he would come into town with all these kids. You know, it's a big change.

MM: Well that was an interesting part of your life, living at Kwinitsa, wasn't it?

JL: Yeah. I mean we were happy, and we were busy.

MM: Was there much of a crew that worked out there?

JL: In the winter we had to lay most everybody off except a few families, Kennedy and Mackenzie, and I forget who else. And we had one deaf-mute. Yeah, he was really a nice guy. He'd come into the store—we had a little grocery store, you see.

If they went to town, they'd load up on groceries. But they always had to buy a few things at our place. I don't know, everybody was working and busy so time went by. Shoveling snow, you know. And now, I haven't gone down there very often, but there's so little snow. God, we had nine feet of settled snow!

MM: Did you play any sports in Terrace, Julia?

JL: Softball. We used to play in Hazelton when I was in high school. Because Jean, my friend after school — one time — there was South Hazelton, New Hazelton, and Old Hazelton. And we were sharing a bat and ball. So we had to make sure that after the game the next person gave you the bat and ball. But anyhow, we didn't have the bat and ball and it was our turn to have a game. So my friend and I walked all the way from Old Hazelton up across that Hagwilget Bridge all the way over to New Town to get the ball after school and back. So we could play after supper. That must be 10 miles! The bridge had washed out, that was in '36 I guess, so we couldn't take the shortcut. So we had to go around.

MM: Interesting. Did you do any fishing in your day?

JL: Oh, up in Houston kids used to fish all the time. Right after school, or weekends. My mother was probably glad to get those fish, you know.

MM: Yeah. Good food. You were involved in community activities in Terrace, weren't you?

JL: In the Hospital Auxiliary and Kinettes.

MM: Do you remember the hospital balls that you used to work on?

LB: Oh yeah, those were beautiful.

JL: I remember. I think the first one we had was in the big hall down there on the park. There was a big hall built in the George Little Memorial Park.

LB: The Civic Centre.

JL: And we had a big ball.

MM: Yeah, down by Riverside Park, as we used to call it, where the school was, right.

JL: It was in the George Little Park.

LB: When the civic centre burnt down, they built a new civic centre and that burnt down also.

JL: They both burned down?

MM: I saw some pictures. I remember the dresses you used to make. You had a theme every year, didn't you? That was the main fundraiser for the hospital auxiliary in those days?

JL: Well, the Kinettes used to have a fashion show. And the Kinsmen used to have something else and we used to help them all the time, too. The Kinsmen and the Kinettes worked together to make money to help the hospital out. Kinsmen — I don't know what their money went for.

LB: I think that the Kinsmen and Kinettes both donated their money to the hospital.

MM: Remember the teas? We used to have a lot of teas.

JL: Oh, yes. There was, I think, a tea in the fall and a tea in the spring. And we used to have a masquerade, too.

LB: Mad Hatter's tea party. Didn't they have a Mad Hatter tea party or something?

MM: Remember in the Odd Fellows Hall, every group used to have their tea or Christmas Bazaar.

JL: And in the Orange Hall.

MM: Where was the Orange Hall?

JL: The Orange Hall was just about where Kathleen's Restaurant was.

MM: What local events do you remember celebrating? Did we have May Day? May 24th was big here.

JL: Yeah, May the 24th.

LB: That was sponsored by the Kinsmen.

MM: Yeah. And then there were logger sports too, in later years. It was in September.

LB: Labour Day weekend. And then, remember, the Kinsmen would wear their underwear and they would play ball? And I remember Mom and Dad have a video of the ball game and there's the

Kinsmen, wearing their underwear, playing ball. And there's a picture of Uncle and Dudley running into a base.

MM: Now, a little bit about the community. Do you have any specific memories of downtown Terrace? Like where you shopped?

JL: Sparkes' had a store, a variety store. And well, we just had Sparkes' and the drug store, Riley's Drug Store. Mr. Riley.

MM: Where was the post office in those days?

JL: The post office was — do you remember where Sparkes' store was? Well, you know the big building on the corner that we always called the Bank of Montreal.

MM: Yeah.

JL: On the corner of Kalum and Lakelse. Well, between that building, going down towards the track, there was Ma Lambly's restaurant, and later the Overwaitea built in there.

JL: So that was the Overwaitea, and Ma Lambly's, and then Emil Haugland's barber shop.

LB: But the post office, it was on Kalum, between the fishing store and the old Rexall building. So it was just right in there, but that was one of the three buildings that burnt down in the '70s.

JL: There was a post office in there? Well, when I came here the post office was on Kalum Street. Between the big black building on the corner that still stands there. And there was Smith's store, or whatever the post office was in there. And Greigs lived upstairs. One of those Greig girls could go out and lean out the window of that post office upstairs. She could yell back and forth to her sister at the house up on the hill. Do you know where their house was?

MM: Park Avenue and Kalum Street?

LB: Where Trigo's is?

JL: They could yell back and forth to each other.

MM: Wow, they had good lungs. Where did you shop for clothes?

JL: Well, sometimes we'd get a trip to Prince Rupert.

LB: Auntie Fern had her clothing store.

MM: Yeah, your sister had her clothing store later, didn't she?

JL: It was '54 when she got her clothing store.

MM: What was her clothing store called? Do you remember?

JL: Fern's Specialty Shop.

MM: Did you shop at the co-op when it was busy?

JL: Oh, yeah, we used to shop at the co-op. And did you know that Bruce Johntsone's name was Bruce Johntson, and then he had it changed to Johnstone? Did they ever tell you that story?

MM: No.

JL: Yeah, probably not. I think this is quite funny. Bruce was talking to George Little, and he didn't like for people to know that he was from Sweden or Norway or whatever. And we always thought it was so funny because he was so Swedish or Norwegian, he looked it and he talked it and everything.

But he didn't want people to think he was. So George Little told him, well you just put an 'e' on the end and it'll be English. So that's how the 'e' got on the end. He had his name changed. And you probably never heard that.

MM: No, no! No, I didn't.

JL: So he had it legally changed.

MM: Oh dear. I never heard that story. Now, what did most people that you know do for work here in the early days?

JL: Well, it was sawmill and logging.

MM: So, your parents were farmers in the early days. But not later years, right?

JL: Early days. From North Battleford, Saskatchewan.

MM: Did any of your family or friends work in sawmills or logging?

JL: They did. My two brothers had a little sawmill and logged in Hazelton. Years ago now.

MM: And, of course, your husband was Gordon.

JL: So, Gordon was tired of living out in the bush anyhow. So we came to Terrace. And, what year?

LB: Well, I guess it was '49 to '50.

JL: Well, George was in grade one, grade two then.

LB: So anyway, Mom and Dad were back in town in either '49 or '50, thereabouts.

MM: And then worked in and around the logging industry all his life, right, Gordon did?

JL: Oh yes. Logging and sawmilling.

LB: Then Dad had the John Deere business for—I'm not sure how many years.

MM: Yeah. How did the community of Terrace interact with Kitselas and Kitsumkalum? When you were younger?

JL: Well, they were pretty small. Kitselas was out there. And Kitsumkalum, they had cars, they had to come to town to shop.

MM: And did you live here during the major floods?

JL: Yeah. We were caught in Hazelton. We had gone up there for the May the 24th weekend. And we ended up having to fly— to go to Smithers, and fly back to Terrace. And Gordon and somebody else got a boat somewhere, because he was worried about the mill down at Kwinitsa. So we stayed in Terrace and Gordon and whoever it was went down that bloody river. It was high and swollen in just a 16 or 18-foot boat. God. Imagine. But he wasn't afraid of it. Gordon just had no fear really of anything.

MM: So that was your impression or remembrance of the flooding. What flood was that?

JL: That was the flood of '36. And snow those first years in the '30s, oh God. It would snow and snow and snow in the winter.

MM: Yeah.

JL: And I think there was a slide here. Oh, I forget how many years ago. And it came down off the mountain. A snowslide. And old Bob Mclean. He was there then, wasn't he? I think so. But we were gone. And when it got to the house, where the house was, it turned, I suppose. The wind that was preceding the slide got the house, blocked it or something, and it turned and went over under the mill and out into the river. And if we had been there, our little kids would have been playing out right in the path of that thing and they'd have probably ended up in the river.

MM: And that's at Kwinitsa?

JL: Kwinitsa. Terrible. And your mom and dad, Lorraine and Lloyd, came down to visit us once and spent the weekend. And we four all got into our bed in the morning. We said "Come on, get in bed with us." So your mom and I in the middle, and males on the outside. Laying there talking and laughing.

M: Having a good time.

JL: Because we did have two bedrooms. So they slept in the spare bedroom, the guest room.

MM: How did the establishment of Kitimat in the '50s impact Terrace as far as you remember?

JL: I don't really remember much about that. Too busy raising kids.

MM: Yeah. Railway went through.

JL: Yeah, there was a railroad, and then later the road. I remember the cadets, we all got together and went to Kitimat. Had a meeting or something and went out on the train. And had a lot of fun.

MM: How has Terrace changed over the years?

JL: Well it grew from just a small little village into a city really.

MM: Alrighty. Let's just leave the community then. Some of these things you'll probably remember. Can you tell us about the Great War Veterans Association hall? Were you around when it was here? What was it, the G W V A…

JL: It was beside the old Royal Bank. On Lakelse Avenue. Bob's store [All Seasons Source for Sports] is on the corner. If you go east, go east, and half a block.

MM: Yeah, there was a hall there called the Odd Fellows Hall.

JL: Yeah. And then later the Odd Fellows Hall I think moved to where the Orange Hall was, near where Kathleen's was.

MM: Do you recall when the military were here? Were you here during the war when the military were in town?

JL: Well, we were in Kwinitsa first. So, God, I can't remember what was that like. But we were in Kwinitsa until about 1950 and I think most of them had gone then. I think so.

MM: So you basically were in Kwinitsa most of the time when they were stationed here. So do you remember the mutiny at all?

JL: No, because I was down there.

MM: Do you remember when the Queen came to town?

JL: Oh yes! We were on the corner of Lakelse and Kalum, and the Queen came to town and rode through. And they paved a little bit of Lakelse and around by the post office, and then back down Kalum, so that's where she went. Just up Lakelse, behind Little's house and your house, and then turned and went around that corner and then down and then back again. And we waved to her.

LL: Yeah, that was cool.

MM: But we got pavement. Our first pavement. Was there any particular person or event that made an impact on your life?

JL: Oh, I don't know. Life just went on. The death of George, of course, that was very sad.

MM: Your son.

JL: Yeah. Otherwise it was a pretty normal life.

MM: As a long-time resident of Terrace, what changes have you noticed?

JL: We used to have more dances then than we have now [laughs].

LB: Our parents were always going to dances.

MM: I know!

LB: And you know, there's no place to dance any more. Well, one place, The Northern. But, I mean, parents back in the '50s, '60s, they were always going to parties whether it was the Kinsmen, the Shriners, whomever.

MM: Do you remember New Year's Eve?

JL: Oh yes. We always had a good dance on New Year's Eve. Either in the Odd Fellows Hall or the Orange Hall.

MM: Yeah. Or the old civic centre. As a kid I remember it being the highlight of the season. Because the dresses. Everybody...

JL: Dressed up.

MM: They'd have a new dress made.

JL: We had the May pole, and all the little girls would dress up and be running around that May pole.

MM: That would be the May 24th. I remember doing that a couple of times. And the May Queen.

LB: Yes! Selling tickets. The kinsmen would have the tickets for the queen, for the girls competing, and you'd go and sell all your tickets.

MM: I remember. I've got pictures of me being a little flower girl. Do you have any advice for the present or future residents of the city?

JL: Keep on working.

MM: Are there any other stories you'd like to share with us, Julia? That we haven't touched on. It's hard to remember all this stuff, isn't it.

JL: Oh, I don't know. We used to just have a wonderful time. I think people just used to get together more when the town was smaller. But now, you hardly ever see anybody. That's one reason I guess I go to Kathleen's. It's kind of nice once in a while. I can help her a little bit and hang out.

MM: Good, well we're pretty much at the end of my questions. So if there's any other stories you'd like to relate Julia, or?

LB: What about your motorcycle ride. Why don't you add that?

JL: Oh. One time Gordon wanted me to ride his motorcycle. And it was too high for me to get on and get my feet on the ground. So he had it running and I got on it in front of their house, and I went all the way out to the high school, across the tracks. No cars coming, or no train. And then along Keith, and across the Kalum Street crossing. Right back up to their house again. And then he caught me. It's a good thing. If I'd have gotten stuck or fallen off or something, it was too high for me to get back on, you know?

MM: Who's motorcycle was it?

JL: Gordon's. He had a motorcycle. That was my motorcycle ride. I used to ride on the back with him. And one time I was on the front and I was steering, I was driving it. And a policemen, I forget whether they stopped us, or we stopped at the corner or what. He said to Gordon, "Your passenger is supposed to be on the back, not the front." Or I guess something like that. And Gord said "I'm the passenger, she's operating the motorcycle" [laughs].

MM: Did you have any other run-ins with the police in the town in those days?

JL: No! I've evaded them. Oh yes, I did! That's right. Up near Vanderhoof I was going along all by myself. I was going to Prince George, or the Okanagan or somewhere. And they have these rest areas, you know? And so this cop had stopped at one and was waiting to catch somebody. And I come flying by, and he came out after me, you see. So he just warned me. I said, I was going up to Prince George and I'm driving my car. But I was speeding and I knew that. But he didn't give me a ticket.

MM: He was a good policeman.

JL: Because up near Vanderhoof there's some nice long straight stretches.

M: There still are.

LB: Up the Hungry Hill.

146

Margaret Li & Charles Li Interview
Interviewed by Marj Brown, 17 December 2013

Margaret Li was born in Hong Kong in 1958, one of five children. When she was six years old, her father passed away and her mother, working as a domestic helper, was left to raise the children. Margaret spent much of her childhood living with her uncle and cousins. Margaret and Charles both describe a simple childhood, making creative use of anything to entertain themselves. Margaret completed high school, worked, and took a dental hygienist course before marrying Charles. In advance of the 1997 transfer of Hong Kong's sovereignty to China, they immigrated to Canada. After a few months in Vancouver, Charles and Margaret moved to Terrace to operate a restaurant. When they took over the restaurant [the Shan Yan] in 1996, the forestry industry in Terrace was slowing down. In this interview, Margaret and Charles describe their early life in Hong Kong, adjusting to life in Terrace, and the challenges of operating a family-owned restaurant.

MB: Where and when were you born?

ML: In Hong Kong, 1958.

CL: I forget mine.

MB: You remember Margaret's? Does he always bring you gifts then, if he remembers your birthday?

ML: Yeah. [Laughter.]

MB: Can you tell me a little bit about your parents?

ML: Oh, actually, my father died when I was very young. I was six and the last baby of the family. I didn't know much about my father. But my mom raised five of us. I've got another four brothers and sisters, but they are much older than me. I did not stay with my mom after my father died; I stayed with my relatives. My mom had to work. For my dad, not much memory, because I was young at that time. I just remember, when I was six, that he passed away.

MB: So, what was your relationship like with your brothers and sisters? Did you live with relatives? And, were your brothers and sisters living with you there too?

ML: No. I lived with my relatives, but not with my brothers and sisters.

MB: So you were alone, being the youngest.

ML: Actually, because at that time, you know, everybody's not that rich. They were poor, right? Especially my mom; the husband dies and she needed to raise five of us. It was so hard for her. So all her brothers and sisters, or maybe my father's side, helped her. So, the five of us were not connected together; each of us went to some of the uncle and aunties. I stayed with my cousin. But my cousin is older than me by so many years.

MB: So, in some ways, would you say you knew your cousins more than your brothers and sisters?

ML: Yeah. I am more close to my uncle and my cousins than to my whole family because my childhood was not with them.

MB: So, what was a typical day like then, as far as your routine and what you did? How early would you have to get up and go to school?

ML: Oh, we woke up very early because the school time was around 8:00 a.m.. Yeah, around eight. And we needed to take a bus to go to school. So, usually we woke up at 6:30 a.m., around 7:00 a.m. … something like that. We had a whole day of school until 3:30 p.m., and then we took the bus back home around 5:00 p.m.. It was a very simple life. And we went to school five-and-a-half days — and a lot of homework.

MB: Was there a school bus?

ML: No. A public bus.

MB: And just one bus? Or did you have to change buses?

ML: We needed to change.

MB: Two buses? Or even three?

CL: Actually, it depended on the route of those buses. There were a few bus lines at one bus stop. It was just like a spider web in Hong Kong. And then sometimes, we missed the right one and then we had to take the other bus and change back to the right one again. But usually, we just took one bus.

MB: So, growing up in Hong Kong, what kind of expectations were there for girls? What were girls supposed to be like when they grew up?

ML: All the generations are a little bit simple. All Chinese people have a very high expectation. Especially — the family — they expect the kid to at least finish high school if possible. Because it's not everybody who could go to college and university at that time. At the very basic, you needed to finish your high school. And you needed to get a job, or get some professional thing. That was a very simple expectation. It's not like you needed to be a doctor.

MB: But you need to do your best.

ML: Yeah. You've got to be a good kid. Not be a gangster or something like that. Simple expectation.

MB: So, what kind of work did your mother do? What kind of work was she in? In those days, in Hong Kong, were women able to get lots of different kinds of work, or just certain jobs?

ML: They could get different kinds of jobs. For my mom, it was a little bit different because she knew some Chinese; she never studied. So, she was a domestic helper at that time. It helped her to have money for all the living costs for the kids, all expenses. So most of the time she stayed in that family's house doing all the domestic jobs.

MB: What was it like just around your neighbourhood?

ML: At that time, we seldom went to the park to play. Because we were staying in a big apartment, you could play with the kids, your neighbours, along the corridor. It is not like nowadays with your neighbour, you go to the park and then play there.

MB: So, the playmates would be the people in the other apartments?

ML: Yeah.

MB: What kind of games would you play in the hallway?

ML: Very simple games. We did not have many toys at that time. I remember when I was a kid, if I got a doll, I would play with it for years. I was so happy. We were using some simple things; you could say it was creative. Just like what he [Charles] tells me. He used paper to make a toy and he played for a week with that. So happy.

CL: You could get a piece of, for example, bamboo. In Hong Kong, we used bamboo. Anything you could get.

MB: When I was young, we had a game we called jacks. There were little metal things and a ball. And we'd go like this, and the little things would scatter. Then you'd throw the ball up... grab one... catch the ball. We played that mostly in the summer. And I was so surprised when one of my friends told me in India she played that. She said, "We had little rocks and a little ball." That was just about like my game. You know, thousands of miles apart, and a game that was very simple and so similar.

ML: Yeah. And at that time, if you had some paper, you would tear a little piece. And you got the ruler — just put that on your hair — and then that kind of electricity made you feel so funny. "Oh! They can stay up!" Just something like that!

MB: The static electricity.

ML: Yeah!

MB: So, what schools did you attend? How was the school system?

ML: Kindergarten was in a separate school in Hong Kong. I think nowadays it's the same, right?

CL: Yeah.

ML: And starting from Grade 1 to Grade 11 — because in Hong Kong, you go to grade 11 — you needed to take exams for everything. Just like here — the provincials — to see who can go to grade 12. After that, you needed to take the exams again. And then you could go to the university.

MB: So, you finished high school, did you?

ML: Yeah. I finished high school, and I went to grade 12, and then I took a dental hygienist course.

MB: And then you guys got married and came to Canada.

ML: We got married, and then we planned to have the baby. We thought, at that time, because Hong Kong had the 1997 incident [Chinese sovereignty] — if you wanted to have a baby and you wanted to give her or him a better education... That's why we decided to move here.

MB: So, how did you meet?

CL: How did we meet? There were a lot of girls [laughs].

ML: I think it was at a wedding, right? Your schoolmate, right?

CL: I think so.

ML: She's a colleague with me. Because at that time, I hadn't taken the dental hygienist course. I just graduated, and then I, like a normal girl, went out to get the job because family couldn't support me. For Hong Kong people, after you graduate, if your family can't support you, you to go to university. So, we would decide to get a job first to help out the family. And for yourself, right?

We still stayed with the family. We're not like here. Nowadays, after we leave high school, we need to move out. But it's so welcome — you stay at home but you're helping the family as well. That time, I think I got an office clerk job, something like that — some kind of job working in the office.

MB: Can you tell me a little about your wedding?

ML: Our wedding was very simple [laughs]. Was just some of our relatives, and some of our close friends. We just had dinner together and then we registered. Just very, very simple wedding. Because we thought: *It's just our thing. We don't need to make a big wedding. Right? We just want to enjoy the night.*

MB: So, how long were you married before you came to Canada?

ML: How long?

CL: '94 minus '83. 11...

ML: Yeah. I think something like that.

MB: 11 years.

CL: And it's still working [laughs].

MB: And it's still working! How did you decide to come to Terrace?

CL: Oh, that was because of my friend. A close friend was running a restaurant [The Shan Yan]. And the first owner — we're the third one — the first owner sold it to another owner. And then, that owner ran it for five years or so. He got all of the information, and knew the previous owner wanted to sell. He checked with me, to see whether we'd like to do it or not. When I was young, I heard a lot of stories about my heritage, my own people. When they were young, they'd go to somewhere like San Francisco, working as a dishwasher in a restaurant or something like that. And I knew a lot of these stories and I never thought that I would be the same. But I think it's okay.

MB: But it's very different when you own the restaurant, than working for someone else.

ML: Yeah.

CL: So we thought, *why don't we try?* Because I was working as a car salesman. It was tough. They had 14 to 15 dealerships around. So people, they just travelled around to bargain for maybe about 50 bucks. That's it. So I said, "okay." And I resigned and we came here.

MB: How long were you in Vancouver before you came to Terrace?

CL: One-and-a-half years.

ML: After we got to Vancouver, a few months later, I was pregnant. Because we decided we wanted to have a baby. And then, I think we moved up here.

CL: Three months?

ML: No, three months is when we came up to check the restaurant. I think it was six to nine months when we came to Terrace at that time.

MB: So Vancouver would have been a big change — small city, fairly cold. And then you came to Terrace, and it was an even bigger change, right?

ML: Yeah.

MB: A tiny city. And...

CL: Cold [laughs]!

ML: It's very different. Because in Hong Kong, even like right now — December — it's still around 10 degrees — something like that.

CL: Sometimes 15 degrees.

ML: Yeah. Right now, it's higher, right? But you can have on a T-shirt, just a cardigan. You will be okay. But here, the first year — I think the first winter in Terrace — I said, "How come it's so cold?" Snowing outside and dark so quickly. Even more short days than in Vancouver. Even in the restaurant, it was so cold! Everywhere it was snowing!

MB: So, where was your daughter born?

ML: In Richmond.

MB: And how old was she when you came here?

ML: Around six to nine months. I can't remember exactly.

MB: Do you just have the one daughter?

ML: Yeah.

CL: It's expensive. She's the most expensive.

ML: [Laughs.] The precious things you've got to say!

MB: How did you find Terrace as a place to raise your family? In your neighbourhood in Hong Kong, everybody expected the children to work hard and study hard. And when you came to Terrace, did everybody think the same way?

ML: I don't think so. I think they're more easy-going. For Chinese people, there is more concern about academic things. But I think in Terrace, they are more focused on the sports, music… It didn't mean they don't focus on the academic, but they like the kids to have music, sport, something like that. Right? It's very different. I think people have a high expectation for their kids as well. But they will let them choose on their own what they like — a little bit different from us.

We have expectations for our girl. Maybe she feels there's a lot of pressure, even if she didn't mention it. But you can feel a lot of pressure because all the kids around her are not the same way. And she feels so different, so left out. And since she has the pressure from the family, she's got the pressure from the kids around her.

MB: Difference between family support, and pressure from the peers, from other students?

ML: Yeah.

MB: What was there to do with children in Terrace? Did you have time to do things with her? Could you go fishing or on picnics?

ML: I'm very sorry because of the job. We ran the restaurant. It was a little bit hard — we tried to have some time with her, but you'd be super tired. I feel sorry for her because these are the things we can't give to her.

MB: So, did she come here after school? Or did she go to daycare?

ML: No. She stayed with the babysitter. We got a very, very nice babysitter who treated her like a daughter. And she took our daughter to school. She helped me to pick her up and she stayed with her, fed her, everything. And then she went home at nighttime.

MB: Did she have children of her own that were your daughter's age?

ML: Not of the same age, but much older.

MB: Oh, much older.

ML: Much older — they treat her like a little baby [laughter].

Shan Yan Restaurant. 2016.

MB: What jobs did you work throughout your time in Terrace? Did you always work here at the restaurant?

ML: Yeah.

CL: 24/7. You work and then you sleep.

MB: So, did your job here help you to get to know customers because they came back? Or did you feel quite isolated?

CL: Customers — they would come back and then we'd be friends. So called 'just to be friendly'. I say hello and they recognize us. We just stay here inside — not much time to talk, a lot of work to do. But friends outside the restaurant, it's quite minimized because we don't have time.

MB: No time. What did you do for fun? Sounds like you went to sleep!

CL: Oh yeah! Sleep is fun!

ML: Sleeping! Sometimes a movie.

MB: What restaurants were popular here over the years?

ML: I think Don Diego's.

CL: Don Diego's.

MB: And there used to be an old A&W drive-in. I think that maybe was closed. Do you know where Sonbada's is? Maybe, I think, it closed before you came here.

ML: I think so.

CL: We never saw that.

MB: And was there McDonald's when you came here?

ML: Yeah. The same old McDonald's [laughter].

MB: I remember when we lived in Hazelton, McDonald's was new. And if we came here to shop in Terrace, we might say to our friends, "Do you want us to buy anything in Terrace?" One of them would say, "Bring me back a Big Mac." I thought, *Big Mac? That's two hours old?* It was very special to have a McDonald's in Terrace in those days.

MB: Did you visit the Lakelse Hot Springs?

ML: Yeah!

CL: One or two times, but it was a long, long time ago. When we still had staff and we could take a few hours off on Sundays. But right now, no. Right now we don't have staff.

MB: What about Lakelse Lake? Did you ever go there?

CL: One time, before we took over the restaurant. Me and my friend went there. When we took over the restaurant, those days were gone [laughs].

MB: Do you play any sports? Or do you recall a Terrace sporting event? Did you ever go to a hockey game here in town? Have you ever hiked up Terrace Mountain?

ML: No. We missed all these good things in Terrace.

CL: The only thing we can do is go around inside cooking. It's hiking already!

MB: Were you involved in any other community activities outside the home, for example, clubs or organizations?

CL: Sorry.

MB: Did you ever have time to go to a meeting at the school?

ML: Very seldom. E.T. Kenney, a long time ago. The first time, they said it was going to shut down, so parents needed to attend. So, he [Charles] went. Besides that, it was seldom. Some of the school activities, like band, if they had performances… not unless it was Sunday. Sunday, we could try to go. But on the weekdays or weekends, I'm sorry we couldn't go.

MB: Did you attend any religious services? Did you ever go to a church or a temple?

ML: No, not here.

MB: How often would you leave Terrace?

CL: Once. Probably once a year.

MB: Once a year. Back to Vancouver? But especially back to Richmond?

ML: No. No. It's just my mom down there. My sister is down there.

MB: Oh, that's nice.

ML: Yeah. Tried to get some time to see my mom.

CL: We just go off to Hazelton, just like everybody [laughter].

MB: How often would you leave Terrace? Like, you said once a year?

CL: Once a year.

MB: And how would you get down there?

ML: Oh, we flew.

MB: Did you go to any local events? Did you go to Riverboat Days?

CL: When my daughter was small, we went. But right now, that don't bother me [laughter].

MB: Yes, when they're small, we know everything and we can do everything. And when they get bigger — "Don't crowd me, Mom!"

CL: I got two bosses: one boss and then another boss!

MB: What do you remember about downtown Terrace? The Co-op was right over here, right?

ML: Yeah. Across the street.

CL: Oh, the mall is new right now with a lot of famous shops inside over there. That's great. And looks brighter. I think better now than the old days.

MB: Where did you buy your food? Did you eat all your meals here?

ML: Yeah.

MB: And where did you buy your groceries? In the old days, when you came here?

ML: In the old days, that was called Overwaitea, right?

CL: Sometimes Safeway, or from our distributors, mostly. See who's got the cheapest spice. And then, if the package is too big, I'm not going to get it myself but order from the distributor.

MB: Where did you shop for clothes or furniture?

ML: Around Terrace.

MB: Any particular place that you always went to or that your daughter always wanted you to go to? In the old days, there was Kmart. And then, what was after that?

ML: Zellers.

MB: Zellers. Was Kmart still here when you came?

ML/CL: Yeah.

MB: Okay.

ML: And then Zellers.

CL: Liquidation World right now. Oh, and that's almost gone.

ML: Yeah.

MB: Did you ever shop much at the Co-op?

ML: Not that much. It was so close — we could just go there and come back, right? But not that much.

MB: What did most people that you knew do for work? Say, most of your customers, what would they be working at?

CL: I don't know. Because most — eighty percent of them — are First Nations. They don't all work. And most of them, right now, are from the camp. Right now, they come in, they eat lots.

MB: Did any of your friends or family work in sawmills or do logging?

ML: Logging. One of the schoolmates of our daughter's family.

MB: And nowadays, you said a lot of the customers are from the camps? What kind of camps are those?

ML: I think it's BC Hydro — that one recently.

MB: Have you watched the forestry industry change over the years?

ML: Yeah.

CL: When we took over — I'm not the lucky one — when I took over in 1996, forestry was going down.

ML: Yeah. The first thing was the '98 shut down, and the sawmill was starting to get problems. Come and go, come and go.

CL: So, if you ask me, it was tough, very tough.

MB: For a long time — not just for a few years.

CL: For the first few years, it was still good, because the First Nations — they still got money. And there was not much entertainment for them. They didn't have to buy so much electronics. So they could spend money eating Chinese food. Sometimes you saw them maybe...

ML: ...Two or three times a week.

CL: Lunch, supper... definitely here. But right now, you might see them, maybe once every two months because they're getting old — can't eat that much. And the second thing is, they have to save money for a cell phone, iPad... So, the majority of money goes for that. Right now it's a tough life for restaurants; they don't need it any more.

MB: So, people's spending habits have changed.

CL/ML: Yeah.

CL: Because, in the old days, Chinese food was a treat. And that was also a treat for the kids whenever they went to town — for the whole family. But right now, no.

MB: This is an interesting question. How did the community interact with the police? Did you ever have to call the police?

CL/ML: Yeah!

CL: And they do a good job. Sometimes we feel sorry because some people are doing damage and some people are drunk. It's good that we are not just the manager but we are also working here, because we have to take care of the work and the food. So we notice if those bad ones come in and have a bad experience here. And then we just ask them to leave, rather than to call the RCMP. So, that would reduce their job. It's less and less a problem.

MB: Have you lived in Terrace during any major floods? How did flooding impact the community? Were you here a few summers ago?

ML: I think it was neat to have the evacuation from the Nass. Our customers were rushing out and saying, "Oh, right now we are evacuating elders." That time, I think it was a serious one, right?

CL: Yeah. Just one or two times.

MB: But you saw the community really trying to help.

ML: Yeah, yeah.

MB: How has the Farmers' Market changed over the years?

ML: Oh. Usually, they had a lot of the grocery things. I think right now, it's a lot of crafts — handmade things — but the groceries less and less.

MB: So, do you notice when the Farmers' Market opens, not so many people come here for lunch on Saturday?

ML: Yeah.

MB: A little bit or a lot?

ML: Yeah, because some of the booths are selling food there. So, when you are walking, you see your friends and then you're eating a bit.

MB: Have you been involved in politics in any way?

CL: We do a little bit, and then argue, "You are wrong" [laughter]. Sometimes about authorities and policies.

ML: Some of the policies you feel, *Oh that is not okay. Why do you do that?*

MB: Do you always vote?

CL/ML: Yeah.

CL: I always lose [laughs].

MB: How have you felt our community and region have been represented? You mentioned that you always lose when you vote. Do you think our local MLA [Member of Legislative Assembly] or MP [Member of Parliament] represents most of the people? Do they speak up for the people of Terrace?

CL: They do. But, this is what I don't really agree with [laughs].

MB: How has Terrace changed over the years?

ML: It is really a big change. I think it's the people who stay in town who are different, so the way you feel is very different. And since then, there's more pressure from all the other things. I think when we first arrived in Terrace, it was more simple at that time. The logging was good, and people had a good job. So they were able to enjoy more outdoor activities — hiking, sports — all that. It was happier at that time. But right now, I sense more pressure. It's not that happy, right? Everybody's got pressure.

CL: Because of the economy. Actually, it's not just Terrace; it's global. I remember when we first came here — for the first few years, when the economy went down — it also went down in Vancouver. That was maybe for one or two years, and then we started to go down. When Vancouver went down, we were still up. And then, when Vancouver was going up, we were still down. One or two years later, then we started to go up. Now it's a problem worldwide. It's down, down, down. And the second thing, which is more and more important, is the teens — they get lazier. They don't like working some of the time.

MB: So, are you disappointed or are you happy with what you've accomplished in Terrace?

CL: Can't say disappointed because everywhere it's the same. And it's okay; I'm still alive. Problems everywhere, every day, so it's okay. It's not disappointing, but it's not, *Oh, I love Terrace!* No, it's just *okay, this is my life.* I have to accept it. It's okay. It's okay. It's not bad or something like that, right? If I was just a worker, not owning the restaurant, maybe I'd feel happier. But because we own a business, we have to think about the business. We have to think about the manpower, it's just this kind of problem. We don't hate people in Terrace, no — we love them. But the point is, because we need to locate manpower too, we need to find some who... feel our passion.

MB: Was there any particular person or event that had a big influence on your life here?

ML: Every year is the same!

MB: As a longtime resident of the Terrace area, what changes have you noticed around town? Have you noticed more business, more empty retail space...?

ML: More businesses have shut down. For a while, some opened and then shut down again.

But right now — okay — we've got a casino. And in the early days we thought *that may be good, because people go over there and then they have to eat, right?* Besides eating inside, they usually just go to nearby restaurants. In the end, we saw the money too. But, it is hard to say, because they've got a restaurant inside, then they may be competition. So, it's hard to say good or bad. It's life.

Charles and Margaret Li in their restaurant. January 2014.

MB: If someone just came to Terrace, what would you want to tell them about Terrace?

CL: Depends on, for example, what kind of job they have — because outside of the Chinese restaurant business we don't know much about that. For just general things, we can talk a bit. The problem is, we're just inside the restaurant every day; we don't get enough experience outside.

My daughter, she knows much more about things than us because she goes to school; she has a community to talk with and we are always inside. We get the information but always have been later than others.

MB: I imagine there'd be the same problem for a lot of people owning family restaurants all over BC.

CL: Yeah. Especially nowadays — it is especially serious this year. You can tell every restaurant in town is looking for employees. Chinese restaurants are usually the toughest to get an employee. It's a different kind of restaurant. If you want to be a waitress and you go to — for example — Mr. Mikes, Boston Pizza, Don Diego's... They know the food or they are familiar with that kind of environment. A lot of people don't know Chinese food. Actually, a lot of people in town never tried Chinese food before. I can tell, right? So we are the worst restaurant to get employees. After they get all, then maybe we can get some. The point is, we get less manpower.

MB: Well, I hope you'll be very busy. So many businesses in town are feeling the same way. I'm glad I had the chance to meet you. Thank you.

ML: Oh, you're welcome.

Maria Allen Interview

Interviewed by Melanie Pollard, 4 January 2014

Maria Allen was born and raised in Mexico City. Maria's early childhood was full of good memories in a house surrounded by wild lemon, pomegranate, avocado, and jicama trees. After grade six, she attended a private school to study commerce to become a bilingual secretary stenographer and bookkeeper. After graduating in the 1960s, she worked at the Ministry of Health in Mexico City to provide for her mother, and took evening college classes. Maria had ambitions to pursue a career in psychology, and completed the first year of college. The year her mother passed away, she met her husband Peter in Acapulco, Mexico. In February 1978, she moved to Terrace to join Peter. During her first days in Terrace, Maria and Peter attended a performance of Latino music from the Andes at the R.E.M. Lee Theatre. There she met a group of people who spoke Spanish, and with her neighbours they started to form gatherings of the Latin community. With the construction of a custom-made gazebo on their property, these gatherings were memorialized as "Gazebo Days." Maria took ESL classes and was hired at McElhanney Consulting Services Ltd. where she worked from 1981 until 1991. Maria was instrumental in starting the hospice palliative care in Terrace. In 2001 she was hired by Skeena Multiculturalism [Project Steering Committee] to develop culturally responsive programs.

MP: So, where and when were you born, Maria?

MA: I am originally from Mexico City, born in 1952 and raised in Mexico City.

MP: So tell me a little bit about growing up in Mexico City before you came to Terrace.

MA: Okay. I grew up in the outskirts of Mexico City. My house was next to a corn field and I was able to live in a very nice outdoors area.

MP: Did your parents farm? Is that what they were doing?

MA: No. Actually, it was our neighbour who had a farm. My dad used to work for a building supplies company. My mom was a housewife.

MP: Are there any memories of growing up where you were that you'd like to share?

MA: Yes. I have good memories of my childhood. My house was surrounded with trees and fruit trees: lemon, pomegranate, avocados, and jicamas — comes from the potato family — which grew wild down there. And we had chickens. It was a really, really nice area to grow up. The children in the neighbourhood played with marbles, and we used to colour the plum seeds to play matatena [jacks], and soccer, jumping a twine rope. All the activities and games were outside sports.

MP: Any memories from the schools you attended growing up?

MA: In the 1950s, in the area where I grew up, there were two primary schools from grade one to grade six. And each school had two shifts: one from 8:00 a.m. to 12:30 p.m., and one from 1:30 p.m. to 5:30 p.m. And one secondary school with trades, grades seven to nine. In the 1950s and mid-1960s, you would be enrolled in university or technical [trades] schools after completion of grade nine.

The primary school I attended, it was an old convent designated as a public school located next to my home. Mexico City is an old city, conquered by the Spanish conquistadores; they took over the Aztec's territory. The Spanish conquistadores built their buildings on top of the Aztecs' buildings; recent ruins were discovered in Mexico City in the 1960s.

I remember when I was in grade one, 1958, we had a president, Mr. Adolfo Lopez Mateos, provided to all school children with breakfast — one cup of milk, one fruit, and a sandwich. And lunch that cost parents 20 cents each. And when parents couldn't afford to pay, it was given to their children for free. This president wanted all Mexican children not to go hungry while in school.

MP: Was it very big?

MA: Approximately 300 children on each shift from grade one up to grade six. My grade six teacher guided me to choose a career. He assigned the class to learn all countries in the world and their capitals, and the main rivers in each country. This teacher pointed out that I have a good memory and encouraged me to pursue a career.

MP: Wow. Neat.

MA: It was nice. I remember after completing grade six [1964] the government closed this school because it became unsafe after an earthquake. Then through the years, the homeless took possession of the rooms. Then the government tore it down and built various apartment buildings on the property and sold them to low-income people.

MP: So you grew up and went to school there. Did you attend college or university?

MA: I did. After finishing grade six, I went to a private school to study Commerce [Bilingual Secretary Stenographer and Bookkeeper]. In 1965, I remember, we didn't have calculators. You had to use your memory for adding and subtracting financial ledger books and financial statements.

MP: So, when you finished all of these courses, you were ready to work?

MA: Yes. This is my diploma. In 1966 is when I graduated.

MP: Wow. Look at that. This is your picture? How old were you when you graduated?

MA: I was 14 years old. Almost 15 years old. And, also, I was ahead one year of my schoolmates.

MP: That's fantastic. And you were finished school at that point?

MA: In 1967, I went to work and my first job was to work for the Ministry of Health in Mexico City because I knew Pitman Shorthand. At that time, shorthand was a very, very in-demand position. I managed to get a very high position with it. When working in the government, I was called to substitute one day as the director's secretary. Then, after that, they hired me just to take and transcribe in shorthand meeting minutes.

MP: Wow.

MA: It was very, very nice. And I was quite fast taking dictation in shorthand.

MP: That's so neat.

MA: I enjoyed my job. After that, I thought to enroll in a college of science and humanities studies, to pursue a career in psychology. Working at the Ministry of Health in Mexico City, the hours of work were from 8:00 a.m. to 3:00 p.m. My first class commenced at 6:00 p.m. and my last class ended at 10:00 p.m. So I got home to do my homework before going the next day to work. Then, I was the only provider at that time.

It was in my first year in college when my dad passed away. My mom and I were just at home. So I stopped my studies as I became the only provider for my mom.

MP: Wow. So you had to work for your family?

MA: Only my Mom and I.

MP: How old were you then?

MA: When my dad passed away, I was 21 years old.

MP: That's hard.

MA: It was hard. I am the youngest of five children. My mom had each one of us every five years. My mom was 42 years old when I was born. So I didn't have much opportunity to enjoy my parents.

MP: They were older.

MA: They were older, yes. Anyhow, I just got my first year in university.

MP: How many years did you work supporting your mom?

MA: Around seven years. The same year I met my husband Peter, my mom passed due to cancer.

MP: Wow.

MA: It is. Then, one day, I was on vacation and I met my husband Peter.

MP: Where did you meet him?

MA: He was vacationing in Acapulco and I was vacationing there too, with my Mom and my girlfriend's family. That is how I met him.

I think it was meant for us to be together. Peter returned to Terrace and we corresponded. Peter used to call me every day. And I used to receive a letter from him, once every week. Then, one day, he asked me in one of his letters to come and see if I would like to live in Terrace. I said, "No. I don't think so. I think you'd have to marry me first."

I was working and I had to give them two weeks' notice. Peter sent me a ticket to Vancouver. He was going to meet me in Vancouver. When I arrived in Vancouver, at the airport, the lady in customs told me, "I have a message for you from Peter. He is coming to pick you up but there is a storm in Terrace and the airplane is delayed. They are trying to bus all the passengers to [Prince] Rupert. Do not move from here. He will come to meet you here. I will tell him where to find you."

I arrived at 3:00 P.M. I didn't understand about the storm because in Mexico City we didn't have storms.

MP: No?

MA: We have winds and stuff like that but I didn't have any clue what they were talking about.

MP: Was it winter?

MA: It was winter. Anyhow, four hours waiting at the airport where the customs lady told me to wait for Peter. She came to see me again and told me that her shift ended and that she was going home. She said, "Do not move from here. I told Peter where to find you so stay here." She was very friendly. Very, very friendly. I think it was one of the translators. Very, very friendly person. She says, "You have to stay here. He will look for you here." Anyhow, I didn't even want to go anywhere, although I was very hungry and hadn't had anything to eat since on board the airplane. I thought, "If I move from here maybe Peter comes and he won't see me." As I'd never been in Vancouver, I was not aware of my surroundings, or where to go.

MP: Did you speak English at all?

MA: My English wasn't fluent but I was able to ask for directions. After nine hours of waiting, I thought the airport was closing. Then Peter arrived close to midnight and he apologized for being so late. He was trying to explain to me what happened. I was so hungry and tired. I just hugged him so hard and didn't want to be away from him.

MP: You had to wait and not eat?

MA: Exactly. So I was telling him, "I'm so hungry." So he took me to a Mexican restaurant to eat. It was after midnight, 1:00 a.m. at the time when we arrived to the restaurant called Pepitas. I will never forget those tacos I ordered. They tasted so good. It was so nice to see Peter again. What a wonderful feeling.

Vancouver was so beautiful. The following day, we flew to Terrace but the same thing; we encountered the same weather. The airplane couldn't land in Terrace and had to land in Prince Rupert.

MP: Oh no.

MA: Anyhow, when we landed in Rupert, I thought to me it was a paradise — beautiful scenery. And I said to Peter, "It's so beautiful. It's just like a postcard." I was taking pictures of the gondola, and the houses we passed by on the bus. And I asked Peter, "Where was Terrace?" And he said, "It's just a two-hour drive."

Then, when the bus passed Prince Rupert and was going by the Skeena River… It's when I started seeing snow and enormous mountains. I was asking Peter, "Are we getting close?" And he said, "Well, not quite." I thought we were heading to the North Pole. I was thinking, *Oh, my God. What am I doing here? I cannot live here.* I looked at Peter, then I thought, *I will try.*

Peter was telling me that in summer it was beautiful, that there were flowers and lots of trees. Everything was warm. I thought, *He's just teasing me. He's trying to convince me to stay here.* Then, it seems to me, that all the way from Rupert to Terrace it took us all day to arrive as it was snowing and the road was covered with snow.

It was a long drive. I couldn't believe it when we arrived to the village of Terrace, population 8,500 people. It was Sunday and I didn't see people walking on the streets. Only a few cars passed by us.

We arrived to the Bench, at 5214 McConnell. It was a small old house, but to me it was beautiful. Beautiful area nearby a college at that time. McConnell Avenue was not paved. The Northwest Community College [NWCC] was few years old.

MP: Oh. Yeah.

MA: Anyhow, in Terrace everything was — there were only a few houses — surrounded by big fields. I really love the area.

My neighbours were very friendly. A few days after I arrived in Terrace, we went to the R.E.M. Lee Theatre to see a group of musicians playing Latino music from the Andes [Peru, Bolivia and Chile]. At the end of this event, I introduced myself to the group of people that spoke Spanish. They welcomed me and were telling me that usually by spring the snow was gone and the weather was getting warm. And then summer was very nice. We exchanged phone numbers and addresses, and Peter and I asked them to come to visit us.

MP: That was when you met the other Spanish-speaking people?

MA: Exactly. Then, they used to come to visit us from Kitimat, New Aiyansh. Only two Mexican women were living in Terrace at that time.

Peter heard that there was a program done by Mrs. Stradynski, a retired teacher. She was teaching adults English as a Second Language (ESL). Peter asked me if I was interested in taking English as a Second Language courses. For sure, I do. So that was my outing twice a week, to go to ESL classes.

In the class were only women, from many countries with different languages. It was really nice when we became very good friends because everybody was very friendly. And Mrs. Stradynski made the class quite fun, asking if we wanted to bring something from our countries to share. Some people brought cookies. I brought tacos. And other occasions, other women brought dresses from their countries to show and tell.

MP: Nice.

MA: We were sharing and talking, and at the same time, we learned the English language. It was very interesting meeting these people. After that, I thought, *Well, I'm going to look for a job*. I don't think I was quite ready for a job because I didn't speak English well enough to work in an office. Plus I have a strong accent. But I don't think people quite understood my accent or I understood as well. I went to apply for a job at 'the centre'. At that time, it was named Canada Manpower. Now, Human Resources Canada.

So, I went there with a copy of my certificates and told them my acquired skills as secretary bookkeeper. I was telling them, "I have all these skills. I want to have a job but I know I need to get more studies, to learn English better." So they say, "Well, look. We have this program. It's provided by the government. It's giving opportunity to new immigrants to learn English and learning skills. Would you be interested?" And I said, "Certainly. Yes."

I was admitted at NWCC to study English writing, to upgrade in business administration. Accounting was not a problem as well as shorthand and typing neither. The shorthand I had is by sound. You write by sound, which is not a problem. It's only a problem when English is spelled different than how it is pronounced. It was another obstacle there for me with shorthand. So I thought I better put it aside and concentrate on accounting. That's why I only took business administration, and upgraded in bookkeeping and typing.

MP: Was that through the college?

MA: Yes. I was paid by the government. It was a nine-month course, plus English. English was my main focus because I needed to be confident in that. What I found is that bookkeeping is the same process anywhere.

MP: Yeah. And you could do it without a calculator.

MA: Exactly. Here in Canada, I learned a 10-key calculator with memory, adding and subtraction. I was very good in math so I concentrated in that area. So, when I finished my courses, immediately I got a job. It was very, very good.

MP: That's great.

MA: But still, my pronunciation — my accent was very strong. Some people found it very difficult to understand me. Even now sometimes, some people have problems understanding my accent. Anyhow, I was hired at McElhanney Surveying and Engineering Company. Because after working for the Ministry of Health, I used to work in Mexico for a surveying and engineering company. I was familiar with sending Telex messages, preparing proposals, and printing plans.

My first manager was a nice person. All the staff welcomed me, and I found it a very friendly environment. I worked there from 1981 until 1991. The reason I quit was because my late husband became ill and I had two kids; my oldest son was 10 years old and my second son was five years of age. I was so stressed out. I couldn't hold my job and all the chores in the house.

MP: That's understandable.

MA: So they finally found the problem with my husband. He had cancer in the head of the pancreas. At that time, the doctor in Vancouver said that it was a rare disease. There was nothing they could do to save him. He went very fast. He passed six months after he was diagnosed.

MP: I'm sorry.

MA: Going back to 1978, after the Latino group that came to Terrace in February 1978, I met my neighbours — Canadian, First Nations people, Germany, Mexico, Bolivia, France, US, Spain. On one of our gatherings, we decided to reach more Latin American people. We put an ad in the local newspaper *Northwest Cities* that May 18, 1980, asking all peoples to come and share Latin music at 5214 McConnell, to bring their tents or motorhomes. And from that day on, every year from 1980 up to 1991, we gathered every year on Victoria Day.

MP: This was the Latin community?

MA: Yes. Mainly Latin American, but was open to anyone who enjoyed Latin music. And every year more people attended this gathering. We only put out a newspaper ad for this event twice.

MP: The first time was just a potluck. From there was the beginning of this Latino American gathering that lasted 10 years?

MA: Exactly. It was our first potluck. And there were quite a few people. We told them to bring their tents, that it's a family gathering so not too much drinking. Because it's also for children to enjoy it. The main focus was that our children learn our culture and how we party, how we gather. Because we were away from our families so we wanted our children to know our culture.

MP: So what would you do to introduce your culture on those weekends when you camped?

MA: Well, the first year when we all gathered, we found out that there were so many artistic people. There was a couple from Chile that used to play charango and also the guitar. Another couple used to sing. Another couple — the man was from Spain and his wife from Colombia — so they have beautiful music, Latino music. So that was the beginning of the gatherings. Everybody was so happy.

We gathered always on Saturday and Sunday. Some people spent overnight and left on Monday. But before they left, they would organize for next year. My husband Peter would say, "Well, if you know somebody that would like to come, tell them to come. We are going to do the same thing. We are going to have a potluck." So then, next time, there were more people. We had the same thing. The kids were having a blast.

MP: Wow.

MA: And they weren't only Latino people. There were people who wanted to share or to see a Latino-type gathering. We did piñatas and it was very nice for the kids and the adults. People volunteered to do games and brought the piñatas. The second year we got organized better. And it got better and better and better to a point where, the last gathering we had, we were probably 160 people including my surrounding neighbours. It was a really nice gathering.

But, what I was going to say is that every year, we got organized better. With the help of other people and my late husband Peter, we made a fire pit. So, in there, one year we cooked a pig, another year we cooked a goat, another year had steaks. Women brought salads or side dishes from their countries to share.

Mornings were always enjoyable because they formed a committee that says, "Okay, the person who gets up early is going to feed the kids." There were so many children. My husband brought a big industrial griddle to cook pancakes, eggs, sausages, tortillas, etc.

MP: Griddle?

Child breaking a piñata at one of the Latino Community Gatherings. May 1987.
Maria Allen Collection.

MA: Exactly. Big griddle with a stove to cook pancakes. And then we used to rent from McDonalds these big containers for the children to have something to drink. Then we all share. We told them, we said, "This is the expense for the pig." And, "This is what we bought for everybody." So we shared expenses and nobody complained about each shared cost. Everybody said, "Sure. No problem."

And it wasn't that much because also the kids were fed in the morning. They were playing all the time. They had games; somebody organized games for the kids. It was a family gathering. It was beautiful. Then, later on, my late husband Peter was very creative. I'm going to cry a little bit…

One of his friends was a carpenter by trade. In 1987, Peter wanted to build a gazebo with a fire pit in the middle. Peter bought a sawmill and cut all the lumber from the backyard (three acres of uncleared land). Peter shared this idea with a group of friends and Ken Berg, a skilled carpenter from Norway, offered to design the gazebo and to be the foreman in charge of the project. And a group of friends gathered every weekend to work, building the gazebo. And before 1988, Victoria Day, this project was completed. The person from Bolivia, he was very artistic. He designed and sent an engraved picture of the gazebo on a piece of cedar and they gave it on that day to Peter.

MP: Was it mostly in Spanish or was there English, too?

MA: There was English and Spanish because some people were married to Latino women and/or men were married from other countries, like Germany, Sweden, Norway, Italy, Spain, Peru, Bolivia, Ecuador, Mexico, Chile, and Canadians. There were all nationalities mixed.

MP: Wow.

MA: And this is one of the reasons we gathered. For children to learn our culture. It was beautiful.

MP: So you did that for 10 years? You'd have these yearly gatherings?

MA: Yes.

MP: And it didn't continue because you and your husband couldn't continue it?

MA: Exactly.

MP: Does it still exist? Did it continue to exist in some form?

MA: After that, I not am aware of any Latino family gatherings as this one was. And they built a gazebo and this is where we used to gather around.

MP: And that's where you'd cook? Or just for fires?

MA: We didn't cook in the gazebo. We just gathered around enjoying the fire and dancing or enjoying singing when somebody was playing instruments.

MP: Oh. Nice.

Carved image of the "Gazebo Don Pedro". Maria Allen Collection.

MA: It was very nice. And it's just amazing how the gazebo was designed. It has very fond memories.

This is what the family Scherre from Prince Rupert said about Gazebo Gatherings: [Maria picks up book and reads]

Not too long ago, my close friend Maria asked me to write something about our reunions in Terrace; also known as "Gazebo Days." These reunions took place during the Victoria Day long weekend. My family looked forward to these events because all our friends would gather at Maria Maximchuk's place.

Everybody would attend with their trailers and tents, and share with us their food, customs, and laughter. We camped together with people with different nationalities; the great majority was from Latin America.

In the mornings, the coffee was always on and someone would prepare pancakes, eggs, bacon, etc. The best part was that people would share new recipes, exchange opinions and have a good time. At lunchtime, we would try new food from different countries and always something special was on the grill.

We Mexicans would bring piñatas for the children, which they had an awesome time breaking. The children also enjoyed playing soccer, climbing trees, and driving the go-cart around the property.

During the evening we had fun singing while someone was playing the guitar. We also danced to various types of Latin American music.

Gazebo Days created a family, a family that kept in touch even after the last celebration, because deep in our hearts it was what we were longing for. Written by Mercedes Scherre and family.

MP: So the gazebo got used for gatherings just for that weekend, or for other times too?

MA: Usually when everybody came, we set up a fire and sat around. But it was originally for Victoria Day gatherings.

MP: That's great.

MA: The kids now, they talk about all the good times that they had there. Not only that but, at that time, it made them closer. The children, they call us aunts. And we adults formed very close friendships because we didn't have family here. Up to now, we are still very close. Some friends have passed away. Some moved away from Terrace. Some we are still in contact. We are only remaining in Terrace, three families.

MP: So it was just this time where there was such a busy, big community in Terrace.

MA: Exactly.

MP: And for those gatherings, would they just be from Terrace or would they come from Kitimat?

MA: They came up from Stewart.

MP: From Stewart?

MA: Stewart, Hazelton, Prince George, Fort St. James, Aiyansh, Smithers, Prince Rupert, Kitimat, and Terrace, as well.

MP: So, it was very special.

MA: It was very big. Beautiful. I have lots of pictures, and I have also a video one of our friends filmed at one of those gatherings. If you want, I can release you a copy of that.

MP: That'd be wonderful.

MA: We always had music and sang songs from our countries. Cecile Alvarez had a beautiful voice and her husband played a guitar. And Tirso and Silvia Morales played guitar and charango, music from the Andes. They developed an album of all the songs that we used to sing there. It was beautiful.

MP: So there's an album somewhere?

MA: I don't know as Cecile Alvarez passed away and her husband moved. But I'm going to ask him if he still has a copy of the songs we used to sing. It has very fond memories from that time. Also, because in 1984, the economy in Terrace was getting very bad. It was the first time that the two sawmills were laying people off. So many people moved and it was a very, very sad time for Terrace.

Some people moved to the south of BC. Some people stayed, but the ones that left always came back for that gathering. It was nice to keep in touch.

MP: That's wonderful.

MA: It was nice. A very nice gathering.

Maria and her husband Peter at one of the "Gazebo Gatherings" in Terrace. May 1986. Maria Allen Collection.

MP: What was it like to raise your kids in Terrace outside of those gatherings, just day-to-day?

MA: My husband was Canadian and born in Kenora, Saskatchewan. His parents were Ukrainian. My children were quite active in sports. In winter, they were skating and swimming. In summer, it was the outdoors, which was soccer or baseball. My older son Lee attended guitar lessons.

MP: Nice.

168

MA: My late husband, Peter, loved gardening. We planted everything — potatoes, raspberries, lettuce, broccoli, tomatoes, cucumbers, carrots. We had a cherry and a plum tree. And chickens. My son Lee used to sell eggs to the neighbours, and the money was for him to keep. It was very nice.

MP: So your kids enjoyed being in the outdoors, too?

MA: Exactly. And Peter was a very, very handy person. He was very good in mechanics so he built a go-cart for the kids. My son and the other kids took turns to have everybody go for a ride. He put it in a very low speed so nobody would get hurt. Then, later on, he built something better. He found a small mini tractor and he made like a train, so the kids could take turns. And then he built a park for the kids to climb. And also built a tree house.

MP: Nice.

MA: It was nice — having those gatherings. The kids had fun and also their parents.

MP: That's wonderful. What about Terrace? What do you remember about downtown Terrace? What was there and how has that changed over time?

MA: In 1978, Terrace was very prosperous. Everybody was employed; there were lots of jobs. Terrace was wealthy at that time. Very nice.

The Terrace Arena provided a skating rink, hockey lessons, and the swimming pool as well. The Terrace Library was small and well-attended. There were two night-clubs — The Red D'Or and Hanky Panky's — and the Skeena Pub. The main groceries stores: [The Terrace] Co-op, Safeway, and Overwaitea. And only one liquor store.

Through these gatherings, my neighbour Kathy Mueller, provided us with information to form the Terrace Multicultural Association. Silvia Morales was a very active participant in multicultural activities in Terrace.

MP: That's wonderful.

MA: Since the Terrace Multicultural Association was established, it has brought together all peoples, including First Nations participating in the annual potluck event. Now all nationalities in Terrace embrace this event.

MP: That's very nice.

MA: When I came to Terrace there weren't as many First Nations people employed in businesses as you see now.

The Skeena Mall was completed in 1978 and the Farmers' Market had only a few local farmers on Saturday morning in summer. There were no need for reservations or fees.

MP: That's a change.

MA: When I was in Vancouver, they had a Hospice Palliative program at St. Paul's Hospital, and I had lots of support down there. I asked my doctor if there was a Hospice Palliative program in Terrace. And she said, "No, there is no hospice in Terrace. But you can start one."

And I said, "I'm not sure I am able to do it." And she says, "Yes, you can."

I phoned the person in charge of the hospice program at St. Paul's Hospital in Vancouver. They directed me to the person responsible of the Hospice Palliative department in Victoria and forwarded me manuals and information on how to form a Hospice Palliative Care in Terrace. And Dr. Hodge introduced me to a group of nurses in the hospital, as well persons from the community interested in this program.

We began our meetings. I provided them with all the information I received from Victoria. One woman was very interested in this program. She was very knowledgeable of legal procedures and policies. She pursued this project further and thanks to her, now Terrace has a Hospice Society.

MP: Wow.

MA: So that was one thing that I think was very nice to have in Terrace.

MP: Absolutely.

MA: In 2001, under the auspices of the Ministry of Community, Aboriginal and Women's Services, I was hired by the Skeena Multiculturalism Project Steering Committee as a project coordinator in the developing of programs of culturally responsive service delivery across all public institutions and private business in Terrace — to promote the benefits of valuing diversity in the workplace. Now the Skeena Diversity has a gathering place for community groups in Terrace.

MP: Yeah.

MA: It was very good. It was a combination of multiculturalism, and also the information that we provided to businesses to welcome diversity in their workforce. Now you can see more First Nations people working in businesses in Terrace. You can see more First Nations people working in stores, public or private offices.

MP: And you saw that as a real change for both the Multicultural Association and that kind of work? People were thinking about diversity issues?

MA: Exactly. Yes. To welcome diversity is good for businesses as well for the community.

MP: That's so neat.

MA: It was very nice. Now I haven't participated anymore because I think I have done my share. I think now is the time for new ideas, new energy. I'm getting older. I think I have done my share to Terrace. I love this community.

MP: That's so neat. It sounds like very interesting work.

MA: Very interesting. I like to meet people and I always respect peoples' culture and ideas.

MP: That's great.

MA: Yeah. I think I've been honoured to have these opportunities, and I took them. Some of this work requires lots of your time. So I'm very grateful that my husband Bill has been very patient with me and allowed me the free time to do what I want to do.

MP: You sort of talked about your life almost in phases. For this next phase of life, what kinds of things are you taking on?

MA: I am still working. I like walking around the Terrace area. And I go to fitness classes at the Terrace Arena. For fun in my life right now, my husband Bill likes the outdoors and we go to the Kalum Lake on the weekends in summer, as well fishing to Kitimat or Prince Rupert. And I enjoy my grandchildren and also teach them Spanish.

MP: Did you ever go to Lakelse Hot Springs?

MA: We did. My late husband's friend, Mr. Cliff, was a friend of the previous owner Mr. Skogland, and a group of friends used to go there to swim. We had a blast. It was very nice.

I remember reading an ad from the Provincial Government asking for a submission of proposals for the development of the hot springs. Mr. Orleans submitted his proposal for the development of the hot springs resort, with a golf course and slides, and expansion of the pools.

The restaurant was very nice. I remember going to the Oktoberfest dinner and dance they had every year. We used to go there quite often to swim and to the restaurant. Sometimes we stayed in the hotel for the weekend.

MP: Since you first came to Terrace and now, have things changed? What were popular restaurants at the time?

MA: Sure. I remember a time when we came here that the City of Terrace was a village. We were only 8,000 people. I should say 8,500. It was very nice.

There was a building supplies store named Omenica, located on Highway 16, now the Creative Zone Store, and the fitness club [Northcoast Health & Fitness] and a new beer place [Sherwood Mountain Brewhouse].

Everybody gathered at that Co-op shopping centre. It had everything — small coffee shop, hardware store, and a gas station. People had a membership and at the end of the year received money back.

Overwaitea at that time was very small. And Safeway has been always there. And the Skeena Mall had a pharmacy and was full of stores.

MP: You shopped there, too?

MA: The Co-op was the big place to go shopping. There was one nightclub for older adults — the Red D'Or, at the Terrace Hotel. Now it is The Best Western and there is not a night club.

It was a big, big gathering. Every Friday, loggers and workers gathered there. It had a big restaurant. The Red D'Or was located downstairs. There was a live band. The Skeena Pub and Hotel, workers went to have a beer. No drink and driving restrictions at that time.

And then there was another hotel. Now it is the Coast Hotel. Also a small hotel, the Slumber Lodge that is now the Bear Country Inn. The Sandman restaurant is now Denny's location. All the truckers used to stop there as they served big meals, people used to say.

The West End store was the only corner store in town located on the corner of Highway 16 and Kenney Street. Across from the store on Kenney Street, the back building was the school district office.

This is a list of all the people who donated some of their time and equipment to build the Terrace arena. [Maria shows a handwritten spreadsheet]. It was amazing. In October of '71, this was the spreadsheet of donations. All handwritten. It is how we used to do bookkeeping, at the time.

MP: All the people who contributed to the arena. That's fantastic. Just a couple last questions. You've done a lot of work thinking about diversity and culture. How did the community of Terrace interact with Kitselas and Kitsumkalum over the years that you saw?

MA: I noticed that people didn't talk or interact in community activities. Now, we do, with events such as Multicultural Potluck, the Salmon Run at River Boat Days, and celebrating National Aboriginal Day. You see all nationalities employed in local business.

MP: That's very neat. What do you think changed?

MA: Having meetings with the community, local business owners and First Nations people.

Facilitating seminars to educate in welcoming and valuing diversity in the community, and the need to interact with each other because it is good for all of us. That's what I think it was to value diversity, so businesses and government offices and the public benefit from this.

MP: Make it work for them.

MA: On one occasion, on one of those projects, our goal was trying to involve so many people from different nationalities. Chief George was in Terrace; there were many people from the different areas gathered at the Kitsumkalum Hall. Yes, it was so neat because we managed to talk about the diversity project.

MP: That's great.

MA: One of the things that I remember, when there was low attendance to meetings, people who attended started getting discouraged. I said, "I'm not going to make a meeting with only three or four people. We have to have at least 15 or 17 people in my meetings, otherwise I will reschedule until we have good attendance from businesses, active people in the community." I needed their support to have their personnel and the community attend workshops provided by facilitators, to train personnel to welcome and value diversity in their workplace.

Just making them participate, to come out of one's shell. Then we all felt comfortable. It was very nice. We had beautiful input in our meetings.

MP: So neat. Your gatherings were so important for the Latino community. Do you remember any events for the whole community, that were important, that you remember in Terrace? Annual events?

MA: Gazebo Days. Latin American reunions that took place during the Victoria Day long weekend in Terrace at Peter and Maria Maximchuk's place. The Multicultural Potluck. Riverboat parade. Christmas parade done by businesses at the Skeena Mall. New Year's Polar Bear Swim at Lakelse Lake.

MP: That's so neat.

MA: It is. And I think this is one of the reasons that Terrace has been very nice. It's a small, friendly community. They just needed to be pulled together and integrated.

MP: That's wonderful.

MA: It was.

MP: Just two more questions. Looking back, when you were a child, what did you expect or hope to accomplish in your life?

MA: You're not going to believe me, but I always wanted to be a singer and to visit many countries in the world. I've always been interested in languages. As a child I always asked myself, why do people talk different? In my mind, I thought people were very smart speaking in another language. I want to be like that. I wanted to know how people thought in other languages. To me, I thought it was something out of my comprehension, hearing other people talk in another language.

MP: Wow.

MA: I don't have the voice. I love singing. I love music from the '60s and '70s. I always want to help people in any way I can, and get married and have children. I enjoy working in my field.

MP: That's perfect. What would you want to share with someone new coming to Terrace?

MA: I always tell them Terrace is beautiful and friendly and is family-oriented and safe. And it has beautiful scenery, and it is the most peaceful place in the whole earth. It is freedom. It's a young city that welcomes your ideas.

MP: That's so wonderful.

MA: I love Terrace.

Norma Morrison Interview

Interviewed by Merilyn McLeod and Margaret-Anne Baxter, 21 November 2013

Norma Morrison was born in Prince Rupert on June 3rd, 1922. One of the four children of local politician Edward Kenney and Leila Brooks (niece of George Little), Norma tells stories of growing up in Terrace in the 1920s and 1930s, and of her adventurous nursing career. Norma briefly describes life during the Terrace mutiny; however, during WWII, she was a student with the Victoria Order of Nursing. After completing her education, Norma worked in various communities in northern Ontario and the United Kingdom, then toured Scotland and Ireland by motorcycle. In 1952, she moved back to BC, and took a public health course at the University of British Columbia. She met her husband Nels in Terrace, where she worked as a public health nurse until she retired.

Note: Interviewer Merilyn McLeod is Norma's niece and interviewer Margaret-Anne (Maggie) is Norma's daughter.

MM: Okay, Norma, I'm going to just start with the questions as prescribed. But you can answer or not answer as you see fit. When and where were you born?

NM: [Laughs.] June 3, 1922. We had to go to Prince Rupert, because there was no hospital here. So if the train was going to Rupert, you went that way. If it was going east, you went to Hazelton.

MM: Did your mother have to go down ahead of time and wait until you came?

NM: I think she went down a couple of days ahead of time — before her due date — because some people didn't go soon enough and they had to take them down by speeder.

MB: The railway speeders? That would have been an exciting trip.

MM: Tell me about your parents. What brought them to this part of the world?

NM: Well, Mother (Leila Brooks) came because she was related to Uncle George.

MM: What relationship was she to Uncle George? That's George Little, right?

NM: Yes, her mother, Grandma Brooks was George's half-sister — complicated family. There was half and half.

MM: And she was Leila's mother, right?

MB: Yep.

MM: And your dad?

NM: He came up from — he was wandering around, I guess. He came up from Vancouver on the boat to Prince Rupert in the early 1900s. The story goes all he had to eat was an onion that fell off the boat [laughs], when he was waiting to come up. And when he laid on the deck all he had was a newspaper for a blanket. [Laughs.]

MM: And that was Ed [Edward] Kenney?

NM: Yeah.

MM: So, how many siblings did you have?

NM: Three. Oh, my sisters: Marjorie, Margaret, Lorraine, myself, and Edward.

174

MM: So there were basically the four Kenney girls, right? And any stories you'd like to tell about getting along with your sisters?

NM: No, we got along fine.

MB: How about the story about doing the dishes? Well, it seems to me there were some stories about you and your sisters being the worst scrappers in Terrace.

NM: Well that was true, too. Apparently we didn't figure we were fighting. We were just being sisters.

MB: What did you do?

NM: Oh, I don't know. It's like everything else. Lorraine was scrubbing the floor once, and Margaret walked across it [laughs], and Lorraine threw the bucket of water at her [laughs]. So she had quite a mess to clean up.

MM: You lost one of your sisters when she was quite young.

NM: Well, there was a virus infection — two people died that year. Can't think of what it was.

MM: Infection?

NM: Uh-hm.

MM: And she would have had a staph infection? Some kind of a bacterial infection?

NM: Yeah.

MM: And why was it so bad? Do you remember why she got this infection?

NM: No. There were only two in the town that got it. And I can't remember her name. But in those days you didn't have any antibiotics.

MM: I always remember that story as she squeezed a pimple. And it got infected. Okay. Anyway, how old was she when she died?

NM: Let me see. I remember my Uncle Stan (Brooks) came to the school (I was in high school) to take me home. So, she must have been in grade 11. She was 17 and died in the Prince Rupert Hospital; there was no hospital in Terrace at that time.

MM: Alrighty, let's go on to happier times. What school did you go to?

NM: Kitsumgallum.

MM: Kitsumkalum?

NM: And it was GAY-lum. It wasn't KAY-lum. And I can never find out why they changed it.

MM: What was it?

NM: Gallum. Kitsumgallum. It was G [gee] instead of a K [kay].

MM: G-A-L-L-U-M?

NM: That's right. I've got proof of it, too. I've got my graduation certificate.

MM: And that's what it says?

NM: Yeah. I've asked natives, and nobody knows.

MM: No? Isn't that interesting? And you were telling us about walking to school in the snow?

NM: We would — for a mile. We had fun. We threw rocks and whatnot. You know, stuff, as a group — walking.

MM: Must have been hard in the winter, though, with the heavy snows. The big kids would drag the little kids through the snow?

NM: There used to be a trail cut across, where the municipal building (at Eby and Lakelse) is now. It cut across there to Munroe Street.

MM: And how about some of your funny stories from school days?

NM: [Laughs.] Oh dear. Yeah, well — Anne Stavous was our teacher, in grade one and two. And one of the girls wet her pants, and it ran down into where the other girl had her lunch, in a paper bag. Anyhow — the next time that this girl had to go to the bathroom, she just got up to go (rather than just putting up her hand), and the teacher said "Pardon, me. Where do you think you are going?" She said "My mother told me if I had to go to the bathroom to just get up and go." [Laughs.] So that's what she did.

MM: What other memories have you got of school, some pranks that you might have played, or, things that you did there?

MB: What about when Mr. [Clarence] Michiel ripped his pants?

NM: He was our grade eight teacher and he told this boy to go out in the hall, because he had sworn. And he went to get the strap, and when he came back the kid had taken off. So Mr. Michiel went chasing after him, he jumped over the fence, which was a barbed wire fence which ran from the school to where Rona [3207 Munroe St.] is; he couldn't catch him. So he came back. He was a real good teacher. And he said "Okay, time to get back to work."

So he turned to write on the board, and everybody started laughing. As he turned quickly to face the class, everybody gave a sombre face. As he turned back to write on the board, everyone started laughing again. Finally this one girl said, "Mr. Michiel, you've got a rip in your pants." [Laughs.] So he felt his pants, and he says, "Okay." He said "Now, I want you to do this, that, and the other thing while I'm gone. I'm going home to change my pants." And so he went back home. And when he came back, he says, "Okay, the fun's over. Now back to work." [Laughs.] Oh, he was a good teacher.

MB: What about Mr. King, the custodian?

NM: Mr. King maintained the school, the furnace, and all that stuff. He was really good to us, too; he helped us a lot. Anyhow, in the wintertime, he dumped the ashes out. There was a big gully between the school and the high school, there. It's all level now. And he'd pour the ashes out there, then at nighttime he'd pour some water on them so it was icy and slippery. We used to all slide down this hill. [Laughs.] He really looked after us well, Mr. King. He helped us with everything. Mr. King had to put the Union Jack flag up every day, and take it down every night.

In those days, there was a dividing line between the right and left of the school yard. The boys played on the left-hand side, and the girls played on the right-hand side. And you didn't dare go across the line up, or anything. You knew you weren't supposed to go across. So, boys mostly played baseball; we played softball.

There was another time. We weren't allowed to go out of the schoolyard at noon hour. We could only go out when we were going home. And for some reason or other, we all went out and down to the railway. I don't know why we went down there. But, anyhow, Mr. Michiel found out where we were — we weren't out in the school yard playing. He came looking for us. And, [laughs] he made us play leap frog all the way back to school. He didn't punish us at all, just made us play leap frog all the way back. [Laughs.]

176

MB: What about your exams during the 1936 flood?

NM: The 1936 flood — we were all sitting out in front of our house — well, not all of us, but, you know, some of us — sitting on the sidewalk. I don't know who came; it wasn't Mr. Michiel. Anyhow he said "Okay, back to school. A man walked in with your government exams." There was no mail coming in because of the flood. We had to write government exams in grade 8. And he said, "This man came in with all your papers, so back to school you go." So, we had to go back and take our exams, which made us really mad. [Laughs.] We thought we'd get away with it.

MM: Oh dear. Any other memories of school that you'd like to share? Now, what year did you finish high school?

MB: It must have been about 1939?

NM: Yeah, I went to Prince Rupert for senior matriculation.

MM: When did you go into nurses' training?

NM: '41. In Victoria at Royal Jubilee.

MM: And what was that experience like?

NM: Oh, it was fun. But if you couldn't stand the discipline, people quit. And, we used to — a few of us, three or four of us — get the same day off. We'd hitchhike down the main road to another town. We'd go just for a certain time. And then we would hitchhike back [laughs].

MM: Where were you going?

NM: Oh, we were just going out to see the country. At night we used to have to put up boards during the war, like, you know, put up plywood in the windows.

MM: Oh, blackouts?

NM: Blackouts. We were two to a room. And we had another girl who was supposed to put the blackouts up. I was getting undressed to go to bed, and a fellow down below was checking to see that everybody had their blackouts up and hollered at us, and [laughs] she pushed me into the closet [laughs]. And then she goes and puts the blackouts up.

MM: Why'd she push you in the closet?

NM: Because I was naked. I was getting undressed.

MM: So was it a tough course — your nursing course?

NM: Oh, no, I enjoyed it.

MM: What kind of hours did you work?

NM: We worked on the wards in the daytime, and went to lectures, too.

MM: Did you get into any trouble there?

NM: [Laughs.] No.

MM: No? You didn't break anything? They didn't charge you for anything?

NM: Thermometers. That's it. Yeah, I broke some thermometers. We were deducted twenty-five cents each thermometer we broke.

MM: How much did you get paid when you were nursing?

NM: Got paid five dollars a month the first year, and seven dollars a month the second year, and nine dollars a month the third year. Boy, were we rich [laughs].

MM: So, when you finished the training at the Jubilee, what did you do?

NM: We went to Duncan [BC], to work in the hospital there. But we didn't like it, so we quit.

MM: You worked in Duncan?

NM: Yes, for a few months. We didn't have any way of getting home (to Victoria) so we hitchhiked and who picks us up, but the matron from the hospital. She bawled us out all the way to Victoria. "You give the nurses a bad reputation." [Laughs.]

MM: You worked in the Rupert hospital?

NM: No, that wasn't in my training days. I was nursing then.

MB: Was that during the war?

NM: Yes.

MM: How long were you in that hospital, Norma?

NM: It wasn't very long? [Laughs.] Anyhow, there was three of us. We wanted to go over to the Salt Lakes, just for the day. This fellow said he'd take us over so we had to pay him. And we paid him full price. He was to come and pick us up in the evening but he didn't come back. We broke into a house, so we could have a place to sleep, and in the morning, the fellow came back. He was drunk as a skunk, so we weren't going to go in his boat. Finally, the doctor and the nurse came over in a boat looking for us. Of course they were all prepared for the worst, you see: blankets, and the rest of it, something to drink, and such. They found we were fine, and we quickly told them our story. So he says, "Okay, get in the boat. I gotta get back. I told them to watch for us and to get the operating room ready for when we get back" (in case we were injured). He says he had some operations to do, so we headed back and the matron told us, "Okay, go get your clothes on and get to work again." They didn't let us have any time off. [Laughs.]

MM: You were right back at it.

NM: It's a good thing that we were rescued; the fellow couldn't get his boat started. But this doctor was very good. He brought him back safely on the right side. He was a good doctor.

MM: You worked with Victoria Order of Nursing (VON)?

NM: I spent a year with them. And then they wanted me to go to Grande Prairie [Alberta]. And I said, "Well, I'm tired. Can I have a week off?" "Okay," they said. So, I went home and took the week off then they phoned me and said, "You are to go to New Liskeard." [Temiskaming Shores, Ontario]. Well, nobody knew where New Liskeard was. They (VON) said "There would be a lady waiting there for you." And that's in Northern Ontario. I had no choice. I [laughs] had to go. So I went by train to North Bay, I guess, where you get off at, and it was getting dark. It took us all day to get there, or more. They put those who were going to go up north in a different train, so that you'd all be together to get off. I guess one fellow figured I looked kind of worried, you know. And he said, "Where are you going?" And I said, "I'm going to New Liskeard." Well, he says, "Come on, I'll take your suitcase. You follow me," and "cause the time you get off this train, the other train going to New Liskeard will probably be gone." So, he took my suitcase, and we went between the two trains. It was dark; we got on the train. It was about seven in the morning when I was to get off at New Liskeard, and there was the lady waiting for me. She took me to her place for breakfast and then across the street was where I was going to be moving. There was no board, just room, but that was fine.

And then I thought, *Oh, my gosh, when we were giving our speech after we'd finished our training at year end, I said there's one thing I won't do, and that is to go to a one-nurse district.* [Laughs.] And that's exactly what I went to [laughs]. The VON didn't tell me that when I went. At the place where I was boarding, there were teachers — two or three teachers — so that was good company. We had to go to a restaurant for our meals. The VON never did tell me why the other nurse left, but the rumours were that she just wasn't who they wanted; the VON was the group that paid you. One of them said to me, "You know, if you want to use the car to go down to North Bay, you're welcome to use it." I was told that that was what this girl was doing, using the car all of the time. [Laughs.] I really enjoyed New Liskeard: it was just a wonderful community. But, I managed all by myself.

Marjorie, my sister, was in Montreal. And I was there when one of the girls that I nursed with said, "How would you like to go to England?" And I says, "Oh boy, that sounds great." She said she had relatives over there and she had a job there, but I didn't have a job. Anyhow, I went with her and they gave me a room, in London, I guess it was. And they said, "Well, we'll see if we can find you a job." Because the girl I was going with, she was going to work in London. So, they finally said, "Well, we have a job for you in Brixton." And that is just outside of London. Of course, I took it. It was great, you know. But, soon we got to it.

MM: What year would that be that you were over there? It was after the war, right?

NM: Yes, it was right after the war.

MM: I'm trying to remember. You brought me back a kilt from Scotland. And I would have been, I don't know, eight or so-so.

NM: It must have been '46 or '47, anyhow. So then we asked if we could go up to Scotland. They put us close together up in Scotland. And we worked there for a while. Then she said, "Let's buy a motorcycle and tour around." They couldn't get over the way we… when we had a day off, we got our days off at the same time. But we weren't in the same office. They'd always ask where we went. And we'd tell them. They said, "You didn't go that far. We never go that far." But anyhow, we bought this motorcycle. And every time we had a day off, we'd go back to my girlfriend's relatives' town, in England. And pretty soon [laughs], the expression down there was, "When are the crazy Canadians coming back?" When we bought the motorcycle, we hadn't a clue. We went out in the road to try and get it started, and we couldn't get it started [laughs], so we pushed it for a ways, and at a garage they said, "Oh, we can't touch that; it's brand new." So we went back out, kept persevering, and finally we got it started. So one of us would go about 30 feet, and wait for the other one to come, then the other one would go about 30 feet. We were going along together and doing quite well, we thought. A truck passed by and says, "You should have an L plate." We just said, "We know it."

MM: So that was quite the trip you had.

NM: Yes. We went up and around Scotland. We'd quit nursing by then and went over to Ireland, because we wanted to kiss the Blarney Stone. When we were coming back to England, we were going to get a ferry across and we got a flat tire. This man comes along and says, "You having trouble?" And we said, "Yes, we have to go to a garage. We got a flat tire." "Well," he said, "Put your motorcycle on my truck and I'll take you." And he took us.

It was getting dark, too, really dark. And he stopped behind a place and says, "You wait here. I'll come back." So we thought he was looking for a garage for us. He came back, and says, "Hurry up. Go get on the train. You'll miss it. I'll put your motorcycle on the train." "Oh, we can't do that. We haven't got that kind of money." "You don't have to. I told them you looked after my mother during the war." So we did as we were told and we got off at the other side just as it was daylight. We had to go down a hill and we still had the flat tire, of course. So I asked the fellow, "Where's the closest garage, we have a flat tire." "Oh," he said, "If you want, I'll put your motorcycle in, if you don't mind sitting with some dead rabbits." "Oh," we said, "We don't care what we sit with." So, anyhow, we got in the back of his truck (he was a delivery man), and he put the motorcycle in.

When we went up, we had the motorcycle insured, and so that didn't make any difference. We got our tire fixed. We were on our way down to Dover. We were on a straight stretch, and along comes a police car and stops us. We thought, *Oh gosh, we're not that bad*. They wanted to know what we were doing and where we were going, and so we told them. "Oh," he says, "You'll never have enough gas to go over there," because gas was rationed over there, at that time. They gave us a whole bunch of their (gas) coupons. So we went down to Dover and went across.

We were going to Paris. And we stopped. We never had a map or anything with us. So, anyhow, we stopped and leaned on the sidewalk and a lady came by and I said, "Can you tell us where we can find a place to stay?" She said, "Well, there's a hotel right in front of you." "No, we don't want that. We want a place where we can meet the people." "Wait, I'll come back," she said. So, she took off back wherever she had come from. When she returned, she said, "Okay, follow me." We followed her to a pub down below where they had rooms up above. The fellow said, "you can go up, have one of those rooms." So we stayed overnight there. Another fellow came over and asked, "Would you like to come for supper at our place?" Well, that was just great. [Laughs.] He kept coming back to see that we were coming. We didn't know where we were going. So, anyhow, he came back and got us, and it was a really good supper. But there was a youngster in a highchair, and I think she was about maybe three years old. They gave us wine. And then they gave the youngster wine, which really floored us. They give you one thing at a time on your plate, so you didn't know how much to eat. [Laughs.] Anyhow, that was fun. So then the next day we took off.

MM: Well, Norma, that sounds like a really interesting story. It sounds like fun. Shall we maybe get back to doing some of the Terrace fun things that you did? Let's talk about when you were back in Canada after that great trip. You met your husband somewhere and you got married at some point after that trip?

NM: After that trip I went home and I worked at the Kenney Dam. Dam construction for the Alcan project. I was with Public Health; they sent me there. You go where they tell you to go. So I went there and I was there for a couple of years, I guess. Anyhow, the fellow who was the head of the dam construction said, "I think you might as well let us hire you," because I was helping them. They'd get me to go out when there was an accident, you know, and take them to Vanderhoof. But I still did the Public Health work, too. Anyhow, I did that. It was more pay[laughs]. Then I went home. '52, I guess it was. The construction was over with and I went back with Public Health.

MM: When did you get married?

NM: '52. Nels came out to the Kenney Dam. I didn't even know he was coming, but he came. [Laughs.] Anyhow, we got married in '52.

MM: Okay. And what did he do here?

NM: Well, I was working with Public Health until I got pregnant. And then I had Margaret-Anne.

MM: You had three children?

NM: I had three children and I didn't go back to work until later.

MM: What about when Margaret-Anne was born — what's the story there? You and your sister both had babies on the same day? (Bruce Johnstone, son of Lorraine and Lloyd Johnstone was also born 21 April, 1955.)

NM: Yes. [Laughs.] That's right. John. John and then Cathy. Cathy, she was the youngest.

180

MM: And Margaret-Anne was born in what hospital? The Red Cross Hospital?

NM: Yeah. They all were. I worked in that hospital, too. That's where I was working, the Red Cross Hospital. I worked until I was eight months pregnant. [Laughs.] You can get a job anytime, anywhere.

MM: So, how did you find Terrace as a place to raise your family?

NM: It was my hometown.

MM: What sort of things did you do with the kids? They had cousins here? What sort of things did you do with your kids here?

NM: Brownies and Guides and Scouts.

MM: The lake?

NM: Yeah, we were at the lake.

MM: Lots of time at the lake. Then, what work did you do while you were in Terrace? What job did you take on?

NM: I went back to Public Health..

MM: How many years did you work in Public Health here?

MB: She retired in '85, I think it was. She worked 28 years or so.

MM: Yeah, that's Okay. Any stories about Public Health that you want to relate? When you were working here?

NM: We had good times. Did you come with us when we went on Halloween?

MB: Halloween?

NM: Yeah. One of the girls had forgotten something at the Health Unit. She went back to pick it up and she drove out where you're not supposed to drive out and the police got her. [Laughs.] I don't know.

MM: Did you enjoy working in Public Health, then?

NM: Oh, yes. It was — we had a great time. We even socialized with the social welfare.

MM: And sometimes you tell stories about running into people and you don't remember them but you immunized them as babies…?

NM: There was one woman: I met her and she had her son with her. Her son was — I guess he must've been about 18 or so — and she said to her son, "Do you remember this woman?" He says, "Yes. She's the one who shot me." [Laughs.]

MM: [Laughs.] Alrighty. Let's move on, then, to what you did for fun. Let's say what you did for fun when you were a teenager in Terrace. For Halloween, what did you do?

NM: Oh, that was just routine but we used to — we had to do the dishes and all that, do our work, you know? And then we went out right away and played out at the barn. We played kick-the-can, paper chase, run sheep run, and there was one fellow that — there were bunkhouses for the fellows that worked in the bush and they'd go to the beer parlour and then they'd go over and watch us playing. One of them even wanted to play with us. [Laughs.] It was funny. My kids — they say, "What did you want to chase paper for, Mom?" So I said, "Well, we went into everybody's outhouse

181

and grabbed some paper — some of it was books or magazines. We'd tear out the page and take it with us and they had to try and find us." [Laughs.] Yes, it was great.

MM: So, what was the story — there was a story about an incident that happened on Halloween.

NM: Oh. [Laughs.] The boys — we all — the girls were in a group and the boys were in a group, you know. The boys went and pushed the railway car a little bit onto the main railway run and, luckily, the train coming from Rupert saw it even though it was dark. It was on the other side of the station that they'd pushed this and, anyhow, of course they had a volunteer helping the police and he saw the boys running and he had a flashlight.

MM: The kids running had a flashlight?

NM: Yeah. Anyhow, this one boy had a flashlight and he put it in the fellow's face so he couldn't see the boys and they managed to run away. But the fellow who had the flashlight got caught. That same night, I had borrowed a flashlight from my dad's store and one of the girls had been taken in at the police station and they were questioning her. I put my flashlight on over there and they said, "You, get over here. We know who you are." So I went over and they were going to take my flashlight and I started crying and said, "You can't take it. I only borrowed it." And they said, "Okay. You go straight home." This was early in the evening. "You go straight home and we'll give you your flashlight back." So they gave me my flashlight back and I went straight home. Then the next day, I guess it was, we heard about this other incident where this fellow had stopped a police helper from catching the boys and they never did anything about who the boys were. But, for this one fellow, they sent him down to Vancouver.

MM: The one with the flashlight?

NM: Yes, and he spent some time in prison. One of the women sent him down a Christmas cake and they wouldn't even let him have a knife to cut the cake. I don't know how long he was in there but he was one of the nicest boys there were in Terrace. The whole town was just flabbergasted.

MB: Wasn't he the minister's son?

NM: Yes. The minister's son.

MM: Wow. Alrighty. I know that your family spent a lot of time at Lakelse Lake. Do you want to tell us a little bit about your time there?

NM: We spent every summer out there at Gruchy's Beach. Came to town once. Dad came out on Saturday nights… we only had our bathing suits on. We never wore any clothes, you know. And when we came to town, our feet would be so spread out (from not wearing shoes). We'd get back into shoes. It still bothers me that none of us drowned. We'd dive under the diving board and all that kind of stuff and I was the one that had to go all along the beach to William's Creek to get water for drinking and to clear up the dead fish. That was my job. And there was another family out there, four boys, and they never went to town.

MM: What family was that?

NM: The Coopers.

MM: They had four boys.

NM: Yes.

MM: And you had four girls.

NM: Yes.

MM: What kind of accommodations — what kind of house did you live in? Like, they weren't cabins, right? They were tents?

NM: No, no, they were cabins. They were real. We had what you'd call the cookhouse, built like that, and then we had the other one that was bigger. It had two bedrooms and a front room. That was it, you know? But, no, no, they were cabins.

MB: That was on Gruchy's Beach?

NM: Yes.

MM: How'd you get there?

NM: The landing there.

MM: The road went to where? What's now the picnic site?

NM: Yes. But the flood took the road out and all the trees came into this lake. Now you have to go around and back to the —

MB: Picnic site.

MM: But you had to go by boat from there to the beach?

NM: Well, that's as far as the road went and everybody had to park their boat there. And you never had any of this stealing. You usually left your boat there and then we'd come around Williams Creek. And then one time Dad was bringing [laughs] a mattress. We were in the boat and the boat was pretty heavy and I guess he decided — because we were all scared, you know — to stop on this side of the creek and put the mattress in the bush. Then he took us around to Gruchy's. Then he went back and got the mattress. We used to swim from that point to the beach to the picnic site.

I don't know. We were so fortunate there was never any drowning or anything. Bears galore, of course. And Mr. McKinney (Department of Fisheries officer) came out visiting one day and I asked him if he'd like to see a bear as big as a cow. And he said, "Oh, that'd be something." He laughed. He just didn't believe it, but he said, "Okay. Let's go." So we went up Williams Creek and there was this big bear pawing this salmon out of the creek and he says, "Boy, you're right. He is big."

MM: In later years, you lived on the lake but not at Gruchy's Beach, right?

NM: Not on Gruchy's Beach. I don't know why we all had to move off of there.

MM: Your father built a place?

NM: Yes. A log cabin. But everybody moved off [Gruchy's Beach] at the same time and I don't know why.

MM: Well, you were squatters, right? You didn't own the property.

NM: No. Nobody could find Gruchy. I think you found him, didn't you?

MB: Yeah. In an insane asylum.

NM: Of course we didn't have that kind of technique in those days, but Dad wanted to buy the part [of the beach] that we were on. And he couldn't. So I guess that's why.

MM: That's why you moved?

NM: Yes. But there was about three or four other cabins there and they moved and some of them moved their house just across the lake. We moved it and Dad gave me the log cabin. But it was getting to the point where you couldn't live in it all year round, you know? So we tore it down and we built a house beside it and lived there all year round. But with the pipes freezing and that, I couldn't manage it, so I moved into town.

MM: So that was some of your reminiscence of Lakelse Lake. Were you involved in any other community activities outside the home? Like clubs or organizations?

NM: Oh, yes. Scouts and Brownies. Search and Rescue.

MM: Right. You did Search and Rescue, yes.

NM: Yeah. What else did I do?

Norma rappelling at Terrace Mountain as part of Terrace Search and Rescue exercises. Terrace Standard Collection.

MB: A million prenatal classes.

NM: [Laughs.] That was my job.

MM: And now you're involved with your church.

NM: Yes, Knox United.

MM: So, we're back again — we jumped around here — what do you remember about Terrace as far as where you got your groceries?

NM: Well, we used to buy them at Sparke's store.

MM: In later years, did you shop at the Co-op?

184

NM: Oh, yes. There was another store up on Lakelse.

MM: Did you have a drug store in the old days here?

NM: Oh, yes.

MB: Riley's.

MM: Mr. Riley?

NM: Yes. Mr. Riley. And then there was Bodine's store there.

MM: Bodine?

NM: Bodine, yes. We'd have a cup of tea and whatnot. Then there was Sundal's.

MM: Sundal's? Yeah. That was on Kalum Street?

NM: Yes. Little Joe had a restaurant there on the corner of Kalum and Lakelse.

MM: So what did most of the people that you knew do for work here, then?

NM: They were all in the lumber business.

Linda Frank (Norbirg) and Norma Morrison in the Terrace Co-op booth, Kitimat Trade Show. Circa 1967. Norma Morrison Collection.

MM: Forestry?

NM: Forestry. Their owner, Pohle, he headed out Kalum Lake Road. And then there was Christy he headed across the tracks.

And that's where all the boys used to work. And then they quit school early. I remember once [laughs], we were going to school and there was a box of chocolates on the windowsill where the boys had their bunkhouse — oh heck, what was on the corner there? Anyhow, they could see us from the mill [laughs].

MB: In the mill.

NM: Yeah. And they could see us. And we went in to get this box of chocolates and there was a dead rat in it. [Laughs.] Oh, gosh. I'm telling you. Yeah, we had our moments, that's for sure.

MM: So, another one of the questions is, where you involved in politics?

NM: Nope.

MM: You weren't, but your father was, right?

NM: Yeah. He was.

MM: So how do you think Terrace has changed over the years, in general?

NM: Oh, the whole world has changed. I mean, people don't say hello to you like you used to. Or eye contact — they're all on these iPods or whatever they are. You know, they walk across the street — there's no respect anymore. This part here was all pine trees. We used to have a trail running through to Braun's Island.

MM: Oh, yeah. Down here on Graham, yeah.

NM: And we used to swim in the pool there but…

MM: By Braun's Island there?

NM: Yeah. There's no pool there anymore.

MM: Were there any annual community events that you remember?

NM: We used to go to Usk every 24th of May, I guess it was annual. And we'd play softball with them and the boys, of course, played baseball.

MM: So you weren't here during the military years in Terrace, right? Were you away when the military were in Terrace?

NM: Yeah, more or less.

MM: So you don't remember the mutiny or any of that? Do you remember the mutiny?

MB: You were telling me you saw the Zombies.

NM: Oh, well, yeah. When they were protesting.

MB: That is what they call the mutiny.

NM: Mutiny, yeah.

MM: So you do remember the Zombies?

NM: It was peaceful, though. It wasn't… you know, it wasn't erratic or anything.

MM: Didn't scare you?

NM: Nope.

MM: No. The rest of the family felt okay about it? They weren't worried about it?

NM: Nobody seemed to be worried about it. It was really peaceful.

186

MM: Yeah.

NM: At least as far as I know, it was.

MM: Okay. Do you remember when the Queen came to town?

NM: Yes. Dad had a two-storey building on the corner of Kalum and Lazelle and we were upstairs and they came down Kalum and turned onto Lazelle.

MM: When you were a child, what did you expect or hope to accomplish?

NM: Oh, I always wanted to be a nurse. I had an Aunt Carrie who was a nurse. She lived to be 104. I don't know how she did it, you know? [Laughs.] She lived in Victoria.

Norma Morrison fishing below the Skeena Bridge, circa 1938.
Norma Morrison Collection.

MM: Aunt Carrie was there when I went into nursing, too.

MM: Yeah. She came. So there you go.

MM: So as someone who has lived here and learned, what would you want to share with people that are new to Terrace?

NM: Oh, just share everything we've got. We've got lots. This is the best place in the world to live. People used to say when they came from the Prairies, "Oh, how can you stand it? You're shut in with all the mountains." And I said, "Yes, but when we go to the Prairies we feel like we're falling apart." [Laughs.]

MM: So those are all the questions they suggested we ask, but if you have any little stories or other things you'd like to tell us, we'd like to hear them.

MB: What was with everyone going out to the bridge? It seems that I look back at all your pictures…

NM: Every Sunday, we'd all go out to the bridge. And when I see people — I've got pictures of them standing up on the top part of it.

MM: Up on the top?

NM: Yeah. Gosh. We never thought anything of it.

MB: What did you do when you went up there? You just hung around the bridge?

NM: Yes that's all. It took us ages to get there because we were jostling around, you know. Didn't Julia (Little née Simpson) tell you about it?

MM: Julia, yeah. She told us that was their entertainment every Sunday. They'd walk to the bridge.

NM: We didn't always walk. We had a horse and buggy. I've got a picture of that and Julia is in it.

MB: That was Edith's little horse and buggy?

NM: Oh, yes. Edith (Little) had a pony and a buggy and she'd always give us a ride. Frequently. And, one day, we were coming up Lakelse Avenue and her house was on fire. Chimney fire — the chimney was burning. Of course we all jumped off and left her with the horse and she took it up to Emerson and Lakelse where our house was and there's trees all along there. And she tied the horse to this tree and she came back crying, "You all left me and it's my house." But she would never let us hold the reins.

MM: It's her horse [laughs]. What kind of fire department did you have here?

NM: Fire department. Oh, that's another story. [Laughs.] Every Halloween the fire alarm went off. Of course, we all knew who it was that did it. He climbed up on top of the hardware store and I don't know how he did it but he managed to get it. And they never did catch him. But it's right across from the police station.

Definitely. He was the nicest kid but he was always getting into trouble; it wasn't serious trouble — it was just things like that. I guess some people would call that serious, but you just had to go and turn the thing off, you know? But oh, he could get into more trouble and one lady who had all these young single boys all our same age, they'd all go to her place to just… communicate, you know? And one Halloween night, they put a small tree down her well. [Laughs.]

MM: Down her well?

NM: That was their joke on her. [Laughs.] Mind you, the next day they took it out. Things like that, you know?

MM: So was your father a fireman in the day? One of the firemen when the fire siren went off?

NM: Oh, everybody went. We did, too. That was the same when the plane came looking for somebody. Everybody went up to see the plane because we'd never seen a plane before, you know? [Mattern Expedition]

MM: Where did it land?

NM: Up on Frank's Field? Yes. On the right hand side. And people carved their name on the propeller and it cracked the propeller. They had to get another propeller.

MM: Oh, really?

NM: Of course, they didn't think that would happen.

MM: No.

NM: Yeah. I mean, fires were our excitement [laughs].

MB: What about when the liquor store burnt down?

NM: Oh [laughs]. Gee. You've got a memory.

MB: You told me all the stories.

NM: The liquor store burnt down and the boys were getting the liquor out of the store and they were hiding it in the trees or —

MB: The snowbank.

Fire at Terrace's local liquor store. Circa 1938. Norma Morrison Collection.

NM: There was some wood stacked up. And, of course, with the snow it broke them. Because they were hot.

MM: More than hot, hot.

NM: Yes. Got a picture of that somewhere.

MM: Well. We've been making you talk for quite a while, Norma. We'll give you a bit of a rest. I think that's pretty good.

NM: I don't know. I hope I didn't talk too much.

MM: No, you didn't. You can never talk too much.

MB: 1947 you were at UBC for a year. Yeah. That must've been where you did your Public Health. You did one year Public Health at UBC.

MM: Okay. Thank you.

Rani Parmar Interview

Interviewed by Linda Lee, 13 December 2013

Rani Parmar was born in Rajasthan, India, in 1946. Rani was sponsored by her husband and arrived in Canada on March 25, 1970. In Terrace, Rani experienced winter for the first time. Her first child was born in 1970, and her second in 1973. She also sponsored her nephew to come to Canada. Rani worked at home looking after the children and the home, and eventually worked at a local motel making beds. With encouragement from her husband and a neighbour who offered to look after the children, Rani enrolled at the local college in the professional cooking program. In this interview, Rani describes her experience working at the hospital as a cook, enjoying the outdoor activities in Terrace, meeting elders at the Kermode Friendship Centre, and her involvement in Terrace and District Multicultural Association. In the latter half of the interview, Rani describes how Terrace has changed over the years.

LL: So, first of all, where were you born?

RP: I was born in India — Rajasthan [State].

LL: Okay, what part of India is that in?

RP: It's in the north part, just beside Punjab.

LL: When were you born?

RP: I was born in 1946.

LL: So what brought you to Terrace?

RP: My husband.

LL: How did you meet your husband?

RP: I never met my husband before we married. We were an arranged marriage and we were engaged for 10 months and we never saw each other, and after the wedding we saw each other after two days.

LL: Wow.

RP: Then we got married and we stayed about three weeks together and then my husband — I was in grade 10 and my husband was leaving for England. After two months, 1967 on January 16, we got married. Then he left India March 11, 1967. He stayed a year and four months in England and then he came to Canada and then he came to apply for me. So it took a long time for the immigration process. I came in 1970, March 25.

LL: So you've been quite a while in Terrace.

RP: Yes, first when I came to Terrace, I don't know, I was reading and dreaming like it would be a nice place and the roads would be all paved and that. But when I came and only the Lakelse and Kalum Streets — those were the only ones that were paved and the rest of them were all unpaved. And we said, "Oh, this is Canada?" [Laughter.] But slowly, slowly… we used to live on Hamer Street. After a few months we moved to Thornhill. Slowly, slowly those roads were paved. Even in Thornhill in 1980 they brought the water — there was no water. We used to have our own well. Sometimes in the summertime the water would go low and then we had to dig it down deeper. Oh that was a heck of a time. Sometimes the water would go low and we tried to have enough for water then we would turn off the taps.

LL: Did the water freeze a lot in the winter?

RP: One time all the pipes were frozen for four days and we went to stay with some other friends 'til we could get somebody to unfreeze — defrost the water. I'll never forget that time. We never had snow back in India and we had snow here. And the first time I loved it and all that.

Rani Parmar in historic costume. Business Expo, April 2014.
Heritage Park Collection.

Our kids were born — in December 11, 1970 — my first child. It was a boy and after a month it snowed like crazy and hard and we were stuck. And we took him to the doctor just to check him out and when we came out we were stuck and it was a heck of a time. We tried to pull out the car and then my husband said, "You go home. I will bring him," but he had to leave the car there. Then he came home but he didn't bring my son home. I said, "What—" He forgot him in the car. Oh, that was terrifying. He went back and got him and he was so relieved. That was my first snow.

LL: So your first year in Terrace — if you think back to it, what kind of feelings did you have? I mean, you came from a country that was very warm to a country that was very different.

RP: Yeah, it was totally different. But I love to change myself and I made quite good friends. And there were some families that were from India so they were living here a bit longer, so I learned things from them and then I made some Canadian friends which helped me to learn things — different ways. It was a totally different experience.

LL: So after you had your first child, did you at all do any jobs in Terrace… did you start work?

RP: No, I never did work because I had to look after the kids and I didn't go to work. I stayed home. My husband was looking after that.

LL: Did you have any more children?

RP: We adopted — not adopted — sponsored our nephew, my husband's nephew, because his mom and dad passed away. When we got him he was nine years old. So he was with us and then because of the kids it was hard to leave them and go to work. I would love to; we needed money, but it was that kids were important, too. After two-and-a-half years, my daughter was born, in 1973 in April.

So I had three kids to look after but we needed the money, so I started working at the motel making beds. That was all fine, then my husband said, "No, you should go to school and learn something instead of doing this kind of job." But my kids were small and slowly my son started going to school and I had my neighbour across the street. She was from Spain and she was helping me and she said, "I will look after your kids and you can go to school."

So I went to school. I went to college to do a little bit of upgrading — English and math. My English is always poor but I was good in math. They were asking me to go for bookkeeping courses because I am good in typing. I said, "No, I think I will learn Canadian cooking." So I went to the college for one year and took cook training. After two to three months I finished my upgrading and took a whole year for the cook training.

LL: So did you become a cook?

RP: I am a cook.

LL: How was that experience?

RP: It was a good experience and I learned a lot and, you know, I liked Canadian cooking. All the spices and herbs I didn't know at all, so it was interesting. It was hard to remember those names and all that and finally I remembered all those names slowly and it was good. We used to have a lot of fun and the instructors were very nice. They were well experienced and they taught it really, really nice in the class and then they showed us how to make things for small portions and the bigger portions. It was good — I learned all the Canadian cooking here.

LL: How did you use your cooking education?

RP: First I got a job at the hospital as a cook, but it was not a full-time job and they called me at five o'clock in the morning to start a six o'clock shift. There were two shifts: one started at six in the morning and one at 10 o'clock. So one week was that and another week was at 10 o'clock.

There were three cooks and one was off all the time — one works in the morning shift and so you start after a few hours and then you help for the lunch and then in the evening you make the dinner. Morning shift you work the breakfast and the lunches. But when they called me at six o'clock in the morning it was hard to go and, where should I leave my kids? If I knew it before then it was easier and could have kept working and I could arrange it before, but it was very difficult to arrange the babysitter in the morning when you don't know when you get called.

So then I started working at the Bavarian Inn Restaurant. I started the 10 o'clock 'til two o'clock shift — so four hours when my kids were at school. So by the time I got home they came home. I prepared for the dinner and all that and I did other things. Then I'd go in the evening shift — six o'clock. My husband was working at Alcan. I picked him up and he was home to look after the kids. Then I worked three hours, four hours, or two hours sometimes, depends. On the weekend it was four or five hours in the evening. It was split shift work; it was not easy, but it was working for the kids and it was good.

LL: So when you came over from India, just to look at your career path here, how did you see your future in Canada in terms of jobs and career? Did you have any dreams about it?

RP: I have a lot of dreams to learn more things so then I can do different jobs. But because of my English, I couldn't do more. And that was my dream but I haven't fulfilled that yet.

LL: Dreams are good.

RP: Dreams are good. What else was I going to say? Then I got a job after a few years when my mom and dad came from India in 1980 so then they could look after my kids. I got a full-time job at the hospital as a cook. So I worked there for many years.

LL: So this is at Mills Memorial?

RP: At the Mills Memorial Hospital. So it was good. That was my permanent job and it was good pay and all that, too.

LL: So how did your career as a cook — how do you see it framing your experience in Terrace? How did it become a part of your life?

RP: I love cooking. I always liked different cultures' cooking — like different ways of cooking. I love to learn it and even watching those shows all the time. I love to be with the people, too. Yeah, it was good.

LL: So that kind of leads into recreation. What kind of things did you do for fun after you arrived in Terrace?

RP: For fun I tried anything. I loved skating — like people skating, oh my God — how do they skate? But I just borrowed some skates and I went for skating lessons. My supervisor took me. I felt odd but I tried anything. I went tubing and all that and everybody said: "you are brave!" but I went for that, too. So I went for swimming even. I am not a professional swimmer but I can float and do small strokes. Any game, anything, is for fun — I love to do it. I love crafts, too — knitting, crochet, like that. And I used to do it a lot but now I don't do it, but I start again a bit because I got hurt. Tendonitis on my elbow, so then I didn't do it for a while. I do it now for a little bit again. But I love to do it — all this crafty stuff.

LL: When you went skating, did you go out to Lakelse Lake? Did you skate at Lakelse Lake?

RP: No.

LL: Swimming?

RP: Swimming, yes I did, at the lake. I was not good, but I didn't go too far. Wherever places I go I always take my swimming suit and go for a swim.

LL: So did you ever go to the Lakelse Hot Springs?

RP: Yes I did many, many times.

LL: Did you go to the old one that was just out in the forest? Before they actually built the building?

RP: Yes, I did.

LL: Can you tell any stories about being out there what it was like?

RP: It was quite fun, like all the other people — I just watch how they do it and I just keep trying to do those things and it was quite fun. It was different. And now it is totally different — a lot of changes, but it used to be Mount Layton Hot Springs, and then they closed it and then it was closed for years. And again they opened it. We used to go every week for swimming with my friend. Even sitting in the hot water was fun. I used to go to the arena here, too, in the swimming pool. I don't go much now because chlorine bothers me.

LL: So you went to the Mount Layton Hot Springs, the old one? What was that one like?

RP: It was fun. A lot of people from everywhere. You know, tourists and all that and the new people coming — they all wanted to go there — ah there is a hot springs, so exciting place.

LL: What about sports in Terrace? Did you play any sports or watch any sports?

RP: Yeah, I watch all the time sports with my kids. I didn't play my own.

LL: Did your children play sports?

RP: Yes, my son always played basketball, badminton, and then he was in soccer. So those sports he was doing them. He loved to go for hockey but we were living a bit too far and I was working at different times. Didn't have time to bring him. But now we are living so close to the arena and my son could go down the hill and go any time if a hockey game comes. But now he always tells me, "Mom…" — he is a teacher in Port Alberni and he goes for hockey there. He learned skating — he teaches adults and they have a hockey team so he goes and play hockey there now.

He said, "Mom, you and Dad, you never let us go." I said it was so hard — it was so difficult at that time for us.

LL: Is that when you were living in Thornhill?

RP: Before there was no arena either. Then they built it, what year was that? There was no swimming pool in the early '70s.

LL: Where was hockey played?

RP: There was no hockey played 'til they built this in, I think, '77.

LL: Were there outdoor rinks?

RP: Yeah, people would make all their rinks, but there was no hockey arena at all. No swimming pool, I think until '76.

LL: What about fishing?

RP: We used to go for fishing — that was fun. First time my husband went with some friends on what is that Lava Lake — 1970, '72. And — Mud Lake. Is there a Mud Lake? I don't know. They went for fishing on the boat — the first time my husband went and he caught 72 lbs. of fish and he didn't know. He borrowed a rod from friends and they helped him to pull it out because he didn't know how. But the fish caught on his net. After that, it was so interesting. So we bought all the fishing rods and we used to go everywhere for fishing. We didn't catch too many — we caught a few small ones but we used to go and have fun. It was so much fun.

LL: So what would you tell your family back in India that you were learning here in Terrace?

RP: Oh they wouldn't understand — I never told them but it was so nice, you know. I went to Australia one time, snorkeling. I didn't know what it was to snorkel and then I learned what it was and I learned how to do it a little bit. And then scuba diving. We put the suit on and I just went in the sea and that was fun. I couldn't go under the sea but I went on the top. I tried to learn — it's good and fun. I try anything.

LL: You have had a lot of experiences. So what about community involvement? Were you involved in any community activities outside the home like clubs and organizations?

RP: Yeah, I just go for multicultural here and I go on different things, whatever is happening. And I just find out the community and I try to go, I try to get a part in it. This way, I meet more friends and do more things. I go to the Kermode Friendship [Centre] a lot, too. And then we joined the Adults Conference and joined the Elders Group. And then once a year — we went to many Elders Conferences in many different places and that is quite interesting and quite an experience.

LL: So tell me something about this Elders Group.

RP: This is Kermode, Tsimshian, and all those people in Gitsegukla and all those. They have the Elders Group and they get together and we do lots of crafty stuff — the last few years we did it but now the coordinator has another job. Now, since last year, there is nobody taking too much part. It was quite a bit of fun. I wish they would have it again and we could do it. Once a month you get together and we do crafty stuff and then we have a dinner together. There are always different families, different houses.

LL: So is this Kermode Friendship.

RP: Kermode Friendship.

LL: Is Kitsumkalum or Gitaus involved at all?

RP: They do maybe their own, but this one is at Kermode Friendship.

LL: What year did you and Nirmal start with the Elders Group?

RP: Six years ago. That was about 2008, I think.

LL: So going back to the Terrace and District Multicultural Association — what year did that start?

RP: 1984.

LL: You and I were in that together.

RP: Yeah.

LL: Where did we have our first gathering?

RP: That was at the Sikh Temple.

LL: Do you remember how many people were at that?

RP: I think it was around 25, 30.

LL: I'm thinking it was actually a bit more.

RP: Maybe more.

LL: About 50 people showed up.

RP: I think there was quite a few.

LL: You must have some stories about the Terrace Multicultural Association that you could share?.

RP: We have a dinner. We are a few on the board and we always have different chores to do. Some do advertisement, then some for the kitchen and then we always get some donations from the stores. A couple of people go to the stores and get that. We phone the restaurants and maybe they can donate some dishes, so all that.

LL: This is all for the Annual Multicultural Potluck Dinner.

RP: And after the dinner is a lot of fun. It's all different multicultural dishes there. First we have the dinner and after that we have entertainment and different cultures. It is quite fun, and amazing things there.

LL: So when you're saying many cultures for entertainment, which nationalities would be maybe doing some of the performances?

RP: Scottish, Philippine, from India, Bhangra and all that, some Irish, and then belly dance, then some songs, singers. What else? It was a lot of fun. Every year that was different people, different performances — lots of nationalities.

Soccoro, Rani Parmar, and Leydi Nobel [l-r] at 'Latin Night', an event
sponsored by Skeena Diversity and held in George Little Park. Also pictured
in the background are Jane Dickson and Nirmal Parmar. August 8th, 2012.
Linda Lee Collection

LL: Okay, very lively. Do you know how long the multicultural dinner has been running?

RP: This year is 29 years. 1984. Next year will be 30 years.

LL: Wow, longevity. That is really good. What local events do you remember celebrating in Terrace? Any local events that happened here that you remember celebrating?

RP: The first time I came in '71, I think was May time in the park. The library was totally different. It was just like a house before. I remember it was green; I think I have a picture or two somewhere. It was like people were a big group and lots of dances and stuff was going on.

That was the first time I saw it. The people were selling stuff, too. It was different. I haven't seen anything in India like that.

LL: This was in May?

RP: It was in May, first time in '71.

LL: Do you think it was for May 1?

196

RP: I don't know — I remember it was in May but I don't remember what the occasion was — I don't remember that. I remember seeing some of that. People were doing all different things.

LL: So were there any other local events that you can remember from the past that you were part of?

RP: Yeah, we have the Riverboat Days, it happens every year. There's the parade; it is so much fun to see. Even my daughter took part in the parade one year. Because she was in the Terrace pageant and now they don't have it. They used to have it every year.

LL: This pageant was for what?

RP: It was for Miss Terrace. So she got a talent award that time. They took part in a parade with all the girls who were involved in the Terrace pageant.

LL: Oh, nice.

RP: Yes, it was quite nice. And then my husband was involved in the Riverboat Days, too. He got to be a Captain two years ago.

LL: Oh, yeah, right, he was travelling in the convertible.

RP: In the convertible, yeah. And then we were in the Diversity, and they were having all the different faces and it was quite nice and I took a part in there, too.

LL: That was Skeena Diversity?

RP: Yeah, it was Skeena Diversity.

LL: I'm just going to go back to the faces, what were these faces — this was in a parade?

RP: Yes, it was in the parade — the head is made from paper mâché and then you had cloth and you put it on your head and you walk — it shows a different character. That's how.

LL: Yeah, different characters.

RP: Oh, kids and adults love it. It was so much fun.

LL: That's great!

RP: We had so much fun. We came first or second that year. We won something like that. First time when I came we had a group for Remembrance Day and all that, too. We never did it in India. Then when we came here we have — I love that Happy Gang Centre. They have a good thing, you know. All the elders get together there and then they do the pancake breakfast and I love that. Once a year they have it at the Fire Hall — the breakfast. That's quite fun, too.

LL: The next thing I would like to ask you is what you remember about downtown Terrace. Like in terms of maybe where you bought your food, shopped for clothes…

RP: You know, when I came first from India, it used to be Overwaitea and now it is Save-On-Foods. And where Overwaitea was is CFTK. That was the Overwaitea store. Then we had a Sears store on Kalum where Don Diego's is and where that fishing store is on the corner of Lakelse and the park and Fish Tales — where the Ev's Men's Wear is?

LL The fishing tackle store?

RP: Yeah, the fishing tackle store. After that was the Sears Store and then the Seven Seas restaurant — that was a Chinese restaurant and then on the corner was a drug store.

LL: There was a Rexall drug store. Wow!

RP: Yeah, and then the Co-op. But they are all gone now. Then the Overwaitea, they moved to where the BC Service — where the liquor store and the BC Access Building is. Where the Skeena Mall is — where the Save-On store is, there was a church. And everything was open except for the church there. We had two weddings that I attended in that church.

LL: Do you remember what church it was?

RP: I forgot the name of that church but it was a church, I remember that. Because I was from India and there were two weddings — you had to rent a place to get married somewhere. In that church and the hall there were two Indian weddings. We celebrated there.

LL: Oh you celebrated the Indian weddings there?

RP: The Indian weddings, yeah. So there were two weddings attended there. So after that — in late '70s, that's where the Skeena Mall comes up.

LL: So what was that change, from what you just described: the church being there and then there being the Skeena Mall?

RP: Then there was nothing and then the Skeena Mall: what a change [laughter]! It was so interesting and the people would come from Kitimat and Prince Rupert. Oh, there is a nice mall in Terrace. Same was where the Bank of Montreal is — where the Tim Hortons is, there was a gas station. A Shell gas station. I remember that was looking like a gas station and then there was nothing much in there and now there is the Royal Bank and Bank of Montreal and all the big buildings and the Tim Hortons — so totally changed.

LL: So before the Skeena Mall, where did you buy clothes or furniture?

RP: There was a furniture store where now is on the Lakelse — what is that, Bruno's store?

LL: Gemma's.

RP: Gemma's now. There was a furniture store. It was called S & S. And there was a furniture store on Lazelle where the Bank of Montreal is — no, the Credit Union building. And just a little bit after there was a small furniture store there.

LL: So that was on Lazelle.

RP: On Lazelle. And at Sears you can buy the furniture.

LL: Were there clothing stores?

RP: There was one clothing store where the Don Diego's is, and around there beside it was a nice big building. There was a clothing store and that was a nice store. I bought a few things there. Then there was a Woolworths and that is where Shopper's Drug Mart is now. After Woolworths is gone and there was a — what was that store, I forgot that name. They are all gone and now it is totally different.

LL: Can you think of any stores that are still around from when you first came that are in the downtown area?

RP: Safeway is there at the same place. They moved around but the sport shop —Big Bob's store [All Seasons Source for Sports]. It used to be in a different place. There was another old clothing store — where is that — across from Bob's store — it stayed for not too long.

LL: So there's been a lot of changes.

RP: A lot of changes, a lot — not many stores stayed. The small businesses, they come and go. And then there was one that we used to go on Lakelse — there was a newsstand and you could buy anything — small stuff — and that used to be and now it's Elephant's Ear. Around there was always small stuff you buy from that store and then there was a nice jewellery store, too. Amico, I forgot this name. Also, Northern Drugs. I loved that store. It had everything — a great variety store.

LL: That first store — that was the Hub.

RP: Yeah, that was the Hub.

LL: An all-purpose store.

RP: And then there was a nice coffee shop that used to be owned by a German lady and that was a nice shop and they used to make nice desserts.

LL: That was in the 4600 block.

RP: Yeah, the 4600 block and then the Lakelse Hotel was there and then the Terrace Hotel. The Terrace Hotel became the Best Western now. And then the Sandman Inn. That one was there when we came. What else? The Kentucky Fried Chicken and the McDonalds, they came in the late '70s. So it was quite exciting and the theatre is always there.

LL: Did you go to the theatre?

RP: Oh, I went lot of times — we used to go and watch movies a lot. Nirmal and I had a date in the drive-in theatre. It was so much fun. They sold popcorn and other fun food.

Ollie's Place at the lake was a great pub and restaurant. It had live music and was a nice place for couples to go for entertainment.

LL: So what did most of the people that you knew do for work over time? Were they in forestry? What kind of…

RP: All the people used to be in forestry — like the people from India, most of them worked in forestry. There were a lot of Punjabi people, but now they have all moved away because the mills closed. I know a lot of loggers, too, but they are all moved away because there is not much logging. Even in Kitimat there was so much going on, too. But now there's not much. Looks like it's going to be changed lots now because of the LNG [Liquefied Natural Gas] and the pipeline or something. I don't know if it's for good or for bad, but I hope something will go good for Terrace.

LL: So did any of your friends or family work in logging or the sawmills?

RP: Just a lot of friends I know, but not the family. My family — my mom and dad came in the '80s and they were here for a long time. My dad passed away in '99. My mom was living on Davis for a long time and she went to India, but she was not well and she passed away this year. My other family, they came here and they moved away wherever the jobs took them. Nobody worked in the logging industry.

LL: What role do you think logging and forestry has had on the history of Terrace?

RP: Logging — it did a lot in Terrace because that's the only two industrial things that were in Terrace. And since they closed, it was not the same thing. And because there were a lot of logs around here but now you can see that, you know. It used to be called Pohle Lumber Industry and it was very small. I remember that time and people — how they used to work hard in the snow. It was very difficult. Then they renovated that industry and it was a very nice, big mill, and then it shut down and everything looked awful around there. Too bad, but what you can do?

LL: That's true, but then it's like you said with LNG and the pipeline — whether positive or negative it doesn't matter — changes again.

RP: Changes again.

LL: So looking at that—so how throughout your life in Terrace how did the community in Terrace interact with Kitselas and Kitsumkalum? What kind of interactions happened over these last 40 years?

RP: All the community used to live in the villages most of the time and you'd never see them — very few in town. They come for shopping and all that — not living in Terrace. But slowly, slowly they come and live in the city and now you can see more and they are a very good people and educating themselves and they are mixing. Even the other nationalities, they come — I know a lot of different nationalities and people. They come and mingle with each other. Which is good and same as the natives, they have a lot of things happening. My husband is very involved with them. So we always enjoy the people. I think it is good for the community—good changes.

LL: More generally, if you want to summarize — how has Terrace changed over the years?

RP: How Terrace changed with the industrial things and with the people? They come and go. Different ways and different things goes on. It is improving the buildings. It is improving with the houses and the roads and all that. But there still needs to be more done in Terrace.

LL: So what would you want to share with people just newly moved to Terrace?

RP: I just tell the new people to come and find out the different organizations — maybe go to Skeena Diversity, it is very helpful — and other organizations. Ask them if they need any help from them. Mix with everybody and whatever is happening in the community you should be involved in those things. If you know something better, teach other people and learn from the people who have been living here long. Which is great. If you don't know that language and all that maybe take your friends who know better English you can interact with them. If you are mingling more they will learn more. I think it's a good thing.

LL: So it's about the people. Could you tell us a bit more about Skeena Diversity? It's been mentioned a few times. What is it?

RP: Skeena Diversity is diversity and the people are from different places and different cultures and they all come. That is what the Skeena Diversity is about. Helping new people out. It doesn't matter where you come from and what you do and things like that.

LL: Do you know when Skeena Diversity started?

RP: I think about 15 years ago. Approximately.

LL: And how has it grown in the last 15 years?

RP: It's grown quite a bit. And they finally have a place and people can come and they have two employees. They are open Monday to Saturday.

LL: Where are they situated?

RP: They are situated on Lazelle. It's across from Terrace Interiors — they have been there a long time. Terrace Interiors is the oldest store.

LL: Rani, thank you so much This has been really interesting.

RP: Thank you.

Raymond Ernest Sande Interview
Interviewed by Mike Folkema, 24 October 2013

Ray Sande, the youngest of four children, was born in 1930 in Prince George. His family was living in Sinclair Mills, a sawmill town 60 miles east of Prince George. Like many families who lived during the Depression, the Sandes moved around the province for work. His parents, Norwegian-Canadians, were both raised in Manitoba, and eventually moved to Alberta and then to Sinclair Mills. In 1936, the family moved to Burnaby, where Ray's father built and ran a lathe mill. A millwright by trade, Ray's father taught him to forge weld by the time he was a teenager. In 1944, his family moved to Terrace, where his father had started a small bush mill company with Jim McKinney and Cece Ruckle. Ray quit school at 14 to work. He discusses the army camp in Terrace during the Second World War, and briefly describes the mutiny. In 1949, he met his wife Colleen, married, and had three children. By 1950, he and his father were operating the sawmill in Terrace for Claire Giggey's Intervalley Lumber. Eventually they purchased the sawmill. They sold the mill to Skeena Forest Products and Pohle Lumber Company in 1966. Ray describes in detail the forestry industry in the late 1940s, including earlier influences such as the Soldier Settlement Act of 1917 and 1919. He also discusses the Sande sawmill business. In 1971, his family bought BC Yukon Air Service and operated the company until 1989. In 1990, he retired and moved with Colleen to Terrace. He describes his wife's involvement in clubs and organizations, and ends the interview speaking about his grandchildren.

MF: Where and when were you born?

RS: I was born in Prince George on September 20th, 1930. We were living in Sinclair Mills and my mother stayed in a boarding house in Prince George for the last part of her pregnancy, as Sinclair Mills was a sawmill town with a first aid man for the mill crew. It is located approximately 60 miles east of Prince George. No road and not much train traffic in those days.

MF: And growing up — your childhood, your youth — can you tell me about your parents?

RS: My parents were both born in the United States. Both Norwegian, they moved to Manitoba and were raised there. They were married in Manitoba, I think in about 1918. They tried farming in Manitoba and raising a few cattle but apparently there was a little bit of a depression in 1922 and they had to get completely out of that. My dad did a bit of well drilling with a friend of his in Manitoba. This is well drilling for water and he worked at that for a few years. Then he got into working in a sawmill, I believe in Alberta. Rocky Mountain House was the first place I know of that he was in the sawmill. And from Rocky Mountain House he moved to Sinclair Mills, BC, which is where I lived for the first six years of my life.

In 1936, we moved to Burnaby, as my father had built a lathe mill and he ran that for a couple of years. All his material was coming from one of the big sawmills, down on the Fraser River. He was using cedar slabs to cut up for lathe and shingle bolts. And he did a couple years. The mills he was getting his cedar slabs from found out he was doing fairly good at it, so they decided to put in their own lathe-making machines. So that dried up his supply and he had to shut the lathe mill down.

So he went to work in the sawmills in False Creek, Vancouver. At that time, he used to take me to the mill with him on weekends. The mill did not run Saturdays and he worked as a millwright. I used to clean up under the mill and once I finished, he let me practice arc welding in the millwright shop.

My father had a blacksmith's forge under the back porch of our house and I was allowed to use it. There was a supply of metal for me to practice with. He taught me to forge weld and how to make eyebolts and forge weld the ends. There was also a vice and a set of tap and dies that I was taught to use properly. I would have been 12 or 13 years old.

He worked there until 1943 and there was a Clair Giggey from Terrace that put an advertisement in the Vancouver Province saying that he had timber here to sell. He was looking for people to come up here to start and run sawmills. My father came up and looked and liked what he saw. He spent the next year, 1943 to 1944, getting all the parts necessary to build a small bush mill and looking for and buying equipment that he didn't have in the used equipment market in Vancouver.

We all moved up here in 1944. My eldest sister died in 1942. My next oldest sister never did

Lakelse Avenue, Terrace. 1948. Ray Sande Collection.

move up here, although she visited. She got married in Vancouver. My next oldest sister — I'm the youngest of four kids — Bernice is living in the Ashcroft area at this time and she came up here and was married to Charlie Houlden.

MF: Okay. So you moved to Terrace initially in 1944?

RS: Arrived here in the summer of 1944 and my dad had two partners: Jim McKinney and Cece Ruckle. So the original company name was McKinney, Ruckle, and Sande.

MF: So they started with the building of a sawmill.

RS: We built a sawmill down on the Remo Road. It was about half mile off the old airport road (now called Queensway), then you turned right and went about three quarters of a mile to the mill site. I was going to school and every afternoon when I got home there would be a list of bolts for me to cut and thread and drifts to cut for holding the timbers together. I decided to quit school after the Christmas holiday. I was 14 years old. We were there for about two years and a nephew of one of my father's partners came up here and started talking about all the wonderful timber there was out of Savona (on the west end of Kamloops Lake) and he convinced Ruckle, (McKinney had left the company because of family problems) that they should go down and have a look at this. And, of course, Dad agreed to go because they were all tied in together in the mill here, and he didn't really want to buy Ruckle out at that point.

So we went down to Savona and started building a mill across the lake from the town of Savona up at a small lake called Red Lake, BC, about 25 miles north of Savona. This mill was under construction when Ruckle wanted to go and borrow the money from M.B. King (a sawmill owner who Ruckle had worked for in North Vancouver) to get a big sawmill built right away.

My father was against this and he asked me if I would come back to Terrace if he bought Ruckle's share of the company (in Terrace). I agreed and Dad stayed in Savona to finalize the splitting up of McKinney, Ruckle, and Sande. I came back to Terrace in 1947 while he was doing that. So I got a job working for John Hagen for a year, I guess.

MF: And did he have a sawmill?

RS: John Hagen ran a sawmill out at Vanarsdol or Copper City, I guess you could call it. It was on the railroad side and they used to bring some of the logs down the river and up the slough into the mill.

MF: How far from Terrace is that?

RS: It's only about six or seven miles up the Skeena.

MF: So is that as far as Usk?

RS: No, it's between Terrace and Usk. At that time there were reaction cable ferries going across the Skeena River at Remo, Copper (approximately one mile this side of the suspension bridge that used to cross the Copper River), Usk, Cedarvale, and Kitwanga.

MF: How long did you work there?

RS: Somewhere between six months and a year, working at Hagen's mill, and then my father arrived back here and we were getting ready to start the mill up. In fact, we did get it started and we were only there for a short time when Clair Giggey wanted us to go into town and run the mill for him (with an agreement that if it worked out we could buy the mill from him). He had a mill right in the middle of Terrace right under where the overpass is now.

MF: When your father and yourself and the rest of the family moved down to Savona, the sawmill that you had in Remo stayed behind?

RS: On the Remo Road — this isn't old Remo, the old Remo Road, it's the first turn off to the right. There used to be a road that went down to where the railroad is now. Ran right through where the sawmill was, so no sign of it anymore.

MF: So it was still there when you came back.

RS: It was still there when we came back; it was all ready to start up and run. So we just got that started when Giggey decided he didn't want to run sawmills any more — he wanted to log. So he asked dad if we would come to town and operate the mill in town (this was a steam-powered mill) under contract, with an option to purchase — which Dad agreed to do. And we operated the mill for Intervalley Lumber (Clair Giggey's company), I guess for two or three years. Then he wanted to get out of the business, including the logging, and wanted us to buy the whole thing, which we agreed to do. And so we purchased the mill in town from Giggey.

I guess it would be somewhere around 1950. We did go down one season to run the old Remo mill for Giggey, as he had taken an order for 40 foot, 10 inch by 10 inch Sitka spruce timbers and some cedar mine plank (used in underground mining). (This mill was built around 1918 and was a steam mill with two boilers and was capable of cutting 40-foot timbers.)

The mill was located on the railroad side of the Skeena between the railroad bridge and the highway bridge over the Zimacord River. The Remo mill was made for bull labour, not very efficient, but in any case, we went down and operated it. It was a steam-powered mill, as was the mill in town when we first ran it. We converted the mill in town to electricity once Alcan got power into Kitimat and BC Hydro built a power line to Terrace. So there was enough power available to power the mill.

MF: What year would that have been?

RS: Oh, I guess it would have been about 1951 or 1952 before the power was in Terrace — I'm not sure on that date.

MF: So as soon as the power came in, you switched your sawmill over to electricity.

RS: As soon as there was enough electricity available to power the mill. Before that, we were only allowed to run lights as there was just a diesel plant put in by the military during the war [WWII]. After the army left Terrace, BC Hydro took the plant to supply power to the town, but it was not large enough for heavy industry, not enough to run a mill. So once they got the transmission line from Kitimat to Terrace and we were able to get a bank of transformers installed at the mill, we converted to electricity. We ran the mill until 1966 and then in 1966 we sold the mill to Skeena Forest Products and Pohle Lumber Company.

MF: Did you have forest timber rights?

RS: We had timber sales.

MF: So you had to auction or had to bid on timber auctions.

RS: You had to bid, but you got replaceable value as long as you're successful in your bid. We did have a promoter who created problems by bidding up timber sales, but he wasn't successful and we were not directly affected as we did not have any sales that came up. I don't know where he came from or where he went when he left, but he made all the operators like ourselves pretty nervous. In any case, in 1966 we just did not have enough timber to run a modern mill, and we were advised by the Minister of Lands and Forests about over-cutting our timber sales (in other words, cutting more than the replaceable volume was in a year). We used to always be able to cut what we could get off a timber sale. It was sold as having so many thousand board feet of timber on it and if we were able to get twice as much, we were allowed to cut that off without affecting our quota (allowable cut). But we received a letter from the Minister of Lands and Forests and he advised us that this was no longer allowed. So that more or less put us in the position of not being able to operate the mill for more than another couple of years if we cut all timber on our Crown grant lands.

The Soldier Settlement Act (1917, 1919) allowed veterans of WWI to purchase land with the help of government loans. Most of the land we held in Crown grants came from that time, but some of the grants were from a later period and I don't know how this land became available to Clair Giggey and others. But we got all our Crown grant lands from Giggey and they all had timber on them. We had about 2,000 acres north of Terrace in Crown grant land with timber that we didn't want to cut then or we would have nothing to sell other than our quota, which the Minister may or may not allow to be sold. So we decided to put the operation up for sale as an operating company with the timber sales and the Crown grant land.

MF: Was the Minister of Forests encouraging smaller outfits like yours to sell out to the big companies?

RS: Well, the Minister of Lands and Forests in 1949 was encouraging everyone to expand and there was going to be no end of timber available for the local operators. This was when Columbia Cellulose was granted the first timber license with most of their timber coming from the Terrace timber area. A few years later MacMillan Bloedel Company (they owned most of the land on the flats in Crown grants between Lakelse Lake and Kitimat, BC) were talking about putting a pulp mill in Kitimat. Well, they decided not, to and they cut all the timber on their grants and shipped it all down to the pulp mills in the south. I believe they allowed all their land to revert to the Crown. A pulp mill was eventually put in by Eurocan.

MF: Yeah, there was a Finnish company involved in there first. I think Ben Ginter from Prince George.

RS: I'll tell you what the score was there. We (the local operators who held quota in the Terrace Sustained Yield area and were applying for timber in the Kitimat Sustained Yield Unit) were all invited by the Minister to go to Vancouver to discuss with him the possibility of building a pulp mill in Kitimat in partnership with a Finnish company. But when we got to Vancouver there was no meeting with the Minister. It was a meeting with Ben Ginter (a businessman from Prince George). There were several of us who walked out of the meeting because we felt that we couldn't deal with Ben Ginter as he was very unreliable. When we first heard about him coming into this area, we were advised by the Prince George Lumberman's Association never to sell him anything because you'd never get paid for it. So it didn't seem sensible for any of the smaller outfits like ours to get involved with him.

MF: The sawmill that you had here in Terrace that you bought from Giggey, how much lumber did it produce on an annual basis?

Sande Lumber Mills, circa 1964. Mill site was near current location of Sande Overpass.
Ray Sande Collection.

RS: On a daily basis it was about 75,000 board feet in one shift. And because we had been told that there would be available timber (which turned out not to be the case and our quota would not cover more than one quarter of that amount) we were in trouble. Things were quite political at that time. There was a timber quota being granted but it seemed to us to be on the basis of who you knew and not on need. We didn't feel that you should have to donate to a political party to get timber. I think that left us with no possibility of getting any increase in our quota. In any case, we did end up selling to Skeena Forest Company and Pohle Lumber.

MF: Okay, and with the sawmill that you had there, I guess it was called Giggey's Sawmill, then it was called Sande's?

RS: It was called Sande Lumber Mill after we bought it.

MF: Did you make any changes to it?

RS: After we bought the mill from Giggey, we operated with the steam plant, but we had trouble finding a class-four steam engineer. So my dad and I both wrote our steam engineer's licence and ran the mill on steam until electric power was available, at which time we completely rebuilt the mill.

MF: You made a reasonable living from the sawmill?

RS: Oh, we were doing well enough with the sawmill.

MF: So you weren't tempted to head somewhere else again?

RS: Oh no, it was going well here. It's just when we were advised that we were in trouble with our annual cut that we decided it would be better to get out of it while we still had something to sell.

MF: Well, around that time, too, wasn't the overpass built, where your sawmill was?

RS: No. The overpass wasn't built until after we got out of the business.

MF: Okay, it was some years afterwards.

RS: Yeah, it was a few years. I'm not sure exactly how long.

MF: With the sawmill, where did you sell your lumber?

RS: Most of our lumber went to the States, although there were times when the lumber market was really bad we did manage to keep the mill running by selling cedar lumber to Eastern Canada. We cut a lot of the mine plant. I believe it was 2"x 9"x11' (used in construction for workers to stand on) and was supported on both ends and could be any height off the ground and had to be a high quality Sitka spruce. Cut a full 2" thick by 12" wide and 16 feet long. We also cut ties for the C.N. Railroad. I believe they were 7"x9"x9' long; also we cut crossing ties up to 26 feet long also for the CN Railroad.

MF: Did you have a dry kiln?

RS: No, we never did have a dry kiln. We shipped the lumber green or partly air-dried.

MF: Did you feel that you were a competitor at all with the existing mills?

RS: Well, the existing mills were mostly the smaller bush mills like we originally built here and they were going out of business because of either not knowing enough about business or not being able to get a market for their lumber. It was a lot harder to sell the lumber here when you had to do everything by telegraph. There was no phone system when we first arrived. So it was pretty hard to sell the lumber unless you knew of a lumber broker to handle the sale of the lumber for you. Dad had connections with a broker so we were okay.

MF: In terms of selling your lumber for the bush mills?

RS: Well, for the bush mills it was hard. By the time we bought the mill from Clair Giggey, there was a telephone service in town and we were able to get a phone in our office and were able to talk directly to the brokers. We used one located in North Vancouver, and she was a lady broker; this was unusual at that time. She sold a lot of our lumber and she also sold through brokers in Seattle, who sold to the American market. Most of our hemlock went to the American market. The scaffold planking, well, that would vary because scaffold plank specifications were in effect in Canada as in the States. So that could be sold either place. But again, most of it sold to the States.

206

MF: Okay, backtracking a little bit to when you first came to Terrace the second time, was that 1944? I guess you were about 13 or 14?

RS: When we come back the second time, would be about 1947.

MF: '47. Okay, the war was over.

RS: Yes, the war was over. When we first came here, the war was still going, and there was a large army camp in Terrace, I believe about 5,000 soldiers.

MF: Do you remember the army camp?

RS: Oh, yes, I remember the army camp. I remember when I was still going to school — I went to school for the first four months they were here. I was in grade nine and they had the… well, what you call the zombie riots in Terrace. It wasn't a riot really, but they had a disobedience of some sort and they marched by the school one day. That's the only time I saw them.

There were planes flying around. This was an advanced training air base. We did have one or two of the airport personnel who used to come down and work in our bush mill, as it was only about two miles from the airport. That would be 1944, 1945.

MF: What schools did you attend in Terrace?

RS: I went to the high school here. I was 14 in September of 1944 and I went to school until Christmas holidays, and I decided not to go to school any longer. I went to work in the mill. I also worked in the bush driving a 1930 three-tonne Chevrolet truck hauling logs on a plank road from the high lead (spar tree) to the mill.

MF: What grade were you in at the time?

RS: I was in grade nine. I never finished grade nine. So I have grade eight education.

MF: I guess that was quite common back at that time.

RS: There were not too many of the kids that went all the way through high school here. But there were a few.

MF: Was there plenty of work back at that time?

RS: Anybody who wanted to work could get a job in Terrace in the early days. I'm referring to as long as we were operating, and we operated until 1966. Yes, anybody up until then who wanted to work could get a job, and I think that lasted for another 10 years according to friends of mine who were still in the logging business here. I left Terrace in 1971 for the Yukon, but I did fly in Terrace for Trans Provincial Airlines [T.P.A.] from 1968 until 1970. We left for Watson Lake, Yukon in 1971.

MF: When did you first get involved with flying?

RS: I started flying here with the first flying school; I guess it would be 1953. At that time, the government was still giving a grant for anybody who would take up flying, because they had been stuck at the start of the last war with no pilots when they needed them, and I guess this was the reason to get some of the younger people involved.

MF: Yeah, it's an incentive. Were there more people that took advantage of that?

RS: I think there were about 12 in the class that I was in and 12 in the next year's class. They ran the school out of Prince Rupert. I think they required a minimum of 12 students before the Prince Rupert Flying Club would operate a school there.

MF: So once you started flying and you got your flying license, did you continue?

RS: Well, I flew here until 1971, and then we went north.

MF: I'm thinking during the period 1954 to '66.

RS: I flew privately from 1954 until 1971. I owned my own planes from 1954 until 1972. The last plane I owned was a Boeing Stearman (this was a biplane used in WWII as a primary trainer). I sold the Stearman to my son Ernie. I did own a Piper PA 12 for about a year after we came back to Terrace. I sold that and then bought a Cessna 180 and then a Cessna 185 in partnership with Ernie, I think from 1991 until 1998.

The first aircraft I owned was a 1946 Aeronca 7AC Champion followed by a new 1959 Piper Tripacer then a new Cessna 172, then a used Bellanca Citabria, then a new 1966 Cessna 180. I sold the 180 to T.P.A. in about 1968.

I purchased a Piper Super Cub in about 1968 and Ernie, my daughter Patti, and I flew the aircraft to the Terrace area. Ernie flew the Super Cub to Watson Lake, Yukon, and we used it in the business for a few years. I also owned the Stearman before we went north and I flew it north after we were established in the business. I had to stop twice for fuel; the first stop was in Stewart where my good friend Bill Ross lived, so we had to take a short flight over town and do a half-dozen loops. The Stearman was acrobatic and wasn't much good for anything but playing.

It was my hobby and I did a lot of flying. I had a plane that I leased to Trans Provincial Air Service in 1968 (a Cessna 180) and they purchased it in 1970. I flew for them in 1968, 1969, and 1970.

MF: Did you use it at all for your business, let's say for logging, did you use the plane at all?

RS: I flew around and looked at timber and the lay of the land for building roads. I knew the timber from the ground and looking at it from the air gives you a different perspective. Although, they did have the, you know, the glass thing.

MF: The stereoscopes.

RS: Yes, they were pretty good but we didn't have any of that stuff. We could go to the forestry and use theirs; they were always helpful here. The local forestry personnel were always really good people to deal with.

MF: How did you do your logging?

RS: We started with horse logging in 1944. We had, I guess we had seven horses when we first operated in Terrace. We sold four or five of them. Four of them I guess when we left to go into the Savona area; we took a couple with us and we sold them down there. When we came back, it was mostly logging with a crane and tractors. We started high leading. We did a bit of high lead logging as well. In fact, I think we operated the first high lead logging operation in the Terrace area. That was probably in 1945.

When we bought the mill from Giggey, we also got a logging contract with Western Plywood Company out of Vancouver. We logged cottonwood on most of the flat ground along the Skeena River between Exstew and Cedarvale. We put a siding on the railroad below Kitselas Canyon between the railroad tunnels and put a fin boom across the Skeena at the lower end of Kitselas Canyon from the road side to the railroad side of the river. We logged with Allis Chalmers tractors and pushed the logs into the Skeena. I and a helper spent the summers for three years with a boat pulling logs off the bars to keep them floating downriver where we caught them with our fin boom below the canyon. We then picked them out of the river and loaded them on log cars. They were then hauled to Prince Rupert and boomed and taken to Vancouver for processing by Western Forest

Products. Our responsibility ended once the logs were loaded on the rail cars. For the rest of the year, we logged everything we could get at below the canyon and trucked the logs to sidings at Terrace, Shames, or Exstew.

MF: Did you have family members running the logging or was that contracted out, for the sawmill?

RS: No, I looked after the logging for the sawmill until we started modernizing the mill, and then I looked after that project and we used people from our crew to supervise the logging. I was managing both the mill and the logging. We bought a few logs the last years that we operated.

MF: So you operated with horses in the forest?

RS: We operated with horses in the '40s up until about 1947. After that we used tractors and we used a crane with a 40-foot boom with a set of tongs on the end of a half-inch cable and we used a tong setter who would pull the line for maybe 150 feet off each side of the road, hook it onto a log so you could pull it out to the roadside where it could be loaded on to the trucks. This worked well on flat ground. A lot of the roads were built using slabs and sawdust. This only worked for the Deep Creek mill, which was located off the road going to Kalum Lake (you would turn off to the right about a half mile before you get to Deep Creek and it was about one and a half miles in, almost to Cameron Lake). We used the same system of logging for logs going to the mill in town, but we did rely a lot more on tractors and we built the roads with gravel.

MF: Okay, what type of trucks did you use?

RS: Well we used International Tandems (trucks that had two sets of axles on the rear of the trucks) or we mostly hauled logs on the back of the trucks (no trailers). We also had had two single-axle trucks and used a trailer with them because we were hauling a lot of 26-foot logs. We specialized in 26-feet lumber because we could get a premium price for lumber 22 to 26 feet long.

MF: The logging, would that typically be done in the wintertime?

RS: We had to shut down for a short period in the spring. The bush roads would break up as the frost came out and the public roads would be closed for any heavy hauling for the same reason. Otherwise, it was done year-round.

MF: Okay, and the sawmill operated year-round?

RS: The sawmill operated year-round.

MF: How did you get the logs into the mill?

RS: The logs in by truck and trailer and we owned the trucks and we owned all the equipment.

MF: Did you have any water storage of logs?

RS: No, we used a dry land sort; the logs and the lumber were piled west of the mill.

MF: So Sande Sawmill was a partnership between you and your father?

RS: Yes, between my father and I and my sisters.

MF: And your sisters?

RS: Yes, two sisters.

MF: Did they work in the business, too?

RS: Bernice worked in the office for a number of years.

MF: And the ownership stayed the same until they closed it?

RS: The ownership stayed the same until it sold.

MF: Once the business was sold in 1966, what did you do after that?

RS: I didn't do much of anything for about two years and then I started flying for T.P.A. (Trans Provincial Airlines).

MF: A fixed-wing aircraft?

RS: Yes, fixed-wing aircraft, mostly Beavers and Otters equipped with wheels, wheel-skis and floats.

MF: Okay, and then you got into your own business?

RS: We got into our own business in Watson Lake.

MF: What year would that have been?

RS: That would have been 1971. We bought BC Yukon Air Service. It was an established company. We bought it from a group of investors and they were having trouble with their manager and not doing as well as they hoped.

George Dalziel started BC Yukon Service in Telegraph Creek and moved his family to Watson Lake, Yukon territory, in 1950. I am not sure how long he operated the company but there were several owners before we bought it.

Dease Lake Airport. Ray Sande Collection.

His granddaughter and her husband are trying to buy the license from Bruce McNaughton, the present owner of the license. I believe they now own the log house and the property and have an agreement in principle to purchase the license. It will be back in the Dalziel family again, the BC Yukon Air Service name and license.

MF: And you operated that business until?

RS: We operated the B.C Yukon Air Service, I guess until 1989. We moved from Watson Lake to Dease Lake in 1984.

MF: Why?

RS: The mining exploration, which was the biggest part of our business in Watson Lake, dried up in 1984. In the spring of 1984 we put out 12 barrels of fuel, whereas in the spring of 1983 we had a contract to fly out 600 barrels. I remember the 12 barrels because I flew them out with the Otter on wheel skis. It was two loads. So the mining exploration business was gone. We hadn't worked for the guide outfitters out of Watson Lake. There was another flying service operating out of Watson Lake and they were doing most of the flying for big game guides.

We had operated a base out of Dease Lake from 1972. Most of the flying there was with resident hunters and businesses during the late summer and fall. It seemed like the best option for us. We built a very nice log house for Colleen and I. We had a 60-foot mobile home on the property that Ernie and his wife lived in.

I think that we were doing better operating with two aircraft out of Dease Lake than we did with eight airplanes in Watson, with just my son and I. He had his aircraft maintenance engineer license so we were able do all the maintenance on the aircraft.

Ray Sande on the dock with BC Yukon aircraft. [Ray is pictured wearing the hat.]
Ray Sande Collection.

MF: You're talking about Ernie?

RS: Yes, I'm talking about Ernie.

MF: So it was the two of you that were...

RS: Two of us, and my wife and Ernie's wife looked after the radios, weighing the loads for the aircraft, helping dock the aircraft, and booking the trips.

MF: There are some seasonal aspects to the hunting, I presume.

RS: The hunting was, I suppose, the end of July through until the first of October. It was a very short season but if you are prepared for it and if you own your equipment it's not a difficult thing to do to make money.

MF: Who did you sell it to, by the way?

RS: We sold the business to Bruce McNaughton.

MF: Okay, and the year was?

RS: Bruce bought the company in 1990. We shut it down and sold the last aircraft in the fall of 1989. Bruce couldn't make up his mind whether he was interested or not, so by the time he made up his mind, we had sold all the aircraft. But we still owned the base and the log house and the license to operate a commercial air service.

MF: You still do now?

RS: No, Bruce bought it in 1990, I guess.

MF: Okay, and then you retired from the flying business at that point?

RS: And then I retired from commercial flying at that point.

MF: So you've been retired since 1990?

RS: Yes, basically.

MF: And this house here on Eby Street, when did you move into here?

RS: We bought the house in the spring of 1989. My wife moved in and I finished up at Dease Lake as soon as we had all the hunters out of the bush about the end of October 1989; I loaded up the last of our belongings and joined her in Terrace.

MF: You mentioned your wife Colleen. When did you get married?

RS: We got married in 1949. I was 18, as was she. I was 19 in September and she was 19 in March. So we were married quite young. Everybody said, "Not going to work." But it did.

MF: And Colleen was from Terrace?

RS: Colleen's from Terrace.

MF: Was born here?

RS: No, she was born in Grande Prairie, Alberta, and they actually lived about 40 miles north east of Grande Prairie.

MF: But she moved here with her family?

RS: She moved here with her family in 1939, I believe. And she had two brothers. One of them died from an enlarged heart not long after they came here. It was something no one knew anything about at the time and he just dropped dead when the three of them, Colleen and her two brothers, were coming back from Lambly's Snack Bar. I was about four blocks from where they lived on the corner where you turn off Park Avenue going to the swimming pool. Her oldest brother, Harold, was in the army. He went overseas to Holland. He was there in the later part of the war and he didn't see too much action. But he came back and was here a few years. He married a nurse who was working in the hospital. They now live in San Diego, California. Or just outside of San Diego.

MF: You had children?

212

RS: We have three children. The first was Ernie. He was born nine months and 10 days after we got married. And then we had Patricia in 1953. She was a pharmacist for Northern Drugs, in Terrace, for many years. My youngest son, Alan, is working at the college as a teacher. He was born 10 years after Ernie. Patti was in between.

Alan is very interested in technology and gold mining. He has a website, hollowaybar.com and must have at least 15 webcams between what he has in the Terrace area and what he has at his friend Scott's placer mining property in the Cassiar area. He is planning on spending his summer working with Scott mining for gold.

Probably the only reason that I have four computers and controllable webcams located under the eaves of my house is that Al is around to keep me out of trouble.

MF: And they would've been up with you in Dease Lake.

RS: Ernie stayed the full time. Patti got married in 1982, and she did not work for BC Yukon. She worked as a pharmacist in Terrace and did visit us in Dease Lake. Alan worked in the office from 1982 until 1984 and then went back to school and got his accounting degree. He never flew for the company, but he got the private pilot's license and also got his helicopter endorsement as did all my family, except my wife. We bought a helicopter and hired an instructor to come up to Watson Lake and we got our helicopter endorsements in 1980.

MF: So you had a helicopter there?

RS: Well, we got the helicopter, but we never used it in the business. After we were endorsed on the helicopter, we kept it for about a year. I flew it from Watson Lake to Terrace, but as we were winding down our flying business in Watson Lake at the time, owning a helicopter among the four of us was just too expensive; insurance costs alone were $16,000 a year. We were able to write part of that off through BC Yukon Air Service as a bonus to Bruce Chapman and my kids and myself.

MF: What do you remember about Terrace — you know, the early years?

RS: Well...

MF: Do you think it was a good place to raise a family, for example? Did it have enough services?

RS: Oh yeah, we felt that Terrace was always a good place to raise a family. I assume it still is, people are still doing it. And the schools were good and there was always work; my kids were never out of work. They've always been able to get work either here, or wherever they would have to go to get it. Ernie moved around a bit more because he got into flying helicopters commercially, so he ended up moving around. He lived in Smithers for a while and as helicopter pilots went where the work was, he was based out of town more often than not.

Bruce Chapman married my daughter Patti in 1982. He had flown fixed-wing aircraft for us in Watson Lake from about 1974 until 1980. He got the helicopter endorsement as a bonus in 1980. The next year he started flying helicopters commercially. Bruce flew helicopters until they had four kids, but he was out of town too much, so he took a year off and got his teaching degree and taught grade 10, 11 and 12 math until he retired in 2013.

MF: Were you involved with any community activities outside the home?

RS: My wife was involved. I wasn't, I was too busy with my work. My wife was involved in hospital auxiliary and she was into clubs, but I never was.

MF: Like what kind of clubs?

RS: Well, she was involved with the Auxiliary, Royal Purple, and the Museum Society, but that was never my thing. I was not quite as social as she was.

MF: Were you involved in any sports or recreational activities?

RS: I never was, no. My dad had a baseball team. The Sande Lumber Mills team that played ball here.

MF: Were they sponsored?

RS: He sponsored it, yup, that's the word I was looking for.

MF: And how long was your dad involved with the business there, right till the time you sold it?

RS: No, my dad more or less lost interest in the business. In the early 1960s, he got involved with a partner in a limestone quarry up on Thornhill Mountain.

MF: So after that, you were running things?

RS: After that, I ran the business.

MF: Did he sell out prior to that, too?

RS: No, we didn't sell out till '66.

MF: I thought maybe your dad sold out, but no.

RS: No, he didn't. He was not actively involved, but he still owned part of the business.

MF: Okay, are there any things that we haven't touched on that you want to add?

RS: No, you were mentioning where the shopping was done in the early days. Well, there was Jim Smith's store; they had everything. They had dry goods and groceries and then there was McAdams Store. They sold groceries and clothing, and there was a butcher shop on Lakelse Avenue. My wife's parents ran a small dine and dance in the second building west on the south side of Lakelse Avenue, just west of Kalum Street. J&M Hardware was located on the northwest corner of Kalum and Lakelse.

MF: What was it called?

RS: I don't recall what the dine and dance was called. There was a dance floor surrounded by booths that would sit four comfortably or a maximum of six. They served what you would call 'fast food.'

MF: What years are we talking here?

RS: Well, that would've been a year before I got married, so I suppose it would've been 1947 and 1948. My wife worked as a waitress in the restaurant for a while. She was working in McAdams Grocery Store when we got married.

MF: Okay, after you retired from the flying business, you moved back to Terrace. Why did you go back to Terrace?

RS: Well, our daughter was here and grandchildren were here. Terrace had been home for us and we always came back. We actually bought a couple of houses in Terrace while we were still operating the flying-in business and Colleen moved down a couple of times, but she could never convince me to leave until there was a bad accident in front of our business in Dease Lake. A Beaver aircraft crashed into the lake in front of our home and my wife was watching. It was an orange Beaver and our aircraft were orange, but for some reason or other she was convinced it was me coming in with the Otter aircraft 9, a larger aircraft than the Beaver (built by the same company and looked similar) that had crashed. So that finished her for being around the flying business. It never bothered her, my flying privately, but commercially she wasn't good with it anymore, so that's probably the biggest reason we left the flying business in Dease. She just couldn't handle it.

Thinking about it now, it worked out well for me, as I got to spend a lot of time with my grandsons. Dan is the oldest; he is an immunologist in Toronto. Chris is a doctor in Edmonton. Jeff is a journeyman carpenter in Terrace and the youngest, Stephe, is a civil engineering technologist based in Terrace. I have a well-equipped shop for both wood and metalworking, and they all spent time doing woodworking projects. They worked together and built a model of the type of crane used in building skyscrapers.

I helped Chris rebuild a Volkswagen dune buggy and paint it. I also helped him build a small racing boat. I helped Jeff overhaul a Jeep pickup and repaint it. I also helped Stephe with several projects. We built a scooter and then powered it with the motor from a whippersnapper. We put skis on another scooter and Stephe repaired and rebuilt a fiberglass boat. My shop is also equipped with 12-inch metal lathe with 48-inch bed and I also have a 250 arc welder with high frequency and has TIG welding capability. Stephe understood working on the lathe and used it on his boat project; he also did some arc welding.

For a couple of years, I took them flying two at a time. We flew to lakes north of Terrace. Most of the lakes were almost at tree line and although the highest lakes were not good for fishing, they were great for hiking and camping. We flew to lakes almost as far north as the Yukon border.

MF: That's interesting that you moved back to Terrace again and retired here. Okay, I think unless you have something else, that covers it pretty well from my perspective. So, anything?

RS: No, not really.

MF: So let's leave it at that then, Ray, and I'll say thank you on behalf of the Heritage Park and hopefully we can add this to the records — the history records for Terrace. Thank-you.

Rhoda Seymour Interview
Interviewed by Estelle Mitchell, 11 December 2013

Rhoda Seymour was born in Kitselas in 1931. Rhoda's grandparents were Emma and Charles Nelson, well-known Tsimshian people who lived in Kitsumkalum. Rhoda grew up in Kitselas with her nine siblings. The family fished, hunted, gardened, and canned. Rhoda remembers fishing with her father and siblings at Kitselas Canyon. Her father built packboards for each one of the children, which they used to carry fish 3-4 miles from Kitselas Canyon to Kitselas Village. At 18 years old, Rhoda married Willard Seymour and moved to Usk, where she raised her eight children. Rhoda's husband was Usk's ferry operator for many years. In this interview, Rhoda talks about her childhood, her grandparents, and raising her eight children. She also recollects riding the Usk Ferry, trips into Terrace, gardening, fishing, WWII, and the Queen's visit.

EM: Tell me again where you were born. You said you were born in the old village, right?

RS: I was born in the village of Kitselas, six miles east of here and I was born on June 24th, 1931.

EM: You just mentioned that there was no hospital there, but what was there at that time — was it a pretty big village at the time?

RS: There were quite a few houses. There were quite a few people living there at that time.

EM: So is that where you went to school as well?

RS: Went to school there, I went up as far as grade eight, then I was supposed to continue my education by coming into Terrace for high school. That didn't happen. So I went as far as grade eight.

EM: So you have this nice picture here that hopefully we can make a copy of. That's you in the picture with some other girls in front of the school [in the old village of Kitselas]? There's a boy here as well. There were boys and girls at the school, right?

RS: Oh yes, boys and girls, mixed.

EM: Grade one to grade eight. Did you like going to school?

RS: One-room school. I liked it, I liked going to school.

EM: Did you want to tell me a little bit about your parents? Were they born around here, grow up around here?

RS: My mom was born in Kitsumkalum. My dad was born and raised in Kitselas. That's where we lived. Right there, growing up.

EM: Did you have brothers and sisters?

RS: I had four brothers.

EM: Were you the oldest — the youngest?

RS: I am the youngest.

EM: So four older brothers?

RS: And I had four sisters. Everyone is gone now; they left me behind.

EM: Oh, well, you're the tough one, the one that is still going. That must have been interesting, the youngest of nine kids. Did you get spoiled?

RS: No, didn't have a chance to get spoiled.

EM: What would have been a typical day — you would go to school — what were other things you would do for fun in the village outside of school?

RS: [Noticeable sigh.] Not much for fun; sometimes we played ball. We mostly worked. We worked hard, doing fish... was our main food.

EM: Did your family have a big garden?

RS: Oh yes, our family had a big garden. Whole family worked on that.

EM: Did you get to pull weeds?

RS: Lots of weeds.

EM: What kinds of things did you grow?

RS: Mostly potatoes. My dad liked to grow everything — turnips, carrots, cabbage.

EM: All those good things that last a bit longer, that you can preserve.

RS: We had a root house there where we kept all the produce.

EM: Underground?

RS: Yes, underground, it works pretty good.

EM: Any fruit trees?

RS: Oh, yes, there's lots of fruit trees.

EM: You got to pick cherries, apples?

RS: Yeah, picked apples, kept them in the root cellar. Kept for a considerable amount of time.

EM: Did you do any canning?

RS: My mom did all that; she does all the canning.

EM: So that and you had fish, your protein. Do any hunting?

RS: Yes, sometimes, get some meat, like deer, or sometimes bear meat, whatever is there.

EM: What about canning meat, is that something you would do?

RS: Yeah, my mom canned meat, too, and smoked some, dried it. They keep for a while.

EM: Lots of work for the kids?

RS: We were always working.

EM: Did you get to go on trips with your parents out in the woods? Hunting trips? Fishing trips?

RS: Fishing trips.

EM: Did you like that?

RS: My dad is very particular about taking us hunting. Because we wouldn't know what to do if we run into something — what we're supposed to do — he has the rifle.

EM: Could be a little dangerous?

RS: So he doesn't take us hunting too much.

EM: But the fishing?

RS: Just fishing. Packed the fish, we did a lot of packing.

EM: Packing it back?

RS: Yeah, on packboards. Dad built one for each of the kids. You know where the Kitselas Canyon is — way up there? That's where my dad goes fishing and then we pack the fish back to the old village, that's about three or four miles down a track.

EM: So you were pretty young when you did that?

RS: It was tough. It was tough. Uh-hm.

EM: You were tough?

RS: Now, I feel all the aches and pains in my body.

EM: Anything else in that community that you would have been involved in as a kid? So you're going to school and you're doing a lot of work. Of course, you didn't have to look after younger brothers and sisters 'cause you were the youngest. Did you do any babysitting for other families?

RS: No.

EM: How long did you live in the village?

RS: 'Til I was 18. I got married at 18.

EM: Then did you move away?

RS: Yeah, I moved out of there and lost my status. I moved to Terrace... Usk, where I used to live, nice place, I knew everybody there, but not anymore.

EM: On the highway side of the river?

RS: The north side, the north side of the river where the railroad track is.

EM: Would you go in and out to Terrace?

RS: Yes, we had a vehicle.

EM: On the old Kitselas road?

RS: No, that's when the highway goes through here.

EM: Did you have to take the ferry?

RS: Took the ferry across and came to town.

EM: What did you come to town for?

RS: Groceries.

EM: Did you have a garden in Usk?

RS: Yeah, always had a garden everywhere. Everywhere I live I have a garden; it's in my blood I guess.

EM: I would think so if you grew up around that. There's still things you can't grow in the garden so you would come to Terrace, coffee and things?

RS: Yes, I still have to come to Terrace.

EM: How was the highway?

RS: Mud, lots of mud on the highway, no pavement yet.

EM: In the 1950s?

Usk Ferry. McRae Collection.

RS: Yeah, in the '50s. Big potholes all over the road. Sometimes we would get stuck in the mud holes.

EM: What kind of car or truck did you have?

RS: A station wagon.

EM: So you would get stuck coming into Terrace? When it snowed, would it be pretty hard to get in?

RS: No, it was better when it snowed, it was easier to get in. It [snow] covered all the potholes because the snowplow went through. It was kinda alright then.

EM: Would there be other things you would do when you came to Terrace, to the movies or sometimes to a restaurant?

RS: Sometimes to the restaurant. If we have the money to spend. All the money goes to groceries. The Silvertip was here, Silvertip Restaurant, on Kalum Street.

EM: It [Terrace] was looking a little different then?

RS: It was starting to grow. Terrace is starting to grow.

EM: Any other places you remember particularly, like the grocery store wouldn't have been Safeway…

RS: Can't remember the name, smaller... right where the Bank of Nova Scotia is, I remember the name: J.H. Smith Groceries.

EM: So, no going to the movies?

RS: No.

EM: The Tillicum Twin Theatre. That's been here for a while.

RS: It's been here for a long time.

EM: Did you have kids — you were talking about when you were living in Usk? You raised a family there?

RS: Yeah.

EM: How many kids?

RS: Six girls and two boys.

EM: Big garden. Lots of groceries. Did you and your husband do any fishing?

RS: Oh yes, we did fishing. He was the ferry operator up there. Did that for quite a few years. Can't remember how many years.

EM: Can I ask your husband's first name?

RS: Willard Seymour.

EM: He was operating the ferry. That would have been something. Did the ferry operate all year round?

RS: Not the ferry, they have a cable car there when the ferry pulled out for the winter season.

EM: So when it [the river] froze up, then there would be cable cars?

RS: And sometimes, we were living up in Usk, we had to walk on the ice, to walk across, that was before the cable car.

EM: You had to walk across. Did you ever drive across?

RS: No.

EM: Tell me about the cable car, how did that work?

RS: There was a tram; you know what the trams are, right? Have a little motor in there, the operator starts it up and then it goes across the cable.

EM: Is it pulling cars?

RS: No, they don't have cars.

EM: No cars there?

RS: There would be people sitting on a little bench in there. The cars are parked on the south side, where the highway is.

EM: So you would come down and sit in this tram, on a bench, then it would be winched across.

RS: Yeah, there's a motor in there that runs the cable.

EM: So how many people could sit on the bench?

220

RS: Maybe three or four.

EM: Not a big thing, but it got you across?

RS: It wasn't a big thing, at least it got you across from one side to the other. It got you across and the car would be waiting on the other side.

EM: Then off you would go to Terrace. Did you ever do any trips going the other way? Smithers?

RS: No, not really.

EM: Down to Rupert?

RS: Only if there's a funeral or something and we know the people, we'd make a trip to Hazelton or something.

EM: Right now when I picked you up — you are living on Kulspai [Crescent]. Do you remember people living there at that time — when you were living in Usk?

RS: No, that's new. I was living in Thornhill when they started up that subdivision where my house is.

EM: You moved from Usk to Terrace?

RS: Yeah, I moved to Usk, then we moved back to Terrace 'cause we had a house on Park, from there I moved to Thornhill, rented a place there.

EM: Then your next move was…

RS: My new house [on Kulspai].

EM: So you were living on Park Avenue then?

RS: Yes, right on this end, the east end of Park.

EM: Is the house still there?

RS: No, that's why I moved out of there. The house was condemned. It couldn't be fixed anymore.

EM: Time to move on, right? Did you ever go to the Hot Springs? Would that be a place you guys would go for an outing?

RS: We'd just go there to look around, then go to Kitimat.

EM: But when you were raising your kids, would you take them to the Hot Springs?

RS: Yeah, we would take them everywhere, but they don't swim, don't stay around long enough to swim.

EM: What about sports, you mentioned in the village that you used to play baseball.

RS: We were just killing time, recess and at lunchtime… then we'd play ball 'til school goes in again. After school, we have to go home and work.

EM: Baseball — that was always a big deal. On Sundays, my parents always had baseball going when they were young. Would you have gone to any of the churches in Terrace?

RS: Salvation Army.

EM: Over on Walsh?

RS: That's where it was. First on Greig, then on Walsh, but now it's on Kalum Street.

EM: Any churches in the village?

RS: There were two, one was the United Church and the other one was the Salvation Army. They're gone now.

EM: Any particular memories of one or the other when you were growing up?

RS: I got married in the big one, the United Church; it was a great big huge church. Had a big fire there. The church burnt down but they managed to save the school.

EM: I've been up to the village but not very much. It's not there anymore?

RS: No, Morris has a picture of that church.

EM: Morris?

Charles and Emma Nelson (Starr), Rhoda's grandparents. Kitsumkalum. 1908.
Yvonne Moen Collection.

RS: Morris Mason.

EM: Somebody from the village?

RS: He doesn't live in the village. I don't know where he lives. He's got pictures. He takes pictures all the time. He must be around in the museum.

EM: Well, again, in these other pictures you did bring this one, you weren't sure who it was [in the photo]. Probably a relative? You would think so if you have her picture. And you're thinking it was taken in Port Essington.

RS: Yea, I'm pretty sure it is Port Essington because of the boardwalk.

EM: And I see a row of little houses all the way along here. This other one, looks like a newspaper article, this is your aunt?

RS: Aunt Miriam.

EM: [Reading from the photocopy of a newspaper article] "Passed away on December 16th at Terraceview Lodge?" but we don't have a date. "At the age of 83 and she was the last surviving child of Charles and Emma Nelson." So this is your mom's sister?

RS: Yeah.

EM: So these are your grandparents?

RS: Yeah, my grandparents.

EM: [Reading] "Charles and Emma Nelson who lived in Kitsumkalum village before the first settlers arrived here." Nice-looking couple. Did you know your grandparents?

RS: I knew my grandmother, not my grandfather. He died when I was still small. I knew her [pointing to photo of Emma Nelson].

EM: Any special memories of her? A hardworking lady, too?

RS: Yeah, hardworking.

EM: Sounds like everybody was.

RS: It says she died when she was 105; she was blind for a few years, for a lot of years before she passed away.

EM: There's a lot of information here. If you want to let Heritage Park take a picture of this…

RS: Yes, read all that, everything… the story is in there.

EM: [Reading] "The couple used to move down to Port Essington for fishing, Emma worked in the cannery in Port Essington." Charles would go out fishing and Emma worked in the cannery. That's an interesting one. I am just thinking — you would have had your own garden. Did you exchange vegetables and things with other people? Now of course, we have the Farmers' Market, of course there wouldn't have been anything like that then?

RS: No, there were no farmers.

EM: So if you had too many potatoes, you'd give them to the neighbours and they'd give you all their zucchini?

RS: We'd put it in the root cellar, in the old village. My dad was still alive then.

EM: In Usk, would you have had a root cellar?

RS: No, just canning.

EM: Maybe a freezer?

RS: Yes, we had a freezer, but we'd find a place to store potatoes.

EM: Do you have any ideas about how Terrace has changed in other ways? What do you think is the biggest change that you've seen?

RS: Skeena Mall.

EM: Getting all those fancy stores in there. Before the mall, you would have had a grocery store, a few other stores? Ladies clothing? Shoe store? A pharmacy?

RS: Yeah, the pharmacy was right on the end of Kalum Street, on the corner of Kalum and Greig. Allan Dubeau was the one that was running that.

EM: Dubeau? Like the French name?

RS: Yes he just passed away, he had the drugstore there. Called it Rexall Drugs. You would go to get... things that were drugstore stuff.

EM: What if you needed to buy clothes or shoes?

RS: We'd find a place. [Laughter.]

EM: Maybe the Simpson Sears catalogue?

RS: Yes, that's right, and Eaton's. I forgot about those guys.

EM: I used to work for Simpson Sears in the catalogue department in Burnaby and it was a big thing. We would take orders from all over BC.

RS: They had a place here too, Simpson Sears — you'd put your order in.

EM: You'd wait a week or two and hopefully it fit! [Laughter.] Where would you would buy bigger things, like washing machines?

RS: No, nothing big like that. There must have been stores here somewhere for that.

EM: Did you have anything to do during the war? You were born in 1931, you would have been pretty young…

RS: I remember — what year it was — I remember the army moved in.

EM: Up where the arena is?

RS: Little Street. That's where the army hospital was, that was our first hospital.

EM: So when you came to town, you would see soldiers in the street?

RS: Oh yes, yes, soldiers all over the place. Even made it up to the reserve, six miles up.

EM: How do you mean?

RS: The old Kitselas village, they would ride motorcycles…

EM: To come and visit, sightseeing?

RS: Sightseeing, I guess.

EM: Any of the boys from the village sign up?

RS: I think there were two that I know of, no three, three guys. They didn't go to war though.

EM: That was a big thing for Terrace when they had a bit of a mutiny. They told them they wouldn't go to Europe, then they changed their mind and said they were. [Laughter.]

RS: Now, that's history.

EM: So your memories are more of seeing soldiers around and noticing that there was something going on?

RS: Yeah.

EM: No fighting in the streets?

RS: No.

EM: I think with all these young men here with nothing to do, there must have been some fights somewhere? Do you remember the Queen's visit to Terrace?

RS: Yeah.

EM: That's how Queensway got its name. Did you get to see her?

RS: I travelled to Prince Rupert to see her. Through one of the clubs in town, the Rotary Club.

EM: You were a young woman by then?

RS: I was. I had kids.

EM: You drove down to see her?

RS: Can't see anything. There were too many people, couldn't see her.

EM: She would have been in a car waving, Prince Philip beside her.

RS: [Laughter.] Oh, yeah.

EM: So you went all the way down to see her…

RS: That club that picks up people had a big bus and that's how we went down. Took my kids down there. We still didn't see her, too many people.

EM: They just paraded down the main street?

RS: Um hum.

EM Well, you got an outing to Prince Rupert. That road was pretty bad, pretty rough?

RS: Yeah.

EM: Took a couple of hours by bus?

RS: I don't know.

EM: People say it took a lot longer to get there then. Is there a particular event, or a particular person that had a big impact on your life? Who would you say was the most important person in your life who had a big influence?

RS: I don't know.

EM: One of those teachers at the school?

RS: Not those teachers. [Laughter.]

EM: Your grandmother? You talk about your grandmother a lot.

RS: There were a lot of people that I like and can't remember their names. Just good friends. Lots of friends.

EM: What do you like best about Terrace?

RS: The new stores that are coming in — interesting to go through them, something new and different.

EM: What was the hardest thing, or the thing you like the least about living up around here?

RS: Too much drinking and drugs; I don't like that.

EM: That's hard for people to live with that in their community. Would you have gone to Kitsumkalum to visit people there?

RS: Oh yeah, lots of relatives, they come from those two there [pointing to photo of Charles and Emma Nelson].

EM: From these — your relatives here.

RS: All the relatives I have at Kitsumkalum are descendants of them. That's where they use to live; they started in Kitsumkalum.

EM: Would they be the ones who moved to Kitselas?

RS: Yes, my dad's always a Kitselas person. They moved to Kitselas when they got married. My grandmother was married before and had 5 kids, all young when her first husband died.

EM: What was your dad's name?

RS: Solomon Bevan.

EM: And he's passed away?

RS: Oh yeah, many years.

EM: What do you think of the village now they have that beautiful kind of museum with all the long houses?

RS: Kitselas Canyon.

EM: Have you been there? What do you think?

RS: Oh yeah, pretty nice, they are sure doing lots of work there, and nice... still not finished... still working... doing other things with it.

EM: Ever go down the walk to the canyon?

RS: Oh, yes, I did and I even climbed up that ramp that they built, on top of the river. I made it up there one time, two or three years ago

EM: Brings back memories?

RS: Oh, yeah [laughter]. I went right down there, to the canyon.

EM: Do you remember seeing steamships go through there?

RS: No, that was before my time.

EM: Sorry, I didn't mean to make you older than you are.

RS: Saw pictures of them.

EM: Anything else?

RS: And I seen those big round rings on...

226

EM: Ringbolt Island?

RS: Ringbolt Island, yeah. Where they pulled the steamships through, they winched them through the canyon.

EM: What about the petroglyphs? Anything you ever heard about those?

RS: I seen pictures. There was one hanging in our administration building, big sheet of rock, pictures on them.

EM: And one is the picture for the library. …You were saying that all your siblings have passed away as well?

RS: Everybody in my family is gone, except me, I am the only one left.

EM: Like you said, you're the tough one, from early on. 105 here we come, like your grandmother.

RS: 106! I'll beat her.

EM: Good stuff. Thank you very much.

Roberta Perry Interview
Interviewed by Andrea Comerford, 21 August 2013

Roberta Perry was born on December 13, 1930, in Prince Rupert. Trying to make ends meet during the Depression, her family moved to Terrace when she was three and a half. There, her family had a hobby farm and her mother opened the popular Corner Snack Bar. Her sister, Freda Diesing, contracted tuberculosis and moved to Kamloops' Tranquille Hospital. It was during her time at the hospital that Freda (a renowned First Nations artist) began doing art. Roberta describes life growing up in Terrace, walking or cross-country skiing to Kalum School, and graduating in a class of four students. She briefly describes the presence of the army in Terrace, in particular one soldier who frequented the Corner Snack Bar for an egg and Prem sandwich. It was at the Corner Snack Bar that she met her future husband. After graduation, Roberta married and had a family. Roberta traveled extensively during her life and has seen many changes in Terrace. With six children, 20 grandchildren and 21 great-grandchildren, Roberta spends her time reminiscing about her travels and enjoying her family.

AC: So Roberta, can you please state your full name?

RP: Well, my first name actually is Mary, but I try and ignore that and just say Roberta Perry [laughter].

AC: When were you born?

RP: I was born on December 13th, 1930.

AC: And, where were you born?

RP: In Prince Rupert.

AC: Why did your family move to Terrace?

RP: Well, it was during the Depression, and the only job my dad had out there was packing coal. He wasn't a big man and it was hard on him. He got a small inheritance from his mother, I believe, and was able to buy 10 acres of land in Terrace and start a little farm. And that's where I grew up, on this little farm down by Braun's Island.

AC: How old were you when you moved to Terrace?

RP: I was three and a half.

AC: Three and a half. So you said you lived on a farm?

RP: Yeah, it was what you would call a hobby farm now. We had our own chickens, cows, and pigs.

AC: How long did you live on that land for?

RP: 'Til 1943 or '44. It was a long time ago. [Laughter.]

AC: Tell me about your parents.

RP: My parents — well, they really did well on this farm during the Depression; vegetables were hard to get. We grew all our own. They were really resourceful; we made our own bacon and ham. It was a really good life. Then my dad became the road foreman. Yeah, we had a good life there. And then, in '43 I believe, my mom decided to go into business, and started the Corner Snack Bar.

AC: Right.

BP: My sister got tuberculosis in '43 and had to go to Tranquille, the hospital for TB patients. She was there for a couple of years and that just left me at home.

AC: Right, and whereabouts was the hospital located?

RP: Tranquille—just out of north Kamloops. I don't think it's there anymore because TB is being done away with now.

AC: So tell me about your siblings.

RP: She was my half-sister from my mom's first marriage. Her name was Freda Diesing and she turned out to be the Native artist. The school [Northwest Community College's Freda Diesing School of Northwest Coast Art] is named after her. And she started her art while she was in that hospital. She started practicing her art and then she went to Victoria and got interested in Native art. So that is what she did with her life from then on.

AC: Right. Back to you coming to Terrace, how did you and your family travel to Terrace?

RP: We had to come by train. That was the only way.

AC: Describe a typical day during your childhood — living on a farm, what sort of responsibilities did you have?

RP: I got up in the morning and milked the cow. Fed the chickens and walked to school — about a mile and a half to school.

AC: A mile and a half!

RP: And in the winter we cross-country skied to school.

AC: Oh really. That must have been nice?

RP: Yeah.

AC: So through rain or shine, you had to walk to school?

RP: Yeah.

AC: Tell me about your school experience.

RP: I went to the Kalum School [Kitsumgallum School] there, for all the 12 years. Seven years, in the one school. And there was a little high school across the gulley. There were 32 of us in grade one. By the time I got to grade 12, there were four of us. My graduating class of '48. [Laughter.]

AC: Okay, so you said your sister was really involved in art. Were you involved in any sports clubs or music groups throughout school?

RP: No, not really.

AC: What kind of hobbies did you have as a child then?

RP: I really didn't have time for hobbies, you know. During the summer, of course, we were working in the garden, picking strawberries. We sold a lot of strawberries. And in the winter, there were other things to do that kept us busy.

AC: So how would you describe yourself as a child?

RP: I was kind of a tomboy.

AC: You weren't afraid of getting a little dirty.

RP: No. [Laughter.]

AC: Can you tell me about your childhood friends?

RP: Well, I didn't have that many. We had neighbours that were mostly our friends because we didn't travel around. There were our friends in school and the neighbourhood kids. In those days, there wasn't any organized sports. There was nothing like that.

AC: Right.

RP: I was in grade five when some people moved from Williams Lake. And one of the girls that was there is still my best friend, and that was from grade five. I play Scrabble with her once a week.

AC: Oh, wow.

RP: She lives up at the McConnell Estates. Yeah, — and her sister who has passed away. There is still Betty and I. There is a picture of us up there.

AC: Awesome.

RP: Judy and Betty and I.

AC: So, do you have any specific memories from school that you want to share — anything that stands out?

RP: Not particularly. I remember when we used to walk to school when I was small, and my feet would be freezing. And the old fellow who was the janitor would take me into the furnace room and take my boots off and warm my feet. I really appreciated that.

AC: But it got pretty cold back then.

RP: Oh, yes. It was a long way for a small child to be going. But, there were no buses in those days, either. Yeah, things have really changed.

AC: Yeah, I'd say.

AC: So, tell me about after you graduated.

RP: I graduated and got married. I had six children. I now have 20 grandchildren and 21 great-grandchildren.

AC: Oh, wow! [Laughter.] Big family, for sure.

RP: Yeah.

AC: So let's talk about your mom's Corner Snack Bar. What can you tell me about it?

RP: It was a meeting place for all the teenagers, and more like bachelors and what-not, and everybody; they had no other place to go so they'd come there. We just served pie and coffee and sandwiches.

AC: So it was quite the happening place.

RP: Oh, yeah, and the girls that worked there were all teenage girls, pretty well.

AC: So, what did the Snack Bar look like?

RP: Oh, it was just a small place with tables and a counter, and it wasn't that big. I think it went in sort of an 'L' shape. We had a Wurlitzer jukebox and the candy counter. I think we might have had five tables, and then the counter with bar stools on it.

AC: So it must have gotten pretty squishy in there at some points.

RP: There weren't that many people around, not like there is now, though.

AC: Did your mom have any special recipes that she made?

RP: She made a lot of cream puffs because during the war [WWII] you couldn't get sugar. That was one thing that took less sugar.

AC: So how would you describe the atmosphere in the Snack Bar?

Judy Houlden, Roberta Perry and Betty Crosina [l-r], outside the Corner Snack Bar. 1948. Roberta Perry Collection.

RP: Oh, it was always happy with the Wurlitzer going! Yeah, it was a good place to be.

AC: You mentioned that the girls who worked there were all young. Did you ever work there yourself?

RP: Oh, yes. I worked there.

AC: So what type of responsibilities did you have?

RP: Well, I got stuck scooping the ice cream for everyone. Because holidays, some of the girls wanted it off — and I always got to work the holidays. [Laughter.] Eventually we got a soft ice cream machine. Was that ever nice! It was the first one in Terrace.

AC: I bet your wrists would hurt scooping an ice cream cone.

RP: I still got good muscles. [Laughter.]

AC: So was it hard with your mom being the boss? Did she have higher expectations for you?

RP: Not really, no. She was a very easy-going lady.

AC: So are there any memorable moments you have at the Corner Snack Bar you'd like to share?

RP: Not really. When the army came it was a little busier.

AC: Yeah, more people coming in.

RP: The only customer I remember is one fellow; I don't even remember his name. We could see him coming and we'd make his sandwiches. He had two egg and Prem [canned meat] sandwiches every day. [Laughter.]

AC: You still remember?

RP: Oh, yeah. I don't know anyone else that ate egg and Prem [canned meat] sandwiches. Well, in those days you couldn't get a lot of things, and Prem was one of those things that was really popular. [Laughter.]

Corner Snack Bar, 1948. Roberta Perry Collection.

AC: Yeah. I bet you got a consistent clientele coming through there. So, you mentioned the military. What was life like in Terrace during the Second World War?

RP: Oh, it got pretty hectic. We had a lot of army around there. But they didn't really bother anybody or anything — except the French army that didn't want to go overseas. They had a riot, or a demonstration. That was kinda scary.

AC: So you said it was a little bit hectic. But how did the presence of the military impact Terrace?

RP: Well, it was good for the businesses. Oh, we had dances and different things like that we wouldn't have otherwise. Mostly it was that the streets were more crowded. It was motorcycles and jeeps and trucks and training all over. Yeah, for a little town it was quite a lot of action.

It didn't make that much difference to our daily life. I was still in school most of the time. When the army was there in '45, I was in high school. I graduated in '48. So I was just a high school kid. But I worked in the Snack Bar after school and on weekends. Otherwise, I can't really remember it being much different.

AC: So as a child, did you understand what was going on?

Geoff and Flossie Lambly, outside Knox United Church. Terrace, circa 1940s. Roberta Perry Collection.

RP: Oh yeah. We were still on the farm when the army was here. We sold strawberries to the soldiers and, once in a while, we had a couple of soldiers down for meals. I remember my mom cooking for them.

AC: All right, so we will move on to reflecting on your life in Terrace. Do you remember what you did for entertainment to keep busy?

RP: Oh, we played a lot of cards and we bowled. There was a big hall down where the curling rink is. The army had built it there. We roller-skated there, and then there was the bowling alley along the side. The soldiers built it there but when they left, of course, the building was still there. So it was our Civic Centre.

AC: Now, I would assume lots of playing outside.

RP: Oh yeah. Baseball and volleyball. Of course, I seemed to be always working and I didn't get too much chance to play. [Laughter.] But I remember roller-skating around that civic centre down there.

AC: So, you worked a lot. How much was the normal wage working at the Corner Snack Bar?

RP: I don't remember. I doubt if I even got paid. I don't remember really what the girls got. It wasn't a heck of a lot anyhow. All I remember is when I came back to town after my divorce in 1950, I started working and it was five dollars an hour.

AC: Wow. [Laughter.]

RP: You know, the prices of everything have gone up so much that five dollars went further [in those days]. I bought this house.

AC: You were saying you lived here for 32 years.

RP: For 32 years. I bought it in 1980. Yeah. I was 50 when I came here.

AC: What dreams and goals did you have when you were a young girl?

RP: I always wanted to travel. And, after I came here, every chance I got, I travelled. You know, I've been all over Europe and Australia. I've been from Inuvik to Costa Rica all the way, in different stages. Yeah, it was good.

AC: So, what is your favorite trip you've gone on?

RP: Oh, New Zealand. It is the place where everything is so different and yet it is something like home. I've never wanted to go to places like China. I wanted to go to places where they mostly spoke English. [Laughter.] And I've been to pretty well everywhere I wanted to go. Now, I can't travel too much with my walker. I can just sit back and remember where I've been.

AC: That's good. So, other than travelling, what's on your bucket list to do?

RP: Oh, just stick around and enjoy my great-grandchildren.

AC: So, during your childhood and teen-hood, were you allowed to date?

RP: Oh yeah. We always had some boys hanging around the Snack Bar. Because it was all of us young girls working there. There wasn't that much to do except go to a show. Go to the theatre.

AC: So throughout school, were there strict rules with the boys and the girls playing together?

RP: Yes, they were separate. Like in the Kalum School there, it was the boys on one side and the girls on the other. In the basement part, our play areas were right separate. Come to think of it, we never thought anything of it. It wasn't until we got to high school that the boys and the girls played on the same baseball teams or whatever.

AC: So what would usually happen if the rules were broken throughout school, playing with boys?

RP: In those days, I can remember the boys getting the strap.

AC: Wow, things have changed. So speaking of boys, did you ever get married?

RP: Yes, I got married. I was married for 32 years.

AC: And how did you meet your husband?

RP: In the Snack Bar. His parents moved up from Prince Rupert to Terrace, and he was working in the lumber mill. We got together and got married. We lived in a little house where the [Park Avenue] Medical Centre is now. That was our land there at one time.

234

AC: So, you said you met him at the Snack Bar? Did he work there or was he a customer?

RP: He was a customer.

AC: So you started to notice him coming in more and more.

RP: Oh yeah. That's about it. [Laughter.]

AC: Tell me about how he proposed to you.

RP: I don't really remember. We just sort of talked it over and we decided that was the thing to do, I guess. He wasn't the romantic type.

AC: So, what about your wedding? Do you remember anything special about your wedding?

RP: We went to Prince Rupert and we were married in the Anglican Church in Prince Rupert. We didn't want to have a big wedding because my mom and dad were so busy. So, we went down there with just our immediate family. And then we went on the train to Edmonton for our honeymoon. All I can remember about Edmonton is going to the big fancy theatres with all the plush and velvet.

AC: When did you get married? What year was that?

RP: In '48. I graduated and then got married.

AC: Let's talk about your mother's Aboriginal background. How big of a role did your Aboriginal heritage play in growing up in Terrace?

RP: Mine didn't make any difference at all to me, until my sister got into this Native art. And in those days nobody even talked about anybody being Native, you know. My mom was just half and I am like a quarter. So I am hardly aware of it. I'm half English.

AC: So, it was just your sister getting involved with the art.

RP: Yeah, since she's been gone, I've had to fill in at the school when they decided to name that art school after her. I've had to go and represent the family.

AC: All right, let's move on to life as a female. Growing up, what kind of expectations were there for girls?

RP: I don't really remember any expectations. We all just went to school and did our thing. Some of them went on to be nurses.

AC: So, did you feel you were equally treated with the boys?

RP: Yeah.

AC: How did your mother cope with running a successful business as well as caring for her family?

RP: By the time she got into the business, we were pretty well grown-up — more of a help than a hindrance. She just loved people and being around them, seeing people every day. On the farm, she was kinda lonely, because we didn't have any real close neighbors or anything. She just loved it when we got into business. They never made any money on it but just kept going. Everything just went back into equipment.

AC: So let's talk about your children. You said you have six children. And what about your grandchildren and great-grandchildren?

RP: Oh, they are scattered all over. I've only got one grandson in Terrace and a granddaughter in Hazelton. She has a nine-month-old baby now. They bring him down quite often, but the rest are scattered all over BC and Alberta.

AC: So let's talk about this article you found here.

RP: 'The Life Chronicle' — it just tells that my mom married Frank Johnson. He was a Swede and they had their first child, Freda. And I had a brother named Frank who passed away when he was 16 from a heart condition. They told him that he had rheumatic fever when he was two years old and they said he would never grow up because his heart was so enlarged. There was nothing in those days they could do about it. I was 14 when he died. The next year Freda got TB, so that's when we decided to go into town.

AC: As a long-time resident of the Terrace area, do you notice anything that has specifically changed?

RP: When we came here, there were 19 licensed vehicles [laughter] and they all had to be brought in by train. Yes. When we moved here, there were no sidewalks. There were gravel streets. Things have really changed. But it is still a nice little town. You know, it's not that big yet.

AC: Have you ever considered moving?

RP: Well, we moved to Smithers for a couple of years, then came back. We had a farm out in Kitwanga — Woodcock — for 18 years. We were actually out there for most of the time. That's where I raised my six kids, was out there. One girl is still on that farm. The oldest girl is in Kitwanga, just on the highway on a farm. My son is still in Kitwanga. So it wasn't bad. My two oldest boys have passed away with heart attacks, and the other girl is in Williams Lake, so I don't see her too often, either. It was a good place to raise kids. They were all quite happy there.

AC: Do you have any advice for the present or future residents of Terrace?

RP: I am not very good at giving advice. No, I think Terrace is just going to be fine. We are going ahead and our crime rate isn't that bad — not what you hear about other in places. And our weather is a lot better than most places in the world.

AC: That's true.

RP: We don't have any hurricanes. Well, the odd flood, but only near the river. We were flooded out in 1936 for a couple of weeks. We had to move out, but we survived that too. I can remember that. I was only six years old, but I can remember we had our garden all planted and it was underwater. And after the water went down, things weren't in rows anymore; there were mixed vegetables all over, but they grew good.

AC: They got their dose of water.

RP: They were well-watered!

AC: Is there anything else you would like to share?

RP: I don't think so. They've got a lot of my mom's things up there at Heritage Park. Like when they had that lady do the Ma Lambly play, and I don't know if it was this coat she's got on. I gave them a purple velvet coat that was her favorite and it hung in the closet here for years. I didn't know what to do with it, so finally I took it up when she came in on that play. So it's up there somewhere.

AC: That must have been nice. Did you watch the play?

RP: Oh yeah, I've seen it twice. She does a really good job.

236

Roberta Taron Interview
Interviewed by Veronica Kurz, 26 August, 2013

Roberta Taron was born in Prince Rupert in 1947. Roberta's mother was raised in Terrace and moved her family back there in 1952. Roberta has a large extended family that resides in the Terrace area, including ties to the Desjardins, Johnsons, and many other early lineages. Roberta married and had five children. After raising her children, Roberta worked as an office clerk until she retired. In this interview, Roberta recollects growing up on South Kalum Street with her mother, father, and 10 siblings. She reminisces about her childhood spent swimming in the Skeena River, playing with the neighbourhood children, going to school, and attending large family reunions. Roberta also talks about the Queen's visit, popular downtown locations, Lakelse Hot Springs, and the racism towards the First Nations and Portuguese communities.

VK: So, first of all, when and where were you born?

RT: I was born in Prince Rupert, in 1947.

VK: And what brought your family to Terrace?

RT: My mom was raised here and my dad decided… They decided to move. So they moved to Terrace in 1952.

VK: Tell me a little more about your parents.

RT: My dad — his dad worked on the Canadian National Railway [CN] and his mother was Scottish. They lived different places up and down the railway; at different times. Up, sort of north of Smithers, there's this place called the Highroad, I think it is.

VK: Oh, the Telkwa Highroad?

RT: Yeah! They lived there and my dad used to tell me that he would ski to school and carry the skis home. Mom's family came here when my mom was four. That was in about 1921. And they came out here because Grandpa Desjardins loved to try new things and to roam. So he came out here first and Grandma came with all her kids later, on the railroad, and set up here.

VK: Excellent. What did your parents do for work?

RT: Well, Mom stayed home. In those days most women stayed home. Dad worked for Terrace Transfer. He was a bookkeeper. He had two jobs because he had a lot of kids. So he worked for Terrace Transfer and he also worked for CN railway. And then when CN railway found out that he was working for Terrace Transfer, they saw that as their competition, so he lost that job.

VK: Did he find a different job after?

RT: Yes. He did bookkeeping for other places. Parker's Motors was one of them. Then in 1966, they moved to Kitimat and he got a really good job there.

VK: How many siblings did you have?

RT: I had 10 siblings.

VK: Ten siblings! So eleven all together?

RT: Yes!

VK: Wow! So what was your relationship all together?

RT: Well, Mom was so busy just doing the cooking, the cleaning, all of that. We were pretty well left to our own devices. It wasn't so much our siblings that were the group; it was more the whole neighbourhood. The whole neighbourhood would do things together after school and at night, all the time.

My siblings — I had two older brothers, two older sisters, and they were pretty close to each other. My younger siblings were kinda young [laughs], so I guess I was kind of a loner in the family.

VK: So, the only one in the middle there?

RT: Yeah.

VK: Okay. Can you tell me a bit more about the neighbourhood? You mentioned the South Kalum gang. Can you tell me a little about that?

RT: Yeah. Actually, about 10 years ago, Terrace had a reunion and there were quite a few of us there from South Kalum Street. We just had so much fun talking about it. We said, "We should have gotten together," which we did.

There were lots of kids in the neighbourhood and most of the moms were at home and it was really a community. Like, the moms were friends with each other, helped each other. It was a lower income neighbourhood. All kinds of different people, so I had friends.

I had one friend whose name was Tally. She was Dutch. Her mom and dad met in the war [WWII]. She was a war bride. And her cousin Leidy — same thing. Who else were my friends in the neighbourhood? Different people that moved different times.

Those were the ones that I remember did a lot together. So, we all had our friends but also we'd often, almost every night, we'd play baseball, or kick the can, or one hundred up. Everyone — like the teenagers, the little kids, the middle-aged kids — we all played together all the time. We had a lot of fun.

And I was telling the people at that little reunion. I said, "One of my fondest memories was listening to our moms call us home at nine or ten at night, you know: 'SANDY! PIERRE! BETTY ANNE!' " And she'd be yelling really loud. But I still love that sound in my head.

VK: All the parents calling you home?

RT: Yeah.

VK: Great. So, what schools did you go to?

RT: I went to Riverside, which was near the curling rink. It had been… a lot of buildings in Terrace were barracks. And so the school was just like barracks. I think it probably was except they were quite long. Anyway, it was a very old building and it was a fun school to go to.

VK: Were there lots of kids at your school?

RT: Yeah. It was a fair size. Our classrooms were probably like 30 kids.

VK: And that was for a single grade?

RT: Yes.

VK: What grades did that school go to?

RT: It went from grades 1 to 6.

VK: Where did you go after Riverside?

238

RT: After Riverside, the Catholic school was built. So for grade 7, 8, 9, and 10, I went to Veritas. And then some of the mothers talked with the principal of the Catholic school. She was a nun, and she talked about sending us to a Catholic school for the last two years. So five of us went out to a boarding school in Saskatchewan run by the same sisters — the Sisters of Saint Joseph.

VK: What was that like — traveling so far from home to go to school?

RT: Oh! You know. At that age — you're 14, 15 — it's a great adventure. And I was terribly homesick, so homesick. But at the same time I'm so glad I went there. It was a great experience. I got to see Prairie people, how they lived. And it was very different from how we grew up. Yeah, it was a great experience.

And I got a first-class education. I found that out when I went to university classes not that long ago. The grounding I had in my education was just so solid.

VK: Wow. That's excellent.

RT: Yeah.

VK: So the people who didn't go over to school in Saskatchewan, did they just stay and finish up their grade 12 here?

RT: Yeah — they went to Skeena.

VK: So, you talked a little bit about memories of school. Are there any others that you wanted to share?

RT: Oh, so many! I have so many memories!

VK: You can write a book?

RT: [Laughs.] I was smart in school but I was also a rebel, so I used to get kicked out of class.

VK: Oh, really?

RT: Oh yeah. I got the strap once.

VK: Oh! They still did the strap back then?

RT: Oh yeah. And they didn't hold back either.

VK: [Laughs.]

RT: I had blood blisters on my hands.

VK: Oh my goodness!

RT: But you know what? Like, it was a priest who did that to me. But he was the nicest man. And I deserved it. I had kind of gotten a little rebellion going, and I had taken off from school and came waltzing back and, you know, thought we'd get away with it. He was really upset. But yeah, I didn't hate him for it. We did all kinds of things back then. You know, life was a lot freer back then.

VK: That's for sure.

RT: You know, kids could go anywhere. I was a girl. I could go anywhere I wanted — by myself. No problems. No worries. And nothing ever happened to me.

VK: Yeah. Definitely different.

RT: I think we were lucky to have lived when we lived.

VK: Definitely. So what was your friend circle like when you were growing up? You had your friend circle living in your neighbourhood — how did your friend circle grow and change through school?

RT: You have your friends at school and you know, you go to their birthday parties and they come to your birthday parties. But we didn't have playdates. Our moms and dads didn't drive us anywhere. We wanted to go somewhere, we had to walk there by ourselves.

And my circle of friends… a lot were cousins. I had one cousin I was really close friends with all through school and we did a lot together. So, it was cousins and then kids that I was in school with. I'd go to their place sometime.

I learned to skate at one of the residents who's been in Terrace here forever. Her name is Linda Frank. She was Linda Norberg. We went to grade school together and I learned to skate at her house, you know. Different things... We had no skating rink. We had no swimming pool. [Laughs.]

VK: So you had to make your own fun?

RT: But I learned how to swim at the river!

VK: Wow. That's nice. So tell me more about your extended family; I know you have a very large family. I know you're related to the Desjardins, Cotes, Kofoeds, Johnstons, Normandeaus, McConnells, and Renauds.

RT: Right.

VK: What's that like growing up with such a large family?

RT: It was a big part of my life. You know, our cousins were our friends. We hung out lots together. As I said, this one cousin and I were best friends.

The moms were so busy. They rarely got together to visit and when they did, you know, once in a while… Maybe a few adults would come over for tea, and they were so happy to be together because it was so rare.

But my Uncle Ted Johnston had — they called it 'The Ranch.' And it was way out on Kalum Lake Drive. He had cows there, and hayfields and that. Anyways, once a year he'd host a family reunion; we called it a family picnic. And we'd all go and they'd have races for us, and prizes for us, and it was just a great day. It was so much fun! Yeah, things like that, you know, were rare. A day or something the adults organized for us. So we really liked that.

VK: Wow! So that was usually once a year that you guys did that?

RT: Once a year.

VK: Wow. So, how many cousins would be at these reunions?

RT: Well, I don't know how many. They probably counted at different times. But, we had about 150 to 160 of us. There would probably be about a hundred cousins there.

VK: Wow! Big event! [Laughs.]

RT: Yes! [Laughs.]

VK: So, can you tell me a little bit more about your grandparents? You mentioned when they were coming to Terrace, but do you know a bit more about them?

RT: Well, Grandpa did different things. He mined. He was usually gone and so Grandma was kind of the anchor of the family, and she was very innovative and had foresight.

240

She had a huge vegetable garden and flower garden, and she would sell fruits and vegetables and flowers at the train station. And she bought land around here. It was really cheap back then.

She bought land in town. She owned the land where the two malls are now. She owned a huge piece up on the Bench, and she owned a huge piece or two out in Thornhill here. She visualized what Terrace has become, really.

VK: When was it that she was purchasing land?

RT: Probably the '30s and '40s.

VK: Wow. So when Terrace was starting?

RT: Yeah. Well, Terrace started earlier than that but that was when Terrace was really starting to become a town.

VK: Yeah, for sure.

RT: Yeah. The Depression didn't really hit up here. You know, the Dirty Thirties? Yeah. 'Cause I used to talk to Mom about that.

You know, in those days, people did their own things… their own food and things like that. And so Terrace was okay, you know, because there was no drought here. They could still sell lumber then, so they did okay.

VK: So a little more self-sufficient.

RT: So, what else can I tell you about Grandma Desjardin? I just really admire her. I think she was a woman of real foresight. And she really worked to get the Catholic Church here.

VK: So did your family identify as French-Canadian?

RT: Pretty much. Mom was. All my aunts were. My dad wasn't French-Canadian, but they were over there working.

VK: Were they able to speak French?

RT: My mom did. She'd speak French to my aunts on the phone when she didn't want us to know what she was talking about. [Laughs.] But we didn't learn. I learned in school and for some reason I caught on pretty easily to French. But no, we didn't learn it when we were young.

VK: How did growing up with a French-Canadian family shape your experience living in Terrace?

RT: I think the fact that we were a very large family was the main reflection that we were French-Catholic. But there wasn't the racism then that people think of now.

The racism was a lot with the men, you know. But in our neighbourhood, we were all alike. And you heard some sort of racist things like 'Wop' and 'Dago'. But to us kids, it was nothing, and by the time we had grown up, that had died right out.

My dad's dad was Italian and he figured it would be better to be known as French. So he changed his name from Larossi to LeRoss, which isn't in any way, shape, or form, a French name. And when my mom was talking to my grandpa she tried to say LeRoss. I can't figure out where that name came from and they didn't know until he died that he had changed his name.

VK: Why did he think that French would be better than Italian? Was there a reason for that?

RT: There was less prejudice.

VK: Okay.

RT: Because I know… I remember when I was pretty young and there were a lot of Portuguese people coming to town. You know, it was kind of a derogatory attitude to them. People were more xenophobic back then than they are now.

VK: So, just a bit more about adulthood now. Did you get married?

RT: I did.

VK: And how did you meet your husband?

RT: Oh! I was working with his sister, in the bank, and they gave me a ride home one day. And that's when I met him, and he asked me out later.

VK: And did you have children?

RT: I did. We had five children.

VK: Wow.

RT: Big family — it was considered a big family. I really enjoyed raising my children.

VK: Did you have boys and girls? Or what was the mix there?

RT: Yes, I had a boy, a girl, a girl, a boy, and a girl.

VK: So what was there to do with children in Terrace?

RT: When my children were growing up, there was actually lots to do. There was all kinds of lessons — swimming lessons, dance lessons, sports, you know. We had a TV. There were no computers or Game Boys. Thank goodness. TV was bad enough. [Laughs.]

VK: So what jobs did you work in your time living in Terrace?

RT: I didn't work when I was raising my children. I had a husband who did not want me to work, so I didn't work. Then I was divorced and I took a business admin course. So I had, you know, office jobs. But I moved away from Terrace for five years and did quite a bit of office work. Came back, did some office work before I retired.

VK: So a bit more about recreation and fun stuff. What did you do for fun in Terrace growing up as a teenager, into your adulthood? What kind of things were there to do?

RT: Sure. Well, we didn't talk about how we used to swim in the river much and that is my absolute favourite memory. The Skeena River has changed course several times since then. But when I was a child, at the end of South Kalum Street, there was a slough. And then there was a bridge across it. And then a huge field. Because of the slough, that huge field was called Little's Island. And they had cattle on there, and there was an old slaughterhouse there.

So you walked about, almost a mile down the dirt road, and came to the river. And every spring, it would be different down there. Sometimes there would be big deep pools of water in the sand and there were gravel bars. But there was always an inlet from the river where we could swim. It had a nice sandy bottom.

It was over our heads in the middle. It wasn't too far across and we all knew — we were all very well-schooled — not to go past a certain point. And you know, no one ever did. That's how well trained the kids were in the days.

242

We were considered lucky in the town because of where we lived in — on the hot summer days, because we had the best place for swimming, unless someone took you to the lake. And I learned to swim down there. It was just wonderful.

I was telling a story the other night about how I had gotten my new school shoes and my mom didn't want me to wear them, and I wanted to wear them 'cause I was so proud of them. Normally we'd walk bare feet in the summertime. We didn't even wear shoes most of the time. So I took my shoes down there and when I went to leave, the shoes weren't there. They had disappeared. And I was just frantic — it didn't even occur to me that someone had stolen them. Nobody did things like that then. But looking back, I mean, they just disappeared. Anyway, so we had to walk home, and it had taken me so long to look for the shoes that we were in a hurry.

Little Island. Anne Anson Collection.

We would never walk across the field. We would always walk on the main road because there were bulls and we were worried about getting chased by the bull. That's a bit of a story, I think. Anyway, so I'm barefoot and walking across this cut hay... It was so sharp, it was like walking across ice picks. And my brothers and sisters played a joke on me. Said, "Run, the bull's behind you!" And so here I am, running across saying, "Ow! Ow!" and so scared. [Laughing.] Such a great memory now. [Laughing.]

VK: Oh my goodness.

RT: And other things that we did... Okay, when I was older, as a teenager, there was usually a dance at the Odd Fellows Hall or somewhere else. And we'd always go to a dance. We went to the movies, and we'd have house parties.

VK: Did you go on dates?

RT: Yes, oh yeah!

VK: What kind of places did you go to?

RT: We had a drive-in — a food drive-in here called the Sportsmen Drive-In.

VK: Where was that located?

RT: It was about where the craft store is. They had the best mushroom burgers and milkshakes — just great. So we'd go there. You know, the normal things. You'd go on a date, go to the movies, and go to the drive-in. They had a drive-in movie here then.

VK: Oh wow. Where was that?

RT: It was down on Keith [Road], toward the end of Keith there. It was a lot of fun!

VK: I bet. What kind of movies do you remember seeing?

RT: [Laughs.] I don't really remember the movies.

Lakelse Avenue, circa 1950s. The Way We Were Collection, via Terrace Public Library.

VK: Just whatever was playing?

RT: There were Elvis movies then.

VK: Oh, really?

RT: Yeah. He made a lot of movies, really. He was my favorite movie actor. I remember one movie, from a little early in my teens. It was called 'Shane.' It was so sad. It was a cowboy movie. It was so sad!

We used to go get to the Saturday afternoon matinee here and it was always a show that kids could watch. Well, I think most shows were those days.

VK: So what restaurants were popular over the years? You mentioned that drive-in.

RT: Oh, we often would go to a place called the Silvertip Cafe. It was on Main Street. What's there now? Nothing. Across the street from Don Diego's. Yeah, we'd hang out there when we were teenagers. We'd sit there and drink coffee.

You know what happened there one night? I wasn't there. One of my cousins was friends — I was friends with this guy too — but they used to have pretty strong drinking parties. So anyway, this guy… His name was Carl. I won't tell you his last name. And they'd been drinking and they went —

244

the Silvertip was a place people went after the bar closed. And for some reason, they had a fight with the Chinese guy who owned it and the Chinese guy followed him outside, and this guy killed him. This Carl killed him.

VK: Really? Oh my goodness!

RT: That was such a shock to all of us.

VK: I can imagine.

RT: He went to prison for quite a while.

VK: Oh my goodness.

RT: My cousin stayed in touch with him.

VK: Wow. So did you visit the Lakelse Hot Springs at all?

RT: Oh yes.

VK: Can you tell us a bit about them?

RT: We were all so excited when Mr. Skoglund was building it. And it was a top-notch place — people would come there from all over the world. He really did well on getting it known. My sister worked out there; she loved it. When she went out there, she couldn't swim at all, and she became a really good swimmer.

VK: What did she do up there?

RT: She worked in the restaurant. She made lifelong friends working there. Yeah, it was a really good group. And we loved going to the hot springs. It was the first place where there was a diving board, and I loved to dive.

There was an outdoor pool, and there was quite a hot indoor pool. And it's never been as nice when they redid it. It was just kept pristine clean and it was just thriving. It was huge. It was the motel, the hotel, and the pools and yeah…. Because Mr. Skoglund — he was a very successful logging contractor — he had a lot of money to put into it.

VK: And did you go to Lakelse Lake a lot?

RT: I do. I love going to the lake. I think Lakelse Lake and the Skeena River are the best things about Terrace. I love the river. I love walking by it. And you know, when I was a kid, we didn't get to go to the lake much — maybe once or twice in the summertime.

When I was raising my children, if I got up and the sun was shining and it was summertime, I would plan to take them to the lake. Because lots of summers there would only be four or five or six days you could do it. And yeah, I always took them to the lake, and now my daughter always goes to the lake. It's a real wonderful place we have. I think there are things about Terrace that are just awesome.

VK: So you'd bring your family out to the lake. Would you ever go with friends and bring all of your families out as well?

RT: Sure, we've had different get-togethers out there. When I was a teenager, there was a huge campsite where the picnic site is. And so, you know, groups of us teenagers would go, and the girls would have one campsite and the boys would have another campsite. And we'd sit on the beach in the evening and then — sometime in the early '60s, maybe 1963, '64 — there was a slide that came out from under the mountain that totally destroyed the campsite.

VK: Can you tell me a bit about sports in Terrace? Did you play any sports or go to any sporting events at all?

RT: When I was growing up, in school, we had a lot of sports. I played baseball. I loved baseball. Then, when I was in Veritas, I was on the basketball team. And we were a brand new team because it was a brand new school, and Skeena [Secondary, now Skeena Middle School] was the only high school. Skeena had a team and then the Civic Centre had a team. So the three teams would play off against each other, and yeah, it was lots of fun. And Veritas won, even though we were the new ones.

VK: Did you get involved with fishing?

RT: Not really. When I was with my husband, sometimes we'd go fishing on the river from Ferry Island. Or we'd go out to the [Prince] Rupert highway. Mostly, I'd just sit there and enjoy the nature. I'm not involved with sports. I've caught a few fish, but it's not really my passion.

VK: For sure. Were you involved in other community activities outside the home like clubs, or organizations, or anything like that?

RT: Mostly connected with church and things like that. I'm… you know, I was a real churchgoer. And I did lots of things to help raise money for different things. One time I went around and spoke about our transition house, the house on the South Side for homeless people. And I spoke to about three church groups and we ended up raising, like, three times as much money as we needed. Because I told them that it was the only one in the whole Northwest area. It was the only place that had homeless people. We did things like that, you know, did lots of fundraising things like mini rummage sales and bake sales.

VK: So, you did attend religious services?

RT: I did. I was a good Catholic and yeah — the priests we had over the years were really good priests. We never really had any of the bad ones here. There was one who had been… It had been said that he was not a good priest. But as far as I know, he was kind of on his last legs when he was here, so he didn't actually do anything.

VK: What local events do you remember celebrating?

RT: May Day — it's Victoria Day now, but we used to call it May Day. And we would have a maypole dance, and to do the maypole dance was such a high point. I did it a couple years in grade school 'cause our school would be really involved in it. So the teachers taught us, you know. You'd dance around and weave a ribbon around a pole — pretty little girls in their pretty little dresses. It was like princess time.

VK: Of course.

RT: [Laughs.]

VK: Was Canada Day a big thing back then?

RT: No.

VK: Not really?

RT: May Day was a big day.

VK: The big one.

RT: It was before Canada got a flag or any of those things. So, it was still kind of the whole British feeling, you know… heritage. I remember when Canada got the flag. I was in grade 11. We all designed flags and one of the kids designed a flag with a green maple leaf on it.

VK: Oh really?

RT: So we were close.

VK: Very close.

RT: Yeah.

VK: Did you have Riverboat Days back then?

RT: No. I'm trying to remember when we did have a parade — maybe it was Canada Day. I just can't remember. I remember when the Queen came to Terrace.

VK: Oh, you were there?

RT: I'm sure you've had lots of memories of that, right?

VK: We have a photo or two of that.

RT: Oh, yeah!

VK: So you were there when she came?

RT: Yes!

VK: Oh, tell us about that!

RT: Well, they paved Queensway Drive because she came. I was standing by a boat near where City Furniture is.

VK: How old were you at the time?

RT: She came in '57, so I was 10. I was standing there with my mom and dad, and brothers and sisters. And she was coming in this convertible, and she was waving, you know — how the Queen waves. And no one was waving back to her. And I knew you were supposed to wave, so I waved and she looked right at me and gave me a wave. I was thrilled! [Laughs.]

VK: That's great!

RT: Yeah. And [Pierre] Trudeau, and Maggie [Trudeau] and Iona Campagnolo came here in the '70s. I used to have pictures of that. That was a big thing. Yeah. It was quite thrilling to actually see Pierre Trudeau. He and I talked. We had a little chat with Margaret Trudeau. My friend said to her, "So, are you enjoying your holiday?" And Maggie said, "Holiday? Are you kidding? This is really hard for me!" [Laughs.]

VK: How have the events changed over the years? Of course, May Day isn't celebrated as much anymore.

RT: Well, Canada got a stronger identity. So Canada Day — it's not that big in Terrace. BC day is the big day in Terrace — congruent with Riverboat days. And Riverboat Days celebrates Terrace.

VK: So, a bit more about the community… What do you remember about downtown Terrace?

RT: I remember everything. I was thinking about how you could take the history of Terrace and start with the river where I swam and then, you know… 'Cause I used to walk to school every day — walked to and from school.

So where Tim Hortons is now was Pongratz corner. The Pongratz lived in the house there. And then just up a little ways from there was Clair Giggey. Giggey was a big… you know, an important guy. He was something in the sawmill. And then the pole yards, just before the train tracks.

That whole block that's kind of semi-industrial now, that whole block was just pole yard. And there were sawdust burners. And there were big bee hive burners, and they were so pretty at night when the sawdust was burning. I used to think, *Oh, a dress in that colour would be so pretty, that sparkly red.*

And then, just across the tracks, was the old Co-op. When I was a kid, they still had the bare wood floors that were soaked in kerosene, and I loved the smell in there. Mostly they sold men's jeans. It was such a boring store to look at.

There was Rexall Drugstore. Sometimes I'd have to go for my mom to pick up a prescription or something. Then there was the Silvertip Cafe.

Across the street was the newspaper office and the Five-to-a-Dollar store — kids' favorite store. It was big. It was huge, you know. It had two floors. And upstairs was clothes and that, and downstairs was everything you could imagine. Mr. Duffus ran it and he was the nicest man, really nice. Everyone knew him. He was the mayor for a while. And his wife was a teacher.

Then was Fred Smith's grocery store, same side as the Rexall. That's where Mom bought her groceries. And we were so poor, you know. She'd have to charge her groceries. And she had known Fred Smith when she was growing up in Terrace, so he was really kind and he would let her charge. And she was always stressing about owing him money.

And then kitty-corner, at Lakelse [Avenue] and Kalum [Street], was the little RCMP [Royal Canadian Mounted Police] building.

Across the street from that was Johnson and Michael Hardware Store.

Oh, and I forgot to tell you about the Terrace Hotel, which was where it is now basically. But it was just a ramshackle old wood building then. And Geeraerts used to have for a while in the late '60s, I guess, a radio show there in the morning.

VK: Oh really?

RT: It was really good! I can remember really enjoying it. Mrs. Geeraerts would be on there talking, just like a morning radio show. Yeah. And then where that big sporting goods store is… Just down from there was the Odd Fellows Hall.

And there were other things along there, but the one I remember was — I'd walk to school that way to go to Riverside, and there was the little cafe everybody knows about that's up at Heritage Park, Ma Lambly.

VK: Yeah. The Corner Snack Bar.

RT: Yeah!

VK: Did you ever go there?

RT: Oh yeah!

VK: What was that like?

RT: Mrs. Lambly, she was a big woman and she'd stand behind the counter, and… You just loved her. Everybody loved her!

248

You know, when I was a kid and I had no money, and I'd go in there and she'd treat me really nicely. And I used to like going in there because she was really nice. And then her husband was really little and kind of wizened. They were really nice people, so popular. And they had a little counter where the checkout thing was and there was candy there. And then down here was a snack bar with stools.

VK: Did you go there when you were in your teens?

RT: I don't think it was there anymore in my teens. I think it was in the 50's, mostly, that it was there.

And the other place that I went to a lot, along there, was… What was the United Church? A church for a while there, you know — the bigger building that was called the public building then. And I don't know if the city had their stuff in there? And the province? Maybe, 'cause I think that I went there for needles, too. But in the basement was a library, and I went to the library all the time.

I had read everything in the library by the time I was in grade 7, I think. Couldn't find anything more to read. You know, in those days, there were classics and there were some really old fashioned books. And so that's what I read.

VK: Where did you guys shop for clothes, or furniture, and that kind of thing?

RT: Well, we didn't shop for clothes. We wore hand-me-downs. We were fairly poor.

Friends of Mom's from Prince Rupert… She lived in Prince Rupert. So we'd be all excited when we got a box of clothes and we'd go through it. And I was kinda heavy, so nothing my age ever fit me. So that's why I learned to sew. I would take, you know, older ladies' stuff and cut it down to fit me. And I learned to sew that way.

Furniture — we never had new furniture. When I was little and we lived in Rupert, we were better off. My dad probably had a better job. And he built a house and it was really nice. But I think he really went into debt, and that's maybe why we moved to Terrace. Maybe he went bankrupt or something. We never really knew. But I remember when Dad had an easy chair, and when Mom got it recovered it was, like, a really big deal.

VK: I bet. Did you shop at the Terrace Co-op?

RT: Actually, like I say, we rarely got new clothes. But once in a while, most people ordered their clothes from Sears. Simpson Sears we called it then, because they were the cheapest. And I remember once, I got a pair of jeans and a plaid shirt, and I was just so excited. Yeah, that was a big deal.

VK: As an adult, what did most people that you knew do for work?

RT: Lots of women worked in the offices. A few women might have taken some sort of unusual kind of jobs. My sister worked for Pacific Northern Gas in the office. And she fought and fought to be able to work out of the office, you know, on a truck, and get paid way better money like the men did. And she managed to do that.

VK: Good for her.

RT: Yeah, yeah. Nurses, teachers, you know.

VK: Did you have any friends or family who were farmers?

RT: Like I said, my Uncle Ted. He wasn't a farmer — partially he was a farmer. But in Terrace, there weren't a lot of farmers. There were some around the corner from us when I was a kid. There was a huge farm, and the people worked really hard, and the lady was bent right over from farming all her life. But most people bought their groceries at the grocery store.

VK: What role do you think forestry and logging played throughout the history of Terrace?

RT: Huge. It's not so huge anymore, but it was the main thing from the time Terrace began right through my marriage. My husband was a faller, and all the best jobs were in the bush — highest paid. And then it ended, you know.

VK: Did you have any other friends or family who worked in the sawmill aside from your husband, or logging?

RT: Working in a sawmill is different.

VK: Or logging?

RT: Yeah, sure. Most of the people we knew, you know. 'Course, we made friends with the guys he fell with and their wives. We were all real good friends. We were like a circle of friends, right.

Yeah, working in a sawmill was completely different. It wasn't as well paid, but it was just great. Because a guy could come to town and have no experience, no training, and he would go to work on — they called it the green chain in the sawmill. That was kind of the 'in' to getting to work there. And yeah, when I was a young adult, before I got married — which wasn't a very long time — it was so easy to get work. A man or a woman.

Me, I worked in a restaurant. I was a waitress. You could quit your job, walk down the street, and get another job in those days. It was no problem getting jobs.

VK: How did the community of Terrace interact, if you know, with Kitselas and Kitsumkalum?

RT: I don't know. When I was growing up there was no division then — I mean, that we were aware of. Like, our neighbourhoods were mixed, our schools. We all went to school together. We were all friends together – 'specially in our neighbourhood. And you know, we weren't really aware then of tribes, and rights, and all those things. It hadn't started yet. It didn't start until the late 60's or early 70's, I guess. Yeah.

VK: How important do you think the First Nations culture was in shaping our community?

RT: I think it's really important. It wasn't important when I was growing up, but it is. You know, I'm really happy that First Nations people have been able to form their own identity and feel good about where they come from — just like any other group would feel. And they're able to feel proud of it, and they get support from it, and that's the way it should be, for sure.

VK: Definitely.

RT: Yeah. The racism I saw in the '50s was not in my neighbourhood, or our mom's. In my mom's, they were all friends. But I saw that men, the working men, were racist. I would hear, you know, racist words, and I never liked them. And my mother was very anti-racist, you know, the opposite of racist. She was aware of that side of things and she really was an example to us — that wasn't okay.

VK: How did the construction of the new bridge impact the community — especially connecting with the South Side there?

RT: It did really bring a lot more business to the South Side. You know, there was nothing here except housing and it was the 'wrong side of the tracks' kind of idea — wasn't really a big deal but it was a little bit.

It was better to live on the other side of Terrace. We Southsiders loved it, loved where we lived! But yeah, when the south bridge came, then of course, it started bringing more businesses in that corridor. And it was Walmart that really changed it a lot.

And low-income housing… That all kind of happened at the same time. So it's a lot more densely populated down there, and there's more crime there now since that whole thing happened. Before that it was very quiet — single family dwelling kind of a place.

VK: Have you lived in Terrace during any of the major floods?

RT: I don't remember any major floods when I was a kid. The major thing that happened as an adult was — there was a huge slide that happened on that [Prince] Rupert highway that killed the eight people. That was really big to all of us.

VK: When did that happen?

RT: That happened, I think, in the 70's. And you know, I knew one of the people that was killed. And it was a real shock because there was a little restaurant in the path of it. And yeah that's some of the people who died.

And there have been more floods in the past — what 10, 15 years? — than before. My sister has flooded badly twice. She lives on Skeena Street.

The flood that happened that was extended all down Graham. We all blamed the City for that because the City built some kind of wall or something out there in the river. I forget, my brain is fuzzy. That changed things a bit because it flooded where it had never flooded before. And where I lived, where I grew up, where I raised my kids, it was considered a floodplain, but it was never ever flooded there.

VK: How has the flooding impacted the community, do you think?

RT: Actually, people were really good. They really pulled together and helped people. You know, I was really impressed in the way people responded in helping people with the flood.

People who get flooded, they are aware that it could happen. They know that they are in a floodplain, and it has flooded before, because it always floods in the same places, you know. And it's terrible and upsetting. But, you know, they are aware that it can happen. They take that risk.

VK: Did you garden or grow fruit at all?

RT: Yeah a lot. I was of the hippy generation. And my mom always wanted to garden, but she never really could because she had a husband who wouldn't plough the ground for her.

And then in the very early '70s, you know, I said to my husband, "I'd like a garden." So we started with a small garden and we got more and more and more. And we gardened about an acre of vegetables and that. We had fruit trees, and raspberries, and strawberries. And we had chicken and geese sometimes. And yeah, we lived pretty close to the land because we'd get a moose every fall. Raised chickens to eat, as well as for eggs. Ate a lot of fish.

I used to can, and jam, and freeze them [laughs], a lot! But it was a good life. It was a really good life. Yeah, I enjoyed it.

VK: Did you ever sell any of the stuff that you grew?

RT: You know what? You couldn't give it away. People were so used to buying stuff clean and debugged from the grocery store. In those days, unless you were some kind of hippy or whatever, I guess, you didn't appreciate home-grown things. Because we were organic; we didn't use any pesticides. We didn't even use any chemical fertilizer or anything.

VK: Did you have friends or family who also gardened?

RT: Not like we did. I had friends who did, you know. It was something that just some certain people really wanted to do and did it.

VK: Do you ever go to the Farmers' Market?

RT: Oh always. I love the Farmers' Market. I think it's one of the best farmers' markets that I've been to in BC.

VK: For sure.

RT: I'm really glad Terrace has it.

VK: Can you talk about how it's changed over the years?

RT: Oh it's really grown. But Terrace, the kind of people who live in Terrace, really embrace that kind of thing, you know. They appreciate the natural kind of things you can buy, homemade things you can buy. There have been people there — like the fudge lady — who have been there forever. The friend of mine, the girl whose yard I learned to skate in, she's there every week. She sews and knits.

VK: Nice. How do you feel our community and region have been represented, on any level — locally, provincially, nationally… that kind of thing?

RT: Well, Terrace has always been NDP. So I think nationally, you know, you don't have a lot of power when you're a minority party. Provincially, we did pretty well when the NDP got into power, but that wasn't for very long.

And of course, you know, Terrace has always taken the backseat to the Lower Mainland. The Lower Mainland — I mean, in some ways, we support them; we pay for their benefits almost, in certain ways. But I'd still way rather live up here. It's worth it. [Laughs.]

VK: Definitely. So, more generally, how has Terrace changed over the years?

RT: It's grown a lot. The personality hasn't changed that much though.

VK: Really?

RT: No. We're from the South side, and there's still a separation — kind of — between who's important and who isn't. And that never changes. But I think each is happy in their own way. I've never been on the important side and I don't really care. So, I wouldn't say it has changed a lot.

I mean, getting the college here has been a huge thing. It's been a real advantage in so many ways to have a college here. Things like that.

VK: So just looking back a bit when you were a child, what did you expect or hope to accomplish in your adult years?

RT: I used to dream of going to New York and becoming a famous author, which is, I mean, pretty trite, I think. One of my daughters dreamed the same thing.

I thought I'd be a teacher. As far as ambition though, I don't think I was ever that ambitious. I don't think you think that seriously about it when you're a child.

VK: Was there any particular person or event that had a major impact in your life?

RT: There have been people. The one that I think of, on the top of my head, is Bishop O'Grady. He was a bishop of the Catholic Church at the time, and he was just a wonderful man who could talk to anyone. He has just the best reputation. He really cared about the Natives before a lot of people did, you know, back in the '50s and '60s and '70s. He was very well known, and loved the First Nations people as well.

Roberta Taron, 2014. Roberta Taron Collection.

And, you know, he was really involved. And he knew me and I knew him, and I was one of how many? He was a bishop of a huge area. But he offered me a full scholarship to university — because he knew I was pretty good in school — if I would agree to be a frontier apostle for five years. I decided not to. I didn't want to commit to it. And that was a good thing because I was very immature. That was really affirming for me for him to do that.

VK: And has anything else had an impact on your life?

RT: I'll tell you one impact. It's just a little thing, but I went away to boarding school and I came back, and I said to my little sister, "Let's go to the Island." She said, "There is no island." I said, "What do you mean!?" And the river had changed its course and destroyed our summer resort. And that really bothered me because it was, like a whole chunk of my childhood had been destroyed. So that was a big thing to me. But that's the only thing that I can think of that was.

VK: Do you have any advice for present or future residents of Terrace?

RT: The advice is to go for lots of walks, and really appreciate where we live. If you've lived in Vancouver and you come up here… I never forget how fresh the air is to breathe here compared to Vancouver. Never mind, you know, China or Korea.

And there's so much beauty here — whether it's raining or sunshine-y or anything, it's a beautiful place to live. To me, that's the best thing about Terrace — just being here. And I mean, I've never been a mountain climber. My mom climbed all the mountains around here. I never have but I can still sure enjoy the mountains, the river, the lake. Yeah, that's the best part of living in Terrace.

VK: Are there any other stories you'd like to share?

RT: I'm all talked out. [Laughs.]

VK: Well, thank you so much.

Roy Nelson Interview

Interviewed by Sarah Komadina, 15 December 2013

Roy Nelson was born in Port Essington in 1925 and grew up in Terrace. Roy remembers his mother raising the children, cleaning, and cooking. She also baked bread for the entire family and sewed most of her children's clothing, all of which she did without electricity. His father had a career in the logging industry and worked for George Little. Roy remembers that his father built a six-room house on Park Avenue. At the age of 15, Roy followed in his father's footsteps and began his career working at Little, Haugland and Kerr's sawmill. Roy never married. In the interview, he states that he was, 'supposed to get married about a half a dozen times,' but 'had lots of fun running away from marriage.' Roy spent time traveling to Vancouver, Seattle, and Montreal. He lived in Montreal for 30 years before returning to Terrace in 1987. In this interview, Roy recollects his childhood, his family, working in the logging industry, and living in Montreal. He also shares memories of the great Terrace flood, George Little and his wife, WWII, and living life as a bachelor.

SK: Do you remember quite vividly what the great flood in Terrace [in 1936] looked like?

RN: Oh yes. I used to see that in the magazines as a joke, but it was no joke what I saw going down the Skeena on the roof. Just below the Skeena Bridge there were a lot of houses. Down the edge of the river, you know. They all got washed out and they were well back from the river. So much land was lost. And the milk farm — what was the name?

They had lots of land down Kalum, just above Kalum Bridge. All their land was just on the river side of the tracks. There were orchards there. And the guy who lived down there too — he had a bunch of sheep but the barn was above the tracks. So he lost land but he didn't lose any animals. Frank's Farm. They supplied the milk for Terrace for many years.

SK: As kids, did you get on that bridge or were you all too scared to go up?

RN: Oh, we were all too scared. It looked like it was ready to go any time because the bridge was just shaking. It's a wonder it's still standing. I guess it was well made.

SK: Were any of your houses affected?

RN: No. My aunt lived down on Kalum Street there. We found a fish in the well because the river was that high.

SK: How long was the river high?

RN: Quite a few days. And we all had to go down to the coast that summer. We all wanted to go because that's the year Mom died. And there were no trains, of course, no trains for a long time.

There was nothing under the track, no land. It was just hanging there. And these gas speeders, they call them… Dad put us on one of them and told the guys where to take us and let us off. He went down the river on a boat, and that is where he picked us up. The river was really high. So much land was lost. The Skeena wasn't that wide.

SK: Before?

RN: It was very narrow and it was all on the opposite side from us. But so much land is lost. Yeah, I'll never forget that. Us kids were saying, "Oh no, we won't go. We won't go up there." But that was the first thing we did. We couldn't wait to get up there. We ran all the way.

I'm glad we did. We got to see it anyway. I stayed up on the road, and that road was packed too. A lot of people lined up watching, waiting for the bridge to get washed out. [Laughs.]

So we never lived down in Kalum. Dad was the only one that lived there and my mother lived down in Port Essington. She went to school there because Port Essington was kind of a big settlement at one time. It was built for the riverboats. It was the main port for the riverboats down at the Skeena.

And it burnt down. I was in Montreal listening to the news and all of a sudden the news cut out. And "What's going on here anyway?" And it finally said, "Port Essington is on fire." I almost bawled, you know. I liked the place — old houses, old style homes — and what a waste.

SK: That's sad. What's your clan Roy?

RN: Raven.

SK: Can you tell me a little about your grandparents and what their role was in Kitsumkalum and how they came [to Terrace]?

RN: Grandpa had a big house down there, and most of the family lived there. But Dad — he was working in town here and so he built a home. Grandpa bought land and then he wanted Dad to live there, and you always did what Grandpa said. [Laughs.]

Anyway, the older girls got married and it was just Dad and me and Bunny. I used to rush home from school to cook for Dad, and then Bunny took over. She couldn't even reach the top of the stove.

SK: Wow.

RN: So Dad built her a little stool and it was good. It was a fair-size stool, just high enough for her to get onto.

SK: So she could cook?

RN: That's what she stood on to cook.

SK: What kind of things did you guys cook?

RN: Regular stuff like everyone else did in Terrace. Of course, in the summer Dad used to go fishing with his brothers and the women put up a lot of canned salmon, smoked salmon, and salt salmon. That I loved. The rest you could have it.

SK: It's so good. So did you grow up in Kitsumkalum or Terrace?

RN: Oh no. I grew up in Terrace. I was born in Port Essington because Mom always went down there in the summer to be with her mother. Grandma was getting old. She wanted to spend some time with her, so Dad would stay in Terrace. He was working there. George Little owned the mill then so Dad started to work there.

SK: The infamous George Little…

RN: And my grandmother worked for him. She would clean house. She would carry that baby Little on her back while she was doing housework. [Laughs.] She told me all this. I can just picture it.

Oh Mrs. Little was quite a woman. Her nose was up in the air all the time. She looked down on everybody. She was the only one that had a car in Terrace and she used to speed it up to scare us kids off, you know, and we would all scatter.

SK: What did the car even look like?

RN: It was a model T, I guess — older than that. A model A…? I don't remember now what the older cars were.

SK: What did your mom do while your dad was working? Did she work as well?

RN: No, not in Terrace here. She was busy looking after kids and cooking, putting up food; Mom was a very good cook and, of course, she had to make bread. She made 12 loaves at a time. She supplied bread for the whole family.

SK: And that would be your grandparents and your aunts and uncles that she would supply bread for? Did you live in a house with your parents or did you live in a house with other relatives as well?

RN: Oh, no. We let Dad build a house and we all lived in our own home, on the acre that Grandpa had bought. The street we lived on was called Cory Road at the time, which is Park Avenue now.

SK: What did the house look like?

Charles Nelson Sr., with Roy Nelson on his lap at Kitsumkalum. Harry Richmond and Charles Nelson Jr. are in the doorway (ca. 1925). Adeline Turner Collection via 'Landscapes in Transition: Perspectives of a Tsimshian Matriarch,' Brenda Guernsey and Adeline Turner, May 2006, Living Landscapes, Royal BC Museum. http://royalbcmuseum.bc.ca/exhibits/living-landscapes/northwest/tsimshian_matriarch/index.htm.

RN: It was a six-room house, and all the lumber Dad bought from Little, Haugland and Kerr. Dad planed the lumber himself, and the shingles — made the shingles because they were all made of cedar, you know.

I used to watch him. There would be a slab there, I guess they were only about that deep. [Shows depth with hands]. And when he was ready, the slab was off and trimmed, then he'd go like that with his thumb. [Shows with hands again.] Up goes the shingle and he'd glance back at me and trim the other side. And it had to be done fast because the machine was fast. And he trimmed his thumb a few times and his thumbs were big. [Laughs.]

SK: How many kids [were there]?

RN: Well there is Charlotte, Addie, and me, and Bunny.

SK: So four?

RN: But there should have been 12 of us; all passed away from the measles when they were very young.

SK: What was that like for your mom?

RN: I think that's why she enjoyed going down to Port Essington to be with her folks. She wasn't very happy here in Terrace. She liked Terrace but the family was pretty hard on her. They expected too much from her because she used to do everything, you know. She'd never buy anything. All the girls' dresses were handmade. My shirts were all handmade.

Mom was a half-breed. She was part Irish, and her father died when she was just a baby. Because she never saw him... She was just too young, you know. Because it was right after she was born that her father died.

SK: Was she born in Port Essington?

RN: She was born in Port Essington.

SK: How did your mom and dad meet?

RN: It was arranged. Them days all the marriages were arranged. But it turned out very good for Mom and Dad. They were a very loving couple.

SK: That's different, hey. So they ended up loving each other. But for other families growing up, did you ever notice tension because it was arranged?

RN: Oh no. Because they all got married… They were all arranged too when they got married.

SK: And so did that carry on in the next generation as well — the arranged marriage?

RN: I was supposed to get married about a half a dozen times. I ran away each time. I wasn't going to go through anything like that.

SK: Did you ever get married?

RN: No.

SK: And so where did you run away to?

RN: I went to Vancouver, Seattle… I was all over.

SK: And you spent some time in Montreal too?

RN: Not at that time.

SK: No?

RN: Montreal. I always wanted to go to Montreal because that was the biggest city in Canada. And I wanted to see the biggest city in Canada.

SK: And you stayed there once you went to see it?

RN: Yeah, well… I had a nervous breakdown after Dad died and my grandmother and old Dr. Mills said, "Roy, you better get away from Terrace. Get away from here. Get away from the family for a while."

I was always working and it seemed like the whole family depended on us. My uncles… none of them worked. They were a lazy bunch. Dad was sure different. He worked hard all of his life.

SK: That makes for fun conversations though. So when you started working in Terrace, what kind of work did you do?

RN: I worked for Little, Haugland and Kerr in the sawmill.

SK: And what job did you do in the sawmill?

RN: First I worked cutting slab wood because the slab would be thick at one end and very thin at the far end. And some of them are very heavy. So there was always somebody around to give me a hand because I couldn't lift them myself. I was only 15 and you were supposed to be 16 before you worked at all.

SK: So why did you start work early?

RN: I quit school. And Mom told Dad, "You make sure he goes right through school." So Dad tried. And he finally gave up and let me quit school.

I went to grade 8. I quit school at Christmas time and I didn't even tell Dad. Addie was living down on Kalum and I went and I hid out at her place.

SK: Did she let you? Did she give you a hard time?

RN: Nope. She was hiding me.

SK: So when you weren't working and when you were out of school, what kind of things did you do for fun?

RN: Oh, there was a lot of things. There was always the park. We used to play ball there. And in the winter that would be all covered with water and we used to get heavy rain falls just before freeze up. And that park there was just all ice. So we used to skate there and we would build a bonfire. And somebody would always bring wieners. Dad always got me wieners to roast. I guess he would do that because Little, Haugland and Kerr had their own store and they used to sell all of this stuff and I would say, "Get some wieners, Dad..."

SK: You would be skating in the wintertime. Did you play hockey?

RN: No. We just skated, chasing each other around. And this was all ice — not here, a little farther going west. But they dug that ditch here just below the Bench and that's what drained the water out of here. This place used to be filled with ducks, geese — in the winter, in the fall, in the spring. As they were going north, they all stopped here to rest.

SK: So with this development that has happened, do you kind of miss what it used to be like?

RN: Oh do I ever! Sometimes I wish I was back in those good old days. [Laughs.] It was a hard life. I know when I started work, I didn't realize it was going to be that hard. And Dad told me, he says, "You know you can't go back once you quit. You got to keep going." I remember him telling me that, so I thought, *No, I got to keep on now. I got to stay working.*

SK: Were you upset that you stopped school and went to work?

RN: Later years... I am paying for it now. I should have went to school. [Laughs.] Because working in the mill... It's not how it is today, you know. It's all push button... those rollers... You pushed the log, put the log on a little thing like a carriage, and then you had your big saws there.

SK: What did downtown Terrace look like when you were growing up?

RN: Kalum Street was the main drag. That's where all the stores were — and hotels. Terrace Hotel has always been at that corner near the tracks. And grocery stores — two big grocery stores... And then there was a hardware store. ET Kenney — it wasn't ET Kenney then. It was something else. And right at the corner on Kalum and Lakelse… It would be the southwest corner … There was a hotel… a bank — Montreal Bank there.

And there was a fishing sports store.

SK: Did you fish growing up?

RN: I did because the family moved down to Port Essington when I was five years old. Dad quit working in the mill here and he moved down with us. Because he had a home that belonged to his father. There was a reserve there at the end of Kalum — Port Essington — so all the natives stayed.

And then that fall I was turning six, because my birthday is on September fourth. Dad had a boat built for himself and that put his finances way back.

At Christmas time we didn't have nothing. Dad couldn't even afford to buy me anything at all. I believed in Santa Claus. And that year, I was told that there would be no Santa Claus. So Mom was crying. "But there will be next year," she said. "We're not going to be like this all of the time. Dad will find work."

Dad did. There is Ecstall River running down by where Kalum is, Port Essington is. It's on the opposite side from the tracks, you know. There was a big sawmill there. It was how everything got built. That is where all the lumber came from that started Prince Rupert. And farther up there was the falls and that's where Rupert got their power from. And it's still there and they are still getting power from it.

SK: So when did you move back to Terrace?

RN: Mom got TB, and her older sister, her children all had TB. And Mom used to go there and help her sister-in-law out. Dad says, "Don't go near that house. Stay away from it."

No. Mom was that kind of person. Anybody that needed help she would go and help, you know. A kid got sick and was throwing up blood; she was just full of blood. Dad really got mad. He said, "We had enough of this. We are going to go back to Terrace." So we packed things up and we moved. Then Mom got sick. We managed to get back to Terrace.

I was… How old would I be then? I was very young, anyway. Yeah. Maybe I was around 7 or 8.

It was hard on Mom and on Dad. When we got back to Terrace, Dad went back to work with Little, Haugland and Kerr. And then he was working for [Clair] Giggey too at the same time. He was hauling poles, cedar poles. This was the centre of cedar pole country. There was lots of money in it, too. They were for all the lights, you know. Those poles were for electricity.

SK: So, did you experience a time without electricity?

RN: Oh yeah. It wasn't 'til the war broke out… Oh by the way, I was called up for the war when I was 18 and half. I went down to the little mountain and, of course, we all were standing in a row. We were given numbers and certain things were handed out to us. I thought for sure I was going to go overseas; I wanted to go. All of my friends, a bunch of us, left Terrace at the same time. All of my chums… They all passed but I got rejected. Because I was very nervous and high strung and they wouldn't take you in the army if you're nervous and high strung. You might shoot yourself or shoot somebody else. [Laughs.]

SK: But not going to war… Now, do you look back on it and go, "That's Okay?" Or do you still wish that you would have gone and gotten selected?

RN: I wouldn't have gotten into the war, but I might have been stationed there, you know, and help get everything settled. Because that's what the soldiers did after. They went there, like Germany… There was always a big army from Canada there, and the States, to keep everything under control.

SK: So what did you do instead? Went back and worked at the mill?

RN: Oh, I was working for Giggey when I got called up, so I went back to Giggey for a little while.

SK: Who was Giggey?

RN: He had a lumber mill too and he had a pole yard.

SK: How long did you work in the mill for?

RN: Oh, that was my first job working in the mill. It's all I did here in Terrace. And anyway… I could have went back to school after the war. Wouldn't have cost Dad anything because when you were off the reserve them days, the government didn't help you. You were on your own.

SK: Was that difficult?

RN: I'm glad we never lived on the Reserve because long before that… the Nelson family were the only ones who still had a house in Kalum, and my uncle Gordon had a house. The whole family would go down there in fishing season and they would can salmon, smoke salmon, salt salmon.

I didn't care too much for salt salmon; it was just a little too salty for me. I liked it, though, when Mom made hash with it. You'd get all the salt out of it. You had to keep changing the water. And it's made with salmon, mashed potatoes, and onions, and a few other things. And I don't know all the spices that Mom was using then but that used to be good. Mom would bake it like a loaf…like a loaf of bread, and it was good. She would make a sauce — especially a carrot sauce — that would be good with the salt salmon.

SK: Do they still make salt salmon now anywhere?

RN: Not that I know of.

SK: A lot of things have changed?

RN: A lot of things changed. Even had a smoke house on Cory Road and when I left here, Addie took the place over because I didn't pay for the land tax anymore. I said, "To hell with it. I'm getting out of here. If they want the land, they better pay the taxes."

So it went up for tax sale and Addie bought it. Addie was working all the time. She was working different restaurants. She was working housekeeping and different jobs. She was with Ed Wulff at the time… So they got together and bought the land, and then they sold it to build a store across the river.

SK: Is the store still there?

RN: It's still there but it's not a store anymore. I don't know what the heck it is.

SK: Did you ever visit the Lakelse Hot Springs?

RN: Oh yeah. There is a big story about that. I didn't tell you about myself…?

As a kid I always had arthritis, you know. I guess I was born with it. When I was going to school here, Dad would carry me a ways to get to the hot springs. He would make a hole in the mud, put me in the mud, and cover me up with it — hot spring mud. Oh, that felt so good.

When Dad took me out of it, I still couldn't stand because I was so weak from sweating. I just couldn't. Dad still had to carry me. But after that I stayed feeling good for quite a while, you know.

Go to school…it's a wonder I got as far as I did. Because I missed a lot of schooling.

Mom used to teach us kids. If any of us had to stay home, she would teach us. Them days, the women never went to high school. Very few women did but Mom went to high school in Port Essington. Because Port Essington was quite a settlement. It had the high school and from grade 1 to 8… So there was two schools there. And the Japanese had their own school and in the big building…

Port Essington was quite a settlement. One part was Native and the English part was where all the stores and stuff were. And then you went down to Chinatown and the Finland town — because there was a lot of Finns there and they all had boats…sailboats then. And you want to see it.

It used to amaze me. I used to stand on the waterfront, watch the tugboats take them out where they were going to fish, and all in a row like that. The wind blowing the sails, you know... Oh, it was quite a sight. I wish I could see it again.

SK: Did you have any children ever? I know you weren't married.

RN: No. I never married, no. But I brought a lot of kids up. I did bring all Addie's kids up.

SK: So you had quite the influence on your nieces and nephews?

RN: Oh yep. Christmas time was a big time, of course — for all of us. I would be busy buying Christmas stuff for 'em. I was eight years old when Bunny was born. Dad more or less brought Bunny up because when Addie got married she had her own house down on Kalum. The house was still there.

SK: Did your mom pass away?

RN: Oh yeah. In 1936. I will never forget that. I wanted to die at that time. I was just a kid, you know. But one of the nurses there that was looking after my mom, held my hand tight. I was trying to get away. I was trying to jump on the coffin. She wouldn't let me go. I cried for days after Mom was buried. Mom was a beautiful woman. You wouldn't even know she had Indian blood in her because her father was a white man, Irish man.

When Port Essington was built a lot of people from Kalum moved down there. And the guy that built the town gave the natives land… And it's still Indian land. So we thought that was pretty good. As far as I know, it's still under the Indian Act, maybe not now… I don't see why it should be because there is nothing there now, from what I understand.

I wanted to go over there and see it when I first came home but was always busy doing something else. I had lots of time, but nobody seemed to want to go over there that had boats.

SK: So you moved to Montreal…what year did you come back to Terrace?

RN: '87.

SK: And when you came back, did it look different?

RN: I didn't reckon the town. The town was a little village. Even the Pentecostal Church was on Lakelse Street… like, where it is now... I don't even know where it is now! It's one of the bigger churches in town here.

SK: So it grew significantly?

RN: Oh yeah. Well, the war broke out. That's when Terrace first started to change.

During the war, this was a big army camp here — up on the Bench, on Park Avenue. That was all army huts. And on top of that, that level where all the homes are, that was all army houses. Up here Terraceview, that was all army houses there. Where else? Well, they had little bits here and there, you know, around town, just on the edge of town.

SK: And you came back and it was blown up. It was expanded.

RN: It expanded right after the war because there was always lots of work here. Mills were busy. Because right after the war, everybody was crying for lumber. So they could build, you know. A lot of lumber was shipped overseas. That's where a lot of it went.

SK: And you came back from Montreal because your sisters were adamant on making sure you came?

RN: Yeah. "Come home. Come home. We want you home."

Oh what a dull life! I was out dancing every night just about and I had to go to work early in the morning, and I would have a hangover. I would just have a little coffee and that was it. And by noon I was always hungry. There was lots of work in Montreal, you know.

SK: Did you learn French?

RN: A little bit of French I remember now... All I can remember are the swear words. [Laughs] Of course, that is the first thing that people learn. And you know, I never swore before I left here. I never swore. Once I got to Montreal, that's all they used was swear language! I boarded with a family there. They were talking and, all of sudden, somebody would swear and they would go on and on.

SK: And you lived there for 30 years and you came home to Terrace. What was that like? Was it an adjustment?

RN: Oh yeah. Because the mall wasn't even there [in Terrace]. The Catholic Church was right there on the corner. And just beyond, past the Catholic Church on Eby, there was a French family. There's a lot of French people here. It was English and French.

SK: And were your sisters quite happy that you succumbed and came home?

RN: I don't know, but I got used to it. I'm glad I came home after a while, you know. I still went out dancing here. I was in my 60s enjoying myself.

SK: Where would you go dance?

RN: In town!

SK: Yeah, but where?

RN: The Legion was going strong and there was the Oddfellows Hall. And there was that hall down on Kalum. We just passed the tracks there…. What's the name of it now…? It's always rented out. When I turned 80, the girls all got together and held a surprise party for me.

SK: Was it awesome?

RN: It's all on tape. I should take that tape down to the Happy Gang and show them.

SK: And so how old are you now?

RN: 88.

SK: 88. So what do you do now? You spend a lot of time at the Happy Gang?

RN: Oh yeah. I joined the Happy Gang right away, anyway, when I came home. There wasn't such a thing as the Happy Gang when I left here.

SK: Is it fun? Do you guys get rowdy?

RN: Oh, we used to. It's dull now as far as I'm concerned! [Laughs.]

SK: There could be more dancing?

RN: There should be. And there is a lot of music and there is a lot of musicians in this town, you know. And you think on weekends they would do that. But no…

The kids run wild. We didn't have time to be bad like that. There was lots of work to be done.

Those days, there wasn't such a thing as power. Everything was wood and coal to keep warm and cook with. I don't know. I liked the woodstove for cooking. Everything tasted good.

SK: Yeah! So when you're living without power, what were the nights like? Was it really dark? Was it comfortable?

RN: It was comfy. Everybody had gaslights…something like that. It was a cloth, a special kind you called a mantle. It was just by gas and then it sparked like this.

And after school, we had to do our homework around coal lamps. I had one because they come in handy if the power is turned off for a little while.

SK: You still have one?

RN: I still had one, but maybe it's gone now, I had it there. I used to keep it there, but it's gone now.

SK: What are some fun stories with your parents when you were growing up?

RN: Oh with Dad... Like I told you, he worked hard all of his life because in the mill days, you had to work hard. And Dad would get off work… We would have our supper and then Dad would sit in his chair and he would fall asleep. He was so tired and he would hear us playing. Then he would come…used to play ball with us. Anything we were doing, Dad would join in too! [Laughs] We had a lot of fun with Dad. I just wish some of the kids had fun with their Dad like I did. Him and Mom sang together in church choir.

SK: What Church?

RN: United.

SK: In Terrace?

RN: Uh-huh.

SK: Were there any popular restaurants that you used to go to?

RN: Oh yeah. There was that Longs... and that's all on Kalum. Like I told you, all the restaurants and stores were all on Kalum and Lakelse. Didn't go very far though on Lakelse coming this way. It didn't go very far. It was mostly all homes on Lakelse then.

SK: Were you in any other sports growing up?

RN: Baseball… I used to like baseball. I played a lot of baseball. There was football but I didn't care for it. I played and I quit. Then I rejoined and quit again. And bowling… I enjoyed bowling at George Little Park, which was where the bowling alleys used to be.

264

SK: What about local events? Do you remember any significant town parties or things like where they are celebrating in the streets?

RN: Twenty-fourth of May was a big day here. First of July, of course.

SK: What was the twenty-fourth of May?

RN: Queen's birthday.

SK: Oh! Sorry.

RN: And Labour day, of course…. And a special train used to come from Rupert to Terrace. People from Rupert came to Terrace. There were baseball players, dancing in the evening. And there was a lot of sports going on. For kids…there was a lot of games for kids. So things weren't so dull, you know. They were lively.

SK: What school did you actually go to when you were there?

RN: See that old school down on the highway there, that old building. That's where I went. It's on the highway. It's part of town. That belongs to the school board, that property. It's used for offices now. There are four big rooms there – grade one and two had one, three four, five six, seven eight. And then just north of that, there was the high school.

SK: One last question I have is, as someone who has lived in Terrace and learned here, what is something you would like to share with someone who has newly moved to Terrace? What do you want them to take away from the community?

RN: I feel sorry for the kids today. All they do is on the computer. There's nothing there. They don't enjoy life like we did. There was so much to do. What would happen if all of sudden — everything, the power, was turned off? What would the kids do? I often think that, you know. What the hell would they do anyway?

SK It would be chaos.

RN: That's for sure.

SK: I think there is a respect difference now, too...

RN: When I was kid. It was like, "Yes Ma'am. No, Ma'am." And then there was the "Sir." And to think I used to pray at the table too! [Laughs.] Now I don't know how to pray. [Laughs.] What a difference. I enjoyed life. I had lots of fun running away from marriage. All the things I did…! [Laughs.]

SK: Six people you ran away from. That's funny.

RN: Mom didn't believe in it, so whatever Mom said went. Dad had to go by it, so he wasn't pressuring me. It was the grandparents mostly.

SK: Were they upset that you didn't go through with any of them?

RN: I guess so. I don't much care.

SK: Life would have been different, hey?

RN: I wonder what would have happened.

SK: It would have been different, for sure.

RN: I worked for over 10 years for Columbia Cellulose here, cruising timber. They taught me the trade and I did a lot better than the kids that took it up in school. All they did was get lost in the bush. We had to go out and look for them. I enjoyed that work. We had to map the country, take elevations.

SK: That was here?

RN: That was what I was doing until I left here, and Dad worked until he got sick. He had heart trouble. That's what he died from.

SK: How old was he?

RN: He would have been 50. He died in '55. He would have been in his late 50s anyway. I'm not sure. And Mom was only 35 when she died. But they died young. Them people died young them days.

SK: What year were you born?

RN: 1925. Good year, good month, good day! [Laughs.] That's why I know how to run.

There's only one girl that I met after all the running was over. She was very pretty. From Rupert. I met her on the first of July, because there was always something going on here the first of July. It was a big day here.

Sarah Komadina and Roy Nelson. December 2013.

Then they had Riverboat Days. I don't even see the kids doing too much. There was always a lot for us to do.

Allen Dubeau and Edith Lofeudo were king and queen on May Day. All dressed up and they both had crowns. They had a special car for them so everyone could see 'em and they could wave to people. They had better floats them days, too. Now they got nothing — all a bunch of big firetrucks tooting their horn.

SK: Not the same.

RN: Things are so much different now. When I think back of my younger days, I don't think I would like to relive them, but it would be nice just to see it.

SK: Definitely.

RN: And my TV. I can't play the movie they took of it, you know. I got it here in the bedroom.

SK: Of your eightieth [birthday party]…?

RN: Yeah, my eightieth. What a time. I have had two big days here.

After that, they had a big party for me at the Happy Gang, I knew that was coming. There's people from all over — from Rupert, up the line and down the line.

SK: It was a special day!

RN: There was a few people that are still alive that I went to school with. Shortly after that, they all passed away. Allen Dubeau just passed away and he's younger than I am. I was even younger than his older brother. He was even younger than I was.

I am an old man. If I'd known things would have gotten this tough, I would have never gotten old, and I would have stayed young my whole life. I locked it up and threw the key away.

I went to big time — this was right after the war — and there was a big hall still where they play bingo now, but way back closer to the river. That's where the soldiers and the army had a big hall there — to practice doing different things, you know. So after the war there was a big dance there. They used it as a big dance hall. Good music too! Full band. Not just like the little thing they have now — just a guitar and violin. Everybody played some kind of music. I never did get into it. I love music.

SK: Music is good.

RN: Music in the family. Dad always played the guitar. Mom played the piano and what do you call this thing…where it stands and…?

SK: The harp?

RN: She had one. But she couldn't take it to Terrace. It was left in Port Essington after they got married. She doesn't know whatever became of it. Bunny is the only who took music lessons, piano lessons, right across from where the old school was.

SK: Is she still in town?

RN: No. In Houston. When I first came, I said, "Why don't you move to Terrace? There is more to do there?" She said, "No. All my family is in Houston."

She has Pam here, Pam is mentally disabled. She lives in one of the group homes here. But then she's got the boys — four boys. And I think they are all married now too. One of them had twins not too long ago. I think Bunny said they are eight months now.

Ruth Shannon Interview

Interviewed by Ed Curell, 18 October 2013

Ruth Shannon was born in Lethbridge, Alberta in 1927. Ruth moved to Kitimat in 1956 with her husband and children. Her husband, Lloyd, was a WWII veteran who was stationed in Europe during the war. Ruth and her family lived in Kitimat for eight years. They decided to move to Terrace due to the construction of their house in 1962. Under the Veterans' Land Act, they were not permitted to build their house in Kitimat, hence were forced to relocate to Terrace. Ruth worked as a stay-at-home mother and was a Welcome Wagon hostess and a Cub leader in the community. In 1965, she began volunteering at the library part time. Later she became a paid employee and was a witness to the library's expansion and development over the years. In this interview, Ruth shares her experiences working at the library, living on Lazelle Avenue, and being witness to the change that has occurred during her time in Terrace. She also talks about outdoor activities she shared with her family such as camping, having picnics, fishing and swimming at the Lakelse Hot Springs.

EC: Where and when were you born?

RS: In Lethbridge, Alberta, on November 14, 1927.

EC: When did you come to Terrace?

RS: In 1962 from Kitimat.

EC: So you lived in Kitimat for...

RS: Eight years.

EC: And you moved to Kitimat in…?

RS: In 1956.

EC: Were you married?

RS: Yes, we had two children when we came to Kitimat and we had one more in Kitimat. Then we moved to Terrace after we had built our house out here. We had a company house in Kitimat and they wouldn't allow you to build under VLA, which is what we did when we came to Terrace.

EC: What's VLA [Veterans' Land Act]?

RS: Veteran's Association. My husband was a veteran.

EC: From WWII?

RS: Yes.

EC: Where was he stationed?

RS: I really don't know.

EC: Was he in Europe?

RS: Yes, he was. He was wounded when they were in Holland and then he was sent back home.

EC: Where did you grow up — in Lethbridge you said, right?

RS: No, we didn't. In the '30s, the soldiers from World War I were sent 150 miles north of Edmonton into the bush because there were no jobs. They were given half a section of land and they had 10 years to put a house and a barn up and be self-sufficient and what not, and it would be considered theirs. That was the prize they got for defending their country. So I was up there until I was 15 and then came down to Lethbridge.

EC: So you went to school...

RS: Up north, and then I finished when I came down to Lethbridge because there was no high school up there; that was why I came down.

EC: Did you attend college or university at all?

RS: No, I didn't, except for the library course out here that I took at Northwest [Community] College.

EC: Did you get married in Lethbridge?

RS: Yes.

EC: Was Lloyd a soldier then already?

RS: He was home from the war by then. That was when I met him.

EC: Did you meet him at a dance or…?

RS: We were a little town of 500. We had a girl's club and as the soldiers came back to that town we would put on a concert and a dance for them. We had a choir and we would sing and we would do skits, and he happened to come one night and didn't get away.

EC: My mom likes to tell the story of meeting my dad because I guess he was kind of drunk and he fell down the stairs into the hall.

RS: She was the one to pick him up.

EC: Were your kids young when you came to Kitimat?

RS: Yes, Gary was just starting school and Patsy was in grade two.

EC: Did you like Kitimat as a place to raise a family?

RS: No, we didn't. We didn't really care for the school system, that was one of the reasons we decided to move them to Terrace and, of course, that was the only place that allowed us to build under VLA at that time as well.

EC: Was Terrace a good place to raise a family in those days?

RS: It was, it really, really was, and Gary was just starting school when we moved here.

EC: So, what were you able to do with your children in Terrace that was different?

RS: Well, it was just an entirely different attitude. Kitimat was a company town. And it was really different than any place we had ever lived. Patsy was just starting high school when we left there. I didn't like what it was doing to her, really. Everybody had such an attitude, so it was good to get her out of there.

EC: Well, we're glad you came to Terrace. And then, what jobs did you work at throughout your time in Terrace?

RS: The library. I was home with the kids until the two oldest ones were through school. I was Welcome Wagon hostess, and then Gary was in elementary school when I started working at the library.

EC: So what year was that?

RS: It would have been two years before. That would have been '65, yes, because the Centennial Museum Library opened in '67 and I was at the little one. You could stand in the middle of the library and shelve the books, you know.

EC: What was the little library? Where was that?

Terrace Public Library, Circa 1967. Heritage Park Collection.

RS: It was just off Kalum where the Senior's Centre is now. It was a little building, just off Kalum and Lakelse, right on that side there where the Happy Gang is, and that yellow/ purple house.

EC: The old police station [TEDA office]?

RS: Yes. You know, I've tried to think of that since. Was that it, or was there one next door to it that they took down when they put up the Happy Gang? I can't remember that, because that looks like it could have been. It was about that size. It even had a children's section, a little nook in one corner.

EC: How many customers would you get if it was only big enough you could shelve the books from standing in the middle?

RS: It was a little bigger than that. But then, when we did start in the new library in 1967 — you know what our opening hours were — two to four, Monday, Tuesday, Thursday, Friday, and seven-thirty to nine in the evening, and then two to four on Saturday. In that great big library, that's all we were open for.

EC: Although it wasn't quite that big in 1967.

RC: Well, no, it wasn't, because it was renovated before the final renovations.

EC: What did you do for fun in Terrace — I mean did you go to see movies?

RC: No, I never did go to the theatre very much. Raised kids mainly, and we had a big garden and Lloyd was a shift worker.

EC: So raising kids was fun?

RS: Yes, more or less. We picnicked and camped and stuff like that. That was really the main thing you do with kids.

EC: Were there any restaurants that were popular through the years?

RS: There weren't very many restaurants at all. There was a Chinese restaurant on Kalum across from where Don Diego's is now and one in the motel. I guess that was all really.

EC: I remember when I came — where Don Diego's is was the newspaper office, and next door to that down toward the Terrace Hotel was a thing called Smiling Jack's Steakhouse.

Ruth Shannon ready for a home visit as Welcome Wagon Hostess.
Circa 1964 - '66. Ruth Shannon Collection.

RS: Oh, then that must have changed, 'cause that was the Sternwheeler and it was high-end where we went at that time.

EC: So you obviously visited Lakelse Lake hot springs?

RS: Yes, the kids took swimming lessons at Lakelse because there was no pool in Terrace.

EC: Do you have any memories of the Lakelse Lake hot springs?

RS: Well, it was always a fun place to go, and a lot of people went there from both Kitimat and Terrace 'cause neither of them had swimming pools at the time. It was always a very, very busy place. They had rooms in later years and we had these friends that used to come in every spring from Edmonton and they had to book in January to get a room to come for a couple of weeks in the summertime. So that's how busy that place was then.

EC: But it wasn't in the same place that the current hot springs is now. Wasn't it slightly toward Terrace?

RS: Yes, because in the early years we drove out from Kitimat and there was no road through to Terrace yet then. Ray Skoglund had it and it was just a great big cement thing with no cover or anything over it. It was the hot springs that he had made into this kind of swimming pool and cemented it in. There were no buildings there at that time and they gradually built them.

EC: Was the water really hot?

RS: It was. Some of the pools were too hot: you couldn't get in.

EC: There was more than one pool there?

RS: Oh yes, and the steam was always rising from them.

EC: Is that the same one where Al Capone was supposed to have...

RS: Well, I guess it would have been. Way back when they had that log hotel, I think it must have been a hot springs back then even, or why would that hotel have been there?

EC: Then what about Lakelse Lake more generally? Did they have the trails and stuff for walking around?

RS: Well, no, because you see, we were still in Kitimat when that slide came and that wiped out a lot of the site there at Lakelse Lake because it slid right into the lake and took the highway with it.

EC: Which site did it destroy?

RS: Well, there was a campsite kind of, a provincial campsite there at the time. I think that is still there. I don't know. I haven't been out there for a long time. But we would go out in the summertime to picnic at Lakelse Lake.

EC: Was anybody killed there during the slide?

RS: I don't think there was any loss of life. Because there just wasn't that many people around there, I guess. We were in Kitimat and we heard it over CBC Radio.

EC: I've seen pictures of the slide...

RS: Yes, then we took the kids out, us and the neighbours — about three couples and their kids — after we heard it on the news. We rushed out there to see it. And there were all these big bubble-ups of blue clay and everything and the kids were picking them up and then of course the next day it slid some more. We thought, *if that wasn't the most ridiculous stunt parents ever pulled.*

EC: Well, you were just having fun with your kids, right? And what about sports in Terrace? Did you play any sports?

RS: I didn't, until I was on the library ball team and you know how great I was on that. But the boys were in ball and hockey and Patsy was in volleyball.

EC: Did you go fishing?

RS: Oh yes, always, we did — all of us actually.

EC: Catch anything?

RS: Yes. I have pictures of me with great big fish.

EC: Were you involved in any other community activities outside the home, any clubs or organizations apart from working?

RS: No, other than Welcome Wagon and Home and School. We had a Home and School then.

EC: What's Home and School?

RS: Where you went to talk to your kid's teacher once a month at night...

EC: So were you doing Welcome Wagon before you started working at the library, too?

RS: Yes, right up until I quit when I started to work at the library.

EC: There must be some interesting Welcome Wagon stories?

RS: Well, there are still a few of the people here actually. Betty Nordstrom, I welcomed her to Terrace, and she had three little blonde kids hanging on to her when I went to see her that day. She was up near where we live now, actually. It was in Gordon Little's apartments or something there — I think they are torn down now, but that was where she and Neil lived when they came to Terrace. And at that time there were so many people coming. Sometimes you would have 30 visits in one week because the logging was a really big thing then and there were so many people coming out, a lot of French people from Montreal coming out to work in the bush.

EC: Were you a church person?

RS: We were, yes. When we built our house on the 4900-block of Lazelle. We were the only house there, and there was an old deserted farm down where the Do-It Building Centre is now. And then there was the fellow down on Kenny that we bought the property from and then later on, they sawed the United Church in half. It was down on Lakelse Avenue and they moved it over a piece at a time and put it on the property, so they were the only other one there until the Masons built their place, and all out behind us was just thick bush right through to the highway. And then, out in front of us, was called Head's Field and there was nobody living there at all.

EC: What street did you live on?

RS: Lazelle Avenue, 4900-block of Lazelle.

EC: So you are right next to the United Church?

RS: To the Masonic Hall now, because that was built in between the United Church and us.

EC: So is that the church that was cut in half and transported there?

RS: Yes, the old part that now they use as a hall was the church that was downtown on Lakelse Avenue in the 4500-block.

EC: When did they do that little move?

RS: Jeepers, that would have been early sixties, I guess. Yes, we moved out there in '62, and we had been there a few years when they did that.

EC: That must have been quite a procedure when they did that back in those days?

RS: Well, you see, there wouldn't have been the power lines there are today. I mean, that's your big problem now with moving anything like that, is your power lines. They moved it on a Sunday. There wouldn't have been a single person on the street.

EC: But you had electricity right, in your house?

273

RS: Yes we did. It came in through from the highway, actually, and when we were building they told us our address would probably be Lanfear because we had to know what it would be to give it to the power company. And we were on well water because there was no water or sewer through. And we had septic.

EC: Was that the same for the whole town in those days, everybody was on well?

RS: Yes, there were a lot of places that didn't have water and sewer and of course no pavement or anything. And that wasn't that long ago.

EC: I know. Were there any local events that you remember celebrating?

RS: The opening of the new library. That was a biggie. And there must have been some others, but they couldn't have been too memorable.

EC: Did they still have the Riverboat Days?

RS: No, I don't think so. I don't think that started that early. What we did used to do was we took turns with Kitimat of celebrating May 24 and July 1. One year we would get one and have the parade and then the next year you would switch. And the parade consisted in those days mainly of logging trucks and horse clubs.

EC: What do you remember about downtown Terrace? This would have been before the mall was built, too.

RS: Oh, yes. Definitely. Yes, that was a big deal when the mall was built. Dick Evans came as manager of Woolworth, and that was when I met Bev. In that space where the mall is, was the Catholic Hall, the Catholic Church. And it burned down. Everybody ran down to that. Ran over the firemen's hoses and things like that. Because that was later on where the mall was built.

Then there was the Maples, a motel right on Lakelse Avenue that Murdo MacDonald ran later on. You remember him. And there was the service station. I remember it well, because right on the corner of Emerson Street where they have that Brolly Park now, that was the service station at that time. And the wife's owner, myself, and Gerry Duffus were on a zoning committee because we didn't like the way they were doing zoning, so we had quite a summer that year.

EC: So you were involved in other community activities.

RS: Well, yes, I guess you could call that a community activity. We would have to go to Council and, I tell you, we had some councillors at that time that really didn't amount to too much. We'd get up there and speak our piece and then they would say, "five years down the road it won't make any difference one way or the other." But it did make a difference at the time.

EC: Where did you buy food?

RS: SuperValu, where M&Ms is now, there was a big SuperValu store there.

EC: That same building that's there?

RS: Right, right along that same way. Fred Smith who used to live on Munthe here and Bob Sheridan ran that at one time. And then Overwaitea came in. It was where the government building sits and that whole thing was a parking lot. The liquor store wasn't there then. I don't remember where it was. I'm sure we had one.

EC: You just weren't a big drinker.

RS: Yes, right, I wasn't interested at that time. I found it since.

274

EC: So where did you buy clothes and furniture and stuff, the same places?

RS: What is now Countrywide was the nice furniture store then even, and it was owned by a local family, I forget their name, and they were a really, really nice family. And what was the furniture store called at that time? I don't remember. And then there were clothing stores, Co-op, one for children's wear [Tots 'n Teens], 5¢ to a Dollar on Kalum Street, Ev Clift's Men's Wear, and Don's Men's Wear. He and daughter-in-law Shirley are still here. They put their name down at the Twin River [Estates]. And we had two really high-end men's stores at that time, and there was Elkin's Ladies Wear on Lakelse Avenue, which was a nice store for women.

EC: Did you shop at the Terrace Co-op?

RS: We were members of the Terrace Co-op.

EC: Was it already here when you moved here?

RS: Yes, it was. It was right on the corner and it was painted yellow, I remember that. Then they built a newer one later on, a bigger one. I guess that was the main store. There was Miller's Men's Wear, too. You know, in those days, men dressed up, like in suits and shirts and ties, all men working in the bank, and teachers in the school. It was a totally different time.

EC: I remember that Gerry Duffus never dressed up.

RS: No, well his wasn't really a dressy store. He had the 5¢ to a Dollar. There was Miller's Men's Wear on Lakelse Avenue, they were a local family. Don's Men's Wear, and Ev Clift's, and there was enough business to keep those three stores going with high-end clothing.

EC: Yes, it seems to me, I mean, I'm not a big shopper for clothes, but there are no men's clothing stores anymore.

RS: Well, there isn't, you see, because, when do you see a man dressed up?

EC: The bank?

RS: Well, not even too often in the bank really, you know. If you went to a dance, you were really dressed up, or a funeral or a wedding. Go to a funeral or a wedding now.

EC: It's about comfort, I guess.

RS. Well, I think it is, you know. When I was with the Welcome Wagon in the '60s — I have pictures of me — I wore white gloves, high heels, and nylons, and there weren't paved streets in Terrace. And out on the end of Johns Road they were putting in a whole new subdivision. Over in Thornhill, as well, just going in there with bulldozers and taking the jack pine out and putting trailers up because there were so many people moving to town, there was no place for them to live. I can remember being out there and sinking up over the top of my high-heeled shoes in just plain dirt and dust, but I still had my white gloves on and my high heels anyway. Now that was foolish.

EC: Well, what did most people that you knew do for work in Terrace?

RS: A lot of it was the bush. I mean, that really employed a lot of people in Terrace at one time.

EC: So, what role do you think forestry and logging played throughout the history of Terrace?

RS: Well, back then, it was certainly its main employer. Up where I live now, in Twin River, was all H-huts left over from the war and they were made into apartments. I didn't realize that until somebody came to sign up last month and she said, "Oh, this was my living room!" It's our office now. She said, "I used to live here!" And she was telling me then that these were all H-huts and people had apartments in them. They were broken into apartments, and then later on, that would have been in the '50s, and then later on in the '60s when the logging was so big, Columbia Cell took that over and that was their offices. And of course, when Twin River was built, they were torn down. The H hut that is still up there is the only one left from the war.

EC: Yes, I mean, it seems to me that when I first came, there were all those old wartime buildings right, they just took them down to build Twin River.

RS: Right, yes. That was where Patsy had her first job, was in that H-hut. I sent her a picture of it right after I moved up there, and she said "Oh, Mom, that's where I had my first job." She was working for Columbia Cell.

EC: So you said you started working at the library in 1965?

RS: Yes, at the old library.

EC: Do you know much about the history of the library before '65?

RS: No, I don't.

EC: Were you using the library when you first came here to town?

RC: Yes, I was, and then I was asked to come and help, because they needed volunteers as I had taken some of my Cubs in as I was a Cub leader. Gary was in Cubs then.

EC: Well, there's another thing you did with community groups.

RS: And I took some of my Cubs in, because they were looking to earn a badge and they had to do so many things. A few of the boys that were interested in getting their badge and asked if there was anyone in there that could explain the workings of the library to them. And the lady that was working that day was Anna. She later moved to [Prince] Rupert, and I can't think of her last name.

EC: Anna Thorsen was her name, I believe.

RS: And so she walked them through the whole procedure and everything, and when we were getting ready to go she said, "if you have some spare time, would you like to volunteer at the library because we really need volunteers?" So I said sure. And so I did.

EC: And what kind of hours did you wind up getting?

RS: One day a week. Our volunteers just had one day a week, even after we moved to the Centennial Library. We had volunteers like Helen Smith and Jenny Smith that lives next door to me now, and they had their days.

EC: So did you work the whole day or would you do an afternoon shift and the evening shift...?

RS: No, we had evening volunteers and afternoon volunteers.

EC: So during a day you would get two hours either in the morning or the afternoon or the evening?

RS: Yes.

EC: Oh, wow. And what kind of things did you do at the library?

RS: Well, in those days we didn't have to catalogue any books because Library Development Commission did all of that. They did our buying and our cataloguing out of Prince George. And then just shortly before Mien van Heek left, she hired Betty Olson to come in. By then, we were buying some of our own and Betty came in and was our cataloguer, doing the same thing she was doing after you came.

EC: Do you remember anything about, trying to get the new library built in '67?

RC: Yes, Hazel Cameron was head of that Centennial Committee and Mien helped her. And Gladys Kerr, it seems to me, had quite a lot to do with it, too. They went around and saw people, all kinds of people, because they needed donations and everything. Then we got in Lower Little Park. I don't know whether you read that on the internet or not about the opening of it. They had all of the locals. Dud Little presented the library with a picture of the founder of Terrace, his father. I think the library still has that.

EC: There's a picture of George Little. I don't know if it's the original one. I don't remember the original one being there when I arrived in '79.

RS: They decided once we moved in, they should pay Mien. So they paid her $50 a month because she lived way out in the bush and she had to drive in all the time. She had a little Volkswagen bug, and she put an awful lot of miles on her car that year when she was running around to talk to everybody.

EC: Did you get paid at all?

RS: Not then. No. Later on, Peggy and I got paid. When I started to get paid I got paid out of the funds, the book fines. Fines were five cents; five cents for adult books and a cent for children at that time. No, it was before I took that library course that they started paying us. I took that library course and if I passed, I got a raise, an automatic raise, 'cause the government paid.

EC: See, I remember that you were always the most interested in collecting fines from people and always wondered if that stemmed from...

RS: That probably had something to do with it.

EC: Was this a project that was well supported by city council?

RS: Well, you know what city council is like, if it's going to cost any money… But the people were certainly all for it. I mean, the library has always had good support from the people of Terrace. It's something that appeals to everybody from the really young to the really old, you know. And yet, when we were trying to raise funds for the arena, we had a great big thermometer down on the corner of Lakelse and Kalum. And they had numbers all up. They kept track of it for the arena of how much they had. And it moved a lot faster than raising funds for the library, I can tell you that. And yet, it just caters to a certain group of people. It just never seemed quite fair, but I guess they had a stronger voice.

EC: What kinds of things was Mien van Heek interested in doing or having done at the library? I mean, she played such an essential role in getting that library built.

RS: She did, she was always, always trying for something more for the library and trying to get more. I remember one time she had a thing going there, people saying what type of books they would like to see in the library, and then if we did manage to get any funds, quite often she would buy them herself, or through the library.

EC: Where did the funds come from? Was it all city?

RS: Well, we must have had some provincial, because, I mean, after we took that course they stepped in and it was them that was giving the extra money for anybody that had the library course. Library Development Commission, I think, got the provincial money because they were the ones buying the books for all of the libraries that came under that umbrella — Hazelton, Smithers, Terrace.

EC: How many people worked there in '67 when they had the new library?

RS: Well, there was Mien and Peggy and I. We were regular, we were working every day then. Every day, two hours. And then we had a volunteer for each day, so we would have an extra person. Mamie Kerby was one, Jenny Smith, and Helen Smith.

EC: So what about children's services? Was it just providing books or did they have story times and all that?

RS: Well, just if we had time to read to them. Something I remember was, we brought the little orange bench from the old library which was the only seating in the Children's Library over there, it was a little orange bench about this long, somebody had made.

EC: Well, it's still there, I think.

RC: Oh, it probably is, yes, because we brought it from that library. And I remember Joe Durando bringing Paola in because he was so keen for his kids to all have good educations. And he was so proud that day. He said "my daughter would like to join the library" and she was so shy, you know, she was hanging on to her dad. And then after that she could come from school and when Joe got off work he would come and pick her up and she would sit on that little orange bench in the Children's Section reading books. She was so, so well-behaved.

EC: I remember you telling me too about the library: after it was constructed, you had to crumple up bits of paper and put them in the cracks. It wasn't the best-constructed building in town?

RS: Paper towel. They had an architect from Vancouver design it. And I mean, what does he know about the weather up here? And when the wind blew, the snow would blow in through the cracks. And many times Peggy and I took paper towel and stuffed the cracks to keep snow out. And those skylights, they were a laugh. I mean they were necessary for lighting but I don't know if they were just poorly done, because they'd flop when the wind blew and they'd leak.

EC: You know, when they redid the library in 1995 and they tore out the walls of the old children's library, in behind were bits of coloured glass, do you remember seeing that? Because there were at least three different colours uncovered, long, tall, to let the light in?

RS: No, because see, that was the museum, when the original library opened.

EC: The children's area?

RS: Yes, and Ed Kenney was in charge of the museum then, but they had trouble getting volunteers, too, so they would just lock it and if somebody from out of town came and wanted to see the museum, one of us would open it and let them in. But it wasn't kept up at that time and the shelves would be dusty and what not, it wasn't very nice, but the entryway was way over on that part, on that end, because they changed all of that in the next renovation. Yes, it was a pretty cold place there. You'd go home at night and your hands would be blue they would be so cold.

EC: Well, it's better now, that's for sure. How did the [the library] community of Terrace interact with Kitselas and Kitsumkalum? Did they bring the communities together, all three of them?

RS: I don't think so. Anybody outside of the Terrace boundaries had to pay to belong to the library.

EC: Even Thornhill, in the early days.

RS: Yes, definitely. And people were resentful. I don't know why. They were living out there so they wouldn't have to pay as much tax, and the library was supported by people's taxes, so why should they have felt they should have it for free.

EC: It's the idea of a library. I think people think of the library as a free service.

RS: I know, I know, because I can remember having conversations with you at times, where you didn't even think we should be charging fines. I didn't agree with that.

EC: How did the establishment of Kitimat in the '50s impact Terrace? I mean, that's before your time, so…

RS: Yes, it was. And there wasn't a road through '57, fall of '57, I think, was when the highway went through.

EC: But even so, your husband worked at Alcan, right?

RS: But we lived in Kitimat then and the only way out to Terrace was by train.

EC: But later on when the road was built you moved to Terrace?

RS: Yes, when we moved to Terrace, of course, the highway was in by that time. And Lloyd drove back and forth in a car pool. They each took turns, drive for a week, and the next guy would drive for a week. A lot of Kitimat people lived in Terrace then.

EC: They still do, I think.

RS: They do. So at one time they even had Allan McGowan, I think it was, drive a mini bus, and he would pick up a busload. But that was the day shift workers. Lloyd was a shift worker so he couldn't do the bus. They did their own driving.

EC: And what about the construction of the new bridge? How did that impact the community?

RS: I don't think that it ever changed a lot of anything. At first, they were going to take out the old bridge, and I know people didn't like that at all, and in fact I even took a picture of it and had somebody do a painting for me, because I thought we were going to lose it. But we didn't lose it. I remember the opening of it, because, of course, Dudley Little headed that up, too.

EC: Was he the mayor at that time?

RS: No, no. For years and years and years, while Bennett was the Premier, Dudley Little was MLA.

EC: So was he from Terrace, Dudley Little, he was a Terrace resident?

RS: Oh yes, he was George Little's son, him and Gordon were George Little's sons. Yes, I can't think of how many years, but it was years and years that he was the MLA.

EC: So then, you've obviously been here during some pretty big floods. Any reminiscences about floods? It didn't impact you where you lived, did it?

RS: No, it didn't really, you know, or anybody that I knew very well, even.

EC: Had they built down in that lower area of Terrace close to the river?

RS: Skeena Street was caught in floods different times, but I didn't even know anybody that lived down there, so it was never anyplace we were, you know, to make a difference. Our big thing in those early years was forest fires, because we had a lot of them. It's been a lot of years since we've had really severe forest fires and if it stayed hot for a couple of weeks, you hated to say, oh isn't this weather just beautiful, because somebody would just cut you down to size and say, "yeah sure and there'll be a forest fire before the week's out," and surely there would be, too. If somebody had thrown a bottle in the bush, the sun off the bottle could start one. And with the trucks going, sparks from them too.

EC: Yes, I know, I kind of wonder, why we haven't had any serious forest fires in the last few years, you know: we've had some beautiful weather.

RC: Well, we haven't, but then the trucks aren't out in the bush, either, you know, like they were.

EC: That was the major cause, you think?

RS: Well, yes, that was one of the causes, anyway, because we never really had that severe a thunderstorm. And then that one [fire] we had was so severe it burned and burned everything off. Then for quite a few years there was nothing to start a forest fire cause all the underbrush was gone and what not. Because it used to be bad. I mean the smoke would be so thick and the sun would just be a red ball in the sky.

EC: Yes, and I've seen a couple of those. So did you garden or grow fruit or anything?

RS: Oh yes, we did. We had lots of fruit trees and we had a big garden, and in fact we gardened years after we needed to be gardening. After all the kids grew up and left home, we were still canning and pickling, and three years later down the road putting it on the compost so you'd have the jars to fill again. Then we started going to the Charlottes every September. That would be just the time we'd have to be canning and freezing, so we decided what are we doing this for? So we quit the garden and went fishing.

EC: Well, did they have a farmers' market then?

RS: I don't think so, not that I ever thought of attending, anyway.

EC: That started in the '80s, right?

RS: Yes, I think that was much later on. Yes, 'cause I can't remember there being a farmers' market.

EC: And what about art in Terrace?

RS: Well, that was the Art Club, where they'd take over the library basement if they would finish it, 'cause it was just an unfinished basement with walls. And so they got all of this what you called hopsacking at the time and they glued it all over the walls.

EC: That was in 1982 or '83 then, as well, right?

RS: Yes. And then they could have it for their displays and what not, and that was what they did. I didn't really care for the walls, but then, we had quite a few local artists at that time and some of them were quite good.

EC: We used to run children's programs down there, too. Gillian did some. Were you involved in politics?

RS: No, never that I can remember.

EC: Except for your stint on the zoning committee. That's kind of political.

RS: Oh, right. But that was kind of against the politicians.

EC: So more generally, how has Terrace changed over the years?

RS: Well, for one thing, some of us were talking about this the other day, it is not the safe place it was back then. I mean, when my youngest grandson, who is now 29, was in elementary school, either his parents or I picked him up and took him to school when he was little. And my kids, I mean, I would never even have thought of that when the children were in school. It took us a year driving back and forth from Kitimat to build our house because we would do it on days off or after Lloyd got off shift, and that whole year all of his tools and our bathroom fixtures and everything lay in that house and the house was wide open. Nothing ever went missing or was damaged or broken or anything. Try that today. That builder's supply just down the street from us in later years, I remember one time my neighbour seeing these fellows after hours with a truck up out beside the fence and one of them was in the fence handing the lumber over and she thought, *this doesn't look right. I mean they're not going to be loading from the builder's supply like that, somebody's there that shouldn't be doing it.* And she called the police and that's what they were doing. They were helping themselves to a load of lumber.

EC: They obviously didn't get away with it though, did they?

RS: No, not that time, they didn't.

EC: So were there any annual community events that you remember?

RS: Not other than the parades. I can't think of anything else.

EC: What about when that first highway came, the first paved road?

RS: Yes, when they first paved that, that was the year the Queen came and they paved from the airport then down the street in Terrace. That's why it's Queensway, because that was paved for the Queen. I can't even think what year that was, when she came. I'm sure you can find that on the internet. Yes, up until then it was just mudsville. [The Queen visited Terrace July 18, 1959, for 40 minutes].

EC: But that was before you, wasn't it?

RS: Yes, we were in Kitimat, I think, when [the Queen] came.

EC: Oh, that must have been a pretty big event, even if you lived in Kitimat?

RS: Yes, but you see, there wasn't the publicity then that there is now. You hear about anything going on the other side of the world now. Back then, we depended all those years on Kitimat, and the first years in Terrace, we depended totally on CBC radio to get any even local news. So we didn't get a lot of local news.

EC: Were you here when the radio station...?

RS: We lived in Kitimat when Fred Weber was trying to do that. In fact, nobody even had TV then you know. We got TV when we were in Kitimat. One shift at Alcan Lloyd was on, they went around and talked to all of the people, because Fred had to be assured that there would be enough people that would take it when it came. People paid $25 down; that was their good will. They put their names down then so they could use that $25 toward a TV set. One of the furniture stores had a truck bring up loads from Vancouver, most of them were used TVs, and then they could take their $25 off of the price.

EC: A used TV? How did that work out?

RS: Well, ours worked out great. We had it for a long time.

EC: Oh, wow.

RC: And they had the pattern, you know, the Indian head pattern that came on first and then TV went off the air at such and such a time. But everybody was thrilled to have it, I can tell you.

EC: I bet, yeah.

RS: And then the station was where it is now. Saturday afternoon it would have been, the school kids could go down and they could dance and they would be on TV and that was the Saturday afternoon program. A lot of them did, too. It was really something.

EC: When you were a child what did you expect or hope to accomplish in your life?

RS: What most kids expect I guess, to get big one day.

EC: And you did that.

RS: One thing, I've been to China four times. When I was a kid, I was always interested in China. In our little school we had a library that contained about maybe 10 books at the most at any one time. But I had an uncle who was a missionary in China at the time, my dad's brother, and he used to write to us all the time and he would tell us that he was going to school over there in a rickshaw to learn to speak Chinese. And so then I was allowed to take the part of his letter that wasn't personal and read it to the class. We had a big map up on our wall that all of the mothers of the community had got together and put in their Nabob coffee coupons. (You used to get a coupon in Nabob coffee, and you could buy things for your kitchen mainly, stuff like that). And they had all put their coupons together and bought us that map for the school. And we found China on that map. That was really the only other part of the world that we knew outside of our little area at that time, and I always thought one day I'd like to go there, and I did.

EC: Four times.

RS: Four times, yes.

EC: So you still must be fascinated with China.

RS: Right, and there's still lots that I haven't seen, too, because it's really big.

EC: Well, it's a huge country. Was there any particular person or event that made an impact on your life? Sounds like your uncle had an impact.

RS: Well, yes, I guess Uncle Clare did, yes, and he was my favourite uncle because I was born on his birthday, so he always said I was his favourite niece.

EC: So as a long-time resident of the Terrace area, what changes have you noticed?

RS: I don't think, other than the fact, like I say, that it isn't nearly the safe place it used to be, it's still a lovely place to be.

EC: It's grown a lot, though, too.

RS: It has, it has, from then, yes. Now it looks like we're going to have another big spurt, too.

EC: Yes, 'cause I mean when you were talking earlier, you were talking about all the roads were gravel or mud, now they're all paved, pretty well.

RS: Right, yes, and I mean it was just so dusty driving around Terrace then. Another thing we used to do in those early years after we built our house: people would drive down that street at such a rate and it would just be clouds of dust, we would take oil and oil the road. Can you imagine doing that? Saved the used oil 'cause Lloyd had always done the vehicles and pour it on the road to keep the dust down in front of your house.

EC: Well, you know, I remember, I think it was in Vancouver when I was there, I have this image of a big truck with an oil tank on the back and spraying oil out the back of the truck. They used to do that when they seal coated the roads. They'd spray oil down and then they'd throw these stones down. They do that still on the highway, don't they, or something like that?

RS: I don't think so. You're not allowed to pour oil around anymore are you?

EC: I don't know. What's seal coating then these days?

RS: 'Cause there's one area up there at Twin River in that corner where there isn't anything built, you know, where you can park your RVs and what not, and that was where the Columbia Cell trucks changed their oil on the ground. To this day, that is polluted.

EC: That's like the old Co-op gas station that had to sit there for years and years, same as the Esso Station where the Brolly Square is now was.

RS: You know, the thing is, people didn't realize the damage that we're doing. It's like when in Kitimat, all the houses in Kitimat had an underground tank, a buried tank, for their diesel fuel to run their furnaces. And some in Terrace did. We didn't have it in ours. We had our tank above ground, which was a good thing because had we had — before I sold that house, I'd have had to have that all taken out of there. But, I mean, at the time you didn't know; you're putting it out of sight and it's fine. We spend so much time undoing the past and apologizing for the past: I mean, you didn't know it was bad at the time.

EC: I know... you have to right those wrongs now, right? I mean, if you know it's wrong, you gotta fix it. Hopefully most people wouldn't do those things. So, as someone who has lived and learned here, what would you like to share with people moving to Terrace? Any advice for people moving here?

RS: Well, I think there's still a Welcome Wagon hostess out there. There was a few years ago, and I mean they're very good at introducing you to the community. They tell you what services there are, and what amenities and what stores are nice to shop at, then give you a letter from your MLA and your MP. [Frank Howard at that time and MLA Dudley Little].

EC: Well, you know, we used to have Welcome Wagon materials in the library just for people to help themselves, right.

RS: Oh really, so maybe there wasn't a hostess then any longer.

EC: I think there was someone, because you could, I think someone who worked for the library also was a Welcome Wagon hostess.

RS: Oh really. Yes, because when I was doing it there were two of us, Grace Fell and I because there were so many people coming.

EC: Grace Fell the florist lady?

RS: Mm mm. Yes, because there were so many people coming. We all had our sponsorships and at the end of each week, I had to type up a report on anybody I'd visited; what the husband did, and how many children there were and this and that, and give it to all the sponsors. And Cliff McChesney was one of my sponsors and he could use that list to go visit them if they wanted a visit from him. Co-op gave them a loaf of bread and a can of soup and, you know, different places gave them little gifts and what not. And I told them what schools if they had children and what services were like for them. So it's a good thing for when people move into a community, it is.

EC: I think it's still around. I would think the bigger a town gets, the more, the further away something like a Welcome Wagon would become.

RS: Yeah, either that or you'd have to have more hostesses.

EC: Like in a big place they'd never know that you were a new person in town, would they?

RS: Well, we kept in touch with the moving companies and with the apartment owners, that was how we did it. One summer I visited the Keystones as many as three times, 'cause people would come and there always seemed to be something empty there. They would take it just until they could find someplace else to live and they'd move on and somebody else would get theirs.

EC: And, are there any other stories you'd like to share?

RS: I can't think of any. Except to say I think we have the nicest public library of any town I've been in.

EC: Thanks to you Ruth.

RS: Well, when I was in Hazelton at the conference in September, our Auxiliary Conference, I went by that little library, you know, that was the boat. Of course it no longer is. It's a museum now. They built a bigger one, because remember when it opened, some of us went up there to it, and it was so lovely. Then within a year they realized it was far, far too small.

EC: That was the boat?

RC: Yes, little paddlewheeler. But it's still there.

EC: Well they've got a new library next door now, and it's really nice. It's beautiful. It's got a little seating area outside looking over the river. It's very nice.

RS: I'd forgotten how beautiful the Hazeltons are, really because I haven't been through them for years, and with having the conference there we went to all parts of it.

EC: Okay, well I think that's all. That's great, thank you very much.

RS: You're welcome.

EC: Talk to you later.

Shannon Mark Interview

Interviewed by Kara Mitchell, 14 December 2013

In this interview, Shannon Mark describes her life in Terrace and Lakelse Lake, reflects on the many recreational activities in the Northwest, and ends the interview describing her involvement in the establishment of Northwest Community College. In this interview, Shannon Mark describes her life in Terrace and Lakelse Lake and ends the interview describing her involvement in the establishment of the College. Shannon grew up in Prince Rupert. She moved to Terrace in 1985 to teach anthropology and sociology at Northwest Community College. Eventually, she built a cabin at Lakelse Lake. Shannon remembers many details of life in the Northwest: driving from Prince Rupert to Terrace for lemon meringue pie at the Silvertip Café, annual traditions like pyrohy at Ukrainian Christmas, and Skoglund Hot Springs.

KM: Where and when were you born?

SM: I was born November 15, 1940 in Bralorne, a little mining town near Lytton. I lived there for just a few years until my mother and I moved back in with my grandparents in Vancouver.

KM: How did your family come to live in the surrounding Terrace area?

SM: I guess it was 1949, in the late 1940s my mother met my stepfather, who is really the only father that I knew. He was a fisherman. They married on Valentine's Day, 1948. And quickly my mother realized that he was fishing in and out of Prince Rupert so she thought it was best we all move there where we could see more of him. And that brought us to Prince Rupert.

KM: That's good. What are your early memories of coming to Terrace?

SM: The first trip to Prince Rupert was by car. It was a gravel road most of the way — I am diverting a bit here — the road through the Fraser Canyon was a single track road with passing spots and if a car came along one of you had to back up to the nearest passing spot to let the other car by. And we continued on up through Prince George, which was just a little tiny town, turn left at Prince George, and through the north, through Terrace which again the highway went right down Lakelse Avenue. The old bridge was there, it was a two-way bridge. You passed trucks on that bridge very slowly and drove right down Lakelse Avenue and that's all I can remember of Terrace. Terrace was a very small town then. Even the Catholic Church was on the main street in town, then on to Prince Rupert.

KM: Oh wow. I knew you ended up working in Terrace at the college. About what time period was that?

SM: I moved to Terrace to work at the college in 1985. I had taught for the college in Prince Rupert before but I came up to Terrace in '85 to a full-time position. But I'd been in Terrace before that.

Well, Terrace has always been a good part of my life. Living in Prince Rupert and for many people who live in Prince Rupert, Terrace is a big part of their life and even more so now with the main shopping hub being here. But growing up in Rupert in the '50s, Lakelse Lake was always a destination place for people to come. Many people would have friends that had a cabin, and cabins were cabins in those days! And my in-laws, the Prystays, had lived in Terrace in the late '30s and '40s and then they moved back to Terrace in the early '60s and bought a hotel. When I was married, we started coming back and forth to Terrace on a regular basis, a couple times a month, on Christmas vacations, and then we built a cabin at the lake. So all our summers were spent up in Terrace at Lakelse [Lake] and visiting with the Prystays in town and the whole Ukrainian community there. And there were other relatives, as well. Jim and Stella Prystay lived up on

McConnell, up near the college [Northwest Community College] and Roy and Iris Prystay lived in town so we would often come to visit them. So that was a lot of connections.

KM: And what about your children?

SM: The cabin at Lakelse was a major part of their life, something they looked forward to as the weather got good enough to open up the cabin in the spring. And then spending the full summer here and coming up to visit their grandparents. Both my daughters live here now and all my grandchildren live here. So although I have gone back to Prince Rupert, which was my hometown, my connections are very strong here.

KM: Have you noticed that the area around the lake has changed?

SM: That has changed greatly because as a young woman building a cabin here, that was exactly what we built. We built it in four weekends and lived in it after that. People were building cabins but in the last 20, maybe 30 years, people have bought what were cabins and have been converting them into homes. That's really what I did with this place right here, that we're sitting in right now—the area we're sitting in right now was the kitchen and the rest of that area over there which is now the dining room was the whole living room. I took the back bedroom and made that into the kitchen. And this became my home while I lived in Terrace.

KM: Were there any longtime Terrace residents who lived in the cabins around you?

SM: Gary Reum lived out at the lake. There were very few people who lived year-round at the lake. There was also John Sarich and they had a big log house down past Oli's Place, Lorraine and Lloyd Johnstone lived down at the lake and ran a float plane business for a while, and the Colthursts developed the Waterlily Bay Resort, but it was few and far between that lived here all year-round. That has changed and a lot of it are people that had cabins and when they retired they turned their cabins into retirement homes and stayed here. Now on this little strip of 11 properties that were all built as cabins, there are about five full-time all year-round retired people living here; oh there's six, seven, eight. It goes on and on.

KM: My uncle did the same thing. He bought a cabin out at the lake in the Yukon in the '70s, and just kept building on to it and that's where he lives now. He retired to his cabin.

SM: Yes. I'd like to tell you what Terrace meant to me as a teenager. A destination date for us was a drive to Terrace to go to the Silvertip Café. So you know where the Silvertip Café was? It was on Kalum Street, just down the hill from the sporting goods store on the west side of the street. The Silvertip Café — we'd drive all the way to Terrace on gravel roads to the Silvertip Café for lemon meringue pie. [Laughter.] You know I remember that so clearly. I was like 16, 17 years old and that's what Terrace was to me in those years.

KM: So they had notably good lemon meringue pie?

SM: They did, they did.

KM: Being so close to the hot springs, did you guys spend any time at the...

SM: At Skoglund? Absolutely, that was a real drawing card, and we're all very sad that the place isn't open to the public now. The natural hot springs were fun to take people to. I have another cute little story to do with that.

We had taken some friends that were visiting from Denmark out to the natural hot springs, not the developed part, but a hot springs nearby in the bush you could easily get to. I think it was November. It was late into the year, because all the trees branches that overhung the outside rim of the hot springs were rimmed in frost. Somebody had built a bonfire. There was a lantern hanging in the tree and there were all these branches crusted in frost from the steam coming up off the hot springs, because it was cold enough. It was just beautiful and these people that had come from Denmark were sitting in the hot water, with this cold air above and it was so beautiful and natural, and in his limited English he said, "When I go back home and tell them about this they won't true it, they won't true it." [Laughter.] So I thought that's it, now I got the message across.

Shannon Mark Collection

KM: That's amazing, that's amazing!

SM: That Skoglund was really quite an attraction with the little pool. You could bring family there and camp. They rented horses and then people grew food. It's been through quite a transition.

KM: How about sports around the Terrace area. Did you take part in any sports, like fishing?

SM: Definitely fishing, water skiing around the lake, whenever anyone had a powerful enough boat. Canoeing—did lots of canoeing on this lake. And the other thing that Terrace was very important for me was the Terrace Hiking Club. I was a member of the hiking club back in the '70s. I was quite surprised when I opened up one of the scrapbooks when I lived here, to find my picture in the first page. I joined the hiking club when I was coming up with my children in the summer and met Peter and Sheila Caddy, who were the organizers then. But anyway the hiking club was an important thing to me and that's something I really missed when I wasn't here because we were very active, every week, and the hiking club even had a separate group that met mid-week. They were a group of senior women that wanted to go on less arduous or slower-paced hikes than some of the real gung-ho younger hikers. Now I'm at that stage that I could be part of that mid-week group and there are some in town now that do that.

KM: How about other community activities like, were there any other groups you belonged to?

SM: Years ago, when I lived here, I was very active in the community from '85 on. But when I was a younger woman coming up to stay at the lake—when you're out at the lake, once you get back out here after shopping or working or something, getting back in the car and driving into town for a meeting is a bit much. So right offhand, I can't think of organizations that I belonged to in those early years.

KM: Okay. Do you remember celebrating any local events? Like Riverboat Days would be a good one in the summer.

SM: No, not too much, but of course, almost every Christmas Eve was up here in Terrace. And the other big connection I mentioned before was the Ukrainian Club, and they had the Luso Hall that they built in the area close to where those Maple Estates are built now, on the west end of it. They had good parties and so we would drive up for those because Mrs. Prystay was quite an organizer for cooking for these things. And of course, we always came up for a traditional Ukrainian Christmas dinner which is the 12 meatless dishes.

KM: Oh.

SM: There's quite a bit of tradition that goes on to do with that so we would always come to Terrace for that. It was always a drive over that very changeable highway between Prince Rupert and Terrace on Christmas Eve. Drive up and probably drive back down that same night around 10 to get back to Rupert for midnight mass.

KM: Oh wow, so tell me which one of these 12 dishes was your favorite?

Lakelse Avenue, 4700 Block looking east, June 1987. Photographed by Andrew Webber. Andrew Webber Collection.

SM: Probably the pyrohy. What most people call perogies, Ukrainians call pyrohy, and it's just like somebody's Christmas cake or their spaghetti: your mother or your mother-in-law makes the best ones 'cause they're the ones you're used to—so Baba made the best ones, with lots of melted butter and fried onions and sour cream, they were favourites.

KM: You still miss them?

SM: Well yes, the commercial ones just don't quite match up.

KM: What do you remember about downtown Terrace?

SM: What I had mentioned earlier, was that downtown Terrace was just Lakelse Avenue, and really the centre of town was more Kalum Street and Lakelse Avenue. So that there were stores on Kalum Street where the Seniors' centre is now, there was the RCMP at the corner there and there's a few stores on either side of Kalum and Lazelle and then again down on, what's the next street south of there, I wanted to say, it's not Keith...

KM: Greig?

SM: Greig, and there were a couple of the hotels, there's still the one there, then there was the Skeena Hotel further up.

KM: Before it burned?

SM: So really there's that little grid over there and the mall, the new mall, drew the town more in the direction westward. But the Silvertip was right in the middle there and north was the sporting goods. There's the Northwest on one side — anyway, you know the one I mean and the florist was beyond that. But that was the main area. And that was Terrace. Terrace was a small town and really just like a little bit of a dust bowl because it is pretty dry and has the reputation for the wind. But I really notice a big difference in Terrace.

Terrace being a hub city — and with the roads now extended up to the Nass and the Highway 37 going up to Dease Lake — Terrace has become a hub for a lot of shopping. And it's developed very well, where the communities around it have not. You know, it's central and so it makes sense to create business here, so I have noticed that there's been a big change in Terrace.

KM: Do you think the role of forestry and logging has played a big part in developing the area?

SM: Well, of course. My daughter married into a logging family, into a contracting family and a lot of their contracts were logging. So yeah, logging has been a big part of Terrace and to me, logging is a good resource to utilize because it's probably our most renewable one and it's disturbing to me to see people criticize that resource. You know we have to be responsible with all of our resources, but of all our resources, that is one that is going to come back within the next lifetime.

KM: Yeah, it grows back quicker than oil [laughter].

SM: Or silver.

KM: You said your daughter married into one of the families. Was it more trucking or sawmills or…?

SM: It's a large contracting company that's involved with logging and road building, and a lot of trucking.

KM: How do you see that industry change in the Terrace area?

SM: Change there is! For a lot of people, their main work was logging, like reaping the logs. Right now, those same contracting companies are not logging much at all, but they are very busy with all of the current development of road-building and clearing and building sites and working on the transmission lines they are putting up north.

KM: In your time that you spent here in Terrace, did you notice a lot of interaction with the people of Kitselas and the people of Kitsumkalum, or is that more like a recent thing?

SM: Each community has its own interaction, and celebrations and politics. They're all busy looking after their own politics and interests. I don't know if that's changed that much over the years. You know, in some ways there's less interaction now, because there's more things going on in each little individual village. The villages have their own band councils, their own halls, their own celebrations. So in some ways, they've become more associated with their own identity and enhancing their own identity as a positive thing, so maybe there's been even less. When there was only one area that had a big hall, that had a dance, everybody from all around came to that hall to dance. And when Terrace was a smaller town, that's the kind of thing you would get. But as a place gets larger, sometimes it's inclined to start getting more specific groups meeting for each activity.

KM: Interesting. How did the establishment of Kitimat in the '50s affect Terrace?

SM: We were all very keen about what was going on in Kitimat, it was a drawing card for people to go see what was happening there and before there was a road there, I can remember a number of times we'd get a group together and take the train down to visit Kitimat and see what they were doing. This instant town created quite a fuss and, of course, it created jobs for all kinds of people. One of my good friends, as a young man, got a job. He was a new Canadian with limited English but he got a job chaining. Maybe it was the rail line down to Kitimat. That would have been in the very early '50s, because I guess it was before the rail line went in. I didn't know what chaining meant but I learned from this person what the chain was and how they measured with this chain that ran the line down. There were jobs opening for people and it was just a haven for new Canadians to come and find work and it just opened up their whole world.

KM: And how did the construction of the new bridge impact Terrace?

SM: That certainly made life a lot easier for getting back and forth from Thornhill and the lake and maybe had a lot to do with people choosing to live out in Thornhill as opposed to in town. I still like going over the old bridge, and last night when I was driving my granddaughter to the play, I told her the story about how this was the only bridge and how it was a two-way bridge when I was a kid and how at the curve, you actually had to stop to inch past a big truck.

KM: But do you think it had anything to do with more people living here out at the lake as well?

SM: I don't know about at the lake, but I think for the development of Thornhill for sure, and not only that but the confidence of living out there — you don't want to be cut off from town if the only bridge has got some problems so it's the security of knowing.

KM: And I can imagine it would have made it a little easier, as I know Terrace has had some pretty big floods over the years as well, so probably the development of the new bridge made people more confident when there was a flood.

SM: I am only speculating — I never lived in the low areas of Terrace. When I was choosing to buy a house, I came very close to buying a place down on Skeena Drive because I like the idea of being right on the view — near the water. But then I had young grandchildren at the time, and the threat of the flood, knowing that those places occasionally were flooded, I thought the river might be a problem. So I chose to live up on the Bench, and then I moved out to the lake.

KM: What part of the Bench did you live on?

SM: I lived on a little road. It was the only house on that road, off Westview, the road above before you get to Heritage Park. You turn right and there's a little branch road off there, called Morris Avenue. I had a house there but since I lived there, there's been a whole subdivision built in behind and above there. I was right backed up against a mountain and adjacent to an old orchard so I had the odd apple tree in my backyard and it wasn't unusual to look out and see Mr. Bruin out in the backyard harvesting my apples and leaving applesauce behind as proof of what he had been doing.

KM: So there weren't a lot of people living up there when you were living in that area?

SM: Well, Westview was completely developed but in behind this Morris Street, there's just this little tiny spur. But now there's a road, not that road itself, but just the next road goes in and there's a whole other subdivision behind.

KM: Other than the apple trees, is there anything else you grew in your yard? Or even out here at the lake?

SM: Oh, I am a gardener. I love gardening, so I have always had a vegetable patch but when I lived in that house on Morris, I used to frequently go out and walk the Terrace Mountain route. It's right behind the house. It's an hour or two's walk in the summer evening. I'd walk that route by myself and it was years later when I was reading the book about "Sheslay Mike," who was a fellow who had gone a bit nuts living out in the wilds north of Telegraph Creek, where he supposedly murdered another trapper. It was a sad story! I found out later that this fellow had been camped up there on the Terrace Mountain trail for months waiting to go to trial. And I had been hiking this trail blithely all by myself with this character. So obviously he wasn't that dangerous a guy — in town anyways.

KM: Wow, wow. How about the Farmers' Market?

SM: Well the Farmers' Market was just starting when I was leaving Terrace. Again, the Farmers' Market was on in the summer and I had long summers off when I was teaching at the college and I would often be away doing what we call professional development during the summer. So for about six years I was working on archeological projects during those four months away from town and so I wasn't around a lot during those days. But one of the persons involved in getting that market started was Lena Chapplow, who is now passed away. She was Lena Mark and was a sister-in-law of mine who grew up in this area and stayed her whole life in this area. Really all my in-laws — and I have two sets of in-laws — were people who spent more time in Terrace than myself.

KM: How about the art in Terrace?

SM: The art in Terrace? Well, I paint a bit myself but I have periods of my life where I'll paint like mad. In fact, when I retired, it was to go to my cabin on the Dease River and paint full time but other things ended up taking my interest. But I used to paint with Maureen Worobey and Gail Sears. There was a group of us that met in a little studio that Maureen had behind her house years ago, so all those people had quite an influence on me. Terrace has produced some wonderful artists and having other models to work with and paint with really has helped Terrace to grow up.

KM: Nice. More generally, how do you think Terrace has changed over the years?

SM: Well, it's changed from a little dust bowl to quite a thriving community. It has a good theatre and we attract good concerts and get pretty good crowds to them. I think Glen Saunders had a really positive effect on the arts in Terrace. I met him when he first came to Terrace; he subleased a house that I was living in at the lake, just down the lake a little further from here, and I saw the attendance at the concerts go from a few dozen to a good house.

The [Terrace] Little Theatre has always been really active, as the McColl family has consistently kept that going. I can remember going to plays in the 1960s when I'd come up to Terrace to visit or be out at the lake. I was very active in little theatre myself as a young person in Rupert so I was interested in what was happening here, too. Terrace has become quite a nice cosmopolitan little town and with the fact that it's in the terrain that it's in, as opposed to Prince Rupert, which is a port city, huddled on rocky shores and a very difficult area to build on.

KM: And hilly, very hilly.

SM: Terrace has a lot of flat open area, so a lot of area to develop on relatively cheaply as you don't have to blast and fill and that kind of thing. So Terrace has become a very nice little town, good shopping, good sports facilities, good arts and culture. Always love the library and the art gallery downstairs.

KM: How about the Queen's visit to Terrace? You hear a lot about that?

SM: I was at the Queen's visit to Terrace in 1959. I have pictures of us sitting on the bank, across from the Legion and now where the seniors' residence is. I sat there with all the Prystays living in Terrace. I have pictures of us sitting there and waving to the Queen going by in her convertible and that's when they changed the name of the road that went up to the airport, in the old days, to Queensway. I forget what it was called before that, can you remember?

KM: I know someone's told me but I don't recall.

SM: …and there's a road, there's a Mark Road that goes off Queensway and that Mark Road was named after an in-law of mine, a Mark family that came to Terrace from Denmark.

KM: Nice, nice. We'll go more into personal things—when you were a child, what did you hope or expect to accomplish?

SM: When I was a child... oh what did I want to accomplish as a child? I don't know, as a teenager I thought maybe I'd like to be a lab technician. When I was a young woman growing up, the options were teacher, nurse, or secretary. That was about it and I thought a lab technician sounded very different and much more interesting to me. But I wasn't very good in math and chemistry, just limped through those courses, so I thought I'd better change my focus. So I went into teaching.

KM: As someone who's lived in the Terrace area, and learned in the Terrace area, what would you want to share with people newly moving to Terrace?

SM: I think first of all, I would want to find out what they wanted to learn, and maybe what I could offer with my interests. I taught anthropology and sociology for years so I'm very interested in the richness of a culture and I suppose what I would want to…I guess the first thing I would say to people coming to Terrace is that they're in the midst of a wonderful environment, the mountains are fantastic for hiking and that was one of my loves and there's rivers to paddle and oceans to fish.

There's also very rich culture that goes back thousands of years in the area and I would encourage people to learn what they can from that. But that's not easy to do because you have to earn your acceptance by another culture and you have to leave yourself open to being able to quietly appreciate what it is that the other cultures know and what they can pass on to people besides just the general interest in their art and their dance and that kind of thing. It's not easy to learn the depths of those cultures because you can read about them from books but it's only through time and making friends that they can see a very real interest, a reality in your interest. That was a hard question.

KM: That was a hard question. Do you have any advice for present and future residents of Terrace?

SM: Same thing, same thing.

KM: Absorb as much from the surroundings as you can?

SM: I mean it's a beautiful area and it's interesting to me to watch so many people of all ages moving away from the north and moving to the more populated Lower Mainland. It's not an area I would want to be in at all, the crowds, the impersonality, the expense, none of that appeals to me. I mean there's many things in a city that appeal to me but I can get those on short term visits. But that's not the majority. People are moving to the city and the young people are going there for jobs but my golly, the cost of living is so high, you wonder...

We have so much to offer and the opposite to that you know is we have space. We have freshness. We have opportunities for people who are willing to put their energy into those. We don't have to spend a fortune on a place to live, or parking. So there's so many wonderful things to take advantage of in our northern small town. You know, see them and enhance those.

KM: I know you worked up at the college so how would you say the role of the college has changed over the years in the area?

SM: The college has changed a lot. Years ago the college was first developed as a vocational school and in the '70s there was a big thrust to make a full-scale post-secondary education available to people throughout the province. The province decided that for this area they would turn the vocational school into a full range college offering university courses, a business school, and some vocational training as well as trades training.

I met a lot of the people that were involved in the initial transformation and some of the people on that board lived in Kitimat and some of them lived in Terrace. I had met some of these people socially but I had a place at the lake, so they started having some of their meetings at my house at the lake so I got quite involved in that.

It was a controversial group because this came out of the NDP government at the time, and the people that were appointed were left-wing and they were interested in developing a college that would enhance the worker mentality and development of unions. That was really very interesting and over the years that changed but a lot of that reputation stuck with the college which was both a positive and a negative depending on which side of the political fence you sat.

Northwest Community College Vocational & Technical Institute circa 1980s.
Photographed by Andrew Webber. Andrew Webber Collection.

But it was an interesting time and I felt privileged to sit in on some of the discussions and to see what the efforts were of some of the people that were trying to develop a college with a little bit of a difference. You know rather than being elitist which a lot of the universities are, they were trying to make this more of an everyman's college. So that was a very interesting part. I was working at the college probably at some of its best times, when there was a fair amount of money available and more courses were being offered. And actually I gather that when I left things were starting to change. Financial cutbacks were coming in and when there's cutbacks, the politics in the organization start to get a little uncomfortable with departments protecting their own area.

Anyway, the college is struggling to stay alive. I think it's very, very important to the young people and to the businesses in the area that we have a thriving college that can move with the times. It's like so many other government-run organizations that become administrative top-heavy and when the cuts come they're so often to the services to the students rather than getting rid of the very expensive people at the top.

KM: Are there any other stories you want to share about your time in the area?

SM: What stories could I share, I mean this is like a history thing so when I think of the early days, Terrace has always been important in the area. When I was a young woman, we used to have to drive to Terrace to catch planes out of Terrace. There had been a time when planes into Rupert were amphibian planes from Sandspit — you landed in the water and then when they decided to build an airport, they stopped the amphibian connection with Sandspit, and we drove to Terrace. I can foresee that that's going to happen again because it's an hour and a half drive, a road that is a much more pleasant drive though a very changeable drive at this time of year. You go from rain to slush, to snow to ice, from that coastal to the interior weather pattern.

I am sure a person if they had time to think about historic things, like off the top of my head, you know the Silvertip Cafe came to my mind and my vision of Terrace in the '50s was of this small, little, quaint little town, not many paved roads but it had that nice lake, and nice rivers to fish in.

KM: And good hiking spots.

SM: And good hiking spots. So it was always a drawing card for a lot of us.

JANET MONSEN'S MOTHER - FIRST MARRIED TO VIC FRSTAY + THEN TO ONE OF THE MARKS (PETER ?)

Wilfred Bennett Interview

Interviewed by Melanie Pollard, 9 December 2013

Wilfred Bennett was born in Kitselas in 1939 and grew up in Port Essington. In 1947, Wilfred's parents, Edward and Lucile Bennett, died in a tragic boating accident while travelling from Prince Rupert to Port Essington. After the death of Wilfred's parents, he was sent to St. Michael's Indian Residential School where he remained for 10.5 years. After school, Wilfred moved to Prince Rupert and worked in the fishing industry. He married Audrey in 1960 and had six children. Wilfred and Audrey lived in Kitkatla for 11 years before moving to Terrace in 1971. Wilfred spent his career working in the fishing and logging industry, as well as working as a First Nation's band manager. In this interview, Wilfred talks about his time as a band manager, changes he has witnessed in the community, traditional First Nations mentoring practices, and how both he and his wife lost their Sm'algyax language in residential school. He also talks about topics such as fishing, hunting, trapping, and the logging industry.

MP: We'll start off with a nice easy question. Where and when were you born?

Kitselas Canyon, 1936. Johnstone Collection.

WB: I was born in Kitselas, February 18th, 1939, and after I was born, my parents moved down to Port Essington, down at the mouth of the Skeena River across from Tyee. I spent well, just about eight years of my life there, just going on to my eighth year when tragedy struck our family. My mom and dad were passengers on my mom's brother's boat — Peter Spalding. My dad was Edward Bennett and my mother was Lucile—Lucy Spalding Bennett (that was her maiden name, Spalding). And January 29, about three o'clock in the afternoon when that happened.

My older brother Lawrence Bennett—my parents, they sent a message through the CBC and they were going to be arriving in Port Essington while the tide was still coming in. But the departure was delayed and my uncle Peter—I don't know what was so important for him to be up in Port Essington that day, but he departed Prince Rupert (I'm not sure what time). They got to Port Lambert and my brother saw their running lights coming up and then disappeared. And when they disappeared, the boat had hit ice, punched a hole in it and it sank. The only ones that made it shore were my Uncle

Pete along with his new infant baby. The next day they had a search party searching along Port Lambert, the Skeena River there. They had people up — searches going through the woods there — and that's when they found Uncle Peter cradling his infant baby at the bottom of a cedar tree. My mom and dad, they weren't found along with Peter's wife, Martha Wesley Spalding, and an older child of theirs, Kenny, and the father-in-law Matthew Wesley. They didn't find them. I guess they had two search parties going on for four days or more there in all the communities — Hartley Bay, Kitkatla, Port Simpson and some up the Nass there were all in the search party. But, they never found them. It was probably in the spring — maybe the better part of April a fellow from Oona River was walking along the beach north and he came across my dad. He found my dad, dried up on the beach there. I believe how that happened was he had drowned and sank to the bottom and the ice was on top of him. So, he was just impeded in the ice. And ice floating up and down the river and then probably went down Standard and at the south end of Kennedy Island and then across towards the north part of Oona River and that's where he ended up. But the rest of the family were never found.

And in — say February, the better part of February, we were sent down to St. Michael's Indian Residential School along with my older brother Sydney Bennett and our cousin Henry Spalding and myself. When I arrived there, I didn't speak English, I just spoke Sm'algyax, and I was fortunate enough to have some of the fellows from Port Essington that went to Alert Bay. There was Victor Jackson, Robert Jackson, Jimmy Jackson, and Raymond Wesley; four of them. I was still able to talk to them in Sm'algyax

MP: You could still speak.

WB: That was in February of '47. Prior to that accident there, I spent the first eight years, well just about eight years, in Port Essington growing up. And my dad — he was a commercial fisherman, salmon during the summer months and in the fall he'd go up Ecstall River where he worked in Brown's Mill. And until the [salmon] cycle, he worked in Brown's Mill until during the spring and summer months. So that carried on until 1947. I did school in Port Essington but it wasn't on a regular basis. I sort of set my own schedule and I'd leave the classroom when I had enough. So I didn't learn too much at the time there. I was eight when I was in Alert Bay [British Columbia] there, residential school. I started up in grade one, from '47 to '57, so ten-and-a-half years I was down there.

MP: That's a long time.

WB: Yeah. Well, I finally came home at the end of August of '57 to Prince Rupert, the only relatives I knew was my dad's younger sister Gladys Grey. We were close to her and her family and they lived in Port Essington at the time. And then my mother's youngest sister Mary Spalding was married to Ken Dobson, that was her married name, Mary Dobson. We were close to Gladys and so I spent a couple of weeks with Mary. And then I had a younger brother. He was in Sunnyside in foster care. His name was Reginald Bennett. The only way I could get there was by train so I boarded the train when I found out where he was and went there. I got off in Sunnyside and checked out to see where he was, and I found him. I stayed with him and then moved out to Kitkatla where Reuben Mason was from and his family. They were just finished their seasonal employment there in Sunnyside. Yeah, when we first got there — we had the Jackson boys, Raymond Wesley.

MP: At school?

WB: At the school there and knew them. Being there it's just a routine on a daily basis. We'd get up, line up for breakfast — after we washed up then line up for breakfast. And then after breakfast we'd be outside picking up anything that was paper or other trash. Kept the grounds fairly clean there and then at nine o'clock we'd go to our classes with all of them at the school. It ran grade one up to grade two and then we went up to the Indian Day School up on the hill on the reserve in Alert Bay there. The day school — so that's where we went from grade three on up until we got to grade seven and then grade seven we went to the high school downtown in Alert Bay there. Grade seven up to grade 12. So I didn't graduate down there. I started school late. Instead of six, it was eight; so three years I'd lost there. I left Alert Bay at grade 10 and came home. But 1950 — there was only one summer, while I was down there, that our older brother Lawrence Bennett, brought Sydney and myself over for the holidays. We spent the summer in Port Essington with our Auntie Gladys.

MP: Was that the only time you came back north?

WB: I stayed there until vacation was over and then we boarded the steamboat in Prince Rupert. Then went back to Alert Bay. And then from there, we remained in school during the summer months up until 1956. I was 17 at the time. So I was a deckhand on the seine boat for one of the fishermen down there along with three other friends of mine from the school. Terry Dudoward, Danny Walkus and Pat Joseph, and myself. Four boys from the school were deckhands on the same boat and there were three other crewmen who were on the boat.

MP: How long did you work there?

WB: Throughout the summer months, so I enjoyed that. We fished around Alert Bay there and then went up around Namu, half way to Douglas Channel. So we spent a couple weeks up there fishing and then headed back down to Alert Bay. By that time, we were just about ready to get back into routine of going to school, high school, down there.

I left Alert Bay in 1957. I was 18 years of age then. I came back up this way, Prince Rupert to live with my Uncle Reuben Mason in Kitkatla along with his wife and family, Grace Mason. They're wonderful people.

MP: And did you get work then at 18…?

WB: Yeah, just seasonal. In 1958, I was hired as a crew member for drag seine down Union Pass. Catch many species but the main species was the chum salmon from July to the end of August. So there was a lot of work in that. I did that for four years, '58, '59, '60, '61, two summers in Union Pass there and then '60 and '61 at Gail Point at Banks Island. That was through June to end of August.

MP: And did you marry?

WB: Yeah. In 1960 I married Audrey and then I spent, let's see—I was 13 years in Kitkatla. We were married 11 years before we moved. It was 1971 when we finally packed up our belongings and loaded them on the boat and headed into Prince Rupert and loaded them on the train and headed up to Terrace there.

MP: So you moved back together in '60-'61?

WB: Yes. So, I was active in the fishing industry when I moved up here. I fished the summer months down the coast there and after the salmon season, I worked for Twin River Timber Logging Company. That was before the salmon season was up — I worked for a couple months then I went down the coast and fished for Port Edward Nelson brothers. After the season I came back home here and then went over to Kitimat to Crown Zellerbach. I put an application there and that's where I was hired on logging, high lead logging; I worked there up until Christmas and then settled down and waited, collecting U.I. [Unemployment Insurance]. In 1977 I got my herring license. February was when we had our boats all tuned up to go herring fishing and we'd start down the straits there at Port Alberni. We'd tie up in French Creek, then we'd haul the boat out of water, and then, instead of running the boat up around into Vancouver Island [British Columbia], we trucked it over to Port Alberni.

That was a lot quicker. We just launched it there. Start scouting around for herring and when they did open it up we'd just fish herring there. When the season closed there, we'd have the boat hauled back out of the water and on the truck and over to French Creek and fish around Texada Island and those other areas around there. We worked our way up to central coast there, up around Bella Bella area, and fish herring there. We then ended up in Kitkatla Inlet. When that was done, the season was over; we had our herring nets all washed down and stored away in the net loft in Port Ed [Edward]. Then we'd get ready for the salmon season. March, I'd go backlogging for a few more months before the salmon season.

MP: All the seasons changing, your work would be changing.

WB: But them days are all gone now, so. Finished the salmon season and then go logging; it's not there anymore.

MP: How many years did you do that?

WB: Let's see. Up '70, '71 then '75. And then I worked for the band, took care of their business part there until '85.

MP: In administration, or what were you doing with the band?

WB: I was, well, band managing. We were a small band. Our population at the time was barely 100 probably, living in Rupert, Terrace and other areas. But now we got about 600 and we got two offices that's going pretty strong.

MP: Pretty different than when you were managing.

WB: Yeah, I remember when we first moved here and Lakelse Avenue down the west end — there where the mall is — I remember the Catholic Church there but it wasn't in use. The trees started to grow around them and they started planning for a mall and they had that all cleared up. From the time we moved up here, it made a lot of difference on the area.

MP: What kind of changes have you seen in what the band was dealing with when you were manager and what you're now doing as a councillor?

WB: Let's see. When Terrace started developing the mall there: one of the big developments prior to that was the grocery store, Overwaitea. I remember when they were located in the corner of — where Gemma's store is. What's that store? Gemma's store. Yeah, the Overwaitea was there and they relocated to where the TK radio station is. That's where the Save-On Foods was, and then they moved down to the BC Access area building there. Then when the mall was completed, that's where they've been ever since. And then we had a Super-Valu Store just down where the M&M Meats and the pet store is, that's where that was.

MP: In the early days when you were managing for the band, what were some of the things you had to do?

WB: Oh, the band started expanding there. There were more houses coming up at the time. '85 we just had, let's see, there was nine houses: eight on Queensway and one on Lowrie Road. And over time, it started adding more and more houses. '80, '85, we built four houses out there. In '86 they built 20 units that filled up that subdivision up on Kulspai and '92, when we developed the Gitaus subdivision there, that started in February. But prior to that, we had Bruno Contracting in the area logging. When that was done, they started pushing in the roads, the access road, and following the blueprint of what the subdivision was gonna look like. The blueprints were developed by Lapointe Engineering. So when the first part of that development was put in, there were 20 units. That was completed just before Christmas. And then, over the years, they started building homes up there. We got about 80-some units up in Gitaus and 35-some odd units down Queensway and Kulspai.

MP: So, big changes.

WB: And during this time, we tapped in to the Thornhill water system when they laid it out and then we were under agreements with them. And we got agreements with them and we got water. Sewer came in in '90, about '97 I think, and we got the garbage pickup, and the street lighting. So all that was tied into it, the Kitimat Stikine Regional District. And then we built our own health centre up in Gitaus there. That was about '97, '98. And so the Health Centre administration was all completed and the following year we put up the fire station. And over time, they developed the Kitselas historic site, and they put up four longhouses down there and carved four totem poles for up on top, and then four down on the end of that trail. Then they built a viewpoint area down at the end of the trail there where you could look at across the canyon to Gitlaxdzawk, the fortress area.

MP: Wow, that's a lot of developments and changes, hey?

WB: Yeah.

MP: Very neat. I'm just going to go back to your family. Did you and Audrey have children?

WB: Yeah, Robert was born 1960 and we had six children: Glenn, Sidney, Cyril, Webb and Sharon. We also lost two. One was 11 months in '66 and '95 we lost our third oldest boy. We also had four granddaughters that we raised.

MP: That's a lot of kids.

WB: Yeah, so…

MP: And how was Terrace and the area for raising a family?

WB: Oh, I think—it's been pretty, I think its great. All the children got their education and they graduated. Glenn here is working in Treaty and was the Chief Councillor for about… was it two terms or three terms? So he's the one who is responsible for putting up the health centre in Gitaus and putting up the firehouse and all. And having all the streets paved up there on Queensway and having a sewer system tapped into the Kitimat Stikine Regional District.

MP: And he was Chief Councillor during that time?

WB: Yes.

MP: So your family was quite involved in administration and government.

WB: I think that's been pretty great. A lot of our other community members that they worked along with, most of them had parts in having the Gitaus subdivision developed; building houses up there.

MP: What did you and your family do for fun?

WB: When the boys were growing up, they joined the hockey program here, and they were in it up until, I guess, after their high school years.

MP: Do you play hockey too?

WB: No, no I wasn't a sportsman.

MP: Not into sports. What kind of things did you like?

WB: I was the sit-in-the-stands guy.

MP: You need those, too. What kind of things did you like to do for fun?

WB: Well, hunting and hunting deer. When I was up in Kitkatla, didn't do too much hunting up here. Not as much as we did down the coast there and I did a bit of trapping up along Kitimat. That's where my trap line is. Right in where that PTP pipeline [Pacific Trail Pipeline] is going in there; a couple miles of it is my trapline. Right in where that was coming in there.

MP: What kind of things did you like to do in Terrace? Were there things in town that were interesting to do or restaurants that were popular?

WB: Yes, we used to watch the local hockey games here with our boys playing hockey; taking their schedules and watching the games. And we parents watched hockey games there. But other than that, with the TV, I have more sports. I watch a lot of football on TV.

MP: Why not? That's great.

WB: I used to watch a lot of hockey but when they had that boycott a couple years ago — I never watched a full game of hockey since.

MP: Did you ever visit Lakelse, the hot springs?

WB: Oh, yeah. We took our grandchildren out there for their birthday parties. They have hot, hot springs. They swam out there.

MP: What was that like?

WB: They enjoyed it. But I'm 74, I'm still active in fishing: halibut fishing, salmon, yeah. I think that's probably the only thing that's keeping me going, even though I had a heart attack two years ago. So yeah, I've just got to take it easy. I got my older boy out on the boat doing heavy work out there.

MP: So, you're still fishing?

WB: Yeah.

MP: That's great. Were you involved in any other community activities?

WB: Well just in, what with the council business — some of the programs. There's not too much sports activities going on the reserve.

MP: Were there cultural events that you were a part of?

WB: No. I was busy just about from the early part of spring till November. So when I came in, I would take in the Riverboat Days parade. We usually go on our vacations in the middle of August 'til the first week of September. Took the grandchildren and the great-grandchildren along with us. So we, our families, are tight-knit. We celebrate birthdays and Christmas. We have Christmas and dinners at our place, even though it is expanded, we still enjoy the home atmosphere.

MP: What are the events you most enjoyed together as a family?

WB: Let's see — we'd take in the Prince Rupert Seafest. We'd take the family down there and take it in. And then when I'm not there, the missus would take them to the Kitimat July 1st parade there and their events. And we'd try to get our granddaughters involved in different activities, but they're shying away from that now. But we got them two great grandchildren, one will be four and three pretty soon, so we enjoy taking them around. Raising them, help raising them.

MP: What do you remember about downtown Terrace when you first moved back?

WB: '71, well there was still lots of trees on the Lakelse Avenue and there was still lots of brush around the buildings on Main Street. And it's just starting to — beautification is making a lot of difference in the area now.

MP: And where did you buy food…?

WB: Well, it was Super-Valu here and Overwaitea and Safeway came in later on.

MP: And where did you shop for other things like clothes or furniture? What was popular in the '70s?

WB: Well T. Eaton's was where we got our furniture and appliances from. And then the clothing store was Ev's Men's Store. But the children's clothing was — we did the shopping in Prince Rupert there. The Stork Shop, where they had clothes for infants up 'til the teens.

MP: And what did most people that you know do for work? What kept people working?

WB: There were loggers working in the bush there and other ones working in the sawmills.

MP: And have you watched a lot of changes in the forest industry over the years?

WB: Yeah, it's just like, I guess — what sort of brought down the industry was the high-tech sawmills, cutting lumber fast and cutting themselves out of the industry. And the companies that were here earlier cleared the areas and I see what they should have done was build the roads to the furthest outreach where they'd have to go out that way and work their way in to the city — not start from around the city. And the companies just cleared the timber out of here. Struggling companies aren't around anymore.

MP: And how did you see the community of Terrace interacting with Kitselas and Kitsumkalum?

WB: Well, Kitselas has always been working great together with [the Regional District of] Kitimat-Stikine and the city of Terrace along with Kitsumkalum. They work closely with Kitsumkalum but we're ahead of them because we have our own land codes and don't have to rely on the Department of Indian Affairs to get any permits to develop our lands. We can just get a consultant or engineer to design an area and we can develop it ourselves. And the Treaty, we got the Agreement in Principle that puts us ahead of other First Nations like the Gitxsan and the Coastal Tsimshian. Kitselas and Kalum, we're both in on that Agreement in Principle so that's where we're ahead and where we're ahead of Kalum is our land codes. We have our own land code. They still have to rely on the Department to get any okay on their development. And that Agreement in Principle is where Kitselas is ahead of those — like I said the Gitxsan, the Coastal Tsimshian, and other First Nations. So I think we get along quite well in most areas there.

MP: Have you lived in Terrace during any major floods?

WB: Just, what was it? '77? And the one not too long ago when Braun's Island was flooded out, my granddaughter's high school and I was part of the sandbagging down there (around 2008?). 1936 was a bad year for the flood. I wasn't born then…

MP: Yeah, absolutely. But the '77 one you said?

WB: Yeah, '77, and then '92, I remember having to shut down the development up in Gitaus because with the heavy rains. I remember the Copper River. The water was just probably six inches from underneath the bridge there.

MP: Did that impact the community in any way?

WB: Nope. Not where I am, and not Gitaus, no. We're fairly high. Kitsumkalum — they're on the lowlands and it affected them a lot there. Where their community hall and administration building is, that's the area that is usually flooded out.

MP: I know that you've been a councillor with the Band, are you right now as well?

Wilfred Bennett Sr. in Kitselas Administration building, May 2004. Photo credit Terrace Standard.

WB: Oh, yeah.

MP: What got you involved in politics?

WB: Over the past few terms there, I wasn't as heavily involved in it as I used to be. And, well, there's kind of a limited amount of development going on because of the financial part. So, hopefully, 2014 to 2015, I'd like to see more houses going up in the other subdivision there—build homes for our members, then half for rentals for non-community members, I think.

MP: That's what got you most interested in politics?

WB: I'd like to see our young people get the training in different areas, heavy-duty operators. I'd like to see them get involved in that. Get their tickets for that and there's other areas they could go in and maybe start their own businesses. They just have to put their minds to work and get at it.

MP: Did you garden or grow any food, your family?

WB: Just fruit trees and berries. No, I guess I'll be just about the age now that I can maybe head out and plant some vegetables and potatoes.

MP: But you had fruit trees and did berries?

WB: Yes, but I've never grown any of those here in Terrace. Even though I got a fairly good-sized yard here on Queensway. I could handle a lot of vegetables.

MP: How have you seen Terrace change over the years?

WB: Yeah, from there it was a bustling logging and lumber town, sawmills and logging industry back then. That was the main industry here and — yeah, logging and the sawmills were the heart of Terrace that kept it going. But when the industries started going down, it really affected it. Other communities along the way were affected, too. That's where I see the change. But even though there's a lot of port expansion happening down in Rupert and there's a lot of trades coming through here — you know, Kitselas was situated in an area where they were able to apply the toll system. Usually it's up river coming down. And I think that's always been in their culture, for the past 11,000 years. And it is part of our culture and I'd still like to see that applied into our Treaty, to get the tolls on the railway, all the containers going through, all the parties going through—pay a toll to Kitselas. That alone should stay in our community and retroactive—back to when the Grand Trunk started coming through. And they did apply that to the Grand Trunk: they did pay some tolls to Kitselas at the time so, I think they should re-instate that. I think we'll be in a good position there.

MP: Couple of other questions. When you were a child, what did you expect or hope to accomplish?

WB: Well, that was the furthest thing from my mind, never thought of that.

MP: You were just a kid.

WB: I was just growing up.

MP: There weren't dreams or hopes you had as a kid?

WB: Well, I think with all the First Nations youth there, they had their mentors, their uncles showing them the way—that's the way it used to be. Uncles would be the ones that would be mentoring the males in the hunting, fishing, trapping, the way of life. They're the ones who'd be gathering the food and would be processing them.

I didn't have a grade 11-12 education, but the education we received in Alert Bay was all academic programs we had to go through. So it was way above the standards the regular classes are getting now. But no, our First Nations were always in the fishing industry. After I finished school and started work as a deckhand, I wrote a letter to the Nelson brothers requesting I rent a boat from them for the 1968 fishing season. That's when I first got to use a boat from them and started commercial fishing from there.

MP: Was there someone that made a big impact on your life?

WB: Let's see. Well, I think I was usually amongst the elders. I was close friends to people that would be at the age of my parents and I was close to them. And those people were the ones who mentored me and everything, even though I wasn't with them on a daily basis. But I'd talk to them and they'd tell me how to fish and set a net and all that.

And same way, when we were on a herring boat, my son was listening to another radio band and they were talking about a big body of herring out at Striker Island and we were all anchored through Reid Pass in the central area. They were just about 10 o'clock, so when I heard that I told my brother-in-law that we were going to pull anchor and we were gonna head out there and wait for the opening. So before I left, I stopped off about three boats from Kitkatla, told them what I heard. I stopped off and told them what was spotted by the aircraft and told them we were going out and asked them if they were gonna be coming out. "Nope, we'll wait till tomorrow."

And the next day we got out there about one o'clock in the morning and we anchored up and waited till they opened up at eight o'clock in the morning. So, we anchored out there, got up and went to where we were going to set our herring gillnets. So, we were all ready for the opening and then the opening happened. We set our gear but after we set we started shaking the herring off the nets. During that time we had about six tonnes of herring and I phoned the guys; Wilfred Jackson and

Johnny Vickers. Told them how we were making out at Reid Pass there and they were still scratching away at home. We had six tonnes delivered to the packer and then, the weather blowing—before the day was over we had 10 tonnes of herring. And they didn't have anything where they were, but they were trying to come…but it was just too rough. So yeah, I listened to the older, experienced fishermen and they helped me along quite a bit.

MP: What would you share with people who are moving to Terrace now?

WB: Make sure they get an education and I think what I see here is mostly truck driving, equipment operators. I would say to get their training for operating the heavy-duty equipment and get all those tickets. I think, once they've gotten that, I think they'd be okay. Because that's the main thing I see here now: there's a lot of trucks. I tried to count how many trucks are coming and going when I'm driving up to Gitaus there. But there's a lot of truck traffic—transport trucks and flat beds towing the equipment. There's a lot of truck driving that's to be done around here and heavy-duty equipment; and trying to get a band to invest in snow removal with snowplough, and sanders, and graters. That's what we need and it's not that they're gonna be sitting around after the winter months; they'll be involved in road development or construction, stuff like that.

MP: Well, we're coming to the end. Are there any other stories you'd like to share?

WB: Let's see. Terrace, our communities in Terrace: Kalum and Kitselas, when the areas of the coast opened up—well, people moved to where the employment was, they worked at the canneries. There weren't too many of them that were involved in the commercial fishing. But Kalum, they have a lot of commercial fishermen in their band there. They got a bunch in Kitselas.

Let's see. Audrey, she's really brought up by her grandparents. She was mentored by her great-grandmother, grandmother and her aunties. Yeah, she learned a lot. Even though she was a residential school survivor, she come home a lot earlier than I did. But that's the one thing that we lost, was our Sm'algya̱x, speaking the language. Even though I was fluent when I went to school, it was all gone when I got there—before I left. But, let's see. She's one person that has lots of knowledge in herself, what she learned growing up and what she learned when she moved here. She was involved in the Terrace Public Library. Yeah. She was the trustee and well, a board member or something anyway—and they're multicultural. She was involved in Crime Stoppers. And she was involved in Skeena Diversity.

MP: That's wonderful. Well, thank you so much for your time, Wilfred. That was very interesting to get to hear your stories and to get this time with you.

WB: Yeah, and oh yeah. There's one that pertains to our, Kitselas and other tribes like where my great grandparents, Philip and Amy Campbell (her maiden name was Musgrave) come out of—they come out of Gitladoiks and we have over 100 members to come out of that particular Campbell family that's still living in Kitselas. So that's one thing that we have going, both of our members are from Gitladoiks tribe there. There was seven tribes that lived up in the canyon prior to the arrival of the Europeans and they all came—they are all situated along the Skeena up this way. And the seven tribes are all in the canyon. I just got to get the names of them.

MP: Well that would be great, to hear more. Thank you, so much.

WB: Okay.

Willy Schneider Interview
Interviewed by Ed Curell, 17 December 2013

Willy Schneider was born in Germany in 1923, in the province of Saxony. After completing training to be an agricultural manager, Willy was drafted into the army and served most of his time on the Russian front during World War II. After the war, he worked as an agricultural manager in East Germany. When he caught wind that the Russian police suspected that he was in 'conflict with their regime and with their government; he fled to West Germany. Willy worked as a farmhand and a horse handler in West Germany for a few years before being married in 1951. In West Germany, there was no future in his profession as an agricultural estate administrator. With no money, limited professional prospects, and a child on the way, Willy decided to emigrate to Canada with his wife. On June 29th, 1954, on his 'daughter's very first birthday; Willy and his family arrived in Calgary. Willy worked in various jobs for five years before being introduced to the financial service industry. He joined Sun Life of Canada in January 1959, which brought him to Terrace. Over the next 50 years in Terrace, Willy was involved with the Terrace Rotary Club (25 years), the Skeena Valley Golf Course, the Railroad Club, the Royal Canadian Legion, and the Terrace Public Library. At the age of 84, Willy wrote and published his autobiography, Such... is Life: The Story of the Trials and Tribulations of an Immigrant.

EC: Okay, so we can get going. I know that a lot of these first questions that were on the list to ask, you have already covered in your book. Because you wrote a book. That must be about five years ago now, right?

WS: Five years, yeah. It was published in 2008.

EC: Five years. Called *Such is Life*. So, it has a whole record pretty well of your history — from birth up to the time when you first came to Terrace. But anyway, we should probably do a little summary so that people who are listening to this, or are reading the transcript, can get an idea of who you were and where you came from. So, where and when were you born?

WS: Well, I was born a long, long time ago, in 1923 to be exact, in Germany, in the former part of Germany that was regarded as East Germany. It's the province of Saxony. And after the war — during which I spent most of my time in Russia — when I came home, there were the Russians again. And I wasn't exactly on the best footing with these people. So I was able to flee from East Germany in June 1946, to the West, and from there on, it developed into a much better life.

EC: I know that's in your book, but that's a pretty interesting story about how you managed to get away.

WS: Well, it was actually in June 1946. Yes, the war was over in '45. There was no Iron Curtain, there was no no-man's land, and it was relatively simple to slip across the so-called border within Germany.

The little village where I worked as an agricultural manager was only about three or four kilometres from the border. So one night I snuck across there. I more or less — I think I should call it — I was fleeing. Because I came back from work one day, when my boss called me in the office, and told me that the Russian secret police — the NKVD — and the German police were there to enquire about me, and they would like to talk to me because they feel that I somehow got in conflict with their regime and with their government, which I did. So without asking any more questions, I found the smallest suitcase I had and put a set of underwear and a toothbrush in. And at two o'clock in the morning, I snuck out. And about three-thirty, four o'clock in the morning, I was in West Germany.

I was a free man, but I was a persona non-gratis because I had no ration cards. I had no permit to acquire accommodation. So with my agricultural background, my background being agriculture, I simply became a farmhand and drifted from farm to farm. It gave me a bed to rest my head on and gave me a table to eat on. And I did that more or less until 1950. In late '50, I heard that the British occupation forces in Bielefeld, where I lived at that time, were looking for a groom — and horses have played an important role in my life so far.

First of all, I was in agriculture. I was involved in breeding and I belonged ever since to the army; I belonged to a mounted troop. So I applied there and it developed, actually, so that I was working for the occupation forces and for the British occupation forces who sometimes could be a little bit difficult to deal with, so to speak. And it developed into a very, very nice, good relationship.

It took me about half a year before we got to know each other. We were mostly dealing with officers and their wives — and after they found out what I knew about horses and my riding abilities, it developed into a very, very good relationship. I had offers to go to Ireland, to England, to look after some of the officer's horses. But that was not my idea of my future, to look after somebody's horses for the rest of my days.

So, by that time, I met my wife. I was married in 1951 in December, and after lengthy debates and exchanging ideas and exchanging how we felt about it — because I wanted to emigrate — it was a very nice surprise when I found out from my wife that she asked, "When and where are we going?" And then it took us approximately two years to get that far. But finally we made it and here I am.

EC: And we're glad to have you.

WS: Thank you.

EC: So, I wonder if you could tell us a little bit about your parents.

WS: Well, it's a sad story. My parents, I believe, married in '21 or '22. It was, I must say, an arranged marriage. Not in the sense that we know it from the Far East, but my grandmother, having been an extremely powerful and strong-willed person, more or less decided who my mother will marry.

There was a big, big café. It was a very famous café, Cafe Troemel in Plauen. And it was known not only in Plauen; it was known in the whole surrounding area. And it was known as heiratsmarkt, the marriage market, where mothers with eligible daughters went there and snooped around a little bit, and showed their daughters, showed their wares, so to speak. And I guess one of these days, she saw this one guy and she reeled him in and they were married in '21.

I was born in '23. And after that my grandmother immediately initiated the divorce, which lasted two years. She hired two lawyers. Her daughter had a nervous breakdown during it, but she was determined to end it. And my father said right from the beginning, "Do whatever you want to do. I am moving away. I am going to Munich. Let me know what I have to do or what I have to pay for." But she still dragged it out for two years. And for that reason I never really got to know my father. And I was brought up not so much by my mother; I was brought up by my grandmother. The slightest thing that I did wrong there was always the stick and backhand. It was not much fun. And I began to dislike her unfortunately, intensely.

EC: So, did you ever see your father again after he left?

WS: Yes, yes. I saw my father from 1929… Let me see. I was about six years old from the very late '20s or '30s. Well, I was — even before — I was encouraged to write him a letter. Now what is a five- or six-year-old writing a letter to a person he knows is his father, but he doesn't know; he hardly knows what he looks like. So that didn't work very well.

But anyway, I wrote letters and they must have been literary masterpieces. And then one day my dad took the bull by the horn and said how would it be if Werner, which is my German first name — it's Willy Werner Schneider — if I came down to Munich and we would spend a couple of weeks in the Bavarian Alps. Well, he drew the big lottery. That was the first and only thing that ever was agreed upon by my grandmother, and off I went. And we did that between 1929, I believe, and 1935 — two or three times. But it didn't get us any closer. It didn't bring us any closer.

I have always been a railway buff. And when I was six years old, my grandfather, who actually really stepped into the footprint of my father… He became my father. He was a great man. I always said to my granddaughters, "If I can be half the grandfather to you that my grandfather was to me I'm going to be a good grandfather." But anyway, he bought me a little wind-up railroad thing just around the circle — and I was just in seventh heaven. So, I remember one of these visits down in the Alps — Schliersee was the name of the village where we usually stayed. My father says "What would you like to have for Christmas?" I said "Really?" He says, "Yes, what would you like for yourself?" "I would like a railway set." Christmas came, and I got a microscope. End of the railway...

And then I saw my father again after the war in summer of '46, and I had seen…needless to say, I survived this war. I should mention there was always in the background, *Why did this happen? Why did I have this strange relationship? Why didn't I have a father and a mother at home to whom I could talk as I saw with my friends and with the young people I went to school with, that I was invited here and there?* Whenever I prodded at home, and Oma was still alive — Oma was my grandmother — and I touched the subject [she'd say], "We don't talk about that. That's the way it is and that's the way it stays and don't ask any questions." Okay.

I took my mother aside one day — I was able to do that — and she says, "Well, we better not talk about that." So I said, "okay." So, when the war was over, I met my mother in West Germany at that time, where my grandfather lives. And I took her aside one day and I said, "Mom, I'm a grown up man now. I have survived this war, I've been shot up, I've been shot at, and I want to know what was going on." And she sort of let it out; there were tears flowing — and Grandma had everything under control, and she was totally under the rule of her mother. Her mother was a goddess and what she said was carved in gold and carved in stone. That's the way it was.

So I said, "okay." I said, "Now I'm going down to Munich to have a chat with my dad," which I did. I went down to Munich and I sent him a telegram that I'm coming down. And even though the railway transport wasn't the most reliable at that time… It was a far cry from what it is today. Anyway, the train arrived within an hour or so of the time I gave him and here he was. He was all dressed up as he always was; he was dealing in cloth for men's wear, for suits, for coats and shirts — very well-dressed.

And so, before we left the station, I said to him, "Just a moment. I have to get myself some cigarettes." And you might find this strange, that I asked at the railroad station. Because cigarettes, you could only buy them on the black market and the black market in the railroad station was in the men's room; it stank to high heaven. There were the shadiest characters floating around and where you could buy. If I remember correctly, one American cigarette was six marks, and the English were five marks.

So he says, "Why do you want to buy cigarettes? Didn't I forbid you to smoke back in 1940?" — I think it was; he visited me once where I worked. And I said, "Yes, yes. I remember clearly." But I said, "Dad. Times have changed. I have grown up. I am no longer the little baby. I have just came from an ugly war. Yes, I smoke. I don't think it will make you feel better…I drink a little bit and I look at women." Well, that was definitely not the right way to start a new relationship with my father.

But amazingly enough, he says, "Well, you're not going in there to buy cigarettes. I can get them for you." I said, "Are you trying to tell me that you're in the black market?" He says, "Well, by no means, by no means. I met this American army chap — just accidentally. We were sitting on the bench and he didn't look too happy: I usually don't look too happy. And we got talking and we entertained the same ideas and whatnot. And he supplies me regularly with whatever I want: coffee and cigarettes and whatnot."

Well, I says, "Is he your confessor?" "Absolutely not!" But anyway…Dad lived a good life. The good chaplain supplied everything. I was only down there…that visit only lasted about three or four days, and we both knew it's not going to happen; we are simply not going to have a father and son type of thing, perhaps go out even for a drink together and slap each other on the shoulder. It would have never entered my mind.

And then that…incidentally, that was the very last time I saw my dad alive. He committed suicide in spring '53. He could not cope with the post-war time. He simply couldn't. I received a letter from him and it ended, and he enclosed — I think he enclosed — 500 marks with it. And he says it was just a little gift. Gisela and I, we were expecting our daughter Barbara. "For your future and whatnot." And he says, "I am going to go on a long journey and you may not hear from me for quite some time." He knew that he was going to commit suicide. And that was the end of my father.

And the end of my mother is much worse, because she got involved in the Russian-occupied zone. She was obsessed. I have to explain…we had a very successful shoe business in our town; we were the third largest shoe retailer in a city of about 120,000 to 130,000 people at that time. We did very well. My mother was sort of running the business. My grandfather already had semi-retired. And my grandfather was also the kind of guy who, if it doesn't get done today, there's a good chance it gets done tomorrow, but let us have a beer first. My mother was entirely different: go, go, go, business, my business, and better business.

So anyway, she got involved with the wrong people. She thought she could build in the eastern zone, where everything belonged to the government. She was under the illusion that she can revive our business, schuhgeschaft, our shoe business. I kept telling her in my letters, "Forget it. It's gone. It's nationalized." Anyway, so she got this offer to manage a store — for a person who apparently had the right connection, had a license, got merchandise — to manage that store for him. And then, sooner or later, he made inappropriate advances of a sexual nature, which my mother declined, of course. So he found himself another lady who was smarter than my mother — which is an ugly thing to say — and before my mother knew it, the police knocked on the door, and from there on it gets grey.

There is nothing carved in stone — no date, no time. I received the telegram from my aunt that my mother had been taken by the police at a railroad station in Plauen in June '46, yes, '46. And then I got another one that told me that she got on the train, which was headed for Berlin, and she was taken off the train before it went into the eastern zone, and then she vanished.

And the last thing… So I began a lengthy, lengthy correspondence with the Red Cross, and a new legal industry began to develop simply trying to find people that were snatched away by the Soviets and sent to some gulag or to Siberia. And that's where my mother ended up. And then, after two or three years of corresponding, I finally got a letter from the International Red Cross in 1961 simply informing me that my mother has died on Russian soil. So that was the end of my family — and I have no brothers or sisters. I'm the last Schneider. When I'm gone, the Schneiders are gone — well, this type of Schneider.

EC: But, I mean, eventually you wound up in Terrace after that pretty fascinating beginning. I mean, you had quite a life and so much of it is detailed in your book.

WS: Well, I think the thing was, I'm a very positive-thinking person. The war was ugly, yes. Millions of people died, yes. But it was over and life still goes on. And then, of course — especially after I met Gisela and we married and we expected a baby — the going on of life became more important. I could not see in West Germany a future in my profession, in agricultural estate administration. Because all the agriculture was in East Germany; that was with the Russians. There was no way that I would go back to the Russians. I would only end up somewhere in the Ukraine.

So, we made that decision — and we didn't know anybody. We had no money, but we thought it was not difficult because at that time — that was in 1900 — we emigrated in 1954. That was in 1952. That's when we first filed our first application for emigration. At that time, the Canadian government advanced you the funds for the journey from the old country to Canada. You had to sign a contract to an employer—mostly farmers—for three years. And that employer would take part of your salary, of your pay — remit it to the government, repaying the funds that they have advanced to me. But unfortunately, when our turn came up, that system was discontinued.

It lasted from April; Canada only took immigrants in from April to October. They didn't want anybody in wintertime. So, we were ready to immigrate, but we had no money. Well, to make a long story short, my wife found a little ad in the local paper that said, "Immigrants. Are you looking for funds for your immigration? Contact so and so." And it wasn't the next city, but I could go in a streetcar. When I came to that building, it was a Catholic mission, and I'm not a Catholic. So I thought, well, there is two ways to handle this: I can turn around and say tough luck and go home, or I go in there and find out, which I did.

I said right in the beginning, "Before we go any further I must tell you, I'm not a Catholic." And he looked me straight in the eye and said, "Did I ask you?" From there on, they had everything together within two or three weeks it was. Everything was arranged: the ship passage, the CPR across the country to Calgary, meal tickets, everything. So on the 29th of June, 1954, our daughter's very first birthday — she was born on the 29th of June — we arrived in Calgary and were in the new world.

EC: How did you wind up in Terrace?

WS: Oh, that's a long story.

EC: Well, the short version.

WS: We make it as short as possible. I should possibly mention that I never thought of Canada as the country of our destination. Never. Canada simply was not known in Europe. And who knew about it? Well, I knew a little bit about it because I was fighting the Canadians the last half year of the war, and I had the position to wind up the German forces; that was all the Canadians. But the opinion of Canada back in those days, in the '40s and '50s, was that it is a northern outpost of the United States, all frozen up, dog sleds and igloos and what not. Civilization was not equal with Canada.

So we met this guy in Iserlohn, from where we emigrated eventually — Big Eric. And we became friends. He was a bachelor — very, very badly shot up in the war. He stepped on a land mine and he'd half torn up his face. Half of his face torn up... terrible. Anyway, we got to know each other and we talked a little bit to each other, and we became friendly. And he being a bachelor, I said to Gisela, "Could I invite him for afternoon kaffee und kuchen on Sunday?" "Oh, by all means. Bring him in." He was really a German gentleman, bouquet of flowers, all beautiful. But when she saw him she just about fainted.

But anyway, to make a long story short, one day he said, "Well, what is a bright young man like you doing in Germany for the rest of your life?" Well, I says, "Don't have to worry about that. We're emigrating." "Oh," he says, "Where to?" "Well," I says, "We are not too clear yet. We don't want to go into a hot country, and I don't want to go to the United States — not that I'm an American basher, or that I don't like Americans. But what I don't like about Americans is their foreign policy, and I just came home from a war. They became involved in Korea and Vietnam and what not." And I said, "I don't want to fight another war," which would have been highly unlikely. But anyway — once burned, twice shy. "Oh," he says, "Don't worry. I know where you're going." "Oh," I said, "And where would that be?" "Well," he says, "Canada."

Canada was a cold country. Anyway, he bombarded me with old magazines and with old newspapers and all the stuff was years old. He was in Canada from '28 to '35, I believe, so the stuff was 15-, 16-, 17-years old. But we were so excited about it. And we saw pictures of the Rocky Mountains and Mount Robson with the highway — not today's highway, but the old winding highway. It looked better from day to day. So I says, "Where should we go?" "Well," he says, "Go west. Don't get stuck in the east. Too many foreigners."

To Eric, anybody non-German was a foreigner, and foreigners were usually no good. So he made it very simple. "Anyway, you go to Calgary." We had no idea where Calgary was; out came the maps. And we looked. Good God! It was the other side of the world. It was close to the Pacific Ocean. "How do we get there?" "No problem. No problem. It can all be arranged." Well, it was arranged so we ended up in Calgary. And here again I give you the short version: things didn't work out in Calgary, so they sent us to BC.

As a matter of fact, at the foot of Fairmont Hot Springs, there was a little tourist camp and ranch. They called themselves 'The Meadows.' Well, we lasted there a little bit. And then I got into the lumber business at these little chipper mills where they pulled them right up the mountains. I heard the guys always talk about down the coast, the big money. I didn't want to ask what that means. But then I developed... One couple, we became very good friends.

I said to him one day, I said "Ted, what does this down the coast big money mean?" "Oh, there are these huge sawmills with these huge trees. And there is, yes, there is big money." "Well," he says, "Willy, you don't think what I think you are thinking?" I said, "Yes, that's where I'm going." Off we went, down to Vancouver. The first job I had was down at the very, very end of Granville Island, a huge sawmill just before you cross the river to the airport. I forgot the name of it.

Anyway, I didn't like that at all. "Do you have camps?" We went to camps. That didn't work. Anyway, then I went into construction and my last job was as rock foreman at the Digby Island airport in Prince Rupert. I was there from April, early April to a week before Christmas. When I came home for Christmas, it was already dark.

We lived in Chilliwack; my family lived in Chilliwack. It was already dark and I had a brush cut, and when I knocked on the door and Gisela opened it, Barbara was hiding behind her. She was extremely reluctant to give me a hug or something, my daughter was. Her mother had to usher her forward and tell her to say hello to your dad. Gisela told me later after Barbara was put to bed, "She said to me, 'I know this man, but who is he?'" And that was the end of construction. I said that's it.

I thought with my background — with a little bit of management, language wasn't too bad — it shouldn't be too bad to get a job in Chilliwack. But it didn't quite work that way. I should mention that in the woods and in construction, I was a witness to three fatal accidents. And that made me realize that it could happen to me. And I have always been insurance-conscious. So one of the first things, when I came back in the new year in 1954, was to get some insurance. I bought some life insurance. And one of the questions is, what is your present occupation. That is what gives the insurance company some idea how I can pay for the premium.

Well, I didn't have a job. So the salesman kept coming back and asking if there was anything new. "No, no, there isn't anything new." He says, "We can't carry on that way. Either I tear up the application and you have no insurance or you have a job." He says, "Incidentally, have you ever thought of selling life insurance?" I said, "You must be out of your mind. Absolutely not."

310

Well, two weeks later, I signed a contract with Sun Life, on 29th of January, 1959. I started out down in the Fraser Valley and I fell flat on my face. And then I got a phone call from an agent, a German agent in Kitimat who knew about me. He phoned me and, "How are things going?"

"Well," I said, "I'm ready to quit." "You're crazy. You come up to Terrace." I said, "Where in the world is Terrace?" I had heard it mentioned in Prince Rupert, when we were building the airport in Prince Rupert. I heard of it, but I didn't really know where it is. "Well," he says. "That's where you are going. We just lost our agent there and you are off to Terrace and off to riches." "Well," I says, "How far is this Terrace?" "Oh, two days driving." "Well," I says, "Al, I haven't got enough money for one day driving." "No problem! Just go down to the bus depot in two days from today and there will be a cheque for $100." I said, "Where is that coming from?" "Never mind. Just go down to the bus depot and there will be a cheque for $100." It truly was — a Sun Life cheque.

So anyway, I came up there and I met the manager in Quesnel, a very rough man, very realistic man, didn't mince words. He was a hard rock miner before he became a life insurance salesman. Some strange characters were drawn to the life insurance industry in those days. So anyway, he says, "Well, let's make it short. You're going out to Terrace, set the world on fire. I don't want to hear any whining. I don't want to hear any moaning or groaning. I just want to hear good news from you, applications for life insurance. You understand that?" I said, "Yes, sir." "Well," he says, "get your ass out of here and go up to Terrace." Well, we came to Terrace and things didn't go very well the first two or three years, but from then on it was all a silver lining.

EC: But your whole family didn't travel up to Terrace together?

WS: They flew up. I arrived here on a drab, late November day— on the 29th of November, 1959, I arrived here in Terrace. There were approximately 4,200 people living here. There was one paved road; it wasn't really paved. It was this cold-packed stuff. That was Lakelse Avenue from the Bank of Nova Scotia to the corner of Emerson. And then, of course, Queensway was paved because the Queen was out here. And it was muddy in the wintertime and it was dusty in the summertime, very dusty. But everything worked out for the best.

EC: So when did you bring your family up?

WS: Christmas 1959. We had Christmas together.

EC: And how did you find Terrace as a place to raise a family?

WS: Ed, I would be a liar if I said that I had a high opinion of Terrace when I came up here. And the reception, business-wise, that I got, wasn't the greatest either. From the general population, great. But the business community made it absolutely clear: just take it easy. We are doing things fine here. We don't need any outsiders here. They made it quite clear. They didn't quite put it in the same words, but they made it quite clear. I'm not going to mention any names. One of them told me, "We don't need you and we are doing fine here." He was in the real estate business and I was hoping he could help me with some accommodation. He says, "You don't need any accommodation. Just go back to where you came from." But the general population, very good, very receptive.

Things took us two years. I don't want to do them again. But they are behind me now — a long, long way behind me. And things worked out just fantastic. I finally was accepted, and I was very well accepted and became the President of the Chamber, the President of the Rotary Club. I was on the Hospital Board. And there was another Board that I belonged to, the Board of Variance. Well, I was well accepted.

EC: What did you do for fun?

WS: Well, I, as most stupid people… golf was one of the first things.

EC: Yeah, well, was there a golf course?

WS: I enjoyed golf. A stupid game. Adult people chasing that little ball because they don't know how to do it; and it ends up in the oddest places. You can't find it.

EC: When was the golf course put in?

WS: Oh, the golf course wasn't there until Mr. Graebler. I think there were only six holes at that time.

EC: What year would that have been?

WS: The golf course was here when I came in '59. I didn't have the time, and quite frankly, I couldn't afford it until the mid-'60s, that I went up there. And, as I said, I think there were only six holes with gravel greens. There was no grass and you put a little bit of oil over it. Then you had to rake it and roll it and what not. But somehow, I got caught with this game, and then it became a nine-hole, then later on it became 18 holes. But it is the people I met up there and the great comradeship up there, great fellowship up there. It's a nice game; it's a very time-consuming game. I had to give it up. I gave my clubs this year to the junior league but I still go up there and have dinner with the boys. I took up skiing. I was involved in the development of every ski hill that was developed since the '60s, out at Kleanza Creek, out at the hot springs.

EC: There was a ski hill at Kleanza Creek?

WS: At Kleanza Creek, yes, there was a ski hill. We built it ourselves and we did all the clearing.

EC: Where was that?

WS: Before you go down the Kleanza River on [Highway 16], a road turns off to the right, before you go down across the bridge, going east. Before you go down that hill, a road turns off to the right, up into the mountains. That is where you went up, and back there we had a little hill. It wasn't very much of a hill. Bill Little donated a tow-rope, so that lasted for about three or four years. And then Ray Skoglund developed that little hill out at the hot springs, directly opposite the entrance. It wasn't very much of a hill, but anyway, it was a ski hill where you could do a little bit of skiing.

And then, I think the manager of BC Tel — I forgot his name but it might come back to me — he was a good skier and he wanted to see something better. BC Tel in those days had much more open pockets than today. He was able to get a helicopter donated by BC Tel, and we got Nancy Greene up here to scout some. We had an eye on a few properties, and she finally decided that Shames would be the one that we could possibly afford to develop, which we did.

EC: Well, no. We had that ski hill at Kitsumkalum first, when I first came here.

WS: Yeah, well. Kitsumkalum first.

EC: I thought that was the one that Nancy Greene was...

WS: Yeah. That's correct. That's correct. No, I still think Nancy Greene helped us spot Shames. Whichever — it was developed. I was in there right from the beginning with Dennis Lissimore, a great optimist. I think his forecasts, especially for population, were a little bit too hopeful and too positive. But then, of course, he couldn't foresee the decline in the economy in this area.

EC: Of course, you know now you that you can't rent or get a place in town so…

WS: Well, three quarters of the hill is still in the timberline, you know. This means you are exposed to any kind of weather, and sometimes it was nip and tuck. And I think, if it hadn't been for the

312

continuous support by a bunch of millionaires here in town, the hill would have folded a long time ago.

EC: So, when you go back to golf… I know that you raised a golfer in your daughter because I've seen her out there bashing the ball all on her own, flying around the course.

WS: Well, she is addicted. That started about four or five years ago, and she became addicted. Well first of all, she adores sunshine; 30-35 [degrees Celsius] is just fine. This is when I crawl into a hole and disappear. Yes, she became a good golfer.

EC: And a skier, too?

WS: Her daughters. Well, Brie has picked it up, the youngest one who is coming back to Terrace here next year. She picked it up.

EC: So what else did you do with your daughter, fun things? What was there to do with children in Terrace in those days?

WS: Well actually, both the girls were deeply involved in figure skating.

EC: Well, these are your granddaughters, right? What about the early days with Barb when you first came here?

WS: Oh, we went out fishing. We went out to the lake. We knew people out at the Kalum River; we knew people there. They had a little dock into the river and we were fishing. I still have pictures actually. There's a little string; there's a little fish hanging on it.

We had picnics and we knew a lot of people. In those days, I should mention, there was a huge German community. I must admit that I became a little bit self-centred and hung around with a lot of Germans. And there was, well, the whole nationality thing. In Kitimat, it was even worse. In Kitimat there was the Portuguese Club, the Italian Club, the French Club, the German Club, and what not, and they hardly spoke to each other. Here in Terrace, we at least spoke to each other.

But anyway, there were lots of things to do: boating and waterskiing on the Lakelse [Lake], hiking; there was always something to do. It's a great outdoor country and we are outdoor people.

EC: Did you go see movies and stuff?

WS: I don't think I have been in that movie theatre in all those years that I am here. I don't think I have been in there more than a dozen times.

EC: Restaurants?

WS: No, no. Well, at one time, when we were new to this country, the western world. But then later on, no, wasn't really.

EC: No restaurants? Were there good restaurants in town?

WS: No, no, no. Good restaurants? Whatever you classify as good restaurants. Now let me see: there was the old Terrace Hotel, which burned down later on. What else did we have? Oh, there was the [Chinese Restaurant- the Silvertip Café], where is now the vacant lot, adjacent to the fisheries store on the corner of Kalum Street and Lakelse Avenue, the fishing supplies.

EC: Right across from Don Diego's?

WS: Yeah, yeah. And it's now an empty lot. There was the Silvertip Café. Silvertip Café was owned by a Chinese family. They were known to have the best Chinese food in town. The father of the owner was a man who weighed about 300 pounds, and he sat in this big chair outside the restaurant all day long. He had this long knife — it must have been at least this long — and he sharpened this knife all day long.

EC: How long, for the record? How many inches?

WS: Oh, at least 20, at least 20. And then he went with his finger over the tip and he put it aside for a while. And then he had this little man in there — he was no higher than five feet, four or five [inches] — could have hidden two or three times behind that big guy. I don't think he weighed a hundred pounds.

And then Friday night and Saturday night, at that time, Terrace had a very, very vibrant logging community. Many of these guys were out in camps and the bush, and they usually came home on Friday night with pockets full of money. They went to the Silvertip Café and whooped it up.

One day, there was one guy, he became a little bit hostile to a woman or something like that. This little guy walks up to him and says, "You no do this here in our place." And he just lifted him up and threw him out on the street. And then I think they beat him up and the police found him in the morning dead. It was wild. It was a wild town.

And then, I can't remember any other… Oh yes, there was a restaurant in the motel. That is, when you come across the bridge from Kitimat, and before you come to Days Inn, which used to be the Alpine House, and Bavarian Inn, the left hand side, there is now a trailer court. There was a motel in there, and it belonged to an elderly couple — very respectable couple. And they had a little bit of a dining room, perhaps six tables. But this was if you wanted to go civilized eating. That would have been the only places at that time.

Doc Robertson took me down there once. There was an officer from a trust company coming up from Vancouver to Terrace, and Doc Robertson worked with that trust company on behalf of some of his clients. He came up and I worked quite a bit with Doc with mutual clients, and he invited me to come along there. It was very nice. We had quite a good meal there and it was a civilized meal. It was a kind of a meal I was used to from Europe.

Speaking of Europe, Canada was a bit of a shock, a culture shock. I mean, we are half the world apart in every respect, especially in the hinterland. I remember that very first job we had at the Meadows, at the foot of the Fairmont Hot Springs. There was no running water; there were no lights; there were no toilet facilities; and not even all the rooms, didn't even have floorboards. Some of the rooms were dirt packed – dirt! And Gisela hated the outhouses; she hated them with a vengeance.

There was a store at the hot springs, the Fairmont Hot Springs store, and somehow the guy — an Englishman, Mr. Wright — took a liking to us. They had water and light and facilities and what not. And Gisela, whenever she could arrange it, when she should go to a bathroom, she could sneak up to the hot springs, to the store. It was about five minutes walk, she would do so. It was a shock. Terrace has come a long, long way.

EC: And the hot springs? You went to the hot springs on occasion?

WS: Well, the hot springs were not very much in those days. Ray Skoglund just began to develop them. He did a good job.

EC: This is late '50s, early '60s, you're talking about?

WS: This is in the early '60s. It was strictly run by his family. There were the two girls and his wife, and he and perhaps one or two hired hands. But it was a family undertaking. It was run well; the dining room was good. Then when he sold it, well, it just didn't live up to the expectation. Let me put it that way. And I haven't been out there — perhaps three times – in all the time that it is under the new ownership.

314

EC: The road from Terrace to Kitimat, was that here when you arrived?

WS: Well, it was the old gravel road through the Jackpine Flats.

EC: I don't know that road.

WS: Yeah, yeah. Well, the old Lakelse Lake Road went through the Jackpine Flats, across Highway 37, where it comes to the highway now. It crossed the highway, went down into the woods, down into the swampy area. That all disappeared when we had that tremor in 1964, I believe. Then they were forced to build a better highway.

EC: Was that when the landslide happened?

WS: Yes, the landslide. Yeah, yeah. It was quite an experience. Was quite an experience. Yeah.

EC: I guess I've seen pictures. That's as close as I've come.

WS: It was everything. Sometimes when I tell my granddaughters how the early days were: "Come on Grandpa, it can't be." It was a different world compared to today — in every respect. Everybody knew everybody. Nobody ever locked the door. It was a totally different society.

The economy of the town, because of the vast amount of merchantable timber around and saw logs — two sawmills, two if not three shifts, six days a week. It was just phenomenal. I remember when Columbia Cellulose, they had their marshalling yard out where they put that new spur in, out in Kitsumkalum, where now, what is the name of the outfit that put the powerline in and they have those blue trucks?

EC: Oh, Valard.

WS: Where their yard is. That used to be the marshalling yard. There were the truckers parked out there, parked all their trucks where all the trains were. There were at least four, if not five, logging trains going to [Prince] Rupert a day. Then Columbia Cellulose, who was up there, that was their office. When it snowed then, they sent a couple of graders out and cleaned the highway to the marshall yard so these guys could get to their trucks. And that was in the headlines of the next paper, which was the *Terrace Herald*, run by Mrs. Fraser. When they did that, it was a big event.

EC: So what about these other community groups — you mentioned a bunch of them earlier — that you were a part of?

WS: Well, the community groups were actually pretty strong and to be quite honest, it possibly shouldn't be done that way. But I guess every salesman does it, at first. After I was accepted by the business community, which was not until late '60, early '61, I joined the Chamber of Commerce in order to find prospects, to make business connections, and then the Hospital Board. Well, let me simply put it this way: after I was established and had both feet on the ground and knew what I was doing, I felt very grateful to Terrace and I thought, there must be ways that I can pay back. Actually, and you know that better than anybody else, I have been involved in community affairs ever since. I was on the Hospital Board, and later on I joined Rotary, spent some 30 odd years with the library. It was rewarding, good fellowship. Met good people.

EC: You were on the board when they were planning on developing that new library in '67?

WS: I was on the board before that. What brought the extension (in '95)… I was sitting on the board, the City called that big meeting where they wanted to develop Kalum Street. They wanted to put all these big apartments up and what not, and they asked all the community groups for input. I guess you might remember that. I think I said to you, "Why don't we enlarge the library?" Great idea. You know the story from there on. As a matter of fact, I think we were the only ones who finished what they suggested.

None of the apartment buildings became reality. That was the time when Terrace switched a little bit, and I think it switched to a certain degree on the demise of Kitimat. In the '70s, the wholesalers began to move up here: E.B. Horsman and all the other people. Besides Prince George and Kamloops, further east and south of us, we became a sort of a supply centre. Whereas Kitimat, where things for the business community went extremely well because of the generosity of Alcan... And I always felt, having been a salesman, I always felt, that many of the merchants in Kitimat in the '70s forgot how to merchandise, how to sell their wares.

And I think Terrace took advantage of that. Terrace Totem Furniture, for instance. They had then the Furniture Barn there, where now the pet shop is in. They delivered all their merchandise to Kitimat, and then, of course, much, much later, Canadian Tire and Walmart came. And that, sort of, was the death toll for the merchants in Kitimat. Anyway, it made life pretty difficult.

Willy Schneider at the ceremony dedicating 'the Willy Schneider Room'
in recognition of his long service on the Library board, circa 2007.
Terrace Standard photo.

But Terrace turned around. Terrace, I think, began to become more aware of itself and its opportunities in this part of the country. After all, we are in that triangle of Kitimat, Prince Rupert, and Terrace. We are the most central one and that has been recognized by many wholesalers and big box stores, as we have realized in the last 10 years. This is when Terrace really grew and then unfortunately, during that same time, the two big sawmills we had, began to collapse, for whatever reason. But I don't want to get into that.

EC: And what do you remember about downtown Terrace — where you bought food, where you shopped for clothes, furniture?

WS: Well, it was entirely different. When we came up here, I don't think, in '59, there was a big box store here. And then Braid Smith began to develop together with Bob Sheridan. Supervalu, where now Mark's Work Warehouse is, they were in there. And then the Overwaitea came in beside the fishing store. The Silvertip Café was gone.

Beside the Chinese café, and where now the fishing tackle store is, there was a small store and it was the Overwaitea. And then she moved into where now CFTK-TV broadcasts. And then they moved into where now the store is. Oh, no, no. And then they made one more move. Oh, yes. They moved where now the government building is, the government service building by the liquor store. They had that end that is pointing south, and then they built their own store.

But before that, Bert Goulet had a little meat store, a little butcher shop beside the theatre. Bob Sheridan had a little gun shop at the corner of Kalum [Street] and Lazelle [Avenue] opposite the — what is in there now? — some sort of a second-hand store or something. Beside Speedee [Office Experts], there was a little store, and opposite him, there was none of this mall or anything. There was an old blacksmith shop that was still there in '59 and disappeared in '60 or '61. And on the corner where now the Bank of Nova Scotia is, there was Michiel and Johnstone Hardware Store.

Clarence Michiel was one of the owners. The store was so old that the main area of the floor where the traffic went over was so bad: there was a big area that was spray painted around and it said, 'Do not step on because you may fall down into the basement,' or something like that. I cannot remember it ever having been repaired.

And then further going on Lakelse [Avenue], going further west, there was a Lion's Drug Store. There was a little alley back up to Lazelle, yeah, to Lazelle, and there was a little drug store. Lion's Drug Store was owned by one man, an elderly gentleman, who was not always open because he was not always able to look after his business. Let's just leave it that way.

Then came Osborne's Guest House, which was finally taken down into the Keith Estates somewhere. Speaking of the Keith Estates, I don't think in '59, I don't think there were more than two dozen houses down there. Was very little. There were no schools or anything down there. There was no hospital down there because the hospital was the army hospital that now has been all torn down here within this year.

EC: And the Catholic Church was where the mall is now?

WS: The Catholic Church was on the corner, where now the parking lot, the west end of the Skeena Mall, is now. And opposite was International Trucks. You know it too. What was the name of the old guy, lived out in…? Well, I guess he's dead now. He lived out at Lakelse Lake, this side of the hot springs. And that was International Trucks.

And then where now the City Hall is, there was a block house. There was an old block house standing there, and right in the front of it was a fire hydrant. And I think it was New Year's night or New Year's morning, '62 or '63, that somebody got really carried away and raced down Lakelse Avenue, smashed right through the fire hydrant, and ended up in the people's living room. The bedrooms were on the back side, and then when they woke up, water was spouting up all over. Oh, it was a wild town sometimes.

EC: When did they put City Hall in there?

WS: Oh, City Hall was put in there in the '70s. Yes. City Hall. The very first City Hall that I knew of was beside somewhere where National Rental car rental is. A little bit on the left, there was an old building also with very wobbly floors. We were not a city then. We didn't have a mayor. We had a — what was it called? — the chief honcho of the council. Because we couldn't call ourselves city, we were still a village. But that was where the City Hall was. That was an old building. And that was taken down and the cleaner moved in, Mr. Smaha. Smaha Cleaners moved in, and built a solid building.

And what else was there? Oh yes. Then, where now the ladies wear store is, Totem Furniture were in there at one time. They moved from there and then they moved down where Don Diego's is. And then they opened the Furniture Barn in the mall where the pet market [Total Pet Land] is and where Mark's Work Wear[house] is. And what else? Of course, the police station, and jail, and library, all in one building. Ten by ten. It was utterly ridiculous.

EC: Yeah, because I talked to Ruth and she couldn't remember whether that little police station on the corner of Kalum and Lakelse, the old police station… you know, the yellow building on the corner there…she couldn't remember whether that whole thing was the library or whether the library was the building next door to that?

WS: There was no next door building. It was all in the same building. It was on the north side.

EC: She said it was so small that you could practically …

WS: I don't think there were more than 200 volumes in there.

EC: Yeah, she said you could practically shelve everything by standing in the middle.

WS: Because the jail was also in there. The jail was facing east. The actual police station was the Chief's little office that faced south. Then you went in from Kalum.

EC: So you never ran for city council. Did you ever think about it?

WS: No. You know my nature better than many, many, many people in Terrace. I wouldn't have lasted.

EC: Too frustrating for you?

WS: Too frustrated and too outspoken. No. Politics is not my game.

EC: Did you shop at the Terrace Co-op?

WS: Oh, yes. As a matter of fact we rented a freezer there. There was the service station facing the hotel, and then there was also an entrance in there. There was a feed store and there were some freezers, and you could rent these little freezers. I think they were about two feet by two feet by two feet. Rented them for $10, or something like that, a year.

Yes, and then we did some shopping in there. There was a little bit of a coffee shop facing the parking lot, which wasn't too bad. You could have lunch or a cup of coffee there. But then, when the other big box stores came in — Safeway and Overwaitea… In my opinion, and I don't want to step on anybody's toes, I think that is where the Co-op didn't keep pace. Well, enough said of that.

EC: But, the Co-op wasn't there when you moved to town was it? They built it.

WS: No. They built it. It was built.

EC: You've been here while the Co-op went up and while it went down.

WS: And went down, yes.

EC: I believe I used to buy my groceries at the Co-op when I first came here.

WS: Yeah, we bought a lot of groceries. Well, it was actually the first big store. Then you got the dividends with it. Speaking of dividends… Those dividends could not be cashed within a hundred kilometers — kilometers or miles — of Terrace. You had to live outside that. Anyway, there was, out in Dutch Valley, there was quite a German community. There was Mr. Hoffman and there was Mr. Bushman, and there was Mr. Roland. And Mr. Bushman, a man in those days in his '60s, walked from Dutch Valley to the Co-op, three times a week. He was all dressed up in Bavarian garb, the whole thing. Spoke hardly any English.

Then there was a rumour that things were not going too well, and somebody must have told him about it. So, he was in there one day, and unfortunately — I was in there one day — he wanted those dividends. Because they did all their shopping at the Co-op, and so he possibly had quite a dividend to come. So, he wanted this dividend and these poor ladies tried to explain to him that he can't have them unless he moves away.

He spots me, and I tried to run away from this. "Come here, Mr. Schneider! Kommen Sie her! Helfen Sie mir!" And I couldn't explain it. Well, I could explain it to him, but he wouldn't…he refused to understand it. Must have spent about half an hour, totally fruitless, useless half hour. But anyway he stomped out of there and he was not a happy man. Yes, there was a clique and they all lived in that neighbourhood.

EC: How did the community of Terrace interact with the Native communities, both in the early days and through the years?

WS: Well, the Native communities… Well, they were there. They did their thing out there in Kitsumkalum or wherever it was. It was a federal affair so we had very little to do with it.

EC: But I have heard it said that, you know, in the later years, like in the '80s, it was the Native communities that kept Terrace afloat really.

WS: Everything, everything, everything changed around when the treaty was signed up with the Nisga'a. BC finally came to its senses and realized that they should have signed a treaty a hundred years ago with these people and we wouldn't have the problems we are having today.

EC: And how did the community interact with the police?

WS: I think great.

EC: All was well respected?

WS: Well, there was… I shouldn't tell you that. I worked at the insurance business both in Rupert and in Kitimat, and also went down into the Bulkley Valley — in [the] Hazeltons and Smithers. And I came back from Kitimat one day, and the bridge, the metal bridge, in those days was two ways. There was no walkway. Was wooden planks. It was two-way traffic. And I came schussing across that bridge, and the sergeant with a couple of his officers was parked there where you could wait for the light. I came schussing over that bridge all over the speed limit. I knew him; we had talked before. I didn't know him really personally, very well, but anyway.

He flagged me down and I rolled down the window and I was not in a good mood. So I said, "What can I do for you?" "Well," he says, "You went a little fast." Well, I looked up to him and I said, "Well, I don't think that's any of your damn business," rolled up the window and drove off. And I must have had…my brain must have shut up there for a while. I came home and I told Gisela about it, and she said, "You did what?" Well, it began to dawn on me that I said "It's none of your damn business" to a policeman. She says, "Tomorrow morning, you promise me, the first thing you do, you go down there and you apologize, and if need be you go on your knees." "Well," I says, "I wouldn't want to get carried away too much."

But anyway, I went down the next morning and actually he didn't see anything extraordinary about it. He only said, "You know, you don't say things like that to a police officer. And you don't do that again, don't you, Willy." He even addressed me as Willy. I said, "No sir." You know, up and out I was.

EC: So, how about the construction of the new bridge? Were you here for that?

WS: Oh, yes. Oh, yes.

EC: How did that impact Terrace?

WS: The new bridge was in the late '70s. It's fitted into the time when Terrace became a sort of a supply centre. There were more people coming in, and there were more business people moving in and more traffic going through. And then we carry it further to the '80s and '90s, and the big box stores came, and then Zellers came, and the Woolworths came. Terrace began to sort of bloom into a second spring or whatever you want to call it.

EC: So more generally, how do you think Terrace has changed over the years?

WS: Well, you know, we had, with the exception of the last two years, we had 10 very, very lean years. It was, I think, best described, and the simplest way to describe this…it was a yoyo performance. It went from next to nothing; they carved it out of the woods here when George Little came walking over the hill there, and saw this, and built it, and called it Littletown at that time. But anyway, it went up. It grew for one reason — that is the woods, the timber resources.

And we all know that they were very, very unprofessionally handled. Because when you have enough of everything, why not waste? It's the same that we do with water today. Sure, we may have the greatest fresh water bodies in the world, so why not waste it?

But Terrace went and the bridge came in. It's up and up and up. And then it collapsed again; the forest industry collapsed and it will never come back to the way it was. It all happened within two or three years. Then for about 10 years, nothing at all happened. The town was flat. And there were businessmen and other people were suffering.

EC: So as someone who has lived here for such a long time, what would you want to share with people who are moving to Terrace today?

WS: Well, if you want to enjoy living in Terrace, you can't be a city child. You've got to enjoy the outdoors because otherwise, it doesn't have too much to offer. Yes, it has a little theatre and it has the art performance that brings us a little bit closer to city life — but not in the city style.

But it is basically relaxed. It is a healthy climate. It is relatively clean air even though we still complain about it. And the one thing, if someone gets in real trouble, the community will line up behind you. It's a great little town. I have lived here now for over 50 years, well over 50 years, close to 60 years, and I'm going to die here, and I will not go anywhere else.

EC: I'd like to ask one last question which is: because you played such a huge role in the library, how did you get involved in the library to begin with and what carried you through all those years?

WS: Well, number one is I am an avid reader. I will not sit down because otherwise I would be reading that book. I sit only down—when I come back from the gym in the morning, I sit down with another cup of coffee. I immediately begin to read. I am an avid reader and we brought a bunch of books with us from Germany. There are some of them out there, and some of them are downstairs. And then I ran out of them, so I had to go to the library, and I liked what I saw. Then I was approached whether I'd want to sit on the Board, which I did, and one thing came to another.

EC: And that was back in the '60s?

WS: In the '60s, yes, the second half of the '60s. And 30 — what is this? — 33 or 35 or 38 years later, I finally called it quits. But I still send them a Christmas card every year.

EC: Okay, well thank you very much Willy. It's been very interesting. I know you could go on for a lot longer. There are some great stories you've yet to tell.

Caledonia Secondary History Class

As part of the *Preserving the Past for the Present* project, we also opened up the opportunity for younger community members to participate. We were interested in fostering intergenerational connections. As part of our outreach, we approached high school social studies and history teachers, inviting them to work with us to involve interested students. Greer Kaiser, the History 12 teacher at Caledonia Secondary, saw a natural fit for her class. She worked with us to shape the interview process into a class project.

History 12 class of 2013/ 2014, Caledonia Secondary School.

To make this happen, we worked with Greer to train the students in interview techniques. We brought digital recorders into the class, and used a double block to practice using the equipment, asking open-ended questions, and using active listening skills. We talked about the importance of capturing stories, the ethical dimensions of informed consent and how we learn and record local history.

We then helped to pair each student with a senior or elder to interview. As much as possible, we wanted them to take the lead and interview someone they were interested in having a conversation with. Many chose to interview a family friend or a family member. Others chose to interview seniors with life experiences they were interested in hearing more about. As we talked and planned the interviews with the class, many students were nervous and a bit apprehensive about the task.

From there, students mostly worked in pairs, and interviewed seniors as a team. Interviews were arranged wherever it seemed most comfortable for all involved: empty classrooms, the public library, in seniors' homes or places of work.

As we talked and debriefed with students after the interviews, we found most were excited, amazed, and humbled by the experience. Many were surprised at how much they had learned, or the meaningful connections they'd made with the seniors.

Here are some of the students' reflections in their own words:

- *It was nerve wracking at first, but I really enjoyed it. Learning about my town is what really made it invaluable to me.*

- *It has broadened my horizons! I learned so much and it has inspired me to dig deeper into Terrace history.*

- *I have learned times are changing and my memories are valuable.*

- *The most significant part of the interview process was the interview itself because I learned about Terrace and also the person I was interviewing. Not to mention, a couple of laughs at the funny stories I was told were a plus too.*

- *Before the interview I didn't know anything about the history of Terrace. I am more interested in Terrace's past and what the future will bring to the people here and the community.*

Reflecting back with Greer, there were many worthwhile outcomes from the interview process. Besides the numerous links to the curriculum, she found local history came alive in a new way for students. For some, their involvement created a 'hook' for further learning. The project also nudged students out of their comfort zones and fostered social and emotional learning. Many spoke about how much they valued the stories they heard as well as the opportunity to sit down with someone they would not have had a connection with otherwise.

Betty Bellamy Interview
Interviewed by Nicole Bellamy & Erin Moore, 30 November 2013

Betty Bellamy was born in Beechy, Saskatchewan, in 1936. Betty met her husband, Allen Bellamy, who was on leave from the Navy, while travelling to British Columbia. They wrote to each other back and forth for a year, and after his discharge, they were married, on November 1, 1955. Betty and Allen had five children—three boys and two girls. They moved to Terrace in 1962. After six years of residing in Terrace, they moved to Usk, where they lived and raised their children for 20 years. They owned and maintained a six-acre garden and were essentially self-sustaining. Living in Usk provided ample opportunity for outdoor activities: Betty recollects her children swimming in the Skeena River and hiking with the Junior Forest Wardens. As a family, they also went swimming at the Lakelse Hot Springs and had picnics at Kleanza Park. In this interview, Betty discusses her children, her childhood, and the changes that have occurred in Terrace. She also talks about downtown Terrace, annual local events, the logging industry, and other stories about living in Usk.

NB/EM: So we're going to start with your childhood and youth. Where and when were you born?

BB: I was born in a little farm town called Beechy in Saskatchewan. And on my birth certificate it doesn't say Beechy. It says township: section, because I was born in the farmhouse where I grew up. I was born in 1936, on September 15th.

NB/EM: How did you and your family arrive in Terrace?

BB: We arrived by car, and that was very scary, because in 1962 the roads weren't paved and they were totally scary. I told myself I was never leaving Terrace because I would have to drive out.

NB/EM: What was your relationship like with your siblings?

BB: I was the youngest of six girls, with two older brothers, and one younger brother. And as far as I can remember, my mom and my older sisters say that I was quite spoiled, but I can't remember that I was.

But it was fun growing up on the farm. There wasn't any TV, very little radio, and it was very limited, because my dad wanted to listen to the news. And if we listened to too many programs during the day, the big batteries that we had for the radio would drain, and we would have to buy a new one. So we used to get heck about that quite a bit.

NB/EM: Tell me about growing up in Beechy.

BB: In Beechy it was quite lonely sometimes, even though there were lots of siblings. The nearest neighbour was probably five miles away and the nearest school that I attended was two and a half miles away. We walked to school winter and summer. Very rarely did we get a ride. It was a one-room, eight-grade school.

NB/EM: What was the name of the school?

BB: It was called Neasen School. Each area had their own school and they were probably about six or seven miles apart. So we used to play ball with the school that was down the road. That was lots of fun!

NB/EM: Do you have any memories of school that you would like to share?

BB: Just that we used to have lots of fun during recess. We would go outside in the summertime and play ball. That was the main thing we did. In the wintertime, there was quite a bit to do. Saskatchewan, where I grew up, is quite flat — some hills but not any big hills. There was a hill a

324

quarter of a mile from the school, and we used to walk over there and sled during lunch recess. That was fun.

NB/EM: Did you attend college or university at all?

BB: No.

NB/EM: Did you get married?

BB: Yes, I did!

NB/EM: Tell us about your wedding and your spouse.

Betty and her family celebrating her 80th birthday: Mark Bellamy, Betty Bellamy, Jody Bellamy, Todd Bellamy, Heather Bellamy, and Craig Bellamy [l-r]. MK Bay Marina. September 15th, 2016. Betty Bellamy Collection.

BB: We were married in 1955, November 1st. My husband was in the Navy. He was going to Vancouver on leave. I was going to visit my sister, with my older sister, by bus to BC, and he was on the same bus. That's how I met him. He took my name and my address. I didn't see him again until about a year and a half later. He was cleaning out his kit bag on the ocean and found my address and he started writing to me. We wrote each other for about a year and a half. I have letters that I got from him, from all over the world. He was discharged in the spring of 1955. We were married in November 1955.

NB/EM: So you must have had children.

BB: We have five — three boys and two girls — all born in different places: Calgary, Saskatoon, Swift Current, Edmonton and Terrace.

NB/EM: How did you find Terrace as a place to raise a family?

BB: It was great. We lived in Terrace for probably six years. Then we bought an acreage in a place called Usk. We lived there for 20 years and raised our five kids there. We named the street we lived on 'Grandview Drive.'

NB/EM: What was there to do for children in Usk?

BB: We belonged to an organization called the Junior Forest Wardens. All of our kids went into the program. It was like a scouting program, but we thought it was superior to the scouts, of course. All the neighbour kids came to the meetings in our basement. Sometimes we had about 15 kids. The parents were really good about participating. Our kids were in band, so we used to make a lot of trips into town for practice. The kids say, now that they've grown up, that it was a really fun place to live. The back of our property bordered the Skeena River, so they used to go down there to play. It was very calm, kind of an eddy. So they'd go and swim down there in the summertime and hike. With the forest wardens, they did a lot of field trips and stuff and went to Prince George for summer camp, every summer.

NB/EM: What kind of jobs did you do?

BB: I was a stay-at-home mom. When I was first married, we lived in Calgary, Alberta and I worked at Birks' Jewellers, until my first son was born. And then, I can't remember. I was so busy raising my kids. Once they left home I worked in a daycare. I kept busy. Let's put it that way. And I was a caregiver for a couple of kids for about four years. We managed Sleeping Beauty Lodge for three years and managed Sparks Place Apartments for six years.

NB/EM: So now we're going to go to recreation. What did you do for fun?

BB: We usually did things as a family: swimming at the Hot Springs, picnics at Kleanza Park, lots of trips to see family in Saskatchewan and Alberta. In 1974, we drove to Disneyland.

NB/EM: When you were younger, did you go to the movies?

BB: No. Well, I was already married when I lived here. So we usually did things as a family. Both of our parents lived elsewhere — mine in Saskatchewan and my husband's in Alberta. We made lots of trips with all five kids — no seat belts, no car seats, no nothing. Took the long trip usually once a year to see our parents. And our kids always seemed to enjoy that, because they were growing up without grandparents in Terrace.

NB/EM: What restaurants were popular here in Terrace throughout the years?

BB: What restaurants? A Chinese food restaurant called Gim's. We went there whenever we could afford it. And for five kids, two adults, we could have a full Chinese food supper for 20 bucks. And that was with drinks and everything. We didn't eat out a lot so it was special when we did. Dairy Queen and KFC [Kentucky Fried Chicken], when they opened, were good.

NB/EM: Did you visit the Lakelse Hot Springs?

BB: We did, many times. It was an important part of our lives.

NB/EM: Can you tell us more about that?

BB: Well, it was always a lot of fun and even today, my grown-up kids are saying it's such a shame that they are not operating anymore. It was one of the very special things we did with the kids.

NB/EM: What about Lakelse Lake in general?

BB: We did occasionally, maybe once or twice a year, go to Lakelse Lake. But because we had our own little recreational place behind our property, the kids were just always happy to be playing outside and keeping busy that way.

NB/EM: Can you tell us about sports in Terrace?

Skoglund Lakelse Hotsprings Resort. Cars parked in front of the outdoor swimming pool, 1959-1962. Skoglund Collection.

BB: We didn't have a skating rink. So most of my kids, when they were older, didn't know how to skate when we did get a rink. We bought them all skates but it was hard to learn and they didn't enjoy it much. Once the ski hill opened, most of the kids enjoyed skiing.

There wasn't really a lot to do as far as sports. We had a Civic Centre — it was where the library is now and George Little Park. It was a huge building where they had events, but it burnt to the ground. So they relocated up on the hill, where it is now.

NB/EM: Were you involved in any other community activities outside of your home, like clubs or organizations?

BB: We were usually involved, as a family, and also myself, personally, in church. We attended the Alliance Church. So the kids went to Sunday school, as they were growing up, and summer camps, and day-to-day vacation bible school. I was usually involved as well: helping out with the ladies group, being the secretary, and always involved with the cooking, because I liked to cook.

NB/EM: Were you involved in any clubs or organizations?

BB: I belonged to the Hospital Auxiliary for many years, and I still work at the gift shop in the hospital. I belonged to an organization called the Leprosy Mission for years. It's an organization that still is involved. There's still a lot of leprosy in other countries, so they're still working with people who are suffering with leprosy, and making it less of a stigma to have leprosy. So I do support that.

NB/EM: What local events do you remember celebrating?

BB: July 1st was always a pretty big event. We went to Kitimat, because they were the ones to have the parade over the years, and Terrace would have Riverboat Days. So it was usually Kitimat for July 1st. It was always a fun time. Riverboat Days was Terrace's big event of the year.

NB/EM: How have the local events changed over the years? Or have they remained the same?

BB: Probably because we have a larger population, they've probably changed. Become more, you know…with the music in the park, etc. It's always really enjoyable. Terrace is really good at putting on a good show. Also, the Farmers' Market on Saturdays is popular. The bands were also an important part of the community.

NB/EM: So, what can you remember about downtown Terrace when it was first built up ,when you first got here?

BB: Well, when we came in 1962, there really wasn't a lot here. That was before the new bridge was built. I remember we did have an Eaton's outlet here for quite a few years, and quite a few stores like Super Valu. And, of course, the Co-op was here.

NB/EM: Did you shop at the Terrace Co-op?

BB: We did.

NB/EM: What kind of items would you be able to purchase there?

BB: Everything. And I still remember our Co-op number.

NB/EM: What did most people that you know do for work, for a living?

BB: Well, it was mostly logging and a lot of different things going on. Of course, there was Alcan. My husband was a heavy-duty mechanic so he worked in construction. He worked away a lot and he was in camps a lot, on big projects in different cities. We weren't really involved in the logging industry, but it was a very important part of the community when we were first here.

NB/EM: Did you have any friends or family that were farmers or had farms that grew produce and that kind of stuff for market?

BB: Not really. We were one of the few. Well, earlier in the years, there were lots of gardens. In Usk we had six acres, and I was known for my strawberries. Every year people would come out and buy strawberries. I had a really big garden because we had lots of kids. We were pretty much self-sustaining out there in Usk. We had chickens, ducks and turkeys.

NB/EM: Going back to the forestry and logging, do you think that they played a large role in the history of Terrace?

BB: Of course.

NB/EM: How have you watched the forest industry change over the years?

BB: Well, it's obvious with the mills closing — like the mill just down here on Keith Avenue. It's actually been torn down. And there's actually only one mill in town now, which is really sad. And a lot of people have been unemployed because of it. It didn't really affect us as a family, but we knew friends that it definitely did affect.

NB/EM: How did the community of Terrace interact with Kitselas and Kitsumkalum?

BB: Not a lot of involvement, I don't think. We had friends that were from the Kitselas band and over the years, we've kept that friendship up.

NB/EM: So, more generally, how has Terrace changed over the years?

BB: Well, it's definitely grown and the streets are paved. Years ago, there weren't very many streets paved — just the main street when we moved to town — so that was a nice improvement, and it wasn't so dusty. And just big buildings, government buildings… The first elevator was at the Terrace Co-op, but now there are lots.

NB/EM: How did the construction of the new bridge impact the community?

BB: Well, it probably helped because the old bridge was quite a bottleneck and it was really scary to drive. It used to be two lanes, with no lights. So you just were very careful when you crossed the bridge. But I think it opened up the south side more with Keith Avenue and the businesses that are there now.

NB/EM: Were there any annual community events that you remember?

BB: The fall fair. I do remember that. Nicole's dad, Todd, had some game birds. Every fall, he would take a load into town, and also chickens and a rooster, and he would usually win ribbons.

NB/EM: When you were a child what did you expect or hope to accomplish?

Betty and Al Bellamy at Seeley Lake in 2005. Betty Bellamy Collection.

BB: Well, as a girl probably, you were expected to get married. And the boys in the family definitely had more involvement in the farm because they were expected to take over the farm eventually. The girls helped with the household chores and cooking and gardening. We were expected to learn all the skills of running a household when we got married.

NB/EM: As a longtime resident of the Terrace area, what changes have you noticed?

BB: Well, I've noticed that when you're in Vancouver, waiting to fly back to Terrace, I used to know everyone. Now it's rare to see someone you know when you're in the holding room. So that's one of the things. And even, you know, going up town and not recognizing as many people as you used to. We used to know everyone. Things have actually improved a lot over the years with the medical centre and the hospital.

NB/EM: As someone who has lived and learned here, what would you want to share with people who are newly moving to Terrace?

BB: Probably that it's a nice place to live, it's a good place to raise a family, and the medical services, I think, are superior. It's generally a safe place to live. Although, that has changed from when we first came here; you didn't worry about locking your doors, where now, you do have to. I used to walk a lot and it wouldn't bother me to walk after dark. But now I don't walk after dark. Things like that.

NB/EM: Are there any other stories that you would like to share just from your experiences living in Terrace, stories that stand out to you?

BB: I would like to tell one story when we were living in the country. My husband was in camp in Kitimat, working on a project there. We had chickens with the chicken coop quite a way from the house. And all of a sudden we hear this — we had actually been in Terrace and came home – we heard this banging in the chicken house. So we went to check and it was a bear. So, of course, we were petrified. He was having fun with the chickens. He was actually having a lot of fun with them.

I was so afraid as my husband was in camp, so it was just my kids and I. I decided that I would drive — and this was probably seven o'clock in the evening — so I drove to Kitimat.

In those days, women weren't allowed to go into the bunkhouses. So my oldest son went in and got his dad and said, "There's a bear in the yard!" So he drove back with us and spent the night watching for this bear. And he didn't show up until, I think, the next day again. The same thing…he was out to get the chickens.

And so, of course, in those days everyone had a gun. My husband thought he would try and shoot. But he didn't have a very good shot, so a neighbour came over and thought he was going to get him. And he didn't have a very good shot, either. He actually shot right through the fence — it was an iron fence — but he didn't get the bear. Eventually someone got it. But that was a little scary for the kids and I. After that we were a little bit nervous in the evenings. But I think just lots of interesting times, with never a dull moment.

Bill Young Interview

Interviewed by Ayleena Ainscow and Lateesha Wigglesworth, 10 December 2013

Bill Young was born in Vancouver in 1923. At the age of 15, Bill began working as a cook along the coast of British Columbia for large logging camps. Bill ended up owning his own catering company and traveled all across Canada and the United States. Bill purchased the Tillicum Drive-in and the Tillicum Theatre in 1967 when he was in Terrace to bid on a catering job. Bill married his present wife, Norma Young, in 1976. He has five children between two marriages. Throughout Bill's time in Terrace, he has been greatly involved in the community. Bill is most proud of his involvement in founding the Thornhill Fire Department. In this interview, Bill discusses his childhood, his active role in the community, and his high school graduation in 2009 at the age of 86. He also talks about the various businesses he has owned and operated in his lifetime.

LW: So, where and when were you born?

BY: I was born in Vancouver, British Columbia, on the first of September, 1923.

LW: How did you or your family arrive in Terrace?

BY: I came up here, actually — being in the catering business — to bid on catering at the Nass Camp for the Columbia Cellulose, Twin River Timber, in the Nass Valley. While I was here, I ended up buying the Tillicum Theatre and Drive-In from Charlie Adam. And then I moved up here with the family to run the theatre business.

LW: Tell me about growing up?

BY: Growing up? Well, I grew up in Vancouver and went to St. Patrick's School, which started with grade 1. Then my mother got sick with tuberculosis and I ended up in an orphanage for some time, and was then sent to the Vancouver Preventorium for tuberculosis (which is now the Sunny Hills Hospital). I went through that and then my dad died in 1937.

The following year, I went out to work in the logging camp as a waiter, or flunky. Worked my way up in the camps and was cooking in various logging camps throughout British Columbia. Ended up as a purchasing agent with the Alaska Pine Company, and then I formed my own catering company and travelled all across Canada, United States. I ended up in Terrace.

LW: Do you have any memories of school that you would like to share with us?

BY: Oh yes. Lots of memories from school.

LW: Any specific ones?

BY: I graduated in 2009. It took me seventy-some odd years to go through high school. That shows how stupid I am.

LW: Did better than most. You still did graduate.

BY: Yes.

LW: Yes. that's good.

AA: Did you marry?

BY: Oh, yes. I got married to my first wife and we adopted two children. There's Jim and Diane. They attended school here in Terrace, at Veritas School, and then both of them, I think, went to the other high school, Skeena [Junior Senior High School]. It was before they built Caledonia [Secondary School].

AA: Do you want to tell me about your wedding?

BY: Weddings? Well, I think I got married when I was 21. I got married at St. Andrew's Church in Vancouver, British Columbia, and I was married for 29 years. After the wife left, I remarried my present wife Norma. Both her and her husband had worked for me for a number of years.

They owned the Bilnor Café in Williams Lake. We've been married now for 37 years. She had three children — so that's five that I adopted, I guess. Now I have twelve grandchildren and last week, I became, for the first time, a great-grandfather.

AA, LW: Congratulations.

BY: Yes.

AA: Can you talk a bit about your experiences of going back to school as an adult?

BY: Oh, gosh. Well, I left school in 1940 during the war and never had the opportunity to finish high school. I was in grade 10 at that time and, as I say, I went out to work in the logging camps.

I worked all over the coast in the big logging camps on the west coast and ended up cooking up at Holberg, which was one of the biggest logging camps owned by the Alaska Pine Company — Walter Koerner. According to him it was the most successful camp they had. So he asked me to leave and go to Vancouver, and take over the operation of purchasing agent, managing 19 camps and purchasing for three or four different hospitals, which gave me a good opportunity.

Then I started my own catering business. I had seven offices across Canada and the United States — 380 employees at one time. And it developed and developed and finally got too big, and I sold it and ended up in Terrace.

The oddest thing happened here: I was on my way to the hospital in Vancouver for medical. Stopped at my old school, St. Patrick's. Pulled up in front of the building and a young Chinese lad comes out and says, "Can I help you, sir?"

I said, "Oh, just looking at the old place: new buildings here across the street, everything built up." I said, "I was the first student in this building." "You were? Wait a minute."

So, he run in and brought out the principal. And he come running out, and says, "Will you come in?" I say, "Sure."

I went in and he says, "We've lost records." He said, "Do you recognize any of these pictures on the wall in the hallway?" I said, "Oh, yes. There's Father Forget, Father Miles, the Sisters all the way down the line…"

"My gosh," he says. "I'm glad you came in. When did you graduate?" I says, "Well, actually I didn't." He says, "What do you mean, you didn't?" I says, "The war came over and I had to go to work." And so he says, "How would you like to graduate on June 23?" I says, "Oh, great."

Anyway, after spending some time with them, I told him I had to leave. He said, "Well, you better say hello to some of your graduating class." I says, "My what?"

So, he took me into the room, which used to be grade 10 and everybody stood up and applauded. I phoned the wife up here and told her what happened, and she told somebody, and the newspapers got a hold of it. Then they took pictures of me and they had the full front page of the Vancouver Province with my picture on it. And we ended up with interviews with the press — CBC Radio and BCTV [British Columbia Television] — in the morning. Then I made a speech to the school assembly on Friday.

Saturday was the graduation with the television cameras. It went on for four days. Well, it was quite an episode — something I'll never forget.

LW: That's cool. So, what jobs did you work throughout your time here in Terrace?

BY: My God.

LW: A lot of them?

BY: Well, in Terrace? I mean, I've pretty well stayed here in Terrace. I started the vocational school catering; started the first feeding facility; and catered Carnaby & Van Dyke. Later, I went up to the Nass Camp and took over that operation — spent 26 years up there. And I was 13 years on the Health Board.

While I was here in Terrace, the house burnt down. So I went out and bought a fire truck and started the Thornhill Fire Department. As I say, I'm very proud of it.

LW: Yes, that's a big accomplishment. So, how did you come to purchase the Tillicum Theatre and the Drive-In?

BY: Well, I was walking down the street and I bumped into Dick Toynbee. He was in the real estate business, Thornhill Realty, here in Terrace. Somehow, we got talking and he introduced me to Charlie Adam. I ended up making a deal with Charlie Adam to buy the theatre — both that and the drive-in. That's how I happened to. Well, from there on in, it's history.

LW: So, why did you add a second theatre?

BY: Why did I add a second theatre? Well, thanks to the management of Adrian Enright, my son-in-law, and son Jim, we are thinking about adding a third theatre.

LW: Really?

BY: Because the theatre business was very, very good in Terrace when I first came here — and then television came out. Television ate into the business. It cut it down considerably. And over the times, it's developed, grown. We've now put in all new sound systems. We had to put in new digital service and 3D applications.

LW: I know everyone was excited about that. So, how have movies changed over the years?

BY: Well, they've changed considerably. One of the biggest things to me — the biggest change in the movie business — was television. It was an odd thing: I got a phone call one day from CBC. They phoned me up and asked me what I thought of the effect of television on the movies. I said, "Well, as long as they keep showing movies like they had last night on TV," I said," I don't think it'll affect us."

He said, "Well, what do you mean?" I says, "Well, you had a picture called Arwa last night on TV." And he said, "Arwa? No, we never had that picture." I said, "Oh yes, you did. It was supposed to be Star Wars."

By the time they cropped it out to fit the television, they had dropped off the beginning and the end of the name. So, I said, "They don't really…." Well, they hung up on me right there. They didn't want to continue that conversation.

LW: So, what's your favourite movie?

BY: Favourite movie? Well, there are so many of them, I guess, I can't... I think The Sound of Music. I think it was one of my favourites that I ever watched.

LW: Yes, that's a nice movie.

BY: And my favourite movie, I guess, was Little Big Man. 'Cause I won the Canadian [Screen] Award in Showmanship in that movie. That was with Chief Dan George in Terrace here.

We had started a yearly presentation of an air show out at the airport. And Chief Dan George came up as an official. I had him and Art Bates and Chief Kitpou on the stage, and presented him with a leather jacket, which he had never had in his life. And the next picture that comes out is Easy Rider and there, he's wearing the jacket that we gave him.

LW: So, how did your career change your experiences in Terrace?

BY: Well, being an extension of the catering business — while I was in the business of feeding and housing, we had to provide everything, which included recreation facilities and movies for the isolated camps.

And we started the Granduc Mine up north. We had the big avalanche there in 1964, and well, that was the month of February. I always hate Februaries. I have just always had unlucky Februaries.

As I say, it was the first part of February that we had the landslide up in Stewart. We lost 26 men — and lost some more men, same month, down on Vancouver Island, Lower Mainland. And the last day, the twenty-ninth, I got shipwrecked and spent three days and two nights out on a log in the Pacific. So, I hate February. Once I get through February, I know I'm good for another year.

AA: Okay. So, when you were younger, what did you do for fun?

BY: For fun?

AA: Yes.

BY: I never really had a lot of fun in childhood. As I say, my father died when I was 14 and I went out to work when I was 15. I was too young to join the service at that time. I ended up a civilian cook for the army signal corps RCSC [Royal Canadian Corps of Signals] and ended up in the Merchant Navy. So, I really did not have the opportunity of growing up and having fun.

AA: What kind of restaurants were popular then?

BY: What kind of restaurants? Well, ours was one of the most popular. We had a steakhouse in Vancouver, a hotel out in Burnaby. Well, there was no McDonalds. None of that was here in those days.

AA: Did you visit the Lakelse Hot Springs?

BY: Oh yes. Ray Skoglund used to own it at that time.

AA: What about Lakelse Lake?

BY: I wanted to build out there but it fell through. We didn't finish at Lakelse Lake. My son Jim — he spends time at the lake with his speedboat. He loves it.

AA: What local events do you remember celebrating?

BY: Local events? My gosh. Well, the opening of the Vocational School in Terrace.

We had, as I say, the Thornhill Fire Department. I mean, that's a big thing, one of my most proud moments. And I can think of, well, so many.

I was head of the music festival here in Terrace; I was president of the music festival for a couple of terms. It used to be called the Terrace Music Festival. I had it changed to encompass more of the Northern Area — changed the name to the Northwest Music Festival. Since that time, the Pacific Northwest Music Festival, I think, is what it is now. But it was sponsored originally by the Knights of Columbus; I was one of the Knights. I was in Rotary Club and Toastmasters, as well. Oh gosh, it was so many years, I can't remember them all.

Bert & Greg Goulet in front of Tillicum Theatre on Lakelse Avenue, fall 1955. Goulet Collection.

LW: What do you remember about downtown Terrace?

BY: Downtown Terrace? Well, I have mentioned a few places: where the Bank of Montreal is now used to be a car lot. [Tim] Hortons was the Masonic Hall. Veritas School used to be across the street where the mall is now. And they moved Veritas up to the present location.

LW: Did you shop at the Terrace Co-op?

BY: Oh, yes. We had to. It was about the only place here we had to shop.

LW: What did most people that you knew do for work?

BY: Loggers mostly.

LW: Yes, lots of loggers. What role do you think forestry and logging played throughout the history of Terrace?

BY: Well, it was the history of Terrace.

LW: How have you watched the forestry industry change over the years?

BY: Well, when I look back and think about the many, many years it was neglected and no trees planted… I could see over to the west coast of Vancouver Island there — Gold River, Jordan River. I had a hotel in Jordan River. Railway logging was quite a deal.

They had stands of cedar. They had stands of hemlock, fir, and cedar, and pine. They had stands of everything in the area. When the market was good in a certain field, well, then they would move up to that, reap that type of log. But, there was no such thing as planting. If that had happened 50 years ago, it would have been another story, wouldn't it?

LW: How did the community of Terrace interact with Kitselas and Kitsumkalum?

BY: I honestly can't answer that. I really don't know. It's always been one community here. After I built the theatre, I was at the door one evening — I always used to wear my tuxedo at the door. A Native came up to me from Kitimat and he says, "Bill." He says, "You sure have a lot of Native people coming to the theatre now, haven't you?" And I said, "Well, what do you mean? I don't really understand." I don't care about being Native or anything else. I mean, everybody here is all one community.

He says, "Oh no, no, no," he says. "People come from Kitimat to the theatre in Terrace now 'cause you hired one of our people." I said, "Well, I never even thought of it that way." And I still never do. It doesn't matter to me.

LW: Exactly. Have you lived in Terrace during any major floods?

BY: None that concerns me.

LW: Okay. More generally, how has Terrace changed over the years?

BY: Well, it's growing. I don't agree with a lot of the stupidity from the city council. Particularly the business of giving free taxes to people who take over houses up on Park Avenue and Lazelle [Avenue] — turn residences into offices and get them paid when all the offices are empty downtown. And the taxes go up on them — on our empty offices even. That's a subject which I shouldn't get into.

LW: Were there any annual community events that you remember?

BY: Well, I remember when I first came up here. As I say, I played the accordion. Up at the old community hall here, we used to have Italian nights — different groups, events, in the old building.

I remember one particular deal: they asked me to be the wandering troubadour with accordion. It was about 40 tables. I got to the first table and, "What would you like to hear?" So they'd want me to play 'O sole mio. So I'd play it — but I had to have a drink with them. And I'd go to the next table and, "What do you want?" Out of 40 tables, I got to about 12, and I couldn't go any farther.

AA: When you were a child, what did you expect or hope to accomplish?

BY: When I was a child…? Well, I always wanted to be a doctor, since I had other friends that I went to school with and they all ended up as doctors. But as I say, my father died, and I had to go out and support my mother and my brother, and that was the end of that.

AA: As a long-time resident of Terrace area, what changes have you noticed?

BY: Well, the streets are paved. I'd been away from Terrace, actually, for 26 years up at the Nass Camp — spent a lot of time up there. And as I say, I've built the theatre in different stages.

It was originally built as one and we spread that out to take in the second theatre. Then we built up over the top of the Quonset hut, and forestry was upstairs. Then we built the back building. I am quite proud of the building, the way it is. It's getting better all the time.

AA: As someone who has lived here and learned here, what would you want to share with people newly moving to Terrace?

BY: Well, I think it is a very good community. It's whatever you want to make of it — and yourself too.

AA: Do you have any advice for the present and future residents of the city?

BY: Well, I think they have to be proud of the town itself. As I say, the original deal here is: all the facilities are here. It's a wonderful place to bring children up.

AA: Do you have any other stories you would like to share?

BY: Oh gosh. I've been very fortunate over the years with my health, and I think that's the biggest thing. As I say, I'm 90 years old now. One of the things, when you get older you… Like, I went to Vancouver… And you get afraid to phone people, you know, old friends, particularly. For instance, I got to Vancouver and I phone up Blackie and Noni —very good friends of mine. And I said to Noni, I said, "How's Blackie doing?" She got mad and she said, "Are you trying to be smart?"

I says, "What do you mean?" She says, "Well Blackie's been dead for three months." I says, "Oh my gosh. I didn't know." "Well," she says, "Why didn't you know? It was in the papers." She says, "All his friends came to his funeral." "Well," I said, "We don't get the paper up here." I said, "I'm sorry. You should have notified me."

I've been known for making puns and jokes, I guess. But, I got another call from another friend. Said, "George died. Are you going to go to his funeral?" I said, "Oh gee. I don't know if I can get away." I was away down south. And he said, "Well, really?" [I said,] "I don't know why I should go to his. He's not gonna go to mine." He got mad at me too.

As I say, the amount of places I've been… I started Gold River Pulp Mill. And I started the pulp mill up at Prince Rupert, the Granduc Mine and Peace River Power Development...

LW: A lot of stuff in the northern area.

BY: I've been all across the country — and I had employees from everywhere — through Vancouver, Vancouver Island, Pickle Crow, Ontario…. I was fortunate enough – well, not fortunate enough.

I guess the most intimidating thing I ever had was making the speech to the Senate in Ottawa to support the Nisga'a Treaty. It would take hours to list the many places, and work, and projects, which I was involved in.

[Second Interview, Conducted by Melanie Pollard, 24 January 2014]

MP: Bill, we've had a chance to chat a little bit, and we've talked a lot about some of the changes you've seen in Terrace over the years. We're up here in your apartment over top of the theatre, looking out. What would the view have been like when you first came to Terrace compared to now?

BY: I first came up here in September, 1967. Across the street was the Veritas school grounds and the Veritas School. The hall and the church, moved to their locations up on Straume [Avenue].

Looking out across the street here, there used to be an old gas station there, the BA station [British American Oil Company]. That's long gone. And all the development of the shopping centre across there, down the other side of the street… I think there were big trees in front of here, what used to be the Slumber Lodge, which is now the Bear Country Inn, I guess. And the whole street has changed. Well, you can see the change in the theatre from some of the old pictures.

MP: You were telling me some stories about when you were building the theatre, the construction of the elevator. Do you want to share that story?

BY: Oh, that was pretty good. I had paid the contractor at the time, Larson, to dig the shaft in preparation for the elevator; had to go down 30 feet. And when we come to open it up, we couldn't find the hole; he hadn't dug it.

So, we had to dig from inside, and two of the boys had come up — three of the Belanger boys said, "We'll dig the hole for you." So they went down about 11 feet the first or second day. And said, "This isn't gonna take very long." Then they hit rock.

We tried to get through the rock but we couldn't do it. Over the weekend, we went to look at it and there was about four feet of water. So I called the city and they come down here. They put in pumps, and were pumping out about 40 gallons per minute.

And Mr. Sande came along and he says, "What's going on here?" I said, "Oh, there's water." And he's laughing; he says, "You'll never pump all the water out. There's an underground river here."

He says, "As a matter of fact, when I had the mill across the street, where the Safeway shopping centre is… I know they used to come by canoe from the Kalum, all the way below the Bench, and down and around here. He says, "You'll never be able to fill that hole up."

MP: It's full of water.

BY: And that's what happened there. I look back and see where our community hall used to be. Everybody used it for functions. That was the place in town. But the theatre was the main place to go before TV.

MP: Where was the community hall?

BY: Where the library is now.

MP: Okay.

BY: And all that block, the curling rink was a Quonset building right behind the community hall.

I look back and see some of the changes, all the way through, up and down the street here, the whole block down where the Tim Hortons is now. Talk about a contaminated spot. That has to be the worst contaminated spot in town. I think Geno paved over the lot and put in a gas station.

MP: You were talking to me about the community centre too. What kind of events went on there that don't happen anymore?

BY: Everything went on there; there was nothing else. Dances… and, I think, I mentioned I played there with the accordion— Italian dinners and events. It was all put on there. But it burnt down and, well, you can see the changes there now.

MP: Do you think something has replaced that community centre — that feeling of everyone coming together?

BY: Well, I think everything is spread out so much now that… At that time, I think, everybody knew each other in town. You meet people in the street, you could say hello and not feel afraid to say hello.

It's not as bad as the city, mind you; the loneliest place on earth, I think, is an elevator. When you get on the elevator, nobody says a word. If you do say something, you're afraid of being charged with molesting.

MP: Just for talking to them.

BY: You used to be able to enter a building and hold open a door for a lady. It used to be commonplace but, heck, you do that now and they say, "I don't need any help!" Things have changed.

MP: You were telling me a little too, about all the renos that have been done here at the theatre. Where have some of your old seats ended up? You've changed the seats here a few times.

BY: Well, the first bunch of seats were donated to the Terrace Little Theatre up on Kalum Street. And a bunch more went to the curling rink and the Church of God in Thornhill.

MP: So, there are movie seats in a few places in town.

BY: I think they're all gone now.

MP: Oh, they're gone now? One of the other things you were telling me a little about was what restaurants were here, when you first came compared to now.

BY: Oh, there were three hotels and two restaurants: across from Augie Geeraert's Old Terrace Hotel and the Lakelse Hotel and Slumber Lodge—a little place on the corner was a nice spot, and across the street, there was the Seven Seas Restaurant next to a pool hall.

MP: Both Chinese food restaurants, you said?

BY: No. One was Chinese; that was the Seven Seas owned by Shan. He owned the place and built the new Shan Yan Restaurant across from the 15 cent store. It was popular, and after hours, there were line-ups. That's all there was here late at night. There were no drive-ins or any of that when I first came here.

The Dog and Suds opened up there, a restaurant in the corner. That's about the only drive-in that was available at that time, too. There was only the one bridge at that time — going across to the other side.

MP: How did the new bridge change town?

BY: Well, the traffic pattern changed with the new overpass. Mr. Little used to be our MLA [Member of the Legislative Assembly] at that particular time. They named the new bridge after him.

MP: And there were a couple of things I wanted to follow up with you, too. You've done a lot of different things in the area in terms of work, but also a lot of different things in terms of community involvement. You just mentioned briefly that you had started the Thornhill Fire Department. Do you want to tell us a little bit about that?

BY: Well, my house on Dorman in Thornhill burnt down and at that particular time, there was no fire protection in the area. Forestry came along and they watered down all around the house, but it burnt up. They were not allowed to service private property. We had a stable out there, had a couple horses. We were able to take some of the stuff that we saved and put it in the stable. A couple days later, somebody broke in the stable and stole that, too.

MP: Oh boy.

BY: I know darn well that, at the time, somebody had robbed the house and set it on fire. I knew that was a fact because I had a big double deep freezer. I had just closed my at the community college, and I had all this meat, and stuff was in there. When I opened up the freezer, there was nothing in it. So, I know somebody had stolen it and set the fire up.

MP: What a shame. So your house burnt down and you decided there needed to be some fire protection.

BY: Well, then I got a call from Vern Ciccone up in Port Edward and he says, "Hey Bill. You know one of you fellas needs a fire truck down in Thornhill?" He says, "We've got one here that we just retired. Why don't you come up and take a look at it?"

Andy Owens — he used to be the Chief here in Terrace — he came with me and we went up to Port Edward and bought the fire truck and brought it back. I remember going out to the racetrack on a Sunday afternoon. I think we circled the track with the fire engine, siren and the flashers, and we ended up getting 23 volunteers for starting the volunteer fire department. William Moving and Storage provided space in their new facility for our fire engine. From that day on, we had some additions put onto it, some extra water tanks.

The trouble is, when we first started, there was no fire protection at all and no fire hydrants anywhere. I remember one of the first fires. I was driving the truck — there was a fire near the golf course and we run out of water. So I'm heading down into town with Chief Best and the boys were helping us. We used to get water on the Terrace side of the bridge, there's a fire hydrant there. They made us use it to fill our truck, and back we go again. This particular time we're coming down there and I hit the amber light — I had the flashers and siren on — but I kept on going. And I get over here and the police gives me a speeding ticket. But I think when it was all explained up there, they very kindly kicked it out. Thank God and the Terrace fire crew for their assistance.

MP: And then you were a firefighter for those years?

BY: Well, I had to. I worked in it for about six to eight months. I ended up as the first captain and it was very interesting. You really have to hand it to volunteers. How lucky we are to have people who spend their time and efforts for someone else. And if you ever want a friend, have a volunteer fireman or woman.

MP: No kidding, eh?

BY: Anybody willing to do that is willing to do anything for you.

MP: Another thing that you talked about was the vocational school.

BY: Oh, the vocational school. Oh that was something else, too, and I often laugh about it. I went up there, first of all, to cater for 16 aboriginal people who took a course in navigation. We put in a building, we fed them, set up the first cafeteria in some of the rooms there and we looked after 16 people. I had beds and put them in a dormitory. It worked out pretty good.

Then we put in a building for a new residence and finished off the new cafeteria. They started a program up there called Adult Re-Education Program and people started phoning in. They said, they wanted to partake in 'Adultery Education.' Well, that name got changed pretty quickly.

Along the same vein, I remember John Pousette. He was city manager at the time. He started a program asking everybody to put 'Terrace is Terrific' on all their envelopes to advertise Terrace. Well, I was down south at the time and I phoned up to John and said, "Can you explain to me a little more about your T.I.T. program?" He says, "My God. Somebody like you has to spoil the project!" And that was the end of that. He said they could no longer promote that. Lots of fun.

MP: What kinds of programs were offered through the vocational school?

BY: Well, they started first of all with mechanical and automotive. But the problem was, they opened this school up here with all the very latest modern equipment. People who had gone through the course here couldn't get a job anywhere else. They couldn't do it manually, because no local companies had the equipment to work with.

MP: Interesting, hey?

BY: But at that time, the only thing that was operating was the automotive, the navigation course and the academic program.

MP: And what was your role in getting that going?

BY: Well, we had to feed the people before the cafeteria and the dorm was finished.

MP: With your business, your catering?

BY: Yes, my catering.

MP: Wow. Well, I don't know if there is anything else you want to add Bill? Those were some additions we talked about from your first part of your interview. I know that you wanted to comment on how many changes you had seen in Terrace over the years.

BY: Well, I don't know. It's…the whole area. The streets are all paved now and there was a lot of gravel at that time. When I first came here, the building, which is now at the back, used to be at the front. Used to be Bert Goulet's store. He was the mayor at that particular time. There was a beautiful big oak tree next door— my wife still comments on that. They were working over at the library at the time, putting a facility in, and somebody said they wished they could move that tree over there. It was all pre-arranged by one of the builders to move it. In the meantime, they were in a hurry to get the addition to the motel and they cut the tree down. So that was the end of that. But it was one of the most beautiful trees.

MP: So have you been happy to call Terrace home after all these years?

BY: Oh yes, of course. It's been good to me. One of the funniest things to me is, I walk in to the stores and people say, "Hi Mr. Young. Do you remember me?" I says, "Not really." "Well, you used to kick me and other kids out of the theatre for throwing popcorn, being noisy and disrupting other patrons. Oh my gosh," he says. "You were pretty tough on the boys in the theatre. I'll never forget it." I've met so many people that I can call friends.

MP: That's neat. Well you've had a lot of opportunities and a lot of interesting experiences over the years.

BY: Yes. I have been very fortunate with my health, a wonderful wife Norma, family, many friends and many memories. Twenty-six years at the Nass camp and Nisga'a hospitality.

MP: Well, thanks so much Bill, for sharing your stories.

Billie Hoving Interview

Interviewed by Sarah Searle, 24 November 2013

Billie Hoving was born in Longview, Washington on September 29, 1931. One of three children, her family lived in a hotel in Portland, Oregon. Raising their children during the Depression, Billie's father worked in various jobs to make ends meet and her mother worked raising the family. In this interview, Billie describes how her Christian faith has shaped her life. Billie followed the example of her pastor's daughter who went to Westmont College in Santa Barbara, California, majoring in education and minoring in Christian education. While a student, she met her future husband, Arthur Hoving. They were married, and while both students, had their first child. Arthur became a teacher, and the family moved as he taught in California, Oregon, and Hawaii. Billie's son Tim Hoving moved to the Terrace area for work, and the family followed. Billie and her family were involved in various volunteer and religious organizations, including the Evangelical Free Church and the Thornhill Fire Hall.

SS: So, where and when were you born?

BH: I was born on September 29, 1931, in Longview, Washington in the [United] States.

SS: And I've been hearing that you remember how you walked, like learned how to walk.

BH: Yes, yes. The first Great Depression was in the '30s. And my mother and dad were married later in life and they wanted a big family. So they had the three of us within 30 months. Myself, I came first, and then my two brothers. My mother was busy taking care of two little boys — babies — and I grew up looking after them.

But we lived in a hotel. My father somehow felt that a hotel was a good place for my mother. And so we lived in a hotel in the upper part of the downtown core of Portland, Oregon, which is a fairly large city in Oregon. And we lived in this hotel. Like, it was my first home. It was a spacious suite.

I didn't learn how to walk until I was 15 months old, and I think I must have been about a year old when we moved in there. And I remember my mother taking me by the hand — and sometimes she had a pencil. And she held on to one end of the pencil and I held on to the other end of the pencil, and we would walk the halls. And she would meet friends in the hallways and would talk to them. And I, interestingly enough, I remember walking. I remember they were dark halls, fairly wide halls, with lovely soft carpeting. And I still have got glimpses, memory, of walking those halls holding onto the pencil talking to my mother or to others.

And from that point on, every time I get into a hotel and be in the hallways, I would feel like I was home. And it took me a long time to realize why. It's because — as a teacher I've learned that — your earliest memories are some of the deepest ones.

SS: So what was your relationship with your siblings like? You said you helped raise them.

BH: Yes, right. Very close. They were 15 and 30 months apart. I was 30 months old. Two little brothers and I just adored them. I mean, we lived in a hotel. Not a lot of places for little boys, toddlers. And we were there for several years. So Mother would let us go down on the street. I was responsible to make sure my little brothers didn't run in to the street. Mother would watch out.

We were living on the fourth floor and Mother could look down and see us. But I mean, they needed exercise. And to this day, I love to walk. And so I would walk my little brothers and make sure they didn't get away from me. Yes, of course…I didn't have to watch them both at once. But finally, just before we left the hotel, it was both at once. But it was good for me, because I grew up learning how to look after others and be responsible.

SS: So, what schools did you attend?

BH: Interesting question. My father, being he was in his 50s and he had three children, was not what you call at the top of the hiring list. And when he married my mother, he was extremely well-to-do. The first car I remember was a Cadillac — a silver Cadillac with a red stripe down the side. But being it was in the Depression, my father just lost everything with the crash of the '30s: one day he was almost a millionaire and the next day he was in debt.

I had a wonderful mother. My parents were Christians, thank goodness, and they did a lot of praying. And my father taught me how to pray and it's amazing. God took care of us. But, finding employment when you are 50 years old or older… My dad was 50 when I was born and then he was about 53, 54, when my brothers were born. As a result, he had a lot of different jobs, going anywhere where he could be employed. He did many different things. Managed a cannery in one place and worked as a sales representative in another place. Ended up in real estate, developing shopping centres; he did very well.

But during these years, I went to eight different schools in eight years. We moved a lot. And the upside is, I learned to make friends rapidly because who knows what might be next. And that was good. But another time, another way, it's hard because you just get friends you feel familiar with and then you're in a different set.

SS: Did it put you out of your comfort zone for a little bit?

BH: Yes. I think I lived there. I really think I live there. And then I had got asthma quite badly when I was around twelve years old, and I was home-schooled for a year. And there was another girl who had rheumatic fever and I couldn't be in a classroom, because if I caught a cold I would immediately go into asthma. I was a fairly sickly child growing up. But I outgrew the asthma and it's made me very, very appreciative.

Back in those days, before modern medicine, they burned the inside of my nose, trying to make me less sensitive to things I was allergic to. And as a result, to this day, I have to really follow recipes very closely. Now they've got much more refined ways that… don't damage people. Be glad for modern medicine and all that they have learned.

SS: I can't even imagine having someone burn my nose.

BH: Oh, I know. I know it. I understand the premise; they want to make it less sensitive like scar tissue. Like I enjoy roses, flowers, but it's sight — visual more than scent.

SS: That's just scary.

BH: But that intensifies my enjoyment of colour. Yes, so there's always a good side. Yes. And thank God for progress.

SS: So on top of that, do you have any other memories of school?

BH: Hmm. One major memory I'm going to share because it explains how I felt as a little girl. I was in a new school and I could run — I was small but I could run — and that was just something special I carried with me. So we were having races, like they do in schools, and I was in a new school. I'd been there only a month or so. We had six of us running together and it was just who could get around the track the fastest. One of the girls was the best runner in the class, and I hadn't picked up on that yet, and the other girls didn't challenge her. But thank goodness it was something I could do well. So I ran, and as I passed her, she fell. And then as she got around the track, she said that I had tripped her, which I would never do. But that was just a real low point for me in school, because everybody was really down on me for doing something that I knew was good.

One other thing from grade eight — a memory from grade eight... Lots of good memories but these were the sad ones. But they shaped me to probably look on the bright side of things. We had a first aid class after school — this is grade eight — and I was the only one who didn't have someone to bandage, because you pair off by twos. I remember that was one of the down ones. But I figured out anything I was going to be good at, I was gonna be good at, and also reach out to others. And if somebody was new or sort of down, I would reach out and be a friend. So there were positives.

SS: I remember growing up for myself. We had these games in gym where we always ran. And I was one of the fastest runners and I just remember running and feeling exhilarated.

BH: Yes, that's the way I was.

SS: You just start off in a standing position just waiting to run and then zoom.

BH: Right, right.

SS: Off you go.

BH: You're free, you're free and you're not held back, you can just go.

SS: Like all your worries are just passed.

BH: Yes, they just float behind you. There's a good verse in the Bible that says, "Forgetting those things which are past, and reaching out for what's ahead." We're always learning. That's the exciting thing.

SS: Yeah, I think if you're going to become a teacher you cannot stop learning.

BH: Oh no, you never do. I'm going on 83 and I'm still picking up and recording. It's exciting. And I'm still adding to the person I am.

SS: Yeah, but when I see your life and what has happened [in your life], I'm just excited for life now.

BH: Oh yes. Every new day is another opportunity and we learn, as you are doing right now, we learn on the mistakes and the joys of other — the ones behind you.

SS: So, as we've talked about your childhood, you growing up and all, what was it like for you to go to college and university?

BH: One thing...I've got to back track to my childhood. My mother was very, very busy with my little brothers. But she put them down for naps and then we would weed whatever property we were on. I would weed with her and that was our time together. I love it. As a result, I love it. I love growing things. I love gardening, flowers, vegetables. Yeah.

And I had a funny mother. She was just delightful. She was my father's secretary. We'd go for a lot of walks, my brothers and I. And she loved snakes, and in California she would have us play with the snakes along the way. And this was my mother! My brothers and I, we didn't... It's funny my mother was the one that was doing it.

And then across the street in Salinas, California, my father was the manager of a cannery there that did apricots, and artichokes, and things like this. And I would go with him to visit the different people the different clients he had that he bought produce off of. But one time I was home with my mother and brothers, and there was a bull across the street. There was a huge fenced area and there was a bull over there, and he was constantly pawing the ground with his foot. And my mother had

344

heard that you wave a red flag in front of a bull, you'll make him angry. So, Mother took a red sweater, went across the street, and there was just barbed wire fence between her and the bull. And we were in a house with a glass door, and my brothers and I were just aghast watching Mother across the street waving this red… And he really got upset! So Mother came tearing back across the street, thank God, and we were just wondering if the door would hold him. But he stayed behind his fence. But with a mother like that, we had some interesting experiences. But oh, she was delightful. She lived to be almost 100 and she was just delightful right to the end and a wonderful example.

SS: So, what colleges or universities did you go to?

BH: Okay. That was good. I was thrilled. I went to all four years of my senior secondary in the same school, which was delightful. Except Mother — afraid that being I'd had asthma — she'd made me wear knee socks, wool knee socks. This was in California! The members of my class remembered me as the girl who wore — and this is like grade eight! — who wore knee socks. Great way to be remembered. Anyway. Okay then. I went on then to graduate, thank goodness, and did well in school, and really, really loved it, and ended up going to Westmont College in Santa Barbara, California.

My pastor's daughter had graduated from Westmont College. It's a four-year liberal arts college. And being my pastor's daughter really liked it, and it was in Santa Barbara, California… Lovely place, lovely place to go. So I went down there and attended four years. And I majored in primary education and minored in Christian education and had excellent teachers.

From then on the college just got more and more respected educationally and it's still going. That is where my oldest brother joined me my second year. And he became very close friends with an Arthur Hoving — and this is exciting — and they were the best of friends. And being I had grown up with my brothers and knew what men basically liked — and they liked to chase girls back in that generation… And the girls were just… Maybe they've always done it, but they began chasing boys. But I kept running and as a result, by the time I met Art, I was getting tired of running and just wanted a friend. So Art and I became very close friends And we always went out with my brother Roger, which was a delightful way to start a relationship.

I was in Santa Barbara, California and I loved to hike, explore. There were a lot of estates — beautiful, beautiful estates overlooking the ocean with gardens. And we would do a lot of hiking on these estates, just thoroughly enjoying it. Getting to know one another on a friend basis was delightful. And one evening Art took me out without Roger, and he asked me to go steady. And I said that I had decided never to go steady with anyone unless I was willing to marry them; and I found out that that was the safest way to live.

And at that point, four of my schoolmates at Westmont College… Pardon me. There were three from the college and one before — one of my bosses while I was earning money to go to college asked me to marry him. And I told him, "No, no, no, no," and I just kept running.

It's interesting. When Art asked me to go steady, I told him that I had decided never to go steady, and I really think that's a wonderful thing. Art still asked me to go steady and wear his class ring. It was called 'going steady' in those days.

And we just blew through to our 59th wedding anniversary, when he gave me this new stove and a dozen red silk roses, which are sitting here in our living room. We began on December 7th, 1941. (Pearl Harbour Day). That's our big anniversary.

SS: I can remember from my childhood seeing you and Mr. Hoving having the best of time in the back of the church.

BH: Yes! We enjoyed everything.

SS: So, you did marry Mr. Hoving. And what was your wedding like?

BH: Oh it was lovely, glorious. Pastor's daughter was my maid of honour and I included another close girlfriend there. I pray a lot. You can see growing up with a father that had different jobs and older, we prayed. We prayed as a family. My father would take care of me. My mother took care of my brother and sister, and I would travel with my father. And during these times in the car he would teach me that God was there and God answered.

So for a wedding dress I prayed — I prayed for everything. I prayed for a dress and I drew the wedding dress, like I'm sure Sarah drew hers someday [The interviewer Becky has a twin sister named Sarah]. I sketched it and I said, "God. This is the dress I want. And you know we don't have much money. I'm working and I'm only getting 90 cents an hour."

I was working for a department store in the display department, which means the windows, and I did the signs for the store. It was just tremendous with a wonderful boss, just great… And he taught me how to letter, how to do signs freehand. And that's before a lot of the printing. So I've had excellent training to be a teacher because I learned how to make these beautiful, beautiful signs and flashcards — whatever a teacher needs to know. So that's good.

But earning 90 cents an hour… And as I said, I went to Westmont College and had to work my way through school, all four years of college. It was good. I did all kinds of things. I dog sat, I did the laundry, I collected the laundry for our dorm, and I also did a lot of the cleaning. My favourite was cleaning the crystal chandelier in one of the main halls of our college there in Santa Barbara. But back to that…

When Mr. Hoving proposed, he took me for a walk, and we were overlooking the Pacific Ocean. And that's when he asked me to go steady and I took his class ring. And then we, of course, had the wedding, which was beautiful.

Prayed about the dress and went to Meier & Frank, a big department store in town. Walked in to the bridal shop and they had two dresses on sale; one of them was the dress I sketched. It had a cathedral train, slipper satin — glorious beautiful dress — and lace down the sleeves and pointed over the hands, and little tiny buttons down the back, from the neck down the back. And I tried the dress on and it was a perfect fit. It didn't even have to be altered — length, anything.

SS: Wow.

BH: I'm used to miracles in my life and this was one of those special, sweet, big ones. So yes, it was lovely and it was glorious going down the aisle. I felt like a princess going down the aisle and one of the happiest days of my life. I was just thrilled.

My father was just developing shopping centres there. Two had bakeries. One of them donated what was called the grooms cake — which is a dark cake — and the other one donated the multi-tiered wedding cake. So expenses for our wedding weren't that much. Just a joy, a wonderful joy of a day, absolute joy of a day.

And right toward the end, just before we left on our honeymoon, my brother — who has quite a sense of humour, a good friend of Art's — he took a chain and attached a tire to the back axle and then in oil based paint, which just doesn't come off. He wrote some of the crazy phrases from that day on the car—we had an older car. So everybody knew we were newlyweds. And we lost the tire going around a corner, thank goodness. Oh dear.

SS: So how did you and your family arrive in Terrace?

BH: That was interesting. I have a brother that worked up here. And like I said, I'm very close to brothers. This was my younger brother. He had moved up here with his wife. He had gotten a degree

346

in forest engineering from Oregon State College and they moved up here with their two children; they had a son and a daughter. And they just loved Terrace.

Both of us were in college. I ended up going five years to college, Art for four years. And then I quit to pay for his last year and also had our first son Tim, while I was in college. About 10 days before finals, I had a wonderful job working on an estate, and thank goodness we were able to pay our bills. The week we graduated we celebrated our second anniversary. Tim was a year old. This was all within one week, and then all the cards coming in; we both graduated at the same time. And we both worked very, very hard. And basically, the last bit of our education, we paid for ourselves. That's a good feeling.

Oh, by the way I graduated. I did say that. Yes, I did.

SS: So, as you mentioned, you have a son named Tim, but who were your other children?

BH: Okay. Tim was the oldest and he was wonderful, because, to make him go to sleep —here we are doing finals and term papers — and to make him sleep, all I had to do is turn a vacuum on. And he's that kind of kid. He never fights what he can't control, which is wonderful, tremendous. And the only time he'd cry was during basketball games. Took him to basketball games. I actually took him to class with me. I had two classes I had to attend and the professor was wonderful. And he was a quiet baby. Thank God for that. And then after Tim came Rick.

We then graduated and Art received his first teaching assignment in Castro Valley, California, and we lived halfway down the side of a canyon. I didn't work— just stayed home and took care of Tim. Art taught — had his first teaching assignment — and it went really, really well. And he was teaching math and science in a junior secondary and trying to think of something that would be appropriate as to progression of life.

We were in a duplex. We had part of a duplex and I remember the neighbour's dog had puppies. And the neighbours — actually they were above us — our landlords, they had two young girls very much like you and Rebecca. It was fun. The three of us watched the puppies being born. In fact — oh glory — she just had them on the driveway. Why? I do not know, but we were right there and each one came in like a plastic bag. We were just fascinated. And so life is just wonderful. It is always a learning experience.

And then the girls got a pet lamb that they kept upstairs – in an enclosed porch upstairs. And we called the lamb 'Lamolin'. And it was fun to watch that grow. Happy memories along the way, often times involving animals.

SS: When you arrived in Terrace, what was Terrace like? Was Terrace a great place to raise a family?

BH: Right. When we arrived in Terrace, we had the three boys. Steve had been born in Lake Oswego, near Portland, Oregon, where we lived. This was just after California. My great grandfather was a steamboat captain on the Columbia River. He had a family home from past generations, which was on the Willamette River [Oregon], which flows to the Columbia.

And so our family history went back many generations there. And there we had the original, beautiful four-storey home, built there on the river. And it sold many, many years later. And we wanted to keep it in the family but a hockey star in the States bought it. It's where the Tualatin River flows into the Willamette River, which flows in to the Columbia. A beautiful place.

And we lived in Lake Oswego for quite a while, and that's where our third son was born, and Art was a teacher there also. Then, when we were there, we decided that Art wanted to move into a different school district. So he sent resumes all over, and the resumes started to come back, and then all of a sudden Art was offered a job in June in Hawaii.

And I had just gone to a seminar on praying and how to do a prayer diary, which I do to this day; been about 40 years now or more. And our teacher said — that the Bible says we can ask for anything: 'you have not because you ask not'. This has been a part of my life since then. So I thought, okay, I have a diary. I love diaries. I'm still keeping one, which is fun. And I asked to go to Hawaii. And here we are with three sons. We had prayed for a girl after three boys, and on Mother's Day, we had Jana, which was just a joy. She was five years old, just ready in the fall to enter Kindergarten. And I prayed that we'd get a job in Hawaii, and one of the deacons in our church had a business in Honolulu, and he needed someone with my husband's ability.

Art's father had been in plumbing and heating. Had a business doing that and so Art was very knowledgeable with his hands and he had the qualifications. So, of all things, we were offered a position in Honolulu, Hawaii, for the summer. And it came with a truck — a small truck — and also a small vehicle and an apartment overlooking Waikiki Beach. Oh glory. And I'll never forget the joy of going there.

It was just for two weeks to start with. But our employer thought so much of Art that he wanted him to stay on for an additional six weeks, which would be like an entire summer for a teacher. Just Art and I had gone initially for two weeks, and then his parents had looked after Tim, Rick, Steve, and Jana.

Then Tim left to work for the summer, working to enter Trinity Western College in Washington. He'd already gone one year. He really liked it and was planning on returning, so he was working for the money to go. He was busy for the summer working in the bush of BC. So, Rick and Steve and Jana came over.

So this is the family we arrived with [in Terrace]. We drove ourselves up. We arrived here with two pickup trucks. And we had a piano — my mother's beautiful piano — to bring with us, and also a pump organ, so it wasn't that easy. Then U-Haul trailers that we pulled. And one of the boys drove his car up. Our older son, of course, was helping to drive one of the pickups. But we did move ourselves up and it worked out well.

We got into Terrace and we came along the Skeena River from the east. And it was when the highway was just going in. We stopped at one point — I would say now is probably Hazelton today. It was a dirt road and very bumpy, and we had come through areas where we went through Native villages with totem poles, so it was a new experience for us. And anyway, this woman came and she was going east; we were going west. She said, "Roll your window down." So we rolled our window down, and she said, "The road ahead is horrific. Be careful!"

And I remember thinking, *Where are we going?* We got into Terrace— this was in June—and the Skeena was really raging and roaring like it is. And I was wondering, *How am I gonna raise three boys with a river like this?* But I knew that my sister-in-law — she was a secretary at one of the schools and my brother was working for Columbia Cellulose and had a good job — and they both really enjoyed it. And their children were the ages of ours, their son and their daughter.

But Terrace, of course, has really changed quite a bit since then, although it was a modern city. And I was delighted with it right from the beginning. My brother and sister, they were somewhere else when we arrived. And we still didn't have a place to live....

But, there was a place they were hoping we might like. It's right where Sarah and I are sitting. And I walked into the house and it had a big stone fireplace just like our home in Oregon — floor to ceiling hearth. It had hardwood floors just like our home in Oregon, and I just felt like I was home. It was just home.

And I went out to the car where our children were sitting and I started to cry. And Rick said, "Why are you crying, Mom?" And I said, "I just know God is gonna give us that house."

And it had a pond and also a creek, which as a child, I had drawn a picture of a pond and a creek. And from the time I was 13 until I was married, we lived in that house with a pond and creek. And this one had the same thing. And just a beautiful, beautiful lawn and a half circle driveway and fruit trees, apple trees, raspberries — just like getting to the promised land. And it was. We're still here and just really loving it. And it had lot of weeds but I love weeding so…

But Terrace was a lot quieter then, but a thriving area, and just the best family area to move into. And as schoolteachers, we were always just happy with this being where we raised our family. And it has changed and grown. But it's still a wonderful family place to live. And with people from all over the world… We are so blessed to be in Terrace.

I know some teenagers wonder if they're not sort of held down, but they're not. They're given a wonderful foundation to live good family lives and enjoy the out-of-doors — and skiing, and hunting, and swimming, and fishing, and ice skating, and snowshoeing and yes. Great. Wonderful. And all these things just have really developed. It's great to see it.

By the way, our boys ended up on Canadian Ski Patrol. That was just a happy time in their life. Our second oldest son was one of the first full-time employed ski patrolmen in the first ski lodge we had here in Terrace. And it's fun to see this also developing. Wonderful place to be educated, to raise a family, and just for a good life.

Evangelical Free Church of Terrace. Original Building. Evangelical Free Church Collection.

SS: So what did you do here with your children? What activities were here in Terrace?

BH: Okay, basically it would be skiing. We skied also in Smithers and Jana learned to ski at six years of age. And like I said, the boys were nine and a half, 12 and 14 years older than that, and they just thoroughly enjoyed this.

They really enjoy the out-of-doors, fishing with their dad. Wonderful fishing areas here: Takysie Lake, which is south of Burns Lake. We found out about that very quickly. Art's father had been told, "stand behind a tree while you bait your hook because fish jump in the boat." And I actually have had a fish jump in the boat behind me and scare me to death. But beautiful trout — healthy.

349

Love to eat fish. So we did. I would say basically fishing and skiing…hiking. Just yes. Really just enjoy the area.

There just wasn't enough light for us to do everything we like to do. If you're family-oriented and love the out-of-doors. Terrace has it! Terrace has done nothing but enhance that, the family values. Far as I'm concerned, medically speaking, we have all these excellent specialist doctors, and this is something else that had progressed. And all these tremendous doctors have been such a bonus for us.

Went to the Evangelical Free Church, just like my brother Alan Nichols did. He was involved with starting Rough Acres Bible Camp, and we just slipped right into that. Spent a lot of our summers at Rough Acres in all kinds of capacities. And Art and I have both been on the board and, I think, every job there: first aid attendant, counsellor… Love teaching archery. And that's another thing — living in Terrace is living on the growing edge. You know, if you're interested in life and 'gungho' to go, this is a very good place to be. And it is still going that way; you've got talents and they are used.

SS: So, what other jobs did you have here besides teaching?

BH: Okay. I was fortunate here to teach. I did substitute teaching with all eight grades at Centennial [High] School. And I also filled in one year for the principal. I freed him to teach because he was a teaching principal. I thoroughly enjoyed that. I taught his grade five/six class but I had the joys of teaching grades one to six whenever they needed me. Watching wonderful young people go through, and some wonderful names that are a part of Terrace like Talstra — teaching their children or their grandchildren.

Then our daughter—she's teaching at Centennial [High] School right now, head of one of the departments. Also, I did calligraphy. But then my life got so busy. I would sell calligraphy. And I was in great demand. I'd taken a class back in the States and I loved it. It was called beautiful writing. It's been a joy in my life because I can make all kinds of things.

SS: So, how did your career help shape your experience in Terrace?

BH: It was perfect — because I had excellent training as a teacher in a Christian college. At Christian college you are really taught to value each life as very special and unique. And that it is your responsibility to bring out the best in each life. And so what better incentive for a teacher? And when you do this, and you pray for children, and you really love them, parents are appreciative and students are too. And it's a joy just to see that a nurturing type of person can make the difference in individual lives. And I've said this and I can't emphasize this enough: Terrace is one of the best places to raise a family.

And you meet people from all over the world and it's just tremendous! And you can have Filipinos and Hindus, and Portuguese, and lovely Native people as your close friends. What a broad foundation to teach the value of an individual.

SS: What a broad community of people.

BH: Yes. Very broad. And it continues to be that, more so and more so. And it's grown that way. I don't think people realize how fortunate anybody who's living in Terrace is. And the way it has evolved into giving the best of today's world plus incorporating all of the joys of yesterday's world. And that's a beautiful mix right here. And the wonderful thing of it is, you could very quickly be any place; you don't waste time in traffic. You can be a lot of different places within a very short distance. And, of course, constantly they are making Terrace better — the Highways Department, everything. Beautifully located. Beautifully situated. And yes, we've never seen a place where the churches got along better either.

Our daughter when she was in senior secondary school, whatever church had the best weekend going for the teens, that's where all the teens would go. And they would move from church to church to church. The year Jana was married, they put on a musical called 'High-Tops.' And they had young people, as I remember, from the Catholic Church and all the various churches. And they used their giftedness, and then this musical was very well received. It was delightful. And Jana was in the middle of it. Happiest as can be as a senior that year Jacques Pelletier proposed to her when she was still 17 years old. But he figured out she was good marriage material. He was seven years older. My husband loved him; so Art gave Jana to Jacques. And if it had been anybody but Jacques… Oh my goodness, my little girl grew up fast.

SS: Well, so what other things did you do for fun? What restaurants did you go to?

BH: Yes, right, right. Being we were teachers, we loved teenagers. We had Bible studies in our home and we would have like an hour of Bible study, and then we would play card games or Scrabble on the floors in front of the big stone fireplace. And we had a group of about 40 teenagers coming. We played what you call 'Ten Letter Scrabble', which is really fun, and 'Fast Scrabble'; we had all forms of it. Trying to help them develop their word skills, which would help them develop in their schooling, and also in the college they would be going to, and help their lives. It was just really fun to be a part of the joy of teaching, a fun way — and just having fun all together.

That's another major thing, as families had to invent their own ways of entertaining each other before the years of television. Television had only been in maybe about five or 10 years when we arrived here. And Art was thrilled because the strap had only been out about five years, and he was thrilled with how well-behaved the students were. Because at that time — and I do not think the strap was used really wrong, just if really necessary — the main thing was the kids knew that if they stepped out of line they were going to be disciplined. So that is something that I am so glad as a teacher that I could put into this.

SS: So, did you visit Lakelse Hot Springs?

BH: Oh yes. And that's exciting, I'm glad you brought that up. They had the initial hot spring, which was just off the highway, just a large pool. That was one of our favourite places to go and take our family. The only thing is, we'd make them sit in the car to make sure that everybody that was using the hot springs at that point were decently clothed — or even barely — which is alright. But occasionally there would be a group there that was just enjoying things in the buff. Part of Terrace's early history, but just the most wonderful place to go to.

We'd go in the winter too. Yes, through the snow and jump in to the hot springs and then get out and make snow angels and jump back in again. Fun, oh fun.

SS: The hot springs were actually just a big pool there?

BH: Just a big pool off the highway to Kitimat— just right close to the highway.

SS: So the hot springs I know about, there's an actual resort.

BH: Yes, sure there is. There's a pool and slides. It was just as you're coming into that area. It was right there, just off the highway. And it was a large pool— just a glorious, hot pool. Big natural pool.

Progress is wonderful. I mean, we live better, healthier lives and we can do more things at once. But there are a few things that have sort of slipped into the past. And it's so exciting to be older and remembering this. And just remember the joy of it again — the joy before computers, which are fine, and cell phones. Brains are so expanding and I'd never be against this. But oh, there are these delightful images we have in our minds of the past, which are just wonderful to hold on to or bridge to, or just remember to be grateful.

Another exciting thing about living in Terrace is getting to know helicopter pilots and how they would go up to these beautiful places. I'm thinking of David Newman who worked with Okanagan for years and bring back just fabulous stories. And at camp… He would come to camp to visit his young people and he would land in camp in his helicopter. It was special.

Lots of really rich, good memories and when they are shared they are just multiplied out. I know you know that already Sarah, it's just so good, just so, so, so, so good.

And oh, a lot of ice skating on our pond. We have a pond and so we would just serve hot chocolate in our house. And just a place for them to come and get warm by the fire, and then they could go back on the beautiful, beautiful pond. And our third son put lights up around them. It was just like magic.

It was just beautiful and I was just thrilled with every single different season because it gave us such joys. And farmers' markets…such a joy. Just all this healthy good food, everybody getting together. Yes, I think everybody's got happy memories of that. Terrace has got some of the richest things, which appeal to so much of us socially, mentally, emotionally, physically... help, everything. Good place to live, good air, good water, good produce, wonderful rich Skeena bottomland, developed really well, and just so good.

SS: So, I don't know much really about Lakelse Lake. How has it really developed in the past few years, if it's developed at all?

BH: We came here with a ski boat, which we built during our last year of college when I was expecting Tim, and we could pull six skiers behind it. If you don't think that isn't fun… It takes somebody really good who is running the boat, somebody really good in the back that's making sure nobody gets tangled up with anybody else, and all six skiers get off.

But the sky's the limit with Terrace, you know? Just enjoying life. And also, we have a man in our church who teaches sail boarding — wind surfing with a sail, just like a surf board with a sail on it. And they started that years ago on Lakelse, and oh, was that ever fun. That's one of my dreams, which I never quite realized I wanted to do. I wanted to do that too. I water ski a lot but never got to do that.

SS: So, what other sports did you do in Terrace?

BH: I think they were mostly involved with water. And skiing, of course; that's not water.

SS: Well, snow is…

BH: Right, it's frozen water. But Art and I both did a lot of skiing — and with Jana too. And, of course, fishing. Just such a joy. Travelling with the Gideons —Art was a Gideon — was all over the world. The Gideons have been to 174 countries. We travelled all over Canada, which was just a real joy. We took Jana with us, from the time she was seven years old. So she's had a very good foundation. And by the way, she also got her papers with Canada. She's a legal immigrant. Wonderful, really good.

SS: So, what other community activities did you guys do outside of the home?

BH: Okay, Art was Thornhill Fire Chief. We bonded with the former fire chief and his wife, and they moved to Quebec and insisted that Art take over as Fire Chief. He did, and this really filled both of our lives. That's where I could use my first aid ticket; I had a double A-ticket. And also my secretarial skills, which were developed.

I got to go to the college, which is a wonderful place to broaden yourself. I took computers and advanced typing, and so I worked in the office areas as well as a full-time fire fighter — first of nine women. And, of course, now women are in all kinds of departments, but that was initially one of the beginnings. A wonderful way to learn here in Terrace.

Also, the Thornhill Fire Department developed a group of men —'cause we were limited as to where we could go. And if there was a fire out of our district, it was so hard to see someone's home burn up with no hope and no one able to respond. So the men made up their own fire department and had a group of additional men that would go to any fire anywhere. And Art inherited this and we just added more trucks and built the fire hall even bigger. And we used the money that we would earn, the money that the men and the women together would earn fighting fires for forestry. And so, we were able to buy more trucks.

And this enveloped our lives. We had parties and all kinds of ways of holding the families together and meeting their needs. And what a joy that was. Like we would have 40 firemen and families — good, just another joy of living in this area, living on the growing edge.

Thornhill Volunteer Fire Department. Billie in centre of photo. Thornhill Volunteer Fire Department Collection.

SS: So, you've been involved with the E-Free [Evangelical Free] Church for many years?

BH: Yes, my brother was on the Board when we arrived.

[Recording cut out]

BH: This is fun.

SS: So, back to forestry...

BH: That's fine. That's excellent. I hate to see the forestry industry diminish at all because it's brought in wonderful families, and given them a variety of work — and kept a variety of people, with different gifts and capabilities, being able to support families. It would be interesting to see what the next phase of Terrace is.

SS: So, as you have watched the forest industry, how has it really changed over the years? Like there was the shutting down of the mill, I know that…

BH: Yes. And that was difficult 'cause when we came it was everything — roaring and full speed ahead. And it's been hard to see it gradually step back, you know, not become as productive.

SS: So, health care and teaching has become more productive than forestry and industry…?

BH: Yes — and a regional area where people can come to have their physical, mental, emotional, social needs met.

SS: Yes. But I do know, as Terrace is one of the darker cities with all the rain that you really do have to grow up here…

BH: …to appreciate it.

SS: Yeah. But you've moved here and you've got to see how Terrace has changed and that's really helped.

BH: And also get an appreciation for the deep values you don't see on the surface.

SS: Do you want to add to that?

BH: Yeah. Well, I mean, I was just at a Christmas party, an early one. And I sat next to a man from Sri Lanka, it's exciting to see people moving from all over the world and to be able to see life from their point of view. Just saying, this is how Terrace, and this is how the world was before computers or cell phones came. Not that they're wrong, but we don't want to lose all the richness of our past that Terrace exemplifies and has been a rich centre for.

SS: So, how did the community of Terrace interact with Kitselas and Kitsumkalum?

BH: Oh, that's wonderful. We were with the fire department and they trained Native people out of the Thornhill Fire Department. That was exciting. And they've — Gitaus — maybe in the last five years, built a wonderful hall at Gitaus, which is right just east of Terrace and east of Thornhill.

SS: How has Terrace changed over the years, in general terms?

BH: Building.

SS: Just expanded structure?

BH: Yes, just expanding. Which is good, because it shouldn't be a closely guarded secret that this is a special place in the world to live, and to work, and to raise a family, and to use the gifts that God has given you. And people are needed up here still; they're still needed and I know we are seeing this in the last year or so. Because it has too much to offer, and there are still trees growing, and there are still programs. They are planting, reforesting... So hopefully it's an industry that's going to reproduce itself.

SS: I know with me, I do see some houses being put in, and I don't like seeing all the trees getting cut down. But I love seeing all the green around Terrace. But it's just great that they're replanting all the trees.

BH: Oh, absolutely! And maybe you haven't seen as much as I've seen, but the [Terrace] Beautification Society should be given a warm pat on the back, and handshakes, and everything else. And kudos. They're doing great because Terrace isn't just growing, it's growing beautifully by people who really care. And they are gifted. So we're fortunate.

SS: So, were there any other annual community events that you remember?

BH: It just seems like Terrace celebrates the seasons beautifully, you know. It's fun to look from one to the next. Right? Right.

Santa Claus comes flying in a helicopter. Just all the funny little things, you know. Just absolutely delightful, just so good… And laying out on – oh, this is so good — laying out on our front lawn with my brothers and our children, growing up watching the Northern Lights or meteor showers. Just awesome. And this is part of the changing of the season and it's something that city [children]—a lot of children—don't see. Because cities are so bright, you don't see it.

SS: I've always heard that you can see the Northern Lights from here, but I've never been able to see them.

BH: At Rough Acres Bible Camp, I was out in between camps in canoes — one of the most exciting nights of my life — with the Northern Lights all around us at Dunalter Lake. Right there, all around us, at Rough Acres Bible Camp. I'm sure it's made an indelible impression on all of our minds, glorious night of Northern Lights.

SS: When you were a child, what did you expect or hope to accomplish in your life?

BH: I was given a verse when I was about 16; how old are you now, Sarah?

SS: I'm 16.

BH: Oh that's interesting. I was 16. I was given a verse and the verse was, "Let your light so shine before men, so they may see your good works and glorify your father, which is in heaven." Isn't that a lovely verse? So that has been my focus.

And it's not just a rock, a pebble being thrown in a pool of water with the ripples going out and disappearing. They're remaining, and they're making other rocks going, and other ripples, and other people are being touched.

That's another thing: our life here in Terrace, it is exciting because of the size of the area. Each life makes a difference. And if somebody has a sorrow, many people in Terrace — the ripples from that sorrow — go out. One person has a joy and I have never seen an area like Terrace that's more giving: for muscular dystrophy, the firemen with their boots taking donations, and people standing out in the cold just getting money for others. Giving, oh, they are so giving.

Terrace has such a heart and that seems to be growing. And I pray that never gets lost in industry and numbers — not that the industry and numbers are bad.

SS: Well, it seems that…in Vancouver there's lots of industry and that's good. But it's not as warm. It's only, like, concrete and windows.

BH: That's true. That's true. And just to launch engineers and doctors, what a wonderful rich area this is. That we are, you know.

And another thing — more missionaries come from this area because people aren't afraid of an area where life can be harsh. Because they were living on the growing edge here anyway, and reaching out and seeing the joy of it and trusting God.

SS: So, another thing from your childhood I was wondering about…what were the expectations that your parents had for you when you were growing up?

BH: My parents—it's interesting—both of them were children of pastors in a church, Methodist and Congregational. But neither one of them became Christians until after the three of us were born.

After the three of us were born, they suddenly became quite serious and thought, *Why do we believe what we believe?* And they really went into it. And a Chinese missionary to China, home on furlough, got ahold of my mother and dad. Dad was asking questions in a meeting and she talked to him and said, "Just start reading the Bible. Both of you start reading the Bible and say, 'God, show us what you mean by it.'" And so she told them to start with the book of John, and that she and her parents — she was a missionary to China — would be praying for them. Billy Graham is a great one for this — and he's still going.

By the way, I was in two different Billy Graham meetings as a teenager and also as a young adult. I was in two of his crusades, which has marked me a lot. And I found the power of prayer there too. But the main thing is, there's not a doubt in my mind just to let God use me and develop me. And even going on 83, I don't see it ending. And my own personal medical physician says I got another five to fifteen years in me. I just wish Art did too, you know. I'm still in shock because I really thought we were gonna have at least another five years.

SS: Well, I know that as I've seen and watched you guys together as I was growing up, you've truly been an example of what it means to be married as Christians. Because I remember reading this verse in the Bible… I can't remember where it was, but basically as a Christian and marrying a Christian, the husband is supposed to love the wife as God loves the church. And your marriage is supposed to be for the glory of God, not for your own.

BH: And also mirroring the relationship between Jesus and the church. He loved them and gave himself for them, and we give ourselves for each other. The two nights before Art died, or passed into heaven, we were both so exhausted. And we laughed and wondered which one of us was gonna die first because we were giving beyond what we could give physically.

And yet, my back doesn't hurt. And he was a big man and I'm a small woman. And my back… The pain I was suffering from straining to get him up and get him where he needed to be without falling, I just marvel at it. It was his love that my back is okay. I can go to bed with no pain. And at this age, I think most seniors, they get a big couch because they hurt. It's because of the love of my wonderful husband — and I was ready to give everything I had. In fact, we were so almost out of it that we were laughing; Art's humour is just so good.

SS: One of the many hopes I have for my life is that I'll be able to find the right person — to love him and for him to love me throughout the years.

BH: Yes! To put you first. And actually, you put God first. And I had a hard time with that one. You love God and obey your husband. And God gives a certain man to us and we are to obey them in everything. But the main thing is to ask God to 'CR'; this is a main focus of mine in life. I'm telling all young people: CR, which means Control the Relationship. This is what I did.

Art was the fifth person to ask me to marry him, and with every person I said. "CR — Control the Relationship". If they're not right, get them out of my life because you are who you put first in your life. Put God first in your life and who's gonna control you? It's exciting. You put chocolate cake first in your life…

SS: …chocolate cake is gonna control you.

BH: I know some wonderful person who did this. Yes, she said, "Don't ever put me in the house with a chocolate cake when there's eight pieces left." We learned from each other in Terrace. That's wonderful; you get to meet a lot of different people. And you can pick and choose what you believe and what you see work. That's why I write books too: to pass it on. As you know, my life is so full. And like a bubble, with a book you can close me up and go back when you have time.

With God and with the bible, and following what the bible says, I have taught seminars on prayer, marriage, and raising children. And I just love it, just love it. Because when God's been so good to you, you just want to share. I've heard Christianity is one beggar sharing with another beggar where to find bread.

SS: So, as a long-time resident of the Terrace area, what other changes have you noticed? And for those who have just recently moved here, what would you like to share with them?

BH: Just to let your life reach out to the new people coming in. And I'm even thinking, like, our Muslim community. Christianity and Muslims and Sikhs — we're not that close at all and yet every person God puts in your path is important. They are a living soul and we need to be ready just to reach out. And I've got some very great, precious Muslim friends.

One other thing is, I have a hope chest I'm going to show to you. I'm making eight of them for my eight granddaughters. And there's 20 different categories: one is love, another is forgiveness, another one is prayer, another one is marriage — everything I've learned, every quote I've gotten.

I've got wonderful thinkers of the world. And there's all quotes in there too — people I've taken these quotes from as well as every Bible verse I've used myself in my own life. And this is my legacy to my granddaughters. They're getting their grandmother in a little tiny carved, wooden hope chest. And that's what's in there. After I'm finished thank-you letters, that's gonna be my next project: putting all these verses and quotes in. They're all in Ziploc baggies for now, 20 of them.

SS: That's exciting.

BH: It's fun. It keeps your life going and I'm never bored. That's another thing—there are so many things up here in Terrace that as kids they don't see it. People don't see it. There's so many things they can develop here and then go out into the world and use it.

SS: Well, thank you.

BH: Oh, you're so welcome Sarah. Really good, bless your heart.

SS: I had so much fun and I can't wait until I tell my mommy and daddy and my entire friends and family.

BH: Oh bless your heart.

Bob Erb Interview

Interviewed by Morgan Belanger and Tanis Lewis, 21 November 2013

Bob Erb was born in Regina, Saskatchewan on July 1st, 1952. His father worked in the propane industry and was transferred to Terrace in 1969. Bob, working in Edmonton at the time, followed his family to Terrace during Christmas of that year. In this interview, Bob describes the next 40 years living in Terrace. He married and had two children, and had a varied life working in forestry, electrical, and in industrial construction work. Bob talks about his work at The Chocolate Shop, a popular burger and milkshake joint in downtown Terrace during the 1970s. He describes his political views, his experience in municipal politics as a candidate for the BC Marijuana Party, and his perspectives on social and economic development in Terrace. In the latter half of the interview, Bob talks about winning the lottery in 2012.

TL/MB: So when and where were you born?

BE: 2:13 P.M. Regina Hospital, 1952, July 1st, which was known as Dominion Day. Now they call it Canada Day. But back in the day, it was called Dominion Day, July 1st.

TL/MB: How did you or your family arrive in Terrace?

BE: My family — my parents, younger brother, and sister — arrived here in '69. My dad worked in the propane industry in Saskatchewan and took a transfer to Terrace. At that time I was living in Edmonton on my own and working at a hardware store. I got a card in the mail saying that they'd moved here.

So I came here Christmas Day in '69. And on that Christmas day of '69, under the old temperatures, it was 40 degrees Fahrenheit, which would translate to about, I believe, 10 degrees. No, five to six degrees Celsius. So it was quite mild. When I left the day before, by Greyhound bus, December 24th, 8 A.M. from Edmonton, it was 40 below and a blizzard.

TL/MB: Did you attend college or university at all?

BE: No, neither one. I did attend Caledonia briefly in the fall of 1970, when I moved to Terrace in March of '70, after my first visit at Christmas. I thought, *hey. This is the place to be.* 40 below in Edmonton. 40 above here in Terrace in 24 hours. I had two weeks' holiday coming up after a year's working at the hardware store in Edmonton, which was March of '70, I had two weeks' vacation coming up.

So I jumped the Greyhound again, and it was 20 below in Edmonton in March, and I got here and it was about 45 to 47 degrees Fahrenheit, which would be close to about 10 degrees Celsius. My two weeks' holiday were up, and I phoned my roommate and my boss in Edmonton and told them I wasn't coming back to Alberta.

It was still 20 below there, and I was here drinking strawberry wine, and smoking Mexican pot, and having the time of my life. I was only 17 and ¾ years old. Off the farm in Saskatchewan for a year and a half that I spent in Edmonton before coming here coming to visit. That stretched into 43 years.

TL/MB: So it kind of grew on you?

BE: Yeah, I hadn't planned on staying this long. You know, the people are great. It's a booming, robust town. Everybody was working. There was just more jobs than people. But it was a one-horse town. It was logging, logging, and logging, and very little tourism. There was a little bit of construction with Eurocan and the pulp mill being built, and the roadwork between here and [Prince]

Rupert. That was a major job, too. So they did get a little bit of employment here, but not sustainable. Little pockets of year after year booming.

TL/MB: Did you ever marry?

BE: I certainly did. I lived in sin with a lady I had met here, and she was actually quite young. She was 17 and I was 23 when we started dating, and we lived in sin for five years, and then got married. And then shortly after had a son. And then a year after him, we had a daughter. They were born on the same day, one year apart.

TL/MB: And what jobs did you work in Terrace?

BE: I worked in logging first year, and the sawmill and with CanCel [Canadian Cellulose Company Ltd.]. It was with Columbia Cel [Columbia Cellulose Company Ltd.]. They had a few different names; it changed before it went bankrupt. Uh, West Fraser or something… Skeena Cel... I did that and the pole sawmill downtown, which would later become whatever sawmill that was. I worked building the new one back in the '80s and it's all bulldozed over. So I did that for about a year, year and a half.

I worked as an electrician apprentice and wired the first A&W here in town, which is now Sonbadas Restaurant. It was a drive-in and under the sidewalk there, there's a causeway, like a concrete service tunnel. That's where all the wiring is for speakers and lights there. And there's a canopy over the top. Cars would drive in. You got your speaker there. You would put your order in. Car hops would come out with your tray and hang it from your car there, with your milkshakes. That was in 1970 when I worked there. And with Omenica Builders, a hardware store. And that was pretty much the first couple of years up here.

And then I got into construction about '73, clearing the buildings and the farmhouse out of the way for the new Skeena River Bridge. The Dudley Little Bridge it's called, where Walmart and Irly Bird and all of that is. It was a farm that was used for a warehouse for a bakery and a bottling. I can't remember if it was the Coke or the Pepsi people that also used the barn as a warehouse. And then we moved the farmhouse from there out to Old Remo, where it still stands today. It was put on a foundation, the farmhouse that was there. Right where Irly Bird and that is now.

TL/MB: How did your career frame your experience in Terrace?

BE: Oh, how did my work frame my experience? Well, I was working in construction and a few years after, I joined the 168 Tunnel and Rock Worker's Union. And it's cement finishing, labouring, specialized construction work in 1977, so I got into industrial sites — Alcan, Eurocan… It was seasonal work mainly. And Rupert pulp mills for maintenance and that.

It was seasonal work. And some people were discouraged, because it's hard to make a decent living and raise a family off of seasonal work. It was great for me. I was always frugal and was a bit of an entrepreneur, and I made ends meet nicely. I don't want to get into detail with that because I had a 14-year argument with Revenue Canada over that. And I won. They lost. And I paid off a friend's bill — $365,000 that they were after him for — just with some of the lottery winnings. So I don't like to discuss that. It was right up my alley, and it allowed me a lot of free time to be with my son and daughter.

They were in the swim club. I was a tee ball and a baseball coach for them for five to six years, and a member of the Blueback Swim Club executive for four to five years. I was vice-president of fundraising, and I got all of the major stores and little businesses to sponsor two swim meets a year and our travel. We were probably the most moneyed up sports team in Terrace at that time.

TL/MB: Oh cool, you were really involved. And what did you do for fun?

BE: Watch NFL football. You know, I had a men's ball team that we started. And when the kids got old enough and couldn't find coaches, I dropped the men's ball team. The wife and I, we played on mixed scrub, and did a lot of camping before kids and after kids. Drank a lot of beer, smoked a lot of pot, and had a lot of good times. I use pot like a preventative medicine, you know. Why wait to get sick before you start taking it? I use it like a multi-vitamin, 15 a day.

TL/MB: Keeps the doctor away.

BE: Yeah. Like I said, I'm 61 years old, and I go in every five years for a physical. And the heart doctor says I have impeccable blood pressure: 113 over 63 with a 46 or 48 heartbeat, which is quite slow. But if you are athletic or have done hard physical work all your life from youth — I grew up on a farm and that — your heart works more efficiently.

TL/MB: So what restaurants were popular over the years?

BE: Well, there's two pizza places that come to mind. The very first pizza place in town is where Gusto's Restaurant is now, across from the Terrace Hotel, or the Best Western, they call it. I always refer to it.

The first place that opened up in 1970, it was called 'The Place', and it was a pizza place. Well, it was the only pizza place. It was a great spot and they did have pizzas there. Later on, it was bought out and renamed The Sternwheeler, and it was a steak and seafood place. And I believe they also had pizza there. I think a buyer took all of those buildings down.

But, we had a little place called The Chocolate Shop, and it was a burger shop on Main Street, across from the Scotia Bank, right by the alley walkway where the old Ev's Menswear store is. You go down the walkway to Greig Avenue and the Shan Yan Restaurant. A little bit on the left, there was a separate business there and that's where we had The Chocolate Shop. It was called The Chocolate Shop after [the Archie Comics]. I don't know if you read Archie and Jughead, Betty and Veronica…

Back in the day, there were three different lengths of women's dresses. There was the mini skirt, the midi skirt, and then the maxi. So we named our burgers the mini, midi, and maxi…So, the quarter pound was the mini, the half-pound midi, and the three-quarter pound the maxi. And then we had three milkshakes: vanilla, chocolate, and strawberry. We had a choice of onion rings and fries. And then we sold a lot of acid and pot. We were, you know, 17, 18, 19.

We opened at about three or four in the afternoon and then closed at about three or four in the morning. We had the jukebox cranked up loud. You could hear it from the Terrace Hotel, which was the Best Western, and over to the Lakelse Hotel, which is whatever…Hanky Panky's and the Coast. But it was always those two hotels, and we were situated right in between. And there was always steady traffic all night, walking from each place. Back in the day, that was the social set focal point of every community — the bars.

We had no colour TVs. Those were space age. Remote controls had a wire that went from the remote to the TV, and that was space age, too. You had one TV channel. We didn't have cable vision up here. We had no VCRs, you know, which is a pre-runner to whatever they call those DVD things or CD things now. I don't know how to run those; I never learned how to run my VCR properly. The only place to go to catch up on the news of the week was at the bars after work. And that's where everybody would go on Friday and Saturday nights. The town was shut down on Sunday. No stores would be open. The stores and service stations were the only thing open.

TL/MB: What were the names of the bars?

BE: Oh, I got rambling. There were two restaurants there, ones that I didn't mention. And one is still in existence: the Bavarian Inn. Their fine dining upstairs was probably the best in town — or one of

360

the two best. And one was Manuel's Restaurant, which was located on the main street, in the area where All Star Shoes is today. There was a Bank of Montreal there, and his restaurant, Manuel's.

He relocated over by Telus, where the Hospital [Auxiliary] Thrift Store is. And they had that five-story building — that brown one here on the corner. The basement was turned into Jezebel's Café, which was a hot spot of Terrace in the late '70s and '80s, as well as the well downstairs. But he had relocated his Manuel's Restaurant, which was above-average dining, like the Crest Hotel, and better, you know. The best dining in the Northwest was the Bavarian Inn. And then the other restaurants… There was a nice Dog 'n' Suds, where they have that little RV park next to Sonbadas [Steak House]. There was a Dog 'n' Suds Drive-In, and they would come out on roller skates. And they take your order, or you would phone your order in. They had the speakers here. You push a button. The menu is all up here. You drive under the canopy and they would deliver it out.

TL/MB: Did you visit the Lakelse Lake Hot Springs?

BE: Rarely. We did lots in the '70s. We were there. And lots in the '80s. It was more kept up at that time. But we used to go there at that time when the motel was all over at the right hand side, and there's a bar and a dining room and horse stables in the back. It was called Skoglund Hot Springs at the time. And I got a bunch of stuff from there that I've picked up from around the province, concerning the hot springs. I put it in a shadow box and traded it to Kelsey [Wiebe, the curator] up at Heritage Park. It's the only Skoglund Hot Springs memorabilia that they've been able to come across.

I have two of the plates and a cushion. It's a purple cushion with gold tassels all the way around, and it has sort of a First Nation face, a happy face sort of thing. And the plates were like that. And then there's a silver serving tray, also, where they did an aerial photo of the facility showing all of that. I put that into the box. I think it's the only history they have — of any artifacts they have actually from it. It was the Skoglund family that had that. Yeah, it was a regular spot.

Then we went to the hot springs that weren't part of the complex. There are a few smaller ones and we would go skinny-dipping and that, drinking the wine after the bars, yeah.

TL/MB: Did you ever visit Lakelse Lake?

BE: Yeah, yeah, always. We always went out to Gruchy's, but that was before there was an entrance. You know where Gruchy's is? That parking lot and that was all that there was — all bush and swamp.

You used to cross the bridge, and where they have the concrete barricades, all the way around the curves, as soon as you get across the bridge, well, there used to be a little road in there, and a couple of little parking lots. And that's where, after the bars, cabarets closed, we would drive down there, half a dozen cars. Then we'd piggy-back the girls, and cross the two creeks, and get out to Gruchy's. That was in the early and mid-'70s, long before it was too popular with anybody. It was a great spot.

Camped a lot at Furlong Bay with the kids. We would camp out there with a few families. For two weeks at a time, it would be six families. We would have the skateboards and the basketballs, and we would get the row of campsites right up front by the parking lot. That way, it was close to the beach and the playground, and they could skateboard and play soccer on the parking lot.

It wasn't near as crowded as nowadays. You didn't have to make reservations and you could stay as long as you wanted, pretty much. And firewood was for free. I think they charged us two dollars a night or 10 dollars a week to camp there.

We would take a pick-up full of firewood, and take it over. We had three sites. Not a hope in hell they would charge you 300 bucks for the firewood we used to get for nothing back in the day.

TL/MB: Can you tell me about sports back in the day?

BE: My sports or sports in general?

TL/MB: Oh you know, sports that you were in.

BE: When I first got here in the 1970s, I played on a mixed bowling team — five-pin bowling. I was a pinsetter out in Saskatchewan; that was before the machines came and did it all. I was the machine: me and my buddies. I think we got a nickel a game, or something like that. And you jump down — they had a little foot lever — and they would put up little pins like that. And you put the pins on them, you know, the bowling pins. Because they had a little hole in the bottom. You could stand them all up, and take your foot off the lever, and jump up and curl up, and then CRASH! And those things are scattering all around you and that. It was a dangerous job, but that was in Saskatchewan in the '60s. And so I did some five-pin bowling here the first year.

We threw together a motley crew full of people. We got the last-place champs. We got a funny statue, where the bowling ball landed on the person's foot — sort of a thing like that. We were so heavily handicapped. They had to give us so many points, you know, give us a 400-point start to the other teams. And we improved all year long, and we ended up winning the playoffs too. And we got a big trophy too. So we got the last-place champs. One time we were called the Happy Gang. I think that was the last team in the early millennium. I think the last team we were called the Smoking Idiots.

Then we played, like I said, mixed baseball. I think there was 100 scrub mixed teams around town. It was really popular in the late '70s and all throughout the '80s. The men's team I played on, and started — the Thornhill Pub team — and managed. Then I went into the kids sports when the kids were old enough. They were always struggling for volunteers and coaches and all that, and I had a coaching certificate. It was actually more fun coaching the kids than the adults. What a bunch of babies the adults were.

One memory of coaching the kids: one of the first years, the first year after tee-ball, there were 17 kids. Everybody wanted to be on our team. I think it's because we bought Dilly Bars after every game and practice. But anyways… You have all these kids milling around you and you have to get them dispersed, you know. And I didn't have any volunteers helping me until later on in the season. You go to first, you go to second, you go to third, you go with this guy — the two of you as a matter of fact — and start throwing the ball. Two over here throw back and forth, you know, pitching. And then the other guy stands up and pitches back, so you know, they practice pitching and catching. Get them going. And trying to get your guys going out in the field here… And then there's this girl smiling, about six teeth missing there, about six years old. "Coach, coach, where's second base?" Okay. So we better get back to square one here! So I get them all lined up, and, "See that. I want you all to run to that base there and touch it. Don't miss it. Touch it and yell 'first base.' And go to that one and yell 'second base.'" And that would become our every day — or every practice. Get them to learn where first, second, third was.

And then other parents… The kids were having fun, and there would be other parents out there. And it was easy once you delegate and get them into different units. Some would be catching balls. Some would be pitching balls. Some would be taking batting practice. And you know that's it – ball!

The main thing was swimming. It was a life skill rather than just a sport. They had to do a sport, and I didn't count swimming. They were in it 10 to 11 months of the year. They had to swim because there you are, at 80 or 90, and save your life or somebody else's.

So my son played hockey. Spent a lot of time at the hockey arena. And my daughter, she — they all did — everything. And they had golf memberships and that. My son liked baseball and hockey.

He was a good swimmer with the Blueback Swim Club. And my daughter swam for 12 years with the Blueback. And she was scouted with some university teams. She was honour roll and honourable mention here at Caledonia. She had national records, provincial records, and regional records, for the 10, 12 and 14 age group, you know.

TL/MB: So how have you been involved in the community over the years?

BE: Oh, I have been an activist with the marijuana thing — and union, construction union job steward. Run for provincial MLA. And I run for civic politics here. I ran for mayor. I believe it was in '02. I think it was…under the Terrace Marijuana Party. I'm the only candidate who has ever run before, or since the '02 municipal election, that ever ran with the legitimacy, or autocracy, or whatever it's called, of a party, or a coalition. Everybody runs in municipal politics as an independent. You have to get into large cities like Vancouver, and then they have little coalitions, and few letter names and stuff like that.

When I ran in the provincial election in '01, I had a couple hundred members signed up to the provincial Marijuana Party in the Skeena riding. And we decided that the people who were registered in Terrace would form another political party called the Terrace Marijuana Party. We had 60 some members — and registered in Victoria.

Bob Erb, 2015.

So when I ran in '02, they asked me what name I wanted on the ballot here. You know, there's Jack Talstra and then myself. I said, "Well, I want Bob Erb, Terrace Marijuana Party, on the ballot." And they said, "Well, we're not sure." I said, "Well, I'm a registered party in Victoria." "Well, we will have to check it out." And indeed I am a registered party and that's who I am representing, so they had to put it on. And there was a big write-up in the Terrace Standard about it. I'm the only one who has run as the Terrace Marijuana Party and they had to put it on the ballot. By law they had to.

TL/MB: What local events do you remember celebrating?

BE: Riverboat Days. I am disappointed there's not a Canada Day celebration here. It's a national friggin' holiday and my birthday too! July 1st. You know Kitimat always has something happening. And also July 1st, my birthday, Canada Day, is formerly known as Dominion Day, and also Cannabis Day. It's a national holiday for the pot smokers too.

As well April 20th, 420, is the demonstration day. And marijuana legalization has 73% to 82% in favor of turfing the marijuana possession laws in BC. We don't want to see our school teachers, the nurses, the construction workers, the retail sales clerks, the waitress, the whoever, drawn in front of the criminal justice system for choosing a joint over a coffee and a cigarette with a newspaper. Or instead of choosing a cigarette and a beer over a hockey game. You know, it's a safer...

TL/MB: So what do you remember about downtown Terrace?

BE: It was a vibrant Terrace, always full of activity. Most of my life in Terrace, I lived in Thornhill. So it was only up until the summer of '74, I believe it was, there was only one option to get into town. And that was the Old Skeena Bridge, the one-way bridge as it is today.

I can recall all the traffic heading into [Prince] Rupert, or all the traffic heading into Prince George. And that came through Terrace. With all the local traffic, it was pretty busy, all the way down Lakelse Avenue, right from where the ambulance shelter is now, all the way down Lakelse Avenue to the bridge. And the Dairy Queen used to be located kitty-corner to the present day Kondolas. And we had line-ups of traffic that far up to the Old Skeena Bridge, which is a mile long, you know. A couple hundred cars, one-way, getting across. That's how busy it was. The town was booming with logging. Plus all the through traffic had to be downtown Terrace.

When they opened the new bridge, the Dudley Little Bridge — and opened the Sande Overpass — it killed all of the businesses from the [Royal Canadian] Legion to Eby Street. Because now, 10 to 15% of the traffic that used to come through Terrace heading to [Prince] Rupert and Alaska Ferries etc., they bypassed Terrace. And same thing with the traffic heading to Prince George. And even Kitimat coming from [Prince] Rupert. They didn't come to downtown Terrace any more. They bypassed it. So it killed a lot of the businesses. And the proof is the Co-op is no longer there. The Best Western, Terrace Hotel, is almost belly under — except for now, you know. None of the traffic from the Skeena Hotel, [it] never rebuilt. The traffic from out of town used to pass downtown Terrace.

We can change that by building a one-way bridge from Ferry Island over to the curling rink, making it one-way downtown Terrace towards Prince Rupert, Alaska Ferries... And make it all so people wouldn't have to use the overpass coming into Terrace from [Prince] Rupert. They could come straight there, you know. You have the campground on the left, the turn-off. You make a turn-off like that to the right, over the railroad track, and come out by the curling rink, straight down Greig Avenue. The through traffic that ordinarily bypasses Terrace to go to Rupert and the ferries now have the option to go to downtown Terrace, stop and gamble at Chances, have drinks at the Legion, or go straight down and stay at the Best Western or the new hotel that's being built on the Co-op property. And, you know, that would take traffic off of the Sandy Overpass. Same thing, put up a big sign heading east over by the ambulance shelter sort of thing, and say hey, Prince George, Kitimat, via downtown Terrace, you know. Not over the overpass. Right over Greig, past the Co-op land— the new hotel, past the Terrace, past the Skeena, up by Chances by way of the Legion. Bang-o there's businesses there that would benefit from that out-of-town traffic. Past the Bavarian they would benefit, the Aspen House or whatever it's called now, that motel there. They would benefit from the traffic going to other destinations that are driving past the businesses going to downtown Terrace.

That would revitalize downtown Terrace.

Well, you continue the millennium trail around, too. It's a great place to watch fireworks off of a one-way bridge like that, coming from Ferry Island into Terrace — wide sidewalk, with pedestrian and wheelchair access, or horse and buggy, that sort of thing, and it makes your overpass. And then you keep the old bridge always green, going out to Thornhill, and to Kitimat, and to Prince George, that way the people of downtown Terrace, instead of like me, can take the overpass, take the Old Bridge. It might be a red light, you know, it's always green going out to Thornhill and Kitimat. That takes traffic off of the Sande Overpass. Those two things, we won't have a crowd at Sande Overpass and it revitalizes downtown Terrace. Just a single-lane bridge; one little bridge. You know, we don't need an overpass out by Frank's Field. You know, it doesn't help the downtown Terrace.

TL/MB: What did most people that you knew do for work?

BE: Logged, and construction, and sold pot. Really. Seriously.

TL/MB: So what role do you think forestry and logging played throughout the history of Terrace?

BE: Well, they created short-term employment, and long-term benefit for a few. By that I mean, they give away all of the logs, and timber, and everything to a few companies. And that was in the '50s and '60s and '70s. Who's they? The people that voted for the Social Credit Government, the Socred government that was in power for 22 years. And then 'they' later become the Liberals. And, you know, a lot of the members. But it was a Socred government of 22 years, you know: W. Wacky Bennett, W.A.C. Bennett and his son Bill Bennett. They gave away all of the logs and timber and that, for jobs. So everybody had two vehicles. Robust economy. And nobody is collecting any of this stumpage fee for any of the big timber on the doorsteps of Terrace.

And every logging community of northern BC, well, they knew 20 or 40 years down the line that somebody is going to have to pay the piper. Because Eurocan, and Kitimat, SCI [Skeena Cellulose Inc.] in [Prince] Rupert… They shut down. Why? Because there's no affordable fibre source close to their mills. Where do they go? Hundreds of kilometers up in the mountains — and getting a poor wood fibre. And it costs tons of money to build roads into the mountains. And then the fuel costs at the time and that, you know… It just wasn't viable any more.

So who benefitted from that was the contractors that had logging trucks and the politicians who got elected year after year after year. And then in 2000, the new millennium, we built a 70 million dollar highway up the Nass. Tax dollars. That should have been built in 1950 and 1960 with tax dollars and stumpage fees.

So the politicians all got their lucrative pensions and were elected for 20 some years. And some lucky people that were in the trucking industry, logging industry, contracting and that… they had the bucks fine and dandy. They got jobs, but it was short term. It wasn't sustainable, you know?

One simple solution: instead of being logging, logging, logging, we could have been logging, logging, and agriculture. This used to be known as the Okanagan of the North before World War I. And then they got all the Japanese out of here and moved them into Alberta and that. But large orchards and farmland around here, great for agriculture, after the War, never got started up. And you go through local history... There's lots of abandoned orchards, for 50 and 60 years, all around the Terrace, Thornhill area.

So land that was logged off, that was suitable for agriculture, should have been turned into agricultural land. Should have grown hemp right on the doorsteps of these pulp mills and they would have had a renewable fibre. The strongest fibre in the world, used for 6,000 years by the Egyptians, Venetians, and Syrians, Babylonians and later the Greeks, and even later the Romans and Persians and all of that. It was the oil of the ancient world, right up until 1850. They made all of the hemp sails, ropes and that. You wouldn't have sailed the seven seas and ocean with cotton and ore sails. It was hemp. And they used it not only for writing, for clothing, for food products, fine oils — a lot of hemp uses. And right up until the petroleum era started in the 1850s. But they could have grown a renewable fibre right on their own doorsteps of these pulp mills.

It would have been a known fibre supply, at a known cost, renewable every year. One year, on this 50,000 acres gets grown. And then that one grows, alternating crops. Same as they do in Saskatchewan or any other place. You know, one year, summer followed and fertilized, and you know it's rejuvenated, and the next year it's replanted. So you would have had — instead of going hundreds of kilometers up into the mountains and you burn fossil fuels and all of that — you could have grown the damn hemp fibre right there.

And that same thing with the plywood mills. They call them OSB [Oriented Strand Board] strand mills, you know. With all that strand and that, they could have grown hemp fibre. And put that mill in the middle of a thousand acres of hemp and without cutting logs down. They do select logging instead of clear-cutting. Great for the whole world's environment. You could have just had hemp, you know. Why is that illegal after 6,000 years of being legal? No scientific evidence. There's no medical evidence to support it. It's ignorance that supports it, not being informed.

TL/MB: So tell us a little more about your role in politics.

BE: Hmm. Well, the biggest social injustice I've ever seen in my adult life is the marijuana prohibition. It's caused more social harm and grief — since I've become an adult, so since 1970 — that I have seen than any one thing has done. It's criminalized. Law-abiding, tax-paying, working citizens that are choosing a safer way to relax than alcohol and tobacco. If you go to Health Canada… I've rounded off figures that 44,000 people die in Canada every year from smoking-related diseases. Something like 12,000 from alcohol-related incidences. That doesn't account for all the misery and injuries caused from alcohol also, and you know, domestic stuff. I think the third highest was about 2,200 deaths annually from prescription drugs and 1,800 deaths annually from all illegal drugs. Something like 40-some deaths from aspirin a year. Twenty-some deaths from caffeine. And a couple deaths from this and that. Zero from marijuana. And people say, "Well, how can that be?"

You know you're smoking it, and smoking it — it's good for yah, and I've given two vast examples — it's like comparing apples to oranges. I get it from all the journals: English, American medical journals. So you can go on site, where they have some studies — some preliminary studies, because it's been banned from doing studies on marijuana because nobody could get legal marijuana from the government to do the studies with. So that's why there's so few studies that have been done up until just recently.

If you have a forest fire, and the smoke from that — it's wood fibre. If you have a house fire, well, that's from paint, and a hundred different chemicals. They both smoke and you breathe the smoke. The composition is different. If you have a can of ginger ale, or a can of beer, you pour them into a glass they are both amber-coloured fluids — both fizz, same delivery system, but different substances. Tobacco — sixty-some carcinogens and they have a poster up there in the doctor's office that tells you about that, and zero [carcinogens] in the marijuana. Go to the health website, that's where I get my information from.

They found in an English study several years ago — it was published, and then this spring I just read one in the *Vancouver Province*. One — from an American study follow-up to the English one — showed that they didn't have any carcinogens in the pot smoke. But they had found in England six years ago — that there's preliminary indications that some of the cannabinoids released in the marijuana smoke by igniting it actually showed possibilities that it could detox some of the carcinogens introduced to your system by tobacco smoke. And then it was reaffirmed six years later with this American study, out of the Eastern United States, showing the same preliminary indications that were first discovered in an English — and those were both published in the medical journals too.

366

They're showing that if you smoke tobacco — well if you smoke, smoke pot. But if you smoke tobacco, smoke pot too, because as the preliminary studies show, it will help get rid of the [carcinogens] and flush that out sort of like the cranberries, or blueberries help detox your liver, to flush the impurities out of your system.

TL/MB: How have you felt the community and the region has been represented on any level — locally, regionally, provincially, or nationally?

BE: Well, I think nationally — Nathan Cullen [current Member of Parliament] — poorly. Caters to a special self-interest group. Especially one thing I can say is the Enbridge thing [proposed Northern Gateway Pipeline]. I forget the name of it. Just read it in the *Province* here a couple days ago. $125 million that they've financed for the Enbridge thing. An American foundation financing the anti-pipeline thing.

Now, why the hell would the Americans not want to see a pipeline go to the West Coast and to the world market? Well, they get all of our oil down to Texas — to their refineries, 2,000 miles from Alberta to Texas. They get our oil for $80 a barrel. The world price is $105 if we get it to the West Coast. Huh, well whose interest is it to not getting it to the West Coast? The Americans. Why is all the money that is financing the Enbridge this and that coming from the States? Why isn't it coming from Canadian outfits?

And the First Nations… They're getting all their money from the American interest. $125 million that the San Francisco foundation — I forget the name of it anyways. But it's just ludicrous that here we've got oil that we import from Venezuela into Nova Scotia to the Irving refinery there. And here we pay $105 bucks a barrel for that instead of having a pipeline going from Alberta out to the Maritimes. They use very poor examples, none of which are very recent. They *blah blah*, this and that. They use the Exxon Valdez, have you girls heard of that? The Exxon Valdez. You might have heard or remember the Exxon Valdez. Well, it sunk in 1981 in foreign waters — a single hull, one big compartment.

It was in a foreign country 32 or 33 years ago — no GPS navigation and all of that which is all standard now and they know that now because they've charted the waters. They didn't have that other stuff charted and that was 30-some years ago. And it was a single hull vessel with one or two compartments, split in four. And, you know, every compartment filled up. Now they've got these compartments the size of a school, about 20 of them. And they're all double-hulled, so if one gets ripped open, it ain't going to sink the ship, because it will fill up with water and it will still float. And they've got all different technologies. They've got GPS. They have pilot boats and all of that, which guide them all in, and so they use that. Poor example: 30-some years ago, foreign country, single hull, 1970s technology, on that 1981 boat.

And then they mentioned Kalamazoo Michigan, the pipeline that went there—foreign country, 1961 pipeline — pardon me, that seems like 53 or 54 years old — in a foreign country, done by foreign workers, with 1950s technology. No, we're all doing much better, nobody wants to see any harm done. So those are two very poor examples. The only two examples they came up with on the spring legislative assembly here, in session when it opened here in session in March — this year, in Victoria.

There's a reporter that asked every city and every MLA that was in there if any of them, regardless of party, who could bring back an example of an oil spill in the past 100 years of mainland BC supply and oil tankers, full of oil, to and from Vancouver Island in the past 100 years, or supply in Haida Gwaii — Queen Charlotte Island — in the past 100 years. Like they don't have an oil well over there to keep their generators going in the past 100 years. They're all diesel-fueled generators since 1910.

That reporter asked that question three times in the first week of it and not a Green, an NDP, a Liberal, not one MLA sitting this spring, through 100 years of newspaper reporting, could bring back one example of ever an oil spill off the coast of BC caused by tankers or barges by Vancouver Island for 100 years or on Haida Gwaii. And now we have 100 years more new technology and GPS, radar, sonar, double-hulled ships, the best trained pilots through here — you know and in fact they have never had an accident yet — 50-60 years of hauling oil and aluminum ore in and out. Also, let alone 100 years of supplying oil to Haida Gwaii or Vancouver Island. So, you know they gotta get the stats right.

You know the prohibition, and it's a minority. I won't go out there. This anti-Enbridge thing… You see a few hundred people there. You do the quick math. There's 30,000 people within 15 kilometers of downtown Terrace, and you go out there and there's only 300 showing up there? That must mean there's 29,000 that are okay with it.

Because you get a vocal minority that go out there and push their views on, you know, the silent majority. It shows okay, you get 300 people that object to it, and 20 of 30,000 people that are okay with it. Otherwise, if everyone objected to it, you would have 20,000 out there and you don't. So don't let them influence your own decisions here. Like — a lot of people want to be on the right side of the thing. Or they don't know what they're talking about, and they also come here with fossil fuels too. None of them are taking horse and carriage.

The Amish, did you hear about the Amish? Living in Detroit or Michigan or that. They go out, walk out to the fields, and do all the work manually with tractors. Do this, that or the other with the oxen, or the horse, or something like that. They build fine furniture by that. And they take it into the country by horse and carriage. They sell it like this, and that, or the other thing. They talk the talk. But they walk the walk too. They do everything without fossil fuels. They have a right to say stuff. All of these people, these protesters, that take the planes, trains, and everything with fossil fuels — I mean really? Walk to these protests like the Amish. You know you can't have both. You can or can't. And there's not a god-darned oil executive or a shareholder — I have shares in a lot of different companies and that, and none of us wants to see our grandchildren, our great grandchildren, or the next generations sacrificed because of our greed. That's not the way it is.

Robin Austin [current member of the Legislative Assembly of British Columbia], you know, he does a little bit better on the governing part because he spoke on our [Terrace District Community Service Society] 420. And he knows very well, 73% of his constituents are in favor of turfing the [marijuana] possession laws.

Nathan Cullen lets his own personal stuff come into view. And the people of the Skeena riding didn't elect Nathan Cullen for his personal beliefs. They elected Nathan Cullen for the federal party's belief. And the federal party, since '78 — NDP — said if elected as the federal government of Canada they'd decriminalize marijuana. That was done in 1978, at the Winnipeg National Convention [of the New Democratic Party]. And every four years they have reiterated that. That will be part of their platform for the next four years until the next election.

So that's something that the federal NDP party has stood up for, and said that they would do. I talk to Nathan Cullen lots about that, and he says that it is something that he is personally not for. And I said, "Nathan, nobody has got you up here, run as an independent. Then see how long you stay elected. Because we didn't elect you for your personal beliefs. We voted for you for your god-darn party's beliefs, which is decriminalizing and legalizing marijuana, which 73% or more of your constituents want. And you're going to sit up here and cater to a small minority group and let your taxpaying, law-abiding citizens be criminalized because it's not bloody great for you right now?" I have very low respect for Nathan Cullen. Much higher for Robin Austin. Jack Talstra [former long-term mayor of Terrace], I didn't have any respect. [Dave] Pernarowski [former mayor of Terrace], so-so.

When I ran for politics in '01, I said, "Hey. For mayor I would lobby the BC municipalities to lobby Victoria." I did a lot to raise awareness for the unfairness of the marijuana possession laws. I did that in '02. I coloured the pamphlets that were sent out in lime green, stating that just in the last year, '12, the Union of BC Municipalities approved that by a vote of 52% to 48% to lobby what I had said 10 years earlier. I'm a visionary. What can I say?

TL/MB: Can you tell us about your experience winning the lottery?

BE: Oh, well. I was none prepared for it, because I've been thinking I was going to win for the past 43 years that I've been buying lottery tickets! So, you know, every time you buy a ticket, okay. You go through your mind with what you're going to do with it. Oh, I didn't win this time. I always buy the Quick Pick and the Extra. I never ever play the same numbers. I think I might have tried that once or twice, but it takes too long. I just Quick Pick and the Extra. And I got it covered for the Wednesday, Saturday [Lotto] 6/49s and the Friday Lotto Max.

So, you know, I did a couple of upgrades. I haven't really done anything much different. I bought some clothes and gave a lot of money away. Gave $7 million to relatives, friends, strangers, charities — most of it to homeless shelters, the wet or dry homeless shelter, and the transition houses, and the food banks, and the hospice society.

You know: $20,000 Happy Gang [Centre], the 649 Air Squad Cadets $10,000, $30,000 to the K'san House [Society], $20,000 to the TDCSS [Terrace District Community Service Society]. I think that's the food bank and that, the Core Store…

And there were a dozen businesses that received funds for Christmas parties. Safeway got $23,000 for 155 employees for gift cards. City West, seventy-five employees and they got about $18,000. And Kalum Cabs, they've got forty-four employees. And All West Glass, Kalum Tire, Wightman and Smith, West Point Rentals, Hair Gallery, and other groups and organizations…

There were the food programs for the schools too. And the Salvation Army got $20,000. And the Hospital Auxiliary got $20,000. And the Regional District got $30,000. $20,000 of that to the Thornhill Fire Station. I don't know most of the guys. And, of course, I give them another $10,000 just for the volunteers and that for their Christmas party. So I gave $40,000 to the Thornhill Fire Department, Regional District, and the volunteers and all of that crowd. Forty thousand bucks for them.

$85,000 for Rosswood Community Centre, for a roof and that. And then, that one family out there: $70,000 for their septic, their addition. Nora and Pat Thompson. Wheelchair ramps. Tens of thousands of people with dentist bills of $300, plus $1,000 bills — different individuals. That lottery money went a lot of different ways.

And, of course, I've got close to one million dollars spent to date on the legalization of marijuana nationwide. I'm sponsoring the Sensible BC petition, which is out right now for referendum. Probably got in excess of $340,000 spent last year on that, and we could top $400,000 by the time it ends.

And then I sponsored the national 420 events in cities across Canada; '13 was the first year. I spent about $150,000 on that. Twenty-four, twenty-six cities… And this year the '14 one, on April 20, we are hoping to have it in 40 to 50 cities, and $150,000 on that. So we can get a national voice and all that, leading up to the 2015 federal election to deter Harper. And then get some sense to get rid of this mandatory minimum [sentence] and to get legalization of marijuana happening.

A perfect example is fourteen years of alcohol prohibition in the States — caused tens of thousands of deaths, poisoned alcohol, hundreds of thousands of hospitalizations from poisoned alcohol, and fourteen years of gun crimes in every neighborhood of every big or small town in the United States. 'Cause of the prohibition, that's what happened. They legalized alcohol after fourteen years — millions of jobs were created in the warehousing, the distillery, the trucking, the retail sales. Millions of jobs in the States were created, collected income taxes, mortgages were bought, taxes were paid on property taxes, increases in the streets, in street lighting, infrastructure, all of that was done. Money was left over — for increased education, health care.

With prohibition, you've got the gangs, and the guns, and that in the neighborhood — and the only money being spent is taking it from healthcare, taking it from education, and putting it into the RCMP. I mean, really, do we need twenty-some year old cops running around with an $80,000 a year income shooting people because they felt threatened with a plastic fork? And then they get two-year suspension on pay, and stuff like that, you know? Like the kid they shot in Houston [BC] a few years ago. He's handcuffed, behind his back, that Ian Bush — that's in Houston, five or six years ago — and they shot him in the back of the head! Killed him. He was handcuffed at a hockey game, they took him to the police station, in Houston BC just down the road here, it happens all the time. Happens all the **** time — the cop felt threatened. And of course the camera was shut off during that one thing. You know he's sitting with some friends out at the arena there, drinking some beer, he's a nice guy — and they shot him in the back of the head and killed him.

TL/MB: When you were a child what did you expect or hope to accomplish?

BE: I don't know. Legalization of marijuana, for sure, as an adult. Yeah, I don't know. If you think of what I was looking at when I was, you know, growing up in the '50s and '60s. Maybe getting someone to the moon? But that already happened. Get somebody back there again? They're talking about that 40 years later.

Just having an ordinary, you know, fruitful life, I guess. I had no great — I didn't want to be an airplane pilot. Certainly did not want to be a cop. I had no interest being a cop when I was a kid, and less so when I was an adolescent.

You know as soon as I found out more about the mentality of the person that it takes to be a cop, and I would think eight or nine out of ten are probably ***** and teacher's pet in school. You know? I remember when I was a kid growing up, you know, and you talk in class — and I'm talking in primary and elementary — they draw a little circle up there, and you have to stand like that with your nose to the blackboard and your heels sticking out, and they would smack you on your calves, your leg — and that was in the Catholic school we went to too. I could [inaudible] them now.

[Laughter.]

And anyways, yeah, they would have two or three of us and then the teacher's pet would be on the floor behind you — and you standing on the tiptoes with the nose touching, you know. Anyways…

TL/MB: As a longtime resident of Terrace area, what changes have you noticed?

BE: Oh geez, you know. The changes have happened so slowly over the forty-some years here, you know. You gotta sorta think back. One of the big changes — when I came here, the first winter I was here, the civic centre burnt down… that's where the band shell is now. And that runs straight down along the parking lot to the outhouses there. There's a civic centre that come across the front of that property towards the library. And then the part alongside the parking lot going by the bathrooms was a Quonset, which is a metal building, sort of like the bowling alley. And that was a curling rink there.

So when the civic centre burnt down in the winter of '70, they said, "Well, the schools are relatively new and they all have gymnasiums and that." They said, "Well, the activities that they build in the civic centre, for a temporary fix, would be put into the gymnasiums of the schools." You know, the adult basketball and adult badminton, and all the other winter sports that you needed the civic centre for. They gave up the roller skating, because after that there wasn't any roller skating here.

So then, instead of building the new civic centre, they will relocate the curling rink, and use that money for the curling rink. So we put the curling rink up there by the ball field where it still stands. And forty-two years later we still don't have a civic centre here, where the youth can hang out and all of that.

They tore down a perfectly beautiful band shell that it took, I don't know, $100,000 and hundreds of hours of volunteer labour material to build that cruddy old one, and there was nothing wrong with it. They could have added on, and put windows or whatever — made it into a spectator's booth, you know, but…

All the volunteers spent all that time and built that thing, and then they tore it down 20 years later. Sorta discouraging for volunteers to come and do a lot of hard work and donate cash, time, for a short-term project like that.

So back to the civic centre... They never did build one, and they moved the curling rink up there and we're still without a civic centre. You know, that's one of the biggest things.

The Dudley Little Bridge, it was a nice thing to do, but sort of short-sighted because it killed the economy of the downtown Terrace, you know, ever since they opened that. For thirty-nine years, you know it's taken away. And the proof is in the pudding.

All the hotels downtown, the Coast which is The Lakelse [now Days Inn], shut down. The rooms... They never kept it up, because it wasn't fiscally viable to keep it up. You don't sink $100,000 per year into a hotel that only brings in $80,000 a year or something like that. And every year it goes down because there is less through-traffic.

And the people that used to travel that highway before they opened the bridge, they know downtown Terrace. And, instead of going over the overpass, they know they can go there. But it's the new travellers that don't know what to expect. Ah, we know [Prince] Rupert is only an hour, so we will camp or stay there. You know, instead of staying here; they could have stayed here.

I think the overpass, the first sheet of ice, the second sheet of ice — I worked on both of those, you know — and the block buildings, are the biggest changes. I guess Keith Avenue build up, you know. The biggest change is the new Dudley Little Bridge and the Sande Overpass. Had the biggest impact on Terrace because it grew some businesses down there. But the only thing, it killed all of downtown Terrace right from the [Royal Canadian] Legion to City Hall. Or really hurt the businesses.

TL/MB: Do you have any advice for the present and future residents of the City?

BE: Promote Terrace. It's a great place to live, a great place to raise a family. There's a great future here, enhanced by all the economic activity brought in by number one, the hydro line [Northwest Transmission Line]. With that, it got power up to several construction projects — a few of them being mines and a couple of them being hydro projects — which is opening up a big area of the province.

We've been waiting here for 43 years for that hydro line [Northwest Transmission Line]. The NDP government back in Dave Barrett's day — the only time they did get in briefly in the '70s — they started a railroad line from Prince George up to the Yukon-Alaska border, and proposed the hydro line. And the railroad line stopped and the Alaskans are crying for it. The hydro line's just getting built and the Alaskans want to tie into it. It ties them in to the rest of the North American grid.

So finally, you know, we're getting that to happen. The north is here on the tip of an economic boom. Because the real estate is going to skyrocket like it did in Vancouver and the Okanagan in just more recent years. Like it's happening in Calgary, and Edmonton. And this is the place to be: you've got the fishing, you've got the skiing, you've got the mountains, and still a low crime and small population. The amenities…you can be in Vancouver in an hour and a half from here by plane. Terrace is it. That's where it's at.

Edward McFadden Interview

Interviewed by Harry Bineham and Luke Whitaker, 28 November 2013

Edward (Ed) McFadden was born in Mannville, Alberta, in 1920. During the Second World War, Ed came to Terrace. He served there as an Air Force pilot in 1944, and returned to Terrace with his family in 1953. He was married in 1941 and had two children, Dale and Lynn. Ed had many jobs throughout his time in Terrace, including: working as an Air Force pilot, as a foreman for the railway and at the Department of Highways. He also worked as the Superintendent for the City of Terrace from 1959 to 1981, until he retired. Throughout his time in Terrace Ed maintained an active role in the community through his extensive volunteer work.

In this interview, Ed shares stories about early Terrace life and what changes he has noticed as a long-time resident. He talks about how Terrace has gone from a small town with little amenities to a city with a 'great future'. He also shares his personal recollection of the longest lasting mutiny in Canadian history, which began on Nov. 25, 1944. During the mutiny, he was the only man in the Terrace Air Force qualified to operate a Lewis Machine gun. Ed was stationed in the machine gun pit overlooking Queensway, waiting for the soldiers to capture the airport.

HB/LW: Where and when were you born?

EM: I was born July the second, 1920.

HB/LW: Could you tell us a bit about your parents?

EM: Well, my parents were farmers, mixed farmers. We had lots of cattle, pigs, chickens, everything. We milked cows and sold cream, you know? Everybody in the prairies sold cream.

HB/LW: So, how did you and your family arrive in Terrace?

EM: Well, we came to Terrace in 1953 by car — it was all gravel highway, too.

HB/LW: Where did you used to live?

EM: Where'd I come from? Oh, well, I come from Mannville, Alberta; that's east of Edmonton.

HB/LW: What made you come to Terrace?

EM: Well, I was in the Air Force. So I was here in '40 to '44. I came here in the spring of '44 in the Air Force, but my family came by car in 1953, and I was hired on when Campbell Bennett put the grade in from Terrace to Kitimat. When the fall came it was freezing, and the Highway Superintendent came along and says, "What are you gonna do this winter?" and I says, "Well, I dunno," and he says, "Why don't you come and work for the highways?" I was a grader operator, so I quit one day and the next day I went to Highways.

HB/LW: Did you have any siblings when you were growing up?

EM: I had four sisters. I was the oldest.

HB/LW: What was your relationship like?

EM: Oh, we got along good. They picked on me all the time, but you know how girls are. We still get along good.

HB/LW: That's good. So tell me about growing up. What was it like in your neighborhood?

EM: Well, we had to walk two miles to school. We got up at five o'clock in the morning because we had to get all the chores done, and walk to school, and I had to milk cows and everything before I went to school. But then, you want to know what we had for entertainment? We had country dances, and there was the local movies every weekend. And, of course, there was hockey: we had an ice rink, an open ice rink. We had baseball parks, two of them. So there was lots to do, you know. And, my god, when you're up from five in the morning doing chores till just about 10 o'clock at night, you were ready to go to bed.

HB/LW: Yeah, you wouldn't really have time to –

EM: — Dirt your boots.

HB/LW: What were the names of the schools that you attended?

EM: Well, I just went to the Mannville School because we were just about two miles from the school, from the town. If you're outside two miles, you went to a country school. So, we went to school in town all the time. But, of course, when I was little, my grandmother had a store in the town of Mannville. I stayed with my grandmother when the weather was bad, and everything. So you want my memories, eh? Well, one thing I remember, I hated Latin. Oh, I hated it. And our teacher was Latin-crazy! There were two boys who wanted to be druggists. So, anyway, he told me one day, he says, "if fish makes brains, Ed, you better catch a whale to eat it."

HB/LW: That's not a nice thing to say. So did you attend college or university at all?

EM: Nope, never did, no.

HB/LW: Did you ever marry?

EM: Yep — I got married in 1941.

HB/LW: Did you have any children?

EM: Oh yes, I have a boy and a girl. Dale and Lynn. They still live here.

HB/LW: Could you tell us a bit more about them?

EM: Dale McFadden, did you know him?

HB/LW: No.

EM: He operated the arena, and was a teacher to start with. And Lynn, well, she was a manager at a logging company here.

HB/LW: So what did you do with your children when they were younger? What was there to do?

EM: Oh, heavens, children had lots to do. There was lots of open land here, you know. And they played: they did everything; they could play baseball anywhere. They're out there, kids playing ball. Well, my son played on the junior baseball team — he was on that. And they belonged to the Boy Scouts. They were Scout Cubs. My daughter was with the Girl Guides. So, of course, they looked after things. I was the head of the Scouts for 12 years. I went to one meeting and ended up there for 12 years — chairman.

HB/LW: So, you said you worked for the highways. What other jobs did you have throughout your time in Terrace?

EM: I guess I came to Vanderhoof to Kenney Dam. I worked at the Kenney Dam for two years, for a hydro project, and then transferred to here. I came over to this job, in 1944 to '45 in the Air Force. In

1953, I had the railway to Kitimat job, then the Department of Highways from 1953 to '59, and then the City of Terrace from '59 to '81, until I retired.

HB/LW: Oh, wow, busy life.

EM: Busy life, yup.

Ed and Nellie McFadden [front row] honored as Riverboat Days King and Queen, 2006. Pictured here with their family: Lynn Apolcer (McFadden), Dale and Gale McFadden [back row l-r]. 2006. Ed McFadden Collection.

HB/LW: So, how did your career frame your experiences here in Terrace — what did you learn from the careers that you did? Did it teach you any lessons in life?

EM: Oh heavens, I guess it did. I guess you have to get along with people. Because I was the superintendent here for the city, I had a lot people working for me. A lot of different types of people, and you have to be very diplomatic. You have all the unions to contend with and all. And you have a council, too, that you have to contend with. All of them didn't know too much about anything except their job on the council — how it operated and was of value. They knew nothing about unions. They thought you could just do anything you liked, but you couldn't.

HB/LW: Okay, so what did you do for fun during your time in Terrace? Like, what did you do in your spare time?

EM: Well, I don't know. Spare time, let's see… I was for seven years the president of the credit union, I was on the co-op board, I was the past president of the curling rink — when we built the curling rink in the George Little Park. Well, there were three of us who organized it, and we did a lot of volunteer work steady, every night. Oh gosh, all the volunteer maintenance for senior citizens up Tuck Avenue — I was one of the volunteer maintenance men up here, and you were called in all the time. Forty years on the church board, and then the Carlton Youth. Then I started the square dance club here, the "Skeena Squares," and I became the caller. So that kept me pretty darn busy.

HB/LW: Kept you in shape.

EM: Oh, it sure did, it was a lot of fun doing the travelling. And then I did the Masonic Lodge chairs, so I was busy with that!

HB/LW: Do you remember what restaurants were popular in Terrace?

EM: Well, in Terrace here there was the Star Café — that was just across from the Terrace Hotel down there. And then there was the one on Kalum Street. It was the Chinese one. We called it the Silvertip. It's the one that burnt down.

HB/LW: When did it burn down?

EM: Oh, it must have been 15 to 20 years ago now. Fifteen years. The Star Café was torn down — torn down or burnt down, I don't know. There was something else around there by Ev Clift's [4605 Lakelse Ave.], a little restaurant in there. And that was the only place to eat at war time here. 'Course after — you know, later on when we came back here — of course there was the Terrace Hotel; there were restaurants all over. It's a lot different. Chinese restaurants.

HB/LW: Yeah, a lot has changed, hasn't it?

EM: Oh, heavens. You can't believe it.

HB/LW: So did you visit the Lakelse Hot Springs?

EM: Yes, we used to go out there all the time!

HB/LW: Oh, really? Could you tell us a bit more about the hot springs and what they were like?

EM: I was with the Highways. I used to grade by there, going to Kitimat, and the people working in Alcan, they got this rash. And I used to see them rolling out in the mud out there. It's called the white mud, and they were rolling in it. And that killed the itch, or whatever it was, cured it or something. But when we went down there first, it wasn't as big as it was after Skoglund took over. He enlarged it and everything. And now this fella's [Bert Orleans] really built it up, you know. And now I guess it's pretty well collapsed again, is it?

HB/LW: Yeah, I don't think it's operating right now.

EM: Well, it was much the same. It was the hot pool and everything. Not too much — just the hot pool down there. It didn't have all the activity stuff and all that. Had a dance hall; they built it later, you know. Some people would come down from Kitimat, but most of 'em were from Terrace. Kitimat had school bus loads of kids come out, you know.

HB/LW: So tell me about the sports that you did in Terrace. I know you said you did curling.

EM: Oh, well, I loved to curl. And I played baseball here in wartime. George Little Park was a baseball park. None of you guys know that. And the curling rink was there, too, you know. On the edge there, where they have the washrooms now for the Farmers' Market, that's where the curling rink was — three sheets. Then, where the sign is there for George Little [Park], there was a community hall — a big community hall that burnt down. And we moved the curling rink — tore it down — and moved down to the present location. We chose the area where the drill hall used to be.

HB/LW: What did most people that you knew do for work?

EM: They were pretty well all loggers. All logging, you know. So logging, construction, that's about all. And teachers and, you know, not much else. Well of course we had a big hospital, but we didn't when I first came here. Course now, now we have one. And then we got all the seniors up there. That nursing home up on the hill there, that was a hospital, an old army hospital. I know, I had my tonsils taken out there. They weren't doctors; they were butchers!

HB/LW: What role do you think forestry and logging played throughout the history of Terrace? Like do you think it made it better? Worse? Or what do you think — how important do you think forestry and logging is in Terrace?

EM: Well, I think I wouldn't have come to Terrace here if I didn't have that to start with. Couldn't get the local men to come in and open the country up. You know everybody if you get a job anywhere in the forestry. Everybody worked at the railroad and then there were a couple sawmills. Ernie Sande had a sawmill, and then, of course, Columbia Cellulose came in with a big sawmill and developed some jobs. Pohle had a big mill down there. And we fought sawdust. Everything was sawdust from that mill, from the burner.

HB/LW: How did the construction of the new bridge change the community?

EM: Well, it made quite a difference on Lakelse Avenue. And, well, it changed. Keith Avenue was built then to accommodate the traffic off of it. When they built the bridge, there was nothing but Keith Avenue there and one or two houses. Well, you can see it now today. Some nuts wrote a letter in the paper here not a year ago, saying that they didn't need that little bridge. The Old Bridge was quite sufficient. Could you imagine the traffic coming down Lakelse now? You can't come out of the A&W or anything! And the mall's there. What's going to happen in the next 20 years?

HB/LW: Maybe make another bridge?

EM: Well, eventually things will change, you know?

HB/LW: So, do you remember any major floods in Terrace?

EM: Well, they had the one down Braun's Island, and the one down on Queensway there. It was quite the flood they had down on Queensway; I can remember all the chickens up in the trees, and they were going around in boats trying to catch the chickens. Braun's Island had quite a flood down there. Some of the South Kalum and Graham Avenue flooded some, too. Every time it ever flooded here, the water's high. But I don't know, everybody survived best with the neighbour's help — that's just how it is.

HB/LW: How has the Farmers' Market changed throughout the years?

EM: When the Farmers' Market started, it was just small, you know it wasn't much. It was mostly just stuff from Old Remo, those farmers out there. And what's the place down there — the one with the old farm just out of town [Usk]? Big farm – big farmers out there. You can see today how the market's growing: it's coming from Smithers, it's coming from everywhere now. There's a demand for the stuff now. Now we've got people selling food, people selling everywhere. It's getting to be quite a show and all. People are coming from everywhere to take part in it, to get something out of it. Oh, yeah, it's quite a deal now.

HB/LW: So, were you involved in politics in any way?

EM: Yes, I was in politics for many years — steady.

HB/LW: So, more generally, how has Terrace changed over the years? Like stores and stuff.

EM: Terrace? Well, when I came here in wartime, there was nothing but plank sidewalks. A block of Kalum and a little block on Lakelse had sidewalks, and that was all. They had no sewer and they had no water; well, they had pumped wells, I guess, 'cause I don't remember there being any wells. Where the Co-op store was, down on that property, that used to be the town sump. All the town would drain in there. I remember when I was here I would look down and there was nothing but stumps. Stuff — everything — was pushed in there, and that's where all the water went. When I came back in '53, I was amazed to see it cleaned up. That's when the Co-op store was started and moved in there.

HB/LW: So were there any annual community events that you were aware of?

EM: Well, of course we have our Riverboat Days, now. But then I don't think we had a heck of a lot. I don't remember too much. A few ball tournaments, I guess? 'Course, there was the curling. We had our curling bonspiels, and of course we had our square dancing club, that was a pretty big club. And we had some pretty big events in high school and that. People came from everywhere to dance, you know? It was big. Logger sports and also the country fair.

HB/LW: Was there like a dance competition? Like a square dance competition?

EM: No, we never had competitions, no. We just had everybody come from Prince George, Ketchikan [Alaska], Prince Rupert; everybody was here. We brought in callers, we brought in extra people, everything. We took over the school, decorated the city, put up posters, banners, and it was quite a do. Oh, it went on for about four days. Yup!

HB/LW: So let's talk about World War II for a sec. What do you recall about the military years in Terrace?

EM: Well, did you want to know about the mutiny?

HB/LW: Yeah, sure, definitely!

EM: Well, we used to play floor hockey with the Army down here; they were the other team, and they had several teams. And Friday night, on the 24th of November, we were playing against them down there in their drill hall. Well, I was a defenseman on a hockey team back in the prairies, and another defenseman was Doug Wheeler, with the Air Force. And we had a couple of smart-aleck officers, and of course everyone down there was scared to touch them when they're playing the Army. But they kept coming down there. So we said, "Well, let's nail 'em." They were about 10 feet from the seats on the edge; spectators. And we nailed them. I hit him, and he [Doug] hit him, and he leapt right out in the seats! And his leg went in the seat, the old seats down there, and they couldn't get him out! They had to go and get some carpenters and stuff, and mechanics, with saws. They said after a while, "let's continue the game!" and we just started to play, and pop bottles started firing at the Air Force. Bang, bang, everywhere. So they blew the whistle and the referee says, "game's cancelled," he was evidently with the sergeant, the referee was. So, they took us up to where the Legion is now, that was the sergeant's quarter. They took us up there, for a beer. So we went up and had a few beer.

The next Saturday morning, we got our supplies from the Army down there. They had all the Air Force supplies. We came down with our truck in the morning, about nine o'clock, and — of course, you guys wouldn't know — but right where the Legion is now, right across there, that's where the gate was. They had a gate that dropped and that's where the jail house was. Jails, police station, everything was there. So we pulled up, and he would come out with his rifle, and he says, "Well, where do you think you're goin?" We said, "Well, we are out lookin' for supplies." And he says, "how long would it take you to get across that Skeena bridge?" "Well," we said, "I guess it would take about five minutes?" And he said, "Well, see if you can do it in three." And we left. Boy, things were hummin' downtown. So then, in the afternoon, we had a power unit up here — on the Bench up there behind Emil Froese's house — in there somewhere. It was just a light for the mountain, beaming, up there for the airport airplanes. They set me up with a truck and two men to pick this up. They figured it would be destroyed, I guess.

So we went up and we got it, and were coming back down Lanfear Hill there. We got into town here, and the boy says, "Oh, it's Saturday — let's have a beer, Ed!" "Well," I said, "I'm in charge of the truck and this equipment here." "Oh, yeah, we'll just have one beer," he said. So I said, "well, okay then." It was about three o'clock or so. So I pulled up — it used to be around where the feed store was — on Kalum there, on the sidewalk. I parked the truck there, and so we started over to the Terrace Hotel; that was the only hotel here, it wasn't much. So, anyway, as we got just about to the door we met an Air Force guy who was Corporal Mackenzie. It was his day off — he was a fireman up at the airport. "Well, fellas," he says, "it's just like a hornet's nest in there." He says, "They've all got rifles, and they're all French, and they're mad," and I said, "I don't know." "Well, look," he says, "there's a table by the door. Get in behind that table with your back against the wall, and if they start, throw the table in front of them so you can get out that door fast." Well, we sat down there, the four of us, had a beer — ordered a beer, we never even got to drink our beer. Crash! Bottles came down, glass behind going out our backs and they're all getting up there, you know — and the admiral, the French one. So, anyway, we just threw the table over like that, guarded the door and took off.

Terrace Mutiny, November 1944. Park Avenue, 4500 Block. Terrace Standard Collection.

So I ran for the truck, one other guy ran for the truck with me, we got in the truck, and made a U-turn up to Lakelse. The third guy, he went up there because, of course, the police station was up there — that yellow building was a police station — so he figured he would be safe there. So then we slowed down, and he jumped in when we got just about there. But I tell ya, it was scary because we didn't know whether they would have Lakelse blocked off past the Legion there to get to the bridge. Anyway, we got out. We got out. But uptown, they had all the people out in the streets, and the French soldiers were marching up and down the sidewalk with their rifles, throwing them everywhere, you know: everyone was scared to death.

Anyway, we got home and well, my friend, he started up Greig Avenue, going to the Star Café. And just as he got out of the hotel and started up there, these two soldiers hit this other soldier over the head with a whiskey bottle, and cracked his head open — he was laying there bleeding bad. And Mackenzie came along, and gosh sakes, these two run like mad, run from him. So he took his coat, and put it under his head, and loosened his collar and everything. And while he was straightening all this up, the two army provost guys come along and picked him up — dragged him up to the jail cell, all the way up to the army jail cell, and threw him in there. They blamed him for it. Now, I never heard whether the guy died or not, but I think he must have. They had a court of inquiry here when he was in jail. They never got him out of jail — my officer's command never got him out — until three o'clock in the morning. And he couldn't leave anywhere, he was on bail in the Air Force. Then the Army came in and the judge. What they did, they interviewed, and had a big court session here. And Mackenzie got off, he was free. I never heard what happened to the soldier, or if they caught anybody that did it, or nothing. We never heard anything. Of course, we didn't get news through the Army at all.

So anyway, we got up to Monday. The Army got the rumour that day: General Pearkes was flying in to talk to them, and settle this mutiny. All these rumours in here that the Army had guns all over, and they had plans to protect the Army and take over. But I never saw any of those guns or anything — whether it was just a rumour, I don't know. It could be. I was just in the Air Force. But anyway, Tuesday, rumour came around that the plane was getting in and, of course, they got all the family people out, the women and kids, 'cause they figured they were going to get bombed or shot up. So they knew they wouldn't do anything if all the people were on the street, in one little block. Anyway, this airplane came in and circled a few times and landed at the airport. First thing you know, a jeep came along. I took my commando training when I was stationed in Kamloops, and when they looked at my records, I was the only one who had any experience with machine guns or anything. So they picked me up and took me out to the machine gun pit, and gave me a Lewis machine gun and said, "The Army is going to attack this airport, but you watch that edge." So I'm in this machine gun pit and I could see Queensway; well, this Army hadn't been there, or the airplane hadn't been landed about an hour and a half, and there were about twenty soldiers headed up Queensway, and they were singing and everything. And first thing I thought: *oh my God here they come.*

So anyway, I'm there to watch and all of a sudden, I see the airplane took off, and the officers and them stayed. They were flying around in a circle a few times — I see them flying over top of these soldiers, and I see them trace bullets over their heads. Well, they just disappeared like ants, and I thought, *oh boy, I'm in this pit here, and these guys are well-trained: they're going to crawl up the railroad track* — or, well, there was no railroad then — *and come up here.* So, my officer command came on, and he says, "What are you going to do when they come over that edge, Ed?" I said, "Well, I don't know," and he said, "Well, are you going to shoot 'em?" "Well," I said, "I don't want to shoot them; they're Canadian boys," and he said, "Well, they're going to shoot you, so you better make up your mind." So I waited there, and I was there until six o'clock at night. No sign of them, they never came. But then, about an hour after that, I saw the officer's jeep go down, and it was this officer who came in to talk to them. It wasn't General Pearkes; it was another officer who came in. And they were going down to the drill hall to talk to them. The jeep was going down — they had a soldier at each door with a machine gun and I guess — I think the officer was driving. And when they got down to the drill hall, well, of course they were armed with machine guns, and they wouldn't let him in the drill hall. They said "You come in here and we'll shoot ya," and he said, "Well, I've been sent here to talk to you fellas: this is a pretty serious offense, and if you don't let me in to talk to you, and you shoot me, there's going to be a lot of you guys shot, too." So then they

380

calmed down and he went in and talked to them. So, I don't know, some of the regiments decided to volunteer to go overseas.

And I don't know, from the people talking there — There was a train going down to Prince Rupert to load them up, and train them with the Prince Albert Regiment and the Prince Edward Regiment. And, of course, the French boys were there with the bayonets marching them off. They marched them on the train and they would march them off. Guns sitting in front of the engine, guns in the machine guns and everything — the train engine. It went on for quite a while, but I wasn't there — I just heard it, and it's on that tape [CBC program on the Terrace Mutiny, from 1974]. Floyd Frank was right in front of his dairy farm, so he was watching a lot of this; he knew a lot about it. But, anyway, I don't know how it settled. We were never allowed — we were out of bounds to go down from the Terrace airport. They didn't want us to get mixed up in it all. Anyway, I guess it all got settled somehow.

HB/LW: So do you have any knowledge of the initial arrival of the Army, and the civil construction workers on the train?

EM: You mean when they first built the place?

HB/LW: Yeah, and when they first came over.

EM: Well, you see the whole riverside down there — that was all army barracks, and well, there weren't that many. There were more soldiers coming down all the time, and up on the Bench, that's where the officers were. That was all officers that built up on Birch Avenue there. Lots of tents they had — well, I guess they had bunkhouses, too. But they seldom brought their wives here. Plus, you couldn't get a place to rent or nothing. Everything was sold down here. There was only one grocery store down here — that was Jim Smith's grocery store on Lakelse Avenue. That was the only grocery store. One little hotel there; it was an antique. It didn't even have washrooms. It just had a bowl in there, and a towel. When we used to run to have a beer, I said "Where's the washrooms?" … "Just go out to that door around there." We went out the door there, and everybody was standing there against the fence! And the train's there, the engineer was blowing the whistle! Yeah. But, you know, they had nothing here at all. As I said, there were the plank sidewalks. You couldn't get in to eat anywhere, with so few people and all. There was just nobody here to work, you know? There wasn't much for schools; at that time, the school was down by Franks' farm at the end of Keith there. And I don't know when they built the other school there on Kenney. I don't remember them building that. Well, my wife was a teacher here.

HB/LW: Okay, where did she teach?

EM: She taught at Riverside there, grade four. She retired after 22 years. But there weren't many students then, either. The biggest entertainment was, well, they had a little orchestra here. They called it the Orange Hall. That's the one on the street there across from Hertz Rentals [National Car Rental] there, beside that place used to be a meat market in there [Originally a Royal Bank building. The Orange Hall was directly to the west of the meat market/Royal Bank]. The United Church was next to it, and we moved the church out to where it is now. It was moved away.

HB/LW: So, how did the Air Force view the mutiny?

EM: Well, you know, people didn't know a lot about it. It was kept pretty secret what we heard, you know? We didn't hear much at all about it. And the Air Force heard nothing. Nothing on the radio: anything we got on the radio came from Ottawa, and they kept it pretty quiet. They didn't want it known. But we weren't too happy about it, because we were all joined up in the Air Force— everybody signed up for the Air Force — and well, lots of guys joined and signed up. Our friends were all over there, my cousins were over there fighting and stuff. These guys were well-trained and they didn't want to go. I knew a lot of the boys here were from my hometown. I didn't know it at the time, but they were farm boys. They would have went if they had to go. But they didn't want to go. And then the French took over there; Quebec was against it, you know. They were told they didn't have to go overseas. Mackenzie King promised them that, until things got desperate over there. And now, there were a lot of good French regiments over there, mind you. They were good regiments, too; they were good soldiers. But a lot of these here — oh, they were officers, and all these guys, big shots' sons up here, hiding them. Keeping them hid! They didn't want them to get hurt. Anyway, I don't know, we got along good with the boys here, you know, until they started the mutiny stuff, and then… We went to the movies, and everything.

Start of Second Recording [Due to some technical problems, some of the initial interview was lost. This second recording was done to capture what was missing].

HB/LW: So I think we're just at the WWII questions. How did the Air Force view the mutiny and why do you think it happened in the first place?

EM: Well, of course, the Air Force were not too involved with it. I just heard — there was a rumour that there was a mutiny going on, and there was going to be a plane coming in with General Pearkes coming in to talk to them and all that. Did you want me to go right back?

HB/ LW: Let's go all the back to where it started, just in case they didn't have the stuff…

EM: General Pearkes was supposed to come in — that was the rumour going around. There were cannons and guns all around Terrace in the mountains. And he would come in with two bodyguards with machine guns. I think it was a Monday or Tuesday. Of course, the Army thought it was General Pearkes coming in. They were going to go right up to the airport, go capture the airport and take him as a prisoner, and then they would have something to bargain with, you see. Use him as a hostage to bargain with. But, anyways, the plane circled a couple of times and then they landed up at the airport. I didn't see anything.

That was about one o'clock or something, so I had my lunch and all of a sudden the CO came out there with a jeep and a Lewis machine gun, and he said, "Come on, you're going out to the machine gun pit out there." And I said, "Well, what's going on?" And he said, "Well, the Army is going to capture the airport and you're the only commando we got here." I had taken a commando course and I could operate a Lewis Machine gun, while nobody else could handle it in camp. So I was there for a while, I would say until about maybe two o'clock.

I saw 20 soldiers marching up Queensway, just about at the log house at Benoits', and I leaned over and I could see them coming up, and then all of a sudden this plane came over their heads and traced their bullets and everything, and boy, they just — they were gone! So, I'm sitting up in this machine gun pit and I thought, *Oh boy, these guys are trained soldiers they're going to be climbing the bank. And I'm sitting here all by myself.* So, the officer had come along and he said, "They may come up that bank, what are you going to do Ed, you gonna shoot 'em?" "Well… I hate to shoot 'em — they're Canadian boys, some of them are my neighbours even." And he said, "Well they're going to shoot you, so you better make up your mind." Anyway, I was there until about six o'clock. I saw the jeep going down with this officer and his two guards, one sitting on each side of the jeep with a machine gun, and they were headed down to Terrace. And so they went down there, but I sat there and sat there and thought, *Well, were they going to come up there or not?*

But at about six o'clock they came and got me and said, "I guess it's not happening." The officer had talked to them [the mutineers] in the drill hall, there by the mall, and they told the drill hall that the officer said he was coming in to talk to them. And they [the mutineers] said, "If you come in, I'll shoot ya." And he [the officer] said, "Well, go ahead and shoot me." He had his two guards there with the machine guns, and he said, "There's going to be a lot more of you fellas die." So they backed down, and he came in there and he talked to them. What he told them about was — I guess that this was a serious event, this mutiny, it's quite a serious event — and most countries, they just take you out and shoot you if there's a mutiny during the war time. But he cooled them down anyways. I wasn't there, so I don't know what he told them, or what took place. A friend of mine back in my hometown was there and told me that he cooled them down pretty fast when he started telling them what it was going to cost — and if they went overseas there would be no charges, so a lot of them had decided to go overseas. But then, of course, the officer came back, got in their plane and they took off. But, really, it was out of bounds to us, Terrace was just about this mutiny started downtown.

But the Air Force, you see, we were pretty well out of it. Except our corporal — I told you before — who was on his day off and went down with us. When he came out of the hotel there, the two soldiers hit this other guy over the head with a beer bottle, another soldier. He was laying there, and he [the corporal] came along, and loosened up his tie and everything, took the tunic off and put it under his head, because Greig Avenue was all gravel — everything was all gravel in Terrace, there was no such thing as pavement in those days.

I told you about the army jails and everything all being up by the Legion. So, they just grabbed him — two police just came up in a jeep and grabbed him — and took him up there and threw him in the jail. And my officer and his helper — they had him until three o'clock in the morning until they got him out of that jail. Went through Eastern Command and Western Command to get him released. And then they had a court case later on; I don't know how soon that was. I never talked to Mackenzie (the corporal who was in charge), because I think they just shot him out of here, put him right out. Because they figured some army guy would be after him, you know, if it was his friend that was killed. And now they never mentioned when the guy died, it's never been mentioned. We never heard on the radio or anything whether the fella died or not. But he must have been or else they wouldn't have the court of inquiry and all the rest of it, and a court martial, and all this stuff. But it's funny; we never heard a thing. We inquired, but nobody ever heard anything. So, we assumed he died or there wouldn't be such a big court case or anything. And the hospital was right up there on the hill, so that's where they took him. It was an army hospital. So I don't know what else, that's as far as we got with the mutiny and the Air Force, because they flew out. Everybody flew out and the Army just disappeared. We weren't allowed to go downtown, so they just slowly disappeared. Closed the camp down and so.

HB/LW: So, how did your family feel about the mutiny and all the soldiers?

EM: Well, my family wasn't here. It was just myself. My wife and family went back to Alberta. So they didn't even know that anything was going on. Nobody ever heard of it. Ottawa never gave any news of it or anything. They never gave nothing out, they didn't want anybody to know what was going on up here. So, what I mean: I don't know if anybody back in Alberta who I talked to knew that there even was a mutiny. Except the boys who came back after the war. Some of them overseas and that were involved. Some of them were probably farmers in that area that left to come home to take off the crop. And, of course the war maybe ended. '44 was the end of the war so… oh, hell, nobody knows anything about it.

HB/LW: So, how did Terrace deal with the large influx of soldiers — so many soldiers in Terrace, how did Terrace deal with that?

EM: Well, there was a boom for them. They never had anything in Terrace here; it was just a little logging show. And then these 10,000 soldiers came in here, and all the people building the huts, and everything, it was the Army's. The officers' place was up on Birch Hill there — that was all officers' quarters. Mind you, there were no buildings here at all for them, so they had to build the great big huge drill hall, built there where the curling rink is now. So all these people were carpenters and that, but they were all housed; you know they had places built for them. In fact, this house next to me that

383

I bought here, that was one of the carpenter's that was up here working. I imagine he built the house with material from the Army.

The Army was first housed in tents. But, you know, you talked to Marie Piffer, didn't you? Somebody did. Well, there was just a little hall down there. They used to have dances down there. And, of course, the Army would come there, but they had lots of shows and stuff at the big drill hall. They had a big drill hall there, a big army base. Well, we used to go down to the shows and all that stuff, and when my wife came down, later on, we went. The Army was pretty well gone; my wife came in after this mutiny, and we used to go to the show. They had a little Bambi, a little deer like that that used to walk up and down the aisles and everybody used to feed it popcorn. I just thought it was wonderful, that little Bambi. I wonder whatever happened to Bambi. I guess somebody cooked him! But, you know, it was something. They had dances in the little hall. They called it the Orange Hall there then. As Marie Piffer said, "Girls, there were about 20 men to every girl so they were pretty happy, they could dance themselves to death."

HB/LW: It's a little harder for you being one of the 20 guys though, hey, all the competition?

EM: Oh, well, we never bought it. We were out of bounds. Nobody from the Air Force could go downtown — well, that is, when the mutiny was on and all that. But we never came down. I don't think too many would come down, because so many were in there dancing and so few girls, you know, they didn't bother.

HB/LW: Wasn't worth it?

EM: No, I don't think so. I mean, I didn't know any of the girls then, I was just 22. And I don't remember any of the guys coming down to the dances. We had parties up at the airport and we invited the girls up there. But the Army didn't come up, they weren't invited. No, we never really got involved, the service down there. You know what would happen, we were all active service and the Army didn't love us too much — the boys — because we figured they should be over there fighting. So we never got involved with them that way. The girls could have them.

HB/LW: Do you remember the Queen's visit to Terrace?

EM: Oh, yes, we were there. My family was there, and my daughter, my son, my wife and I were sitting on the sidewalk by the post office when she drove by. Yep, she just wisped right by like that. I think she wasn't really in it, I don't know. I think it was quite the event because they paved the roads! Paved some of the road. They didn't want the Queen to get dusty. Oh, yeah, I remember that. But I don't remember a celebration afterwards. I guess we just went home.

HB/LW: When you were a child, what did you expect or hope to accomplish in your life?

EM: Oh that's quite something when you're a child. It's like you folks, too, you know; you kind of wonder now what you're going to do when you go to high school. What's your future? You haven't got a clue. But we were farm kids, and everybody on a farm was a farmer. So that's what you did. You just farmed, you know. But, as I told you before, my mother's brother was a professor at the university in Edmonton, and that was my ambition, to get an education.

My dad was just as happy to keep me at home cleaning barns and stuff, you know. He didn't care. But Mother, her family was well-educated, and you go to school; you get that education. And that's the whole thing, I tell ya, everywhere you go. I had grade 12, and in the Air Force you would be surprised how many boys never had more than grade eight. Like all the guys working at the airport, and all that stuff. But, of course, to be a flyer, you had to have grade 12, and I was aircrew. I was slated for that, and it happened to be that Pearl Harbor happened when I was at Field, coming through to Kamloops on a troop train. So, all us western boys were kept on the west coast, back and forth. I was up at radar stations and everything and, of course, Kamloops was the ammunition centre/supply centre for the west. That's why we were sent right up from Trenton, Ontario. Because it's all in that valley there, it's all tomato plants. It was all run by Japanese. They figured, anyway, there would be lots of spies in there. And there probably was; I don't know. But, we never found any, of course. They chased 'em out pretty fast. Closed all the Japanese and moved them out to Alberta, Saskatchewan.

HB/LW: So as a longtime resident of the Terrace area, what changes have you noticed?

EM: Oh, well, heaven's sakes. Like I argue with my son: when I came here into Terrace, there were seven lights in Terrace. When you're up on the hill, there were seven lights. Go up there and look now! There was no pavement, there was no nothing. There was no water system, no sewer system to speak of, you know. Well, it's a city now. You come from a city. When I took over as work supervisor, our water supply for the Army came from Eby Street. Just up Eby Street there, there's a pump house; it's a big spring. That supplied the water down some of the streets, but the Army didn't have houses or anything. They just went across with wood stave pipeline down right to the army bases. Well, after I took over for some of the years, that wood started to rot out. So somebody's backyard all of a sudden found the water shooting up, and you couldn't shut it off anywhere! There were no blueprints, no nothing, where it was. So then, of course, all the water system had to be changed. And the sewer systems had to be put in, fire hydrants, everything. So we've become a city now. They can say what they like. I don't know what the population is, maybe 16,000?

HB/LW: 20,000?

EM: You know? So, I mean, the way things are going now, the power, the mine, it's going to keep growing. And we've got lots of land here, whereas Kitimat and [Prince] Rupert are at a disadvantage, because it's pretty hard to do anything in that rock up there. But here, we've got lots of land. And we're going to have industry in here, because where there's power, there's industry, and it's going to come, it just takes time. But I was just arguing yesterday: "Ah Ed, nothing's going to come in here." "Ah," I said, "you guys said the same thing when they put the Dudley Little Bridge in there." Why, I talked to some of these local people and they said, "Oh, waste of money, there will never be anybody driving into Terrace already, they don't need that bridge!" Well, could you imagine if that bridge wasn't in there now? My God, it would be solid cars all the way downtown! You'd never get over that old Skeena Bridge. Now, if it goes down, if something happens, and they have to do something to it, the whole city would be out.

Well, I see a great future in Terrace. Not in my day, at my age, but if you take 50 years from now, 100 years from now. Hell, 50 years ago, Kamloops was nothing, Prince George was nothing, and now they're pretty good-sized cities. We used to go to Kelowna, and there was nothing much there. But you fellas don't know. Don't you see — your generation don't realize that, but the older generation they said, "Oh, well it was all forestry, and now there's no demand for the forestry," and all this stuff. Well, there's a demand for it but they've priced themselves right out of it. You can get it cheaper anywhere else, you know? Kitimat is all union now, and you can't run a business. They just run you out of town if you don't join the union. But they're all over here in Walmart shopping. On Saturday you can't walk in the place hardly, and it's not unionized.

HB/LW: So as someone who has lived and learned here, what would you want to share with people newly moving to Terrace?

EM: Oh, well, I think, you see now, it's all new people here. And, of course, I talked with them all when I was on my job with the city. I knew everybody; all the business people and everybody, you know. Oh, I'd say there's a great future in Terrace; it's not going to happen overnight or anything. There's going to be industry up by the airport; there's going to be stuff up here. You've got to realize Vancouver is just about plugged now. Look at the traffic on the TV! They're just about bumper to bumper, and you can't even go out for a walk now: she's going to get killed or raped or something.

So, I mean, it's a really nice place here, I would say. Until it gets to be a bigger place, too, then you have problems coming. We had quite a few problems down in the park here, too, but now they've cleaned that up, they cut the brush out and everything and cleaned it up. So they're not drinking, and fighting, and feuding in there, like they used to. They moved up somewhere else. But people are getting all educated, and things have changed. I mean — me right now, I'm in a different world than when I was your age. Absolutely different world. There was no such thing as TV or any of that stuff. You guys walking around with all this stuff — you never even heard of it. Cars were extinct, mostly horses, and you know. Heaven's sakes, and the restaurants are pretty modern. There was really nothing, when I got here, to speak of, you know. A little church, a few little churches and we didn't even have a bowling alley; there was no theater to speak of.

HB/LW: Alright, I think we got everything we missed the other day. Thank you for your time.

EM: So you make a movie out of that, we will all go to Hollywood!

Gord McConnell Interview
Interviewed by Matthew Simpson, November 2013

Gord McConnell was born in Vernon, in 1939. In 1954, at age 15, Gord moved to Terrace with his family. Gord became a sports enthusiast at a young age, playing sports such as track and field, floor hockey, basketball, and volleyball. Gord married Aveline and had three children. When he finished school, he worked for a telephone company for four years. His career then took a turn when he went into business and opened up Sight and Sound in 1962. Throughout his life, Gord has been greatly involved in the Terrace community, taking part in the development and operations of many sporting organizations and programs. In 2004, Gord received The Order of Terrace, which is given to those who have significantly served the community. In this interview, he recalls growing up, playing sports, and swimming at Lakelse Hot Springs. He talks about the Queen's visit, the logging industry, popular downtown locations, his community involvement, and many other topics.

MS: So, Gord, where were you born?

GMc: I was born in Vernon, in the Okanagan, 1939, May the 15th.

MS: What were your parents like?

GMc: My parents were very supportive in everything that I did. I moved out of Vernon when I was 14, so I spent most of my life in Terrace. Then my father came up here to work in the forestry industry. He moved us up here a year later.

MS: So, you arrived in Terrace for forestry. Did you have any siblings?

GMc: No I am it — single.

MS: Would you mind describing a typical day in your household?

GMc: Well, we arrived in the fall of 1954 and I was in grade nine. We lived right by the Legion Hall and so I got up in the morning and walked to school. In those days, the grades eight to twelve were all over where the School Board Office is now. In fact, it was in the Resource Centre, that old building.

MS: What was the name of that school?

GMc: It was called Terrace High School. Then we moved from there in January, 1955. That was when Skeena School opened. The interesting thing about the old school is that it didn't have a gymnasium; it had a basement that was underneath the school at ground level and that was the only place under cover.

MS: Growing up, what kind of expectations were there for boys?

GMc: In those days, most of the people worked in the woods industry — I would say maybe 50, 60, 70 percent of the boys didn't graduate because they went to the mill, or the woods, because they could make good money there. They were leaving at 16. So, consequently, at the end of grade 12, you only had a few boys left graduating.

MS: So, did you go and work in the mills or anything?

GMc: No, I didn't. I worked in the woods industry in the summertime, when I was a student. I did that. My after-school job in high school was filling the gas tanks on work vehicles used by Columbia Cellulose, which was the biggest woods operation.

MS: Growing up in your neighbourhood, what did you do for fun?

GMc: I played a lot of sports; I was really into the sports. There was a lot of sports available. We didn't have a gymnasium other than the school gymnasium, but we had a swimming pool at the hot springs. We had a curling rink back in those days. The golf course was just beginning. They were clearing the land for the golf course. There was a certain amount to do, like helping clear the land, and some boys learned to play golf as the course progressed. There was a lot of hanging around downtown in the local coffee shop and whatnot. So it was good.

MS: So, the school that you attended was just by the School District [Office] and Skeena. Was Skeena all the way to grade 12? There was no Caledonia?

GMc: No, mind you there weren't a lot people in grade 12. When I graduated in grade 12, I think there were 26 people in that class.

MS: Over two hundred people in grade twelve now. Do you have any specific memories of school that you would like to share?

GMc: It was a good time, because the school had so very few students in it. We pretty well knew everyone there. It was a tight-knit community. When we moved to the new school, we finally got a gymnasium, so we were all learning how to play basketball and we used to take trips to Prince Rupert. In the springtime we took trips for track and field to Hazelton, and we played volleyball. We had a house system in those days in the school, an intermural system — so that was pretty cool.

MS: Did you attend any university or college?

GMc: No, I didn't do that.

MS: Did you marry?

GMc: Yes, I married a girl that I went to school with, actually. But we went our separate ways after high school. We got back together again when she completed her nursing training and then came back to Terrace.

MS: Do you want to tell me about your wedding at all?

GMc: There wasn't much to tell. Her family was here for many years, and I was really involved in the athletics and sports in town and knew lots of people. In those days, I had just started my business and she knew lots of people through the hospital. So, we had a very, very small wedding — about 14 people — and it was obviously an eventful day. Anyone that has gotten married — it is eventful.

MS: Did you have any children?

GMc: We had three children, two boys and a girl. They were all born in Terrace and they all left Terrace to go farther afield. Our son came back, years later. One daughter ended up in the Northwest Territories, in the Arctic Circle, for 25 years and the other one went as far as Labrador. So we have a grandson who was born in the Northwest Territories and we have two granddaughters who were born in Labrador City, Labrador.

MS: Did you find Terrace a good place to raise a family?

GMc: Yeah — excellent. Where we lived, there were lots of young people there, too. It was right on Park Avenue, so the kids could walk to school. They only had to go a block and a half to go to school. We had lots of pick-up water fights and we had lots of kick-the-ball. We'd go down to the park and kick it around — soccer games — it was a great place for a family, a great neighbourhood.

MS: So, what jobs did you work at in your time in Terrace?

GMc: Well, that's fairly easy. When I went to school, I had a part-time. During the summertime I worked in the bush doing quite a few different things. When I got out of school, I was very fortunate. I applied to work at the BC Telephone Company. I got the job and I was with the telephone company for four years. My supervisor at the telephone company, he was opening up a store in Terrace and he asked me if I would be interested in doing that. I never worked in a store before but I thought, *Well, why not.* So I did, and that was 52 years ago. I've been here 52 years doing this, managing a retail store.

MS: Right on, that's awesome. So how did your career really frame your experiences in Terrace?

GMc: In the early days, I was still involved in sports, and involved in the community helping operate the civic centre sports programs. That was centred around the community. It was a good place to bring up children with lots to do if anyone put out the effort. We were really involved in the school band programs; we've done that for a long time.

MS: The concert in the park and all the bands coming into Terrace and stuff — that must have been a pretty cool experience, too.

GMc: No, that was much later on. That was done the last twenty years. I did lots and lots of things in those days. Probably the people in Terrace that are around the 65 age group, we probably taught most of them how to swim. We didn't have the pool in Terrace, but they had one at the hot springs then, so we bussed people every Saturday. We had a bus going back and forth from the civic centre to the hot springs. So we taught probably a hundred or so kids to swim every section. They were separated into age groups and we had three buses running every Saturday.

MS: For fun, you played a lot of sports.

GMc: One of the interesting things about hockey: in those days we didn't have an ice arena, so we played floor hockey. You probably played it in school. Well, floor hockey, the way we played it, was with a felt puck. It was really quite hard, and it was six inches in diameter. We used to play at the civic centre and the games used to be broadcast – the radio was just starting at that time. So they broadcast that and we used to go back and forth to play against Kitimat. I am not sure exactly when we got the ice. But we must have got it in mid 70s, I would guess. That put an end to floor hockey.

MS: So, where did you go for dates when you were a teenager?

GMc: There wasn't much choice there. We had a movie theatre and we had the sports. There were teen dances, and there was an organization called 'Teen Town' that I was quite active in. They put on a fair amount of stuff, so that was just about it. Kitimat first came to pass around 1953 but there wasn't any road in there for a long time. So you couldn't go there by car. Of course, in those days the road to [Prince] Rupert was in such tough shape that it took you three to three and a half hours to get to Rupert. But, anyway, we made our own fun with family and friends.

MS: So, what restaurant was popular over the years?

GMc: I think the most popular one — in the early days, in the late '50s — was the Corner Snack Bar and that was right across from where the National Rental place is; on the corner there right across the corner from Kondolas [Lakelse Ave. & Atwood St.]. That was the place, and we had a couple of different drive-through and drive-ins. They were situated around. There wasn't anything in those days that was franchised — it was all local people.

MS: So you visited the Lakelse Hot Springs quite a bit. What was it like back then?

GMc: Well, the Lakelse Hot Springs has had quite a few things happen to it. There was a fellow here that is really well known and he did a lot of work, him and his family at the hot springs. They had the hot springs pool and it was not situated where it is now. It was across the parking lot, actually.

They had a hot pool and an outside pool, and that's where we taught swimming. It was sort of interesting, because all of the instructors were around the edge of the pool and, of course, it wasn't covered. We have a lot of pictures of people with umbrellas teaching swimming. Of course, the water was nice. It went through quite a few transformations, but Ray Skoglund and his family did a really good job of looking after that.

MS: Were you involved in any fishing?

GMc: No, I wasn't a fisherman — I never got to be a fisherman.

MS: Did you see any changes around industry throughout the years?

GMc: Recently, of course, the forest industry has been in tough times. They are coming back now. At one point we had a pulp mill in Kitimat and one in Rupert, so it was really a booming place as far as forestry is concerned. There is still logging, of course, but it is not as robust as it was, that's for sure.

MS: Were you involved in any community activities outside of the home, like clubs and organizations?

GMc: Yeah, I was involved in the beginnings of quite a few organizations: the Terrace Basketball Association, Youth Soccer, Minor Soccer and of course, the swimming. And I played a lot of sports myself. It was a great time playing sports.

MS: What local events do you remember celebrating?

GMc: Well, one of the events early on that was really something for the town was the visitation of the Queen when she came to Terrace. In fact, you may or not know that Queensway was named because of the Queen coming here. That used to be the road that took you to the airport. She got off the plane and came down Queensway, and they paved it for that reason. The only pavement put down was for this occasion, the first in Terrace. Then she went across the Old Bridge and down Lakelse Avenue and turned where the Coast Inn is. She went to the post office, around the block, onto Lakelse Avenue and back to the airport. But there were probably 15,000 people that day and they were from all over the place. She didn't go many places, just Terrace, so we had people down from the north and people from Kitimat, Rupert, Hazelton, and all over the place. Yeah, it was a banner day when the Queen came to Terrace.

MS: So, you saw her?

GMc: Yeah, I did.

MS: That was actually cool. Do you remember anything about downtown Terrace from your childhood?

GMc: There weren't any chain stores to speak of. There were all individual stores. It was home grown, you know. Instead of Overwaitea, we had Fred Smith Grocery Store. And we had individuals that had grocery stores and other retail stores. There really weren't any chains to speak of at all.

MS: Did you shop at the Terrace Co-op?

GMc: Terrace Co-op was very, very popular. It was the biggest store in town. Of course, they carried a whole variety of different things — anything from fish hooks, to food, to petroleum, to gas, you name it.

MS: It was the first super-store.

GMc: It was.

MS: Where did you shop for clothes and furniture?

GMc: Furniture: the fore-runner of furniture was Western Home Furnishings. As far as clothes were concerned, for me personally, there was a fellow that came to town that opened up a men's wear store and it was called Godden's Men's Wear. That was a long, long time ago in the '50s and early '60s. He was an interesting fellow. He and his wife ran the store and he was community oriented.

Gord McConnell's basketball team. Gord pictured in plaid shirt on the right. Gord McConnell Collection

MS: What did most people that you know do for work — like, the mill?

GMc: Most of them were all involved in the logging industry in some capacity and if they weren't involved in the logging industry then they were a support for logging. That was pretty well a one-town thing. The advantage that Terrace has always had, though, was its geographic location — it is the centre. But at one time, the bigger shopping was in Kitimat. That changed when the Hudson Bay moved out. The Hudson Bay had a big store in Kitimat and a lot of people from Terrace went there. The Trigo building in Kitimat used to be the Hudson Bay Company.

MS. What role do you think forestry and logging played throughout the history of Terrace?

GMc: It was the history. Everything really hinged on logging. A whole generation went into the logging business and some of them are still in there — they are driving trucks and loaders and there's lots of work. Columbia Cellulose was the major one. It was a lot of individual people that had a Cat, or had a couple of Cats, or trucks. There were also little places around — small sawmills.

MS: How have you watched the industry change over the years in forestry?

GMc: Well, of course, when they cut back the forest industry, big things happened. First of all, we lost the pulp mill in Rupert. Then we lost the one in Kitimat and, of course, that resulted in there being no place to put the chips or the sawdust, so that really was a crunchy thing. And then, the logging industry really went down when the price of lumber went down. And, of course, more recently, the pine beetle epidemic. That didn't affect us too much locally, because we don't have a lot of pine, thank goodness. But even at that we had a hard time; when the sawmills quit, of course, we are still sending out whole logs. But now that we have the new Skeena Forest Products open again, it looks a lot brighter than it did in the last 20 years or so.

MS: How did the community interact with the Kitselas and the Kitsumkalum?

GMc: Well, when I went to school, there weren't that many people from the Native community that were going to school because a lot of them were going to residential schools. But we have always had a good relationship with the Native community. When we were playing sports, we would go to Aiyansh and Greenville and play sports there and they'd come down here. I'll meet somebody in the mall my age and we can reminisce about the crazy days we had playing soccer. So, it was good.

MS: So, how did the community interact with the police?

GMc: In the early days, the policemen were the ones that had their own basketball team and they were in the league playing basketball. And, you know, it was a small town and everybody knew everyone else. I didn't see any problems with the police.

MS: How did the establishment of Kitimat in the 1950s impact Terrace?

GMc: Well, initially, it didn't impact it right away because there was no way to get there. Then they put in the railroad. The railroad was in there a couple of years before they put the road in. In fact, when the people came out on their days off from Kitimat, they would all hop on the train and they would come to Terrace. Eventually things got a little rowdy. They wouldn't let them stop in Terrace and they went to Rupert. [Laughter.] So that was sort of interesting. It did have a big impact and, of course, we still have lots of people in Terrace. A good percentage of their workforce in Kitimat live in Terrace.

MS: How did the construction of the new bridge impact the community?

GMc: I think it was very, very necessary. They had a little trouble building it because the first time they put the piers in the middle of the river it was high water. They had to get the piers out of there and start over again. But it had a huge impact. And then there was talk about closing the old bridge — I don't know how serious that was. Anyway, there was a big uproar to leave the bridge in because if something ever happened — an accident — we had no way to access the other side of the town. As it turned out that was a very wise thing — if you've ever had to get across early in the morning or in the late afternoon — that bridge traffic piles up.

MS: So, have you lived in Terrace during any major floods?

GMc: The really bad floods were in the forties. I missed those, but we were here for the flood that happened three or four years ago. The river would have to come up a major amount before it would really affect the town, that's for sure.

MS: It's more the river outside of town than the stuff coming into Terrace that's affecting it.

GMc: When we opened our store in November, 1962, the mall store, two days after we opened we had some really stormy weather. November is when we get a lot of rain and if we are going to flood, it will be November (as well as the springtime). The water cut off many of the bridges. We lost bridges between here and Kitimat, and between here and Hazelton, and between here and Rupert. So it was pretty catastrophic at that time.

MS: Did you have a garden at all?

GMc: My parents didn't have a garden because we lived in an apartment. We had a garden after we were married — a nice garden, and we now live at the lake and we have one out there. We've had a garden all the time — vegetables and flowers.

MS: How was the Farmers' Market and how has it changed throughout the years?

GMc: Well, it certainly got bigger, for sure, and it's been a real bonus for a town our size. The Farmers' Market is exceptional. It really is. It's by far the biggest one around and it's been going for a long time. The people that are in there now, organizing it, keeping it going, are the people that started it. Now it's grown into something that is a real tourist attraction, and for everybody.

MS: What role has art played in Terrace throughout the years?

GMc: I think it's been an active community all along. They have had art shows, and I see that fairly recently there are murals going up on the buildings. I think that is a really neat idea. The Terrace Little Theatre has had a long history and has been well known for the amateur theatre productions in town.

MS: Were you involved in politics in any way?

GMc: That is something I wasn't involved in at all. It didn't really interest me too much and I was involved in so many other things. I never really got involved in politics.

MS: How important do you think First Nations culture has been in shaping our community?

GMc: Well, I don't think it was shaping our community that much in the early days, but it has gotten stronger and stronger in the last twenty-five years and it has made a huge difference. The culture back in the fifties, they used to bring eighty-piece bands out of the Nass. They were fantastic — in fact, one or two of them went to play for the Queen in England. They had to go down the river, down to Kincolith and then catch a boat to Rupert and then back up here again. When we had a band festival, and we did have some in those days, it was a case of which Native band was going to win because no one else had near the numbers they did.

MS: Have you felt our region has been represented, regionally, provincially, nationally?

GMc: The problem, when you have a community where we are, is we're fairly isolated compared to the lower mainland. When you talk to people in Vancouver, the earth ends at Hope. They don't really know where it is. What I find really discouraging is when I'm in Vancouver and anyone asks me and I say I'm from Terrace and I ask them, "Have you ever been? Do you know where Terrace is?" More often the case, they don't know.

MS: You tell them Prince George, 1000 miles north.

GMc: I think you are better off, especially if you are talking to Americans or non-Canadians, you can tell them you are 130 km as the crow flies from Alaska. They understand the Alaskan part of it. I think a lot of it is population and that is something we have to live with, that's all there is to it. But now, of course, with all the activity going on in this part of the world, they are paying a lot more attention to us now than they ever did, that's for sure.

MS: More generally, how has Terrace changed as a community over the years since you have been here?

GMc: Obviously it's not as close-knit as it was before, because there are just that many more people. But there are lots of people organizing things. I think we are in pretty good shape. There is the odd blip that happens in politics or whatever. We've got the Millennium Trail. We've got a whole bunch of things that are volunteer-driven — River Boat Days, I think that's a good example. So, I think we are in pretty good shape as far as that is concerned. People are concerned about the community — I think it is a good community.

MS: You probably don't have too many memories of WWII and stuff?

GMc: No, I can't help ya. I can't go back that far.

MS: Do you recall anything of the military's presence in Terrace?

GMc: No, I don't. The only thing I know about the military is they were gone when I was here. When I first arrived in Terrace in '54 or '53, they still had the Red Cross Hospital here and that hospital was taken over from the military and that was up there by the Aquatic Centre. It was just the next street over. Then they built the airfield here, and that's why we have such a large airfield, because of the military. But that hangar, that old hangar at the airport, there were two more of those: one of those was on top of the bench and the other one was down by the ball diamond. One of those at the ball diamond was the old civic centre. There was a basketball court in there. There was a bowling alley, and right next door to it was a bunch of buildings that were army buildings, army barracks. That was where the elementary school was — it was called Riverside School. Then a fire came along, and burnt down the school and the civic centre.

MS: When you were a child what did you hope to accomplish in Terrace?

GMc: You know, I didn't have any long-term goals. I'm sure, like a lot of kids, they are involved in their life and it rolls along and you played. I didn't have any long-term goals.

MS: Was there a particular person or event in Terrace that had a big impact on your life?

GMc: I don't think there was one person in particular. There were a few people: that would be somebody like Bill McRae. I don't know if you know Bill at all, but he would be a wealth of information for this area. He would be in his nineties or so. He would be marvellous. So I got to know him pretty early on and then Ernie Gooden. He had Gooden's Men's Wear and because it was so small, and my dad was in business, I was able to talk to a lot of these people. No one jumps out of the page, but there were lots of them that we knew personally.

MS: As someone who has lived here and learned here, what would you share with people new to Terrace?

GMc: Well, I think for one thing — the number one thing when you live in the north — is you have to adjust to the climate and that is the toughest part. Once you figure out that: you aren't in the big city, and you don't have the variety of things to purchase, but there is a wealth as far as Terrace is concerned. In five minutes you can be in the wilderness — where else do you get that? If you go down to Graham Avenue we've got farms. It's probably three minutes from town. That doesn't happen very often. So, there is space. I think space is the big thing. I think you want to use it and take advantage of it. There are lots of things to do — the difference being that you have to participate and you have to go out and find it. You can't go to basketball or the Lions Games or anything else. You got to put something in to get something out. We've been in business for a very long time and the people are very friendly and they are all willing to help. I think it's a great place.

MS: Do you have any advice for the present and future residents?

GMc: I think the thing is going along pretty well. I think it is important that the people who come in know where the Native community lives and where the Sikh community lives. I mean, everybody is mixed in together and I think that has been a good thing, and certainly we would like to see that continue in the future.

MS: Thanks a lot for this interview.

Jim Allen Interview

Interviewed by Kenan Kinney and Noreen Sandberg, 27 November 2013

Jim Allen was born in Ireland in 1934. As a young adult, Jim lived in London for three years, which is where he met his wife, Josephine. They immigrated to Canada when Jim obtained a contract with the Catholic Church to help build school churches in the Northwest. During his time in Terrace, Jim worked as a painter and a plasterer. He also worked for the government and owned a bed and breakfast on Braun Street. Jim was a long-time member of the Royal Canadian Legion and was part of the Knights of Columbus. He was also the creator of the local tourist attraction, Tiny Town, which is a miniature replica of his hometown Youghal in Ireland. Tiny Town began in Jim's front yard of his home on Agar Avenue, but can now be found located beside George Little House. In this interview, Jim talks about how he met his wife, how he arrived in Terrace, his career, fishing, and playing soccer. Jim also shares stories about obtaining his Canadian citizenship, saving the lives of two people, and the changes he witnessed as a long-time Terrace resident.

KK/NS: Where and when were you born?

JA: I was born in Ireland, 1934.

KK/NS: And how did you and your family arrive in Terrace?

JA: I came by boat and train. I came to Montreal [Quebec], and then I got the train from Montreal straight through to Terrace?

KK/NS: Okay, and what was that like?

JA: I tell you, when you had no money, it was pretty hungry. Yeah, it was rough — it was rough. Seemingly it was different, right enough, but then you had no money to go out and buy. Generally, you got the grub at the railway stations; it was cheaper than on the train. But now, you don't get any grub at railway stations anymore. That has changed completely. You just have to get the food on the train.

KK/NS: So, why did you come to Canada? Why did your family come to Terrace?

JA: Well, unemployment back there. Although I wasn't unemployed. No. It's pretty hard. I left home just like this — overnight. And I was in London [England] the following day, and the following day I was working.

So I was in England for three years, and that's where I met the wife. She was engaged to a guy, and I didn't know that. But, anyway, we were working in this building, and she was working on the other half of the building. It was a big store, like Walmart. So, I was doing my little bit, working away like a trooper, and then decided to go into — it was called Little Woods, the name of the store, and they sold everything just the same as Walmart. Anyway, I hit the ice cream counter and there was this little English girl there, and I got talking to her. Then one fine day, I thought, *Oh, I'm going to stay,* and I said, "Where do you come from?" and "What do you do?" She was wearing a dress and she had the run of three counters. She had to look after three counters: she had the ice cream counter, like I called it, the doughnut counter, and the jewelry counter. You know, altogether different, and she had staff on the ball, you know? So that was that. Anyway, it took me a little while, you know, after getting a few ice creams, back and forth — you know how it goes. So I asked her out! And I said, "Would you like to go to the movies?" The show, that's what they're called, right. And, "No, no," and "That's Okay." I didn't think nothing of it.

Anyway, we were working real tough, real hard; we were classed right in next door. So, to make a long story short, I went back in one day and I said, "Why don't you want to go to the show? Is there something wrong with me or something?" "No," she said, "I'm engaged." "Oh, you are, eh?" I said. "I'm sorry, I'm sorry." But, anyway, the boys started bugging me, "Oh, you couldn't get a date in there." I don't know how it happened — I just said to her casually, "What about going to the show tonight?" She hesitated, and she said, "Okay." After the show, and a week later, I asked her out again, and bingo! I don't know what happened between herself and the boyfriend, but at that time I went and bought a bed, you know.

On a Saturday night — a Saturday evening — it was show time. I had asked her right up. But she lived in another part of England, so she had to come by double-decker bus; all I had to do was run up, right from here to Misty Rivers. So anyway, I can't believe it: there she is on the top floor, looking down below! Anyway, so I had a girlfriend after that. Then, a week or two later, we went to the show, and then we went dancing. We did a lot of dancing; we were right into the dancing.

So anyway, we were not going to that dance hall because her ex-boyfriend would be there, and a bunch of his buddies — they'd jump me. I would never have a chance in hell to protect myself. Mind you, I was in good shape. I was in real good, good shape. A runner — I used to run. I ran against the best of them in Ireland — We were champions, yeah. And football, the same way. Oh yeah, I was right on the ball.

But, anyway, we were having lunch outside because where we were working there were jackhammers and everything, and there was a lot of dust. We put up a bench, and we sat down, and a couple of buckets in the clank, and we were having lunch. Never took any notice, and then all of a sudden there was this guy, and he stood in front of me, and he let fly. He got me right there in the nose, busted my nose, and I nearly went right through the big plate glass window that was behind me! Then I gave him — it was only one blow and he was gone, he was across the street. But that's the first time I seen him, and I can't see what my wife saw in that guy, because he was a big slob. Even the manager at Little Woods, where she worked, didn't like him. Whoever was around never liked him. But he was a farmer — he had property back in Ireland, and I guess my wife Jo — we call her Jo (Josephine) — thought, well, I'm set for life. I had nothing, just nothing.

That was it. So about six months later, we got married, and about a year and a half after we had Delores, and then we went back home to Ireland, for a holiday. But then, in the meantime, I got in contact with the Catholic Church. You would know all about this — they were looking for people to help build the school churches at the time, right through from Prince George. I volunteered, and I was accepted because I was a half-decent tradesman, even then. I was a painter, and a plasterer, aye.

Everything was set up — visas, everything. Everything was going great — but her mother had a heart attack and she died. The day we were leaving was the day the funeral was on. And somehow or other at the funeral, I got over to this side, when I should be at this side. But the wife, you know, just got twiddled around a little bit. Anyway, it was decided that I'd leave on my own. I had to jump over the grave to get to the other side, because there was a big bunch of people over and around the grave. I just jumped with my little baby, who was two or three months old, to give her a hug. She was in rough shape.

So, anyway, I ran down the road to get the train to go from there to Dublin. Then I had to get from Dublin [Ireland] to Liverpool [England], get the big boat in Liverpool, and then we left Liverpool the following morning and arrived in Montreal 14 days later. Seasick as saw — yeah, it was rough! Oh my God, there was just as much water up there as there was down below, I think. So I arrived in Montreal and I was met by the Sisters of Charity, and they put me on the train, and then seven days later I arrived in Terrace.

The train didn't go that fast in those days. It stopped at every station, and at some stations it would stop for two, three hours. I had money but somewhere along the line it just gradually disappeared. Eventually I arrived in Terrace and I was supposed to be met by so-and-so. I didn't know who I was meeting, anyway. There was only three or four tracks, and that's where the train stopped, out on the fourth or the fifth track, so to get off the train, you had to cross over the railroad tracks. There was no station. There was nothing. That's the beginning of Terrace.

And on the way in, on the other side of the Skeena Bridge, I said to the porter, "Where is Terrace?" He says, "We're coming close to it." Before that, before I left home, we were up in Dublin at the Canadian Embassy, and the guy at the Embassy, the immigration officer — he didn't feel like an immigration officer, but a real smart guy — he said, "You're going to Terrace?" "Yeah." I explained to him the school and everything, and he was quite, "Yeah, yeah, yeah." Anyway, I arrived there. Oh, he says, "Terrace is a growing town, it's a growing town." He had never been to Terrace. The same guy had never been to British Columbia, but Terrace is a growing town to him, which it could be, but I didn't know. So I asked the porter, "What kind of town?" "Oh," he says, "Only a s**t town." I said, "No, it's a city!" And he said, "Well, who told you that?" I said, "The guy at the immigration office in the Embassy in Dublin!" He said, "Oh, yeah, well, you'll find out tomorrow." Which I did.

So anyway, that's where I wound up, behind the Catholic Church on Lakelse — the main drag — in a barn. There was bales of straw there, and that was that. The deal with the Catholic Church and stuff went sour — they weren't ready. Things were not up to par. I should have stopped off in Prince George and things would be different, but I didn't know. My instructions were to go to Terrace. But anyway, from thereon in, the following morning — which would be Sunday morning — I went to church right next door, but with no money, not a cent, flat broke. What am I going to do, you know? I went to church, and I looked at everybody, and not anybody looked at me, but that didn't matter that much. I was kinda down — very down, very down. There was mice, everything, in this s**t hole. Maybe if I had a rough life at home, I would— Anyway, this went like that.

So, Monday morning came around and I started to inquire, "Where would a guy get a job?" So, in not very long, I was doing a little paint job here and a little paint job there. There was not too much going on; no construction going on. It wasn't the city I was expecting to see; it was only a shack town, a few little buildings, the main street. And it's not much better yet, since they built the hotel and all that. There was houses over by where the hotel is now, there was living quarters.

KK/NS: And which hotel was that?

JA: On the main drag. The main street there — Lakelse — it might be called something different now. And that was that. Anyway, there was an addition going on to the Co-op. The first addition going on to the Co-op. So I got in on that, and that job kept me going until Christmas Eve. It was a real good job. The contractor was a nice guy, and everything worked out good there. And then in the meantime, I was doing a little bit of painting, whatever there was around.

Then eventually the wife came out, and she came out by plane. I had to go up to the airport and get her off the plane, and brought her home to a beautiful building — a hay barn. Yep, that's what we had. But, anyway, from there we moved to Kalum Street where the courthouse is now — the law courts. There was a building there and we moved into that. It was not anything better than the one we left, but it had a proper bed and stuff. We had a baby, so it was kinda — no clothes, no blankets, you know? We moved the bed when it rained. The rain came right through; it didn't come through in the hay barn. From there, we moved to another shack down where the medical building is now. And the guy's name — what was that guy's name? Harvey Doll. I used to call him the Mayor of Terrace. We lived there for a while, and then we moved again down to the Maple Autocourt. That was a little motel right across from the Catholic Church, right across the street, where what you call it? Name out a few of those little stores right across there where the barber shop is?

KK/NS: Is it where the—

JA: Mr. Mikes! A little motel, a bunch of cabins, there's no such thing as a hotel. Motel. You had a great big stove, that's how you did your cooking, and we had toilet — an outside toilet — which you had to go to. We hung in there for the whole winter. And then things started to improve. Then they were building the post office — it was called the federal building, but it was the post office. So I got in on that, because the plasters came in too early from Vancouver. 90% of the craftsmen that came in to do work were either from Kitimat or from Vancouver. And in those days it was mostly all plaster, no gyprock. In my time it was all plaster. So I got in on that. That was a good job, too. They all went back because they weren't ready. They weren't ready for me, either. But stop and start. So that winter, I ended up pulling off lumber off the green chain at Sande's sawmill. Down by the overpass; under the overpass. That was a number one job but it was hard going — hard, hard, going. I worked there for a whole winter and summer, and then I quit.

Then after that, I used to get in there every winter, every fall, and I would work over winter. It was good; it was really good. The people that worked there, that owned there, were number one, number one. And the two sawmills, Pohle Sawmill and, on the other side, Sande Sawmill, are the people that built Terrace, and donated wood. And you never hear them, Sande or Pohle. You only hear the Littles — they did this, they did that. As far as I'm concerned in my period of time, they did not. But these people, the sawmill, they donated wood and whatever.

KK/NS: Is that why it's called the Sande Overpass?

JA: Yeah! That's why it's called the Sande Overpass. There was a sawmill right underneath there, a good sawmill. Then they ran out of lumber through business deals with some other people in Terrace. You know, not good, not good. So they had to spend thousands and thousands of dollars fixing it up. When they went to get the lumber, they were told they couldn't get it no more. It was given to someone else, somebody else. But they were sure they had these lumber rights, timber rights, and they were told to go elsewhere. I won't mention who got them. So then it was going.

I guess in the meantime, we had a couple more kids. Yeah, a couple more kids came along, and I went to the Catholic School, Veritas.

KK/NS: And where was it located at the time?

JA: Right beside the church. Right down.

KK/NS: And that was downtown, where the mall is?

JA: Yeah, right across from the mall. Yeah, that was there. So, eventually, the school — that's over there now — was moved over there, and then the convent was there, too. So we moved the convent over also, to where the convent — the Father told you he tore down the convent, he got rid of that. He shouldn't have gotten rid of it, I'm against that, but it don't matter. But, anyway, that was torn down, and the school they added, that was that. I did a lot of work for the school. I plastered the school, I plastered the convent, and what else? Okay, so that brought us up to about five years, I would say.

One time back in London, I made a vow — I wouldn't say a vow, a promise — to the wife. No more running, no more football, because I went to play a game after mass on a Sunday and she went home with baby, and I would be home within a couple of hours. But, anyway, we played the game, and then there were these other guys came up to me and said, "Jim, how would you like to stay and play against this other team from Australia?" You know, a different style of football. And I said, "No, I've got to go home. The wife will kill me, you know? I've got to get home." So, anyway… "Ah, heck, sure. I'd love to play against those guys." So I stripped back and put on my uniform again, did okay, so we beat them anyway. I couldn't believe it but they were rough — very, very, very, very rough.

Anyway, on the way home now, seeing as I didn't know my way around in London, I figured I would get on this train — the tubes, they're called, underground tubes. So, I would get on this one and it would drop me off there. So, anyway, I got on the wrong one, and instead of going home, I was going up to the airport, the London airport, when I started inquiring. I said, "What's the next stop?" and "Where is Kilburn [England]?" "Oh, you're going in the wrong direction." So I had to get out, take the train back, and go back to Kilburn. Anyway, by the time I arrived home, it was 10 o'clock. Here's a guy who was supposed to be home at 10 o'clock in the morning, only playing a game of foot! By the time I got home, oh boy, she was wild. "This is no good! This is not happening again!" My, oh my, oh my.

So, anyway, she cut me and she threw me out the door. I was sitting out there and then the landlord said, "What are you doing there, Jim?" I said, "Oh, Mother is pretty mad. I was supposed to be home at 10 o'clock, 11 o'clock around, but now I just arrived." So anyway, okay, he started laughing. "Oh you'll have a lot more than that." I was sitting there an hour, an hour and a half. Figured she has cooled off a little bit, you know? Just as I went to open the door, she was opening the door, so to straighten things out. Then I made a promise. I said, "I know it's not going to work out. It would break my heart to quit but I will do it." So anyway, I quit the running and I quit the football.

We jumped the gun here and we're back in Terrace. I was going looking at a job, and I think there was a couple of the kids with me, so where will we live? On Eby Street — south Eby, just up here. We went up to Kenney Street and then you turn down, and here are all these guys playing soccer, you know? It was kind of funny; more or less. I pulled over to the side of the road. "Oh kids, let's stop here for a minute, and see what's going on." I parked the truck and they got out, and they, you know, ran down the sideline, and I got to go in after those monsters.

Anyway, a ball came, and it landed right in front of me, so I went and I picked it up and I just took it to where the goal posts were, you know, and I let fly. Oh, first time, it felt good, you know, and I drove that thing nearly through the goalkeeper. Anyway, one guy said, "Oh, we're just picking a practice team. You want to?" "Oh, no, no, I haven't kicked a ball in nearly five, six years now." So I said, "Ah, put me in goal, I'm not so good with this soccer business and I'll stop a few goals, here or there." I did good. So anyway, I was working for the government where the Knox United Church is now — right uptown just across from the furniture store.

Yeah, anyway, the government agent was the coach of this football team that he had me in. I didn't know who they were. But anyway, he came out to me, and he says, "You were kicking ball the other night and were pretty good. You play football before?" I said, "I did, but I didn't play soccer, something like soccer — scary football, you know, kick the ball up, kick it and get rid of it." "Okay," he said. "How long have you been in Canada now?" "Oh," I said, "I've been going on five years at least." He said, "You wouldn't play with the other team." Pohles had a team, the Co-op had a team, and they were good. A lot better than today. I shouldn't say that, I might be making a wrong statement, but they were good. They were from Europe: there were Dutch, a few Hungarians, and they were good.

So anyway, he said, "Jim, I will make you a Canadian citizen if you play with my team." I said, "Oh, you can't do that?" he said, "Oh yeah, I can do anything. I am the government agent." He could be king as far as I'm concerned, what a government agent meant to me at the time — it didn't mean a thing. He says, "You go home and get the wife and however many kids." So I went home and told the wife we would keen up a little bit and I told them we would become Canadian citizens. "What the heck you talking about, man?" I said, "Yeah, we're going to be Canadian citizens." But I said, "I got to play soccer. Is that okay with you?" "Okay, okay."

We met up and it was about 100 degrees and it was a flat roof, still flat roofs, and in that building it was about 200 degrees. Oh, it was horrible. Anyway, he had all the literature and everything, and bing, bing, bing. He said, "Let's go out on the sidewalk." It was a wooden sidewalk, not concrete, so we sat down, with the odd truck, odd car going by — you know, not as busy as it is today. We took allegiance to the Queen and everything, and we signed this, and we signed that, and now he says, "You be over there for practice tomorrow evening, six o'clock, and everything will work out all good." I said, "If I don't go, will you cancel that?" "No," he says. "You're in now. You're okay."

So I went over for practice, and to make another long story short, about three months later, I got this big brown envelope — oh a big brown envelope for James Allen. Oh my! And it was from the Ministry of Immigration in Ottawa, sealed and signed. Judy LaMarsh was the Minister of Immigration, and she sent me a very nice letter congratulating us on deciding to become Canadian citizens. At the side of the street. Today to become a Canadian citizen, you've got to be nearly a university student to pass all the exams and questions. It's unreal. Even today, I wouldn't be able to pass those, because I wouldn't have the education, you know? You've got to study for weeks, and weeks, and weeks. Anyway, that's how we became Canadian citizens.

So, then my back started to go on me, so I was slowing down considerable. And okay, we got a job up at Skeenaview [Lodge], or Terraceview. Skeenaview was what it was called then. At that time, there was about 350 seniors who came down from Vancouver. They were closing a facility some place in Vancouver, so they thought this would be an ideal spot. They would fix up these buildings, which were army buildings. I got a job in that and I was doing pretty good — I worked there for two years or something. But like I said, the winters were very, very cold. I was working on firewalls to separate the rooms, lock the doors, just in case they have a fire. So at lunchtime this particular day, it was cold and icy, and the little sidewalk that they had down by the side of the hill, Skeenaview hill — it wasn't a sidewalk, it was just a trail — oh, it was unreal. Dangerous.

But at that particular time there was a lot more money floating around, and these old guys used to get five dollars a month out of their pension, which was pretty good. It's the other way around today, if you had five dollars they'd steal it from you — the government, you know? But they got five dollars. Some of the guys gave it to the nurses and to the people who take care of them. Some of them stuffed it up, and then they would go downtown and jump on the bus and head to Prince Rupert, and then they would start looking for them and stuff, and then there were the regulars that went to the Terrace Hotel.

Like I said, it was after Christmas — freezing cold, freezing cold — so I was going home for lunch and I had this truck and everything, and I was going a little too fast, because here was one of these here guys, George. I knew them all. They used to help me — they were my helpers — oh, they were really good, some of the old-timers. Some of them, there was nothing wrong with them — only a little, and they used to help me. But, anyways, this guy was going down the hill, and I couldn't stop, because even the road then at 12 o'clock in the day was sheer ice. You couldn't even jam down the brakes.

Anyway, I figured I would go down and turn around at the end of the street on Tuck Avenue. It's closed now, but not at that time. There were three or four cars that went by, and I had full view that this old guy hasn't been in any of those cars, so they couldn't stop, but they wouldn't stop anyway. So I went up nice and slow, what the heck, he must have gone back up, you know? But he couldn't have gone from there up to the top of the hill in that short period of time. So I went up the hill and I turned around and then I just cruised down, nice and slow. I figured this is where I passed him and no more than about another 40 or 50 yards further ahead would he have got there. I went to go lay on the brake, and I was crawling at the time, but I just skidded across the road.

I jumped out, and I start looking over the ditch like this, and I heard some grunting, some moaning. Right enough, there was this old guy who fell over the stump, fell over — anyway, but he was down below. So I jumped down and I dragged him up. To make a long story short, there were cars on this

400

side, and cars on that side, and they were rushing home, like everybody else. I had this old guy and my poor back — I could barely lift a cup up at the time — but I dragged him up, and I went to put him in the cab, but he didn't want to go in the cab. So I got enough strength that I just picked him up and threw him into the back of the pickup, the back of the truck, and that's where he stayed. "Don't move." But, to turn around then, I either had to go this way or that way, and it was unreal: the more I would move, the more I would slide. It was unreal.

I would say about an hour down the road, he would be a goner, so I saved his life. When I got mobile, I got kind of mad at the people at either side of me, because you know what they started doing? They started beating their horns, which wasn't very nice, and that kind of got me, and gave me enough strength to get him into the back of the truck. When I got back turned around and got straight, I just dumped him off at the kitchen door, no questions asked. I said, "You go in there and warm up, see you later, bye." No one hardly knew hardly anything about it. So that was one life I saved. So that was that — I saved one man there.

So after that I had a big back operation in Kitimat, which I nearly died out of but survived, and then my friend came out one morning, and asked me to drive her down to this Fisherman's Park. And I said, "Why do you want to go down to Fisherman's Park?" "Well, I was down there with my brother, he's in from Toronto, and I left my purse down on the rocks, and I hope they're still there — would you drive me down?" So I said, "Yeah, sure, no problem." I jumped into the truck, got her into the truck, and bingo. Got her down and drove right down into the park where they put the boats in, you know, while they do their boat signs now, but that was on this side.

KK/NS: And where is Fisherman's Park again, sorry?

JA: Down on Kalum [River]. It was in mid-summer — but I wouldn't say summer — the tail end of May, coming on first week of June. That river was going pretty good, flowin', flowin' real good, but anyway, what the heck is keeping her? You know, she just ran down in front of the truck, underneath the bridge — so I figured she must have been all the way over there, and I was getting kinda — *Ah, she should be back,* you know? And then, all of a sudden, there was water right up into the parking area. All of a sudden, did I see something bobbing up in the water? *Yeah, yeah* I think — *that's Pat!* So I had to spring into action again. I had to run down about maybe 20-30 yards and bail out into the river and there was two guys going getting — I don't know what they were doing, working for CN [Canadian National Railroad] or something.

Anyway, they were standing there and there was a big log going by and it was passing by and she was going right behind the log and I was up the hill. And I was ready to be taken off my feet — I reached out behind the log, the log that kept me afloat, and as she was passing by I got ahold of her by the big toe. She had sandals on and I will always remember her big toe, and I had to try to get more strength to pull her in. And a good thing that log was there, because the two of us would be gone. So I got her in — then I was there to pull her in, and then I dragged her in the rest of the ways. That was scary. I saved another life. That life would have been gone for sure. I don't know about the old guy up at the Skeenaview Hill, but that was good going. Then after that I worked day in, worked day out. Kids grew up, played soccer.

KK/NS: And how did you find Terrace as a place to raise your family?

JA: Oh, great. Great! Couldn't find a better country. It doesn't matter. Terrace — yeah, great, excellent.

KK/NS: And what did you guys do as a family?

JA: We did fishing. Lots of fishing, lots of soccer after that. Fishing, and soccer, and the whole shebang.

KK/NS: And did you attend any sporting events in town?

JA: Not really, no. I was always working, and I was working out of town, too. Well, we built houses. Does that mean anything? We built houses.

KK/NS: Where did you work out of town?

JA: Dease Lake, Telegraph Creek, all those places up north when I was with the government. I got promoted to foreman. The guys used to tell me what to do and here I was foreman! Oh yeah, I was workin' up. But real early, I got into Stewart, went in by ship and we plastered the new courthouse they built in Stewart. That was '57, '58, or '59. I was only here a couple of years when that job came up. Stewart then was going helter-skelter: they had a big mine going in there, the Granduc Mine, and there were lots of people at that. That's the way it is in Stewart. It's up and it's down. It's up one minute, and now it's down to about 200-300 people. Yeah, there was about 3000 people, and they were all Australians. Mostly all Australians. The weather in those days, it used to be really cold, and snow. Then you get four or five feet of snow in one dump, and that happened in the '70s, in '75, oh yeah, a lot of snow. Then the town gradually built, over at McConnell Street. That's where the town really started to grow, subdivision after subdivision. Oh, do I keep on going? I'm running out of —

KK/NS: I'll give you some questions. Were there any restaurants that were really popular in Terrace that they had here that they don't have anymore?

JA: Yeah, they had the Terrace Hotel, that when they first opened up, they were about four feet out on the main street — so when the Co-op was built, and when they surveyed streets, they had to tear down the restaurant and move it elsewhere, so that's where the restaurant was. Then there was another Chinese restaurant, and a pool hall, just on the main drag there between Kalum and whatever that street is by the Co-op there. And then there was a drug store at the corner that isn't there no more. And that was there for years, and the coffee shop restaurant was good, and the pool hall. It wasn't a big one, but the guy that owned it, he won money in the pools, and he left overnight. He won 649, or one of them. Main street consisted of Jerry Duffis' five-to-a-dollar store. That all changed now, and it's not there anymore. The sporting store took over from that place where the five-to-a-dollar was. It belonged to Jerry Duffis. There was no town hall when I first came here — they built that in the '70s, where the town hall is now.

KK/NS: Did you visit Lakelse Lake a lot? Was it a very popular spot for recreation?

JA: Oh, yeah. Always, the kids used to go there every day. I wouldn't say every day, but I used to drive them out there, and then I used to leave them out there in the evening and go back to work. Then I would go pick them up with the wife and the kids. And then on the way out, when I would go pick them up, I would meet one guy here, another guy over here, another guy screaming at the other guy. Yeah, always, it was fun. No, they never got into the skating or hockey. Never got into that, no. It was always fishing, fishing, fishing — fish all over.

KK/NS: And where would you guys go fishing?

JA: Lakelse, Kalum, all different places, you know.

KK/NS: Find water, find fish?

JA: Oh yeah, it was good fishing then. Good fishing then. I was a big game hunter for a couple of days. That was another story. Want to hear about my game hunting? Now the boys took me in at Sande's Sawmill, they took me in. They were senior guys — veterans — and they took me in, and they understood where I was coming from. I was pretty innocent, you know. They used to give me the gears, so they told me to go out and get a rifle, and you can shoot whatever you want to shoot. Well, I didn't know any difference, you know, so I went and I got a rifle, a 3-0-3. I said, "What do I

402

do now, fellas?" "Well, you can go out on the highway and you'll see the goats and everything running around on the side of the road." Well, yeah, sure, ah heck.

I went out there one day, I could see the goats — bingo — but the mountains were way back in the bush, and you had to go all the way out in the bush, and then I came back in. I said, "No, I seen them, but I couldn't shoot them. They were too far away." Anyway, this evening I went out by Frank's Field, by the college, and there were a bunch of geese, a bunch of wild geese, and they were all sitting in the field where they all sit today, and there were cows and calves, in there at the time. And Frank's Field it was called; they still call it Frank's Field. So, I decided I would take out a goose, so I fired and shot the goose. I don't know if I got the one that I aimed at, but there was such a large flock of them, you couldn't miss, anyway. So I jumped over the fence — it was a wire fence — and there was kind of a trail there. It wasn't like the road that's there now.

So anyway, I came out with my goose, really proud, and the first guy that comes along on a bike is the game warden. Not a lie. He stopped and said, "You shot a goose." "Yeah, yeah!" "Oh my," he said, "I'm the game warden. Where's your license, tags, everything?" I had nothing. I had only five or six shells. I said the boys in the sawmill told me just to go ahead and do that. "Who are the guys at the sawmill?" So I told him, oh, they were good guys. He went down the following morning and went right through them and told them off.

That fall, later on, we went on a moose hunt, so I was kidding around, but then I had a tag. I knew the score. I had learned. This Finn Ferguson, he said, "Hey Jim, you want to go out to Remo? We might get a moose," and I said, "Sure, we'll go." So I jumped — didn't go home for lunch or dinner — I just jumped in the truck. Right underneath the trestles in Queensway here was this huge moose standing at the side of the road. Finn said to me, "Get the rifle, get the rifle!" I said, "No, you can't shoot that thing." He said, "You can, you can, that's a moose!" And I said, "No, it's a horse!" "No, it's a moose!" So anyway, I let fly, and I hit the moose right in the forehead, I can always remember that, and that moose went up on his back legs just as high as this ceiling, and landed right in the middle of the road. Bingo.

So we got a moose, and what are we going to do here? "Well," Finn said, "We've got to get it out of the middle of the road. If the police come by, we're in trouble." The two of us couldn't even budge that thing. "What are we going to do now? We have to wait until somebody comes by and gives us a hand." And you know who were the first people to come by? The policemen. Sergeant Phillips and another guy. The other guy was in full uniform, he was in for some kind of special thing and he was driving him up to the airport to get him on a plane. So Sergeant Phillips said, "What are you guys doing with a moose in the middle of the road?" "Oh, I shot him" He said, "Fell out there?" I said, "No, no, I didn't shoot him right in the middle of the road. He was right out there, and bingo, and I shot him, and he landed — yeah." He said, "If that moose is right there in the middle of the road on my way back, I will charge you." Okay. "By the way," he said, "there was another cabby and nobody will come out. They're all rushing to the airport, nobody coming the other way. They're all going up."

We couldn't budge it. We had no knives to do anything with it. We never figured we were going to ever get a moose so close to Terrace, right underneath the bridge. So anyway, Sergeant Phillips came down and there was the moose still right in the middle of the road and us still standing over it. He said, "We have to get it off of the road, fellas." So with him, the three of us, we got it over about a couple of inches and that's about it. So we put word out with Mike Stormicky — he used to work in the sawmill and he had worked on moose and stuff like that, cleaned out quite a few. So he came and we cleaned out the moose right in the middle of the road. That's where the moose got cleaned out. So to make a long story short, Sergeant Phillips got most of the moose, he got three quarters of the moose. We didn't like moose meat at the time, so we got a few pieces of the moose, but he was quite happy at the time. He was the only policeman in town — only one policeman. He was a really good guy.

KK/NS: And how did the community interact with the police?

JA: Oh, good. I could tell you another story about Sergeant Phillips.

They used to have fights every weekend when they came in out of the bush. It was just like being in the army. They used to walk out into the bush, up north.

KK/NS: The police?

JA: No, the guys that were working in the bush. They used to stay in the Terrace Hotel and they used to stay in the Skeena Hotel. French Canadian guys used to stay in the Skeena Hotel, and the Ukrainian guys used to stay in the Terrace Hotel. There was a vast difference between those bunch, you know. The guys at the Skeena Hotel were pretty rough. Every weekend, every Monday morning, I had a job, because if there were five doors going into a room and they wouldn't be unlocked or open, they would take a chainsaw and cut it open and watch, and that's how they got by from room to room. Every weekend, every Monday morning, Tuesday, I was patching. And that's how I learned to be a half decent carpenter. And that was that.

The other guys, they were good. The Ukrainian guys, they were pretty good. But these guys were French Canadians. That was there and sometimes they got into a big fight. Sergeant Phillips would get in there between those guys and with one hand he would pick up one guy and plop them down and say, "You stay there — if you move you will be in jail for your lifetime." He would have to break them up, and they respected him. Little different today — they call these cops in — but these guys they didn't like him at the moment.

KK/NS: Do you remember any local events that went on over the years. Like Riverboat Days?

JA: Oh, I did but that's gone.

KK/NS: Okay, let's talk about the new bridge. Do you remember the new bridge being built?

JA: Yeah, it was the NDP [New Democratic Party] that built the new bridge, but I'm no good at dates. Like I said, the minister, Dudley Little, he swore black and blue that he would never allow a new bridge, but then, the following year, there was a new bridge built by the NDP. I didn't get in on that. No, that was a different situation, but that was what happened there. But just imagine the situation: the guy swore black and blue in the government, so I don't know what came over him — but he was that type of guy, anyway. That's all I know about the new Skeena Bridge, and, boy, they need it today. The traffic that goes back and forth over that bridge is unreal. And the Old Bridge, too.

KK/NS: And before that, the only way of getting into town was the Old Bridge?

JA: Yeah, and I went through the Old Bridge one time — it was a wood deck — and half a clasp, bingo, whoop, a big splitter of cedar came right up in between my two legs, and right through the bottom of my truck — my car. I was with the wife at the time. Yeah, that was the type of bridge it was. But yeah, those things happen. Yeah, that was another incident.

KK/NS: So, how has the forest industry changed? Was it a lot better back then?

JA: Oh, yeah, well, forestry was the main industry here, you know. Everybody worked in on it. But I wasn't in that, mostly in construction.

KK/NS: Yeah, you built half the town!

JA: That is one thing I can be proud of. I worked my butt off in every shape and form, and helped everybody in every shape and form. Orangutans, rich, little, all. You know. But I worked in houses winter and summer — when they were there, when I was there to do it — and I was there right up until years ago, almost. Nope, I'm really proud of that, because I can drive up any street — Jim, you stuck with this house, you stuck with that house, you did class training, you painted in there. Yeah. I had a good crew. It wasn't a very big outfit, but I had alcoholics working for me. Two alcoholics. Good guys, but some days they were really bad. Some days they didn't pan out at all. Yeah, they were good guys.

KK/NS: Do you think art has been very important in Terrace?

JA: It's improved a little bit, but I don't know, I'm not really into that either, you know? No, I don't.

KK/NS: Do you think the First Nations have helped shape Terrace and make it the way it is?

JA: Don't you get me started. But we go back — we go back, okay. We go back when I first came here. The two best guys who worked at Sande's Sawmill were two First Nations guys from Telegraph Creek. Yeah. They were doing the two hardest jobs there, and I'd been on the same saws as they were, and I would be killing myself and I wouldn't produce anything, and a lot of the white guys there. When they were missing on the one day, things slowed down to a crawl. And one of them guys died on the railroad tracks and one of them went back to Telegraph Creek, and I don't know what became of him.

KK/NS: Have you lived here during any major floods?

JA: No, only the one we had here about 20 years ago. It wasn't a major flood, but it was enough to cause damage down to Graham Avenue along the way there. Yeah, I worked in a house down there. Its basement was flooded right up to the windows. Water was coming right through the windows in the basement. All along Graham Avenue got it — but outside of that, no.

KK/NS: Okay, and I don't know when the Queen's visit was, but were you here for the Queen's visit?

JA: Oh yeah, the Queen's visit. Yeah, we were here for the Queen's visit. Yeah, I think I was a Canadian citizen then! It was great, that was great; there were a lot of people out for that particular thing. She came out on Main, turned down Kalum Street, by Terrace Interiors, back out, and that was the visit to Terrace. Everybody was jumping up and down.

KK/NS: And have you ever visited the Farmers' Market?

JA: I used to when the wife was around, but no. A little bit of groceries I get at Safeway.

KK/NS: Has it changed much? Or is it relatively similar?

JA: Oh yeah, yeah, it's changed considerable. But it was a little more friendlier years ago, when there was business.

KK/NS: Has the content changed from what it was years ago?

JA: Yeah, I think so, I think so.

KK/NS: Was it more of produce?

JA: Yeah, there was more — I think there was a lot more — because the country was more wide open, you know? A lot more going out in Remo today. Now everyone is working. Why spend time farming to barely make ends meet? A good, steady job is better.

KK/NS: And did you go see any shows over the years?

JA: Oh yeah, every Saturday night with the kids, at the Tillicum. That's where we went every Saturday night. Never missed it, unless we already saw it three or four times.

KK/NS: Do you remember a drive-in being around this area?

JA: Yeah, that was down behind the back of another house we had. Down here on Braun Street, we sat there night in and night out, two nights a week or three nights a week. And that was okay, too. The same guy owned that, the same guy that owned Tillicum — Charlie Adam, a Scotsman. Cheap, but good. Yeah, a very good, good guy.

KK/NS: And were you involved in any politics in anyway?

JA: No, no, I don't get involved. I'm not very smart.

KK/NS: Were you and your family involved in any community activities? Like clubs, organizations or something?

JA: No, I'm in Knights of Columbus. I was involved for 40 years now.

KK/NS: Did you have any friends that were farmers or anything?

JA: Farmers? Nearly everyone was a farmer, and there was banks back then. They're more professional now. I've slowed right down, not like I used to.

KK/NS: And did you grow any — did you have a garden, or grow fruit?

JA: The wife used to have beautiful flowers and stuff. When it came to the vegetables, that was up to me, and I would do good for a little while, but then I would forget about them.

KK/NS: And as a last thing, as a long-time resident of Terrace, what changes have you noticed?

JA: Very first one I'll say — and people don't believe me — that's the weather. The weather is number one, when I tell people there 60 years ago, 45 years ago. It was just like being in Iceland, it was unreal. Like that day I saw the old guy, the ice was just like this, you know the centre of the road, honestly, and that was at 12 o'clock in the day. Today it's just like midsummer as far as I'm concerned; there's no ice. Well, there's a little ice, but not like that. There was a sheer of ice like a skating rink. And the wind from up north — the wind come down from the north, I tell you. And snow, even now we get snow, but it's nothing compared to then. Week in, week out, we had snow, snow, snow, shovel, shovel — good exercise. Change in the weather, that's number one. What else? The town has grown; it's not as friendly as it used to be. No way is it in anyway as friendly as it used to be. Everybody knew everybody and everybody helped everybody. Now if you help somebody — if you do — get help.

KK/NS: I remember you were telling me one time about the road out here.

JA: Oh, yeah, the roads were bad, over here on Keith Avenue, the main — I wouldn't call it the main street at the time, but it was very important. Right in front of those buildings, Blakeburn's buildings, Blakeburn Road there, with the freight outfit there. You couldn't go there certain times of the year. You would disappear behind frost heaves. You would get stuck there, and someone else comes along and he gets stuck, and somebody else comes along, he helps and he helps, and everybody helps each other. People used to run up — if they were free — they would run up to Pohle's Mill there, and they would get 2x12 scaffold planks, come down, jack up the truck, and that's how you got by. You got by. That's how people helped in those days, you know?

KK/NS: And the roads, they weren't paved?

JA: No, they weren't paved. Not in those days, no. There were roads down this way — Medeek — and all these other streets, they were just trails. Celanese — that's the logging outfit — had better roads out in the bush than we had, but we survived. We survived. Yeah, we didn't know any better. Kitimat Highway was good, rough.

KK/NS: And that wasn't paved, either?

JA: Oh, it was paved, yeah. It was built and paved at the same time, but narrow and bends and stuff, but now it's improved like a real highway. I didn't work on that. I drove that back and forth to Kitimat, for jobs. Quite a few accidents on it. We survived, survived, survived. Survived by the Skeena Bridge. The first time they had lights on that bridge, had no brakes on the truck — and slamming into the vehicle in front of you! Went over the side, went down, over the railroad tracks and nearly into the river. That was a close one, oh, yeah.

KK/NS: And I think you mentioned to me a while ago, you had opened up a bed and breakfast or something? Just down on the corner.

JA: Oh, yeah, down on the corner [Braun St. & Keith Ave.]. That was working out real good. That's when Mother came down with the cancer. That was right when we had started up. We were in business for about eight, nine months, and then one bright day she was informed that she had cancer. But we were doing really good. You know, it's a funny thing: about six weeks back I got a phone call, and there was this guy at the other end. He says, "Mr. Allen, have you still got your bed and breakfast? Dew Drop Inn?" That's what we called it: Dew Drop Inn. And I said, "No, that went down five or six years back, we're only just more or less." "Yeah," he said, "Yeah, I stayed with you guys for about a week   awesome — you guys were real good." The wife was 100 per cent, but then as soon as she got sick, everything went down.

KK/NS: And did you build that building?

JA: Oh, yeah, and we built this house, too. Yeah, we built the house up by the hospital — right across from the hospital. We built one on Eby Street — built two actually — the first one I ever built was on Eby Street. I didn't know what I was doing, but it's still standing. It's still there, and when I sold that place we got $7,000 for it. $7,000! I can't believe it, and today the average little house is over $200,000, $300,000, $400,000. That house is still standing, and the family that moved into it is still into it, ever since. We moved next door. We just had two lots. That was on South Eby. Never lived on that side of the town, always this side, up there by the hospital.

KK/NS: Do you mind if I ask about the little Irish village that you built? Tiny Town?

JA: Tiny Town? All that's left — and on the way out, you can have a look at it — is the lighthouse, and that will go up with the rest of the tiny town. That was good, too; that was really good. After we moved out on the corner there to here, that was when Mother was sick, you know, and I was more or less babysitting here and looking after her, you know? That worked out real good, and we had lots of tours, and I was helping the town to grow and everything, and I had tours coming. I never got much help there, either. Never got any help to talk about. If I got help, maybe I would have nearly stuck it out by myself, but I came out one day and I said, *What's the use? What's the use? I don't know why I'm doing this*, so that's when I went downhill — after that, anyway. I lost all faith. I wouldn't say I lost my faith, but I didn't see why I should — when people in the tourist business didn't know where the place was. So that would just give you an idea of what I was up against. And then I had a building instructor up on my backside when I was building it, every day of the week. He had nothing else to do, and he would check me — I swear to God, it was like I was building skyscrapers or something — "Tear down this, tear down that."

KK/NS: Yeah, I just remember I came there with my grade school and our class went around and looked at everything, and it was the neatest thing.

JA: Oh yeah — that lighthouse and the two boats are out there, we can have a look at them on the way out.

KK/NS: But how did you get started on that?

JA: How did I get started on that? It's a very simple thing, like everything else. We moved from over there to here, and I was figuring I would put a little pond out front by the front door, so I started digging there with a shovel — you know, the size of the table, and put a pump in. Anyway, this lady came along, at lunchtime and said, "Mr. Allen, would you ever build me a small dog house?" I said, "How small?" "Oh, about this big." I said, "How big is the dog?" "Oh, about the same size as Daisy." I said, "Okay, okay, I'll do that. In three or four days, come back." But she never did come back. When I had it built, I set it up on the pile of dirt coming up from the pond. It looked okay there — a dog house right by a pond. The wife sticks her head out the window one day and says, "Jim, what are you ever going to do with that dog house?" I says, "The lady's got to come back. She said she would come back within the week, and now it's been two months and she hasn't shown up." "Oh," she says. "She's either left town or dropped dead. Do something with it."

Jim Allen in front of Tiny Town. 2007. Photo credit: Jennifer Lang.
Terrace Standard Collection.

So, anyway, that's what I'd done. I took it down, brought it down and into the garage and cut a few things this way, cut that way, and added a few more, and I put two chimneys on there. Instead of having two nice little roundy doors like that, I put one door, put in the lit windows, brought it out. And when it was finished, I put it up sitting on the same mound of dirt. When I brought it out, I said, "Mother, come and see your new dog house." "Why did you build another one?" "No," I said. "I didn't build another one." So she looked out the door. "Oh my God! It's like a cottage back home." Exact words, you know. Her face lifted up. "Oh, that's beautiful. You should build a couple more like that." Within an hour, friends of ours had just got back from Scotland and Ireland, and as soon as they got out of the truck, they said, "Bingo! Jim, we seen dozens of those little houses back in Ireland and in Scotland. We traveled north and south." That's what started it all, and then I did something else, and something else. And a couple of my ex-buddies, they came along, and, "Oh, you should do this Jim, you should do that." That's when it developed into what it did.

I was not a pack rat. You know what I mean by pack rat? You go and you drag stuff and fart around and tear it apart. No, I just go to Rona — Terrace Builders at the time — and buy, buy, buy everything. And then I tell people I tied in $66,000 on that. They don't believe me, but I know, I know it was $60,000 tied up in that. There are two boats out there, you know. And, bingo, big Queen Mary there: I paid $20,000 straight labour plus my labour, and all the material that goes into it all, all the bits and pieces — winter project. And the guy who was helping me, I gave him $1,000. You know, so that would just give you an idea. I wasn't cheap, by any means. All those buildings, but the clock gate, will be all lit up now in the next 10 days. You guys drive by, you can have a look at it, come in and have another cup of tea.

KK/NS: As someone who has lived here and learned a lot, what would you want to share with people newly moving here?

JA: There's lots of advice I could give to them, but if you want to get ahead? It's not much good sitting in the pub, not much good going around to all the different places enjoying yourself. You've got to hustle and that's all there is to it, and when you have a maid — which I'll never have — you can sit back. That's the only thing.

Keith Maher Interview

Interviewed by Noreen Sandberg and Kenan Kinney, 15 November 2013

Keith Maher was born in Vancouver, in 1938. One of seven children, Keith attended New Westminster Secondary School. He worked at BC Buildings Corporation at Riverview Hospital until 1988. Keith was offered a promotion and transfer to Terrace, and in 1988 he and his wife Joyce [Oviatt] moved to Terrace. Keith worked as the Superintendent of Services [at BC Building Corporation] and at various retail locations until retirement. In this interview, Keith describes the transition from Vancouver to Terrace, the changing economy in Terrace, and the community.

KK: Were you born in Terrace, BC or were you born somewhere else?

KM: No, I was born in Vancouver.

KK: What was it like in Vancouver growing up?

KM: Oh, I was born 1938, which was just a year before Canada entered World War II. And it was a pretty uncertain time in and around Canada, because we had no idea whether the war was coming here or what was happening. And news was slow and far between. Technology was not what it is now.

NS: Most definitely. And how did you come to arrive in Terrace?

KM: I worked for BC Buildings Corporation at Riverview Hospital. I was offered a promotion and transfer to Terrace. That was in 1988.

KK: What was your job?

KM: Superintendent of Services.

KK: Was that a promotion when you came up here?

KM: That's the job I was offered.

KK: Did you have any brothers or sisters?

KM: I have one brother and one sister.

KK: What was it like growing up?

KM: Pretty busy house, there were seven of us.

NS: Pretty big family. How was your job when you first came here? What was your first impression of Terrace?

KM: Culture shock.

KK: How different was it?

KM: Very — from Vancouver. I'll tell you a little story that will emphasize it. Just after we arrived here — my wife and I — we wanted to go out for dinner. We'd heard the Bavarian Inn was a top notch restaurant in Terrace. Being from Vancouver, we got all dressed up like we would to go to a good restaurant in Vancouver. Walked into the Bavarian and my God — everybody's in jeans and t-shirts! So, that gives you an idea of what it was like.

KK: In Vancouver where you grew up, what was the schooling like?

KM: I graduated from high school in New Westminster. New Westminster Senior Secondary; that was a long time ago.

NS: And throughout your time in Terrace, did you stay with that job?

KM: Until I retired.

NS: What did you do for fun? Or do in your spare time?

KM: I'm more or less a homebody. My entertainment is pretty much at home. There's not many places to go to in Terrace, entertainment-wise.

KK: What year did you arrive in Terrace?

KM: The spring of 1988.

KK: Was there anything specific you want to talk about — coming to Terrace — or any good memories?

KM: Well, I like it here or I wouldn't have stayed — once I got used to it!

NS: Got used to the culture shock over Vancouver?

KM: Completely different pace of life here than Vancouver, for sure.

NS: What do you remember about downtown Terrace when you came here? Is it much different than it was before?

KM: Yes. It was a lot busier around downtown Terrace than it is now. When I walk around downtown I see an awful lot of retail space empty, and I think the major cause of that is decline in forest industry. That not only took the knees out from under the forestry but a lot of spin-off industries too.

NS: And, talking about forestry, what role do you think forestry and logging played throughout the history of Terrace? How much of an impact do you think it had on the town?

KM: I say that Terrace exists because of it.

KK: How long did you work here?

KM: BC Buildings Corporation. They were the landlords to the government. They owned all the Provincial Government office buildings in the province.

KK: So, how long did you work for them?

KM: Let me think. I worked for Ministry of Health until 1978, and then all the maintenance type work was taken over by BC Buildings Corporation [BCBC] and it was a rollover transfer from Ministry of Health to BCBC.

KK: What other kinds of jobs did you have in Terrace?

KM: I worked for Home Hardware for about a year and a half, until they closed down. After that, I worked for Early Bird for about a year and a half, and then after that I fully retired. I thought it was about time.

NS: Over the years, did you go to any local events in town and around?

KM: Not really, no. Can't think of any off-hand, no. Riverboat Days, of course; everybody goes to that.

KK: What kind of businesses were here that aren't here anymore?

KM: River Industries was one that the decline in forestry put an end to. And a lot of the parking business — parking and heavy machinery businesses. Kenworth Trucking for one. They are gone. What's the other trucking company — Excel — they're just about gone completely.

NS: And there is a decline of stores, like you said before. Terrace used to be quite busy downtown and now it's not.

KM: Well, it's not really. There's been a lot of small businesses that just came and went. Seems one comes in and two go out. Well, look at where Ev's Menswear was, that's still vacant for years.

NS: Yeah, it has been.

KK: Do you know how long ago the Terrace Co-op closed down?

KM: When did that close down? That's got to be six or seven years ago, I think.

KK: Do you know — was that around when you got here, or how long has it been in Terrace?

KM: I don't know how long it's been here. It was going when I came here, it was in full business.

NS: Do you ever leave Terrace? Like go on trips or explore the area around here?

KM: Yes, my job took me all the way from Kitimat to Atlin on a regular basis, and from Queen Charlottes [now Haida Gwaii] to Burns Lake, usually once a month.

KK: Sounds pretty fun.

KM: Oh, lots of…

NS: Driving.

KM: Too much. Trip to Atlin in the middle of winter from here is not fun.

NS: Before you moved up here for your promotion, did you ever come up here before — around the area — or was it completely new to you?

KM: No, I haven't. Except for one time many, many years ago, my father was stationed — he was in the army — he was stationed in Prince Rupert, and my mother, my older brother, and I came up. That was in 1943, and there was no road yet.

NS: There was no road.

KM: There was no road yet; you had to come up the coast by boat to Prince Rupert.

NS: Do you remember much about that trip?

KM: Not very much, no. It was a long time ago and I was pretty young. I think I was about five or six years old.

KK: Do you remember the kinds of things you and your family would do when you were growing up, when you were young?

KM: Such as?

KK: Just recreation.

KM: Recreation? We pretty much made up our own. When I was a young kid, "high tech" was radio. That was it; there was no television. If you wanted a story, you took a book and read it.

NS: Talking about being new to the area, how — when you travelled around, how was your experience driving up and around here?

KM: Very interesting. Going from here to Atlin, it was all kinds of little places along the way. That's a real interesting part of the country 'cause in Atlin, Carcross, most of the buildings look like they're turn of the century buildings — seriously.

NS: And for me — that must sound so silly — I don't actually know where that is, so could you explain how far it is from here or where it is close to?

KM: Well, if I was going to Atlin on a business trip I would probably leave Terrace in the morning — give you an idea. Probably arrive in Dease Lake around three/four o'clock in the afternoon, depending on the road, and I'd stay overnight in Dease Lake. The next day I'd leave there early, and drive to Whitehorse, and stay over there for a night, and if I got on the road real early the next morning I could make it to Atlin and back to Whitehorse in a long day. And then do the same thing on the way back.

NS: So it's fairly far north?

KM: It's in the far northwest corner of BC — you have to go in to the Yukon and over, then back down into the top northwest corner of BC.

KK: Was there any kind of restaurants or businesses that you think were really important to Terrace that are still around today, or that were here for a short while and made a difference but now they are gone? You said about the forest industry, but do you think there was anything else, or was the forestry industry the only thing about Terrace?

KM: Oh, I'm trying to think now. Home Hardware was a good business to have in Terrace. It really was. And oh, let me think, what else? River Industries — losing that, I think, had a big impact on a lot of industries because they were very much oriented to forestry and heavy industrial, and I really think that had quite an impact.

KK: Did a lot of people leave when it went?

KM: Well, a lot of people left when forestry declined, and a lot of businesses that were associated with it left.

NS: And how have you seen Terrace change? Even if it's the littlest thing over the years from when you first arrived here.

KM: Economics when I first got here were quite good. And then — I don't mean to sound political or anything, but in the '90s the NDP [New Democratic Party] came in. And it was a real economic decline — seriously. Serious economic decline. It's coming back now, the economy is improving now, and that's primarily due to mining I think, and that's generating a lot of income.

NS: And you think it'll — 'cause the mining is starting up again — do you think it will further help Terrace and bring new businesses in?

KM: Yup, it will.

NS: Bring more people to Terrace?

KM: Yeah, I think so. And I think it already has with the power line — this new power line that's going in. That's brought a lot of people in. And Alcan expansion has brought in a lot more people in industry.

KK: The hot springs — how different was it when you got here?

KM: It was an operation. I don't think that it ever lived up to its potential. Where else can you go swimming in the middle of winter — and in the kind of winters we have? And with that kind of potential, it should have been exploited and developed and it never has been.

KK: Yeah, it's closed now.

KM: Yeah it's closed down completely now.

KK: Lakelse Lake has always been a — well, just, is there anything you can say about it? Has it been a really popular spot for people to go?

KM: Oh, yeah, it is beautiful. I was out there quite a while ago now. A winter day, it was a real cold winter and the lake was frozen over completely. It was just like a sheet of glass, for a change there was no wind. There were hundreds of people out on the lake skating.

NS: Over the years have you visited Lakelse Lake or the hot springs?

KM: The odd time, yup.

NS: And has Lakelse Lake always been a popular spot over the years?

KM: Yeah, a very popular spot. Particularly in summers like we had this year.

NS: Yeah, it was a really hot one this time.

KM: It was, and surprising — it's staying reasonably warm for this time of year.

KK: Get some cold nights every so often. Were sports a big thing in Terrace?

KM: Not as far as I'm concerned, no. I suppose it is to some people but I'm not really into sports.

KK: Terrace — the town, the area — has it ever been sports inclined? Has it been a very popular thing for the people in general?

KM: Not from what I've seen, no. I think Kitimat is more sports-minded because it's primarily European heritage, I think, in Kitimat.

NS: You said you were more of a home person, but have you ever gone fishing or hiking around the area?

KM: I don't fish. I don't fish. I don't hunt. I don't like salmon, so I don't go and catch it.

KK: Was there any kind of traditions or celebrations, or any kind of a band events that Terrace used to have but doesn't anymore?

KM: Not that I can remember. No, I can't think of any that I'm aware of. There probably are some people that have been here longer than I have that might know.

KK: You said the forest industry has been very popular. So, you think there's any other kinds of work or jobs that people had that was popular other than forestry?

KM: The mill.

KK: The mills?

KM: Yup, that hurt badly. Of course, the decline in forestry led to that and that deleted a lot of good paying jobs in Terrace.

KK: So, the economy in Terrace just mostly revolved around that?

KM: Yup, pretty much in one way or another. Pretty much forestry-related.

414

NS: Do you have any stories that you can remember from your experience in Terrace so far, over the years? Besides there being no road.

KM: Yeah, the first time I made a trip up north from Terrace through my job — Highway 37 North hadn't been seal-coated and my first trip up there, I think was in May. It took me I think 14 or 15 hours from Terrace to Dease Lake. The road was nothing but mud, frost heaves and snow eight feet high on either side. That same year I went — on my way back, I went in to Stewart, and driving down the main street off Stewart was driving through a tunnel, literally. There was snow 30 feet high on either side of the road — so high it was curling over the top of the road. And trying to find places — I'm not familiar with the place, right, and I've got this list of buildings that I have to find. It was an adventure! You couldn't see anything. You're driving along and there might be a tunnel, but where it's going, what building it's going to, you have no idea.

Heavy snowfall in Stewart, B.C. Stewart Museum Collection.

KK: Gotta make some new maps!

KM: Yeah.

NS: Did Terrace ever have similar winters — compared to Stewart, or compared to up north?

KM: Yeah. I can remember one morning... I went in to work at eight o'clock, and it was three or four inches of snow on the ground when I got to work. About five o'clock that afternoon it was 36 inches of snow. It snowed super heavy all day! When I had to try and find my car, it was buried under mountains of snow, so I just said to my boss, "I'm gonna leave my car here and take a truck home."

NS: And where was that in town [BC Building Corporation]?

KM: That was located on — do you know where the convoy supply is?

KK: I don't.

KM: On Keith Avenue? Our office was just across the street from the mill.

NS: Oh, okay.

KM: Just this end of the mill.

NS: And is it still there?

KM: The building is still there, I don't know who is using it now but we moved from that building to that new building that's just on this end of the overpass — you see it off to the right.

NS: Oh, okay.

KM: From there BCBC [BC Building Corporation] ceased to exist.

NS: So it's...

KM: No more.

NS: No more anymore. Talking about your job again, how did your job frame your experience of Terrace? Did it help your view on Terrace or...?

KM: Yeah, it did. Yeah, it was a good job and it paid well. Certainly gave me an opportunity to see a lot of the north country.

KK: Since you've been, here have there been any kind of natural disasters, like floods?

KM: Earthquake.

KK: How bad?

KM: We all remember that!

NS: Yup.

KK: When was that?

KM: That was this year. You don't remember that one?

KK: Yeah, I remember that one. I was just wondering before, was there anything before that — floods or earthquakes?

NS: Floods or snowstorms or...

KM: It flooded — when was that, about four years ago. It flooded pretty good.

KK: Yeah, around that time; we were on the news. Has the Farmers' Market always been here?

KM: As long as I have, yup.

NS: And have you visited it over the years?

KM: Oh, yeah.

KK: Has it changed very much?

KM: Yeah it's changed considerably. When I first went there, it was a lot more of a farmers' market, now it's getting to be kind of a hobby show.

KK: Did lots of people farm or have little gardens or just grow food?

KM: I don't myself, but I guess there's a lot of people in and around Terrace that do.

NS: And when you first visited the Farmers' Market you mentioned that it was very — like an actual farming-oriented, and now it's more of a hobby thing. What kinds of things were there at the Farmers' Market to make it more farmer oriented?

416

KM: Fresh fish, fruit, vegetables; there's not much of that left anymore. More home-canning and home-baking than what it implies: "Farmers' Market."

NS: Over the years have you known many people that have farmed, or do you think there has been a decline in the farming around here?

KM: I haven't known anyone who had farmed any large scale. I've known a few people who've had small gardens, but not on a large scale.

KK: Has art been very strong in Terrace? Like have you noticed any kind of art?

KM: Yeah, I think so. Native art particularly is quite prominent.

KK: Have you ever been involved in politics in Terrace?

KM: Nope. Don't want to be— bad subject.

KK: When you were younger, did you know what you wanted to be or was there anything you hoped or expected to accomplish growing up?

KM: Didn't really know what I wanted to be but I knew all along I was mechanically inclined and I was gonna end up doing something like that. Something working with my hands.

NS: And how have you felt our community has been represented either provincially, or hopefully, or, on any level really?

KM: Pretty well, I think. All in all, I'd say it's represented pretty well. I'm not overly impressed with our city council but we do have a strong political representation in Terrace in Robin Austin [MLA for Skeena]. He's a pretty savvy guy.

NS: Yeah, overall good guy.

KK: When you were growing up, were there any childhood heroes you had, or anyone who inspired you?

NS: Yeah, I worked for a man many years ago when I first left school. I guess I was about sixteen at the time; didn't know what I was gonna do, just kind of bumming around. And he said, "Well, why don't you come and work for me, and I'll give you an apprenticeship and teach you the hardwood flooring business?" So okay, I'll give it a try. So I worked for him for, I guess, eight years. Hard work. He was an old Frenchman from Winnipeg.

KK: Do you remember his name?

KM: John Glouex. John Batiste Glouex was his name.

KK: For anyone who's moving to Terrace, or anyone who's just coming here, is there any kind of advice you'd give them or anything you want to tell them?

KM: I guess that depends on what kind of work somebody is intending to do. You kind of have to come here and fit in with what there is. You can't — I don't think you can be very inventive about what you are going to do. It's got to fit with the community and economics and — if it's here, come and do it. If it's not here don't try and bring it here. I think that's — maybe that's what's happened to a lot of the small businesses in town. They just didn't fit with the community and bailed.

NS: And what would you say for new people to expect when they come here? Like the pace of life or the weather compared to other places, you know?

KM: Take what you get, kind of. I mean we all complain about it, but we aren't gonna change it.

NS: That's for sure.

KK: Any other kind of stories you want to share?

KM: About Terrace?

KK and NS: Yup.

KM: Tell you a little interesting thing. When my wife and I were moving here, the company paid all our expenses, of course, to come here. Had two weeks to find a place to live. And at that time that Alcan expansion — Alcan-Completion was going on and we looked high and low in newspapers, radio ads, everywhere. There wasn't anything anywhere — in Terrace, or around Terrace — to rent, so we had to buy a place, and tell me about hectic! Two weeks I'm supposed to be here to buy, to go to work. So I was flying back and forth to Vancouver. Find a place here, now back down to Vancouver to arrange a mortgage, back to Terrace. What a headache, I tell ya. Finally got all this settled — we had to buy a place out in Copperhead Estates. That was as close to town as we could find anything that was reasonable. Thank God, they did pay all our expenses.

NS: For sure.

KM: Then we got this all arranged, bought the place, and the owner couldn't move out for two weeks. So, here we go — we stayed two weeks in the Bear Country Inn before we could get moved in there. Lots of fun.

NS: And was the Bear Country Inn located in the same spot as it is now?

KM: Exactly the same place.

NS: Has it changed over the years?

KM: No, I don't think so. It's pretty much as it was.

NS: And how was living in Copper Estates?

KM: It was interesting. I knew a lot of people out there. It was nice. When we got used to it, a lot quieter then where we had come from — Vancouver. We wanted to be a bit closer in to town, so we sold that and moved closer in.

NS: And where did you move in town, if you don't mind me asking?

KM: Lived over on Sande Avenue for quite a while.

NS: Oh, okay.

KM: Then this — reading the paper one day, and this place was advertised in the paper. Well, I think, *I'll go over and have a look and see*. I did. Got ahold of the guy that was selling it, and I said, "What are you asking for it?" "$7500," I said, "Okay, maybe do a deal here. I'll give you $7000." "Okay." Now when I first came in all I could see was out this window 'cause the guy that was selling it, he lived way out in the range and he said, "Well I'm not gonna come into town unless you're really interested. Go and have a look at the place." And I looked in here and all this furniture was in here and I phone him up and I said, "Yeah, I'm interested, but what's the story on all the furniture?" "It goes with the trailer." It sold.

NS: Got yourself a deal.

KM: Yeah, for sure.

KK: Nice furniture too, it's all in good condition.

KM: Yup, well it is. It was all brand-new when I bought it eight years ago. It was brand-new. I said, "That's fine," it sold. That three-piece sectional, La-Z-Boy chair, brand new queen-size bed.

NS: Wow, that must have been a real bargain.

KM: It was. The only drawback was, it needed a new roof bad. So I did that, and then I changed it from gas heat to electric. Best move I ever made.

KK: Save a lot of trouble in the winter.

KM: Saves a lot of trouble and it's a lot cheaper than gas. A whole lot cheaper.

KK: Bit more back on the personal stuff. Were there any popular dating sites in Terrace?

KM: I don't know, you're asking me? You guys should know!

KK: I wasn't alive back then!

KM: Well, you're a heck of a lot younger than I am.

KK: It was worth a shot.

KM: Seventy-five!

KK: Back when you were here, maybe places you and your wife went on a date.

KM: Usually to a restaurant, if we went out at all. We used to go to the Northern [Inn] quite often for dinner. Other than that, I don't think in the time I've been in Terrace, I've ever been inside a theatre.

KK: Never?

KM: No, I haven't. Not one for show — I'd sooner watch a movie at home.

NS: My mom's the same way.

KK: More comfortable.

KM: Well, it is.

KK: Have you noticed the theatre changed from the outside? Have you seen any differences in it?

KM: Not a bit.

KK: Not a bit?

KM: Not a particle. Same as it was 25 years ago.

NS: And one more thing about the Skeena Mall — I know a bunch of stores are getting into there now, but is it any different than it was back when you first came here?

KM: It was a lot busier when I first came here than it got to be. It's picking up again now, with the new stores, but what it desperately needs is some place to eat.

KK: Yeah, it took all those away.

KM: But it's coming back now, with the renovations and some new stores in there. But it's declined to the point where it might as well have been bulldozed. Surely dead.

KK: Has any First Nations Societies had a large impact on the community, like in Terrace?

KM: I think so, yeah.

KK: In what ways?

KM: Art, for one thing. The Nisga'a Treaty impacted Terrace considerably, I think. Economically, and being economically independent, I think put a lot of money into the community.

KK: Anything else you want to ask?

NS: I don't think so, I think we covered everything.

KK: All right, thanks Keith.

KM: Anytime buddy.

Marilyn Dahl Interview

Interviewed by Amy Bjorgaard and Ben McDaniel, 4 December 2013

Marilyn Dahl was born in Prince Rupert, in 1944. She was six years old when she moved to Terrace, then a town of 500 people. After graduating from Skeena School, Marilyn attended the School of Nursing at Jubilee Hospital in Victoria. There she met her husband Robert Dahl, and worked as a nurse for nine years until her mother became ill. They moved north to Terrace, where Marilyn worked at Terrace Interiors, a business started by her parents. Her husband worked at the Skeena Sawmill and Freightliner. In this interview, Marilyn Dahl describes the political representation of the Northwest region, recreational activities, and the economic development of Terrace. She describes what people did for fun in Terrace, from visits to Lakelse Lake to the Fall Fair and Strawberry Social in the former Odd Fellows Hall. Some of the notable events she describes include: the opening of Kitimat and the visit of Queen Elizabeth II.

AB: Where and when were you born?

MD: I was born in Prince Rupert on August 3, 1944.

AB: How old were you when you arrived in Terrace?

MD: Six years old.

AB: Tell me about growing up here.

MD: Well, I grew up in Terrace most of my life and we lived down on the 4800 block of Park. Terrace was a very small town when we moved here — approximately 500 people.

AB: What schools did you attend?

MD: I attended Riverside Elementary School and then Skeena School from grade seven to 12.

AB: Where was Riverside?

MD: It was down on School Street, approximately where the new curling rink is now.

BM: How many kids were in that school, approximately?

MD: I don't really have any idea. It went from grade one to grade six.

BM: Were there enough children for specific classes?

MD: No, we were all in separate classes and there was an annex part of the school that was another building out the back of the original Riverside School.

They were very good years and we did lots of sports in elementary school; we'd go outside and play ball. When we were in grade six we had five different teachers because the teachers would come and then leave. They had a hard time getting teachers here. Mrs. Clifford, who was my grade four teacher, I remember her really well — she was very nice. The schools were very cold in the wintertime; there wasn't much heat.

AB: Did you attend college or university at all?

MD: I went away to Victoria and attended Jubilee Hospital to do my nursing in their school of nursing. My training was for three years, and then I nursed for approximately nine years, until my mom got ill.

AB: Did you marry?

MD: Yes — I married in Victoria to my husband Robert Dahl.

AB: Did you have any children?

MD: Yes, I did. I had Teri my daughter and Ron, my son. Just the two.

AB: What was it like raising your family in Terrace?

MD: It was really good. There was lots for kids to do. We got the arena and the swimming pool when they were just two or three years old. There were a lot of sports they were involved in: baseball, softball, hockey, any kind of school activities that had sports.

BM: So, between when you grew up in Terrace and when you were raising children in Terrace, did you notice a large change of what was available for kids to do, as far as schools and activities went?

MD: Lots, because when I grew up we had no pool — we had a curling rink. There was a lot of high school curling in those days, which was right in this park over at the library, and it had three sheets of ice. A lot of kids curled in those days. It was a big sport.

AB: What other jobs did you work throughout your time in Terrace? You were a nurse.

MD: I worked at Terrace Interiors, which my mom and dad started 52 years ago and I sort of ended up there when my mom got ill.

BM: Was that the first store of its kind in Terrace?

MD: Yes, it was.

AB: How did your career frame your experiences in Terrace?

MD: My nursing — I really enjoyed and I worked in all areas of the hospital. I was involved in different things at the hospital and after that it was just normal activities.

AB: What did you do for fun? Did you go to any movies?

MD: Yes, we did. Every Friday night we went to the Tillicum Theatre. We did a lot of travelling around when the basketball team went to Rupert. Hazelton would come down here. You'd have pot luck dinners in school that we cooked. There was lots of after school activities like volleyball and basketball.

AB: Where did you hang out with your friends? Did you go on any dates?

MD: Well, there was a civic centre right here too. We had lots of — it was called Teen Town, and we had dances. Most of the kids would end up at our house. We had parties — we were always busy doing something.

BM: Do you think there is a large shift in behavior between teenagers when you were a teenager and teenagers when your own children were teenagers?

MD: I don't really think so — I think we did pretty much as many things as my kids did except for the extracurricular, like having the pool and hockey. We did a lot of outside skating up by the cabbage field in Dejong Crescent. We'd walk up there. The Horseshoe would always flood, and so you'd crawl over the barbed-wire fence and find a big puddle to skate on. We got to Lakelse Lake lots in those winters.

AB: What restaurants were popular over the years?

MD: Well, when I was really young there was the Travellers' Cafe on Lakelse and the Corner Snack Bar, right across from Tilden where we all hung out, and the old Terrace Hotel. We'd go there after school and have something to eat — a bunch of kids. Those were pretty much it.

AB: So did you visit the Lakelse Hot Springs?

MD: Yes, I worked there as a chambermaid and I also taught swimming lessons out there.

AB: How long did you work there as a chamber maid?

Gloria Williams and Rebecca Chasteauneuf (school peers of Marilyn Dahl) skating in front of Curling Rink in Little Park. 1957-59. Sundberg Collection.

MD: Probably when I was in grade 10, 11, 12. I'd work every summer up there. Well, we lived at the lake all summer. We'd just move out there and live out there, so most of the time I was walking from Johnstone's cabin. I'd take my boat up there — [with] Marilyn McLeod, she is now — and we'd walk to the hot springs, because she and I worked there together.

AB: What about fishing, do you have any memories about fishing?

MD: Yeah, we did lots of fishing. We used to go down the Lakelse River and fish — us teenagers and kids, a bunch of us would go down there. And we'd go down to what's now Fisherman's Park and fish. I'd walk along the railway bridge partly to Remo and do some fishing. Yeah, lots of fishing.

BM: Did very many other families spend the whole summer living at the lake?

MD: Yes, there was a lot of us lived out there in the summer so we had lots of — in those days we called them beach parties. Kids from Kitimat would come, so we might have 50 kids or more.

BM: Did the teenagers from Terrace and Kitimat fraternize together?

MD: Yeah, lots! And then we used to go to [Prince] Rupert for a week. We used to call them Easter holidays. We'd go there and they had a huge curling bonspiel. There was maybe sixty-some rinks and kids from the area and it was always lots of fun.

AB: What local events do you remember celebrating in Terrace?

MD: There used to be a Strawberry Social when I was really young in the old Odd Fellows Hall across from Urban Colour. You'd go there with the older people and the strawberries would fill a whole cup, they were so big! Everybody in town would go. And the Fall Fair was always a big thing in those days.

I think it was put on by the Board of Trade, just like the Chamber of Commerce, and everybody in town would go and hang out. Just eat strawberries and whipped cream that you got from the farms. They'd bring down really heavy cream and whip it up.

AB: Has the Fall Fair, or any of these events, changed over the years?

MD: I think they've pretty much remained the same — managed to keep it pretty good, the same.

AB: What do you remember of downtown Terrace?

MD: There was not a lot of stores — no malls or anything — but you always managed to find a good selection of whatever you were looking for and everybody was very friendly. Like Ev's Mens' Wear, you'd go in there. I remember going to the Co-op with my dad when they had bulk cookies and stuff, and you always got to have a cookie.

AB: Where did you do your clothes shopping or furniture shopping?

MD: It was Western Home Furnishings in those days — it's Totem Furniture now, I believe. Clothes shopping was where North Coast Anglers is. There was a clothing shop in there; can't remember what the name of it was. And there was Fern's Specialty Shop around Urban Colour.

AB: What did most of the people you knew do for work?

MD: Most of the people worked in stores or they were loggers or farmers.

AB: Where were the big farms located in Terrace?

MD: Some were down on Braun's Island. I remember going there to get corn from Miss Mitchell's farm. We'd take a big gunny sack and get a sack of corn up on the Bench, most of them were up there.

AB: And what role do you think forestry and logging have played throughout the history of Terrace?

MD: A huge part, because that's what built the town originally and that's what everybody worked at. Everybody could get a job, which was some ways good and some ways not, because a lot of the kids stayed here and worked in the bush. There were a lot of injuries in the bush in those days because it wasn't monitored as well.

AB: Did any of your friends or family work in sawmills or do logging?

MD: Yeah, my husband did. He worked for years at Skeena Sawmill and worked for Freightliner. Most of our friends did — worked in the bush.

AB: How have you watched the forestry industry change over the years?

MD: Well, it's pretty much gone now. Everything is exported, whereas before we had all the mills. There was lots and lots of little mills. There was Sande's sawmill, McGillis and Gibbs — lots of little mills — plus the big mills… like Skeena Cellulose was the big employer.

AB: How did the community of Terrace interact with Kitselas and Kitsumkalum?

MD: I don't know. In those days we were all in school together and they came from down at Kitsumkalum and Kitselas… more isolated in those days. I never remember going there, but we'd go down to Kitsumkalum lots and fish with the kids and stuff from down there.

AB How did the establishment of Kitimat in the 1950s impact Terrace?

MD: It was a big boon to the economy when Alcan came. My mom and dad went to Kitimat on the first train, and a bunch of the Terrace people went over, and they had a big party over there and came back. We used to go over there to the dentist and different things; once they put the road in we'd go over. They had very good shopping, and so people would go over there and shop in their nice stores.

AB How did the construction of the new bridge impact the community?

MD: I guess it made a lot of difference, but everybody managed with the old bridge. I remember the time they were re-decking it and we had to drive onto the railway bridge and go across the river and I would lay down in the back of the car when they did that. [Laughter.]

AB: Have you lived in Terrace during any major flood?

MD: Just the one in 1978 when it flooded. But not any other — like the 1936 one, I wasn't here.

AB: Did you have a garden?

MD: We did. My mom had a garden, quite a big one, for a few years.

AB: Did your neighbours have a garden as well?

MD: Our neighbours, where we live now, always had a garden.

AB: Have you ever been to the Farmers' Market?

MD: Oh yes, lots.

AB: How has it changed throughout the years?

MD: It's become bigger and different quality of stuff, I think — different products.

AB: Were you involved in politics in any way?

MD: No; my dad was. He was involved with the school board and different things like that.

AB: Can you expand with your father on the school board?

MD: He was the longest elected chairman of any school board in Canada at one time. He was on the school board for approximately, I believe, 24 years.

AB: How have you felt our community and region has been represented?

MD: By politics?

AB: Locally, regionally, provincially, nationally — how do you think it has been represented?

MD: I think it has been represented well over the years. We've had some very good people represent us and have got a lot of... it was Dudley Little, when he was Social Credit member [provincially], that got the new bridge. He also got the road into Kitimaat Village for the people. He was very good and he looked after — when he was in Parliament, he would take any of us who were students. I went a couple of times to the opening of the Parliament. He would take us and some of my friends and that was good.

AB: And more generally, how has Terrace changed over the years?

MD: It's become busier. It used to be a little place, where everybody knew each other and got together, and now it's changed that way. Now we've got a lot more businesses, bigger businesses, a mall and things like that.

AB: Do you remember the Queen's visit to Terrace?

MD: Yes, I do. I stood on the main street and I have a blurry picture of her. My mom had sort of got roped into helping with the Girl Guides and she was in the parade — I don't know what you call it. I guess, where you all stood up — and they walked along and my mom talked to the Duke of Edinburgh. He came over and talked to her and she just about fainted! But then, when the Queen went by down the main street, they just sort of sped, so you couldn't really see her very well.

AB: Looking back, when you were a child, what did you expect or hope to accomplish?

MD: I don't know, my mom just always told me whatever I did, I was leaving Terrace because I had to go to a bigger place, because I had to get a career of some kind.

AB: Was there any particular person or event that made an impact on your life?

MD: I don't really think there was one special one that I can think of.

BM: Would you say that your parents showed encouragement of a career? Was that uncharacteristic of that time, or did you see that as well in your peers?

MD: No, you saw it lots. Some kids stayed here, but a lot of us went away. I know one of the students — Robert Kerby, he was quite smart in school — he became a famous scientist and stuff. There were a lot — one of the Kirkaldys, who was a lot older than me, he was a famous scientist. There's quite a few people in Terrace that have gone — there was a lot of us in school that went away.

AB: As someone who has lived and learned here what would you want to share with people newly moving to Terrace?

MD: That it's a really good place to raise kids. I think the people here are very friendly. It's different than a lot of cities. You know if you go up town, people always talk to you, and you talk to them or at least they smile at you. Whereas, you walk up town in a city you never find that. It's good for kids.

AB: Do you have any advice for the present and future residents of the city?

MD: Just look after it the way it is and watch it grow, and hopefully it will grow into a good city.

AB/BM: Well, thank you.

Mario DaCosta Interview
Interviewed by Mercedes McNeil and Jaden Kluss, 23 November 2013

Mario DaCosta was born in Coimbra, Portugal in 1953. In this interview, Mario describes the forestry industry, the development of Kitimat, and the relationship between the Non-Indigenous and Indigenous communities of Terrace. His father came to Canada labouring on Quebec farms for $2.00/day. In the 1950s his family moved to Kitimat and lived in bunkhouses during the building of the Alcan aluminum smelter. Mario learned to operate heavy machinery at an early age, as his father was an entrepreneur in the logging business. Mario describes the town's activities, including the Dog 'n' Suds drive-in and the Fair setting up in George Little Park once a year. He recalls watching Bugs Bunny Hour on one of the town's first TVs. In the latter half of the interview, Mario describes the forestry industry as central to the development of the town. As a manufacturer of high value tonewood for guitars, he continues working in the forestry industry.

Mario DaCosta (left) and Mercedes McNeil, (interviewer and step-daughter to Mario, right). Photos provided by Inge DaCosta.

MM: Where and when were you born?

MD: I was born in Portugal in 1953, in a little house — my Grandma's house, actually. I was born at home in a place called Coimbra, Portugal.

JK: How did your family arrive in Terrace?

MD: My father was part of the first immigration process that came to Canada. He was on the first boatload, as they say. He, and I believe about a hundred other Portuguese, came over to work. They had a shortage of labourers in Quebec at the time, so they imported immigrants to work on those farms. And they were supposed to work there for two years, if they were allowed into Canada. I believe the rate was $2.00 a day for working on the farms.

MM: Tell me about growing up in your community.

MD: We grew up between here and Kitimat. Originally we had come to the north and we were living in Kitimat for the building of Alcan. So, we lived in the bunkhouses that they had down there; and they had these huge, almost army barrack bunkhouses when they were building the Alcan smelter. They imported all the Portuguese and the Italians and the Greeks out of Montreal and Toronto to come and work there. And so, my father was part of that first wave that came to Kitimat.

JK: Can you tell us about what schools you attended here?

MD: Yeah. I went to Cassie Hall [Elementary], Veritas Catholic school, and Caledonia [Secondary School].

MM: Do you have any memories of those schools that you would like to share?

MD: Well, Cassie Hall… not really. Veritas Catholic School was a little different. They believed in corporal punishment and I was tuned up a lot there, to say the least.

JK: What jobs did you work at in Terrace?

MD: Predominantly logging. My father was an entrepreneur in the logging business. And basically, I learned to operate heavy equipment at probably the age of 10 or 11. So, that's what I did.

MM: How did your career frame your experiences in Terrace?

MD: Well, mostly I left for a long time. But I always missed Terrace. I like the weather —I know that's crazy, but I kind of like the rain and the snow. And coming back, I wanted to take the knowledge I'd gathered out there in the world and put it to use in a way here to create employment for myself. In the logging industry, you had to use the latest technology to have a business — in a model of what amazon.com was doing, which was to sell widgets on the internet.

JK: What restaurants were popular over the years in Terrace?

MD: The Dog 'n' Suds and the A&W drive-in. That's basically… if you've seen those old fifties and sixties movies where you go to the drive-ins and, you know, people on roller skates and stuff? We had that all here. We had all the guys with their hot rod cars driving around. And on a Saturday night, we would go to the pool hall down there. Restaurants — there was a good little Chinese restaurant down there by the pool hall.

MM: Were you involved in any community activities outside of the home?

MD: Not really. 'Cause in those days, there was a lot of building houses and that kind of stuff. We had some property down on Molitor [Street], so basically we'd come home from school and we'd work on building our house or clearing land. And then, as I got older, I'd be out in the bush logging.

JK: What local events do you remember celebrating?

MD: Well, one of my favorites was when the fair came to town. George Little Park used to be where the fair grounds were. That was always fun and exciting. And it was a good time, it was neat.

MM: What do you remember about downtown Terrace?

MD: Downtown Terrace was rustic, to say the least. It was where the Co-op used to be — it's gone now obviously. There used to be a second-hand store there. I remember we got our first television set from there — I remember the TV station coming to town. I remember us all going over to the neighbour's house, who got one of the first TVs, and they had television from four o'clock to five o'clock. And they'd close their curtains and all the kids would lay down on the living room floor and watch TV for an hour. And they'd play the Bugs Bunny Hour. So, that was things I remember of the past.

JK: What did most people you knew do for work?

MD: Everybody was basically involved in logging or sawmills; it was all forestry-related. We were in the logging industry or the trucking business and so forth.

MM: So, given that, what role do you think forestry and logging played throughout the history of Terrace?

MD: Logging has a major part in the development of this community. Unfortunately, that's going by the wayside as we move more towards ecotourism and getting the natural resources out of the ground.

We're leaving forestry behind, in the sense that this area is extremely steep ground, which makes it expensive to log. And the wood is over mature, which means that we have a high volume of pulp. And since there are really no pulp mills closeby and 60 percent of your timber is pulp, it makes it very inefficient to log in the old ways. My Spruce Tonewood is the world's largest direct to the guitar builder company.

JK: How have you watched the forest industry change over the years in Terrace?

MD: Well, forestry, as I said, has deteriorated due to a lack of market. And in a sense, since we've gone electronic, we really don't have much demand for a pulp industry. We've lost both of our pulp mills — the one in Prince Rupert and the one in Kitimat. And not many people are buying newspapers. And without newspapers and newsprint, the high price that they used to pay for pulp just isn't there anymore. It's cheaper for them to send raw logs overseas and have workers in Indonesia make pulp, rather than do it here. Because here it will cost us about $500 a ton. There they can do it for $200 a ton and still export the logs there. What I do is manufacture high value tonewood. It's about specialty wood products.

MM: How did the community of Terrace interact with the Kitselas and Kitsumkalum?

MD: Well, I don't really remember very much about that except for the fact that we had a lot of Native youth in the area. A lot of my friends were Native. We didn't treat them any different than we'd treat anybody else, and they didn't treat us any different.

JK: How did the community interact with the police?

MD: With fear. [Laughs.] The police were always highly respected and feared. Because if they came looking for you, they were looking for you. And luckily, they were never looking for me because I never did anything — I was afraid of them. The police were respected in this area and really kept the community well-balanced — and kept the problems to a minimum.

MM: How did the establishment of Kitimat in the 1950s impact Terrace?

MD: Well, hugely. First of all, it brought in a large immigration population that would never have come to the area if it hadn't been for Kitimat. And with that, you saw a great diversity of cultures interacting and mingling. And the old pioneers, for instance, were pushed aside and the non-English speaking immigrants started to populate the area.

MM: How important do you think the First Nations culture has been in shaping our community?

MD: I think you have to reverse that question and ask how we shaped their community, in the sense that we brought our technology, our habits — good and bad — and we influenced their community. Here's an example. You know, we live by time. Time is very important, as you know, to Europeans. Everything is on time — "Do it in time." And the Native community has a different aspect of time. Yet we've imposed our system of time on them, which I think disturbs their sensibilities of heritage.

JK: Have you lived in Terrace during the major floods? How did the floods impact the community?

MD: Actually, I was working for Global TV on the one down there. Was it not Braun's Island? It was down off the Kalum River there.

I think the floods are an ongoing thing. If you're going to build in the flood zone you should be building on stilts — you're not going to hold the water up with sandbags, because when that river lets go, it lets go. And with the greater snowfall happening now, and faster melt, you're going to continue to see floods on a regular basis — and even more drastic floods than we've seen before.

MM: Did you garden or grow fruit? Did any of your neighbours, friends, or family?

MD: We gardened at Safeway. [Laughs.] No. We weren't really agrarian or agricultural. Portuguese are more predominantly fishers and explorers. We only garden if we have to — I hate to weed!

JK: Can you tell us how Terrace has changed over the years?

MD: Terrace has become more central to being the hub of the area. It's where people come to go shopping. It's where people interact with government. It's where people have higher education opportunities. It's the hub, or the center, or the spoke to all the outlying communities. So, Terrace has become that, which it originally wasn't. Prince George was always the hub. Now we've become the hub here in the northern point of British Columbia.

MM: Were there any annual community events that you remember?

MD: Summertime — we had summer and we had winter! Yeah, you know. We had the Santa Claus parade. That was always fun. I think we had May Day. Those sort of things.

JK: When you were a child, what did you expect or hope to accomplish?

MD: I expected and hoped to be able to do what I've done: have a good life, try to be honest and straightforward and truthful. And those are things that were instilled in me by my mother and by the school system.

MM: Was there a particular person or event that made an impact on your life?

MD: Particular person or event… Events I remember were the assassination of John Kennedy, Martin Luther King… and the Beatles on the Ed Sullivan Show. These are things that if you take into account — the Beatles on the Ed Sullivan Show — that was huge, because it completely changed the culture of Terrace. Because all of a sudden, all of us teenagers, you know, wanted to have bell-bottom pants and paisley shirts and high-heeled boots. And you know, the culture of what kids did also changed. You saw a lot of the beginning of drug use and so forth coming into the community at that time, due to that particular event.

JK: As a longtime resident of the Terrace area, what changes have you noticed?

MD: Well, we've remained extremely conservative, so there hasn't been a lot of change in that sense. Our political systems here are very conservative. Our city government is very conservative. You don't see, for instance, any casinos — like you see in Prince George and in Vancouver — coming into this area. Because the government won't allow it. The local governments won't allow it. And that's probably a good thing.

MM: As someone who's lived and learned here, what would you want to share with someone new to Terrace?

MD: It's rural. You can't always get what you want, but you'll always get what you need.

JK: Do you have any advice for the present and future residents of the city?

MD: Don't be afraid to work. Be creative. Think outside the box. And whatever you do, do it the best that you can, and it will pay you back.

'Na Aksa Gyilak'yoo Learning Centre

'Na Aksa Gyilak'yoo was another school that thought the project was a natural fit. Principal Colleen Austin, Natasha Obzera and the rest of the staff worked to build the interview process into their curriculum and to make the interviews a class project.

Once again, we took the interview training to the classroom. This time, the students ranged in age from as young as nine up to 16. They practiced doing interviews with each other and tried their hand at using the recording equipment. Most signed up to interview elders from their own families; others chose to talk to an elder they were interested in learning more about. Some worked in pairs and did the interviews as a team; others worked by themselves with support from teachers and family.

Again, there were a variety of outcomes from the project. We heard that it was especially meaningful that young people were involved in collecting stories from their own community and their own families. Although some students were very young, they took the project seriously. They saw the importance of asking, of listening, and of recording stories.

One family member shared how the project had been especially meaningful. Her mother/grandmother passed away after the project wrapped up. As the family prepared for the memorial, she referred to the oral history collected and recorded by the matriarch's teenage great-grandson in the eulogy. She said it was very special that the great grandson had been able to contribute in this way.

Staff and students of 'Na Aksa Gyilak'yoo School, 2013-2014. 'Na Aksa Gyilak'yoo School Collection.

Elaine Pigeau Interview

Interviewed by Estin Pigeau & Kenny Christiansen, 18 December 2013

Elaine Pigeau was born in Summerland in 1946, and moved to Yellowknife, NWT. Her father worked at the Con Goldmine [Consolidated Mining and Smelting Company of Canada], in Yellowknife. Among the colourful characters she describes in Yellowknife was a priest who would go into the pub on Saturday night and buy a round for the house if everyone agreed to come to church the next morning. She attended school in Grey Creek in the Kootenays, completing her high school years in Summerland. She later trained as a nurse and moved to Terrace with her husband in the 1980s. In this interview, Elaine describes her early life in BC, and the economic and social development of Terrace.

EP/KC: Where and when were you born?

EP: I was born in Summerland, BC in the Okanagan in 1946, but shortly thereafter moved to Yellowknife, Northwest Territories.

EP/KC: How did you, or your family, arrive in Terrace?

EP: We arrived here 35 years ago when my husband and I moved from Vancouver for his work.

EP/KC: Tell us about growing up.

EP: Well, when I was growing up, my younger years, were spent in Yellowknife. My dad worked at the Con Mine [Consolidated Mining and Smelting Company of Canada] which was a gold mine in Yellowknife. And we grew up on the edge of Slave Lake, which was a pretty exciting time. I remember some of the characters when I was growing up. We had a local doctor who used to bring his Saint Bernard with his whiskey keg to visit us. We had a priest, Father Gathy, who used to go into the pub on Saturday night and he would buy a round for the house if everyone agreed to come to church the next morning. And he was also a magician. I remember he used to pull coins out of my ears and out of my nose and things like that. So, it was pretty exciting.

EP/KC: What schools did you attend?

EP: I attended school in Grey Creek, which is in the Kootenays, until grade 10. And then we moved back to Summerland. I attended the rest of my high school years there.

EP/KC: Do you have any memories of school that you would like to share?

EP: Oh dear, yes. I remember one time the teacher went out of the classroom and we locked all the doors and hid in the cloak closet. And he was pounding on the door saying, "Let me in, let me in!" And we were all yelling, "Come on in Mr. Selby, come on in." And of course, he couldn't get in because the doors were locked.

EP/KC: Did you attend college or university?

EP: Yes.

EP/KC: Did you marry?

EP: Yes.

EP/KC: Did you have any children?

EP: Yes, I had one.

EP/KC: What was the child's name?

EP: Danielle Pigeau. And that's my grandson [points to Estin Pigeau].

EP/KC: What jobs did you work throughout your time in Terrace?

EP: Oh, my time in Terrace was spent full-time working at the hospital. I just received my 35-year award the other day.

Mills Memorial Hospital. McRae Collection.

EP/ KC: How did your career frame your experiences in Terrace?

EP: Well, I guess because of the nature of my work, I got to meet a lot of people in town and still know a lot of people in town. I remember somebody visiting me from Vancouver one time, and I was walking down the street and every person I passed said "Hello Elaine!" And they were like, "Well, do you know everyone in town?" "Almost!"

EP/KC: That sounds like something I would say. What did you do for fun?

EP: In Terrace? For fun we went to the lake. We socialized with friends, went golfing.

EP/KC: What restaurants were popular over the years?

EP: Dog 'n' Suds. Many, many years ago we used to go there on weekends and rolled down our window, and somebody would come out, come running outside and take our order and then they would come out and put our tray on the window. That was probably one of the most interesting restaurants.

EP/KC: Did you visit the Lakelse Hot Springs?

EP: No, we didn't visit the hot springs at all. We just went to the lake.

EP/KC: What about Lakelse Lake more generally?

EP: Lakelse Lake? Yes. We went swimming out there in the summer. We went camping, socialized with friends out at the lake.

EP/KC: Tell us about sports in Terrace.

EP: Sports in Terrace. I don't know a thing about sports in Terrace. I didn't have anything to do with sports in Terrace. Oh, that's not true — the hospital had a baseball team. We were called Mills' Staph, like the bug.

EP/KC: Were you involved in any other community activities outside the home?

EP: Not really that I can think of.

EP/KC: What local events do you remember celebrating?

EP: What local events do I remember celebrating? Gosh. Riverboat Days, I guess. And I can't remember anything else. I was always working.

EP/KC: What do you remember about downtown Terrace?

EP: Downtown Terrace was a lot smaller than it is now, and the stores were a lot different. I remember there was a magazine store on Main Street called the Hub. And they used to sell all kinds of books and magazines, and all kinds of funny little toys and things like that. It was a great place to go.

EP/KC: Did you ever purchase anything?

EP: Oh, always.

EP/KC: What did most people that you know do for work?

EP: Well, most people that I know worked either in the logging industry, the fishing industry, or health care.

EP/KC: Sounds like pretty big jobs.

EP: They were big jobs. Fishing, when we first moved here — in Prince Rupert, fishing was the main work. And the fishermen then — there was lots of fish, so the fishermen used to make a lot of money. I can remember going to a hotel in Prince Rupert one time after the boats had come in, and the fishermen had the bathtub full of crab.

EP/KC: So fishing was the biggest in the community?

EP: Fishing and logging.

EP/KC: What role do you think forestry and logging played throughout the history of Terrace?

EP: Huge, huge. I can remember seeing the logging trucks coming with huge logs on them. Just absolutely huge. I mean, the logs today look like little toothpicks compared to the logs back then.

EP/KC: Were there any accidents that you heard of while logging?

EP: Oh, there were all kinds of accidents. I remember quite a few people that I knew that worked out in the bush that were killed out in the bush.

EP/KC: Tragic. Prayers go out to the families… How have you watched the forest industry change over the years?

EP: Well, like I say, forestry is much less now. Fallen off through the years. The sawmill was shut down for long periods of time. And, like I said, the logs were much larger in the old days. They were much more plentiful.

EP/KC: So, just basically saying there's not many big trees left anymore?

EP: Well, I imagine there's some out there. But, I mean, there's certain restrictions on logging today because of the future of the industry — it is much more regulated today.

EP/KC: How did the community of Terrace interact with Kitselas and Kitsumkalum?

EP: Good question. I don't really know. Because I don't know that there was a lot of interaction back then. I can't really think of anything.

EP/KC: More generally, how has Terrace changed over the years?

EP: Terrace has changed over the years in the fact that it's gotten much larger. In the fact that we are kind of like a satellite community with many communities around us that we interact with and we serve. I think that the relationship with the other communities has grown over the years.

EP/KC: Were there any annual community events that you remember? What were these like?

EP: All I can think of is Riverboat Days. You know, there weren't as many events back then as there are now.

EP/KC: Do you remember the Queen's visit to Terrace?

EP: No. As a matter of fact, I don't remember the Queen's visit to Terrace — I was probably working!

EP/KC: It's such a small town. Looking back, when you were a child, what did you expect or hope to accomplish?

EP: When I was a child, what did I expect to accomplish? It's really funny because we lived way out in the boonies. We basically didn't have a lot of social things happening. So I think, basically, it was just to finish school and just to find out what was out there; just traveling.

EP/KC: That's pretty cool. As a longtime resident of Terrace, what changes have you noticed?

EP: The growth in the community; the public spirit has grown greater over the years.

EP/KC: What would you want to share with someone newly moving to Terrace?

EP: That it's a great town. That it's a friendly town. It's easy to make new friends. The shopping is improving somewhat. And it's a good place to raise kids.

Harvey Wing Interview

Interviewed by Toni Wing, 18 December 2013

Harvey was born in Port Essington, in 1941, the second youngest of seven children. His father was from Canton (Guangzhou), China and his mother was from the Kitselas First Nation. The family moved to Port Edward in 1951. His father owned a lighting plant that provided power to the local school and a store where he sold gas and stove oil. He packed fish and worked other jobs to support the family. Harvey attended various schools in Port Edward, Port Essington and Prince Rupert, finally deciding to work after completing grade eight. He moved up to Terrace in the early 1990s, after the Kitselas Band reissued his status, and worked at Muks-kum-ol Housing in janitorial services. In the latter half of the interview, Harvey responds to questions about life in Terrace, from the impact of flooding, to the changes he's noticed in the town over time.

TW: Where and when were you born?

HW: Port Essington, British Columbia, 1941, March 18.

TW: Tell me about your parents.

HW: My dad was from Canton, China. He came to Canada — I don't know what year it was, but he met my mother, they married, and I don't know what happened. They had a problem and they split, and we moved to Port Edward in 1951. My mother was down in Vancouver. She moved back in, I don't know, 1989 or somewhere around there. My dad was in the hospital for a few years, and I can't remember the year that he left us. There were seven of us in the family; I was the second youngest.

TW: What was your relationship like with your siblings?

HW: Oh, well we grew up and lived together in Port Edward while we were going to school. And when they got a job and got married they all moved in to [Prince] Rupert. My oldest sister — I think she didn't go to school very much, and I don't know where she ended up. But she's down in the Interior now somewhere and she had a very big family. She married Dougie Wesley. My oldest brother — he's deceased now — he was married. He had a house fire in Rupert where he lost three kids. And my second oldest sister, I guess, had a daughter in New York and she's married to a fella from there. My youngest sister, her husband is deceased and he was a fisherman as well.

TW: Describe a typical day in your household during your childhood.

HW: Well, there wasn't really that much. My dad was out working, and he had two other fellas looking after us to make sure we had breakfast and lunch. We had to go to bed at a certain time and we were up early to have breakfast and we did go to school in Port Essington. My dad had a lighting plant that gave the school power. He owned a store — he had pool tables in there and also sold a little bit of gas, oil, stove oil. And everybody seemed to get along really good when I was young — no trouble.

TW: Growing up, what kinds of expectations were there for boys?

HW: At that time, there was nothing but fishing. When we lived in Port Essington, that's all there was. My oldest brother, I guess he moved to Rupert and went to school there, and then I'm not too sure if he went down to Vancouver for school, but he was down there a few years. I'm not too sure, two of my sisters went to Chinese school, but how they did or anything else I don't know.

TW: What did your parents do for work?

TW: My dad was a storeowner, a fish packer, and I guess he used to boom logs. When the booms broke he used to go out to look for logs to tow back in. He did a lot of things to try to make a few dollars; raise us kids.

HW: Tell me about growing.

TW: Well, in Port Essington, where I grew up, and Port Ed [Port Edward], all we did was run around. We never stayed home. There was no TV, only radio. And all we did was run around all the time — we got a lot of exercise! In the summer, we had to go and help my dad collect fish. So, we were on a camp that the company gave to my dad to use. I had a very good young life, I thought.

TW: What schools did you attend?

View overlooking Port Essington, circa 1926. Port P351.2, photographer unknown.
City of Vancouver Archives.

HW: Well, I only got grade eight education. I attended two or three schools in Port Essington, two in Port Ed and three in Rupert: Conrad, King Edward, and Booth. So I almost went to a school for every grade that I grew up.

TW: Do you have any memories of school that you would like to share?

HW: Nope, because I was always in trouble I guess.

Unknown Voice: Why were you always in trouble?

HW: I don't know; I guess it was the way I looked. The teachers were picking on me. Whenever they asked a question and I answered, and if it was the wrong answer, they didn't like it.

TW: Did you attend college or university at all?

HW: Nope. Like I said, I only got grade eight education. I only went to grade nine at Booth and I wasn't learning anything and me and the teachers were having nothing but trouble, so I just walked

438

out. It was easier for me to go to work than stay in school and learn. And at that time, that's what most of the kids did, helped their family.

Harvey at home in Port Edward. 1961. Faith and Harvey Wing Collection.

TW: Did you marry? If so, tell me about your wedding. How did you meet your spouse?

HW: Well, I just seen her in a café and she looked real cute. So I went to go with her and have been with her ever since. All of my kids, they all graduated — I can say that much. All of my kids have graduated and hopefully the grandkids are going to now.

TW: How did you find Terrace as a place to raise a family?

HW: Well, I got my status back and the band phoned me and asked — they wanted me to move up. They would build a house [for me]; so I agreed and now I'm up here.

TW: Why did you lose your status?

HW: Well, through the government. They took the status away from women when they married a non-Indian person, such as my dad who was Chinese. So she lost her status. And by her losing her status, I didn't have one.

TW: What was there to do with children in Terrace?

HW: Well, on the weekend I only took them out to the lake to go swimming. The wintertime, they went to the complex up here to go skating or swimming in the swimming pool. Otherwise, they were just wild.

TW: What jobs did you work throughout your time in Terrace?

HW: In Terrace all I did was work for Muks-kum-ol [Housing Society], where my daughter was working. I worked there for a couple of years and then that was it. Janitorial work mostly.

TW: How did your career affect the way you saw Terrace?

HW: When I got here? I guess I moved here in 1991 or '92, and I've been here ever since. The house is paid for. And I'm still here, also living on the Reserve and my oldest daughter is down in Rupert — a hairdresser. The second oldest is in Terrace here working at the Bank of Nova Scotia; the third is here working at the Kitselas Band Council. She's worked a few other places but I don't know the names of the places.

TW: What did you do for fun?

HW: Well, for me, there wasn't very much to do. I used to go and help anybody that I could, go hunting, fishing when I was younger — and party most of the time with everybody else!

TW: Where did you go to see movies?

HW: Oh, I used to go to movies when I was down in Port Ed. But they started getting so expensive, and you couldn't even really hear what was going on, because the people that also went to watch made nothing but noise and I didn't enjoy it, so I didn't go anymore.

TW: Where did you go for dates?

HW: Mostly in the bar.

TW: What restaurants were popular over the years?

HW: Well, in Rupert it was the Galaxy or Imperial; West-End and when we got to Terrace I guess — the first few years it was Tim Horton's. And then the Sandman Inn, but most of the time now we just cook at home.

TW: Did you visit the Lakelse Hot Springs?

HW: Yes, my kids would like to go out there all the time, and I took them there usually on the weekends. I didn't go in myself, but we just sat in the waiting room or the bar part while we were waiting for the kids.

TW: Can you tell us about the Lakelse Hot Springs?

HW: Oh, we used to go out there one or two o'clock and stay there till four-thirty, five o'clock. Most of them just used to go on the slide and they'd swim, and when they got tired or the time was up they all came out and we came back home. Either stopped off at one of the drive-ins, or pick up chicken or burgers or whatever.

TW: What about Lakelse Lake, more generally?

HW: That, I don't know.

TW: Tell me about sports in Terrace.

HW: Sports? Well, my grandkids were into soccer and basketball. I didn't watch them play basketball very much, but used to go watch them play soccer; whenever the weather was good. I wouldn't go and watch them if it was raining.

TW: Did you ever play any sports?

HW: I played basketball when I was younger and still going to school in Port Ed, but that was it.

TW: What about fishing?

HW: Fishing — I did that most of my life and I worked with my dad packing fish. Then I started gill netting. After gill netting, I did some shrimp fishing with another person, crab fishing for a couple of days; taking somebody's place, halibut fishing, herring. I've been doing that for a few years, worked on the rolling kelp pond, herring pond. Yup, until I was retired.

TW: Were you involved in any other community activities outside the home? Like clubs or organizations?

HW: Well, I used to belong to a bowling club in Rupert when we were there. But when we moved up here to Terrace, I didn't go bowling or anything. Nope, I usually just hunt with my grandkids on the weekends in the fall.

TW: Did you attend any religious services?

HW: Only when a person was deceased or a marriage, and that was all.

TW: What local events do you remember celebrating? Have they changed over the years or remained the same?

HW: Well, there was just the parades we go to in Terrace here — Riverboat Days — and if the weather is good we go down to Rupert to watch Seafest and get involved with them down there.

TW: What do you remember about downtown Terrace?

HW: It's changed quite a bit since we moved here in 1991-92. The mall is expanded, and a few of the drive-ins have changed spots and got a little bigger. The schools have changed quite a bit. There used to be four or five of them right around Terrace, now I think there's only four or three.

TW: Where did you buy food?

HW: Usually Safeway or Save-on [Foods], [Real] Canadian Superstore.

TW: Where did you shop for clothes or furniture?

HW: That part I don't do nothing about; the wife does everything.

TW: Did you shop at the Terrace Co-op?

HW: Yes, I did. I used to go in there and I had an uncle that used to — I had to drive up there every Saturday almost to get his haircut! And he'd go up there and meet a few of his friends and then I'd pick him up again later on that night; and that was it. I didn't really shop too much for anything.

TW: What did most people that you knew do for work?

HW: Well, up in Terrace here, most of them were loggers. When I was down in Port Ed and Rupert, they were all fishermen. For a few years I was with my brother-in-law abalone diving, when they still had licenses out for it. And working in Port Ed with Jack. I helped build boats with him.

TW: Did you have any friends or family who were farmers?

HW: Not that I know of.

TW: What role do you think forestry and logging played throughout the history of Terrace?

HW: Well, at one time it was the biggest industry in town, but I don't know what happened. The market wasn't buying the wood anymore and forestry went down. They used to have a big mill here, but that disappeared and now they have a small one — but it's not that great for logging anymore either.

TW: How have you watched the forest industry change over the years?

HW: Well, like I said, I was only in fishing, so I didn't really worry about forestry or anything else.

TW: How did the community of Terrace interact with Kitselas and Kitsumkalum?

HW: Well, they're both Tsimshian and they both belong to the territory here. How they moved here I don't know. But I know they're supposed to be like brothers between the two villages anyways.

TW: How did the establishment of Kitimat in the 1950s impact Terrace?

HW: Well, they had quite a bit of workers from Terrace here working on the [pulp] mill when the mill got started. They had workers that I know of from Rupert and Port Ed. They used to come up Sunday night on the train. I think they called it the Skunk because at that time diesel fuel just came in and it smoked so much, it smelt awful every time it went by. So they called it the Skunk.

TW: How did the construction of the new bridge impact the community?

HW: That's this one over here? Well, it got them a few dollars selling rocks to CN [Canadian National Railway]. CN was the one that put the bridge in so they can take their train cars in and load them up and then take them back out. And it's supposed to be the best rock there is in BC; the hardest rock in BC.

Faith and Harvey Wing. Faith and Harvey Wing Collection.

TW: Have you lived in Terrace during any major floods?

HW: Well, they weren't big floods. There were floods that were supposed to happen back in — well, that last one was in 2007. Yes, we helped sandbag for a place down at Zymacord, Clifford Bolton's place. We sandbagged all around there and when we finished there it wasn't very much left to do.

TW: How did flooding impact the community?

HW: Well, it made everybody get together and stock up on a little bit of grub, and I guess they were all prepared to drive up the hill or wherever. But it didn't really affect us that much here — it was up, but not enough to really have people evacuated.

TW: When you were a child what did you expect or hope to accomplish?

HW: Well, at that time, I didn't have any ambition but to play around and try to go to school. But like I said, me and the teachers didn't get along, and I left school and worked and that's all I did for the rest of my life.

TW: Was there any particular person or event that made an impact on your life?

HW: Nope. I just seen people and if I had a hand, knowledge to help them, I did. Otherwise, I just did what I was supposed to do; run around and be wild like you kids are nowadays!

TW: As a long-time resident of the Terrace area, what changes have you noticed?

HW: Well, the highway itself, the tracks CN has fixed to get more transportation through from the new port in Rupert. The highways because of all the trucks going back and forth, they had repaired it and the sawmill started up again; so that's helped a bit.

TW: What would you want to share with people newly moving to Terrace?

HW: I don't know. There's not very much for anybody to do nowadays. Unless they got an education and that's what I've been telling my kids, grandkids, "Go to school; learn." But they were just like me when I was young — they wouldn't listen!

TW: Do you have any advice for the present and future residents of the city?

HW: The mayor in Terrace right now seems to be doing a very good job. And the Band Council and the Band Manager down here on the Reserve; they're also doing a really good job. So I'm too old to do anything right now but sit back and watch. To me, they are doing a very good job.

Mildred Roberts Interview

Interviewed by Tracy Sam, 26 November 2013

Mildred Roberts was born in Port Essington, in 1931. Mildred's parents, James and Selina Bolton, were originally from Kitsumkalum. Though Mildred grew up in Port Essington, she remembers her family seasonally migrating to other locations for fishing and hunting resources. Her family would begin the new year (January) in Baker's Inlet, where Mildred's father had a logging claim and a trapline. Baker's Inlet provided an abundance food, including mussels, sea cucumbers, clams, spring salmon, and crab. The family would also hunt for deer, mink, squirrels, marten, seal, and weasels. If Baker's Inlet froze, they would move to Merrik Island for halibut and seal. Otherwise, come April, the family would travel to Arthur Island for the halibut run in May. Arthur Island also provided them the opportunity to gather herring eggs and seaweed, which they would trade for soapberries and blueberries with the Gitxsan people. From there, they would return to Port Essington to gillnet and work in the canneries. Mildred recalls working at the cannery from the age of 12 to 19. In the fall, they would travel to their final camp in Ecstall to dry coho and hunt mountain goat, porcupine, and bear. In this interview, Mildred discusses her move to Terrace in 1963, the Port Essington canneries, Japanese internment camps, and her childhood travelling to seasonal hunting and fishing grounds. She also shares stories about hunting, food preparation, and exploding seal meat.

TS: So, Grandma, can you tell me about where and when you were born?

MR: I was born in Port Essington, August 20, 1931 — Spokeshute.

TS: Can you tell me about your parents?

MR: My parents were James and Selina Bolton. And they were from here, Kitsumkalum.

TS: How did you and your family arrive in Terrace?

MR: We moved up here on August 22, 1963. We came up by train. Oh, no, we didn't — the first time when we came up to visit, we came up by train.

TS: And how was the train then?

MR: It was good; they dropped us off right down the road here.

TS: Really?

MR: Yup.

TS: You came up with all your kids.

MR: Yup.

TS: How did they like the train?

MR: They liked it, they were excited about it, and they were going to a city — a big city they never heard of.

TS: So in 1963, my mom was four.

MR: She was just turning four — she was three — in October, she turned four. Richard just turned six.

TS: Wow, that's cool.

MR: Stella was nine, Steve was 10, and Don was 11. And I just turned 32, two days before that.

TS: I'm almost 32. Wow. And, so you said that it was the first time the kids had come to the big city. Did you guys pack up everything when you moved here?

Mildred Roberts. Roberts family collection.

MR: Not the first trip. The first trip we made, we just looked over the place. Grandpa came up, before that, and started working on the house. This house came from Kitimat. And it was a duplex. There were two.

TS: Oh, really? So, where's the other side?

MR: That side's one unit, and this side's one unit, and they had to open this up, but it was cut in three pieces to move them here.

TR: Wow, and where did the houses come from?

MR: Kitimat City.

TS: Oh, really? How did that work out?

MR: They built the houses there when they first started — little motels, like little cabins. And then, I guess, they were selling them out by '62 and Benny stepped in. He was a councillor. He started working on it and got Kalum to purchase the houses. The cabins, there were 12. So 24 in all, because these places are two. Except the bigger ones: Benny's, Stanley's, Winnie's. And there was another one that was just one big house.

TS: Really? So at the time when they brought the houses, was this the only road into Kalum — with the 12 houses?

MR: They just put this road in — this used to be a logging road. There was a lot of logging going on here in Kalum and down by the ball field. There were two cabins on that side and one on this side; that was the contractor's little cabin. And Winnie and them moved into one and Stanley and Sara moved into the other.

TS: So, was Victor already here, too?

MR: No, the Spaldings were here, but they lived uptown. And Clifford and them were here, too, but they lived uptown. That was it. The next house that went up was Clifford's. He worked on it — they moved it in, and they started working on it. Then the Spaldings, because they were renting uptown. And Benny and them were up here, but they had that little house — that's at the back of his house there, and then they moved Benny's house in. That's all the houses there were when we came up. And they started bringing them in and putting them together. They put two cabins together for each household.

TS: How was that?

MR: There were four little motels in each row, and ours and Harold's were together. And then they split that in half, and Harold got two units and we got two units. They brought in another one that Alec and my dad had — theirs was together.

TS: That's hard to imagine.

MR: The people were really working. It's the women that were doing the carpentry before we moved up.

TS: What were the men doing?

MR: They were working on some of them, and some of them were logging and working uptown.

TS: I know my dad worked for Free Lake. What kind of logging companies were around then?

MR: Free Lake. It was mostly Columbia Cel [Columbia Cellulose Company Ltd.] — Columbia Cel, that came in first. And they took over all the logging licenses. So, people had to work for Columbia Cel — all the logging, they had contractors. But Haugland's was one of the ones going when we moved up here. It was going when my boys started working.

TS: So that was Don and Steve?

MD: Richard, and your dad, and Ernie.

TS: Okay, that rings a bell.

MR: The boys from here — Jeffery, George, Stanley, and Joey — were working with Columbia Cel.

TS: So that was in the '60s then '70s then?

MR: 1963, when we moved in and when we did make the big move — our final move when we came up — we had nothing in the house. We left everything in [Port] Essington, because we'd be going down in the summertime. So the only money we had — Grandpa ordered all the furniture, fridge, stove, washing machine, TV, two bedroom suites and bunk beds and beds for the boys. And we already had chesterfields and the tables. But it was good to have a washing machine.

TS: You didn't have a washing machine before?

MR: I had that gas-powered one. But we had to pack water. Here we had running water. We had an indoor toilet.

TS: How was it, coming into something like that where you did have the running water and indoor toilets?

MR: It was good. There was a lot of dust, because they did a lot of work on the yards. And big tractors were running back and forth and they were working on the other houses, so it was quite dusty. That first day we were here, we slept on the floor. We did have the blankets but we had no beds. So we just slept on the floor, but it was so warm. It was so hot. It was nice in Port Essington — it was cool. And then we moved up here and it was hot, really hot — couldn't stand the heat almost.

TS: Oh, that's so interesting. I kind of knew a little about that. So, how much do you think Grandpa spent on all the furniture then?

MR: I don't know how much he spent, but he cleaned out our little bank account. And then he was so sick that he couldn't go to work, and we were broke, and he was depending on his fishing catch that summer. That's why he wasn't worried. But there was a big loss; strikes. So there was no money, but the company was good enough to give him an advance. So we were able to move on that. And we found that going to the stores here was so good. We could buy a 25-pound bag of flour for 99 cents. Yeah, 99 cents.

TS: Wow! And what was it when you used to shop in Prince Rupert?

MR: About five dollars.

TS: Really? Wow!

MR: Well, we shopped in — we got what we could in Prince Rupert at the end of fishing, and we would blow all the money, most of the money he made, on grub for the winter. He did a lot of hunting, so we survived on that.

TS: Wow. So did he have a trapline or a hunting spot around the area?

MR: His trapline is up at Kwinitsa, across from Kwinitsa [Feeks Creek].

TS: Oh, I've heard Don talk about that. Is that where Don built the cabin?

MR: Yeah. So his trapline was there, but he went fishing in the summertime. That summer was bad for a strike. A strike lasted all summer. Usually, it lasts just as soon as the fish hits — the company gives in — but this time they didn't.

TS: What were they striking over — the prices?

MR: For prices. And at first we didn't want to move. But Benny and them came down and they said there'll always be jobs here. There's gonna be jobs for quite a while. And there were jobs but Grandpa really couldn't work because from packing all the stuff and moving, his back was so bad that he'd be just laid up as soon as we got up here. He could hardly move just sitting down. Then he had a hard time getting up; then he'd go into muscle spasms. That was from his vertebrae trouble. And my stomach was really bad with ulcers. So Grandpa didn't really want to leave Essington; I didn't either. I was giving the kids correspondence. Then they asked my dad what he'd do. Then my dad said, "I'll be here as long as Don's here. If Don's gonna stay for the winter, then I'll stay. And if Don moves, then I'll have to move too." And my dad's health wasn't very good; he was getting weaker. So Don decided that maybe we should move, so he'd move, too. We have the house down there so we can go back and forth.

TS: So did he move?

MR: Yup.

TS: Where did he stay?

MR: They stayed with us for a couple of weeks. They stayed behind in Essington for a while; they were the last to leave. Finally they got the food they wanted, and dried some coho and got some fish, and they moved. Laura and Shirley stayed with us here.

TS: How old were they?

MR: They were going to high school. And Bob stayed by Alec's, by Clifford's.

TS: He was still a lot younger?

MR: If Don was 11, Bob was 13. He's two years older than Don. Shirley was 4 when we got married. Bob was two. So how much older is Shirley than Bob?

TR: Two years? So, she would have been 15?

MR: Laura was 17.

TS: Wow! It's hard to imagine them as teenagers.

MR: They stayed here for a while. They shared Stella's room with Stella, and Bob stayed with Clifford.

TS: Where did Clifford live?

MR: Where Billy and them are. That was his house. And then after my dad moved up, their house wasn't ready, so they stayed here for two weeks.

TS: All right. I know we just talked a little bit about some of your siblings. It sounds like you and your siblings were pretty close in helping each other out the whole time. So where did — where was Irene?

MR: Irene and them were in Port Edward. They bought a house in Port Edward.

TS: Okay.

MR: They already moved away after the fire — after the fire in Essington. Anybody that was planning on moving back to Essington already moved away.

TS: Really? Wow!

MR: Serena moved out after that.

TS: Okay. During a typical day in your household, what types of things would happen in your house? I guess in Essington or here.

MR: In Essington, there was a lot of work. We had to pack water in, but it wasn't really that much then, when we moved down to the other house. We lived in the company house for a while. Grandpa and them's house burned down — not all the way down, but they left it. So they moved into one of the company houses that the Japanese had. And the Japanese were shipped out during the war. They sent them to a camp. And then people moved into the cabins. People came from the canneries and they moved in. So that was good; we had more people living in Essington.

TS: That's good. So, how many people lived in Essington at its biggest?

MR: At its biggest, in my time, it was maybe about 200. But it was bigger than that before my time. There were the canneries and then the companies put up cabins, and people came in to work in the canneries from up the line — up Gitxsan area, Nisga'a people from all over. Some would just stay there; the Lockerbys stayed, and the Browns stayed. There were some from Kitselas that used to move down there and after the cannery was over, they quit. 1936 was the last time the cannery operated. And that was the last cannery. There were three canneries in Essington.

TS: Which ones were those?

MR: Skeena Commercial, Cunningham's, and another one that turned to B.A. [British-American Cannery] after. So that was the only one that was going then, that I remember. Like I was really young, but I remember we did live in a company house right up the hill from where our house is in Essington. We saw the workers coming in from the cannery. And the great big store, Kamida's store, right close by, that was the best part. The next year we moved down — my dad was building a house which was never finished, and we moved into the kitchen part.

TS: Just the kitchen?

MR: Just the kitchen part we lived in. We left all our stuff in the other room, which was supposed to be a dining room/living room and a bedroom and upstairs, but he was too busy logging and trapping that we never lived in Essington. We lived out there year-round. We'd go from one camp to another. Like in the fall, we'd go up to Ecstall [River] to dry coho. That's our fall camp.

TS: How would you dry it?

MR: We smoke it in the smoke-house and when they're half-dry they take them in and dry them in the house. To live in a house that smells fishy all the time — but it was a nice smell. And then they dry them. When they're dry they take them down and pack them up and make room for more. So we lived in Ecstall until almost Christmas sometimes.

TS: Really?

MR: It all depends on the weather, you know, when it freezes. As soon as it starts freeze then we roll up our beds and off we go.

TS: Oh really? And where would you go?

MR: Back to Essington. We would drop into the school for a little bit and we're always allowed to take part in the Christmas concert, even just stand there and sing.

TS: So, how many kids were at the school?

MR: There were a quite a few, maybe about 20.

TS: There was that one that was going around with all the names on the bottom. Is that one of the Essington school students?

MR: That was the public school. That other one was the Indian day school. That's where I went. There was the public school — that was where the white kids went. And the Indian day school on the reserve that only the Indians could go to. That's where I started school. But I didn't go very far, because we were camping all the time. Sometimes my dad would leave us behind to go to school, but it never worked out: we were never happy, we were never happy to stay behind. So we'd go, pack up and move. Everybody got their own box of clothing.

TS: So, when you were staying in the Ecstall camp until Christmas, did you guys also get clams and cockles?

MR: Not up Ecstall. You don't get clams up there. That's freshwater. You only get fish, and we'd get mountain goat, and bear, and porcupine. My grandmother clubbed a porcupine one time and they built a great big fire and the guys, they threw it right on the fire, and they scraped the quills and the fur off. They burnt it off, and chopped it up, and they had a big fire outside with a big pot hanging over the fire — put the meat out there, and cooked the meat outside. There was a picnic table and we sat around there and ate the porcupine.

TS: What does it taste like?

MR: Like porcupine. But you can taste — you know if you burn something? Like you burn the feathers, and the fur, and the quills on it — then it's got a different taste. You burn the skin, but I can't describe how it tastes. But if you skin it, they say it's almost like chicken. But we never skinned it. They burn it.

TS: That's probably the easiest way,

MR: Well, that's the old way.

TS: So, did you guys trade any of your hunting stuff for anything you prepared for other goods?

MR: Not fish, 'cause there was nothing to trade with around then — around there. There weren't many people there, and my grandparents moved. My dad's whole family — there were two cabins there in Ecstall and a great big smokehouse and they got their fish. My grandma had one half of the smokehouse and my mom had half.

TS: So then, you were little when you started learning that? How young were you, or did you just do it your whole life?

MR: I did it my whole life. Like my dad said, I was just a baby. See, I was born in August. We usually moved around the end of August. So I was just a wee baby when I moved up Ecstall. If you ask me where I was before I was a month old I'd tell you, "hanging under a tree." Ecstall, my dad said. I'm hanging there — the flies biting me up, I guess, when they were building the cabin.

TS: And so, you had your older siblings?

MR: Yeah. There's Rena and Harold that was older than me then. And then after a while, there's Billy Clifford and I don't think I would ever make it to Ecstall. We quit moving to Ecstall then.

TS: What year was that around?

MR: Alec was born 1942. I can't remember Alec being up Ecstall. Maybe he was, because we did move up there — I think 1944 when we really quit moving up there. We came up here, went up to Lakelse Lake. We lived up there for two weeks and mom dried some coho and made some üüsk — that's the stinky eggs. We came down with a bunch of half-smoked fish and passed it around and caught the train — went up to Kitselas and brought some up there to Mel Bevan's mother and grandmother. She gave it to others, but to Mel Bevan's grandmother and mom, they gave a whole dozen jars of preserves. So, for vegetables, there was cauliflower and jarred carrots.

TS: Is that different — because there wasn't a lot of farming?

MR: Yeah, that was different: there was no farming in Essington. My grandmother was the only one that had a potato farm. And her neighbour, Edith Starr, Louise Starr's mother, she had a little potato farm there too. And they both had black currants and red currants, rhubarbs and gooseberries. Then from Ecstall we stayed home for a while 'til after Christmas. We went to school. Then after Christmas, right after Clifford's birthday on January third, the next day, we're gone — we moved out to Baker's Inlet.

TS: And that's further out?

MR: That's way out in the ocean. And, well, there's the picture there with my grandmother and I walking the beach.

TS: So Baker's Inlet. What would you guys do in Baker's?

MR: Lots; there's lots to do there. Right below the house, we could roll around and fish for shoals. They look like little fish, like flounders. But they don't call them flounders. They're shoals. They look like halibut, but they're small. You can fish right there. Mom would cook us a whole flounder. And my grandmother and I were picking mussels there. We'd go home, cook it up for lunch. And another thing we could get below the house was sea cucumbers. When the tide's up, we were allowed to go in the skiff as far as we could see the bottom. We didn't go past that — it's pretty deep. They told us there's monsters in it. And so we didn't go past where we couldn't see the bottom. And we moved out to Baker's Inlet and my dad had the logging claim there. He did logging and he trapped. He went out and put his traps out around November and he'd just run back and forth.

TS: So what would he trap?

MR: Mink, martens, weasels, squirrels; or else Harold trapped for squirrels. In the inlet there we got lots of food, we got deer, seal, flounders that I was talking about, and crabs, and clams, and my dad would troll. He'd get spring salmon and he'd troll where we had lots of food. We were never hungry. And there was always canning, clams, and cockles. We never, ever canned mussels or things like that.

TS: Could you?

MR: You could, yeah, you can jar them.

TS: But they're just too good?

MR: Yeah. Because they were right out — we could pick them and eat them. But not in the summertime. If it's clams and mussels, they'll jar them and then when the jars are full, they dry them. Forgot what they call them.

TS: So, since we were talking about food and all the food you have harvested — what is it like going from having fresh food like the fresh mussels and preparing all your food to what we have today where food is so easy to get? Or maybe — what was it like when you moved to the big city and there were more restaurants?

MR: The restaurants won't do you any good unless you have money. And money was scarce with us. We did have a little treat now and then, hamburger and anything what we cook ourselves. Like it was so different what we had. I just couldn't see myself having to pay for seaweed and crabs and things like that, when we used to just pick them and eat them.

TS: Yeah. That's amazing. I think, right now, we take it for granted that it's there, but…

MR: The food we ate you guys will never eat because you didn't grow up on it. Like from Baker's Inlet, sometimes it freezes in there too and then we packed up and moved to another island. We called it Felix Island and it was Merrik Island. We have a nice cabin, and there used to be fox farmers on there. But the only thing is there's no outhouse there. We'd go down the beach. No water close by — we had to go far when the tide's out, then we'd go way up the creek to get water. If it's nice then we used the skiff and went to fill the pails. And there at Merrik Island we'd get halibut, we'd get seal.

We could go down the beach and pick Chinese slippers — that's 'yaans [chiton] — great big things, kind of like reddish-brown. And one time, my grandmother picked 50 pounds. And we stayed out in the shed — there was a big fireplace in there that you could put a big boiler on and you could cook out there. It was a great big sack — just the roof, there was no siding, it was nice — you could hang your washing there and dry it. My grandmother and I stayed in there, and we cooked all the Chinese Slippers we picked and kept sending some in the house for people to eat; when they were too full, they hung them up and dried them. They dry things like that because the men went hunting and mountain climbing — they liked to take things they could chew on and not fall apart in their pack.

TS: So they have it like a jerky?

MR: Yeah. And then they took most of the dried stuff. They didn't take too much because they couldn't carry too much.

TS: And if they caught something they had to take it all back.

MR: And they ate some of it. If they took bread it was fried bread, because fried bread don't fall apart. And this is something they can stick in their pockets, little packsack. Because they never came back without game; they stayed out till they got something.

TS: How many people would usually go hunting together?

MR: About three or four. Up Ecstall my dad said, "See that mountain over there? At night time they're going mountain climbing, at night time you look up that way." So we did, and we saw their fire. They started a big fire. If they got a mountain goat right away — what they did is they ripped out the — there's fat inside that you can rip out. It's just like lace, it looks like this, but in big chunks. They put it on a stick and roasted it over the big fire and that's what they ate so they didn't starve. They didn't eat too much or drink too much. That's the story of Waax.

When your husband's up the mountain, you know that's the first thing they'll eat, is the fat. So the women are not supposed to drink cold water. There was a Waax standing on the mountain someplace down the road, and if you do drink water your husband turns to stone. They freeze, the fat freezes them.

TS: I think you told me that one before.

MR: And then the Waax was feeling that he was starting to change, then he knew what his wife did — I forgot his wife's name — then he hollered down the mountain and he told his wife to eat some fat and drink some cold water and lay over this big boulder of rock. She did and she froze. And I saw it.

TS: Oh really? So both of them did.

MR: He's standing on the mountain — you can see the man standing there with his axe and his hat and the pack on his back. After a while his hat grew in to a tree. Something broke off, somebody said something broke off. The pack I think. Never seen it. I tried to see it, to show it. Grandpa always slowed down so we could see it. And when my dad took us up the Skeena years ago to try and get some fish and we walked along the tracks. I can't remember if the highway just went up.

TS: What year was that?

MR: 1944 or '45. It was one of those years. 1944 we came up here. So it must have been '43, '44 or '45. We walked up and the cabin was gone, somebody burned it down. But he took us to show us where Waax was. It's right beside the highway. They blasted it away. I was looking for it and we couldn't find it.

TS: Let's see. I think we've been talking for a long time.

MR: I just finished telling you about the other camps. You want me to make it fast?

452

TS: Oh, don't make it fast! Tell me about the camps.

MR: Like the Merrik Island, we lived there with no toilet. Then the foods we got there and my dad was logging but he ran back and forth to Baker's to check his traps. And then from there we moved to Laxbishuunt, that's Arthur Island. We'd move there and he'd get his halibut gear ready. He'd have to sand his traps, sharpen them.

TS: So when does halibut start?

MR: Halibut starts in May. So that's why we moved there in April and he got everything ready. Once in a while we got into herring eggs — we dried herring eggs, and salted them and everything. As soon as we had our food, he'd load up his boat and go into Essington and give them away.

TS: Who would he give them away to?

MR: To anybody who came down. He said, in no time at all, a bunch of women were down with little bags to put their herring eggs in. After we got all ours, then he loaded up the boat quite a bit. Then they'd do that in May. We'd pick seaweed, we didn't dry it — and they'd run in and give them out. And one time when we did that, it was Nate and Verna — dried seaweed and they sent us a bunch of salmon berry soup. That's one thing we always missed when we were out there. And then they picked some and sent it out to us.

That's how we trade. And the herring eggs and the seaweed — Mom traded it with the Gitxsan people. They had caked soapberries and rolled in the cake. They come in flats. They had great big long ones, and they rolled it up and gave it away — about that thick and that big. Seaweed — they traded seaweed and they had berries like that too. And so Mom traded, Mom would give them seaweed and they'd give her soapberries or blueberry.

TS: Oh really, wow, that's nice.

MR: Then from Laxbishuunt — the seaweed, the end of May. Then we moved back to Essington; my dad was getting ready for gill netting. And we sometimes — later on, we started moving to the cannery. To work in the cannery.

TS: So how old were you then, when you were going to the cannery?

MR: I was 12 when I first worked at the cannery, at NP [Northern Pacific Cannery]. And the next year I worked as a cashier. And I stayed there 'til I was 19, in 1951.

TS: Did you get paid?

MR: Yeah.

TS: How much did you get paid?

MR: My very first paycheque — I remember it was 85 dollars. That was lots of money. I gave my mom 50 dollars and I kept 35 dollars. I bought quite a bit of clothes. I bought a winter coat and winter boots and shoes, underwear.

TS: Wow, 85 dollars.

MR: Eighty-five dollars — 50 cents an hour. I wasn't supposed to work; I was supposed to babysit. We moved down to the cannery; Mom was gonna work. But Irene and them were taking a walk down the cannery so I tagged along. Then Dave Spalding — that was the foreman — gave them aprons and boots and I took over the work, and he gave me some, too, so I took them. Sent us to work, so I went to work. When I went home, Mom was really mad. I didn't even pay attention to her; I was busy worried about my time. And I said, "Gee." I said, "I've worked four hours and nobody marked my time yet." Then Mom finally laughed.

TS: So you said you were 12 then? That's so crazy to think.

MR: Then Mom went back to Essington. Irene and I stayed. Then, before the cannery stopped working, they took me home — they took me home before my birthday. Then Irene stayed by herself.

Mildred Roberts. Roberts family collection.

TS: Was she married or still single then?

MR: She was single — having a good time ! And the next year I went to Cassiar. We moved to Cassiar. Then again, I got work, and Mom didn't, and she was mad again.

TS: Did you give her more money?

MR: No, she didn't get to work. Her and Irene went down — I was supposed to babysit — and then I guess they asked Irene if she was still looking for a job to wash fish, and Irene said, "No, my sister." So they said, "We'll call your sister down." So Mom had to go home. But then she got a babysitter — I can't remember who the baby was. Laura, no, not Laura. There was just Clifford and Alec that were home.

TS: Was that in 19…

MR: 1945. Laura was born in '46. Alec was born in '42. So there was just Alec and Clifford. So I think they just stayed alone or my dad took them.

TS: We were talking about the cannery and you were working, so was that in '46?

MR: '45.

TS: '45.

MR: Then the next year Laura was born, and then Shirley. But I can't remember if mom moved down again after Shirley was born. Maybe she didn't.

TS: To Cassiar?

MR: Yes, she did because she had Mini to babysit and she had Laura. Because there was Shirley and Laura, and I can't remember when she finally quit going. 1951, was last time I worked. Bobby was born in 1950, so maybe 1949 was when Mom last went down. And then she had Bobby and I stayed with my grandmother. I was gonna stay with my grandmother but I ended up staying with Nita [Anita Ridler] and Verna [Verna Inkster]. Nita and Verna were gonna work, but they couldn't get ready. They just finished camps with my grandmother. Then I stayed alone in that house. The next year I stayed with Meryl, then I got married, then Grandpa came down.

They came down early in the morning and they were drunk. We went to work and went home at lunch time, and they had all my things tied in a sheet. They packed my stuff: they were moving me back to Essington. But that was the last year I worked. Then I got married after that, so that was the end of my working. And then we just lived there — Grandpa did a lot of hunting. We lived on deer, geese, mallard, and scal. He'd get a seal, he'd cut off the nose, and he'd give it to Vicky to go sell it. Eddy and Henry were buying for four dollars each.

TS: What would they do with it?

MR: Bounty. They used to pay bounty for seals. Because there was too many and they were killing off the fish. So when they got a seal, you didn't only get to eat the meat: you cut off the nose and sell it.

TS: So you got to make money off a seal?

MR: Yeah. You could get a case of milk with that, or a bag of flour, or a whole baloney. But we lived — we had a lot of seal meat. Like Grandpa chopped up two one time and in this little shed — it wasn't very high, a little bit higher than Grandpa — and then we put racks up there to hang the seal meat in and then he sat in there and started a big fire. What he didn't think of, was the fire melts the fat.

TS: Oh. And then everything started melting and dripping?

MR: And then it blew up. I was walking down the road to see what he was doing and he was running up with his seal meat and they were on fire. The fat melted and it exploded. The seal meat that was hanging up was burning and on fire.

TS: Oh, no. So he was trying to get them out?

MR: He was running back and forth taking them — threw them into the snow. They tasted good. I ran down and told him to wait he had a spark on his hair. Then they went around passing his barbequed meat — people liked it.

TS: They started a new trend.

MR: So we ate a lot of seaweed. A lot of geese, a lot of mallards, a lot of deer. Then Grandpa was starting to go out with Eddy or Sam to go halibut fishing or go clam digging. But he was able to go out with the others too, so we had clams and cockles. Seaweed — I told him, "We should go out and get some seaweed." He didn't know the way and I told him I knew the way. The tide was low so I didn't know my way. I saw a lot of big rocks and got scared.

TS: How old were you then?

MR: It was after we were married. I was about 21, 20. After Steve was born, then I couldn't go any place. When it was just Don, I was able to go away, but we always left him behind with Vicky.

And then I'd go picking seaweed. We went out one time, spent the night. We picked a whole bunch of sea prunes at Kennedy Island. And we cooked them right on the boat as soon as we'd get them.

TS: Really! How did you cook them?

MR: You boil water. It's good if you use the seawater, and they come out soft. They never get hard-boiled. You throw them in, cook them, as soon as the skin peels off, you take them out. You start cleaning them, and get the shells. There's little shells around the back, just like butterflies. You clean that out, and dip it in oolichan grease — ech — and you dry them. You can dry them, too. We were sitting on top of the boat, and I looked up, and there's two wolves standing there just watching us. I told Grandpa, "look at those two wolves!" and he looked, and he couldn't see it. I looked, and I couldn't see it again. They disappeared.

TS: Really?

MR: And yet, they were still standing there. After a while, I quit seeing it again.

TS: Wow. They were just watching? That's scary.

MR: Saying 'ech', I guess. [Laughter.] Looking at us.

So that's how our life was in Port Essington. And when we moved into Terrace, we didn't get all that stuff. We had to depend on the store. We had to buy what we were going to eat.

TS: So, the store, the one you were talking about, is that the Co-op that they had?

MR: The Co-op. There was one store, one big store. There were other little stores scattered. There was Thompson's Hardware Store. It had quite a bit of things in there, except food. There was Dafron's Store; there was — I forgot the name of the drug store; Terrace Drugs, I think. There was the Silvertip Café, Chinese food. And not too many, not too many things. Where the shopping mall is, there was all trees. And there was a theatre, like a big barn, where Gemma's is. They cleared that place and started putting Woolworth's in. I think that was the first big store. That's the first big mall, that a lot of people started going there, because it was so handy to run through the mall. Then, Co-op — sure enough, Grandpa still shopped at the Co-op. I'd go wherever there was a big sale.

TS: Yup. [Laughter.] Other than Co-op, then, what was the next grocery store that came in?

MR: Overwaitea was here when we came. I don't know if Safeway was. Supervalu, there was a Supervalu. I can't even remember if they were here when we first came. I know Overwaitea was here.

TS: Really?

MR: It's where that radio station is, across from the post office.

TS: Is that where the pharmacy — the drug store — was, too?

MR: The drug store was — you know that little building across from where Co-op is, right at the corner?

TS: Yup.

MR: That was the Terrace Drugs. There was another drug store right next door to the post office. Munson's — Munson's Drugs.

TS: Okay. I remember hearing that before, that there was a pharmacy there.

MR: And then, the corner from the post office, there used to be a cherry tree standing there.

TS: Really? Which corner? Where the laundromat is?

MR: No, going up, up towards the park. I don't know why they chopped it down.

TS: To make room for the dentist's office?

MR: And the post office in the park, it was right behind, right beside it, a small little place.

TS: What happened there?

MR: They moved to a bigger location and that was — where did they move from? Up on Tuck, I think.

TS: Up on the Bench?

MR: No, up on Tuck.

TS: Oh, the post office. Okay.

MR: And then they built that great big grey building past the police station. That was the Indian Affairs.

TS: And the police station was right at the corner on Lakelse, that little building.

TS: The one that was yellow. Oh, okay.

MR: And then they built a bigger one. And then they built another one, a bigger one, right next door.

TS: So then, did they just move into the new police building when they gave the totem pole in '85?

MS: I can't remember when they moved in. A lot of things I remembered way years back, but after a while, I quit remembering. I quit remembering just when that happened. After a while, I almost forgot what it was like going through Terrace. The trees, things, and then all of a sudden the shopping mall there. And the other one where Safeway — I think that's where the first one was. That's where Woolworth's was?

TS: Yup.

MR: And then they built the other one.

TS: Wow. It must have been a lot different. Were the mills already up at that time? The whole Skeena…

MR: Yup, the mills were up. The mills were the main thing that kept Terrace going. The local logging and the mills. And then Columbia Cel took over everything and then they shipped their logs out. They went to Watson Island [British Columbia] and that was the beginning of the downfall of Terrace. The private loggers started losing their licenses. Like Grandpa and them always had a license to log. My dad did. Felix and Ruby did. Sean/John Wesley did, from Port Essington. They all lost their logging license — they can beachcomb.

TS: And take any logs left there?

MR: Yup, but they couldn't go and cut any more logs. Columbia Cel took the whole thing over. There were a lot of jobs in Terrace with the logging. People moved up from Essington, I think. The first one, I think, that moved up was Joe Wesley.

TS: So, when was that? In the '50s?

MR: Yup. Herb Spalding, and Irene and Gus moved up here, but then they moved to Port Edward. Mom and Howard moved up here for a while, and then they moved to Port Ed.

TS: Wow. So if you weren't a logger, then you were still a fisher?

MR: Yeah. The ones that wanted to stay fishing, they went back down to Port Edward.

TS: Wow.

[Voices in background. Man says something in Sm'algyax̱.]

MR: So, there's no way to make money any more. Fishing was cut. Like, they used to fish from six o'clock Sunday to six o'clock Friday. After a while, they start cutting the days. After a while, by the time Grandpa quit fishing, he'd fish about two days, and sometimes they didn't catch any fish.

TS: Oh, really. Just because he didn't have enough time, or the fishing was low?

MR: Not enough time. They cut the fishing down to one day, two days, and that's why he quit, because there was hardly any use, him going all the way down there. The fisheries were putting a lot of demands on the boats — how to fix your boat — and costing a lot of money, and not making enough — not enough time to make money.

TS: Wow. That's too bad.

MR: Then he had the chance to work around here, so he just quit. He just quit fishing.

TS: That's too bad.

MR: He had to let his boat go, because it would cost him money to keep it. It would cost him money to leave it on the dock and to repair it, so he sold it really cheap.

TS: Who did he sell it to?

MR: Some young couple bought it. He sold his A1 fishing license really cheap. When he could have got $45,000, he sold the boat and license and all for $6,000.

TS: Really?! That's crazy!

MR: Mm-hm. I think it hurt him, that time, but he didn't say anything about it. Because he could have sold the boat and then this company said they'd take the boat when fishing's over. Use it for the summer, and bring it in at the end of the summer. So that was going to be his last year using the Kara Lee. Then he fished, and then that company wasn't there any more — that was going to buy it.

TS: Oh, no.

MR: So he sold it. Right after that Tio phoned to tell Don to hang onto that license. He'd found a buyer. $45,000. And he already let it go.

TS: Oh, no.

458

MR: So that was the end of the Kara Lee.

TS: So what year was that, then?

MR: That was '75.

TS: Okay, wow.

MR: See that picture where he's standing on the boat? That was that year. Jim and I went fishing with him that year.

TS: Oh, really. Wow. So what year was Jim born?

MR: '68. Then he rented a boat one year, and fishing was so bad that he just gave it up.

TS: That's too bad. Wow.

MR: Because his back was so bad. I forgot what year they fixed his back. That year Willie was born. That day Willie was born, that's when he had his operation. I forgot what year. Sometimes he couldn't move, because his back was so bad — his vertebrae was worn right down to the nerve. They fixed it and he was able to work again.

TS: Wow. So, he was in the hospital, at Mills Memorial?

MR: In Kitimat. Dr. Kuntz operated on him. So he had two operations on his back. One on his back, one on his neck, and then there was going to be two more. He cut off the bone out of his hip to graft.

TS: Really? Wow! That's something.

MR: But he was able to go back to work again. He worked for Kalum, and then he worked at the hatchery.

TS: And I know he was the Chief?

MR: Just two months, and then he stepped down. He couldn't take the hassle. And Steve got in.

TS: What year was that?

MR: I think it was '75. '75, '76. In the '70s.

TS: And so, then he was working for the hatchery, and I remember going to the hatchery, where we'd all go up there together and picnic.

MR: That's the time I ran away from everybody. I took off with Grandpa. They looked all over for me. [Both laugh.] Then they ran up.

TS: Every time you're gone, then we look everywhere.

MR: Mm. That was a nice day. I found some pictures.

TS: Did you? I remember seeing all the fish, all the little fry, and feeding them.

[Man's voice in background.]

MR: That's about it.

TS: Yeah, I think so. And we could do this again. I like hearing your stories. It brings it all into perspective.

Victoria Roberts Interview

Interviewed by Damian Bohn, 18 December 2013

Victoria Roberts was born in Port Essington in 1932. Throughout her life, Victoria experienced and witnessed racism toward First Nations peoples. When she was a child, the two schools operating in Port Essington were intended to segregate Aboriginal and Non-Aboriginal students. When Victoria first attended school, she remembers not being able to speak English and not being permitted to speak her native tongue. When Victoria finished school, she worked various jobs in the fishing industry, as a school janitor, and as a farmer. Victoria had a common-law partner and three children. In this interview, she discusses her childhood, visiting natural hot springs, living in Kitsumkalum, and her various volunteer positions in the community. Victoria also shares stories such as how the Kitsumkalum people were required to move a burial site due to the highway's proposed path cutting through Kitsumkalum's burial grounds.

DB: Where were you born?

VR: Port Essington.

DB: What year were you born in?

VR: 1932.

DB: Could you tell me about your parents?

VR: I was born, and I never knew my father. My mother left home, and then my grandparents brought me up. So, I don't know much about my parents. It's always my grandmother.

DB: Can you tell us about your grandmother then?

VR: I don't know. She's just old. She was only about 70 years old when she passed away, and my grandfather was younger, and he still wouldn't let me go back to my mother because the man she was living with was drinking too much. I just stayed on with them.

DB: How did you arrive in Terrace?

VR: Well, people started moving away from Port Essington. Some moved to Prince Rupert, some moved up here, and then the Kitsumkalum Band decided they were going to move all the members up here. There were only 17 lots cleared and this was lot number one. Then it goes down that way. But that's the number that I give if I call a cab or ambulance or something. We lived here — I lived here ever since. I don't remember the year. But we just went down to Port Essington and fished, and then after the fishing season was over, then we moved back up again.

DB: What was your relationship like with your siblings?

VR: Oh, good.

DB: Can you describe a typical day in your house when you were younger?

VR: I don't really remember. We had a big house in Port Essington, but then it burnt down so we moved to one of the cannery houses where the Japanese lived. But then the Japanese all got shipped out during the war.

DB: Growing up as a kid, what kind of expectations were there for you when you were younger?

VR: I don't remember. There were two schools in Port Essington. One that they called Indian Day School, and one supposed to be white students. But there were a lot of different-skinned Indians [in both schools]. I don't know what year they joined us together.

DB: Can you tell us a bit about how your community was growing up?

Victoria Roberts and her Grandfather Joseph Roberts coming back in a canoe from beaver hunting. Don and Mildred Roberts Collection.

VR: I don't know. We just walked around; there was nothing there. Like, here, if we want to go to a theater to go see a movie, then we go. But in Port Essington, they don't have anything like that. There's just a band hall and basketball hall. And some of the guys used to play basketball. And then some people throw a party and then they open up the band hall. If somebody gets married then they have a dance in that hall. There wasn't that much going on. You just walk around, walk around.

DB: What school did you attend?

VR: Well, first of all, the Indian Day School, they called it. Then, I don't know what they called the other school: it was a white school. But I knew they were all different-skinned Indians — except for one student: he was white. My grandmother wanted to send me to residential school, and my grandfather said, "No, as long as she knows how to write, she will be good enough" and that's what I always say, when I go writing.

DB: Do you have any memory of your school that you would like to share?

VR: Nothing, I guess. When I first started going to school I didn't understand a word of English at all. When somebody — a white person — talked to me I didn't know what they said. Like, if a

461

Chinese man comes and talks to me now, I wouldn't understand, and that's the way it was. And when my grandmother sent me to the store, she just said [to get] what they call it. It took the storekeeper a long time to understand what I wanted. If we used our own words on the school grounds, while we were going to our own Indian Day School, for each word you said you would have to stay in five minutes.

I don't know how that teacher got the time to sit with me — because I didn't understand a word of English, and the older girls, they picked on me. They spoke to me in our language and said "You can say it and we won't tell." But they were counting how many words I say, and [I had to] stay in school after hours, for about three or four hours. I don't know where the teacher got the time to stay, to sit with me. Because I didn't understand a word she said.

DB: When you grew up, did you go to college or university?

VR: No. I went as far as grade eight, and I walked out of school.

DB: When did you get married?

VR: I never got married, just lived common-law with their father. Because I didn't want my name to end with Bolton. I wanted to keep Roberts. I was doing that register to send in, and I registered as Roberts too.

DB: What jobs did you work at through Terrace or in Port Essington?

VR: In Port Essington it was mostly nets. And I was the school janitor, when they had to order in the stove oil, those big 45-gallon drums. You order them for 50 cents for each drum. Steve and Don were little guys and they helped me roll them up. But I had to stand 'em up, and I had to put a plank up like that, and then roll the top end, and that's why I got a bad back. I did too much lifting. Then I worked on fishermen's nets. George Brown used to pay me three dollars an hour. Then a big thin woman, Elena, she said if I worked on her net she'd pay me four dollars an hour. So I said, "okay." I left George's and then next time I saw George he said, "I will pay you five dollars an hour," and then that's when Elena gave up trying to hire me to work on her nets.

I made lots of money at five dollars an hour. Fishing was only Sunday, Monday, Tuesday, and then it ends. George told me to wait for him six o'clock Tuesday, because that's when he's going to rack his net and start working on his net. And I used to do Gus' net too. He got a new net and we had to cut all the sinkers and — whatever they call it, the cork off. Then they put the lights on the wharf and I had to work on the net there. I made 33 dollars on one net. Then up here, I worked for Samson — he was on Bruce Freeman's chicken farm, that's where I worked. I worked transplanting trees and picking potatoes, and lots of heavy work like that. I had to keep bending over to pick the potatoes. They just plowed the ground, and then we picked the potatoes for two dollars an hour. Some got paid a dollar fifty an hour — because you're a brown — to pick up the potato, put it in the hand, and in the bucket. And so he, Boychuck, said, "that's picking it twice."

And then every little job that came along, I'd go working. I used to do nets for where they [did] fish testing — [testing] how much fish comes up. That was 11 dollars an hour. And that's why the hole is up there, because — They're shallow, the nets. I took it in and worked till midnight on it, repairing it. And then if I woke up four o'clock and I got up, and I did all kinds of little jobs, I wouldn't have to go on welfare after Cindy's father passed away.

DB: Did you have any children?

VR: Three: Cindy, Wayne, and Gary. But I lost Gary to cancer. I forgot how old he was. He kept working on the roofs, and in the sun — that's what we blame. Started with a little dot on the side of his cheek and soon it was getting bigger, so I asked him, "Gary what's that growing on the side of your cheek?" "Oh this one?" he said, "Don't worry about it." And that's where the cancer started.

DB: How did you find Terrace as a place to raise a family?

VR: It's good. It's close. I used to just walk to town, shop at Co-op, and then walk home again. They delivered. But then they built that store James is working in now. It was not that kind of material they used to build the one we got now — the big posts about this round, to haul it up because the roof was caving in. So, they had to put big iron bars to pull it together. Then the road — highway — ran through the graveyard, it's all graveyard up there. And they had to move some of the graves. The government paid Kitsumkalum one million dollars.

Then Steve said we had to count all the members from Kitsumkalum. They lived in Prince Rupert, they lived in Vancouver, they lived all over the place. It wouldn't be worth really anything, so they were thinking about building a hall. But then the government told them that it would cost them a million dollars to build a hall; I forgot how many thousands of dollars to keep it up. And I was the one who jumped up and said, "Oh, we will fundraise! Go ahead and build a hall, we'll fundraise!" But I think the store is the one that is paying for the lights and heat. And the store I worked in, for many years, it was just arts and crafts. And then, we had somebody coming in to make up the grocery list, what we were going to sell. So I worked there for a long time, until I collapsed. And then that was my end.

DB: What did you do for fun?

VR: Nothing. Nothing that I can remember.

DB: What restaurants were popular over the years?

VR: I don't know.

DB: Did you visit the Lakelse Lake Hot spring?

VR: I never ever went up there, and I never saw what it's like. But we had one down the river almost close to Port Essington — we used to go there with the morning tide. We would stay up there all day with the kids. And that's where three young people — I think they were from Terrace — that just drowned, just got lost. I think they're from Terrace. I don't know what they're going to do. That was just this year. Then I thought of all the years we spent playing around there.

DB: Can you tell me about the sports in Terrace or Port Essington?

VR: I don't know anything about sports in Terrace. In Port Essington they play ball, they play basketball, and things like that. Because it's always just quiet there. Not much going on in the wintertime; they just have parties and things like that — When the older people say, "Well, it's a little quiet we better make some tea and invite everybody." And it's coffee that they make, not tea, I think. But, "Give them some tea."

DB: Did you play any sports?

VR: No, I never do any sports, no.

DB: Were you involved in any community events outside the home?

VR: Well, I guess you could say I did a lot of things, down that hall here. I used to do loonie auctions for the kids' Christmas presents. It takes two loonie auctions to pay for their Christmas presents and all the food. And the last one I threw, I was in the hospital when they were doing that loonie auction. I had lots of other things that I picked up here and there. It's an all-year-round job, but I just like to see the kids being happy and things like that.

DB: What local events do you remember celebrating in Terrace or Port Essington?

VR: You know, just some people married in Port Essington and everybody goes. And here I don't go to anything, because usually I'm too tired after working long hours at the store.

DB: What do you remember about downtown Terrace?

VR: Oh, you know, I used to just walk uptown. I don't drive. Even if I did have a car, it takes only two dollars to get a cab, and go uptown, and come back. But it's a whole lot more now. I just walked around town and shopped and then walked home, because Co-op used to deliver the food.

I was just thinking back — we were in the same grade, and his father was saying he was a hard worker. George was the one who took him wherever he was going to do something. And he can do it, he's one hundred percent fine. He's the best drummer. When the orchestra in Port Essington had a dance, George would bring them down and somebody would take him home after the dance was over. He's on the beach sawing, sawing wood.

They had the best house in Port Essington, and they were the only ones who could buy a little power plant. They had electric lights in their house, and they had a fridge in their house that they got ice cream in. It came on the train; the ferryboat brought it over for them. We all went running, buying it.

DB: What did most people that you knew do for work around Port Essington or Terrace?

VR: Well, like I said, in Port Essington, all the fishermen, I worked for them. Moving the big oil drums and doing the fishermen's nets.

DB: What role do you think forestry and logging played through the history of Terrace?

VR: I don't have any idea.

DB: How did the community of Terrace interact with Kitselas and Kitsumkalum?

VR: I don't know about Terrace. But Kitselas people and Kalum people, they get along together, they don't try to fight with one another. And if something happens and we know them, we go over there. They do the same when something happens in Kalum.

DB: More generally, how has Terrace changed over the years?

VR: I guess there's more stores. But I don't go to most stores anymore. And then we started getting our mail out there in that little mail shed. But when I got my post office box — we were still paying for it up town, because I just asked him today.

DB: How important do you think the First Nations culture has shaped our community?

VR: I never think about it. So, I don't know.

DB: Were there any annual community events that you can remember? What were they like?

VR: Well, I don't really know. They used to have that salmon barbecue, but they wouldn't do it this year because there's no fish. And that's the only time I was involved in the workforce. But somebody took over now — and now almost everything that's going on, she's taking over everything. I just don't have the strength to help anymore anyway.

DB: Do you remember the queen Queen visiting Terrace?

VR: No.

DB: When you were a child what did you expect or hope to accomplish?

VR: I don't know. I guess I never thought about it; I just kept growing up.

DB: As a longtime resident of the Terrace area, what changed over the years that you have noticed?

VR: Like I said, I don't go around town very much. I just don't know. I guess there's more stores, that's all. 'Cause there used to be a church where Safeway is right now. There were trees that way, and they cut down all the trees. And then, the store started pressuring the church there too, and they moved that.

Preserving the Past for the Present:
An Oral History Project

Coordinated by Melanie Pollard

A Project of Heritage Park

Preserving the Past for the Present © 2017 Terrace and District Museum Society

This project is funded in part by the Government of Canada's New Horizons for Seniors program.

ISBN-13: 978-1494743680

ISBN-10: 149474368X

Front cover: Skeena Bridge photo, Heritage Park Collection.

Published by Terrace and District Museum Society, Terrace, BC, Canada. Printed by CreateSpace.

Library and Archives Canada Cataloguing in Publication

Pollard, Melanie, coordinator
    Preserving the Past for the Present: An Oral History Project / Terrace and District Museum Society. Coordinated by Melanie Pollard.

(History)
Includes index.
Issued in print and electronic formats.

ISBN-13: 978-1494743680

ISBN-10: 149474368X

1. Terrace, BC—history—20th century.